CURRENT STUDIES ON THE INDUS CIVILIZATION

RIHN-MANOHAR INDUS PROJECT SERIES

Current Studies on the Indus Civilization

VOLUME IX

Edited by

TOSHIKI OSADA
HITOSHI ENDO

MANOHAR
2012

An earlier version of this work was published under the title
Linguistics, Archaeology and the Human Past (Occasional Paper 12)
in 2011, by Indus Project, Research Institute for
Humanity and Nature, Kyoto, Japan

This revised edition is now being
published as RIHN Library No. 17, 2012

ISBN 978-81-7304-859-3 (Series)
ISBN 978-81-7304-948-4 (Vol. IX)

Published by
Ajay Kumar Jain for
Manohar Publishers & Distributors
4753/23 Ansari Road, Daryaganj
New Delhi 110 002

Printed at
Salasar Imaging Systems
Delhi 110 035

CONTENTS

PREFACE

It is my pleasure that the publication of the ninth volume of *Current Studies on the Indus Civilization* is imminent. I sincerely thank all the contributors of this volume, especially Professor Asko Parpola who is one of the most eminent scholars in this field since the 1970s.

This year is the final year of our Indus project. Although our budget was limited, Ramesh Jain of Manohar Publishers & Distributors agreed to publish this book as one of the RIHN-Manohar Indus Project series. My sincere gratitude to him and his team at Manohar.

This volume contains mainly Professor Parpola's papers and his colleague in Helsinki University, Professor Juha Janhunen's papers concerning several animals, i.e. crocodile, ass and unicorn. These animals' motifs are found not only in the Indus seals but also in the several mythological literatures from Eurasia, including India. Their discussions about these animals' motifs are very interesting for me. Please enjoy reading them.

Personally I knew Professor Juha Janhunen since the early 1980s because he was a visiting scholar in my university, Hokkaido University. So I am very happy to contribute his paper to this *CSIC*.

The third contributor to this volume is Professor Ajithprasad of the Maharaja Sayajirao University of Baroda, Gujarat. His paper deals with issues related to the early Chalcolithic regional tradition of north Gujarat in western India. He was a Visiting Fellow at the RIHN twice and had contributed earlier also to *CSIC*.

In the end, I thank Hitoshi Endo who did excellent editorial work on the volume.

Toshiki Osada

osada@chikyu.ac.jp
Professor and Project leader
Indus project
Research Institute for Humanity and Nature
Kyoto, Japan

Crocodile in the Indus Civilization and later South Asian traditions

Asko Parpola
University of Helsinki

Abstract

In order to penetrate further into the little understood Indus script, this study examines texts associated with depictions of the crocodile in the Harappan 'sacrificial tablets'. In contrast to the vast majority of Indus seals, these tablets provide a clear connection between inscriptions and their accompanying iconography. Laying the ground for that study, the first half of the paper collects and analyzes data on crocodiles available in later South Asian traditions[1].

Three species of crocodiles are found in South Asia: the marsh crocodile, the saltwater crocodile, and the long-snouted crocodile. The long-snouted crocodile is sometimes confounded with the South Asian river dolphin, which likewise has a long and narrow snout. This paper begins with a zoological description of these animals.

An etymological examination of important words for 'crocodile' in South Asian languages follows next. The long-snouted crocodile predominates in Harappan iconography; its two primary names, Hindi *ghaṛiyāl* and *kumhīr* (with their cognates, including Sanskrit *ghaṇṭika-* and *kumbhīra-*), have a Dravidian origin. These names are derived from Proto-Dravidian appellations of the distinctive bulbous protuberance on the tip of the crocodile's snout (understood in folk etymology as 'pot', Sanskrit *ghaṭa-* and *kumbha-*). Even after the extinction of the long-snouted crocodile in the lower Indus Valley, Sindhi retains the word *gharyālu*, though it has changed here — but not elsewhere — to denote the 'Indus river dolphin'. Special attention is paid to references to crocodile in Old Tamil literature, the most important source for ancient Dravidian phraseology.

Cults, traditions and conceptions connected with the crocodile in historical South Asia are surveyed, chiefly on the basis of the folk religion studies of William Crooke. This section concludes with a summary of the tribal crocodile cult of southern Gujarat, recently documented by Eberhard Fischer and Haku Shah (1971). This cult involves the creation of wooden images of crocodiles fixed upon poles. A Mature Harappan painted pot from Amri, featuring two long-snouted crocodiles with a pole-like extension projecting ninety degrees from their lower bodies to what could depict the ground, strongly suggests that Gujarati tribals have preserved a local religious tradition that is 4,000 years old.

Finally, representations of the crocodile in Harappan seals and tablets are examined on the basis of the collected material. Several new Proto-Dravidian interpretations for Indus signs are proposed, strictly following the methodology and premises put forward in my book *Deciphering the Indus script* (1994). The results support and widen previous findings.

It appears that the Harappans worshipped the crocodile primarily for the sake of fertility, and that the cult even involved the sacrifice of the firstborn child (as one finds in the Śunaḥśepa legend recorded in Vedic texts and in cult traditions reported as recently as the early 19th century in North India). There is also evidence that the concept of the heavenly crocodile attested in the Veda is predated by the Harappan interpretation of Ursa Major.

THE ZOOLOGICAL BACKGROUND

Crocodiles: some general characteristics

All crocodiles are cold-blooded. For this reason, they must bask in the sun in order to be able to move, to hunt and to breed. Basking with the mouth open is a way to control body temperature; this practice also dries leeches and allows birds to rid the crocodile of such parasites. The crocodile is mostly active at night, while much of the day is spent sleeping, either basking or submerged in the water (Whitaker 1986: 151).

The crocodile is structurally adapted to aquatic life. Nostrils are located at the tip of its snout, so that breathing requires only this part of the body to be lifted out of the water. Nostrils and ears are closed with flaps when the crocodile is submerged, while a transparent third eyelid enables it to see underwater. Because folds in the tongue and palate prevent water from entering the lungs, it can open its mouth underwater. It normally comes to the surface to breathe several times per hour, but can stay under for hours without breathing (Daniel 1983: 8; Whitaker 1986: 151; Murthy 1995: 17).

The crocodile can smell, hear and see very well. It also detects prey by tactile (and possibly chemical) receptors. Adult crocodiles eat fish and, in most cases, mammals as well. They usually approach their prey by stealth and then either leap at it or make a fast grab with the jaws. After lying motionless at the drinking holes frequented by buffaloes or deer, the crocodile will use its mighty tail to deliver a swift blow to an unsuspecting animal, seize the prey, and then drag it to the water to drown it. If the victim is too large to be swallowed whole, it is twisted and repeatedly shaken until torn to pieces. Crocodiles do not need to eat every day, and take less food in cool weather (Whitaker 1986: 151; Murthy 1995: 17). The continued survival of crocodiles for 190 million years may be partly due to their ability to live "on the edge of two life zones, water and land, and being able to find their prey from both zones" (Daniel 1983: 8).

Crocodiles swallow stones: a 3.5 m long mugger had about 1 kg of stones in its stomach, while a 5 m long gharial contained about 4.5 kg foul-smelling stones. It is popularly believed that the number of stones in its belly tells the animal's age (Daniel 1983: 11-12, 15-16).

In accordance with the general pattern of reptiles, crocodiles have a long body and long tail but short limbs. They are excellent swimmers, moving with lateral strokes of their powerful tail, while fore and hind feet are held close to the trunk. They may "high walk" short distances on land, raising their body well above the ground, moving with a slow, waddling gait (Figure 71). More often, however, crocodiles move on land by sliding on their belly, using their legs as propellers. The dead body of a crocodile may twitch and quiver for many hours after it has been killed (Daniel 1983: 8-9, 12; Whitaker 1986: 151).

The male has a single penis situated within its vent or cloaca, which has a longitudinal opening. Located within the cloaca is also one of its scent glands; the other is found on the crocodile's throat. These glands assume more importance in the breeding season (Daniel 1983: 8, 11). Crocodiles mate in the water with "a complicated ritual of bubble-blowing, circling, and head movements" (Whitaker 1986: 151). About six weeks later the female lays eggs, which hatch after two or three months. Both eggs and hatchlings up to the age of one or two years are the prey of birds, snakes, jackals, mongooses, and other animals (including humans, who believe that crocodile-eggs possess aphrodisiac properties) (Whitaker 1986: 151; Maskey and Mishra 1982: 185).

Crocodiles are protected against enemies by their scaly skin. "The skin of the back is armoured with bony plates arranged in transverse series. The tail, similarly armoured, bears two rows of serrated scales which merge before the tail end" (Daniel 1983: 8). Crocodile skin is in great demand for use in leather clothing and accessories. Such demand has led to ruthless hunting of the crocodile since the early 20th century, making it an endangered species. In India, the killing of crocodiles has been prohibited since 1972 (Whitaker 1986: 151). This prohibition has led to problems, however, especially in the monsoon season when river flooding enlarges the water habitat of the crocodiles and in some places brings them into close proximity with densely populated urban areas (Vyas and Bhatt 2004).

The three species of crocodile in South Asia

Today the global population of crocodiles (or rather, crocodilians) is divided into three genera: true crocodiles (Crocodilidae), alligators and caymans (Alligatoridae), and gavial (Gavialidae). In South Asia, there are three species of crocodile, "which the Anglo-Indian persists in calling *alligators*" (Crooke 1906: 110). Alligators (having two species, with one in China) and caymans exist mainly in America; both are separated from crocodiles by the arrangement of the teeth. The appellation 'alligator' originated from the Spanish word *el/al lagarto* (from Latin *lacerta* 'lizard') (Yule and Burnell 1903: 13b).

The mugger, or marsh crocodile

The mugger or marsh crocodile (*Crocodylus palustris*, Lesson) (Figure 1) is broad-snouted and stocky, the full-grown adult being about 3.5 m in length and about 200 kg in weight; it is the most common species in South Asia. It is olive and black in colour, with yellowish white on its underside. The mugger was once found throughout the subcontinent in rivers, lakes, ponds, reservoirs and marshes, but has died out over large areas. In summer, muggers can travel great distances in search of water, at which point they dig burrows in the banks of rivers and lakes to cool themselves. They live in groups of up to thirty animals with a strict 'pecking order', large males being dominant. Subordinate males signal submission by raising the head, thereby exposing their throat. In breeding season, the female digs a 50 cm hole and lays between 15 and 50 eggs, usually at night. Two or three months later, sounds from the eggs tell the mother crocodile that it is time to dig up the covered clutch. She will gently carry the hatchlings to the water in her jaws (Daniel 1983: 10-12; Whitaker 1986: 152).

Marsh crocodiles mostly eat fish, but larger individuals may attack any animal that they have a chance of killing. While man-eating is not common, there are anecdotal statements to the contrary. Crooke (1906: 111), for instance, refers to one beast that was shot, "from the stomach of which were taken 30 lbs. weight of gold, silver, copper, brass, and zinc, all women's ornaments." Such finds, however, are mostly due to the mugger's habit of eating corpses that float unburied in the river (Daniel 1983: 11; Whitaker 1986: 152). The marsh crocodiles on Salsette Island, Mumbai, have been recorded to feed on the fruit of the fig tree (*Ficus glomerata*).

The saltwater or estuarine crocodile

The saltwater or estuarine crocodile (*Crocodylus porosus* Schneider) (Figure 2) is a widely distributed species from South Asia to Australia. Its typical habitats are tidal estuaries, lower reaches of the larger rivers, and coastal mangrove thickets. The saltwater crocodile is the largest existing reptile—specimens over 8 m have been found, but the average length is closer to 4.5 m (weighing approximately 400 kg). Larger individuals can take humans as prey. While saltwater crocodiles are sleeker than the mugger and lack the four distinct post-occipital scales that the mugger has on its neck (Whitaker 1986: 151-153), these two species look so much the same that they are "difficult to distinguish in the wild, without

Figure 1 Marsh crocodile. Photo Karunakar Rayker 2004 (from Wikipedia Commons)

Figure 2 Saltwater crocodile. Photo Molly Ebersold 2004 (from Wikipedia Commons)

Figure 3 Gharial. Photo Petronas 2008 (from Wikipedia Commons)

Figure 4 Gharials in S. Antonio zoo. Photo Greverod 2007 (from Wikipedia Commons)

Figure 5 Gharial in San Diego zoo. Photo Bo link 2006 (from Wikipedia Commons)

considerable experience". They share the same name in most Indian languages (Daniel 1983: 8 and 13-14). Their feeding habits are similar as well, but the saltwater crocodile is more solitary, and constructs a mound nest of leaves and grass (about 1 m high) instead of a hole (Whitaker 1986: 152-153).

The gharial, or long-snouted crocodile

The gavial, or long-snouted crocodile (*Gavialis gangeticus* Gmelin) (Figures 3-4), also known as the gharial, is the only surviving species of the genus Gavialidae. It is found only in the Indian subcontinent. The gharial adult male has an average length of 6 m, while the female is slightly smaller. Its colour is olive, spotted with dark brown patches or stripes. It has bulging, cat-like eyes and a long, narrow snout, by which it is easily distinguished from the other South Asian crocodiles. The males have a prominent excrescence on the tip of the snout, which is believed to enhance virility and the value of which drives hunting of this critically endangered animal even today (Maskey and Mishra 1982: 185) (Figure 5). The bulb at the tip of the snout of the male gharial is hollow and consists of special masses of erectile tissue that can swell to close its nostrils[2]. Males are said to use this snout protuberance to hook onto the female's snout for leverage when mounting in the act of mating (Daniel

1983: 16). Breeding males also hiss loudly, with the protuberance possibly acting as a resonator (Daniel 1983: 15). The gharial is hunted for its hide and also killed by fishermen, who consider predators of fish as threats to their economic success (Majupuria 1982: 150).

The original range of the gharial included all of the major rivers and tributaries from the Indus in Pakistan[3] to the rivers of northern India and Bangladesh, extending as far south as the Mahanadi in Orissa. Increased use of rivers by humans has reduced its wild habitat to a few river stretches in Pakistan, India and Nepal. Today it is mainly found in the Chambal, Girwa, Rapti and Narayani rivers of the Ganges system. Recently on the verge of extinction, the species continues to be very endangered (Maskey and Mishra 1982: 186; Daniel 1983: 15; Whitaker 1986: 153; Murthy 1995: 20).

One reason for the gharial's precarious situation is its need for a specialized habitat. Gharials inhabit deep pools in big rivers, where fish are plentiful; they use sandbanks for basking and nesting. "The gharial is the most aquatic of all crocodiles, coming to land only for egg-laying" (Murthy 1995: 20).

Gharials are almost exclusively fish-eaters. They snap their long, narrow jaws sideways to catch passing fish, which are then swallowed by several backward jerks of the head. While the gharial tends to be very timid and "darts into water at the sight of man" (Murthy 1995: 20), breeding females will charge and bite intruders that approach the nest. "There is no record of the gharial ever having killed a man" (Murthy 1995: 20).

"They are social and live in groups usually made up of a single adult male, several females and several sub-adults. As with other crocodilians, the young live apart after a one- or two-month nursery period. 40-80 eggs are usually laid, in nest-holes on river banks. Gharials may fail to breed where there is excessive disturbance..." (Whitaker 1986: 153). Less than one percent of young gharials hatched in the wild actually survive to reach a length of about 2 metres, at which time they become immune to predation (Singh 1978).

The South Asian river dolphin

On account of its long and narrow snout (called a rostrum), the South Asian river dolphin (*Platanista gangetica*, Lebeck/Roxburgh 1801) (Figure 6) is conflated with the gharial in some vernacular names. Given this confusion, the river dolphin is briefly described here as well.

Dolphins are among the most intelligent animals in the world, with a streamlined fusiform body highly adapted for speed. The horizontally placed, halfmoon-shaped tail fin, called a fluke, is used for propulsion. Pectoral fins, together with the tail, control direction. Dolphins breathe through a blowhole on top of their head, inside of which is a round organ called the melon, used for echolocation. "Dolphin copulation happens belly to belly and though many species engage in lengthy foreplay, the actual act is usually brief, but may be repeated several times within a short timespan... Dolphins are known to have sex for reasons other than reproduction... Sexual encounters may be violent..." (Wikipedia 2009/12 s.v. Dolphin).

The Indus river dolphin found in the Indus River and its tributaries (the Beas and Sutlej in Pakistan)

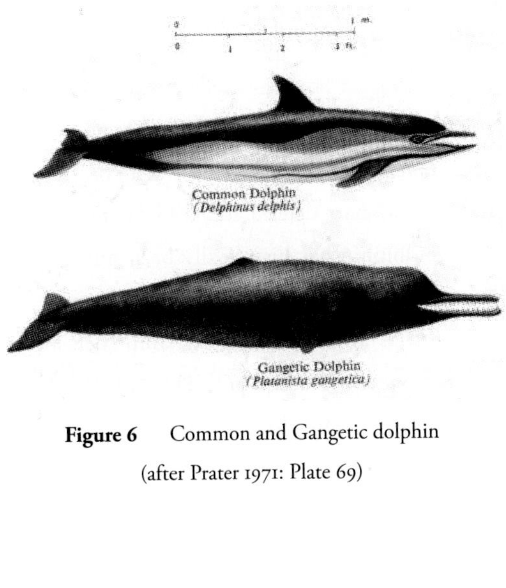

Figure 6 Common and Gangetic dolphin (after Prater 1971: Plate 69)

was originally regarded as a separate species (*Platanista indi*), but since 1998 has been considered as a subspecies (*Platanista gangetica minor*) of the South Asian river dolphin. The other subspecies, the Ganges river dolphin (*Platanista gangetica gangetica*), is primarily found in the Ganges and Brahmaputra rivers and their tributaries in India, Bangladesh and Nepal. The two subspecies have not interbred for hundreds, if not thousands, of years. The South Asian river dolphin is an endangered species. In dictionaries and non-zoological literature, it is often mistakenly identified as a porpoise.

The South Asian river dolphin is generally about 2 to 2.6 m long, with females being larger than males. Like the gharial, it also has a long, narrow snout with a large number of sharp, conical teeth. This rostrum thickens at the end; its teeth, which may vary in number from 27 to 32 on either side of each jaw, are visible even when the mouth is closed. Its eyes are about the size of a pea and virtually blind. On the dolphin's back, one finds a small fleshy lump in place of a dorsal fin. Its colour ranges from dark brown to black.

River dolphins are usually encountered on their own or in loose groups. During the monsoon, they can be seen in tidal areas, although they do not enter the sea. At this time, river dolphins are known to advance through the water in series of leaps.

The Gangetic dolphin usually rises to the surface to breathe for a few seconds before submerging again for a minute or so. Its jaws are well adapted for browsing on bottom-dwellers (e.g., shrimp and catfish), but it also hunts carp and other types of fish via echolocation. Life in turbid waters has resulted in an evolutionary deterioration of its vision.

The dolphin has historically been hunted with nets and harpoons. Its oil and meat are used as a liniment, as an aphrodisiac, as lamp fuel, and as bait for catfish. (Prater 1971: 313-314; Wikipedia 2009/12 s.vv. Dolphin and Ganges and Indus River Dolphin) Dolphin fat has many uses in the traditional Indian medical system (Lüders 1942: 70-72).

The scientific name of the South Asian river dolphin is derived from its description by Pliny, H. N. 9,15: *in Gange Indiae platanistas vocant rostro delphini et cauda, magnitudine autem XVI cubitorum* (Lüders 1942: 61 n. 3 points out that Pliny exaggerates the dolphin's length).

SOUTH ASIAN VERNACULAR NAMES OF CROCODILES

Words for 'crocodile' cannot be reconstructed for the Indo-European and Indo-Iranian protolanguages. This is not surprising, given the fact that crocodiles never lived around the Pontic-Caspian steppes where these protolanguages are likely to have been spoken (Mallory 1989; Anthony 2007; Parpola 2008). Crocodiles were not found in the Black Sea, the Caspian and Aral Seas, or the rivers feeding these seas (Figure 7). Coming from the Eurasian steppes to the Indian subcontinent via Central Asia, Aryan speakers are thus unlikely to have brought inherited words for 'crocodile' when they entered South Asia in the second millennium BCE. This is borne out by the following examination: the only words for 'crocodile' that can be shown to have an Indo-European etymology are descriptive terms recorded by lexicographers or rarely used in literature. An exception is Sanskrit *grāha-* m. (literally 'grabber'), which is of Indo-European origin; it does not, however, have extra-Indian cognates with the meaning of 'crocodile', and denotes other beasts of prey as well (e.g., 'shark', 'snake').

On the other hand, crocodiles were certainly native to the areas inhabited by the Early, Mature and Late Harappans, which comprised almost all of present-day Pakistan and northwestern India from Kashmir to Maharashtra, eastwards to around Delhi. It is in this area that Indo-Aryan speakers first

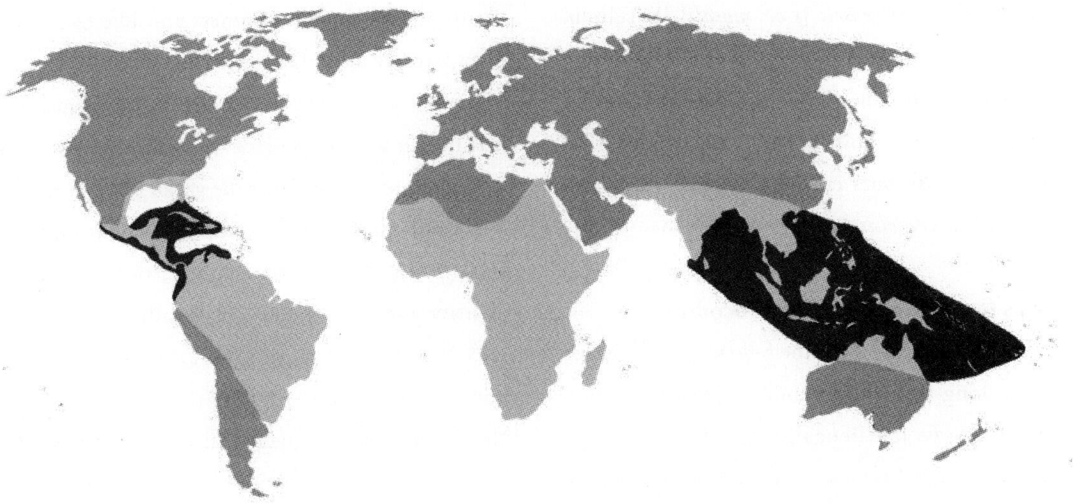

Figure 7 World distribution of Order Crocodilia. Map Wikipedia Commons 2007 (after data from Cogger and Zweifel 1998)

became acquainted with crocodiles and undoubtedly began importing their native names into Indo-Aryan. For this reason, an etymological study of the vernacular names of crocodiles can help answer the vexing question of the language family to which the chief idiom of the Harappans belonged. At the current time, there are three possibilities: (1) Dravidian, (2) Austro-Asiatic, (3) and an unknown substratum. As the following analysis shows, the most important words for 'crocodile' in South Asian languages (except for the admittedly unclear Sanskrit *makara-* and its cognates) have a Dravidian etymology. Austro-Asiatic, on the other hand, does not seem to have any relation to the terms for 'crocodile' used more widely in South Asia. There is only one clearly Austro-Asiatic term.

Proto-Muṇḍa **tajan* or **tajal* 'crocodile'

The only native Austro-Asiatic word for 'crocodile', recorded by Pinnow (1959: 73 no. 31, 263 no. 336, 286 no. 374b, 349 no. 495g), is **tajan* or **tajal* '(broad-headed) crocodile': Santali *tajan*, Muṇḍari *tajan*, Ho *taen*, Sora (Savara) *'tañal-ən*. This word has apparently not been borrowed by Indo-Aryan or Dravidian languages.

Sanskrit terms for 'crocodile'

[Monier-]Williams' *English-Sanskrit dictionary* (1851: 14a and 147a) s.v. 'alligator' lists Sanskrit *nakra-*, *grāha-* and *kumbhīra-*; for 'crocodile', it lists *nakra-*, *kumbhīra-*, *ālāsya-* ['poison-mouthed'], *mahāmukha-* ['big-mouthed'], *dvidhāgati-* ['one who goes in two ways, amphibios'], *asidanta-* ['having sword-like teeth'; actually the word is *asidaṃṣṭra-*], *jalaśūkara-* ['the boar of water'], and *jalahastin-* ['the elephant of water']. The last seven terms (from *ālāsya-* onwards) are rarely occurring descriptive terms that do not require further study. Important terms missing in these two lists are Sanskrit *makara-*, *ghaṇṭika-*, and *śiśumāra-*.

Terms for the marsh crocodile and the saltwater crocodile

According to Daniel (1983: 10), the marsh crocodile is called *muggar* [i.e., *magar*] in Hindi, Gujarati and Marathi, *kuji khumbhira* in Oriya, *kuhmir* [i.e., *kumhīr*] in Bengali, *muthalai* [i.e., *mutalai*] in Tamil, *muthala* [i.e., *mutala*] and *cheengkani* [i.e., *cīṅkaṇṇi* 'alligator, crocodile', literally 'bleary-eyed', Gundert 1872: 367a] in Malayalam, *mossalay* [i.e., *mosaḷe*] in Kannada, and *moseli* [i.e., *mosali*] in Telugu. According to Daniel (1983: 13), the local names for the saltwater crocodile are the same as those for the marsh crocodile in most Indian languages. In Oriya, however, the saltwater crocodile goes by a different name (*Baula kumbhira*).

Terms for the long-snouted crocodile

Daniel (1983: 15-16) lists the following local names for the long-snouted crocodile: "Hindi *Gharial*; Bengali *Mecho* [cf. Bengali *māch* 'fish'] *kumhir*; Oriya *Thantia kumhira*: male *Ghadiala*, female *Thantiana* [cf. Oriya *thuṃṭi*, *thuthi* 'snout, chin', *theṇṭa*, *thaṇṭa*, 'beak', *tuṇḍa*, *tuṇḍi*, *ṭuṇḍa*, *ṭhuṇḍi*, *ṭhuṇṭhi* 'lip, chin, beak' in Turner 1966 no. 5853 and Sanskrit *tuṇḍa* 'beak, trunk, snout']; Bihari *Nakar*, *Bahsoolia nakar*; Nepali *Chimpta gohi*, *Lamthora gohi* [Nepali, Oriya and Marathi *gohi* 'crocodile, alligator' < Sanskrit *godhikā-* < *godhā-* 'lizard', Turner 1966: no. 4286 and below]."

Sanskrit *gōdhā-* or *gōdhikā-* 'monitor lizard, gecko; crocodile'

Taking up the last-mentioned (and rather marginal) etymon first, Sanskrit *gōdhā-* f. and its cognates are sometimes used for 'crocodile' in modern Indian languages. Primarily, however, the word means 'lizard'. This topic has been thoroughly studied by Lüders (1942: 23-50) in his fairly exhaustive examination of all instances (since the Rigveda) of Old and Middle Indo-Aryan literature where *gōdhā-* is attested. Lüders comes to the conclusion that most occurences describe the monitor lizard (*Varanus monitor* = *Varanus bengalensis*), often mistakenly called 'iguana' or 'leguan'. When *gōdhā-* or *gōdhikā-* appears as an aquatic animal (cf. Amarakoṣa 1,10,22), Lüders (1942: 33-34) suggests that it refers to the water monitor (*Varanus salvator*), which in the past may have been more widely found across the Indian subcontinent than today. With the exception of the desert lizard (*Varanus griseus*), other monitor lizards are also good swimmers and like to stay in the water (see also Hawkins ed. 1986: 357-360 and 378-379). Lüders (1942: 35-36) further points out that the diminutive *gōdhikā-* f. obviously refers to a smaller lizard, in particular the gecko (*Lacerta gecko*). This word appears in the compounds *gṛha-gōdhikā-* and *āgāra-gōdhikā-* 'house lizard'; the lexica even identify *gōdhā-* as gecko (Halāyudha 2,79 *godhā muśalikā proktā*; Vaijayantī 150,51 *godhā musalī*). Lüders' conclusions support the evidence of the Neo-Indo-Aryan languages, in which the majority of cognates (see Turner 1966: no. 4286) carry either the meaning of 'iguana' or 'lizard' (other singular glosses include 'venomous lizard', 'chameleon', 'an animal like a snake', or 'a long insect with two horns in front and able to contract itself'). Turner records the meaning 'crocodile' or 'alligator' only for Nepalese *gohi/guhi* and Marathi *gohi*, but Lüders (1942: 34) also adds Urdu *gōh/gōdhi* as an Indo-Aryan loanword in Kannada. Lüders (1942: 35) does not deny that the word *godhā* has been used to denote 'crocodile' in some Neo-Indo-Aryan languages. He points out that the monitor lizard is a large animal that lives near water like the crocodile, but he emphatically stresses that *godhā* never had the meaning of 'crocodile' in the older literature.

Lüders (1942: 43-50) argues at length that *godhā-* should be parsed as *go-dhā-* (with the meaning 'cow-sucker'). He takes the word to be of Indo-European origin, approving of Fick's etymology that links it to Latin *būfō* 'toad'. This hypothesis is fully endorsed by Paul Thieme (1965: 211-212). Turner takes 'cow-sucker' to be a popular etymology, with the more original form preserved in Sanskrit *gōlaka-* m. 'lizard' (cf. *gṛhagōlaka-* m. 'house lizard', attested in Mārkaṇḍeya-Purāṇa 15,24), *gōlikā-* f. 'lizard' (which appears as a variant reading for *gōdhikā-* in Bāṇa's Kādambarī, as well as in the compound *gṛhagōlikā-*, *gṛhagaulikā-*, *gṛhakōlikā-*, etc.; see Lüders 1942: 36 n.1), and *gaulī-* f. 'lizard' (in the Pañcatantra). This latter etymon (Turner 1966: no. 4324) comes from

Ὁ Γάγγης ὁ παρὰ τοῖς Ἰνδοῖς ῥέων,

Κροκοδείλων δὲ παιδεύει διπλᾶ γένη· καὶ τὰ μὲν αὐτῶν ἥκιστα βλάπτει, τὰ δὲ παμβορώτατα σαρκῶν ἐσθίει καὶ ἀφειδέστατα· καὶ ἔχουσιν ἐπ' ἄκρου τοῦ ῥύγχους ἐξοχήν, ὡς κέρας. Τούτοις [τοι] καὶ πρὸς τὰς τῶν κακούργων τιμωρίας ὑπηρέταις χρῶνται· τοὺς γὰρ ἐπὶ τοῖς μεγίστοις τῶν ἀδικημάτων ἑαλωκότας ῥίπτουσιν αὐτοῖς, καὶ δημίου δέονται ἥκιστα.

Figure 8 Aelianus (N. An. 12,41) on the two kinds of crocodile in the Ganges (after Jacobs 1832: 283)

Dravidian (DEDR no. 1338), as Turner as well as Burrow and Emeneau both note, and Lüders (1942: 36 n. 1) already acknowledges:

Tamil *kavuḷi, kauḷi-* 'lizard'
Malayalam *gauḷi* 'lizard, especially *Lacerta gecko*'
Kannada *gavuḷi, gavaḷi* 'house lizard'
Kodagu *gavḷi* 'big lizard'
Tulu *gauḷi* 'a kind of lizard'
Telugu *gauḷi* 'lizard'
Gondi *gūwhal* 'a poisonous lizard smaller than the monitor', *goyhal* 'iguana'
? Brahui *glūnṭ, gulōnṭ, klōnṭ*, in *garrī-glūnṭ*, etc. 'rough lizard' (*garrī* 'mangy'); *tāzī-glūnṭ*, etc. 'common lizard (*tāzī* 'greyhound, swift animal').

Hindi *ghaṛiyāl* m.

Gavial, the current name in zoological literature, is a corrupt form of Hindi *ghaṛiyāl*, probably due to clerical error (Yule and Burnell 1903: 366; Crooke 1906: 110-111; Lüders 1942: 35).

Hindi *ghaṛiyāl* has cognates in other Neo-Indo-Aryan languages as follows (Turner 1966: no. 4422), with all except the Sindhi term denoting the long-snouted crocodile:

Sindhi *ghaṛyālu* m. 'long-snouted porpoise' [i.e., 'Indus river dolphin']
Nepali *ghaṛiyāl*
Assamese and Bengali *ghāṛiyāl*
Oriya *ghaṛiāḷa*
Hindi *ghaṛyāl, ghaṛiyāl, ghariār*

The name is explained as follows: "Adult male with a large pot-like cartilaginous mass on the tip of the snout, hence the name Gharial (*ghara* = pot)" (Daniel 1983: 15; see also Maskey and Mishra 1982: 185 on the belief in its potency, one of the main reasons why this animal has been hunted). As early as Aelianus (c. 170-235 CE), this distinctive feature of the gharial has been known (De natura animalium 12,41): "The Ganges which flows in the country of the Indian people ... breeds two kinds of crocodiles [κροκοδείλων]; one of these is not at all hurtful [ἥκιστα βλάπτει] ... and they have a horn-like prominence on the tip of the nostril [καὶ ἔχουσιν ἐπ' ἄκρου τοῦ ῥύγχους ἐξοχήν, ὡς κέρας]" (Yule and Burnell 1903: 14a) (Figure 8). It is thus quite likely that the ghariyal was named after this feature.

Hindi *ghaṛā* m. 'pot' has cognates in many Neo-Indo-Aryan languages (in West Pahari, Bengali and Oriya the word is identical with Hindi). These can be traced back to Sanskrit *ghaṭa-* m. 'pot' (first attested in Sūtra texts and Manu) and its diminutive *ghaṭaka-* m. 'pot' (first attested in Somadeva's Kathāsaritsāgara) (Turner 1966: no. 4406). In the opinion of Manfred Mayrhofer (2001: III, 167), the etymology of this word attested rather late in Indo-Aryan has not been satisfactorily explained.

This explanation of Hindi *ghaṛiyāl* seems to be corroborated by the fact that another word used for the gharial, Sanskrit *kumbhīra-*, can likewise be derived from a word denoting 'pot', namely Sanskrit *kumbha-* m. (see also the lexically attested *kumbhin-* m. 'crocodile', literally 'one having a pot'). Sanskrit *kumbhá-* m. is attested as early as the Rigveda, and is related to Avestan *χumba-* 'pot' and probably Greek κύμβη f. 'drinking vessel', κύμβος m. 'dish, bowl' (Mayrhofer 1992: I, 370). That said, these 'pot' explanations seem to be folk etymologies. In both cases, the gharial's name does indeed appear to owe its origin to the "protuberance at the muzzle" (Yule and Burnell 1903: 366b), but with a different etymology.

As the nasalized ā of the first syllable in Assamese and Bengali *ghā̃ṛiyāl* 'alligator' confirms, these words are related to Sanskrit *ghaṇṭika-* m. 'gavial', which is attested c. 1550 CE in Bhāvamiśra's Bhāvaprakāśa (Turner 1966: no. 4422; McGregor 1993: 284a; Mayrhofer 2001: III, 168). Mayrhofer (2001: III, 168) argues that the etymology of Sanskrit *ghaṇṭika-* m. 'gavial' has not been sufficiently explained. But Turner (1966: no. 4422) is undoubtedly right in linking *ghaṇṭika-* with Assamese *ghā̃ṭ* 'protuberance on the snout of an alligator'.

Turner (1966 and 1985: no. 4420) connects Assamese *ghā̃ṭ* 'protuberance on the snout of an alligator' with the following words:

- Sanskrit *ghaṇṭikā-* f. 'uvula'
- Lahnda *ghaṇḍī* f. 'adam's apple' (in Awāṇkārī dialect also 'soft palate')
- Panjabi *ghaṇḍ* m., *ghaṇḍī* f. 'adam's apple'
- West Pahari (Koṭgaṭhī dialect) *ghàṇḍu* 'throat'
- Hindi *ghāṃṭī* f. 'throat, adam's apple, uvula, soft palate'
- Nepali *ghāṃṭi* 'throat' (loanword from Hindi)
- Gujarati *ghāṃṭɔ* m. 'throat', *ghāṃṭī* f. 'adam's apple'
- Marathi *ghāṃṭī* f. 'throat, adam's apple, larynx

According to Turner, etymon no. 4420 "belongs to the group listed s.v. *kaṇṭhá-*." I agree with the etymological connection, although I do not accept his etymology for Sanskrit *kaṇṭhá-* 'throat' (Turner 1966: no. 2680) or his conflation of this word with the other etyma in no. 2680. In my opinion, the word **ghaṇṭa-*, *ghaṇḍa-* 'throat, adam's apple' (mentioned above) and the word *gaṇḍa-* 'goitre, boil, bodily protuberance' (mentioned below) semantically match Sanskrit *kaṇṭhá-*, which seems to have originally referred to 'throat' rather than to 'neck'. The following cognates with these meanings are listed in Turner 1966: no. 2680a:

- Sanskrit *kaṇṭhá-* m. 'throat, neck' (since Śatapatha-Brāhmaṇa)
- Pali *kaṇṭha-* m. 'throat, neck'
- Prakrit *kaṃṭha-* m. 'neck'
- Gypsy (Palestinian dialect) *kand* 'throat'
- Gawarbati and Savi *khaṇṭi* 'throat'
- Lahnda (Awāṇkārī dialect) *kadhlī* 'neck-strap'
- West Pahari (Bhalesī dialect) *kaṇṭh* m. 'collar of shirt', *kaṇṭhi* f. 'sheep with a black neck'
- Kumaoni (Gaṅgoī dialect) *kānⁱ* 'neck' (Turner alternatively derives this word from Sanskrit *skandhá-*)
- Oriya *kaṇṭhā* 'throat'
- Hindi (poetic) *kāṃṭhā* m. 'throat'
- Marathi *kāṃṭheṃ* n. 'neck'
- Sinhalese *kaṭa* 'throat, mouth',
- Sikalgari *kaṇḍa* 'neck' (Turner notes that this word has been contaminated by Sanskrit *skandhá-*)

It appears that both Assamese *ghā̃ṭ* 'protuberance on the snout of an alligator' and the words for 'throat' that Turner connects with it are related to Sanskrit *gaṇḍá-* m. 'goitre' (attested since the Aitareya-

Brāhmaṇa), 'boil' (attested since Suśruta) and *gaṇḍi-* m. 'goitre or bronchocele' (Wilson 1819). These have the following cognates in Middle and Neo-Indo-Aryan (Turner 1966 and 1985: no. 3997; note that I have omitted unrelated words from his list):

Pāli *gaṇḍa-* m. 'swelling, boil, abscess'
Prakrit *gaṃḍa-* m. n. 'goitre, boil'
Sindhi *gani* f. 'hump of bullock', *ganri* f. 'bubo', (Kacchī dialect) *gaṇḍho* m. 'swelling resulting from a contusion',
Lahnda *gannh* m. 'boil'
Panjabi *gann* m. 'protuberance round navel', *gannī* f. 'swelling on eyelid'
West Pahari (Bhiḍḷàī subdialect of Bhadrawāhī dialect) *gaṇḍ* n. 'infectious ulcer of sheep and goats', (Jaunsārī dialect) *gān* 'mumps'
Kumaoni *gān* 'goitre', (Gaṅgoī dialect) *gāṇ* 'hump', *gāṇi* 'testicle'
Nepali *gāṃṛ* 'goitre'
Assamese *gāṃr* 'boil'
Bengali *gāṃṛ* 'protuberance round navel'
Sinhalese *gaḍuva* 'boil, abscess, *gaḍageḍiya* 'boils and pustules', (Maldivian dialect) *ganḍu* 'ulcer, swelling'

For the following cognates, Turner reconstructs **gaḍḍa-* as the protoform instead of Sanskrit *gaṇḍa-*:

Kashmiri *gaḍur*ᵘ m. 'goitre, bronchocele' (Turner alternatively derives this from Sanskrit *gaḍula-*; see below)
Hindi *gaḍḍā* m. 'lump, swelling, boil'

As Turner suggests, the following two lemmata (Turner 1966: no. 3977 and 3978) are undoubtedly also related:

(1) Sanskrit *gaḍu-* m. 'excrescence on neck, goitre, hump on back' (Kātyāyana's vārttika 3 on Pāṇini 2,2,35); cf. also *gaḍu-kaṇṭha-* 'having a swelling on throat, goitrous' and *gaḍu-śiras-* 'having a swelling on the head' in Patañjali's Mahābhāṣya on Kātyāyana l.c., *gaḍula-* 'humpbacked' in Ṣaḍviṃśa-Brāhmaṇa 4,4, and *gaḷu-nas-* or *gaḷū-nas-* 'having a swelling on his nose', as an epithet of Ārkṣākāyana Śālāvatya in Jaiminīya-Brāhmaṇa 1,316; 1,337; 1,338, as well as Jaiminīya-Upaniṣad-Brāhmaṇa 1,38,1 (Mayrhofer 1992: I, 458)
Pali *gaḷa-* 'boil, swelling (?)'
Sindhi *gaṛhu* m. 'boil, abscess'
Lahnda (Awāṇkārī dialect) *gàṛ* 'boil, abscess'
Panjabi *gaṛ* m. 'boil, abscess'
Bengali and Oriya *gaṛu* 'swelling of any gland, goitre, hump on back'
Marathi *gaḷūṃ* n. 'boil'
(2) Sanskrit *gaḍulá-* 'humpbacked' (Ṣaḍviṃśa-Brāhmaṇa 4,4), *gaḍura-* 'humpbacked' (lexical), Sanskrit *gaṇḍula-* 'humpbacked' (lexical)
Pali *gaṇḍula-* 'humpbacked'
Khowar *gurūḷi* 'goitre, goitrous'
Kashmiri *gaḍ°r*ᵘ 'goitrous', *gaḍur*ᵘ m. 'goitre' (Turner alternatively derives this from **gaḍḍa-*; see above)
Oriya *gaṛuḷa*, *gaṛura* 'humpbacked'
Sinhalese *gaḍula-* 'humpbacked'

Lüders (1942: 56 n.3) has connected Sanskrit *gaṇḍa-* 'swelling' with the name of another animal distinguished by a big excrescence on its nose, namely the rhinoceros. Mayrhofer (1992: I, 459) dismisses this explanation as a folk etymology. Nonetheless, Mayrhofer (2001: III, 151) does consider that the following Indo-Aryan names for 'rhinoceros' (Turner 1966 and 1985: no. 4000) were possibly borrowed from a non-Aryan source:

Sanskrit *gaṇḍa-* m., (Śukasaptati), *gaṇḍaka-*m.

(Bāṇa's Kādambarī), *gaṇḍa-mṛga-* m., *gaṇḍāṅga-* m. (lexical)
Pali *gaṇḍaka-* m.
Prakrit *gaṃḍaya-* m.
Assamese *gā̃ṛ*
Oriya *gaṇḍā*

With a protoform **gayaṇḍa-* (Turner), ? hypersanskritism < **geṇḍa-*:

Kashmiri *kö̃ḍ* m.
Sindhi *geṇḍo* m. (according to Turner, this is a loanword on account of g-)
Panjabi *gaiṃḍā* m., *gaiṃḍī* f.
West Pahari *geṇḍɔ mɪrg*
Nepali *gaiṃṛo*
Hindi *gaiṃṛā* m.
Gujarati *geṃḍɔ* m., *geṃḍī* f.
Marathi *geṃḍā* m.
Maldivian *genḍā* (explained to be a loanword from Hindi)
Cf. also Tamil *kāṇṭā-mirukam, kaṇṭakam* (Winslow et al. 1888: 1143b) and Malayalam *kāṇṭā-mṛgam* 'rhinoceros'

The phonetic differences between Sanskrit *ghaṇṭa-* 'throat, adam's apple, uvula', Assamese *ghā̃ṭ* 'protuberance on the snout of an alligator', Sanskrit *gaṇḍá-* m. 'goitre' and the related Indo-Aryan words meaning 'swelling (of glands), boil, tumour' and 'hump on the back', and Sanskrit *kaṇṭha-* 'throat' can be explained by the supposition that they are ultimately loanwords from Dravidian, which does not distinguish between aspirated and unaspirated or between unvoiced and voiced consonant phonemes. In Proto-Dravidian, stops were word-initially unvoiced, but became voiced or spirantized between vowels and voiced after nasals (unless they were geminated, in which case nazalization was usually afterwards lost).

An excellent Proto-Dravidian etymology for these words is offered by the root **kaṇṭṭV-*, which is attested in all sub-branches from Tamil to Kurukh (DEDR 1148):

Tamil *kaṭṭu* 'to harden, consolidate, congeal, coagulate, be congested (as the throat), swell (as a boil, tumour); n. boil, abscess, tumour; firmness, strength
kaṭṭi 'clod, lump, concretion, anything hardened, coagulated, boil, abscess, enlarged spleen, foetus'
Malayalam *kaṭṭa* 'lump, mass, clod', *kaṭṭi* 'what is condensed, solid, ingot', *kaṇṭi* 'lump, concretion', *keṇṭa* 'a hypochondriacal disease'
Kota *kaṭy* 'solid lump', *geṇḍ* 'round lump or ball (food, butter), growth in abdomen'
Toda *koṭ-* '(blister) to form, swell'
Telugu *kaṭṭu* 'to gather, collect, become hard', *gaḍḍa* 'lump, mass, clod, clot; boil, ulcer; island'
Gondi *kaṭ* 'spleen', *gaḍa* 'clod', *kaṭṭ-* '(fruits) to form', (Koya dialect) *gaṭ pāpe* 'adam's apple' (*pāpe* 'throat')

An ancient derivative seems to be Proto-Dravidian **kaṇṭṭal, *kaṇṭṭay* 'bulbous root, bulb-like fruit' (DEDR 1171).

Sanskrit *kumbhīra-* m.

The other words for the gharial that at first sight seems to be derived from Sanskrit *kumbhá-* 'pot' (Turner 1966: no. 3317; also see above) are:

Sanskrit *kumbhīra-* m 'crocodile, long-nosed alligator' (attested since the Mahābhārata), *kumbhīla-* m. (lexical), *kumbhin-* m. (lexical)
Pali *kumbhīla-* m. 'Gangetic crocodile'
Prakrit *kuṃbhīla-* m. 'alligator'
Nepalese *kubir* 'crocodile'
Assamese *kumbhīr* 'alligator, crocodile'
Bengali *kumbhīr, kumīr* 'alligator, crocodile'

Oriya *kumbhīra, kimbhīra, kumbhīḷa* 'crocodile'
Hindi *kumhīr* m. 'long-nosed alligator'
Marathi *kuṃbhīr*
Sinhalese *kimbulā, kimbuḷā* 'crocodile'

This etymon seems to be parallel to that of *ghaṇṭika-* (from *ghaṇṭa-* 'swelling on the long nose of the crocodile'), in that it appears to be etymologically connected with Old Indo-Aryan **kumbha-* 'elephant's frontal globe' (in Sinhalese *kumbutalaya*; Turner 1966: no. 3314), *kúmba-* m. n. 'thick end (of a bone or club)' (attested since the Taittirīya-Samhitā; Turner 1966: no. 3307), **kubba* and **khubba* 'hump on back, any projection on the body' (distributed widely in Neo-Indo-Aryan in Turner 1966: no. 3301 **kubba*; see also no. 3300 Sanskrit *kubja-* 'humpbacked'; for **khubba* see no. 3904 and 3903 **khubja-* 'humpbacked').

One also finds an excellent Dravidian etymology here as well; that is, Proto-Dravidian **kumppV* 'to form into a heap or pile, heap up, gather, increase, swell, be full; heap, pile, mound, hump of a bull, protuberance, swelling, knob', which is attested throughout the language family from Tamil to Kurukh and Malto (in the DEDR divided into three related etyma):

(1) = DEDR 1731
Tamil *kuppam, kuppal, kuppai* 'heap (as of manure), mound, multitude'
Malayalam *kuppa* 'heap of dirt or refuse'
Kota *kip* 'heap of weeds, rubbish'
Toda *kïp* 'rubbish'
Kannada *kuppe, guppe, koppal* 'heap, pile, dung-hill', *kuppu* 'to heap up'
Kodagu *kuppï* 'a dropping of dung'
Tulu *kuppè, guppè, kippè, kompa, kompè* 'heap'
Telugu *kuppa* 'heap, pile, dungheap', *guppu* 'to place in heaps or lots', *kopparamu, kopparincu* 'to increase, rise, swell', *goppu* 'small elevation in a field', *gubbali* 'mountain, hill'
Kolami *kupp kal-* 'to gather'
Parji *kuppa* 'stack, mound', *kopp-* 'to be full', *koppa* 'small hillock'
Gadaba *kuppā* 'heap', *kop-* 'to be full', *kope* 'hill'
Gondi *kuppa, kupa, guppa* 'heap, stack', *gubbal* 'hillock', *kupāhanā, kupā kiyānā* 'to gather, collect'
Konda *kupa* 'heap (of grain)', *kumba* 'small conical heap', *koparam* 'hump of a bull'
Pengo *kupa* 'heap, stack', *kupli* 'mound of earth', *gomoṇ* 'hump of ox'
Manda *kupa* 'heap', *kupki* 'to fill', *gupeṛ* 'hump of ox'
Kui *kupa* 'hillock', *kopa* 'hump, cow's hump'
Kuwi *kuppa* 'stack', *kūpa* 'mound', *kupli* 'hillock', *gu'u* 'hump of ox', *kuppu ānai* 'to overfill'
Kurukh *xoppnā, xoprnā* 'to form into a pile, heap up'
Malto *qope* 'heap, pile; to heap, pile up'
(2) = DEDR 1741
Tamil *kumpam, kumpal, kumpi, kumpu, kuvavu, kuvai, kuvāl, kūvai* 'heap, pile, collection, assemblage, group, mound', *kumi, kuvi, kuvavu, kūppu* 'to heap up, be heaped up, piled up conically, accumulate, hoard up, gather, crowd'
Malayalam *kumi* 'heap (as of rice), stack, pile', *kūmpal* 'heap', *kumiyuka, kumikka, kumekka, kuvika, kuvikka, kūmpikka* 'to heap, heap up, be heaped together, assembled'
Kota *gub* 'group of people', *gubl* 'crowd, herd'
Toda *kubïl* 'herd', *kupy* 'crowd, herd, bunch'
Kannada *gumi, gummi, gummu, gumme, gumpu* 'heap, crowd, multitude' *gubaru, guburu* 'thickness (of foliage), crowdedness'
Tulu *gumpu, gumi* 'heap, flock, crowd, multitude, group'
Telugu *kuva, kuvva* 'heap, pile, *gumpu, gumi* 'crowd, multitude, group', *guburu, gumuru*

'thickness (of foliage), cluster'
Kolami *gum* 'assembly', *gum er-* to assemble'
Naiki *ghuma er-* 'to assemble'
Parji *kum-* 'to heap on to'
Gondi *gum ki-* 'to assemble, collect'
Konda *kumba* 'a small heap conical in shape', *kuma* 'heap'
Kuwi *gombu, gōmbu, gumomi* 'heap', *gumbra, kumbra* 'clump of trees'

(3) = DEDR 1743, cf. also the Pengo and Manda words for 'hump of ox' above
Tamil *kumiẓ, kumiẓi* 'knob (as of wooden sandals), boss, stud, pommel, hump of an ox', *kuppi* 'ferrule (e.g., on scabbard, horn of ox)'
Malayalam *kumiẓ* 'knob, pommel; mushroom', *kuppi* 'brass knob on tip of bullock's horn'
Kannada *gubbi* 'knob, protuberance', *kuppu, guppu* 'an abnormal globular excrescence of the body', *gubāru* 'swelling'
Tulu *gubbi, gubbè* 'stud, ornamental knob, button'
Telugu *gubaka* 'knob, boss, stud', *gubba* 'knob, boss, stud, protuberance, woman's breast, *guburu* 'protuberance', *kuppe* 'knob'
Konda *koparam* 'hump of bullock'

Proto-Dravidian ***mōc-alay / *moc-alay* 'crocodile'**

From DEDR 4952, one finds:

Tamil *mutalai, mutaḷai, mucali* 'crocodile'
Malayalam *mutala*
Kota *mocaḷ*
Kannada *mosaḷe, masaḷe*
Koḍagu *mosale*
Tulu *mosaḷe, mudale, mudaḷe, mūdale*
Telugu *mosali*
Kolami (Kin.) *moseli*
Parji *mōca*
Koṇḍa *mōdi, mūdi*
Kurukh *bōca*
Malto *boce*
Indo-Aryan loans from Dravidian:
Sanskrit *mācala-* 'crocodile', *musalī* 'alligator, house-lizard' (both only lexically attested)
Prakrit *muduga* 'a kind of crocodile' (*grāhaviśeṣa-*)

This Proto-Dravidian etymon may be derived from a verbal root preserved only in North Dravidian **mōc-* 'to cut (meat), to cut up into convenient pieces any object too large for use' (DEDR 5130). This verb, which describes quite well what a crocodile does after catching a victim that is too large to be directly swallowed, seems to be related to the Proto-Dravidian verbal root **mōk-/mokk-/*mok-* 'to eat, to eat greedily in large mouthfuls, eat voraciously, devour, gobble, swallow' (DEDR 5127 + 4897). Tamil has derived *moci-* 'to eat' from this root.

This word for 'crocodile' may originally have been a compound involving two roots, the latter being Proto-Dravidian **alacu*, **alay* 'to shake or agitate in water (e.g., to rinse clothes or vegetables)' (DEDR 246), which is undoubtedly related to the root **alaṅku/*alakku*, **alay* 'to move, shake, wave, go to and fro for an object, roam, wander' (DEDR 240). This etymological interpretation, however, necessitates a slight revision of Krishnamurti's Proto-Dravidian reconstruction (2003: 13, 531), which is **mōc-V-ḷ- / *moc-V-ḷ-*. The compound nicely complements the first verb by describing the characteristic behaviour of the marsh and saltwater crocodile noted above (i.e., victims caught on land are dragged to the water and swallowed whole, while large prey is torn to pieces by means of twisting and shaking motions).

***Mutalai* and other terms for 'crocodile' in Old Tamil texts**

Old Tamil provides the oldest source material for

the Dravidian language. The following references to crocodile in Caṅkam literature (Lehmann and Malten 1992) are quoted here in an alphabetical order of the texts in which they appear. When available, I have added existing translations; though these are not always literally accurate, they do provide additional context.

Aiṅkuṟunūṟu 5, 4-5 *mutalaip pōttu muḻu mīṉ ārum / taṇ tuṟai yūraṉ*
"... a cool bay where a male crocodile eats fish whole" (Hart 1975: 181)

Aiṅkuṟunūṟu 24,2 *piḷḷai tiṉṉu mutalaitt avaṉ ūr*
"and crocodiles that eat their young live in his town" (Hart 1980: 19)

Aiṅkuṟunūṟu 41,1-2 *taṉ pārpput tiṉṉum aṉpiṉ mutalaiyoṭu / veṇ pūm poykaitt avaṉ ūr eṉpa ...*
"People say that in his region there is a tank in which there are unloving crocodiles which devour their young ones and there are white flowers too." (Jotimuttu 1984: 177)

Akanāṉūṟu 3,1 *iruṅ kaḻi mutalai mēen tōl aṉṉa*
"like the hide on the crocodile of the great salt river"

Akanāṉūṟu 18,3 *karāan tuñcuṅ kall uyar maṟi cuḻi*
"whirlpool rising and dashing against rocks upon which crocodiles are basking"

Akanāṉūṟu 72,7-9 *āṟē arumara piṉavē yāṟē / cuṭṭunarp paṉikkuñ cūr uṭai mutalaiya / kaḻaimāy nīttam kal porut iraṅka*
"The paths there are difficult. In the river are terrible crocodiles that men shiver to think of. It roars against rocks with its torrent and breaks the poles of boatmen." (Hart 1980: 114)

Akanāṉūṟu 80,1-2 *koṭun tāṇ mutalaiyoṭu kōṭṭu mīn vaḻaṅkum / iruṅ kaḻi*
"great salt river where the fish with a horn (i.e., sharks) live together with the bent-legged crocodile"

Akanāṉūṟu 301,6-7 *nīr vāḻ mutalai āvitt aṉṉa / āṟai vēynta arai vāyc cakaṭattu*
"in a rush-mat thatched wagon, the chamber door of which gaped like the crocodile that lives in water"

Kalittokai 103 (102),17-21 *peru muraṇ muṉpiṉ pukal ēṟu pala peytu / arimāvum parimāvum kaḷiṟum karāmum / peru malai viṭar akatt oruṅk uṭaṉ kuḻīi / paṭu maḻai āṭum varai yakam pōlum / koṭi naṟai cūḻnta toḻūu*
"And many a belligerent bull of acclaimed prowess; a cloud of dust-smoke rose up therein, making the arena look like a cavern in a massive hill covered with rain-clouds, wherein are huddled up a lion, horse, elephant and an alligator." (Murugan 1999: 441)

Kuriñcippāṭṭu 256-257 *oṭuṅk iruṅ kuṭṭatt aruñ cuḻi vaḻaṅkuṅ / koṭun tāṅ mutalaiyum iṭaṅkaruṅ kāramum*
"The black and bent-legged crocodile that lies in wait in whirlpool's dreaded waters deep, the alligator..." (Chelliah 1962: 215)

Kuṟuntokai 324,1-2 *koṭuṅ kāṉ mutalaik kōḷ val ērrai / vaḻi vaḻakk arukkuṅ kānalam perun turai*
"Skilled at taking their prey, crocodiles with curving legs keep men away from the grove-encircled waters." (Hart 1980: 80)
"bent leg crocodile taking strong male / way wander- tearing- seashore-grove[am] big ghat by the big ghat of the seashore grove, where the

murderous, strong male of the bent-legged crocodile tears apart what wanders on the way" (Wilden 2010: II, 727)

Malaipaṭukaṭām 90-91 *irai tērnt ivaruṅ koṭun tāṉ mutalaiyoṭu / tirai paṭak kuẓinta kall akaẓ kiṭaṅkin*

"Now hear me when I speak of the king's old town far famed. Round it are moats with water deep In which live bent-legged crocodiles that seek Their prey, and walls that seem like sky-high hills." (Chelliah 1962: 297)

Malaipaṭukaṭām 211-212 *uṟavuk kaḷiṟu karakkum iṭaṅkar oṭuṅki / yiraviṉ aṉṉa viru ṭūṅku varaippiṉ*

"There is a path along the river wild that runs through forests as dark as the night in which live crocodiles that swallow up great elephants. There too are whirlpools, ponds and pits. To walk along this path is hard." (Chelliah 1962: 305)

Naṟṟiṇai 287,6 *nāma mutalai naṭuṅku pakai yañcāṉ /*

"fear crocodile shiver- enmity fear-not-he without fear of the shivering enmity of the fear[-ful] crocodile

[note 988: *naṭuṅku pakai*: here actually the Tamil is imprecise (as is poetic licence); in fact the enmity should be one that makes shiver]" (Wilden 2008: II, 633)

Naṟṟiṇai 292,7-8 *karuṅ kaṟ kāṉ yāṟṟ aruñ cuẓi vaẓaṅkuṅ / karāam pēṇāy iravu variṉ*

"black stone forest river- difficult whirling wandering-alligator esteem-not-you night come-if you who don't care for crocodiles, that roam the difficult whirling of the forest river with black stones" (Wilden 2008: II, 643)

Patiṟṟuppattu 53,8-9 *kōḷ vaṉ mutalaiya kuṇṭu kaṇṇ akaẓi*

"(the fortress has) moats in the depth of which are crocodiles strong at catching (prey)"

Paṭṭiṉappālai 239-242 *talai tavac ceṉṟu taṇpaṇai eṭuppi / veṇ pūk karumpoṭu cen ne ṉīṭi / mā yitaẓk kuvaḷaiyoṭu neytalu mayaṅkik / karāaṅ kalitta kaṇṇ akaṉ poykai*

"The spacious tanks round which once grew the blossom white of the sugar-cane, the yellow rice, the lily long with petals black, and neythal bloom and where the crocodile revelled, are now o'evergrown with argu thick and korai grass. The fields and tanks made waterless are so confused that stag with rugged horns with hinds now freely leap about the place." (Chelliah 1962: 43)

Puṟanāṉūṟu 37,7-10 *karāaṅ kalitta kuṇṭu kaṇṇ akaẓi / iṭaṅkaruṅ kuṭṭattuṭaṉ ṟokk ōṭi / yāmaṅkoḷpavar cuṭar niẓaṟ katūuṅ / kaṭu muraṇ mutalaiya neṭunīr ilañci*

"... you had the force in battle to destroy the ancient capital, with its walls shielded in bronze, its cavernous moats crowded with alligators, its pools of deep water where vicious crocodiles collect in the dark ranges of the bottom and rush up and snap at reflections of the lights that men who are standing guard hold high in the middle of the night! ..." (Hart and Heifetz 1999: 30)

Puṟanāṉūṟu 104,3-4 *tāṭ paṭu ciṉ ṉīrk kaḷiṟ aṭṭu vīẓkkum / īrppuṭaik karāatt aṉṉa veṉṉai*

"You warriors! Take care of yourselves! Let us tell you my lord is like a crocodile who in shallow water muddied by the playing of children from the city, can drag in, bring down, and slaughter an elephant, with the water only knee deep! ..." (Hart and Heifetz 1999: 72)

Puṟanāṉūṟu 283,4 *māṟu koṇ mutalaiyoṭ ūẓ māṟu peyarum*

"... a hungry crocodile for whom a snake is no more than a shrimp ..." (Hart and Heifetz 1999: 167)

There are three words for 'crocodile' in Old Tamil texts. As they are sometimes mentioned together, they have been assumed to represent different species. However, the gharial is not found among the three crocodile species found in South India. Sex and age differences may also be involved (cf. *karāam* and *maṇṇan* below).

(1) *mutalai* (see above).

(2) *iṭaṅkar*. This word does not seem to have cognates in other Dravidian languages; while several etymologies are possible, none are obvious.

(3) *karāam, karām, karā, karavu* 'male crocodile' (Tivākaram: *āṇ mutalai*) (TL 1928 II: 745ab). It is very probable that these words (especially *karāam*) are derived from Sanskrit *grāha-* 'crocodile', as suggested in the *Tamil Lexicon*. An alternative possible etymology is the Proto-Dravidian root *kara* 'to conceal, hide, disguise, lie hidden; to deceive, steal', from which Tamil derives *karavu* 'concealment' (DEDR 1258).

Tivākaram's lexicon (3, 196 *kiñcumāramum iṭaṅkarum karāmum iṅku ivai vaṉmīṉum mutalai ākum*, quoted in *Varalāṟṟu*... 2002 IV: 2180a) mentions two more Tamil words for 'crocodile':

(1) *kiñcumāram* in Jaffna Tamil (attested in the lexicon *Yāẓppāṇattu māṉippāy akarāti*, TL 1938 Suppl. 222b; see below on Sanskrit *śiśumāra-*).

(2) *vaṉmīṉ* (an Indus counterpart will be suggested below, in the final portion of the Indus section).

While no further Tamil items are added under crocodile and alligator by Winslow *et al.* (1888), the following words for Malayalam are given by Zacharias (1933):

(1) *mutala* (see above).

(2) *nakram* (see below).

(3) *cīṅkaṇṇi*. This compound (also *cīkaṇṇi*) literally means 'bleary-eyed'. It is also recorded as belonging to Tamil, but the citation refers to a work by a Tamil who lived in Trivandrum (TL 1929 III: 1473a). The *Malayalam Lexicon* (1985 V: 458) records also *cīṅkaṇṇi-vēṭan* 'crocodile hunter' as a subcaste of the Malavēṭas. (See below, in the final portion of the Indus section, for an Indus counterpart)

(4) *maṇṇan*. According to Gundert (1872: 780a), "a small alligator *taṭākamaddhyē maṇṇan kramēṇa mūtt aṅṅ oru nakram āyi.*" The quotation means: "The *maṇṇan* in the middle of the pool, having gradually grown there, became a *nakra*." As *maṇṇu* means 'earth', the etymology supports the first meaning given by Gundert for *maṇṇan*: "earthy = stupid" (cf. Tamil *maṇṇaṉ* 'clod-hopper, dullard, stupid person' and *maṇ-ṇ-āvāṉ* 'fellow doomed to go to dust, a term of abuse' (TL 1933 V: 3033a)).

In addition, Gundert (1872: 321a) offers an additional Malayalam word for 'alligator' (i.e., 'crocodile'): *kōḷmutala* = *kōḷttala* (*paital āyuḷḷ oru kōḷmutala*, in Kṛṣṇagātha), which he further correlates with Sanskrit *grāha-*.

Sanskrit *mákara-* 'aquatic monster', 'crocodile'

Sanskrit *mákara-* m. (attested since the Vājasaneyi-Samhitā) 'aquatic monster', 'crocodile'; the meaning 'crocodile' is certain

Figure 9 Makara at the gateway of the Bharhut Stupa (c. 100 BCE) (after Kramrisch 1954: Plate 19)

in Pūrṇabhadra's Pañcākhyānaka and Śukasaptati, where a *makara-* with the name *Karālamukha* is found lying on a sandy beach with its mouth open (Lüders 1942: 65)

Pali *makara-* m. 'sea-monster', 'porpoise' (Lüders 1942: 72)

Prakrit *magara-*, *mayara-* m. 'shark', 'aquatic beast'; according to the Jaina text Paṇṇavaṇāsutta (Bombay 1928: 43b-44a), there are two kinds of *magara*: *soṇḍa-magara* and *maṭṭha-magara* (Lüders 1942: 80)[4].

Sinhalese *muvarā*, *mōrā* 'shark', (Maldivian dialect) *miyaru* 'shark'

Hindi and Gujarati *magar* m. 'crocodile'; these are loans from Prakrit or Sanskrit on the basis of the preserved *-g-*; in Hindi also *magar-macch* m. 'crocodile', and, as a loan from Sanskrit, *makar* m. 'a sea-monster; crocodile; the zodiacal sign of Capricorn', Old Hindi (Brajbhāṣā) *makrī* f. 'female crocodile' (McGregor 1993: 780b, 781b)

Sindhi *maṅgar-macho* m. 'whale', *maṅguro* 'a kind of sea fish'; the original meaning seems to have been preserved in Baluchi *māngar* 'crocodile', which is a loanword from Sindhi. Turner (1966: no. 9692) considers this to be a non-Aryan etymon, comparing it to Santali *maṅgaṛ* 'crocodile' (although this may actually be a loan from Indo-Aryan). Bloch (1930: 739) thought that *makara-* might be related to *nakra-* (discussed directly below).

The origin of Sanskrit *mákara-* and its cognates remains unclear. Although New Indo-Aryan *magar* is widely used for the 'broad-headed crocodile' (which includes both the marsh crocodile and the saltwater crocodile), this is not the only meaning of the word: 'shark', 'whale', and 'a kind of fish' are also attested. As the god of the ocean, Varuṇa uses the *makara* as his vehicle. And in the ocean, one finds the saltwater crocodile as well as dolphins, sharks and whales. In Indian art (for a survey, see Vogel 1929-1930; Coomaraswamy 1931 II: 47-56), the *makara* appears as a mythical marine monster with a crocodile-like head (having a snout with many teeth), two or four feet, scales, and a tail (which at its base resembles that of a crocodile, but then ends in a caudal fin). In early iconographic examples, one finds the makara with ears and "horns or fleshy feelers extending backwards from the end of the long snout" (Coomaraswamy 1931 II: 48) (Figure 9). In the Indian zodiac, which is of Near Eastern origin, the *makara* corresponds to Capricorn (which is represented in Mesopotamia as a goat with the tail of a fish). While Kāma, the Indian god of love, is connected with the crocodile, the totem animal of the goddess of love in Hellenistic culture was the dolphin.

Sanskrit *nakra-*, *nākra-* 'crocodile'

Sanskrit *nakra-* m. 'crocodile, alligator' (attested since Manu), *nākra-* 'a kind of aquatic animal' (Vājasaneyi-Samhitā)
Pali *nakka-* m. 'crocodile'
Prakrit *ṇakka-* m. 'crocodile'
Kumaoni *nāko* m. 'crocodile'
Hindi *nākā*, *nākū* m. 'crocodile'
Sinhalese *naku* 'crocodile'

According to Turner, the Kumaoni and Hindi words are associated by popular etymology with *nāk* 'nose' < **nakka-* (cf. Kumaoni *nakku* 'long-nosed'). Following Bloch (1930: 739), Turner (1966: no. 7038), as well as Burrow and Emeneau (1984: no. 3732), derive the Indo-Aryan etymon from Proto-Dravidian: **nek-V-ḷ-* 'crocodile' (DEDR 3732; reconstruction of Krishnamurti 2003: 13, 529), although this Dravidian word is attested rather narrowly:

Kannada *negaḷ*, *negaḷe* 'alligator'
Tulu *negaḷu* 'alligator', *negaru* 'a sea-animal, the vehicle of Varuṇa'
Telugu *negaḍu* 'a polypus or marine animal which entangles swimmers'

This word might be derived from the Proto-Dravidian root **neka-* 'to rise, fly, jump, leap' (DEDR 3730), from the crocodile's habit of jumping to catch its victim.

Sanskrit *śiśumāra-*, *śiṃśumāra-* 'dolphin' and 'crocodile'

Sanskrit *śiṃśumāra-* m. 'South Asian river dolphin' (Rigveda 1,116,18: together with a bull, it is yoked to the chariot of the Aśvins to allow it to proceed by water as well as by land), 'crocodile' (Suśruta, probably already Pañcaviṃśa-Brāhmaṇa 8,6,8-9 and Śāṅkhāyana-Āraṇyaka 12,6), *śiśumāra-*, *śuṃśumāra-* (Vājasaneyi-Saṃhitā), *śiṃśuka-*, *śiśuka-* m. 'an aquatic animal' (Mahābhārata), 'dolphin' (lex.), *śiśūla-* m. 'dolphin' (Rigveda 10,78,6), *śuśulūka-* m. 'a demonic creature' (Rigveda 7,104,22)
Pāli *suṃsumāra-*, *susu-* m., *susukā-* f. 'crocodile', 'dolphin'
Prakrit *suṃsumāra-*, *susumāra-* m. 'crocodile', 'dolphin'
Kashmiri *sūsᵃmār* m. 'dolphin'
Sindhi *sesaru*, *sīsār*, *sīsar* m. 'large crocodile', *sūnsar* (and *bhulan*) 'river dolphin' (Lüders 1942: 70, on the basis of *Fauna of British India, Mammalia*, p. 590)
Lahnda *sisār* m. 'crocodile', *sinsār*, *sansār*, *sīṃsār* 'gharial'
Punjabi *sansār* m. 'crocodile'
Hindi *sūsmār*, *sūs*, *sūis* m. 'dolphin'
Kumaoni *sus*, *suis* 'dolphin'
Nepali *sus*, *suis*, *sos* 'dolphin'
Assamese *χihu*, (Prater 1971: 313:) *hiho*, *seho*, *huh* 'river dolphin'
Bengali *śiśuk*, *śuśuk*, *śiśū* 'dolphin'
Gujarati *sasumārūṃ* n. 'aquatic animal', *susvāṛ*, *susvāḷ*, *sosvāṛ*, *sosvāḷ* f.
'crocodile'
Marathi *susvar*, *susar* f. 'crocodile'
Konkani *śisari* 'crocodile'

Loanwords from Indo-Aryan in Nuristani include:

Waigali *ċuċumī* 'lizard'
Kamdeshi *ċaċᵊm* 'large lizard'

Loanwords from Indo-Aryan in Iranian languages include:

Tajik *šušmār* 'lizard'
Baluchi *šūšmār* 'large lizard'
Ormuri *šūšmār*, *samsīšʳī* 'large lizard'
Pashto *samsara*, *samsāra*, *sīmsār* 'lizard'

Loanwords from Indo-Aryan in Dravidian languages include:

Tamil (Jaffna dialect) *kiñcumāram* 'crocodile'

A very thorough analysis of *śiśumāra-* and its cognates appears in Lüders 1942: 61-81; on pp. 69-70, the meaning of 'crocodile' in Gujarat and the Deccan is supported by the fact that these areas lie outside the distribution of the river dolphin (Turner 1966 and 1985: no. 12426).

The word *śiśumāra-* literally means 'baby-killer'. The transformation of *śiṃśumāra-* into *śiśumāra-* can be explained by folk etymology, but the reverse is difficult to substantiate (as the nasalization in *śiṃśumāra-* is never found in the word *śiśu-* 'child'; see Turner 1966: no. 12476 and Mayrhofer 1996: II, 641). Therefore, it is assumed that the earlier attested *śiṃśumāra-* is the original form, based on some unidentified non-Aryan source, in which case *māra-* might be a contraction from *makara-* (Lüders 1942: 80-81; the *māra-* < *makara-* development was proposed already by Coomaraswamy 1931 II: 52 n. 2). We shall return to this etymology in the section on Indus civilization.

Sanskrit *culukin-*, *culūpin-*, *culumpin-* 'dolphin'

Another, albeit only lexically attested, group of Sanskrit words for 'porpoise, dolphin' (see Somadevasūri in his Yaśastilaka II,216,2 *culukī* = *śisumārī*, and Lüders 1942: 62 n. 2) includes the following: *culukin-*, *culūpin-*, *culumpin-*. There is no doubt that Burrow (1948: 367) has correctly connected these with Sanskrit *ulupin-* and *ulapin-* 'porpoise', deriving them from Dravidian (cf. Kannada *uṇaci-mīnu* and Telugu *ulaca-mīnu*, *uluca* 'porpoise' (DEDR 602))[5]. The ultimate etymology of these words may be the Proto-Dravidian root **cul-* 'to move about, go round, wander about' (DEDR 2693).

Sanskrit *grāha-* 'crocodile', 'snake'

As Lüders (1942: 63) has noted, Sanskrit *grāha-* is an indefinite expression. Literally meaning 'grabber', from the root *gra(b)h-* 'to grab-', it is of Indo-European origin and related to English *grab*. In female gender (*grāhi-*), it occurs as early as the Atharva-Veda (3,2,5; 3,11,1; 6,112,1-2; 6,113,1 and 3; etc.) in the sense of 'seizure' causing illness; the masculine *grāha-* is found in this meaning in the Brāhmaṇa texts (ŚB 3,5,3,25; 3,6,1,25). In classical Sanskrit, *grāha-* denotes a beast of prey living in the water (rivers, lakes, or the sea). Besides 'crocodile', it also means 'shark' and 'water-snake' (Böhtlingk and Roth 1858 II: 862-863).

Referring in chapter 38 to the Indus (i.e., "the Sinthos River, mightiest of the rivers"), the first-century CE Greek text "Circumnavigation of the Red Sea" states: "An indication to those coming from the sea that they are already approaching land in the river's vicinity are the snakes [ὄφεις] that emerge from the depths to meet them; ... the snakes called *graai* [γράαι]" (trans. Casson 1989: 73). The text clearly quotes Sanskrit *grāha-* (there is no intervocalic *h* in Greek), having 'snake' in meaning. From maritime reports from the 18th century, Casson (1989: 187) cites "Carsten Niebuhr, [who] writing of his voyage in 1763, reports...that his approach to India's west coast was carried out with the greatest safety thanks to 'viele kleine Schlangen, 12 bis 18 Zoll lang, auf der Oberfläche der See...'" The "Circumnavigation" also reports water snakes off the Persian coast (chapter 38); the Gulf of Kutch, where they are "huge and black" (chapter 40); the Gulf of Cambay, where they are "smaller and yellow and golden in colour" (chapter 40); and the Malabar coast, where they are black but "shorter and with dragon-shaped head and blood-red eyes" (chapter 55). Crocodiles are not indicated here, since the text refers to crocodiles in chapter 15 (monitor lizards are probably meant) and chapter 30 (in addition to vipers and huge lizards)[6].

In Old Tamil, Sanskrit *grāha-* has become *karāam*, *karām*, *karā*, *karavu*, all of which denote '(male) crocodile' (see above).

SOUTH ASIAN CROCODILE CULTS AND CONCEPTIONS

William Crooke (1926: 376-377 et alibi) collected a wealth of data on religious conceptions and customs related to crocodiles in South Asia. Below I have supplemented Crooke's data from some other sources and organized it by subtitles.

Gods and spirits connected with the crocodile

The Makara "is well known as the vehicle of Varuṇa and the banner of Kāmadeva, and it is significant that these deities are sometimes identified; and as the vehicle of various Yakṣas and Yakṣīs, and of the river-goddess Gaṅgā" (see Coomaraswamy 1931 II: 47 and pp. 53-56, where the Moon is also mentioned as having a makara vehicle; on makara as the vāhana of Varuṇa and Gaṅgā, see also Mallmann1963: 233). According to South Indian texts, Gāṅgeya-Subrahmaṇya (this appellation was given to Skanda because of his birth in the Ganges) has the makara as his vāhana (Gopinatha Rao 1916 II: 441; Liebert 1976: 91, 166). Skanda corresponds to Tamil Muruku, who is simultaneously the god of war and the god of love (for the Harappan origin of Skanda and Muruku, see also Parpola 1994: 225-239). According to Daniel (1983: 12), "the crocodile is the vehicle of Niridhi [i.e., Nirṛti 'Destruction'], the regent of the SW point of the compass."

Among the Hindu gods included in the pantheon of Tantric Buddhism is Varuṇa (also called Samudra 'Ocean'). While sometimes seated on a moon that is supported by a snake, more commonly he has the makara as his vehicle (Mallmann 1975: 437). In Japan, one finds more than 700 shrines to Konpira, a deity of the sea, who assures marine safety, successful fishing, and avoidance of misfortune. The Japanese name Konpira, also Kubira, goes back to Sanskrit *kumbhīra-* 'crocodile'; in Buddhist texts, this name is (among other things) used for one of the twelve Yakṣa generals (Thal 2005; Teeuwen 2006; Edgerton 1953: II, 187b; Lokesh Chandra 2002: VI, 1757b-1760a). There is another deity in Tantric Buddhism associated with the makara (Mallmann 1975: 6): of Vaiṣṇava origin, Madhukara ('Honey-maker') is represented as a young man holding a banner with the image of makara (*makaradhvaja-*) and having a parrot vehicle (*śuka-ratha-*); these are all characteristics of Kāma, the Hindu god of love (Mallmann 1975: 234-235; on the iconography of Hindu Kāma, often identified with Pradyumna, the son of Kṛṣṇa Vāsudeva, see also Mallmann 1963: 47-48).

One reason for the crocodile's association with the god of desire is undoubtedly its voracious appetite. The crocodile is a personification of sexual desire, not only in India but also among African tribes (Ganslmayr 1969).

An earring in the shape of a crocodile (*makara-kuṇḍala-*, *nakra-kuṇḍala-*) is worn in the right ear of the fierce form of Śiva (Rudramūrti), as well as by Viṣṇu (Liebert 1976: 166). Crocodiles are regarded as abodes for the souls of ancestors (Majupuria 1991: 194). And the crocodile is regarded by Hindus as "an ally of a magician" (Majupuria 1991: 194).

Eating of crocodiles

"Though some Hindus worship them, the fishing tribes have no scruples about eating them, in spite of the unsavoury taste of their flesh. Sir S. Baker (Wild beasts and their ways, chapter xiii) says: 'I have eaten almost everything, but although I have tasted crocodile I could never succeed in swallowing it. The combined flavour of bad fish, rotten flesh, and musk is the *carte de diner* offered to the epicure.'

The Kanjar gipsy of Behar rejects beef, but loves crocodile flesh; and so do the Irulas of Madras, the jungle tribes of the Central Provinces, the Mor fishermen of the Indus, and the Malláhs and Koch fishermen of Bengal" (Crooke 1906: 113).

"One sub-caste of Dhīmar fishermen in the Central Provinces must kill and eat a crocodile at their marriage, and the Sonjharas or gold-washers, catch a crocodile alive, worship it, and when the rite is done they let it return to the river (R. V. Russell, *Chhindwāra Gazetteer*, Allahabad, 1907, i.75)" (Crooke 1926: 377).

"[T]he liver of a crocodile is used as a charm and its various viscera are used in medicines" (Majupuria 1991: 194).

Dread of the crocodile and its use for defence in moats and for execution

"Crocodiles... are dreaded for their habit of attacking men and animals" (Crooke 1926: 376). "Crocodiles have been utilized in India to prevent the escape of prisoners from forts, in moats of which they used to be preserved. Captain Hervey describes the fort of Vellore as guarded in this way by Hyder Ali. Tavernier, writing of Bijapur, says of the king's palace: 'What causes the approach to it to be difficult is, that in the moat which surrounds it, and which is full of water, there are many crocodiles.' General Mundy gives a similar account of the fort of Barabati, near Cuttack; and the old traveller, Caesar Frederick, describing Pegu in Burma, says: 'It is a great citie, very plaine and flat, and four-square, walled round about, and with ditches that compass the walls round about with water, in which ditches are many crocodiles.' These creatures, according to Sir H. Yule, were there as late as 1830" (Crooke 1906: 111-112).

Old Tamil texts speak of crocodiles guarding the city in the moats surrounding the walls (see above).

According to Aelianus (N. An. 12,41), being "most voracious and cruel eaters of flesh, Gangetic crocodiles are "used as ministers of vengeance upon evil-doers; for those convicted of the greatest crimes are cast to them; and they require no executioner" (Figure 8).

Killing of crocodiles

"Crocodiles and alligators are usually worshipped by Hindus. Anyone who kills a crocodile is supposed to take the form of a crocodile after death. ... Killing of a crocodile is considered to be a serious crime ... Crocodiles are only killed when they show hostility to man" (Majupuria 1991: 194).

"There is an interesting story about a crocodile and an elephant. Once an elephant stepped into a lake to quench his thirst. After drinking deep, he took water in his trunk and gave it to his wife and children. At the same time, an angry crocodile attacked him. The struggle continued. The elephant grew weaker. Therefore, he prayed to Vishnu, the Supreme Being. Vishnu seated on a Garuda, with attendants or devas immediately appeared at the site. He cut off the neck of the crocodile with his discus (chakra) and saved the elephant. It is described that the elephant was a Gandharva in his former life, who was cursed by a saint on being disturbed by the former. This saint Rishi was reborn as a crocodile. Gandharva was born as an elephant. It also indicates that the sensual pleasures are taken away and, therefore, salvation is essential" (Majupuria 1991: 194). Gajendramokṣa, or 'the release of the elephant king' (from the clutches of a crocodile), is an important motif of the Kathakali theatre of Kerala.

Crocodile and human sexuality and fertility

The protuberance on the tip of the male gharial's snout is believed to be a potent medicine for virility: "The male gharial bears an outgrowth, called the '*Ghara*' in the local vernacular, on the tip of its snout. Since superstitious belief attributes various mystical powers to this *ghara*, males are often killed to collect their snouts" (Maskey and Mishra 1982:

185) (Figure 10).

"At the tank at Khán-Jahán Ali in Jessore young married women feed the monsters [i.e. the crocodiles] in the hope of being blessed with offspring" (Crooke 1906: 112).

"Women in performance of a vow used to throw a first-born son to the crocodiles at the mouth of Hooghly in the hope that such an offering would secure them additional offspring (H. H. Wilson, *Essays*, ii. 166 f.; Ward, ii. 318 f)" (Crooke 1926: 377).

Ward provides uniquely detailed testimony on the practice of this cruel custom in the beginning of the 19th century, when the British had not yet stopped it. Ward's work was first published in 1811 (in four volumes comprising 2055 pages). Crooke quotes its second edition as having two volumes, the latter of which came out first (in 1815). Both of these were printed at Serampore in Bengal. Having accessed the third edition in four volumes (printed in London in 1817-1820), I found several relevant passages that partly overlap and partly complement each other. Because the topic is important for the present study, I quote them all in extenso, modernizing the transcription of the Sanskrit:

"There are, however, many mothers among the Hindoos, who, in fulfilment of a vow to obtain the blessing of children, offer the first-born to the deity to whom this vow has been made. These offerings are frequently made by drowning the child in the Brahmaputra, a river on the eastern side of Bengal. In these immolations the mother encourages her child to pass into the stream beyond its depth, and then abandons it, remaining on the bank an inactive spectator of the struggles and cries of her expiring infant. These 'children of the vow' used also to be offered at Saugar Island; and here the Hindoo mother was seen throwing her living child into the mouth of the alligator, and watching the monster whilst he crushed its bones and drank its blood! The Marquis Wellesley peaceably and successfully prevented these immolations, by sending a small party of Hindoo sepoys down to the spot at the annual festival held on this island" (Vol. I, p. xl-xli). "The people in some parts of India, particularly the inhabitants of Orissa, and of the eastern parts of Bengal, frequently offer their children to the goddess Gangā. The following reason is assigned for this practice: — When a woman has been long married, and has no children, it is common for the man, or his wife, or both of them, to make a vow to the goddess Gangā, that if she will bestow the blessing of children to them, they will devote the first-born to her. If after this vow they have children, the eldest is nourished till a proper age, which may be three, four, or more years, according to circumstances, when, on a particular day appointed for bathing in any holy part of the river, they take the child with them, and offer it to this goddess: the child is encouraged to go farther and farther into the water till it is carried away by the stream, or is pushed off by its inhuman parents. Sometimes a stranger seizes the child, and brings it up; but it is abandoned by its parents from the moment it floats on the water, and if no one be found more humane than they, it

Figure 10 Snout of the male gharial (photo Bo Link 200)

infallibly perishes. The principal places in Bengal where this species of murder is practiced, are, Gangā-Sāgara, where the river Hoogly disembogues itself into the sea; Vaidyavatī, a town about fourteen miles to the north of Calcutta; Triveṇī, Nadīya, Chākdah, and Prayāga" (Vol. IV, p. 122).

"There are different places of the Ganges where it is considered as most desirable for persons thus to murder themselves, and in some cases auspicious days are chosen on which to perform this work of religious merit; but a person's drowning himself in any part of the river is supposed to be followed with immediate happiness. At Sāgara island it is accounted an auspicious sign if the person is speedily seized by a shark, or an alligator; but his future happiness is supposed to be very doubtful if he should remain long in the water before he is drowned. The British Government, for some years past, has sent a guard of sepoys to prevent persons from murdering themselves and their children at this junction of the Ganges with the sea, at the annual festivals held in this place (Vol. IV, p. 116-117).

"In the year 1806, at this place, I saw a brāhmaṇī (dripping with wet and shivering with cold) who had just been prevented by the sepoys from drowning herself; — and during my continuance there I heard of several mothers who had been prevented from murdering their children" (Vol. IV, p. 117, n.1).

"In the eastern parts of Bengal, married women, long disappointed in their hopes of children, make an offering to Gangā, and enter into a vow, that if the goddess will give them two children, they will present one to her: and it is not uncommon for such women to cast the first child into the river as an offering; but it is said, that at present some relation or religious mendicant stands ready to preserve the life of the child. The mother cannot take it again, but this person adopts and provides for it. These offerings are made on the tenth of the moon in Jyaiṣṭha, and on the 13th of Caitra" (Vol. III, p. 275).

Crocodiles in temple tanks, especially at Magar talāo near Karachi

"The Hindu temples are usually constructed on the banks of various rivers and tanks where these reptiles are found. Therefore, devotees have been offering food to these sacred animals which were tamed by the priests" (Crooke 1906: 112).

"The Rája of Jaypur protects them in the lake at Amber, and will not allow a shot to be fired in their neighbourhood)" (Crooke 1906: 112).

"[A]t the tank at Pír Pokhar, near Pandua in Bengal, one of them [crocodiles], called by the name of Fateh Khán, "Lord of Victory", when called, comes to the surface and is fed" (Crooke 1906: 112).

"Buchanan-Hamilton ([quoted in Martin's] *Eastern India* [1834], iii.59) describes a tank at Purneah in Bengal dedicated to a saint, and inhabited by a pair of crocodiles which are identified with the saint and his wife. When deprived of the usual victims supplied by the pilgrims they became exceedingly voracious, and just before the traveller's visit carried off a young man who was watering a buffalo. 'The natives, far from being irritated at this, believed that the unfortunate man had been a dreadful sinner, and that his death was performed (sic) by the Saint merely as a punishment'" (Crooke 1906: 112).

"The dangerous nature of the reptile has invested him, like the tiger, with sanctity. Tame crocodiles are protected and fed in many places, as in the famous Magar Taláo, or 'Crocodile Tank', near Karáchi" (Crooke 1906: 112) (Figure 11).

"Crocodiles are often kept in semi-captivity, usually in association with a religious establishment. Notable among these is the Mugger Pir at Karachi in Pakistan" (Daniel 1983: 12, with reference to Moses 1948).

"At Magar Talāo, 'crocodile tank', near Karachi, in connection with the cult of Pīr Mango, who

Figure 11 Feeding of crocodiles at the Magar Talão of Mango Pir in 1878 (from http://www.ourpakistan.vze.com)

Figure 12 Mango Pir in 1850 (from http://www.ourpakistan.vze.com)

caused a stream to trickle out of the rock, tame crocodiles are kept and fed by pilgrims (R. F. Burton, *Sind revisited*, London, 1877, i. 92ff.; E. Balfour, *The cyclopaedia of India and of eastern and southern Asia*, Madras 1858, i. 838f)" (Crooke 1926: 377).

Approximately 700 years ago, there lived a Hindu dacoit named Mango Pir, who was notorious for looting caravans. Impressed by the teachings of Baba Farid, he converted to Islam. Pleased with Mango's devotion, Farid gave him the title of Pir. He went on to become a saint revered by Hindus and Muslims alike. While the crocodiles gifted to Mango Pir came either from Baba Farid or the Sindhi saint Lal Shahbaz Qalandar, the story goes that they were originally the lice of the saint, which turned into crocodiles when dropped into the pond (Baloch 2004: 12) (Figure 12). The practice of feeding crocodiles in pools attached to shrines in Sindh undoubtedly go back to local Hindu tradition; this seems to be reflected in Mango Pir's Hindu background.

The tribal crocodile cult of Gujarat

"The crocodile is worshipped as an object of terror. In Baroda the crocodile god, Magar Deo, is worshipped once a year to protect men and animals from the attacks of these monsters, and also as a preventive against illness. The deity is represented by a piece of wood in the form of the animal, supported on two posts (Dalal, i. 157)" (Crooke 1912: 9a).

"Some of the wild tribes in Baroda, to avert injury to men and animals as well as sickness, worship Magardeo in the form of a piece of wood shaped like a crocodile and supported on two posts (J. A. Dalal, *Census Report: Baroda*, Bombay, 1902, i. 157) " (Crooke 1926: 377).

In 1969, Dr. Eberhard Fischer (of the University of Heidelberg in Germany, later of the Rietberg Museum in Zürich, Switzerland) and Shri Haku Shah (of the Tribal Research and Training Institute at the Gujarat Vidyapeeth) documented in fair detail this crocodile cult in southern Gujarat. Unaware of Dalal's reference, they believed that they had discovered a previously totally unknown cult. In one year, they made three field trips, visiting by jeep more than fifty villages of the Choudhri, Gamit and Vasava tribes in the tribal areas of the Surat District. In their documentation of sanctuaries, they researched the way in which wooden statues of these crocodile gods were made and interviewed oracle priests (*bhagat*) and other informants on their significance. The results were published in 1971 in a jointly authored booklet entitled *Mogra Dev: Tribal crocodile gods*. The most important findings are summarized below.

Worship of the crocodile gods is both communal and individual. The principal reasons for communal worship include asking for boons of cows and milk, as well as offspring and good crops. Residents of Devalpada village explained: "The cows from this village were not giving milk and they were not having calves. After installing this crocodile, we got milk and calves." In Amba village, people said: "This crocodile has been installed because the people did not get sons. The tiger was eating their cattle and the crops were spoiled. The (crocodile) god proved good and true. All twelve months they worship the crocodile." And one person interviewed in Jamkhadi said: "Four buffaloes have come to my house. They have been sent by *hela mogra* ['cool crocodile']. (The god) cool crocodile comes walking and gives. Human beings drink milk." Another added, "Man's life is like mogra's life. That is why we offer milk to the crocodile as well" (Fischer and Shah 1971: 39-41).

For individuals, getting children is the most common reason to install crocodile icons. An informant from the village of Singhpur told: "This man had no sons. When he was old (about 70 years ago), in his dream the crocodile-god said: 'Put me,' and the man got the crocodile made and installed." In Sakerda village, one finds similar anecdotes: "One woman was getting no son. She took a vow that she would install a crocodile and worship it after having born a son. That was before 45 years. She got a son and installed this crocodile." And, "Manyo Bhondo had no sons. When he had got his first son, he installed the crocodile. That son is still alive" (Fischer and Shah 1971: 39).

The crocodile god also helps with sorcery and illnesses. A resident of Bhatvada village explained: "If a ghost or a witch has entered someone's body, he will worship. When such a person has become alright again, he will relieve himself of the vow taken when ill" (Fischer and Shah 1971: 41).

One finds another mode of worship in the villages near Mandvi, where Chodhris install undecorated, one-headed crocodile icons. They usually do this once a year, during the time of *maha amas* (i.e., *amāvāsya*, the new moon) in February. Carved by the village carpenter, the crocodiles are not worshipped before they are installed. When the crocodile is erected, a goat is killed and wine is offered. The priests and others drink wine as well (Fischer and Shah 1971: 38). In addition to wine, milk is among the major offerings to the crocodile.

When the researchers expressed their wish to have a crocodile image for the museum, a bhagat hesitatingly agreed to carve a crocodile after being promised the raw material (i.e., a block of wood taken from a teak tree ritually felled for this exact purpose), the articles necessary for the installation ceremony, and a fee for his work. The carved crocodile had to be formally installed, even if it was going later to a museum. This was considered essential by the bhagat. In the evening, a plot of ground under a tree near a broken well was cleared and leveled. After the crocodile was placed on a support post, it was taken down and sprinkled with water, and then fixed again to the post. The bhagat muttered to the crocodile a formula in Gujarati, ending with the words "goddess crocodile, we offer you worship." He then sprinkled grain on the crocodile and deposited another handful of grain in a shallow depression in the center of its body. A coconut was offered, broken on a stone and placed near the post. A cock was held in front of the post, before being taken away to be killed by a helper with a sickle. Vermilion and oil were mixed in a bowl, and then smeared with coconut fibres on the crocodile and the post. Women from neighbouring houses gathered around the crocodile and sang a marriage song to it, describing the new owner as the bridegroom, come to fetch Hela Mogra to his village. Then rice was once more offered to the crocodile, wine was poured on the ground in front of it, and the bhagat uttered: "If children are asked, give children; if money is asked, give money; if grain is asked, give grain; if service is asked give service;

give everything asked for. We offer you worship, gift of chicken, gift of coconut, gift of rice, offering of wine is given." The cock was plucked, cut into pieces and roasted. After the liver and heart were offered to the crocodile with a few drops of wine, the participants feasted on the chicken and drank the remaining wine (Fischer and Shah 1971: 18-32).

The majority of wooden crocodiles were found in the bountiful sanctuaries of Dudhmogra (Mandvi Taluk), Devlimadi (Songadh Taluk) and Devmogra (Zagbara Taluk). Often, however, just one or two crocodiles remained in sanctuaries. These tended to be located not in the immediate vicinity of the village, but at a remove, near places where other gods or ancestors were worshipped. They were always found near fields, rarely by a creek or pond, and usually beneath a group of trees or a roof supported by wooden posts (covering the crocodile to keep it cool) (Fischer and Shal 1971: 13, 17). Most of the icons were old, showing signs of a lack of care (Figure 13). This reflects the gradual discontinuation of the cult (Fischer and Shah 1971: 17). To a few crocodiles, however, offerings of cocks, grain, food or money had been recently made.

The icons have two basic forms. The Chodris of the Mandvi Taluk erect a relatively realistic crocodile with one head, a body, and a tail. The body, which is octagonal in section, is usually only ornamented with grooves (imitating reptile scales). As the crocodile revolves on its post, it is thought to be alive, able to see with its eyes and turn around. The mouth of the crocodile should point towards the sunrise; if it points to the north or the sunset, it is believed that something bad will happen. There are also stories of it biting hands that have been put into its mouth (Fischer and Shah 1971: 13-14, 17) (Figure 14 and 15).

The Gamits and Vasavas also make wooden crocodile figures mounted on poles, but these usually have one body and a crocodile head at both ends. The body, which is square in section, is ornamented with reliefs or chiselled motifs (Fischer and Shah 1971: 15) (Figure 16). The most common ornamental motifs are the sun and crescent moon (Figure 17), followed by two horse riders separated by a standing figure (Figure 18). Aquatic animals are also common (Figure 19), while less frequent motifs include birds and cattle.

The description of two-headed icons by Gamit informants in the village of Ghoda (near Songadh)—"*Mogra* is a couple by itself: one side is male, one side is female" (Fischer and Shah 1971: 38)—suggests that an older tradition of two crocodile images was supplanted. "The fact that quite often two crocodiles are standing together was explained in Karoli: 'There must be two. As we are men and women, we have to install two'" (Fischer and Shah 1971: 37). One is reminded of Francis Buchanan Hamilton, reporting from Purneah in Bengal at the beginning of the 19th century about a water tank "dedicated to a saint, and inhabited by a pair of crocodiles which are identified with the saint and his wife" (Crooke 1906: 112).

"In some places, however, the crocodile can be accompanied with a pole instead of a second crocodile... Chhania Holia explains it [like this]: 'This *khambh*, pole, was installed together with *mogra*, crocodile. It is called *mogra nu jodu*, crocodile's partner (pair). *Khambh* is husband, *mogra* is wife. It was like this in the old sanctuary as well... It is the same with human beings in the house: it needs a couple'" (Fischer and Shah 1971: 38).

The pole tends to be of the same height as the crocodile, square in section, chamfered and terminating in a spherical form. (Fischer and Shah 1971: 16) In this sense, it bears great resemblance to the shape of linga statues!

The installation ceremony ends with *sindur* being applied to the crocodile and the post, women singing a wedding song of the crocodile goddess, and general feasting (Fischer and Shah 1971: 30-31).

Figure 13 Dudhmogra crocodile sanctuary
(after Fischer and Shah 1971: Plate 3)

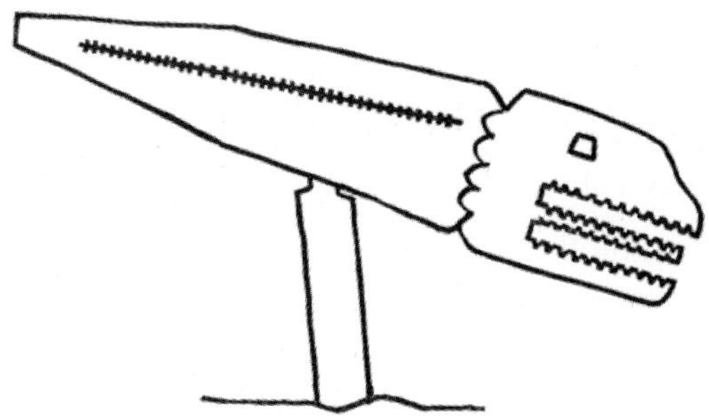

Figure 14 Tailed crocodile image on a pole
(after Fischer and Shah 1971: 14)

Figure 15 Devlimadi crocodile sanctuary
(after Fischer and Shah 1971: Plate 2)

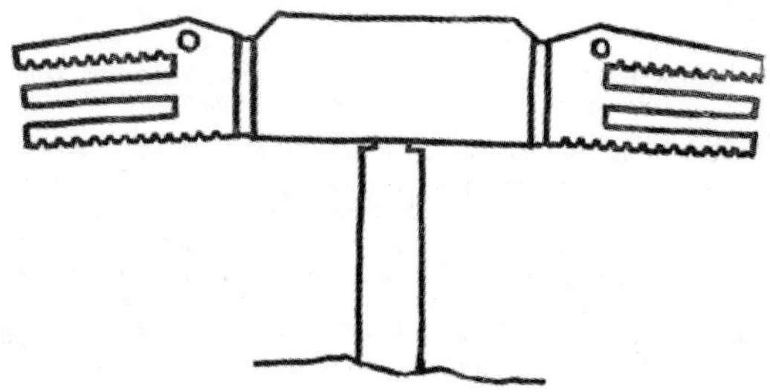

Figure 16 Two-headed crocodile image on a pole
(after Fischer and Shah 1971: 15)

Figure 17 Jundaria Vadia crocodile sanctuary
(after Fischer and Shah 1971: Plate 9)

Figure 18 Riders carved on a two-headed crocodile image
(after Fischer and Shah 1971: Plate 10)

Figure 19 Fish and other watery animals carved on a crocodile image
(after Fischer and Shah 1971: Plate 17)

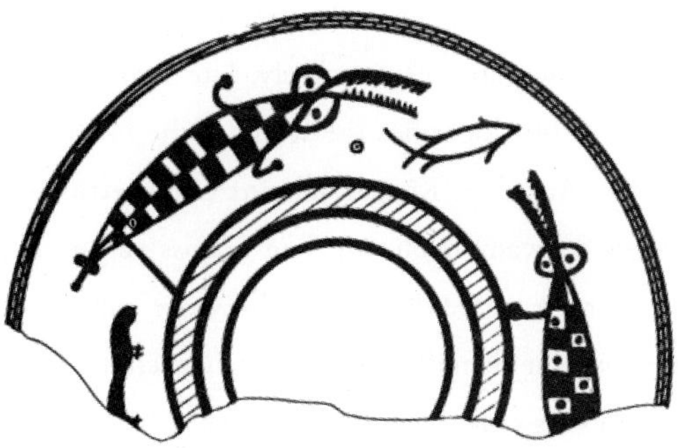

Figure 20 A Mature Harappan painted pot with two gharials set on poles. from Amri III (after Casal 1964 II: Figure 75 no. 323)

Fisher and Shah report many legends connected with the history of the crocodile cult and its origin, a number of which are shown in carvings on the two-headed crocodile images. From these, the researchers came to the following conclusion: "The tracing of tribal cultures of Gujarat to prehistoric findings, seems to us out of place and in a future analysis we shall show, that elements from these tribal cultures tend more to be degenerated forms of much later traditions rather than stagnated primitive cultures" (Fischer and Shah 1971: 7-8).

CROCODILE IN THE INDUS CIVILIZATION

Harappan background of the Gujarati crocodile cult

This position by Fischer and Shah is in direct opposition to that of Sir John Marshall who, after quoting beliefs and practices historically connected with crocodiles in South Asia, came to the following carefully formulated conclusion: "The foregoing facts respecting the present-day worship of these animals afford, of course, no proof that they were similarly worshipped five thousand years ago. In a country, however, which is as conservative as India, particularly in regard to its religious cults, these facts are not without real significance; and when we find, as we do, that most of the elements which make up this prehistoric religion [of the Indus Civilization]—so far as we can at present analyse them—are perpetuated in later Hinduism, we are justified in inferring that much of the zoolatry which characterizes Hinduism and which is demonstrably non-Aryan, is also derived from the prehistoric age" (Marshall 1931: I, 73).

Marshall, of course, was not familiar with the studies of Fischer and Shah, which would be published forty years later. But evidently Fischer and Shah did not know about the artifacts excavated at Amri in the lower Indus Valley by Jean-Marie Casal (Casal 1964 II: fig. 75 no. 323). In particular, one incompletely preserved Mature Harappan painted pot depicts—in addition to a fish, a small circumpunct and an indistinct (animal?) figure—two long-snouted crocodiles with pole-like extensions projecting at a ninety degree angle from their lower body to a painted border that can be interpreted as the earth (Figure 20). When I included the picture of this potsherd in my book *Deciphering the Indus script* (Parpola 1994: 180 Figure 10.1e), I wondered what these extensions might be. I looked in vain in Casal's excavation report for an explanation, but he does not discuss the motif in any detail. When studying Fischer and Shah's work on the Gujarati crocodile cult, however, this puzzling potsherd came to mind. The Gujarati crocodile images installed on poles clarify this unique Harappan picture perfectly. Not only did Gujarat belong to the Harappan realm, but the tribal peoples living in its remote jungle villages are the most likely to have preserved stagnated prehistoric cults. In my opinion, we have clear proof here that the Harappan religion has survived even four thousand years after the collapse of the Indus Civilization. It goes without saying, therefore, that I fully endorse Sir John Marshall's view that "most of the elements which make up this prehistoric religion ... are perpetuated in later

Hinduism," including "much of the zoolatry which characterizes Hinduism and which is demonstrably non-Aryan."

Crocodile on Indus seals and tablets

The crocodile is depicted four times as the main heraldic animal on Indus seals, all of which come from Mohenjo-daro (M-292, M-293, M-410, M-1223). One of the seals is broken and has nothing but the crocodile left (M-1223). Another seal, of the rectangular type, has no script but a crocodile with a fish in its mouth, drawn in the same way as the 'fish' signs of the Indus script (M-410). In both cases, the crocodile appears to be the gharial. In addition, there is also a seal with a tiger as the main heraldic animal (M-1923) that features carvings of the gharial on both sides (Figures 21-25).

Although the crocodile is relatively rarely depicted in the Indus seals, it appears to have occupied a fairly central position among the sacred animals of the Harappans. In some moulded tablets, which have two slightly different variants (see M-440 A and M-1395 A in Figure 26 and 27), the crocodile is the central figure and much larger than the other animals surrounding it.

Fertilization of a human female by gharial

On the A side of Indus tablet H-180 (Figure 28), according to John Marshall (1931: 52), "a nude female figure is depicted upside down with legs apart and with a plant issuing from her womb." For Marshall, this appeared to be a "striking representation of the Earth Goddess with a plant growing from her womb." When the tablet was published in the Harappa excavation report, this interpretation was followed by Vats (1940: I, 42) and later by many others. Mortimer Wheeler (1968: 106), however, speaks of "a nude woman upside down giving birth to what has been interpreted as a plant but may equally well be a scorpion or even a crocodile." Iravatham Mahadevan (1977: 796 no. 70) posits that the tablet depicts "a crab (?) issuing from her womb." Alternatively, Ute Franke-Vogt (1991: I, 90) identifies the scene as the birth of a turtle: "Aus dem Körper scheint ein Vierfüssler, dessen Schwanz noch mit dem Schoss verbunden ist, geboren zu werden. Möglicherweise handelt es sich um eine Schildkröte." But the direction of the animal's legs clearly shows that what is touching the vagina is not the tail, but a long snout. This apparently reveals the gharial in the act of fertilizing the woman.

We have already seen that folk belief ascribes phallic properties to the protuberance on the tip of the male gharial's snout. Among the native names of gharial, Daniel (1983: 15-16) lists Oriya *thantia kumhira*, with *thantia* deriving from Sanskrit *tuṇḍa-* 'beak, snout, elephant's trunk' (see above). Sanskrit *tuṇḍa-*, attested since the Atharvaveda, is a loanword going back to Proto-Dravidian **tuṇṭam*, **toṇṭam*, **cuṇṭu*, **coṇṭu* 'beak, snout, elephant's trunk, pointed mouth of an animal' (DEDR 3311 and 2664). Proto-Dravidian had a homophonous word for 'penis', which in Tamil and Malayalam is represented as *cuṇṇi*, in Kannada as *tuṇṇi/tuṇṇe*, and in North Dravidian Kurukh as *coṇḍō* (DEDR 2666).

The gharial as 'embryo-maker': Indus signs no. 340 and no. 91

The reverse side of tablet C-34 from Chanhu-daro (Figure 29) shows several male gharials (with a swelling on the snout), together with fish. The long inscription on the obverse includes sign no. 354, which is clearly associated with the crocodile (and is discussed below), and a sequence of signs no. 340 and no. 91. This same sequence of signs is also used to conclude the four-sign inscription on a set of copper tablets from Mohenjo-daro (Figure 30), listed as A3 in my classification (Parpola 1994: 111); the first two signs are interpreted below as *val mīn* 'strong fish' = 'crocodile'.

Sign no. 340 (Figure 31) consists of two

M-292 A M-292 a

Figure 21 Indus seal M-292 (after CISI 1: 71)

M-293 A bis M-293 a

Figure 22 Indus seal M-293 (after CISI 1: 71)

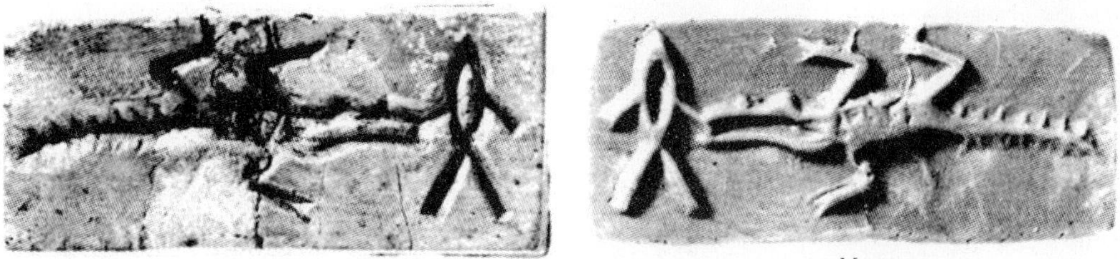

M-410 A M-410 a

Figure 23 Indus seal M-410 (after CISI 1: 98)

M-1223 A M-1223 A bis M-1223 a M-1223 C M-1223 F M-1223 B M-1223 D M-1223 E

Figure 24 Indus seal M-1223 (after CISI 2: 151)

M-1923 c M-1923 a M-1923 b M-1923 e

Figure 25 Indus seal M-1923 (after CISI 3.1: 83)

M-440 A

Figure 26 Indus sealing M-440 (after CISI 1: 108)

M-1395 A bis M-1395 B

M-1395 A ter M-1395 B bis

Figure 27 Indus sealing M-1395 (after CISI 2: 186)

Figure 28 Indus tablet H-180 (after CISI 3.1: 398)

components, each of which occurs separately on its own. One of these is sign no. 337 (Figure 32); I have interpreted "intersecting circles" as 'bangles' or 'earrings' = Proto-Dravidian **muruku* (DEDR 4979) = **muruku* 'boy child, young man' (DEDR 4978) (see Parpola 1994: 226-230). Sign no. 337 has been modified in ligature no. 340 by placing three strokes (either slanting or vertical) in the middle of the three spaces within the two "intersecting circles". In my opinion, these three strokes stand for sign no. 143 (Figure 33), "vertical strokes arranged into a triangle" representing the traditional South Asian 'kitchen fireplace consisting of three stones placed so as to make a triangle' = Proto-Dravidian **cullV* / **cūl* (DEDR 2857; Turner 1966: no. 4879; Parpola 1994: 216-217, 298). This seems to function as a rebus for the Proto-Dravidian homophone **cūl* 'pregnancy' (DEDR 2733) in the two-sign sequence 'fireplace' + 'bangles' (Figure 34), which could stand for '(the god) Muruku of (i. e., causing) pregnancy'; I now prefer this interpretation to my earlier suggestion of 'pregnancy bangles' used for protection (Tamil *cūl kāppu*), which are ceremonially given to the expectant mother during her first pregnancy in Tamil Nadu (cf. Parpola 1994: 218). United in a single sign in ligature no. 354, these components **cūl* + **muruku* suggest the meaning of 'pregnancy-baby' = 'embryo, foetus'.

In my list of signs (Parpola 1994: 72), sign no. 91 (Figure 35) occurs quite frequently. Because such frequency makes this an important sign, I have worked for decades to understand its pictorial significance. Some variants of the sign consist of a vertical rod that terminates in extensions, varying in number from three to five, either in a slanting row where the straight extensions become shorter and shorter, or arranged symmetrically on both sides of the central rod (usually with a little curve, making the variant with three extensions look like a trident). Because the number of extensions almost never exceeds five, I have often thought that the sign originally depicted the forearm ending in a hand with five fingers, which then became simplified in number. The common five-extension variants look a great deal like the Archaic Sumerian sign for 'hand'. The rare variants with more than five extensions start lower, however, giving the impression of a tree stem with branches.

The sign could, therefore, denote a Proto-Dravidian word that had both of these meanings, like **taṇṭa/*taṇṭu* 'arm' (DEDR 3048) and **taṇṭa/*taṇṭu* 'stalk, stem of plant, trunk of tree' (DEDR 3056). It could also serve as the pictogram for other words with similar meanings, like Proto-Dravidian **kay/*key* 'hand, arm' (DEDR 2023), which was originally (as noun-verb; see Krishnamurti 2003: 196) the same as the Proto-Dravidian verbal root **kay/*key* 'to do, make, create, cause, perform' (DEDR 1957) (for the semantic relationship, cf. Sanskrit *kṛ-* 'to do, make' and *kara-* 'hand', literally 'the doer, maker'). While the latter alternative would support the sign's high frequency

Figure 29 Indus tablet C-34 (after CISI 1: 336)

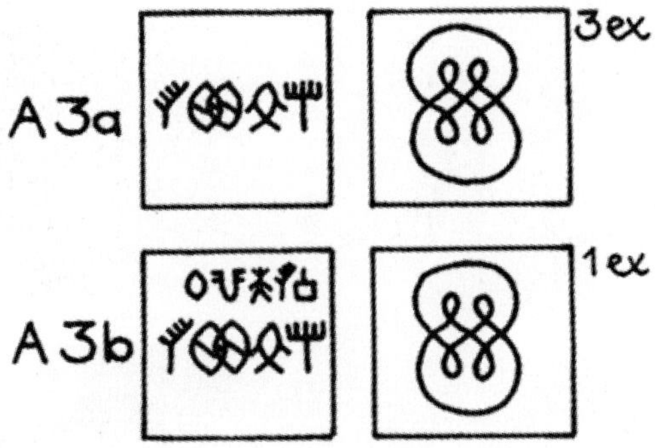

Figure 30 Copper tablets of type A3 from Mohenjo-daro (after Parpola 1994: 111, Figure 7.14)

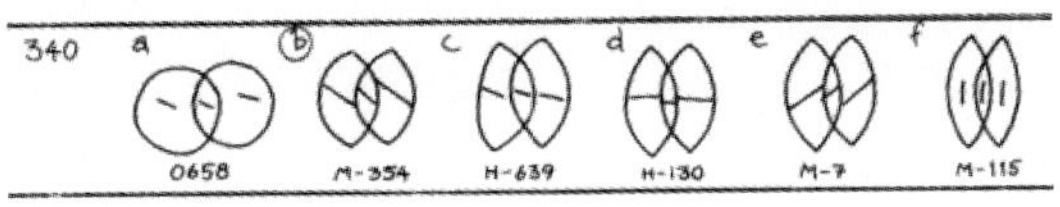

Figure 31 Indus sign no. 340 with variants (after Parpola 1994: 77, Figure 5.1)

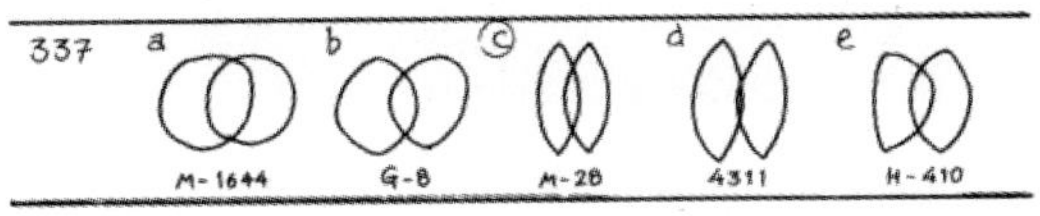

Figure 32 Indus sign no. 337 with variants (after Parpola 1994: 77, Figure 5.1)

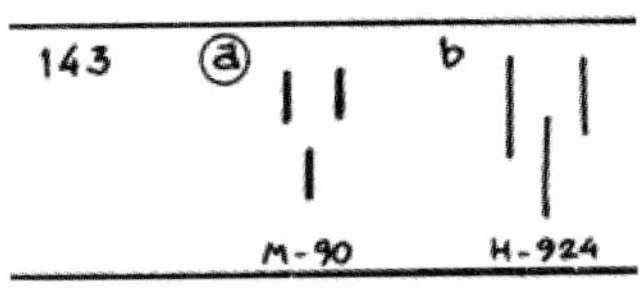

Figure 33 Indus sign no. 143 with variants (after Parpola 1994: 73, Figure 5.1)

Figure 34 Modern impression of the Indus seal H-147 (after Parpola 1994: 228 Figure 13.6)

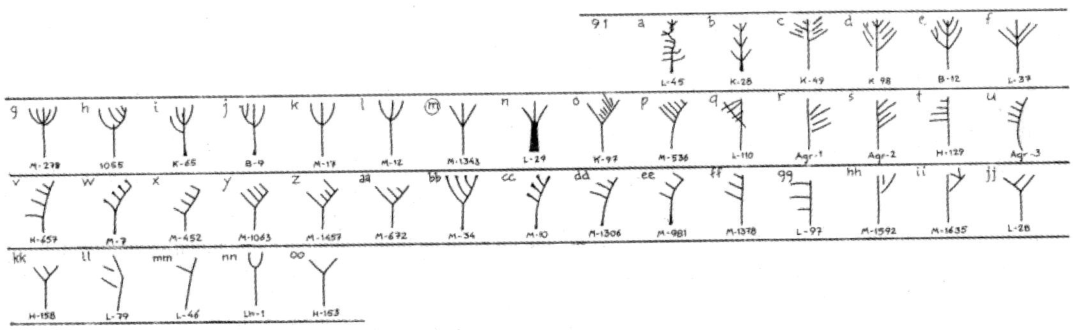

Figure 35 Indus sign no. 91 with variants (after Parpola 1994: 72, Figure 5.1)

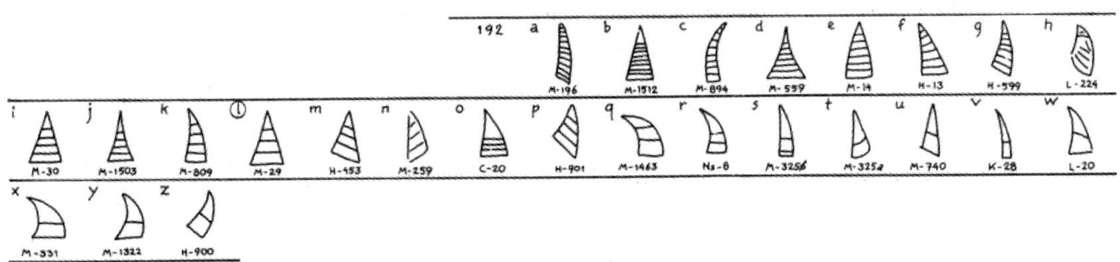

Figure 36 Indus sign no. 192 with variants (after Parpola 1994: 74, Figure 5.1)

Figure 37 Indus seal M-1135 (after CISI 3.1: 378)

Figure 38 Indus seal M-276 (after CISI 1: 381)

of occurrence, this tentative interpretation must be tested further[7].

In line with these suggested interpretations, the crocodile (*val mīn*) would be called 'foetus-maker' in the copper tablets of type A3 (note that the two signs make a noun phrase in the additional line of text in the variant A3b tablet, also associated with the crocodile; see Figure 30) and in tablet C-34. Although the exact word meant for 'embryo' in this phrase remains open to interpretation, I was struck by the fact that *kaṭṭi* is found among the Tamil words for 'foetus'. The specific meaning 'foetus' seems to be recorded in Tamil alone, but the word is derived from Proto-Dravidian **kaṇṭṭV* 'clod, lump, concretion, anything hardened, coagulated, boil, abscess, swelling, tumour, round lump or ball (of food, butter), etc.' (DEDR 1148). This is the same etymon from which Assamese *ghāṭ* 'protuberance on the snout of gharial' and, accordingly, Sanskrit *ghaṇṭika-* and Hindi *ghaṛiāl* are derived.

Harappan counterpart of Hindi *ghaṛiyāl*: Indus signs no. 192 'rhinoceros' horn' and no. 134 'seven'

In Harappan sign sequences specifically connected with the gharial, one would expect to find the word that provides the main etymology for the name *gharial*: namely Proto-Dravidian **kaṇṭṭV* 'swelling, lump, boil, abscess, protuberance' (whence Indo-Aryan *gaṇḍa* 'swelling' and *ghaṇḍa-* 'protuberance at the tip of ghariyal's snout'). Resembling the glans penis, the protuberance clearly has phallic significance. Indeed, Proto-Dravidian had a similar word for 'penis', **keṇṭV*, which has survived only in Kota (*geṇḍ*), Kannada (*geṇḍe*) and Gondi (*gēṭ* 'sexual intercourse') (DEDR 1949). See also Proto-Dravidian **kaṇṭan* 'a strong, manly male person, the male of animals' (DEDR 1173).

As we have seen, Indo-Aryan *gaṇḍa*/**geṇḍa-* also denotes 'rhinoceros', a South Asian animal distinguished by the large excrescence on its nose. Just like the male gharial's snout protuberance (which Aelianus compares with a horn), the "horn" of the rhinoceros is a phallic symbol that is in high demand as an aphrodisiac. The variants of Indus

Figure 39 Copper tablets of type B5 from Mohenjo-daro (after Parpola 1994: 111, Figure 7.14)

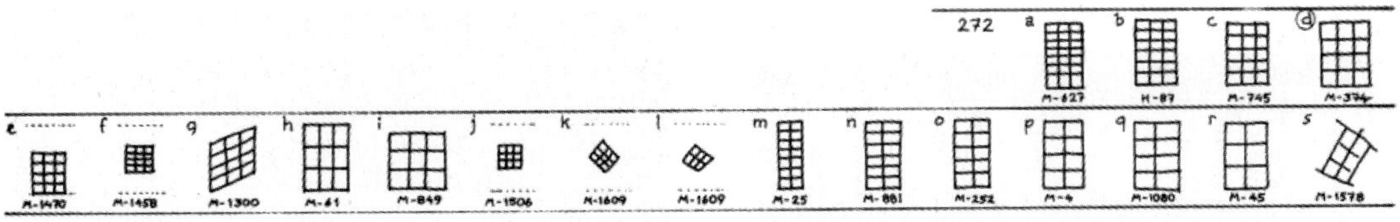

Figure 40 Indus sign no. 272 with variants (after Parpola 1994: 75, Figure 5.1)

sign no. 192 in my list (Parpola 1994: 74) (Figure 36) suggest that it depicts the "nose horn" of the rhinoceros; cf. the actual depiction of the nose horn on the seals M-1135 (Figure 37) and M-276 (Figure 38) from Mohenjo-daro. The copper tablets from Mohenjo-daro constitute a category of inscribed Harappan objects where the iconographic motif is demonstrably connected with the accompanying text. Only one type of these copper tablets depicts the rhinoceros; its inscription begins with sign no. 192 (Figure 39) (Parpola 1994: 110-112 and Figure 7.14 no. B5).

The second sign (no. 272 in Parpola 1994: 75; Figure 40) consists of a rectangle or square, which is divided in various ways into smaller parts. It could very well stand for Proto-Dravidian **tuṇṭṭi-* 'to cut into pieces, tear up, divide' and **tuṇṭṭam*, **tuṇṭṭu* 'piece, bit, slice, section, division, compartment, small plot of field' (DEDR 3310), which has a matching homophone in Proto-Dravidian **tuṇṭṭam* 'beak, bill, nose, snout, elephant's trunk' (DEDR 3311). Together the two signs would make a compound **kaṇṭṭV-tuṇṭṭam* '(animal) having a protuberance on its nose'; while this compound is hypothetical (its survival from Dravidian languages cannot be attested), it can be compared to Greek *rhīnó-kerōs* '(animal) having a horn on its nose', and to such Sanskrit compounds as *vakra-tuṇḍa-* 'having a curved trunk' (one of the names for Gaṇeśa, the elephant-headed god).

Another possible meaning for sign no. 272 is 'animal', cf. the latter part of the Sanskrit compound *gaṇḍa-mṛga-* 'rhinoceros'. A good candidate would be Proto-Dravidian **māku-* 'animal, beast'. This meaning is retained in Tamil *mā-*, which is used especially for horse, hog and elephant; in most Dravidian languages, however, it specifically denotes 'deer, antelope, stag, sambar' (being in this respect very similar to Sanskrit *mṛga-*), as well as 'bull' (in Kodagu) or 'horse' (Telugu; cf. also Nahali *māv* 'horse') (DEDR 4780). This word has a (likely even etymologically related) homophone, which parallels the iconic meaning of sign no. 272: **māku-* 'net' (found in this shape in Tamil); although this etymon is attested in South Dravidian alone, it can be posited as Proto-Dravidian on the basis of having been borrowed into Sanskrit (Mahābhārata, Kālidāsa) in the forms *vāgura-* 'net' and *vāgurika-* 'hunter, deer-catcher' (which correspond to Tamil *mākular* 'hunters' and Kannada *māvuliga* 'man who uses nets for catching deer, etc.') (DEDR 4790; for the *m-/v-* and *-m-/-v-* alternation, which

H-174 A

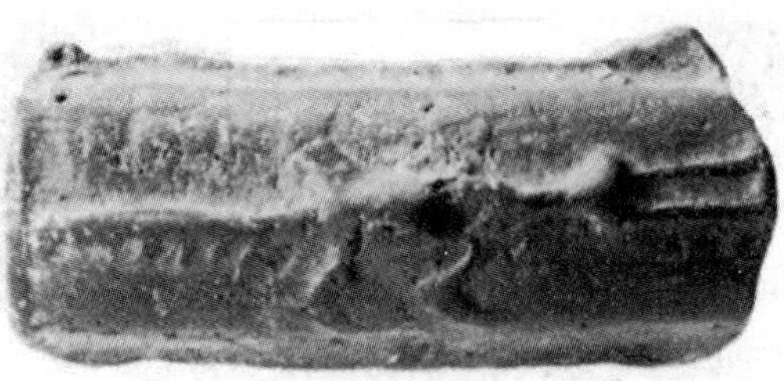

H-174 B

Figure 41 Indus tablet H-174 (after CISI 1: 207)

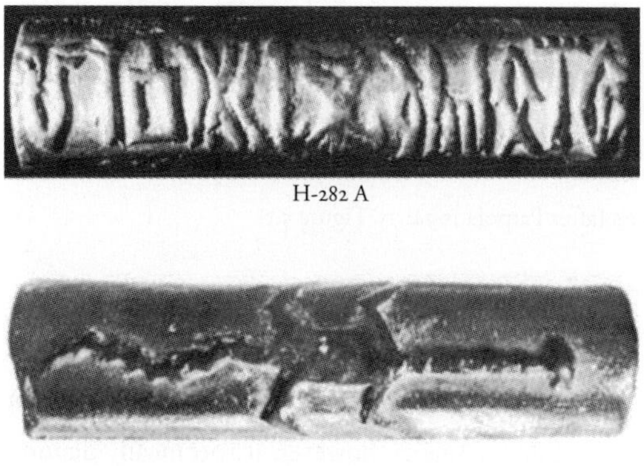

H-282 A

H-282 B

Figure 42 Indus tablet H-282 (after CISI 1: 223)

M-482 A

M-482 B

Figure 44 Indus tablet M-482 (after CISI 3.1: 387)

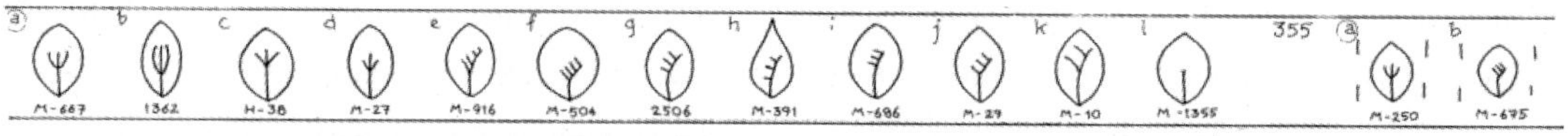

Figure 43 Indus signs nos. 354 and 355 with variants (after Parpola 1994: 77, Figure 5.1)

is frequent and quite widespread in Dravidian languages, see Zvelebil 1970: 125-128). Further confirmation is necessary, however, to provide a sensible interpretation for the frequently occurring sign sequence of no. 272 and no. 272.

Sign no. 192 begins with the inscription on the obverse of tablet H-174 (which has many duplicates), while the reverse shows the gharial (Figure 41). Sign no. 192 is followed here by sign no. 134, which consists of seven short vertical strokes and undoubtedly represents the numeral 'seven' (Parpola 1994: 73 and 81-82). 'Seven' was **eẓu*, **ēẓu* in Proto-Dravidian (DEDR 910). This may have served as a rebus for the Proto-Dravidian verb **iẓu*, **eẓu* 'to draw, pull, drag along the ground' (DEDR 504 a). In the present context, a likely derivative is the verb **iẓa* 'to creep, crawl, slide along the ground' (DEDR 508), whence Malayalam *iẓava*, *iẓa-jantu*, *iẓa-jāti* 'a creeping thing, reptile' (*Malayalam lexicon* 1970 II: 416-418). Therefore, the sequence of the two Indus signs probably means 'reptile with a protuberance (on the snout)'[18].

Gharial as '(fish) catcher': the Indus sign no. 354 'fist'

The crocodile is more common in the Indus tablets than the seals, with numerous cases of duplicates. Most common are long round tablets with a gharial (with a long narrow snout that broadens at the tip) on one side; the other side has a long inscription, which seems to be connected with the beast (see H-282 in Figure 42). Focusing on three signs in particular, I would like to suggest an interpretation.

The first sign, no. 354 in my list (Parpola 1994: 77) (Figure 43), consists of a circle inside of which is sign no. 91 (interpreted above as 'tree stem with branches' and 'arm or hand with fingers'). The graphic of sign no. 91 appears the same when placed within the circle and when occurring on its own without any circle. When placed inside the circle, it is possible that this sign depicts 'hand closed into a fist'.

Looking at Indus tablet M-482 (Figure 44), it is possible to connect this sign (provisionally interpreted as 'fist') with the gharial. The reverse of the tablet contains nothing but a gharial with a fish in its mouth; on the obverse is a swastika, a tree, and a three-sign inscription. The first of the three signs is the one that could depict 'fist'. It is followed by the most common sign in the Indus script, which usually appears at the end of an inscription or a noun phrase. Paintings on Early Harappan pottery (see Parpola 1994: Figure 7.4 on p. 106) suggest that this second sign (no. 311 in my list) depicts a 'bovine head' with horns and ears on either side (Parpola 1994: 104). Likely expressing Proto-Dravidian **ā, ān* 'cow' (DEDR 334), it could denote either the Proto-Dravidian masculine singular marker **-an* identifying human and divine beings (without the added nominative marker **-tu* reconstructed for Proto-Dravidian but dropped in Proto-South-Dravidian; see Krishnamurti 2003: 210-217) or the Proto-Dravidian possessive genitive suffix **-al-ā* (Krishnamurti 2003: 233-235; Parpola 1994: 188, 261; 1997: 169-172).

I suggest reading the 'fist' sign in Proto-Dravidian as **piṭi* 'fist' (this meaning is found in many languages), from the Proto-Dravidian root **piṭi* 'to catch, grasp, seize, capture, hold' (DEDR 4148, attested from Tamil to Gondi). The gharial is a fish-eater; as seen on the reverse side of the tablet, the gharial has a fish it its mouth. The root *piṭi* is used for 'catching fish' (in Tamil *mīṉ piṭikka*). The root can be understood to mean 'to catch fish', even when the word 'fish' is not explicitly mentioned (cf. Tamil *piṭipāṭu* = *mīṉ piṭipaṭukai* 'capture of fish' and *piṭikāraṉ* = *mīṉ piṭikkiṟavaṉ* 'fisherman' in Jaffna Tamil) (Winslow 1862: 769).

Heavenly 'fish catcher'

The 'fist' sign occurs very often, like the 'crab' sign, in the beginning of sequences that contain one or more 'fish' signs. As both the 'crab' and the 'fish' signs frequently seem to have an astral meaning (Parpola 1994: 179-272), there is reason to suspect a similar significance in this context. An astral connotation is suggested also by the fact that the crocodile and the fish (appearing either in the crocodile's jaws or somewhere nearby) are placed above (as if in the sky)—not beneath (as if underwater)—a row of various mammals on a number of Harappan tablets (cf. M-489 A and C in Figure 45). Given the likelihood of astral meaning for the 'fist' sign, it is very interesting that the verbal root *piṭi* is used in connection with eclipses (cf. Tamil *kirakaṇam* [< Sanskrit *grahaṇam*] *piṭikkiṟa vēḷai* 'the time of an eclipse') (Winslow 1862: 769).

In Indian folk-belief attested as early as the Atharvaveda (19,9,10), eclipses are thought to be caused by an invisible planetary demon called Rāhu, who is imagined to be a heavenly reptile that swallows the sun or moon. Rāhu's invisibility is reminiscent of the crocodilian habit of lurking beneath the water while hunting prey. As noted by Mayrhofer (1996: II,450), Rāhu's character matches the traditional explanation of his name from **rābh-ú-* 'grasping, holding', derived from the Sanskrit verbal root *rabh-* (which in meaning agrees with Dravidian *piṭi*).

In South India, diseases like the common cold

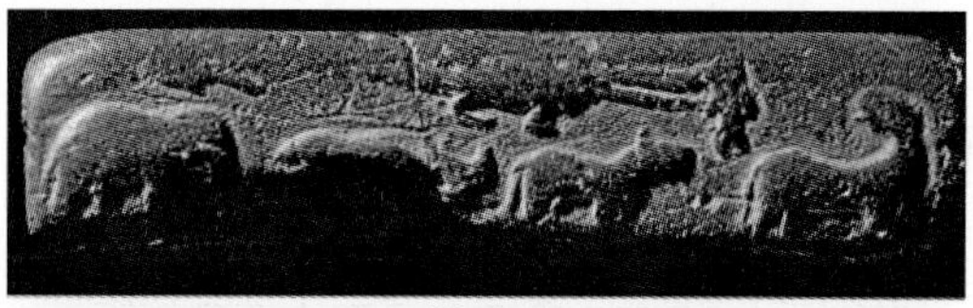

M-489 A

M-489 B

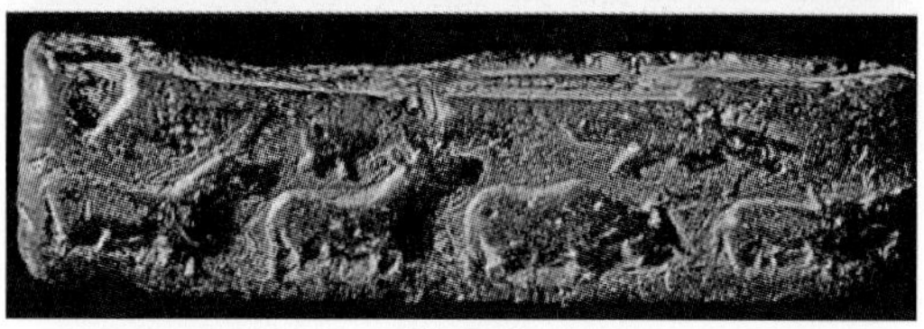

M-489 C

Figure 45 Indus tablet M-489. After CISI 3.1: 400)

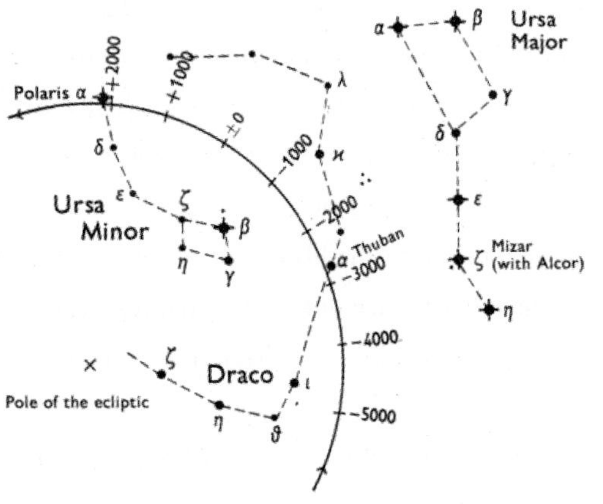

Figure 46 Circumpolar stars (after Parpola 1994: 243, Figure 14.4, based on Liebert 1969: 168)

are often ascribed to ominous planets (Tamil *kōḷ* = Sanskrit *graha-*) 'catching' (Tamil *koḷ* = Sanskrit *grah-*) people by means of invisible lassoes (Parpola 1994: 232-233, 237). At least in Tamil, the root *piṭi* is also used in the sense of catching cold (cf. *eṉakkuc caḷi* [= Sanskrit *jaladoṣam*] *piṭittuk koṇṭatu*, Fabricius 1972: 697). Sanskrit *grāha-* m. *grāhī-* f. 'crocodile' and *grāhi-* f. 'demoness binding people with slings of disease and death' are derived from the root *gra(b)h-* 'to grab, catch, hold'. Like Rāhu, they appear to be translation loans from Dravidian.

See also Tamil *karantuṟai-kōḷ* 'phenomena of the heavens, sometimes visible and sometimes not, which are generally regarded as ominous, such as *irāku, kētu, parivēṭam, vālveḷḷi, vāṉavil* (Peruṅ. uñcaik. 58,57) (TL 1928 II: 743a).

Heavenly crocodile in the Veda and its Harappan background

The Taittirīya-Āraṇyaka (2,19) speaks of a heavenly crocodile called Śākvara (*divyaḥ śākvaraḥ śiśumāras*), whose tail (*puccha-*) has four sections (*kāṇḍa-*). The prayer constituting worship of Brahma (*brahmopasthāna-*) begins with the words *dhruvas tvam asi, dhruvasya kṣitam*, and ends with *namaḥ śiśukumārāya*. This prayer should be muttered at dusk while facing the region of the pole star (*dhruva-maṇḍala-*). As it says, he who knows this heavenly crocodile, the lord of all beings (*bhūtānām adhipatir*), will conquer death and gain the world of heaven (*jayati svargam lokaṃ*). In a discussion of the śārkara sāman, the Jaiminīya-Brāhmaṇa (3,193-194) calls the sage Śarkara by the name *śiṃśumāra-* when he ascends to the heavenly world (*svargaṃ lokam udakrāmat*). This word appears to denote the dolphin, as it refers to an ocean animal (*śiṃśumāro vai samudram atipārayitum arhati*) (Lüders 1942: 66-67). But *śiśumāra-* means both 'dolphin' and 'crocodile'. In Taittirīya-Āraṇyaka 2,19,2, the limbs of the heavenly *śiśumāra-* are equated with different deities. At least in this text, the animal must be a crocodile and not a dolphin, since it is said to have forelegs and hind legs (cf. Lüders 1942: 67-68)[9].

The heavenly crocodile of the Harappans seems to have been Ursa Major, which in Old Tamil is called *eẕu-mīṉ* '(constellation of) seven stars'. Above I suggested that **eẕu* 'seven' (DEDR 910) in the Indus script probably served as a rebus for **iẕu*, **eẕu* 'to draw, pull, drag along the ground' (DEDR 504a), from which the Malayalam term for 'reptile' is derived. In this case, *eẕu-mīṉ* could have been understood to also mean 'reptile asterism'. According to Viṣṇu-Purāṇa 2,9,1, the heavenly form of the God Viṣṇu (which appears in the form of a *śiśumāra-*) includes the pole star in its tail (*tārāmayaṃ bhagavataḥ śiśumārākṛti prabho / divi rūpaṃ harer yat tu tasya pucche sthito dhruvaḥ*). If such was already the case in Harappan times, then the tail was curved as seen in the gharial depicted on Indus seal M-292 (Figure 21), with the pole star (Thuban) added to the seven stars of Ursa Major (Figure 46).

Evidence for Harappan child offerings to the crocodile god

Both the crocodile and the dolphin are included in the fauna of South Asia. The concept of a heavenly crocodile with its tail ending in the pole star was likely inherited from the Harappans. The

Vedic tradition has preserved a similar (though not identical) concept of Indo-Iranian origin. Albrecht Weber (1853: 237) pointed out that the Sanskrit proper name *Śunaḥśepa* 'Dog's tail' has a counterpart in Greek Κυνόσουρα 'Dog's tail', which describes the asterism of Ursa Major (Scherer 1953: 176-177). For this reason, Weber suspected that the famous Śunaḥśepa legend has an astral aspect. The 'Dog's tail' is near the pole star, where the tail of the heavenly crocodile ends. In the Rigvedic hymn 1,24, which is ascribed to Śunaḥśepa, there seems to be a reference to the pole star and its connection with the god Varuṇa: in verse 7, Varuṇa is said to hold a heavenly banyan tree up in the sky. This seems to reflect the Harappan concept of the pole star, preserved in the Old Tamil compound *vaṭa-mīn* 'north star' (which also means 'banyan-star'), represented in the Indus script by the sequence of the signs 'fig' + 'fish' (see Parpola 1994: 234-246, especially 245-246).

The oldest version of the Śunaḥśepa legend is in the Aitareya-Brāhmaṇa (7,13-18). A sonless king called Hariścandra ('Yellow moon') is advised to approach the god Varuṇa. The god grants Hariścandra offspring, but demands in return that he sacrifice his firstborn son as an offering. The king succeeds several times in postponing the sacrifice, on grounds that the boy is not yet fit, until Prince Rohita turns sixteen and finally comes of age. Rohita refuses to be sacrificed, however. Taking his bow and arrows, he departs for the forest[10]. To punish Hariścandra for breaching his vow, Varuṇa inflicts him with dropsy[11]. Hearing of this, Rohita purchases a Brahmin boy named Śunaḥśepa from his parents, in order to use him as a substitute victim. Śunaḥśepa's own father is prepared to perform the sacrifice. Bound to the sacrificial stake, as his father approaches with knife in hand, Śunaḥśepa prays to the gods. As he is released, Hariścandra is simultaneously healed.

For good reason, this legend has been compared to the biblical story of Abraham and his readiness to offer up his son. It is also taken as evidence that the practice of human sacrifice once existed in ancient India (see Müller 1859: 408-419 and 573-588; Weber 1868; Parpola 2007). In my opinion, the Śunaḥśepa legend reflects Harappan traditions, although some elements have been replaced with their approximate counterparts in the Indo-Iranian tradition. One such replacement is the correspondence between Śunaḥśepa and the tail of the heavenly crocodile. Another is Varuṇa as the name of the fertility god who grants offspring and demands the first-born son as an offering.

There is no question that Varuṇa hearkens back to the extra-Indian Indo-Iranian tradition (Parpola 2005). Varuṇa's Rigvedic association with the banyan tree is confirmed by the Gobhila-Gṛhyasutra (4,7,24), which states that "the banyan is Varuṇa's tree." Yet Varuṇa cannot have originally been the god associated with this tree, which belongs to the flora of South Asia and, as can be seen in Harappan iconography, enjoys a prominent position in the religion of the Indus Civilization, particularly in fertility cults (Parpola 2004). Varuṇa was chosen as a replacement because, as a divine king and god of the waters, he was closest to the respective Harappan deity. In the early Vedic texts, Varuṇa is the "lord of waters" (*apāṃ pati*) in a very wide sense; his domain includes the ocean, the rivers, the heavenly and underground waters, and oath water (Lüders 1951-1959). In later Hinduism, Varuṇa came even closer to his Harappan prototype. In the Mahābhārata, he is not only "the lord of waters" (*apāṃ pati, jaleśvara*) but also "the lord of aquatic creatures" (*ambhasāṃ pati, yādasāṃ pati*). In Old Tamil texts, Varuṇa is the god of the ocean (*kaṭal*), of maritime tracts (*neytal*), and of fishermen; in later Tamil texts, he is "king of the ocean" (*kaṭaṟ-kō*) and "the god of waters" (*nīr-k-kaṭavuḷ*). In later Indian iconography, Varuṇa uses the makara 'mythical sea monster' or 'crocodile' as his vehicle (Figure 47). Crocodiles are further connected with Varuṇa as the beasts due to be offered to this god in the Vedic horse sacrifice (cf. Maitrāyaṇī Saṃhitā 3,14,2 and Vājasaneyi-Saṃhitā 24,21: *varuṇāya nākrān*).

It is significant that as recently as 200 years ago, in a fertility cult that included elements resembling the Śunaḥśepa legend of Varuṇa, one still found in India the practice of offering first-born children to crocodiles. Above I have quoted the testimony given by William Ward, from which it appears that these offerings of the first-born were made to the goddess Gaṅgā, not to Varuṇa. There is a connection with Varuṇa, however, revealed by the two preferred dates for these sacrifices.

The first date (the tenth day of the waxing moon in the Jyaiṣṭha month, which coincides with the culmination of the main festival of the goddess Durgā, the *daśaharā*), commemorates Gaṅgā's descent from heaven (Ward 1817-1820 III: 269). On this day, celebrations include "worship of the inhabitants of the waters, as the fish, the tortoises, the frogs, the water-snakes, the leeches, the snails, the makaras, the shell-fish, the porpoises, etc." (Ward 1817-1820 III: 270). He adds, "Persons escaping dangers of water present offerings to Gaṅgā, as well as to Varuṇa, the Indian Neptune" (Ward 1817-1820 III: 271).

The other date is the 13th of the waning moon in the month of Caitra; this day is especially sacred if the moon is in conjunction with the asterism of Śatabhiṣaj, which is presided over by Varuṇa. Then it is called Vāruṇī, and "the merit arising from bathing at this lucky moment is supposed to be very great" (Ward 1817-1820 III: 271-272; Kane 1958 V.1: 405-406). For Indo-Aryan speakers, river names have feminine gender. Accordingly, rivers are goddesses. However, it appears that the Harappans worshipped rivers as masculine gods (see below), as did the Mesopotamians.

Sacrifice of children to a crocodile deity appears to be attested in an unpublished moulded Indus tablet from Dholavira in Kutch, Gujarat (Figure 48). One side of the Dholavira tablet depicts two crocodiles, one with a fish (or a child?) in its mouth; these two crocodiles accompany the encounter of two partly anthropomorphic, partly animal-shaped Harappan divinities. The other side of the tablet has an Indus inscription of six signs[12] and a kneeling man with a child in his hands; it is unclear if he just holding the child in the air or piercing it with a pointed object. In any case, the man's kneeling posture resembles that of a man in moulded tablet M-478 (Figure 49), who is extending what looks like a sacrificial vessel to a sacred tree. The accompanying text in M-478 contains a sequence of signs no. 131 (four short vertical strokes = 'four') and no. 296 (U or V-shaped 'sacrificial vessel'), apparently recording the presentation of four vessels filled with unspecified offerings (Parpola 1994: 109). In moulded tablet M-453 (Figure 50), a kneeling worshipper on the left side extends an offering vessel to an anthropomorphic deity seated on a throne, while another kneeling worshipper on the god's right side raises his or her hands in adoration or prayer; behind both worshippers is a raised cobra with its hood expanded.

The reverse side of moulded tablet H-172 from Harappa (Figure 51) shows the gharial swimming in the midst of four fish while eating a fifth one. The obverse has an inscription that ends in Indus sign no. 306 (U-shaped 'sacrificial vessel', modified by sign no. 376 being added inside it) . As mentioned above, I have interpreted the preceding sign no. 337 (intersecting circles, Figure 32) as 'earrings' or 'bangles' (which are important in South Asian fertility cults) = Proto-Dravidian **muruku* (DEDR 4979), an exact homophone of Proto-Dravidian **muruku* 'boy child, young man' (DEDR 4978). Muruku is the name of the principal god of the Tamils, a counterpart of Vedic Rudra and Hindu Skanda, both of whom are called *Kumāra* 'boy child, young man' (Parpola 1994: 226-230). Hence tablet

Figure 47 God Varuṇa on makara (after Majupuria 1991: 194)

Figure 48 Moulded Indus tablet from Dholavira, Kutch, Gujarat (sketch by Asko Parpola)

Figure 49 Indus tablet M-474 (A side) (after CISI 1: 115)

Figure 50 Indus tablet M-453 (B side) (after CISI 1: 386)

H-172 A

H-172 B

Figure 51 Indus tablet H-172 (after CISI 1: 207)

H-172 may record a child sacrifice to the crocodile god.

That the crocodile god should demand offerings of children sacrificed by their own parents may have its basis in the male crocodile's habit of eating its own offspring, something that is expressly mentioned a couple of times in Old Tamil texts. The Tamil word *piḷḷai* used in this context (Aiṅkuṟunūṟu 24: *piḷḷai tiṉṉu mutalai*) means human as well as animal offspring. In part two of the Ganges series produced for television by BBC Bristol in 2007, it is shown that the gharial male can also eat its newly born offspring. The same is probably true of the South Asian river dolphin: "Male Bottlenose Dolphins have been known to engage in infanticide." (*Wikipedia* in December 2009 s.v. Dolphin) Sanskrit *śiśu-māra-* has been understood to mean 'baby-killer' by classical Indian authors such as Vasubandhu and Sāyaṇa. In his commentary on the Taittirīya-Āraṇyaka, the latter glosses the word as follows: *śisūn mārayati mukhena nigiratīti śiśumāro jalagrahaviśeṣaḥ* (Lüders 1942: 81). This straightforward and literal interpretation of the word may actually be the correct etymology. In any case, the heavenly *śiśumāra*'s connection with Śunaḥśepa does support the traditional Indian etymology.

The Harappan god of water and fertility

Above I suggested that Varuṇa, as the Vedic "lord of waters", has replaced the Harappan water god and adopted his emblems: Varuṇa is associated in the Veda with the pole star, the banyan tree, and the crocodile, all of which appear to have been very important Harappan symbols of divine kingship (Parpola 2004). One face of the three-sided moulded tablet M-2033 from Mohenjo-daro (Figure 52) has the image of a seated anthropomorphic deity with a horned crown, flanked on either side by a gharial and a fish. The fish, which has a phallic shape and boasts phenomenal rates of reproduction, is an important symbol of fertility in South Asia, as well as an aphrodisiac. In Tamil, Varuṇa is called *mīṉ-ūrti*, 'having the fish for his mount'; usually the mythical water monster makara is mentioned as Varuna's mount. Another Indian deity who rides on the makara is Kāma, the god of sexual love. Kāma also has the emblem of fish in his flag. Fish is the most important aquatic animal, of course, and as such is a symbol of water. In the Vedic horse sacrifice, fish are offered to the waters (Maitrāyaṇī Saṃhitā 3,14,2 *abdhyo matsyān*). Fish also appear within the rivers that issue from the body of the Mesopotamian water-god Ea / Enki; praised as a phallic god, he spreads water as his fecundating semen on the soil (Figure 53).

On an unprovenanced cylinder seal likely made in Mesopotamia by a Harappan craftsman (Figure 54), one finds a deity on a throne who is wearing a crown of buffalo horns topped by banyan leaves; the god is flanked on both sides by a fish. This cylinder seal also features a hooded and horned snake on either side of the deity, instead of the crocodiles found in tablet M-2033 from Mohenjo-daro. Beneath the throne are two water buffaloes drinking from a trough. Buffaloes are also beasts associated with water, as they have to bathe every day. In a Kot Diji-type Early Harappan pot from Burzahom in Kashmir, the water buffalo is depicted in the water (Figure 55). Water buffaloes are mentioned only once in the Vedic ritual literature after the Rigveda: they are offered to Varuṇa (Maitrāyaṇī Saṃhitā 3,14,10 *varuṇāya mahiṣān*). In later Hinduism, the water buffalo is associated with Yama as the god of death; Yama resembles Varuṇa in several respects, but most obviously in his role as Dharmarāja (cf.

Figure 52 Indus tablet M-2033 (B side) (after CISI 3.1: 109)

Figure 53 Impression of an Akkadian cylinder seal showing various gods, among them the water god Enki (after Parrot 1960: 193, Figure 237)

Figure 54 Impression of an unprovenanced Indus-style cylinder seal in the Louvre (AO Collection De Clercq I.26) (after Parpola 1994: 186, Figure 10.10)

Figure 55 Early Harappan (Kot Diji) pot from Burzahom (Period I B), Kashmir (after Kaw 1979: 224 Figure 4)

Figure 56 Indus seal M-304 ("Proto-Śiva") (after CISI 1: 382)

Varuṇa as Samrāj guarding Ṛta). In its incarnation as Mahiṣa Asura, the water buffalo is also connected with Śiva, the dying and resurrected husband of the goddess Devī who defeats it.

The buffalo demon Mahiṣa Asura is the prototype of a valiant warrior. In battle with the goddess Devī, it goes through many metamorphoses, taking the shape of one strong animal after another (including lion and ending in man). I have compared Mahiṣa's transformations with those of the Vedic creator god Prajāpati. Seeking to multiply himself and generate offspring, this primeval Man (*puruṣa*) approached his own daughter. The daughter tried to escape, changing from one kind of female animal to another, while her father gave chase by assuming the shape of the corresponding male. In this way, all of the different animal species were created. The myth stresses that all male animals are manifestations of the singular primeval male, the creator god Prajāpati. In my opinion, the same concept prevails in the Harappan 'Proto-Śiva' seal (Figure 56), where the seated buffalo-horned deity is flanked by four powerful male animals: rhinoceros, elephant, buffalo and tiger. All of these animals seem to represent the mighty god depicted in the center in anthropomorphic form. (Parpola 1994: 184-190; 1992; 1998; 2002; 2004; 2007)

Crocodile and the Indus sign depicting 'buffalo-horned man'

Indus sign no. 7 depicts 'man wearing horns', which in some of the variants are clearly those of the buffalo (Figure 57). On the basis of what was discussed above, I would like to propose that this sign stands for Proto-Dravidian **ēṟu* 'male animal with remarkable physical strength'; in particular, the word refers to the buffalo and the bull (but also tiger, lion, pig, etc.) (DEDR 917). This word is derived from the Proto-Dravidian root **ēṟu* 'to rise, ascend, climb, increase (in price or quality), multiply, be much, abound (in number, weight or measure), be more than enough' (DEDR 916). In Old Tamil, the variant *ēṟṟai* is also used for the male crocodile (*mutalai*) in Kuṟuntokai 324,1 (quoted above). In such instances, *ēṟṟai* 'male' is preceded by the attribute *kōḷ val* 'strong in killing, strong killer'; taken as a whole, the phrase is an apposition to the foregoing animal name *mutalai*

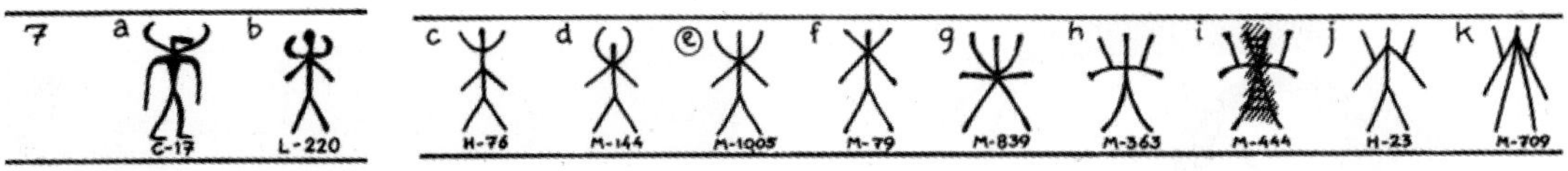

Figure 57 Indus sign no. 7 with variants (after Parpola 1994: 70, Figure 5.1)

(for this interpretation, see Cāminātaiyar 1962: lii: "*mutalai... itan̲ āṇai ēr̲r̲ai yen̲r̲al marapu*"; for example, it is common practice to call the male crocodile *ēr̲r̲ai*). The very same phrase follows in apposition to the characterization of the male tiger in Kur̲untokai 141,5 (*kur̲uṅkai yirum pulik kōḷ val ēr̲r̲ai*), occurring in four other places in Caṅkam literature (Akanān̲ūr̲u 171,9; Aiṅkur̲unūr̲u 216,1; Nar̲r̲iṇai 36,1; 148,9).

While the moulded Indus tablet M-450 (Figure 58) has broken, enough survives to show that both sides were originally identical and contained, from right to left, the image of a crocodile and an inscription with four signs. The last two signs frequently occur together in this position, but the distinctive first two signs probably refer to the crocodile deity depicted on the tablet. The second sign is the 'buffalo-horned man' discussed directly above, which can be read as **ēr̲u* 'male animal with remarkable physical strength'. Supposing that Old Tamil *val ēr̲r̲ai* 'strong male' is an important formulaic phrase inherited from Proto-Dravidian and demonstrably used to designate the crocodile, there is a fair chance that the first sign (sign no. 101) stands for Proto-Dravidian **val* 'strong' (DEDR 5276).

In the Old Tamil poetic formula *kōḷ val ēr̲r̲ai*, the phrase *val ēr̲r̲ai* is preceded by the word *kōḷ*. Traditionally interpreted to denote 'killing' (Tamil *kolai*), it is derived from the verbal root *koḷ* 'to grab' (TL 1928 II: 1202a s. v. *kōḷ*[1], 11). Thus, Hart's translation of 'taking prey' is more faithful to the original: the expression corresponds to Sanskrit *grāha-* (from the root *grah-* 'to grab'), which is used for the crocodile and other beasts of prey[13]. In the Indus texts, sign no. 88—the 'crab', mostly commonly depicted without feet in order to emphasize its pincers (Figure 59), interpreted as denoting Proto-Dravidian **kōḷ* or **koḷ* (Parpola 1994: 232-239)—occasionally precedes the phrase *val ēr̲u* 'strong male' posited above. Even more commonly, it precedes the phrase *val mīn* 'strong fish, crocodile' (see below).

M-450 A

M-450 B

Figure 58 Indus tablet M-450 (after CISI 1: 110)

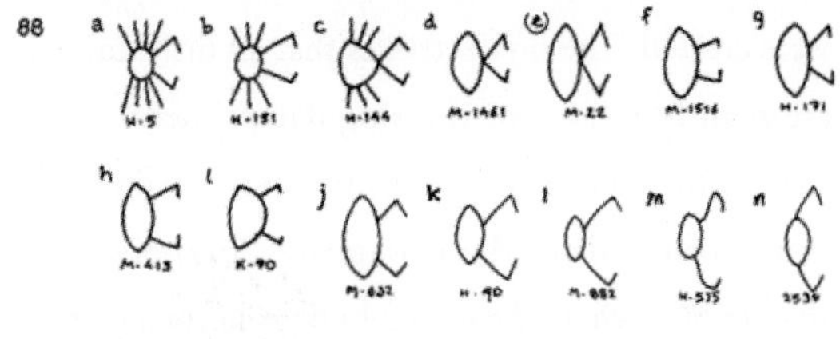

Figure 59 Indus sign no. 88 with variants (after Parpola 1994: 71-72, Figure 5.1)

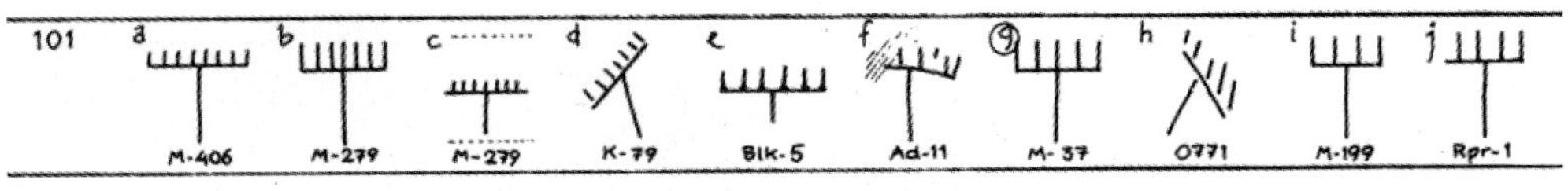

Figure 60 Indus sign no. 101 with variants (after Parpola 1994: 72,Figure 5.1)

Tamil *val-mīn* 'crocodile' and the Indus sign possibly depicting 'fish gig'

Sign no. 101, found at the beginning of the crocodile-related inscription in tablet M-450 (Figure 58) and provisionally read as Proto-Dravidian **val* 'strong' (DEDR 5276) on the basis of an Old Tamil poetic formula, is very often followed in Indus texts by the plain 'fish' sign (interpreted in Proto-Dravidian as **mīn* 'fish' and 'star'). The suggested readings **val* and **mīn* produce the Tamil compound *val mī<u>n</u>* (with sandhi, *va<u>n</u>mī<u>n</u>*). Literally meaning 'strong fish', this is recorded in Tivākaram's ancient lexicon as one of the words for 'crocodile'[14]. The antiquity of the compound is supported by its attestation in Tulu as well (though the *Tulu lexicon* edited by U. P. Upadhyaya only vaguely defines it as 'a kind of fish'). Moreover, this sign sequence occurs in the beginning of the inscription in the long moulded tablet H-282 and its many duplicates, perhaps the most important type of tablets depicting the gharial in iconographic form (see Figure 42). The sequence is here preceded just by the aforementioned 'fist' sign, interpreted as Proto-Dravidian **piṭi* 'catch(ing fish)'.

Sign no. 101 (Figure 60) consists of a vertical rod topped by a horizontal (sometimes slanting) rod with a row of upwards pointing spikes (usually five, but sometimes more and seldom less). What does this sign depict?

Perhaps the first thing that comes to mind is 'harrow' or 'rake'. In Dravidian (and many other) languages, names for this agricultural tool (such as Tamil *palli*, *palaki*, Kannada *halive*, *halike*, *halube*, *halaku*, and Telugu *palu-go<u>rr</u>u*) have been derived from the word for 'tooth', which in Proto-Dravidian was **pal* (DEDR 3986). It is true that in some Dravidian languages, words with an initial *p-* have variants beginning with *v-* (cf. Tamil *paṇṭi* and *vaṇṭi*, *palappam* and *valappam*, *pāṇali* and *vāṇali*, etc.). Although one can actually posit the variant *val* 'tooth' for Tamil on the basis of Tamil *va<u>nr</u>i* 'pig' from *pa<u>nr</u>i* 'pig', since this word is derived from *pal* 'tooth' (the wild pig being distinguished by its tusks), this variation cannot be projected to Proto-Dravidian for the word **pal* 'tooth' on the basis of the available linguistic evidence.

The Indus sign could also represent the fishgig = 'a pole with barbed prongs for impaling fish' (Collins English dictionary) (Figure 61). This many-pronged fishing tool is used by the local fishermen of the Chambal river, featured in the *Ganges* television series (2007). The fishgig serves thematically as an attribute of the gharial, which uses long and very narrow jaws with numerous sharp teeth (Figure 62) for fishing. The slimness of the snout enables the gharial to jerk it swiftly sideways, thereby impaling fish with its teeth. One of the words for 'harpoon' in Tamil (Winslow *et al.* 1888: 621) happens to be *vallayam*, which has cognates with identical meaning (e.g., Kannada *ballega* and Telugu *ballemu*). Use of the fishgig requires considerable strength; the *Tamil Lexicon* (1934 VI: 3528a) suggests that the Tamil word is derived from *val* 'strong, strength' + *ayam* < Sanskrit *ayas-* 'iron'. The latter component would be of post-Proto-Dravidian origin[15].

The Harappan river god

Indus sign no. 175 consists of two vertical and wavy or bending lines (Figure 63). That the wavy and

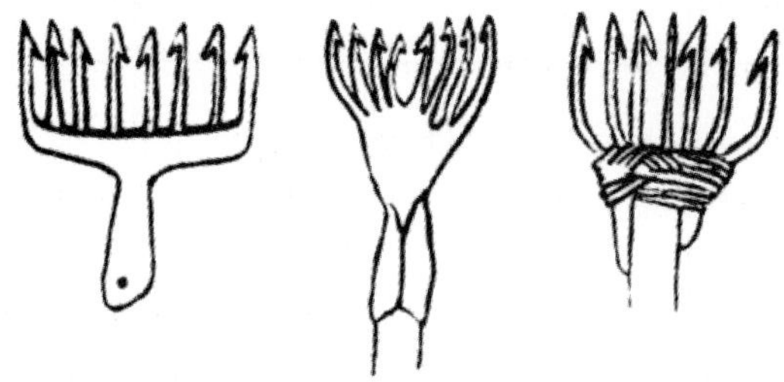

Figure 61 Fish-gigs (after Vuorela 1964: 8)

Figure 62 Gharial feeding. ARKive photo G 34691 (courtesy of Olivier Born / Biosphoto)

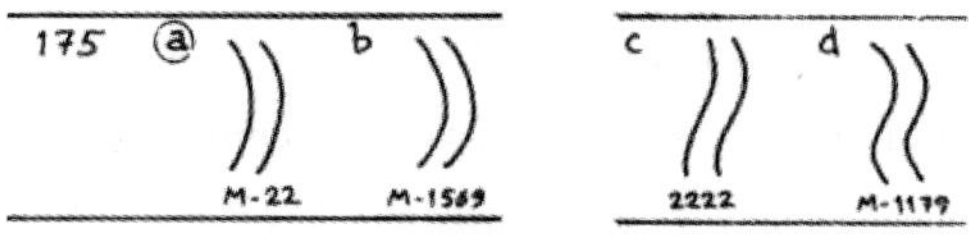

Figure 63 Indus sign no. 175 with variants (after Parpola 1994: 73, Figure 5.1)

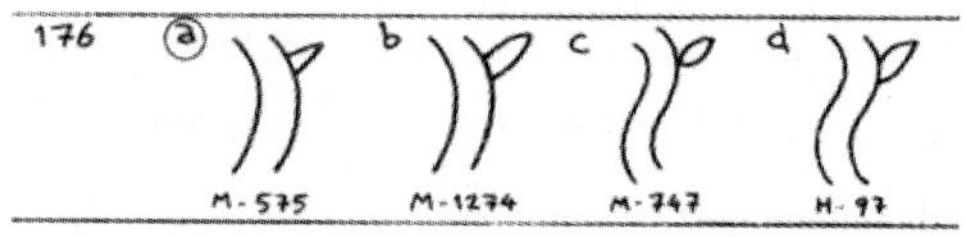

Figure 64 Indus sign no. 176 with variants (after Parpola 1994: 73, Figure 5.1)

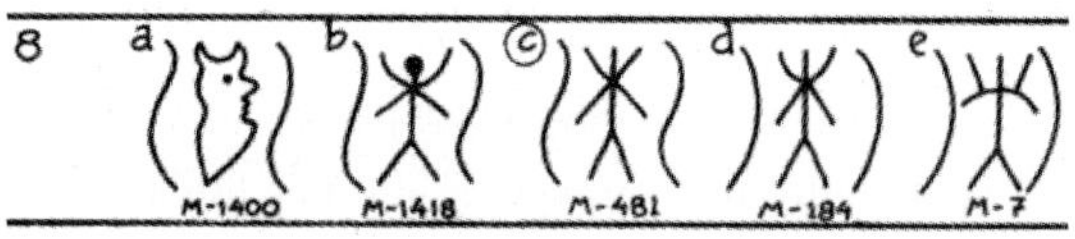

Figure 65 Indus sign no. 8 with variants (after Parpola 1994: 70, Figure 5.1)

M-481 A

Figure 66 Indus tablet M-481 (A side) (after CISI 1: 115)

bending signs are allographs of one and the same grapheme is confirmed by the presence of the same variation in ligatures of this sign in which either an extra element is added to one of the lines (sign no. 176; Figure 64) or another sign is inserted between the two lines (sign no. 8, discussed below). The basic sign (no. 175) is similar to the Sumerian pictogram for 'water': it appears to depict a meandering river. It may have expressed the basic Proto-Dravidian word for 'water', most probably **nīr* (DEDR 3690a). In sign no. 8 (Figure 65), this hypothetical 'water' sign, split in two, surrounds sign no. 7 depicting 'buffalo-horned man' (read above as **ēṟu* 'male animal with remarkable physical strength'). Sign no. 7 likely functions here as a phonetic indicator, showing that the sign for 'water' (no. 175) denotes 'river' in this context; the Proto-Dravidian word for 'river' was **yāṟu*, **ēṟu* (DEDR 5159). This phonetic indicator functions simultaneously as a pictorial symbol, since the 'male' in the 'river' stands for the crocodile. In later Indian iconography, the crocodile represents the river Ganges as the vehicle of this river goddess (Viennot 1964; Tandon and Biswas 1986; Stietencron 1972; 2010). That sign no. 7 ('buffalo-horned man') functions as a phonetic indicator rather than a part of a compound in the ligatured sign no. 8 is supported by the fact that sign no. 8 is followed by sign no. 7 in some Indus texts: this noun phrase would mean 'the male of the river' (that is, the crocodile).

An elaborate pictorial representation of sign no. 8 may be seen in Indus tablet M-2033 (Figure 52), which shows a vertical wavy line on either side of the central god and his crocodile and fish

M-1429 A

M-1429 B

M-1429 C

Figure 67 Indus tablet M-1429 (after CISI 3.1: 386)

H-1932 A

H-1932 B

H-1932 C

Figure 68 Indus tablet H-1932 (after CISI 3.1: 264)

emblems. In Mesopotamian iconography, the river is represented with fish swimming in it; as mentioned above, such a river flows out of either side of the water god Ea (alias Enki) (Figure 53). That sign no. 8 represents a Harappan deity, presumbly the 'river god', is confirmed by Indus tablet M-481 (Figure 66). On the obverse of this tablet there is a kneeling worshipper with a pot of offerings in his hand, which is extended towards sign no. 8. The first part of the inscription contains a sequence of sign no. 354 'fist' and sign no. 311 'bovine head', which I already proposed can be read in Proto-Dravidian as **piṭi-y-an* 'catcher (of fish)' as a name or attribute of the gharial and the heavenly crocodile that causes eclipses (Rāhu).

The heavenly 'overseer'

The 'fist' sign begins the inscription on the three-faced moulded tablet M-1429 from Mohenjo-daro (Figure 67). The next phrase in this text contains a sequence of sign no. 130 'number three' and sign no. 60 'fish' (without diacritics), read as **mu-m-mīn* '(asterism consisting of) three stars'. This is the Old Tamil name of the calendrical constellation *mṛgaśīrṣa-* (Parpola 1994: 194), but it is possible that it originally denoted another three-starred asterism, the *(apa)bharaṇī-*. This latter constellation is expressly connected with the waters, the fireplace consisting of three stones, the womb, and Yama (the god of death); in turn, all of these seem to represent King Varuṇa, the Vedic counterpart of the Harappan water-god (see Parpola 1985: 78-101; 1994: 211-218).

The next phrase in the inscription of tablet M-1429 contains a reduplication of Indus sign no. 358 'dot-in-circle', which is interpreted as Proto-Dravidian **kaṇ* 'eye' (DEDR no. 1159) or **kāṇ* 'to see, look' (DEDR 1443). In reduplication, the signs connote the noun phrase 'overseer' (found in Tamil *kaṇ-kāṇi*).

"This would be a fitting epithet for Varuṇa, who is probably meant in ṚS 10,129,7, which speaks of an 'overseer (*ádhyakṣa-*) of this (world) in the highest heaven'. Varuṇa is the 'thousand-eyed' guardian of the cosmic order, and looks down on the earth with the eye of the sun... in other Vedic texts, the sun and moon are the eyes of the highest Brahma ... The two other sides of the amulet [M-1429] suggest that the text relates to the water-god of the Harappans: one side has the picture of a boat, the other an alligator [read: long-snouted crocodile]. Both designs refer to water, which is the realm of the god Varuṇa. Varuṇa is the 'lord of aquatic animals', including the crocodile (# 10.2), and the boat is explicitly connected with Varuṇa in Ṛgveda 7,88,3" (Parpola 1994: 215).

In Taittirīya Āraṇyaka 2,19, the heavenly crocodile is called "the lord of all beings (*bhūtānām adhipatir*)", an appellation which further supports identification of this **kaṇ-kāṇi* 'overseer' with the

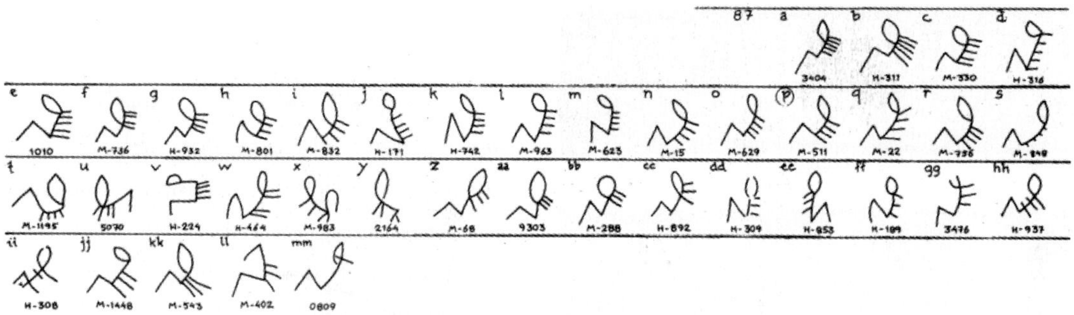

Figure 69 Indus sign no. 87 with variants (after Parpola 1994: 71, Figure 5.1)

Figure 70 Indus sign no. 86 with variants (after Parpola 1994: 71, Figure 5.1)

Figure 71 Mugger's "high walk" (after Whitaker 1986: 151)

Harappan predecessor of Varuṇa.

Snake and crocodile: A reptile with feet

In tablet H-1932 from Harappa (Figure 68), this phrase consisting of the duplicated 'dot-in-circle' sign and read as **kaṇ-kāṇi* 'overseer' occurs before sign no. 87 (Figure 69), which is formed from sign no. 86 (Figure 70) by adding linear extensions on one side; in the great majority of cases, one finds four extensions but, in a few cases, there are five or three. In 1934, Piero Meriggi suggested that sign no. 87 depicts 'horse'. The domestic horse was introduced to South Asia in the second millennium BCE, however, making this pictorial identification unlikely. I have commented on this as follows:

"Some variants of the basic sign (Figure 5.1 no. 86) rather suggest an enraged cobra with expanded hood; moreover, the number of the added strokes (Meriggi's 'feet') is not always four, and they are sometimes placed as if they represented hair" (Parpola 1994: 59).

I still believe that the basic sign should be idenfied as a snake. But looking at the graphic variants of sign no. 87 derived from it, I now support the interpretation of the extensions being 'feet'. Normally there are four extensions, sometimes arranged into two pairs (i.e., front legs and back legs). The very few exceptions with three or five legs are likely just carving mistakes. My guess is that the sign depicts a reptile with legs (i.e., the crocodile). That the legs are sometimes placed close to the 'head' is due to the crocodile's legs being closer to its head than its tail (Figure 71).

H-1932 is a three-sided tablet. One of the sides depicts a crocodile; another side has the text IIU, which likely means 'two pots (of offerings)'[16]. It appears that the main aim of the "sacrificial tablets" was to obtain offspring. On the basis of its great frequence on the "sacrificial tablets", sign no. 87 probably indicates the deity that was most frequently supplicated for this purpose. Given all of these reasons, as well as the evidence presented in this paper, I propose that this sign renders the principal Proto-Dravidian word for 'crocodile', **mōcalay*, **mocalay* (DEDR no. 4952).

Sign no. 86 'snake' and sign no. 87 'crocodile' mean different but related things. They can occur together, as well as next to each other. Both have phallic connotations and both are associated with fertility cult worship. Moreover, both occur

M-1418 A

M-1418 B

Figure 72 Indus tablet M-1418 (after CISI 2: 191)

H-396 A

H-396 a

Figure 73 Indus seal H-396 (A) and its modern impression (a) (after CISI 2: 263)

frequently in connection with other signs associated with the Harappan god(s) of water and fertility, especially those discussed in the present paper (e.g., tablet M-1418 in Figure 72).

The bleary-eyed beast

Seal H-396 from Harappa (Figure 73) is a large one, suggesting that it may have "belonged to" a divinity, in whose name it was used by priests. Although the first part of the inscription has broken off and is missing, the last five signs survive. An interpretation for the first three has already been posited above: Dravidian **piṭi* and **val-mīn*, both of which refer to the crocodile. The remaining two signs form a compound-like sequence that recurs in seven other inscriptions, five times at the end of an inscription (M-205, M-370, H-568, H-602, H-797) and twice in the middle (M-396, H-639). Dravidian readings have been suggested for both of these signs, no. 175 (see Figure 63) = **nīr* 'water' and no. 358 'dot-in-circle' = **kaṇ* 'eye'. The resulting compound **nīr-k-kaṇ* literally means 'water-eye'. The compound is attested in Tulu (*nīruda kaṇṇu*, with the genitive marker added to the first member);[17] its meaning in that language is 'the big one of the three hole-like outlets on the top of a coconut' (Upadhyaya ed. 1997: IV, 1802a): the word *kaṇ* in Dravidian languages means not only 'eye', but also 'hole, opening' (DEDR 1159). In Tamil, *mu-k-kaṇ* is used both for 'coconut' and 'three-eyed' deities like Śiva (TL 1936 VI: 3217a). In this particular Harappan context, however, the word **nīr* 'water' probably has the following sense attested in Tamil: 'humour of the body, as serum, lymph' and 'pus' (cf. also *nīr-k-koḷ* 'to feel heavy with cold, as the head; to suppurate, form pus, as a tumour', *nīr-p-patumam* 'a disease of the eyelids', and *nīr-p-pāyccal* 'irrigation from a river; discharge of serum from a sore, of water from the eyes, of mucus from the nose') (TL 1931 IV: 2299b, 2301b, 2304b). Thus **nīr-k-kaṇ* 'water-eye(d)' is synonymous with Malayalam *cīṅkaṇṇi, cīkaṇṇi, cīyaṇṇi* 'an alligator, crocodile', literally 'bleary-eyed' (Gundert 1872: 367a; *Malayalam Lexicon* 1985: V, 456b, 458b), from *cī* 'putrid matter, secretion of eyelids' (Gundert 1872: 367a) < Proto-Dravidian **kī* 'pus, snot; to rot' (DEDR 1606).

Conclusion

In consideration of all the evidence, quite a number of Indus signs associated with representations of the crocodile on the Harappan 'sacrificial tablets' (and by extension in other texts) can be correlated with expressions that the Dravidian languages have for 'crocodile'. To a reasonable degree, these new interpretations satisfy iconic and linguistic requirements; to some extent, they also support each other. Corroborating the method and premises of earlier interpretations, they open up new avenues for further penetration into the Indus script. That said, we must remain on the lookout for opportunities to further prove or disprove these hypotheses.

Notes

1) This is a revised and much enlarged version of a paper presented at the international symposium on "Harappans in Gujarat" held in Bhuj, Kutch, Gujarat, 28-31 January 2010. I am much obliged to Dr Albion Butters for careful language checking.

2) See www.gharialconservation.org/gharials; for the phallic snout of the ghariyal, see also Murthy 1995: 20 and Benton 2006: 152-4, with Figure 7.13 and references.

3) According to Aristobulus, a very trustworthy companion of Alexander the Great, "crocodiles, neither numerous nor harmful to man, are to be found in the Indus" (Strabo, Geography 15,1,45, transl. Jones 1930: VII, 79).

4) Prakrit *soṇḍa* = *suṇḍa* (Sheth 1963: 932c) comes from Sanskrit *śauṇḍa-*, both of which mean 'addicted to drink' (Turner 1966: no. 12650); for the Prakrit word, Sheth (1963: 911c) gives the additional meaning of 'skilful'. Prakrit *maṭṭha-* is derived from Sanskrit *mṛṣṭa-*, both meaning 'rubbed, wiped, washed, polished, clean, pure; delicate' (Turner 1966: no, 10299; Sheth 1963: 668b); in addition, Sheth (1963: 668b) records a Prakrit homonym meaning 'inactive, slow, lazy'.

5) For the occasional loss of *c-* in South Dravidian, see Krishnamurti 2003: 121-125; cf. Mayrhofer 2001: III, 36 and 195.

6) For various kinds of South Asian air-breathing sea snakes, which are highly venomous and have completely adapted to life in the sea (and are often mistaken for eels, and vice versa), see Murthy 1995: 34-39 with Figure 14-20.

7) Above all, a meaning must be found that convincingly explains a noun phrase found, on many seals, often alone. The sign that probably depict 'hand, arm' is preceded by a numeral whose value varies. A good possibility is **taṇṭu* 'to collect (debts, rents, taxes, etc.), to pay off (debt)' (DEDR 3054); the meaning recorded in Tulu, 'to put forth the hand to receive anything', suggests that the verb goes back to **taṇṭu* 'arm'. The number preceding the 'hand, arm' sign can be an abbreviation for 'x number of pots (of sacrifice or taxation)': in tablets M-494 and M-495, it is preceded by UUU (Parpola 1994: 83), with the sequence UUU being equal to '3' + U = 'three pots (of sacrifice or taxation)' (Parpola 1994: 109).

8) A special development of the meaning of the root **iẓu*, **eẓu* 'to draw, pull' (attested only in South Dravidian) is **iẓu*, **eẓu* 'to gasp for breath as from asthma, to breathe hard as a dying person, to pant' (DEDR 504 b). This may be relevant as well, as breeding gharial males hiss loudly, with the protuberance possibly acting as a resonator (Daniel 1983: 15).

9) Lüders (1942: 66-69) argues that the heavenly dolphin of the Jaiminīya-Brāhmaṇa represents the original tradition, while *śiśumāra-* in the Taittirīya-Āraṇyaka means 'crocodile' because this text was composed outside the distribution area of the river dolphin in South India. However, already in Pañcaviṃśa-Brāhmaṇa 8,6,8-10 and Jaiminīya-Brāhmaṇa 1,176, *śiśumārī-* denotes 'female crocodile' rather than 'female dolphin', as these texts describe the animal lying in a narrow place of a river with an open mouth, waiting for prey that she can swallow. A river dolphin hardly lies for any length of time, much less with its mouth open. On the other hand, an open mouth is characteristic of a basking crocodile; examples are mentioned in Jātaka texts (Lüders (1942: 77-78). Caland (1919: 67-69, #62) first thought the dolphin was meant here—, and Lüders (1942: 66) followed him—, but Caland (1931: 177-178) later changed his mind to his view to crocodile. Lüders (1942: 70 n. 2) admits that *śiśumāra-* could mean 'crocodile' in Śāṅkhāyana-Āraṇyaka 12,6,28: *nainaṃ pramattaṃ varuṇo hinasti na makaro na grahaḥ śiśumāraḥ*. Note that the dangerous aquatic beasts mentioned here are connected with Varuṇa.

10) The name Rohita, which means 'the Red one', appears to refer to the rising sun.

11) This also appears to have astral significance, as the crescent moon may be thought to suffer from dropsy.

12) This phrase, consisting of the repeated sign no. 142 (Parpola 1994: 73), 'roof' over 'number one', occurs relatively rarely in the Indus texts; however, twice (in M-650 and L-98) it precedes the phrase of signs nos. 101 and 60, read below as *val mīn* 'strong fish = crocodile'.

13) Cf. also the compounds *kōḷ-mutala* = *kōḷttala* 'crocodile' (attested in Malayalam) and *kōḷ-ari* 'lion' in Tamil (TL 1928 II: 1202c from Piṅkala's lexicon) and ancient Malayalam (Gundert 1872: 320a, quoting Payanūr pāṭṭu and Rāmacaritam). The latter component is a loanword, from Sanskrit *hari-* 'yellowish; m. lion' (Böhtlingk 1889 VII: 258c).

14) The crocodile is occasionally included with fish in Indo-Aryan texts, too (Lüders 1942: 63 and 72-73).

15) Tamil *vallayam* and its cognates might be related to other Indo-Aryan words denoting 'fish-hook', which on account of their relatively late appearance (first in Suparṇādhyāya 17,2 *matsya iva biliśaṃ jagrasāno*, then in the epics) and great variation have been believed to be loanwords from a non-Aryan language (Mayrhofer 1996: II, 226; Turner 1966: no. 9123); a Munda origin was once proposed by Kuiper (1948: 94-95), but Kuiper himself later admitted that the related Munda words (Munda *bāṛsi, bansi* and Sora *bāṛsi* 'fish-hook') are loanwords from Neo-Indo-Aryan.

In detail, the Indo-Aryan evidence is as follows:

Sanskrit *biliśa-* (Suparṇādhyāya 17,2; Mahāvastu iii,259,2 and 260,16, with variant reading *billaśa-*), *baḍiśa-* (Mahabhārata, Rāmāyaṇa, kāvya), *valiśa-*, *vaḍiśa-baliśa-*, *baḍiśa-* (lexica)

Pali *balisa-*, *baḷisa-*, Prakrit *biḍiśa-*, *baḍisa-*, *barisa-*

Hindi *vaṛis, vaṛiśī*

Old Awadhi *banasī*

Kumaoni *balsī, balchī*

Nepali *balsi, balchi* (whence *balche* 'barbed')

Assamese *barahi*

Bengali *baṛis, baṛsi, baṛsā, bāṛsi*

Oriya *baṛisa, baṛisi, banasi, banisi* 'fishing-rod and line' (whence *banasiā, banisiā* 'angler')

Marathi *bansi*

Singhalese *balasa, biliya, bili-kaṭuva.*

If 'fish-gig' rather than 'fish-hook' is indeed the original meaning, I suggest reconstructing Proto-Dravidian **val-l-icam*, from Proto-Dravidian **val* 'strong, strength' (DEDR 5276) and Proto-Central-Dravidian **ic-* 'to strike, beat, thrust into or through, spear, spit, impale' (DEDR 425). On Proto-Dravidian *-*c*- [-*s*-] > -*y*- > -*g*-, cf. Kannada *ballega*; Krishnamurti 2003: 148-149.

16) Here the text is written from left to right; this is not uncommon in these "sacrificial tablets", though the normal direction of writing is from right to left (Parpola 1994: 107-110).

17) Adding this marker is optional, as seen in the case of the southern dialect Tulu compound *nīruta kaṇi* 'water canal' (versus *nīrukaṇi* in northern dialects).

References

Aelianus, Claudius (1832) *Aeliani De natura animalium libri septemdecim*. Verba ad fidem librorum manuscriptorum constituit et annotationibus illustravit Fridericus Jacobs. Jenae: Impensis Friderici Fromanni.

Anthony, David W. (2007) *The Horse, the Wheel, and Language: How Bronze-Age Riders from the Eurasian Steppes Shaped the Modern World*. Princeton: Princeton University Press.

Baloch, Waseem (2004) 'Manghopir, Karachi, Pakistan, and crocodiles', *Crocodile Specialist Group Newsletter* 23 (3): 12-13.

Benton, Catherine (2006) *God of desire: Tales of Kāmadeva in Sanskrit story literature*. Albany: State University of New York Press.

Bloch, Jules (1930) 'Some problems of Indo-Aryan philology', *Bulletin of the School of Oriental Studies, University of London* 5: 719-756.

Böhtlingk, Otto (1879-1889) *Sanskrit-Wörterbuch in kürzerer Fassung* I-VII. St. Petersburg: Kaiserliche Akademie der Wissenschaften.

Böhtlingk, Otto und Rudolph Roth (1852-1875) *Sanskrit-Wörterbuch* I-VII. St. Petersburg: Kaiserliche Akademie der Wissenschaften.

Boulenger, George A. (1890) *The Fauna of British India,*

including Ceylon and Burma: Reptilia and Batrachia. London: Taylor and Francis.

Brehm, A. E., O. Schmidt and E. L. Tachenberg (1876-1879) *Brehms Thierleben: Allgemeine Kunde des Thierreichs.* Zweite umgearbeitete und vermehrte Auflage. I-X. Leipzig: Verlag des Bibliographischen Instituts.

Burrow, Thomas (1948) 'Dravidian studies VII: Further Dravidian words in Sanskrit', *Bulletin of the School of Oriental and African Studies, University of London* 12: 365-396.

Burrow, T. and E. B. Emeneau (1984) *A Dravidian etymological dictionary.* Second edition. Oxford: Clarendon Press. (= DEDR).

Burton, Richard F. (1851) *Scinde; or, the Unhappy Valley.* Vol. I. London: Richard Bentley.

Burton, Richard F. (1877) *Sind revisited: with notices of the Anglo-Indian army; railroads; past, present, and future, etc.* Vol. I. London: Richard Bentley and Son.

Caland, Willem (1919) *Das Jaiminīya-Brāhmaṇa in Auswahl: Text, Übersetzung, Indices.* (Verhandelingen der Koninklijke Akademie van Wetenschappen te Amsterdam, Afdeeling Letterkunde, Nieuwe Reeks 19: 4) Amsterdam: Johannes Müller.

Caland, Willem (1931) *Pancaviṃśa-Brāhmaṇa: The Brāhmaṇa of Twenty Five Chapters, translated.* (Bibliotheca Indica, Work 255) Calcutta: The Asiatic Society of Bengal.

Cāminātaiyar, U. Vē. (ed.) (1961) *Pattuppāṭṭu mūlamum maturaiyāciriyar pārattuvāci naccinārkkiniyar uraiyum.* (1st ed. 1889) 6th ed. Madras: Kabeer Printing Works.

Cāminātaiyar, U. Vē. (ed.) (1971) *Puṟanāṉūṟu mūlamum paḻaiya uraiyum.* (1st ed. 1894) 7th ed. Madras: Dr. U. V. Swaminatha Aiyar Library.

Cāminātaiyar, U. Vē. (ed.) (1957) *Eṭṭuttokaiyuḷ mūṉṟāvatākiya Aiṅkuṟunūṟu mūlamum paḻaiya vuraiyum.* (1st ed. 1903) 5th ed.. Madras: Kabeer Printing Works.

Cāminātaiyar, U. Vē. (ed.) (1957) *Patiṟṟuppattu mūlamum paḻaiya vuraiyum.* (1st ed. 1904) 8th ed.. Madras: Kabeer Printing Works.

Cāminātaiyar, U. Vē. (ed.) (1962) *Kuṟuntokai.* (1st ed. 1937) 4th ed. Madras: Kabeer Printing Works.

Casal, Jean-Marie (1964) *Fouilles d'Amri* I-II. (Publications de la Commission des Fouilles Archéologiques: Fouilles du Pakistan) Paris: C. Klincksieck.

Casson, Lionel (1989) *The Periplus Maris Erythraei: Text with introduction, translation, and commentary.* Princeton: Princeton University Press.

Chelliah, J. V. (1962) *Pattupattu: Ten Tamil idylls, translated into English verse.* Tirunelveli: The South India Saiva Siddhanta Works Publishing Society, Tinnevelly, Limited.

CISI = *Corpus of Indus Seals and Inscriptions. 1: Collections in India*, edited by Jagat Pati Joshi and Asko Parpola, 1987. *2: Collections in Pakistan*, edited by Sayid Ghulam Mustafa Shah and Asko Parpola, 1991. *3: New material, untraced objects, and collections outside India and Pakistan*, edited by Asko Parpola B. M. Pande and Petteri Koskikallio, *Part 1: Mohenjo-daro and Harappa*, in collaboration with Richard H. Meadow and Jonathan Mark Kenoyer, 2010; *Part 2: Global supplement*, in preparation. (Annales Academiae Scientiarum Fennicae, B 239, 240, Humaniora 359) Helsinki: Suomalainen Tiedeakatemia.

Cogger, Harold G. and Richard G. Zweifel (eds.) (1998) *Encyclopedia of reptiles and amphibians.* 2nd ed. San Diego: Academic Press.

Coomaraswamy, Ananda K. (1928-1931) *Yaksas* I-II. (Smithsonian Institution Publications 2926, 3059) Washington, D. C.: The Smithsonian Institution.

Crooke, William (1906) *Things Indian, being discursive notes on various subjects connected with India.* London: John Murray.

Crooke, William (1912) *Dravidians* (North India). Pp. 1-21 in: James Hastings (ed.), Encyclopaedia of Religion and Ethics, Vol. 5. Edinburgh: T. and T. Clark.

Crooke, William (1926) *Religion and folklore of northern*

India. Prepared for the press by R. E. Enthoven. London: Oxford University Press.

Dalal, Jamshedji Ardeshir (1902) *Census of India 1901, Report*. Vol. 18: Baroda, Part I. Bombay: Government Central Press.

Daniel, J. C. (1983) *The book of Indian reptiles*. Bombay: Bombay Natural History Society and Oxford University Press.

DEDR = Burrow and Emeneau (1984)

Edgerton, Franklin (1953) *Buddhist Hybrid Sanskrit grammar and dictionary* I-II. New Haven: Yale University Press.

Fabricius, Johann Philip (1972) *Tamil and English dictionary, based on Johann Philip Fabricius's "Malabar-English Dictionary" [1779]*. 4th ed. Tranquebar: Evangelical Lutheran Mission Publishing House.

Fischer, Eberhard and Haku Shah (1971) *Mogra Dev, tribal crocodile gods: Wooden crocodile images of Chodhri, Gamit and Vasava tribes, South Gujarat (India)*. (Art for tribal rituals in South Gujarat, 1) Ahmedabad: Gujarat Vidyapith.

Franke-Vogt, Ute (1991) *Die Glyptik aus Mohenjo-Daro. Uniformität und Variabilität in der Induskultur: Untersuchungen zur Typologie, Ikonographie und räumlichen Verteilung*. I-II. (Baghdader Forschungen, 13) Mainz: Verlag Philipp von Zabern.

Ganges. TV series in 3 parts (54 minutes). BBC Bristol, (2007)

Ganslmayr, Herbert (1969) *Das Krokodil im Kult und Mythus afrikanischer Stämme*. München: Dissertationsdruck.

Gopinatha Rao, T. A. (1914-1916) *Elements of Hindu iconography* I-II. Madras: Government Press.

Gundert, H. (1872) *A Malayalam and English dictionary*. Mangalore: C. Stolz, Basel Mission book and tract depository.

Hart, George L. (1975) *The poems of ancient Tamil: Their milieu and their Sanskrit counterparts*. Berkeley: University of California Press.

Hart, George L. (1980) *Poets of the Tamil anthologies: Ancient poems of love and war*. (Princeton library of Asian translations) Princeton: Princeton University Press.

Hart, George L. and Hank Heifetz (1999) *The four hundred songs of war and wisdom, an anthology of poems from classical Tamil: The Puṟanāṉūṟu, translated and edited*. (Translations from the Asian classics) New York: Columbia University Press.

Hawkins, R. E. (ed.) (1986) *Encyclopedia of Indian natural history*. Delhi: Published on behalf of the Bombay Natural History Society by Oxford University Press.

Jotimuttu, P. (1984) *Aiṅkuṟunūṟu, The short five hundred (Poems on the theme of love in Tamil literature), An anthology: Translation with introduction and notes*. Madras: The Christian Literature Society.

Kane, Pandurang Vaman (1941-1975) *History of Dharmaśāstra (ancient and mediaeval religious and civil law in India)* I-V. (Vol. I in 2 revised edition) (Government Oriental Series, B 6) Poona: Bhandarkar Oriental Research Institute.

Kaw, R. N. (1979) 'The Neolithic culture of Kashmir', pp. 219-228 in D. P. Agrawal and Dilip K. Chakrabarti (eds.), *Essays in Indian Protohistory*. Delhi: B. R. Publishing Corporation.

Kramrisch, Stella (1954) *The art of India: Traditions of Indian sculpture, painting and architecture*. London: Phaidon Press.

Krishnamurti, Bhadriraju (2003) *The Dravidian languages*. Cambridge: Cambridge University Press.

Lehmann, Thomas and Thomas Malten (1992) *A word index of Old Tamil Caṅkam literature*. (Beiträge zur Südasienforschung 147) Stuttgart: Franz Steiner Verlag.

Liebert, Gösta (1969) 'Beitrag zur Frage des Polarsterns in der altindischen Literatur', *Orientalia Suecana* 17 (1968): 155-170.

Liebert, Gösta (1976) *Iconographic dictionary of the Indian religions: Hinduism - Buddhism - Jainism*. (Studies in South Asian culture, 5) Leiden: E. J. Brill.

Lokesh Chandra (1999-2005) *Dictionary of Buddhist iconography* Vol. I-XV. (Śata-Piṭaka Series, 601-

616) New Delhi: International Academy of Indian Culture and Aditya Prakashan.

Lüders, Heinrich (1942) 'Von indischen Tieren', *Zeitschrift der Deutschen Morgenländischen Gesellschaft* 96: 23-81.

Lüders, Heinrich (1951-1959) *Varuṇa* I-II. Aus dem Nachlass herausgegeben von Ludwig Alsdorf. Göttingen: Vandenhoeck and Ruprecht.

Mackay, Ernest J. H. (1943) *Chanhu-daro excavations, 1935-36.* (American Oriental Series, 20) New Haven, Conn.: The American Oriental Society.

Mahadevan, Iravatham (1977) *The Indus script: Texts, concordance and tables.* (Memoirs of the Archaeological Survey of India, 77) New Delhi: Archaeological Survey of India.

Majupuria, Trilok Chandra (ed.) (1982) *Wild is beautiful: Introduction to the magnificent, rich and varied fauna and wildlife of Nepal.* Lashkar, Gwalior, Madhya Pradesh: M. Devi.

Majupuria, Trilok Chandra (1982) 'Reptiles', pp. 147-177 in Majupuria (ed.) *Wild is beautiful: Introduction to the magnificent, rich and varied fauna and wildlife of Nepal.* Lashkar, Gwalior, Madhya Pradesh: M. Devi.

Majupuria, Trilok Chandra (1991) *Sacred animals of Nepal and India.* New revised edition. Lashkar, Gwalior, Madhya Pradesh: M. Devi.

Malamoud, Charles (1977) *Le Svādhyāya, Récitation personnelle du Veda: Taittirīya-Āraṇyaka, livre II, texte traduit et commenté.* (Publications de l'Institut de Civilisation indienne, Série in-8:o, 42) Paris: Institut de Civilisation indienne.

Malayalam lexicon (Malayāḷa mahānighaṇṭu): A comprehensive Malayalam-Malayalam-English dictionary on historical and philological principles published by the University of Kerala, I-. Trivandrum: University of Kerala, 1965-.

Mallmann, Marie-Thérèse de (1963) *Les enseignements iconographiques de l'Agni-Purana.* (Annales du Musée Guimet, Bibliothèque d'Études, 67) Paris: Presses Universitaires de France.

Mallmann, Marie-Thérèse de (1975) *Introduction à l'iconographie du Tāntrisme bouddhique.* Dessins de Muriel Thiriet. (Bibliothèque du Centre de Recherches sur l'Asie Centrale et la Haute Asie, 1) Paris: (en vente) Librairie Adrien-Maisonneuve.

Mallory, J. P. (1989) *In search of the Indo-Europeans: Language, archaeology and myth.* London: Thames and Hudson.

Marshall, John (ed.) (1931) *Mohenjo-daro and the Indus Civilization* I-III. London: Arthur Probsthain.

Marshall, John (1931) 'Religion', pp. 48-78 (Chapter V), in Marshall (ed.) *Mohenjo-daro and the Indus Civilization* Vol. I. London: Arthur Probsthain.

Martin, Montgomery (1838) *The history, antiquities, topography, and statistics of eastern India; surveyed under the orders of the supreme government and collated from the original documents at the E[ast] I[ndia] House.* I-III. London: W. H. Allen and Co. [Based on the surveys and reports of Francis Buchanan Hamilton (1762-1829).]

Maskey, Tirtha M. and Hemanta R. Mishra (1982) 'Conservation of gharial (Gavialis gangeticus) in Nepal', pp. 185-196, in Majupuria (ed.) *Wild is beautiful: Introduction to the magnificent, rich and varied fauna and wildlife of Nepal.* Lashkar, Gwalior, Madhya Pradesh: M. Devi.

Mayrhofer, Manfred (1992-2001) *Etymologisches Wörterbuch des Altindoarischen* I-III (Indogermanische Bibliothek, Reihe 2: Wörterbücher) Heidelberg: Universitätsverlag Carl Winter.

McGregor, R. S. (ed.) (1993) *The Oxford Hindi-English dictionary.* Oxford and Delhi: Oxford University Press.

Meriggi, Piero (1934) 'Zur Indus-Schrift', *Zeitschrift der Deutschen Morgenländischen Gesellschaft* 87 (N.F. 12): 198-241.

Monier-Williams, M. (1851) *A Dictionary, English and Sanskrit.* London: W. H. Allen & Co.

Moses, S. T. (1948) *Crocodiles in India.* (Bulletin 15) Baroda: Department of Fisheries.

Müller, Max (1859) *A history of ancient Sanskrit literature, so far as it illustrates the primitive religion of the*

Brahmans. London: Williams and Norgate.

Murthy, T. S. N. (1994) *Illustrated encyclopaedia of the reptiles of India*. Delhi: B. R. Publishing Corporation.

Murugan, V. (1999) *Kalittokai in English translation with critical introduction and glossary*. Chennai: Institute of Asian Studies.

Pacupati, Ma. Vē. (ed.) (2010) *Cemmoẓit tamiẓ*. Tancāvūr: Tamiẓp palkalaikkaẓakam.

Parpola, Asko (1985) *The Sky-Garment: A study of the Harappan religion and its relation to the Mesopotamian and later Indian religions*. (Studia Orientalia 57) Helsinki: The Finnish Oriental Society.

Parpola, Asko (1992) 'The metamorphoses of Mahiṣa Asura and Prajāpati', pp. 275-308, in A.W. van den Hoek, D. H. A. Kolff and M. S. Oort (eds.) *Ritual, state and history in South Asia: Essays in honour of J. C. Heesterman*. (Memoirs of the Kern Institute, 5) Leiden: E.J. Brill.

Parpola, Asko (1994) *Deciphering the Indus script*. Cambridge: Cambridge University Press.

Parpola, Asko (1998) 'Sāvitrī and resurrection', pp. 167-312, in Asko Parpola and Sirpa Tenhunen (eds.) *Changing patterns of family and kinship in South Asia*. (Studia Orientalia 84) Helsinki: The Finnish Oriental Society.

Parpola, Asko (2002) 'Pre-Proto-Iranians of Afghanistan as initiators of Śākta Tantrism: On the Scythian/Saka affiliation of the Dāsas, Nuristanis and Magadhans', *Iranica Antiqua* 37: 233-324.

Parpola, Asko (2004) 'From archaeology to a stratigraphy of Vedic syncretism: The banyan tree and the water buffalo as Harappan-Dravidian symbols of royalty, inherited in succession by Yama, Varuṇa and Indra, divine kings of the first three layers of Aryan speakers in South Asia', pp. 479-515, in Arlo Griffiths and Jan Houben (eds.) *The Vedas: Texts, language and ritual*. (Groningen Oriental Studies, 20) Groningen: Egbert Forsten.

Parpola, Asko (2005) 'The Nāsatyas, the chariot and Proto-Aryan religion', *Journal of Indological Studies* 16 & 17 (2004-2005): 1-63.

Parpola, Asko (2007) 'Human sacrifice in India in Vedic times and before', pp. 157-177, in Jan N. Bremmer (ed.) *The Strange World of Human Sacrifice*. (Studies in the History and Anthropology of Religion, 1) Leuven: Peeters.

Parpola, Asko (2008) 'Proto-Indo-European Speakers of the Late Tripolye Culture as the Inventors of Wheeled Vehicles: Linguistic and archaeological considerations of the PIE homeland problem', pp. 1-59, in Karlene Jones-Bley, Martin E. Huld, Angela Della Volpe, and Miriam Robbins Dexter (eds.) *Proceedings of the Nineteenth Annual UCLA Indo-European Conference, November 2-3, 2007*. (Journal of Indo-European Studies Monograph 54) Washington, D.C.: Institute for the Study of Man.

Parrot, André (1960) *Sumer*. Translated by Stuart Gilbert and James Emmons. (The arts of mankind, 1) London: Thames and Hudson.

Pinnow, Heinz-Jürgen (1959) *Versuch einer historischen Lautlehre der Kharia-Sprache*. Wiesbaden: Otto Harrassowitz.

Prater, S. H. (1971) *The book of Indian animals*. 3rd ed. Bombay: Bombay Natural History Society.

Raghu Vira and Lokesh Chandra (eds.) (1954) *Jaiminīya-Brāhmaṇa of the Sāmaveda*. (Sarasvati-Vihara Series, 31) Nagpur: International Academy of Indian Culture.

Scherer, Anton (1953) *Gestirnnamen bei den indogermanischen Völkern*. Heidelberg: Carl Winter - Universitätsverlag.

Sheth, Hargovind Das T. (1963) *Pāia-Sadda-Mahaṇṇavo: A comprehensive Prakrit-Hindi dictionary with Sanskrit equivalents, quotations and complete references*. 2nd ed. (Prākrit Text Society Series 7) Varanasi: Prakrit Text Society.

Singh, L. A. K. (1978) *Ecological studies on Indian gharial Gavialis gangeticus (Gmelin) (Reptilia, Crocodilia) with special reference to growth rate*. (Ph. D. thesis) Bhubaneswar: Utkal University.

Stietencron, Heinrich von (1972) *Gangā und Yamunā: Zur symbolischen Bedeutung der Flussgöttinnen an indischen Tempeln.* (Freiburger Beiträge zur Indologie, 5) Wiesbaden: Otto Harrassowitz.

Stietencron, Heinrich von (2010) *Gangā and Yamunā: River goddesses and their symbolism in Indian temples.* New Delhi: Permanent Black.

Tamil Lexicon. See TL.

Tandon, O.P. and T.K. Biswas (1986) *Ganga in Indian art.* Varanasi: Bharat Kala Bhavan, Banaras Hindu University.

Teeuwen, Mark (2006) 'Review of: Thal 2005', *Japonica Humboldtiana* 10: 227-230.

Thal, Sarah (2005) *Rearranging the landscape of Gods: The politics of a pilgrimage site in Japan, 1573-1912.* Chicago: The University of Chicago Press.

Thieme, Paul (1965) 'Drei rigvedische Tierbezeichnungen', *Zeitschrift für vergleichende Sprachforschung* 79 (3-4): 211-223.

TL = *Tamil Lexicon, published under the authority of the University of Madras* I-VI and Supplement (1924-1939) [I edited by K. V. Krishnaswami Aiyar; II-VI and Supplement edited by S. Vaiyapuri Pillai.] Madras: University of Madras.

Turner, Ralph L. (1966) *A comparative dictionary of the Indo-Aryan languages.* London: Oxford University Press.

Turner, Ralph L. (1985) *A comparative dictionary of the Indo-Aryan languages: Addenda and corrigenda*, edited by J.C. Wright. London: School of Oriental and African Studies, University of London.

Upadhyaya, U. P. (ed. in chief) (1988-1997) *Tulu lexicon: Tulu-Kannada-English dictionary* I-VI. Udupi, Karnataka: Rashtrakavi Govinda Pai Research Centre, M. G. M. College.

Varalāṟṟu muṟait tamiẓ ilakkiyap pērakarāti (Glossary of historical Tamil literature) I-IV. Cennai: Cānti cātaṉā.

Vats, Madho Sarup (1940) *Excavations at Harappā* I-II. Delhi: Manager of Publications.

Viennot, Odette (1964) *Les divinites fluviales Ganga et Yamuna aux portes aux sanctuaires de l'Inde.* (Publications du Musée Guimet, Recherches et documents d'art et d'archéologie, 10) Paris: Presses Universitaires de France.

Vogel, J. Ph. (1930) 'Le makara dans la sculpture de l'Inde', *Revue des Arts Asiatiques* 6 (3): 133-147.

Vuorela, Toivo (1964) *Kansatieteen sanasto.* Toinen, uudistettu painos. Helsinki: Suomalaisen kirjallisuuden seura.

Vyas, Raju and Snehal Bhatt (2004) 'The mugger (*Crocodylus palustris*) population, problems, panic and rescue operations in and around Vadodara city', *Crocodile Specialist Group Newsletter* 23 (3): 6-9.

Ward, William (1811) *Account of the writings, religion, and manners, of the Hindoos, including translations from their principal works* I-IV. Serampore: The Mission Press.

Ward, William (1815-1818) *A view of the history, litterature, and mythology of the Hindoos: including a minute description of their manners and customs, and translations from their principal works.* Second edition, carefully abridged, and greatly improved. I-II. Serampore: The Mission Press.

Ward, William (1817-1820) *A view of the history, litterature, and mythology of the Hindoos: including a minute description of their manners and customs, and translations from their principal works.* Third edition, carefully abridged, and greatly improved. I-IV. London: Black, Parbury, and Allen.

Weber, Albrecht (1853) 'Zur Geschichte der indischen Astrologie', *Indische Studien* 2: 236-287.

Weber, Albrecht (1864) 'Ueber Menschenopfer bei den Indern der vedischen Zeit', *Zeitschrift der Deutschen Morgenländischen Gesellschaft* 18: 262-287. Reprinted in A. Weber, *Indische Streifen* 1 (1868): 54-89. Berlin: Nicolaische Verlagsbuchhandlung.

Wheeler, Mortimer (1968) *The Indus Civilization. Supplementary volume to The Cambridge History of India.* Third edition. Cambridge: The University Press.

Whitaker, Zai (1986) 'Crocodilians', pp. 151-154, in R. E.

Hawkins (ed.) *Encyclopedia of Indian natural history.* Delhi: Published on behalf of the Bombay Natural History Society by Oxford University Press.

Wikipedia. http://en.wikipedia.org/wiki/

Wilden, Eva (2010) *Kuṟuntokai: A critical edition and an annotated translation of the Kuruntokai* I-III. (Critical texts of Cankam literature 2: 1-3) Pondicherry: École Française d'Extrême-Orient and Chennai: Tamilmann Patippakam.

Wilden, Eva (2008) *Narriṇai: A critical edition and an annotated translation of the Naṟṟiṇai* I-III. (Critical texts of Cankam literature 1: 1-3) Pondicherry: École Française d'Extrême-Orient and Chennai: Tamilmann Patippakam.

Wilson, H. H. (1819) *A dictionary; Sanscrit and English: translated, amended and enlarged, from an original compilation prepared by learned natives for the College of Fort William.* Calcutta: printed by Philip Pereira, at the Hindoostanee Press.

Wilson, H. H. (1862-1871) *Works of the late Horace Hayman Wilson*, collected and edited by Reinhold Rost I-XII. London: Trübner & Co.

Winslow, Miron, J. Knight, S. Hutchings, and L. Spaulding (1888) *English and Tamil dictionary.* Third edition, enlarged, improved and romanized by C. Appaswamy Pillai. Madras: Higginbotham & Co.

Yule, Henry and A. C. Burnell (1903) *Hobson-Jobson: A glossary of colloquial Anglo-Indian words and phrases, and of kindred terms, etymological, historical, geographical and discursive.* New edition, edited by William Crooke. London: John Murray.

Zacharias, Tobias (1933) *Anglo-Malayalam dictionary.* 2nd edition, revised and enlarged by Oliver F. E. Zacharias. Mangalore: Baptist Mission Press.

Zvelebil, Kamil (1970) *Comparative Dravidian phonology.* (Janua linguarum, Series practica, 80) The Hague: Mouton & Co.

On the Asiatic wild asses and their vernacular names

Asko Parpola (1-6) and Juha Janhunen (7-10)
University of Helsinki

1. Introduction: On the equids excavated at Gonur and in ancient Mesopotamia

The basic monograph on wild asses, Gertrud and Helmut Denzau's *Wildesel* (1999), has gathered and digested fairly comprehensively the available scientific and historical information on this endangered group of animals[1]. Our objective is to contribute some complementary data by focusing on sources not readily studied by zoologists, namely the linguistic evidence of vernacular names of the different varieties of the Asiatic wild asses and related textual documents. But as we also want to congratulate our friend Viktor I. Sarianidi on his 80th birthday with this paper[2], we begin with a "Bridge of Asses"[3] to connect our topic with his work.

When Katherine Moore examined the animal bones excavated at Gonur (near Merv alias Mary in Turkmenistan) in 1989, she found

> "no evidence from Gonur that domestic horses were used during the Bronze Age. They certainly could have been present, however, without their bones being deposited in the trash heaps that were sampled for this report" (Moore 1993: 168).

She did find evidence for another equid:

> "The wild half-ass or onager (*Equus hemionus*), called *kulan* in Central Asia, is the native equid of Turkmenistan. Its populations are small and endangered today, but it would have been much more widespread in desert regions in the Bronze Age... The wild kulan were hunted for meat, as their bones are fragmented, marked by cuts, and burned. The specimens of jaws all indicate that they were from mature animals, one more than 8 years, and one more than 19 years... The one limb bone, a metatarsal, appeared to be from a young animal, between 1 and 2 years..." (Moore 1993: 167-168)[4].

Richard Meadow had the following to say of his brief field study in 1990:

> "All the equid specimens, identified as donkey principally on the basis of the small size of the bones, were found in room 262 and could have come from a single, not fully mature, animal.... as they come from the south mound, they presumably belong to Gonur Period II or early in the second millennium BC" (Meadow 1993: 73)[5].

Since those times, Viktor Sarianidi has continuously excavated at Gonur and discovered in its cemeteries the remains of as many as eight equids (cf. Sarianidis 2008: 265-266 and 410-413 with Figures 222-226). Sarianidi speaks of these as horses, which is reasonable in view of the fact that he has found at Gonur (burial #2380) a bronze mace-

Figure 4 Domestic ass alias donkey (*Equus asinus*) in England
(photo (from Wikipedia) 2004 by Adrian Pingstone)

Mongolic terms for the Asiatic wild asses discussed in the present paper.

2. The species and subspecies of the Asiatic wild asses, their historic and current distribution, and the possibility of their domestication

The equids, or horse-like animals (from Latin *equus* 'horse'), are divided into horses, zebras and asses. The asses in turn are divided into two genetically and geographically distinct groups.

(1) The African ass (*Equus africanus*) includes two wild subspecies, surviving in Somalia and in Nubia, while the wild ass of the Atlas region is extinct. The subspecies of domesticated ass or donkey[11] (*Equus asinus* L.) (Figure 4) belongs to the African group of asses. Major work on the origins of the donkey is currently being done by Fiona Marshall, who in her detailed "first synthesis" (2007) comes to the conclusion that the ancient Egyptians domesticated the Nubian wild ass by 4000 BCE, there being archaeological evidence of the donkey from Egypt from 4000-3500 BCE, while the earliest archaeological evidence from the Near East (ancient Anshan alias Tal-e Malyan) is from 2800 calBCE[12].

(2) the Asiatic wild asses comprise two species, the hemione and the kiang.

At this point, before going to the subspecies of the Asiatic wild asses, it seems useful to consider some general terms connected with the asses and their etymology. The majority of European languages have got their words for 'ass' from Latin *asinus*, first attested in the dramas of Plautus (cf. Walde 1938 I: 72-73; Brugmann 1907-08: 198-199; Buck 1949: 172-174 nos. 3.46 and 3.47.5). Greek *ónos*[13], which is attested c. 1200 BCE in Mycenaean Greek (*o-no*), is connected with Latin *asinus*, and both are regarded as loans from some Western Asiatic source (**asnu?*) related to Sumerian AN.ŠE or AN.ŠU 'ass' (cf. Frisk 1970 II: 397-398; Gamkrelidze & Ivanov 1995 I: 480-482). Used without any qualification, all these words denote domesticated ass or donkey. In this paper we use 'ass' without further qualification as a "neutral" subgenus term which may refer to the wild or domesticated ass.

Greek *hēmí-onos*, literally 'half-ass'[14], denotes the 'mule', i.e., the sterile hybrid of ass x horse. In modern zoological usage, English *hemione* is used of one species of the Asiatic wild asses in the sense of 'half-ass', because in size it is between the domestic ass and the domestic horse, and also because it looks more horse-like than the donkey. Because 'half-ass' originally refers to the mule as an animal half ass and half horse, we prefer to speak of 'wild ass' rather than of 'half-ass', although many zoologists use 'half-ass' without 'wild' in this sense. In this paper, 'wild ass' without further qualification means 'Asiatic wild ass'.

The Greek word for 'wild ass' is *ónagros* (in Strabon 7,4,8, etc.), from the older noun phrase *ónos ágrios* 'wild ass' (see below on Herodotus 7,86 and Xenophon, and cf. Risch 1949: 286-287)[15]. In modern zoological usage, English *onager* is used especially of the Persian subspecies of the hemione.

The map in Figure 5 (after Feh *et al.* 2002: 63, Figure 5.1) shows the historical and current range of

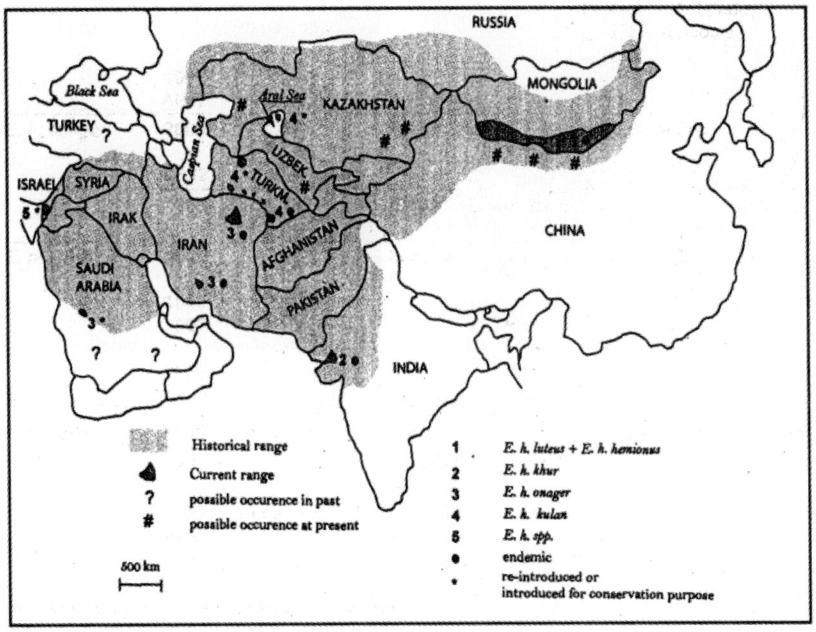

Figure 5 Map showing the historical and current distribution of the Asiatic wild ass (after Feh *et al.* 2002: 63, Figure 5.1)

Figure 6 The Syrian wild ass (*Equus hemionus hemippus*) in the zoo of London (photo (from Wikipedia) 1872 by Frederick York)

Figure 7 The Indian wild ass (*Equus hemionus khur*) (photo Gertrud and Helmut Denzau)

the Asiatic wild asses (a more exact coloured map at the end of Denzau and Denzau 1999 shows also the present and former distribution of the African wild asses, and of the prehistoric European wild ass).

The four to six currently recognized subspecies of the hemione (*Equus hemionus* Pallas 1775) are the following (cf. Feh *et al.* 2002; Groves 1986; Denzau and Denzau 1999: 14-47):

Small-sized (about 100 cm at withers):

- The Syrian wild ass (*Equus hemionus hemippus*) (see Figure 6) is extinct since 1927.

Medium-sized (about 108-120 cm at withers):

- The Indian wild ass alias *khur* (*Equus hemionus khur* Lesson 1827) (see Figure 7) "was formerly widespread in the arid

Figure 8 The Transcaspian kulan (*Equus hemionus kulan*) (photo Gertrud and Helmut Denzau)

Figure 9 The Mongolian khulan (*Equus hemionus hemionus*) (photo Gertrud and Helmut Denzau)

zone of north-west India (including present Pakistan), west towards Syria[16], and through much of Central Asia. However, it is now limited to the Little Rann of Kutch (Saline Mudflat) in Gujarat, India. It probably became extinct in Baluchistan and the extreme south of Pakistan, on the Indian Border, during the 1960s" (Feh *et al.* 2002: 63), endangered.

- The Persian wild ass alias *onager* (*Equus hemionus onager* Boddaert 1795) survives in Iran (very small populations in four protected areas: Touran in the Semnan province, and Bahram-e-Goor in Fars, Kavir, and Kosh-Yeilagh); it is critically endangered.
- The Transcaspian wild ass alias *kulan* (*Equus hemionus kulan* Groves and Mazák 1967) (see Figure 8), survives native in the protected area of Badkhys in Turkmenistan, and rehabilitated in some other areas of Turkmenistan, in Kazakhstan, Uzbekistan and the Ukraine; it is in dramatic decline and critically endangered. This is possibly the same subspecies as the onager.

Large-sized (about 110-130 cm at withers):

- The Mongolian *khulan* alias *dziggetai* (*Equus hemionus hemionus* Pallas 1775) (see Figure 9) lives in northern Mongolia; it is vulnerable.
- The Gobi *khulan* (*Equus hemionus luteus* Matschie 1911) lives in southern Mongolia and northern China; it is vulnerable. "It is possible that... *E. h. luteus* (whose localities are all within a fairly restricted area) is simply a localized sample of a unitary Mongolian race living in extreme desert conditions" (Groves 1986: 27).

The Tibetan wild ass alias *kiang* (*Equus kiang* Moorcroft 1841, formerly *Equus hemionus kiang*) (see Figure 10), has three subspecies: *Equus kiang kiang*, *E. k. holdereri* and *E. k. polyodon* (cf. Denzau and Denzau 1999: 16-18, 20-21; 139-163). The kiang is now widely accepted as a species of its own on the basis of molecular studies (Shah *et al.* 2008). Even so, in its external appearance the kiang is closely reminiscent of the hemione, and the local peoples of the Tibeto-Mongolian region do not distinguish it terminologically from the Mongolian and Gobi *khulan*[17]. The kiang is the largest of the Asiatic wild asses (about 140 cm at withers).

Some general issues relating to the Asiatic wild ass may best be discussed in this chapter. For one thing, the Asiatic wild asses are considered the swiftest and most enduring of all equids:

Figure 10 The Tibetan kiang (*Equus kiang*) (photo Gertrud and Helmut Denzau)

> "When chased, they [the Indian wild asses] run at 48 to 51 km/hr, a speed which can be kept up over a considerable distance. They always run out into the open salt flat when disturbed (Ali 1946). ... All authors agree on the onager's speed and stamina. Ali's timed speeds from Kutch are in fact the slowest records for the species! Solomatin (1964) states that onagers in Badkhys can run at 60-70 km/hr and keep it up for 10 km — and can go for much longer at 40-50 km/hr. A female caught in Iran (Mohr 1961) was chased for more than three-quarters of an hour at 45-48 km/hr..." (Groves 1986: 38).

When sending a specimen of the Indian wild ass to the Zoological Gardens of London in 1873, Captain Henry Lowther Nutt described its capture as follows:

> "I ran it down on the Runn of Kutch. I was riding hard after it for three hours and five minutes, and the estimated length of the chase was forty miles. I rode two horses, as I had discovered from the 'puggies,' or watchers near the Runn, that, if the animals were disturbed from where they were, they would probably make for another place some twelve or thirteen miles distant. I was, therefore, able to post a fresh party of horsemen, and a fresh horse for myself, at the place further on; and true enough the herd did make for the spot indicated, so that the running was taken up and continued with fresh horses, and in this way the capture was effected, but even then not until both my horses, which were in good order at the time, had been ridden to a stand still. This will give you an idea of the speed and endurance of these animals" (Quoted in Tegetmeier and Sutherland 1895: 23).

The swiftness of the wild ass is mentioned by the ancient Greek authors, cf. Xenophon (Anabasis 1,5,2): "The asses, when pursued, would run forward a space, and then stand still — their pace being much swifter than that of horses", and Aristotle (Historia animalium 6,36): "these half-asses are exceptionally swift of foot" (cf. Potts 2002: 107).

H. H. the Thakor of Morvi State in Kathiawar, close to the Rann of Kutch, had as one of his favourite amusements riding down wild asses. The following is extracted from the report given by J. L. Harrington, Assistant Superintendent of Police at Kathiawar:

> "The rides which ended in captures usually lasted about three hours; speed varied from a walk to a spurting gallop; the going was execrably bad, being chiefly ground covered at high tide by the sea, and consisted for the most part of mud, in which the horses sank fetlock deep, necessitating the greater portion of the chase being done at a walk. The distances covered in the different runs varied from twenty to twenty-five miles ... Some twenty wild asses, big and small, were captured in these rides. When captured, the wild asses were extremely vicious, bit and kicked, and

> it was found necessary to rope them before they could be led away. The statement that no varieties of the Asiatic wild ass have ever been domesticated would be deprived of some of its effect could your readers see the wild asses in the paddocks at Morvi. Though some of the captures remained excessively vicious, others became quite tame, and were ridden and driven just like tame donkeys. The young ones are as tame as dogs, and extremely fond of being fondled and played with" (Quoted in Tegetmeier and Sutherland 1895: 26-27).

It is still often said that the wild ass was never domesticated. This seems to need the qualification that while the species remains undomesticated, individual wild asses have been broken in. "Considering their size and sturdiness and their potential as draft animals, efforts have been made to break them [the Indian wild asses] in and also to breed mules from them for use in mountain transport by the Army, but they have not been successful" (Hawkins 1986: 26). This recent statement contrasts also with one made 150 years ago by Edward Blyth (1859: 251), who could report "that the experiments which have been systematically carried on, now for several years, by the Acclimation Society at Paris, have been attended with considerable success in breaking in *Ghor-khurs* [Indian wild asses], which have been bred there for a series of generations, and that these animals are now daily mounted and ridden".

The Roman author Claudius Aelianus (c. 170-240 CE), in his work on the nature of the animals written in Greek (*De natura animalium*) states in chapter (16,9):

> "In India, there are herds of wild horses and wild asses. They say that when the asses cover mares, these submit to it, enjoy the intercourse and give birth to mules that have a tawny skin-colour, and are very good at running, impatient of the yoke and otherwise skittish. They catch them (i.e. the wild asses) with traps for the feet, and it is said they are then taken to the king of the Prasians[18]. And they say that those captured at the age of two years do not refuse being broken in, while older ones (in their vicious behaviour) do not differ at all from harsh flesh-eating beasts.[19]"

Valentin Ball (1885: 285-286) told that in his time wild asses were often taken for wild horses, and that Indian wild asses were still caught in Rajasthan and sold to local princes (cf. Karttunen 1997: 179). Indeed, in the Bikaner desert of Rajasthan, "Once only in the year, when the foals are young, a party of five or six native hunters, mounted on hardy Sindh mares, chase down as many foals as they can succeed in tiring, which lie down when utterly fatigued and suffer themselves to be bound and carried off... these men regard the sale of a few *Ghor-khurs* annually as a regular source of subsistence" (Major Tytler quoted by Blyth 1859: 240). Similarly in Baluchistan, "The foaling season is in June, July, and August; when the Beluchis ride down and catch numbers of foals, finding a ready sale in the cantonments for them, as they are taken down on speculation to Hindustan" (Blyth 1859: 240). General Sir Samuel Browne is quoted saying that captured wild asses were tame pets "seen at every station of the Punjab frontier force... These animals, however, strenuously resisted being saddled, possibly from not having been broken-in when young"; but "one was known to Sir Samuel Browne as having been perfectly broken, and as being habitually ridden by a Belooch chief named Beeja Kham" (Tegetmeier and Southerland 1895: 29).

It seems quite credible, then, that individual wild asses were domesticated and/or crossed with the donkey in antiquity (cf. Potts 2002: 107). Herodotus (7,86) states that the Indian soldiers

Figure 11 Indian subjects bringing an ass as a gift to the great king. Persepolis (photo 2005 by Asko Parpola)

fighting in the Persian army of Xerxes in 480 BCE had chariots drawn by horses and by wild asses (ὑπὸ δὲ τοῖσι ἅρμασι ὑπῆσαν ἵπποι καὶ ὄνοι ἄγριοι, *hupò dè toîsi hármasi hupêsan híppoi kaì ónoi ágrioi*). That wild asses were imported from the Indus Valley to the Persian Empire is backed up by the Persepolis reliefs of the *apadāna* stairway, which show subjects from the 23 provinces of the empire bringing gifts to Xerxes. The 18th delegation is unanimously identified as consisting of three men from India, i.e., the province of Hinduš (Sindh). Two of the men bring as a new year's gift to the great king an ass-jack (Figure 11). This ass, which has the height of a horse, is hardly an ordinary domestic ass: it is supposed to represent a wild ass for the royal park, on the basis of the Assyrian reliefs depicting a royal onager hunt (cf. Walser 1966: 94-95; the Assyrian reliefs are reproduced in Denzau and Denzau 1999: 185).

Onager x donkey hybrids were apparently bred to pull war-cars in ancient Mesopotamia (cf. 1). The Kharaputta-Jātaka (no. 386) speaks of 'sons of an ass' (*kharaputta-* in stanza 80) from Sindh as yoked to the chariot of a king in ancient India[20]. According to Kumar *et al.* (1963: 51), "In India two types of donkeys are met with: the Small Grey Donkey and the Large White Donkey... The latter is light grey to almost bordering on white in colour and is commonly met with in Western Pakistan (Baluchistan and Sind) and in Gujarat State (Kathiawar). Its average height is 11 hands." In colour, size and geographical distribution, the "Large White Donkey" mentioned here agrees with the Indian wild ass[21]. According to Watt's generally very reliable *Dictionary of the economic products of India* (1890 IV: 297), "A specially fine breed [of the domestic ass] occurs in Kathiáwár, of which the Hálár or Jhálávád white variety is one of the strongest and largest." Similar superior breeds are reported from Iran and Central Asia (cf. Potts 2002: 105-106).

3. The Indian wild ass (*Equus hemionus khur*) and the Indus Civilization

The Indus Civilization (2600-1900 BCE) had a script which, with its around 400 known graphemes, can be assumed to be a logo-syllabic writing system, as all other early writing systems in existence around 2500 BCE. The presence of Dravidian loanwords in the earliest preserved historical document of South Asia, the Rigveda (c. 1200-1000 BCE), combined with the presence of a North Dravidian language (Brahui) in the Indus Valley and Baluchistan, makes Proto-Dravidian the most likely alternative for having been the main language of the Indus Civilization. Starting from these two basic hypotheses, I have proposed cross-checked Proto-Dravidian phonetic readings for some two dozen Indus signs. Various signs with the basic shape of 'fish' occur very frequently on the Indus seals. Because fish is never spoken of in the seal texts of Mesopotamia, which had trading relations with the Indus Civilization, the 'fish' signs are likely to

(a) M-93 A (b) M-93 a (c) M-1097 A (d) M-1097 a (e) M-290 A
(f) M-290 a (g) M-290 a bis (h) M-78 A (i) M-78 a (j) M-926 A
(k) M-926 a (l) H-1934 A (m) H-2029 A (n) H-2031 A

Figure 12 Naturalistic variants of the Indus script sign 46 (in the sign list of Parpola 1994: 70-78) (from CISI 1-3/1)

express phonetic values. Proto-Dravidian **mīn* 'fish' (DEDR no. 4885) is homophonous with Proto-Dravidian **mīn* 'star' (DEDR no. 4876). Many signs occurring immediately before the plain 'fish' sign, as well as diacritical marks modifying the 'fish' sign (e.g. a 'roof' over 'fish') can be interpreted in the same way, and the resulting compound words are attested as names of heavenly bodies in the earliest surviving Dravidian literature, Old Tamil texts composed in South India in the early centuries CE (See Parpola 1994) .

In a recent paper (Parpola 2009a: 61-64), I suggested one further Dravidian interpretation along these lines. A sign that depicts 'a hoofed animal's hind leg' occurs once (in the seal M-1690) before the plain 'fish' sign. It thus agrees with the attestation of Old Tamil *tāḷ* 'leg' as a star name in Puṟanāṉūṟu 395 (cf. Hart 1975: 73), while the cognate word *tōḷ* in the Toda language denotes 'thigh of animal's hind leg' (cf. DEDR no. 3185). I ended the examination with this conclusion:

> "Thus *tāḷ* may well be the right reading for the 'hind leg' sign, but it should be tested against other contexts. One such context is the seal M-290, which is promising in this respect that here the 'hind leg' precedes a sign that can be pictorially recognized: it depicts an animal with large upright ears and an upright tail ending in a tuft of hair, either dog or (more likely) wild ass. But in South Asia, the latter animal exists only in Kutch and Baluchistan, and is hardly mentioned in any old text, Indo-Aryan let alone Dravidian." (Parpola 2009a: 63-64)

In spite of these pessimistic expectations, I wanted to see if this track would lead anywhere, and for my part, this is the raison d'être of the present paper[22].

(a) M-416 A (c) M-516 A (e1) M-1282 A (e2) M-1283 A (g) M-1336 a

(b) M-416 a (d) M-516 A bis (f1) M-1282 a (f2) M-1283 a (h) M-1341 A (i) M-1341 a

Figure 13 Schematic variants of the Indus script sign 46 (in the sign list of Parpola 1994: 70-78) (from CISI 1-2)

Figure 14 Male and female Mongolian wild ass (photo from Denzau and Denzau 1999: 131)

The mammal sign of M-290 (no. 46 in the sign list published in Parpola 1994: 70-78, Figure 5.1) occurs nine times in Mohenjo-daro and nine times in Harappa (all occurrences in Harappa are moulded duplicates of one and the same text: H-1934, H-1935, H-2024, H-2026 to H-2031 in CISI 3:1). The more realistic renderings of this animal are shown in Figure 12 (a-n) comprising 14 photographs of the sign, in five original seal stamps and their modern impressions, and in three of the moulded tablets from Harappa. From these illustrations it can be seen that the animal has relatively high legs, an upheld relatively long neck and a relatively big head with large upwards or sideways pointing ears but

(a) (b)

Figure 15 An Indus seal stamp (a) and its impression (b), with the wild ass as its heraldic motif, excavated at Kanmer, Kutch, Gujarat, in 2009 (photos by (a)Indus Project of RIHN, (b)Jeewan Singh Kharakwal)

no horns, and an upright tail ending in a tuft. The same characteristics are found in the less realistic, simplified variants of the sign illustrated in Figure 13 (a-i)[23]. Comparing these characteristics with several books of South Asian animals I had come to the conclusion that the animal is most likely to be the Asiatic wild ass. The tail of this animal ends in a tuft, but it was not held in an upright position in any of the pictures accessible to me.

Wishing to consult an equid specialist, I sent the images in figure 12 to Richard Meadow. His comment was (personal communication, 18 March 2009):

> "I would agree with your assessment, with the proviso that the body and neck usually seem to be striped, which is not hemione-like... the hemione or wild half-ass is known from the archaeological record from at least Baluchistan through Gujarat."

I replied that the "stripes" could just indicate "body" (its roundness). Meadow in turn (personal communication, 19 March 2009) sent me "a picture of a hemione from the wonderful book by Gertrud and Helmut Denzau (1999), Wildesel, Stuttgart: Jan Thorbecke Verlag. Except for the male organ, the animal on the left is quite like the images you sent." This picture, which in my opinion clinches the identification, is reproduced in Figure 14.

Evidently, the upright tail of the wild ass expresses a state of excitement. In Figure 14, the excitement is sexual, but in Harivaṃśa 57,16 (see 6) the tail of the ass demon Dhenuka is up on account of enragement.

In later South Asian tradition, the ass is prominently involved in punishments concerning illicit sexual behaviour. Thus a student of the Veda who has broken his vow of chastity should offer an ass (*gardabha-*) (cf. Āpastamba-Dharmasūtra 1,26,8; Gautama-Dharmasūtra 23,17; Vasiṣṭha-Dharmasūtra 23,1) and in this sacrifice the cut-off portion to be eaten by the sacrificer should be taken from the penis of the ass (cf. Kātyāyana-Śrautasūtra 1,1,13 and 17; Baudhāyana-Dharmasūtra 2,1,30-35)[24]. The Manu-Smṛti (11,122-123) instead prescribes that the guilty student should for one year wear the skin of the ass and proclaim his lapse while begging for his food.

One of the main characteristics for which the

ass is noted is its power of fertility. For instance, in an early charm for virile power (c. 950 BCE), the male organ is asked to grow as great as that of the rhinoceros (*párasvant-*), that of the elephant, that of the ass (*gardabha-*) and that of the horse (Atharvaveda 6,72,3). In this verse, the big size of the male member connects the ass and the rhinoceros. These two animals are associated with each other also in the copper tablets of Mohenjo-daro. Identical inscription on the obverse links the Indus sign depicting the wild ass on the reverse of the tablets M-516 (see Figure 13 c-d) and M-517 with the rhinoceros illustrated on the reverse of the tablet M-1481 (cf. Parpola 1994: 110-111, with A11 and B5 in Figure 7.14).

This correspondence between the script sign depicting the wild ass and the iconographic illustration of the rhinoceros raises the question: why is the wild ass not illustrated in the iconography of the Indus seals and tablets, while so many other real and mythical animals are?

There is one likely explanation for the scarcity of the wild ass as a heraldic animal in the Indus iconography. The wild ass was too ominous an animal to be represented in amuletic art, which may have had as its *raison d'être* wishes for prosperity and welfare. The sounds of dogs, asses, jackals, vultures and crows forebode evil (Atharvaveda-Pariśiṣṭa 61,1,8), and Vedic recitation is to be suspended when dogs are barking, asses (*gardabha-*) are braying or jackals are howling (cf. Āpastamba-Dharmasūtra 1, 10, 19; Gautama-Dharmasūtra 16,8). Dreaming of camels, pigs, asses etc. forebodes evil (cf. Mānava-Gṛhyasūtra 2,14,11). In Rāmāyaṇa 2,63,14-16, Bharata's dream of a man driving an ass-chariot is explicitly stated to portend death[25]. In spite of its fecundating power, the ass[26] is an animal connected with Nirṛti, the goddess of Destruction, the guardian deity of the inauspicous direction of southwest. It is to her, Nirṛti, or to Yama (the god of death) that the ass is to be sacrificed in breaches of chastity, and this in the wilderness (*araṇye*) (cf. Vasiṣṭha-Dharmasūtra 23,1; Baudhāyana-Dharmasūtra 2,1,30-35). The main reason for the ass's connection with destruction and death is, I suspect, the habitat of the wild ass, the lifeless salt desert. Indeed, in the Dhenukavadha myth (see below, 6), the wild ass is compared to the god of death (Antaka).

The discrimination of the wild ass as a heraldic animal in the Indus seals and tablets was not absolute, however. Soon after the first version of this paper had been written, J.S. Kharakwal in the Kyoto meeting of May 2009 presented the first Indus seal to have the wild ass as its iconographic motif, published here in Figure 15. The seal had been excavated shortly before at Kanmer in Kutch, in the very area where the wild ass is still living. The wild ass must have been a very important animal for the Harappans living in Kutch. The wild ass sign appears to be hand-written on the reverse of one of the three "passports" of clay found at Kanmer (which all have the impression of one and the same seal on the obverse but a diffent hand-written text on the reverse) (Figure 16); here the wild ass sign is followed by the 'herring-bone' (backbone with ribs) sign (no. 108 in my sign list), as is the probable allograph of the wild ass sign (no. 47) in a seal from Khirsara (Figure 17), another site in Kutch.

In any case there was no taboo against the depiction of the wild ass in the Indus script and terracotta figurines, for seven terracotta figurines representing an equid have been excavated at Mohenjo-daro. The best of them (now in the National Museum of India in New Delhi) is shown in Figure 18[27]. Some scholars have taken it as a representation of the domestic horse, but as pointed out by Ardeleanu-Jansen (1993: 173) all the figurines are more likely to represent the *Equus hemionus khur*.

Bones of *Equus hemionus* (khur, onager) have been identified in Baluchistan and Sindh at several sites (Rana Ghundai, Mehrgarh, Nausharo, Sibri,

Figure 17 Modern impression of the seal Krs-1 from Khirsara, Kutch (after CISI 1: 357)

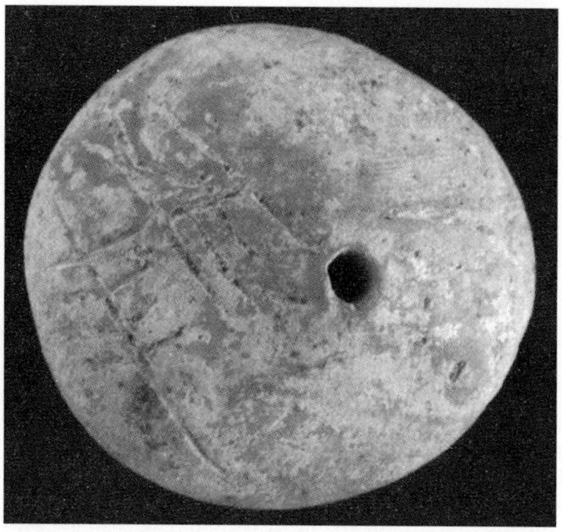

Figure 16 Reverse side of a clay "passport" from Kanmer, Kutch, with incised signs depicting (from right to left) 'wild ass' and 'herring-bone' (photo by Indus Project of RIHN)

Figure 18 Terracotta equid statuette from Mohenjo-Daro now in the National Museum of India, New Delhi. Note that the tail and ears are broken and the legs are modern restoration
(photo NMI (from Chakrabarti 2004: 18 Figure 14))

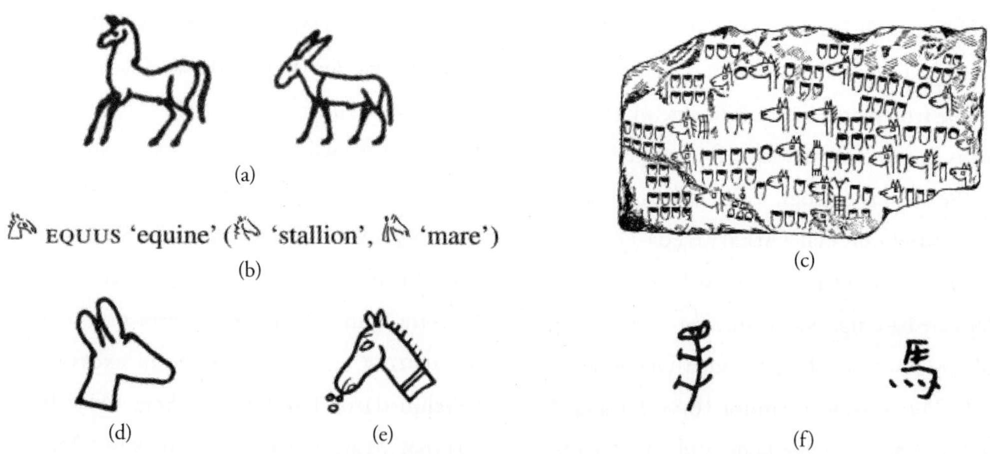

Figure 19 Signs depicting equids in various ancient scripts

(a) The signs for 'horse' and 'ass' in the Egyptian hieroglyphic script (after Gardiner 1957: 459 nos. E 6 and 7)

(b) Sematographic 'horse' signs in the Mycenaean Linear B script (after Bennett 1995: 128, table 7.2)

(c) 'Equid' signs on a Proto-Elamite tablet from Susa (Scheil 1923: table 17 no. 105; after Hinz 1969: 222, Abb. 7)

(d) The sign for 'ass' in Archaic Sumerian script (after *Naissance de l'écriture* 1982: 75)

(e) The logographic 'horse' sign in the Hittite (or rather Luvian) hieroglyphic script (after *Naissance de l'écriture* 1982: 116; cf. Melchert 1995: 121 table 6.1)

(f) The character depicting 'horse' in the archaic (oracle bone) and modern Chinese scripts (after Boltz 1986: 427, Figure 1 no. 11; also in DeFrancis 1989: 97 Figure 17)

Pirak, Sohr Damb/Nal, Balakot) from the earliest Neolithic levels (c. 7000-6000 BCE) down to the Harappan and Late and Post-Harappan times; the evidence from Mohenjo-daro and Harappa is uncertain (cf. Meadow 1988: 41-43; Possehl 1999: 186; Benecke and Neef 2005: 82-83). Wild ass bones have been identified at Surkotada (all three periods), Dholavira and Shikarpur in Kutch and at Kuntasi and Rojdi in Kathiawar; bones with cut marks and charring have suggested hunting of the wild ass for food (cf. Possehl 1999: 186; Thomas 2002: 413)[28].

The domestic horse (*Equus caballus*) and the donkey (*Equus asinus*), on the other hand, are with certainty attested (osteologically and in depictions) for the first time in post-Harappan times, from the second quarter of the second millennium BCE onwards, at Pirak on the border of Baluchistan and Sindh, and in the Swat Valley (cf. Meadow 1988: 41-43; Possehl 1999: 185-189; Meadow and Patel 2002: 400-402; Thomas 2002: 411-413). It is true that some scholars have identified horse bones at Harappan sites, e.g., Sándor Bökönyi (1997) at Surkotada in Kutch, but these are borderline cases between the horse and the wild ass, and must be excluded as uncertain (cf. Meadow and Patel 1997; 2002: 401).

With regard to the Indus sign identified as representing the wild ass, Richard Meadow (personal communication, 19 March 2009) points out that it does not depict a horse, as the tail is quite different, and there is no significant mane or forelock. I would like to add the length of the ears, which are longer (187-210 mm) in the khur than those of the horse (on the average c. 150 mm), but not as long as those of the donkey. The enlarged ears function as heat-dispersing devices also in a number of other mammals living in extremely hot desert conditions like the wild ass; thus "compared to other hare species inhabiting cooler climates, both hare species ... found in Pakistan have especially wide and large ears" (Roberts 1977: 10).

The wild ass depicted in the Indus sign can be compared with the signs depicting equids in other writing systems (see Figure 19). (a) Of the horse and donkey signs in the Egyptian hieroglyphic script, the Indus sign is more like the donkey. (b) In the Mycenaean Linear B script, the 'horse' and 'stallion' signs show the mane, the sign for 'mare' is without mane. (c) A Proto-Elamite tablet from Susa records 185 equids[29]; according to the hypothesis of V. Scheil, the animals with upwards pointing mane hair are stallions, those with downwards pointing mane hair are mares, and those without mane are foals (cf. Hinz 1969: 222-224). (d) The archaic Sumerian script has no sign for 'horse', only one for 'ass' (no mane or forelock; the ears are long). (e) The sign for 'horse' in the Hittite hieroglyphic script has mane. (f) The mane is shown also in the Chinese sign for 'horse', from the oracle bone script of the Shang period down to the modern character (馬 , now simplified as 马).

4. Proto-Dravidian names of the Asiatic wild asses

How did the Harappan people call the wild ass? The whole latter half of my 1994 book is devoted to demonstrating that the principal language of the Early and Mature Harappan people, and the only one they used in writing in South Asia, was Proto-Dravidian. Now there is a word denoting 'ass' (i.e., 'donkey') that is widely distributed in Dravidian languages: Tamil *kaẓutai*[30], Malayalam *kaẓuta*, Kota *kaṛt*, Toda *katy*, Kannada *kaṛte, katte*, Kodagu *katte*, Tulu *katte*, Telugu *gāḍida*, Kolami *gāḍdi*, Naiki *gāṛdi*, Parji *gade*, (S) *garad*, Gondi (G., Ko.) *gāṛdi*, Kuwi *gāṛde* (DEDR no. 1364). Bhadriraju Krishnamurti (2003: 12) reconstructs **kaẓ-ut-ay* for Proto-Dravidian, and asserts that Proto-Dravidian speakers knew the donkey.

This is anachronistic, if the Indus Civilization was Dravidian-speaking and if Proto-Dravidian dates from the early third millennium BCE, as Krishnamurti (2003: 501) thinks probable, since the donkey was introduced to South Asia during the first half of the second millennium BCE. One solution to this dilemma is that **kaẓutay* originally denoted 'the wild ass', which was known to the Indus people, and that this native term was afterwards transferred to the domestic ass.

Assuming that **kaẓutay* originally denoted the Indian wild ass, I am tempted to suggest an etymology for it. The word could be a compound literally meaning 'the kicker of salt desert'. The first component would be Proto-Dravidian **kaẓ(i)* 'saline soil' attested in Tamil *kaẓi* (in Puṟaṉāṉūṟu 48,3), *kaḷappu, kaḷar* (in Kuṟaḷ 406), Malayalam *kaẓi, kaḷar*, Kota *kayḷ-*, *kaḷc-*, and Brahui *kallar*; if inherited from Proto-Dravidian, the Brahui word should be **χallar*, so *kallar* is a reborrowing from Indo-Aryan spoken in the Indus Valley: Sindhi *kalaru*[31], Lahnda *kallur*, Punjabi *kallar* — these words have no cognates in other Indo-Iranian languages, and are loans from Dravidian **kaḷar* (cf. DEDR no. 1359; Turner 1966 no. 2954; Burrow 1967: 41)[32]. This word describes exactly the habitat of the Indian wild ass: "The typical habitat of the Indian wild ass is the flat salt desert" (Hawkins 1986: 25). This applies to the Asiatic wild ass at large: "In summary, *Equus hemionus* lives in flat desert country such as salt flats or gravel plains" (Groves 1986: 38). The Bible refers to "barren land (salt flats)" and the mountains as the habitat of the wild ass (Groves 1986: 42). "Xenophon saw wild asses (*onoi agrioi*)... He certainly means onagers, since they were on a flat treeless plain covered with wormwood" (Groves 1986: 43). The Persian term *χar-e-daštī* or *χar-daštī* for the 'wild ass' (cf. Steingass 1892: 450b, 453b; Platts 1884: 487b) likewise mentions its habitat: *dašt* 'desert, plain without water' (Steingass 1892: 526a)[33]. Salt desert, *kavir*, is the special habitat of the onager, and *Dašt-e Kavir* is one of its protection areas in Iran.

The second component would be Proto-Dravidian **utay* 'to kick', attested in Tamil *utai*, Malayalam *uta, utayuka, utekka*, Kota *od-*, *ov-*, *o-*, Kannada *ode*, *odi*, Tulu *dankuni*, ?Gadba *uyt*, Malto *utese, usete* (DEDR no. 616). The word is used of a kicking animal, e.g., in the Tamil compound *utai-kāl(i)* 'having a kicking leg' = 'a cow that kicks when milked' (TL 1926 I: 417a). The wild ass stallions fighting viciously for a mare in heat offer a dramatic sight when they, "rearing up on their hindlegs, use hooves and jaws in attack" (Salim Ali quoted in Prater 1971: 228)[34]. Asses are proverbial kickers, and this feature figures also in the Purāṇic myth of the killing of the ass demon Dhenuka (see 6). "When captured, the wild asses were extremely vicious, bit and kicked ... some of the captures remained excessively vicious" (Harrington quoted in Tegetmeier and Sutherland 1895: 27, see above 2). The one-year old wild ass run down six months earlier in 1873 by Captain Nutt (cf. 2) "bites and kicks at everyone that approaches her but her own syce" (Tegetmeier and Sutherland 1895: 25).

That **kaẓutay* "might have referred originally to the Asian half-ass" has already been suggested by Southworth (2005: 269), who locates Proto-Dravidian in South India, more exactly in the Southern Neolithic culture, which flourished in northern Karnataka and southwestern Andhra Pradesh (Southworth 2005: 229-287; cf. Figure 20). Because the archaeobotanically documented plants utilized in the Southern Neolithic strongly correlate with the Dravidian plant vocabulary, Dorian Fuller (2003) has proposed that the Southern Neolithic was Dravidian speaking. Fuller and his colleagues have also published radiocarbon dates showing that the Southern Neolithic flourished around 2500-1500 BCE, and that its beginnings go back to the early third millennium BCE (cf. Fuller *et al.* 2007).

There are some serious difficulties with

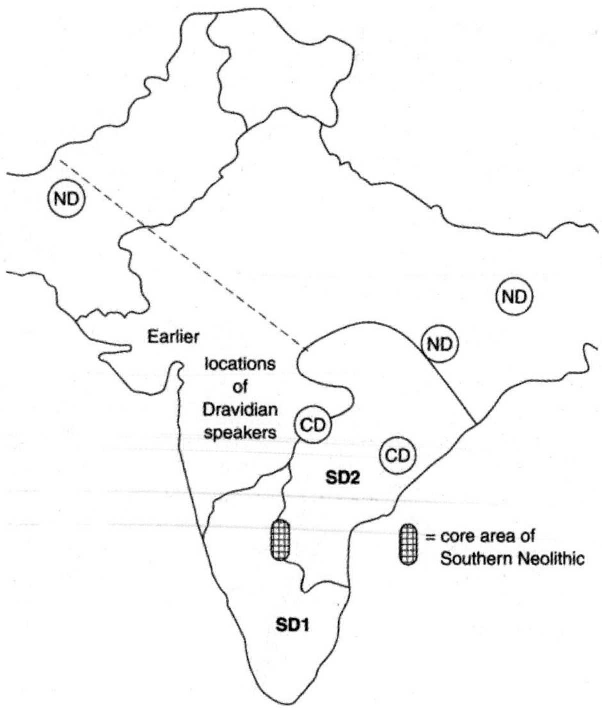

Figure 20 Approximate locations of Dravidian subgroups and the core area of Southern Neolithic (after Southworth 2005: 244, Figure 8.3)

Southworth's hypothesis that Proto-Dravidian was spoken in Southern Neolithic. For one thing, the implied northward expansion of Dravidian from South India is in no way reflected in the archaeological record. On the contrary, the general cultural spread both before and after the Southern Neolithic (in the Chalcolithic and 'Megalithic' periods) is from the north(west) to south. It appears that livestock and plants diffused to peninsular India from the first agricultural villages of Gujarat and Rajasthan (c. 3500-2500 BCE) (cf. Fuller 2006a: 30-31; 2006b: 182-188). P. Ajithprasad and Vasant Shinde (personal communications, January 2010) both mention the narrow-necked globular bowls as a specific trait connecting the Southern Neolithic to the Deccan Chalcolithic cultures. Recent archaeological research derives the beginnings of the Deccan Chalcolithic cultures from the Early Harappan cultures of Gujarat, Haryana and Rajasthan. It is now widely agreed that Early Harappan cultures of Baluchistan and southern Indus Valley (Amri-Nal) spread to Gujarat and Haryana (Anarta) as early as 3500 BCE, and that these Early Harappan cultures, while spreading further to become the Deccan Chalcolithic cultures, continued their existence in Gujarat side by side with the Mature Harappan culture that arrived in Gujarat after 2500 BCE (Ajithprasad 2002; 2010). Parallel to this southern expansion was the eastward spread of Early Harappan cultures (Tochi-Gomal) from northern Indus Valley to Cholistan and Haryana (Hakra) (Uesugi 2010). Proto-Dravidian was therefore spoken in the Early and Mature Harappan cultures, and its disintegration started with the southward and eastward spread of Chalcolithic cultures (cf. Parpola 1994: 171-174). The Southern Neolithic is likely to have spoken Proto-South-Dravidian, or perhaps rather its substratum overlaid by Proto-South Dravidian speakers who came from the northwest with the

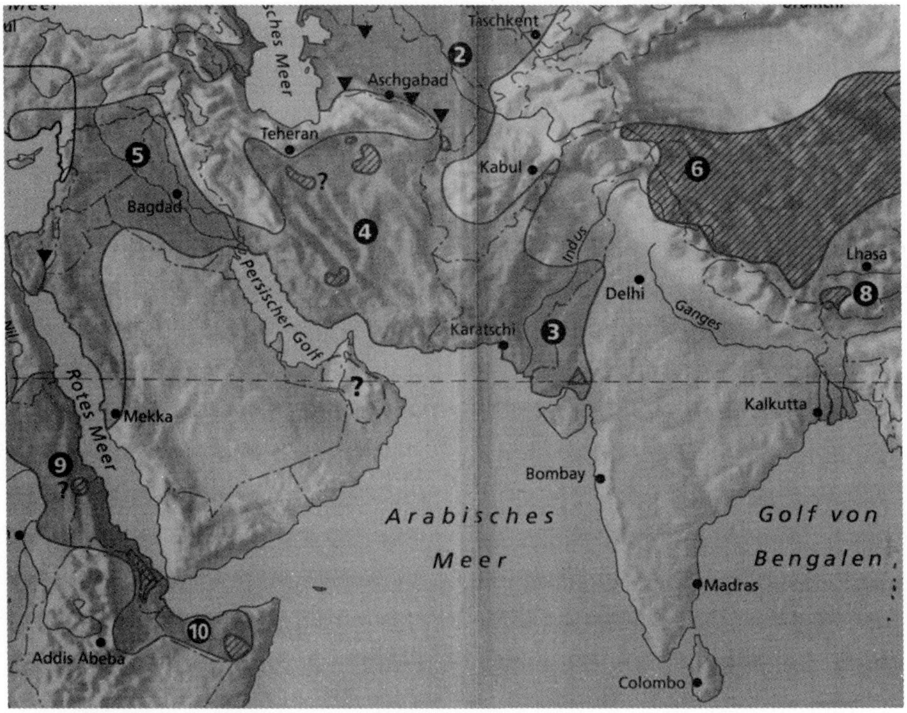

Figure 21 Previous and present distribution of the wild ass in and around South Asia (after Denzau and Denzau 1999: cover map)

'Megalithic' culture which succeeds the Southern Neolithic around 1500 BCE.

Also the reconstructed early distribution of the wild ass, which in South Asia[35] does not extend south of Gujarat or east of Rajasthan (Figure 21) contradicts Southworth's hypothesis that Proto-Dravidian was spoken in the Southern Neolithic culture. Southworth (2005: 270) is aware that the presence of words referring to equids conflicts with placing Proto-Dravidian in peninsular India. He tries to mitigate this by noting that "equid bones are attested at Hallur in Karnataka as early as 1600 BCE". This evidence, however, postdates the Southern Neolithic and relates to the introduction of the domestic horse[36]. The donkey undoubtedly came to South India in the wake of the horse.

If Proto-Dravidian **kaẓutay* originally denoted 'wild ass', this was possible only in the Harappan realm, which coincides with the third and second millennium BCE habitat of the wild ass. The term could have been transferred to denote the somewhat similar-looking 'domestic ass' also just in the Greater Indus Valley, the habitat of the wild ass, through which the donkey was introduced to South Asia from the west c. 1600 BCE. That this really did happen is confirmed by the most common term for the donkey in the Rigveda, Sanskrit *gardabha-*, which has been plausibly explained as an early Dravidian loanword by Burrow and Emeneau (DEDR no. 1364). This implies that the borrowing took place in or around the Indus Valley before 1000 BCE, and that the Indo-Aryan animal name suffix *-bha-* was added to **garda* < **kaẓ(u)tay*. Mayrhofer (1992 I: 473) objects to this Dravidian etymology for *gardabha-*, because the word is so ancient in Indo-Aryan, and because the hypothesis involves the addition of an Indo-European suffix to a Dravidian loanword; in his opinion the etymology is "not clear". However, it is significant that *gardabha-* has no cognates in Iranian languages[37].

And although as an animal name suffix *-bha-* is of ancient origin (cf. Greek *élaphos* 'deer'), it was still productive in Old Indo-Aryan (cf. Debrunner 1954 II.2: 746-747 #591a). Not only is it found in another Rigvedic word for ass, *rāsabha-*, but, though yet another Indo-Aryan word for ass, *khara-*, is without this suffix, it has been added, together with the deminutive suffix *-ka-*, in **kharabhaka-* 'hare' (= a small animal resembling the ass in that it has long ears), the Old Indo-Aryan basis of Nepali *kharāyo*, Oriya *kharā*, *khariā*, *kherihā*, Marathi *kharehā* and Hindi *kharahā* (cf. Turner 1966 no. 3823). Cf. also classical Sanskrit and Pali *karabha-*, *kalabha-* 'young elephant or camel' (cf. Turner 1966: no. 2797, also for New Indo-Aryan cognates), which in all likelihood is composed of *kara-* m. 'hand' + the suffix *-bha-*, and originally denotes the elephant, a South Asian animal, cf. Sanskrit *hastin-* 'elephant' < *hasta-* m. 'hand' + possessive adjective suffix *-in-* (cf. Mayrhofer 2001 III: 62).

Although Sanskrit *gardabha-* m. 'ass', like Tamil *kaẓutai* and its cognates in other Dravidian languages, in most of its occurrences undoubtedly means 'donkey', in some cases it seems to denote the 'wild ass', which probably was the original meaning of the etymon. Thus Brockington (1984: 89) notes that while the donkey is called *khara-* in the Rāmāyaṇa, the word *gardabha-* in its single occurrence denotes *Equus hemionus* Pallas. This identification, obviously based on the colour of the animal, appears to be correct. The single occurrence is in 3,22,1, where "a rumbling storm cloud" (*mahāmeghas tumulo*), "ruddy as the wild ass" (*gardabhāruṇaḥ*), "rained water red as blood" (*śoṇitodakam abhyavarṣat*). Pollock (1990 III: 133) translates "mule-gray", but *gardabha-* is not 'mule' (in Sanskrit 'mule' is mostly *aśvatara-*[38]) and *aruṇa-* is not 'gray' but 'red, ruddy, reddish-brown, tawny, light brown'.

One of the native terms for 'the Indian wild ass' is (Hindi) *khar-gadhā*: the compound is not found in Hindi and Urdu dictionaries (Platts 1884; McGregor 1993; Varmmā 1990-93), but it is recorded in this sense in 1832 by James Tod in his monumental description of Rajasthan (*khur-guddha* in Tod 1914 II: 264, normalized into *khar-gadhā* by William Crooke in Tod 1920 III: 1306), and in 1834 (spelt *khur-gudha*) by Alexander Burnes, who during his survey of the Indus region had observed the wild asses in the Rann of Kutch (cf. Denzau and Denzau 1999: 55-56). The compound goes back to Sanskrit *khara-gardabha-*, which is not found in any Sanskrit dictionary, either, but is actually attested in Matsya-Purāṇa (perhaps 400 CE)[39]. In chapter 118 this text lists wild animals and plants in Himalayan foothills where the river Airāvatī (modern Ravi) has its source (verse 2). After rhinoceroses and wild boars, verse 61 mentions "swift-going wild asses" (*turaṃgān kharagardabhān*). In view of the location given, this may refer to the kiang, the Tibetan wild ass.

'Wild ass' is likely to have been the original meaning even of the following Dravidian words for 'horse' (recorded in DEDR no. 1711a): Tamil *kutirai*[40], Malayalam *kutira*, Kota *kudyr*, Toda *kiθïr*, Kannada *kudire*, *kudure*, *kudare*, Kodagu *kudïre*, Tulu *kudurè*, Telugu *kudira*, *kudaramu*. In Tulu, the word also means 'grasshopper' and 'lock of a gun' (this meaning is found in Tamil and Kannada as well) and 'catch of an umbrella': these secondary meanings support the derivation (suggested by Burrow and Emeneau) from the Proto-Dravidian root **kuti* 'to jump, leap, shake, jolt, gallop, trot' (DEDR no. 1705, attested from Tamil to North Dravidian Kurukh)[41]. That **kutiray* indeed goes back to Proto-Dravidian is suggested by its unexpected presence in the Dardic language Tirahi: "One curious Tir[ahi] word ought to be noticed. The resemblance between *kuzᵊra* 'horse' and Tamil *kudirei* and other Dravidian words is too striking to be accidental." (Morgenstierne 1932: 21; cf. also Fussman 1972 II: 111).

In 1929, Tirahi was spoken in three villages southeast of Jalalabad in Afghanistan; its speakers had been expelled from Tirah in Pakistan (southwest of Peshawar) by Afghans a couple of centuries earlier (cf. Morgenstierne 1932: 20; Bashir 2003: 857). According to Morgenstierne (1965: 138-139), Tirahi is "probably the remnant of a dialect group extending from Tirah through the Peshawar district into Swat and Dir ... connected with Kalam Kohistani and Torwali, but retaining forms of a Lahnda type". It belongs to the 'Dardic' group of "those Northwest Indo-Aryan languages which, because of their isolation in the mountains of the Hindu Kush, Swat and Indus Kohistan, the Karakorams and the Western Himalayas, have retained ancient and developed new characteristics different from the I[ndo-]A[ryan] languages of the Indo-Gangetic plain... Dardic languages on the whole underwent fewer of the major M[iddle] IA phonological and morphological developments than plains IA" (Bashir 2003: 821-822). The Dardic languages alone among the New Indo-Aryan languages have preserved traces of the Rigvedic gerund in *-tvī*, which in later Vedic occurs only a couple of times (cf. Tikkanen 1987: 76-90, 252-253). Phonologically it seems possible that Tirahi *kuzᵊra* preserves, from early Old Indo-Aryan, a Proto-Dravidian loanword **kudira-*, cf. Tirahi *az* 'today' < Old Indo-Aryan *adya* (Fussman 1972 II: 75-77), and the preservation of final *-ra* of Old Indo-Aryan *cukra-* 'vinegar' in several Dardic languages (cf. Fussman 1972 II: 45-47).

5. The Persian and Indian wild ass in Iranian and Indo-Aryan languages

Among the other Sanskrit words for 'ass'[42], the word *rāsabha-*[43] is mainly restricted to Vedic (1000 BCE+), and even in Middle Vedic texts mentioned as an archaic expression[44]. It seems that *rāsabha-* has at least in some early contexts denoted the wild ass. In particular, I have in mind its role as the animal pulling the chariot of the Aśvins. The Nighaṇṭu (1,15 *rāsabhāv aśvinoḥ*) and the Bṛhaddevatā (4,125 ed. Tokunaga = 4,141 ed. Macdonell *rāsabhaḥ sahito 'śvibhyāṃ*) consider the *rāsabha-* as the very animal of the Aśvins, in spite of the fact that these divine twins are associated with the horse (*aśva-*) even in their name, and that they are the charioteers *par excellence* (cf. Zeller 1990: 109-112). The Aśvins are asked to yoke a single *rāsabha-* to their chariot in Rigveda 8,85,7[45]. In 1,34,9 the single *rāsabha-* to be yoked is called *vājin-* 'swift'; and according to Rigveda 1,116,2, a single ass won a thousand (cows/verses) for the Aśvins in Yama's prize-contest[46]. In another divine race described in Aitareya-Brāhmaṇa 4,7-9, the ass-chariot (*gardabha-ratha-*) of the Aśvins defeated the mule-chariot of the fire-god Agni, the cow-chariot of Uṣas (the goddess of dawn) and the horse-chariot of Indra (the god of war and thunder). It seems quite likely to me that the Aśvins as the foremost gods of chariot-race[47] won the race because they used an animal that beats even the horse (cf. 2)[48]. In the Rāmāyaṇa, "a simile compares an ass's gait disparagingly to a horse's (2.98.6a = 6.116.5a); on the other hand, among the presents which Aśvapati gives to Bharata on his departure are swift, well-harnessed asses (2.64.20, not however in most N. mss.)" (Brockington 1984: 89).

In the North Dravidian language Brahui spoken in Baluchistan and Sindh the wild ass is called *gōr*. This is a loan from the Iranian Baluchi language, which is spoken by most Brahui speakers (cf. Rossi 1979: 193 no. H379). 'Wild ass' is *gōr* in Middle and New Persian and Urdu as well, and as a Persian loanword in Kurdish (cf. Horn 1893: 209 no. 938). Pashto *γyara* f. 'wild ass' may come from **γwari* (+ *-a*) as a metathetic reflex of **gaurī* (cf. Morgenstierne *et al.* 2003: 34). In Persian, Gōr (Arabicized as Jūr in al-Ṭabarī's *History*, #857) or Bahrām-e-Gōr is also the name of the Sasanid king Bahrām V (421-438/9), famous on account of his passion to hunt this graceful and swift animal[49], recounted by Firdausī in his Šāhnāma (26,8 and 32,8) and by other poets. Some of the poets, like Omar Khayyam, play in their verses with the homonymy of the Persian words *gōr* 'wild ass' and *gōr* 'grave' and 'desert' (see Denzau and Denzau 1999: 195-197; cf. Steingass 1892: 1101b).

In Persian, 'wild ass, onager' is called also *gōr-χar* (Steingass 1892: 1102a), where *χar* is the Persian word for 'ass, donkey' (cf. also *χar-gōš* 'hare', literally 'one that has the ears of a donkey'). Middle and New Persian *χar* has cognates in Younger Avestan *χara-*, Khotanese Saka *khara*, Sogdian (Buddhist) *γr-*, (Manichean, Christian) *χr-*, and practically all Neo-Iranian languages[50]. It corresponds to Indo-Aryan *khara-* 'ass', which is not found in the Rigveda, nor elsewhere in older Vedic literature excepting the single occurrence in the 20th book of the Paippalāda-Saṃhitā of Atharvaveda (20,39,2), which does not have a counterpart in the Śaunaka version of the Atharvaveda, and is likely to be of later origin. Otherwise the oldest references are in a late passage (cf. Keith 1909: 17) of the Aitareya-Āraṇyaka (3,2,4), and in the Kātyāyana-Śrautasūtra and in Pāṇini's grammar, neither of which predates the Achaemenid period; in Prakrit, *khara-* is attested in the Niya documents of Sinkiang; among the modern languages, the distribution of the cognates is limited to the Nuristani languages of Afghanistan, and the Dardic Neo-Indo-Aryan languages of North Pakistan and Kashmir, and to Neo-Indo-Aryan languages of Pakistan and Western India[51]. It is debated whether Indo-Aryan got the word from Old Iranian (which seems most probable), or whether it goes back to Proto-Indo-Iranian **khara*; in either case the word is likely to be a loanword, possibly from Semitic: Akkadian (at Mari in Syria) has *ḫārum, ajarum* 'donkey stallion' (cf. Mayrhofer 1992 I: 447).

The name *khur*[52] for the Indian wild ass comes from the scientific name *Equus khur* (now *Equus hemionus khur*) given to it in 1827 by the French biologist René-Primevère Lesson. Lesson's source was the short anonymous article entitled "Der wilde Esel", which was published in the encyclopedic journal *Isis* (edited by L. Oken in Stuttgart) in 1823 (cf. Denzau and Denzau: 55). Wishing to check how the name was spelt in Lesson's source, I dug up the article, which confirmed my suspicion that *khur* is an Anglicized spelling of *χar* or *khar*: "Dieser Esel, den die Eingeborenen *Khur* (die persische Benennung dieses Thieres) nennen, ist bedeutend dauerhafter wie der zahme Esel..." (*Isis* 1823, Siebentes Heft, col. 764).

The Persian compound *gōr-χar* has a counterpart in Hindi *gōr-khar*. This compound is not in McGregor's Hindi dictionary (1993)[53], possibly because Platts (1884: 923b) recorded it as a Persian loanword: "*gor-k͟har* (or *k͟har-e-gor*), or *gor*, s. m. 'The ass of the desert, the wild ass, the onager'". This is under the lemma "*gor* s. f. A grave, tomb; in P[ersian] also 'a desert'." Persian (and Baluchi, Brahui and Urdu) *gōr* 'grave, tomb' (associated with the homonym *gōr* 'wild ass' by Persian poets) is however a Semitic loanword in Persian (cf. Horn 1893: 210), and as an etymology for *gōr-χar* 'wild ass' this word is excluded by the Indo-Aryan cognates.

James Tod in his 1832 work on Rajasthan mentions *gorkhur* as one of the local appellations for the 'wild ass' (thus Tod 1914 II: 264; in Tod 1920 III: 1306, normalized into *gorkhar* by William Crooke). The only known Middle Indo-Aryan reference mentioning *gōra-khara* is in the fourth Upāṅga of the Jaina canon, Pannavaṇāsutta (Prajñapanā) which describes the various forms and qualities of the living beings, written in the Ardhamāgadhī language by the monk Ārya Śyāma alias Kālaka in Ujjain c. 79 BCE (cf. Jaini 1979: 60; Glasenapp 1925: 95; 99; 43). Chapter 1,71 briefly enumerates the one-hoofed animals (*ega-khurā*),

4797 (29) Gāura-kharaḥ 〔蔵〕Rgyaṅ
〔漢〕棗騮馬、野騾 〔和〕中央亜細亜に
多く産する野馬の一種なり

Figure 22 Mahāvyutpatti 4797 in Sakaki 1916

including the *gōra-khara*[54]. The Prakrit dictionaries translate this 'a kind of ass' (Sheth 1963: 302b "gardabh kī ek jāti") or 'white ass' (Ratnachandraji 1923-38 II: 653a "*śveta-gardabha; safed gadhā*. a white ass"). As the author resided in Ujjain, this should be the Indian wild ass, the khur. But Sanskrit *gaurakhara* in Matsya-Purāṇa[55] 118,58 probably denotes the kiang, the Tibetan wild ass, since it occurs in the same description of wild animals of the Himalayan foothills around the source of the Ravi river as the already cited occurrence (in verse 61) of *kharagardabha*. Immediately before *gaurakhara*, the verse 58 mentions elephants in rut, water buffaloes, bison bulls, yaks and Kashmir red deers[56] (*tathā mattāṃś ca mātaṅgān mahiṣān gavayān vṛṣān | camarān sṛmarāṃś caiva tathā gaurakharān api*). The kiang is undoubtedly meant also in the single occurrence of Buddhist Hybrid Sanskrit *gaura-khara-*, attested with the Tibetan translation *rgyang* (the source of the name *kiang* used of the Tibetan wild ass, *Equus kiang*) in Mahāvyutpatti (no. 4797), a ninth century text compiled at the order of the Tibetan king Khri lde srong brtsan (the edition by Sakaki has Chinese and Japanese 'glosses'[57], see Figure 22)[58].

Many sources[59] mention as the Hindi name of the Indian wild ass *ghor-khar*. The aspiration is probably not a mistake, but a folk-etymological transformation. I assume the proper spelling to be *ghoṛ-khar* 'horse-ass', although such a compound cannot be found in the Hindi and Urdu dictionaries. What can be found is that Hindi *ghoṛā* 'horse'[60] appears in the contracted form *ghoṛ-* or *ghuṛ-* when it is the first member of a compound (cf. Platts 1884: 938b; McGregor 1993: 292b, 289b). Reference has already been made to Ball (1885: 285-286) who says that the Tibetan wild ass was often taken to be a wild horse in his time[61].

The important lexicographic work Yaśastilakacampū of the Jaina author Somadevasūri, who wrote in AD 951 in Ujjain, records *gaura-khura* and *khara-khura* in the sense of 'wild ass' (cf. Schmidt 1928: 178b, 163a). The latter member of these compounds is clearly Sanskrit *khura* 'hoof', which has survived in this meaning in the New Indo-Aryan languages, mostly in the form *khur* (cf. Turner 1966: no. 3906), but used here in the sense of *khurin-* 'hoofed animal', although this meaning is not elsewhere attested for *khur(a)*. In spite of Mayrhofer's doubt (1992 I: 454), Sanskrit *khura-*, first attested relatively late in Vedic literature (Aitareya-Āraṇyaka and Śrautasūtras), is likely to be a Dravidian loanword in Indo-Aryan (as suggested by Burrow and Emeneau in DEDR no. 1770, which records in the meaning 'hoof' Tamil *kuracu, kuraccai*, Kannada *gorasu, gorise, guruse*, and Telugu *gorija, gorise, gorije, korije*).

The oldest occurrence of *gaura-khara-* in Sanskrit is in the Vasiṣṭha-Dharmasūtra, which perhaps dates from the 2nd century BCE. In 21,1-3 this law text contrast three varieties of ass according to their colour in its prescription of punishments for illicit sex, associating these varieties with three social classes[62].

> "1. If a Śūdra has sex with a Brahmin woman, he should be wrapped in Vīraṇa grass and thrown into a fire. The Brahmin woman's head should be shaved and her body smeared with ghee, and she should be paraded on a highway

naked and seated on a black ass [*kṛṣṇakhara*][63]. 'In this way,' it is stated, 'she becomes pure.'
2. If a Vaiśya has sex with a Brahmin woman, he should be wrapped in tufts of Lohita straw and thrown into a fire. The Brahmin woman's head should be shaved and her body smeared with ghee, and she should be paraded on a highway naked and seated on a yellow ass [*gaurakhara*][64]. 'In this way,' it is stated, 'she becomes pure.'
3. If a Kṣatriya has sex with a Brahmin woman, he should be wrapped in Śara grass and thrown into a fire. The Brahmin woman's head should be shaved and her body smeared with ghee, and she should be paraded on a highway naked and seated on a white ass [*śvetakhara*][65]. 'In this way,' it is stated, 'she becomes pure.'
4. The same punishment applies to a Vaiśya who has sex with a Kṣatriya woman
5. and to a Śūdra who has sex with a Kṣatriya or a Vaiśya woman" (Transl. Olivelle 2000: 437)[66].

Here the *gaura-khara-* is contrasted with the *kṛṣṇa-khara-* 'black ass', the darker, gray donkey (see Figure 4).

The Indo-Aryan cognate of Persian *gōr* 'wild ass, onager', Sanskrit *gaura-* (attested since the Rigveda, c. 1000 BCE), is primarily a colour term, meaning 'white, yellowish, fair-skinned, pale red', and these are the basic meanings of the cognates also in Middle and New Indo-Aryan languages (cf. Turner 1966: no. 4345). Etymologically the word seems to mean 'cow-coloured', as it probably is derived with the suffix *-ra-* from *gav-* 'cow'[67], although the long grade ablaut in the beginning is unusual (cf. Mayrhofer 1992 I: 503). On the Iranian side the only cognate with the colour meaning is Baluchi *gōraγ* 'gray, white'; does this attest for an Indo-Iranian origin, as Mayrhofer thinks, or is the Baluchi word loan from Indo-Aryan **gaura-ka-*, which is the basis of New Indo-Aryan *gōrā-* (in most languages)? And if so, has *gōr* as the name of the wild ass in Iranian also its origin in Indo-Aryan? The etymon is not attested in Old Iranian, neither as a colour term nor as an appellation of an animal.

Indo-Aryan *gaura-*, on the other hand, is attested not only as a colour-adjective but also, since the Rigveda, as a substantive denoting an animal. In this meaning the standard interpretation has long been, not 'the wild ass', but 'the gaur or Indian bison (*Bos gaurus* C.H. Schmith, 1827)'. This is indeed the meaning given for Sanskrit *gaura-* (m.) in all dictionaries and text translations. Originally, of course, *gaura-* denotes a 'fair-skinned (cow-coloured) animal'. For the wild ass this is an apt characterization, for although the skin colour varies somewhat according to regions and seasons, at least the Indian subspecies is described as "fawn or pale chestnut in colour" (Hawkins 1986: 25). For the Indian bison, *gaura-* is less apt as a colour term: "A newly-born Gaur is a light golden-yellow which soon changes to fawn, then to light brown, and so to coffee or reddish brown, the colour of young bulls and cows [see Figure 24]. Old bulls are jet black [see Figure 23], their bodies almost hairless" (Prater 1971: 243). According to Prater (1971: 243), the Hindi name for the Indian bison is *gaur* or *gaur gai*, while in Marathi (the only other Indo-Aryan or Indo-Iranian language mentioned by Prater) the bison is called *gaviya* or *gawa*. Now, *gaur* is a borrowing from Sanskrit in Hindi, having the following meanings: "1. Adj. white, pale; pale red. 2. fair-complexioned. 3. m. the gaur (a wild ox)" (McGregor 1993: 281a). Prater's *gai* is Hindi *gāy* [< *gāvī-*] 'cow' (McGregor 1993: 263). Turner (1966: no. 4096) records Nepali *gaurī gāi* 'wild buffalo' as a borrowing from Bihari. The ancient Sanskrit term for '*Bos gaurus*' is *gavayá-* m., which according to Turner (1966: no. 4095) survives in Pali *gavaya-* m. 'species of ox', Prakrit *gavaya-*, *gaüa-* m. 'species of wild ox' and Marathi *gavā*, *gahū* m. '*Bos gavaeus*'.

Figure 23 Adult Gaur bison (*Bos gaurus*) (photo Gertrud and Helmut Denzau)

Figure 24 A newborn calf and a slightly older calf of the Gaur bison (photo Gertrud and Helmut Denzau)

The identification of *gaura-* with *Bos gaurus* has from the beginning been based on the observation that it occurs together with *gavaya-*[68], implying that both are bovids. "As the Vājasaneyi Saṃhitā (xiii.48) expressly mentions wild (*āraṇya*) *Gauras*, they must usually have been tame" (Macdonell and Keith 1912 I: 241-242) is an additional assumption. Similar considerations prevail with regard to the *gavaya-*, which the dictionaries and translations take as a different species, *Bos gavaeus*[69]. Nowadays the term *Bos gavaeus*, however, does not refer to a different species, but is used of the tamed variant of *Bos gaurus*, resulting from its cross-mating with the domestic cow. It will become clear from the following that *gavaya-* and not *gaura-* is the Vedic term for *Bos gaurus*.

The word *gavaya-* occurs in the Rigveda just once, in 4,21,8c *vidád gaurásya gavayásya góhe*, which speaks of "the hiding place of the fawn bison". I think it is more natural, and in line with the above mentioned New Indo-Aryan names of the Indian bison, to understand *gaura-* here as an attribute of (a young) *gavaya-* than to take it (as Geldner does in 1951 I: 447) asyndetically as a reference to a different animal species on the basis of their co-occurrence as names of separate animals in later Vedic texts. The rest of the verse mentions the mountains and the rains, and these fit the bison which is "by nature shy and timid animal" (Prater 1971: 244) and prefers "foothill tracts of sub-humid or deciduous forest" but exists also "in hill zones with moderate to heavy rainfall" (The IUCN Red list of Threatened Species 2008).

The Middle Vedic texts (which date from c. 900-600 BCE) on several occasions refer to a set of five domestic (*grāmya-*) animals, the males of which are immolated as sacrificial victims: 1. man (*puruṣa-*), 2. horse (*aśva-*), 3. cow (*go-*), 4. sheep (*avi-*) and 5. goat (*aja-*). These five domestic animals are correlated with, and contrasted to, a set of five wild (*āraṇya-*) animals[70].

The Aitareya-Brāhmaṇa (2,8) explains that the gods first slew man as a sacrificial victim. When man had been slewn, his sap or sacrificial qualification (*medha-*) went out of him and entered the horse, which became fit for sacrifice (*medhya-*). From the slaughtered horse the *medha-* went to the cow, and so on. Those from which the *medha-* had gone out they dismissed and they became the following impure animals, which may not be sacrificed nor eaten: 1. *kiṃpuruṣa-*, 2. *gauramṛga-*[71] 3. *gavaya-*, 4. *uṣṭra-*, 5. *śarabha-*.

The Śatapatha-Brāhmaṇa (= ŚB), in its description of the great fire altar ritual (7,5,2,14-36), tells that the heads of the above enumerated five domestic animals are placed in the fire pan, which is laid in the centre of the first layer of bricks for the fire altar. The human head is put in the middle of the pan, the head of the horse and the sheep on the north side and the heads of the cow and the goat on the south side. Then the priest recites mantras addressed to Fire at the heads[72]. He thereby removes from the victims the distress (*śuc-* 'burning heat') that they felt at being slewn, and directs this evil to enter the corresponding wild (*āraṇya-*) animals.

At the human head the Fire is asked not to harm this two-legged animal (*dvipādaṃ paśum*); its burning heat should go to the *mayu-* animal, which according to the ŚB is the *kiṃpuruṣa-*[73]. At the horse's head the Fire is asked not to harm this one-hoofed animal (*eka-śaphaṃ paśum*), the racer, neighing among the racers; its burning heat should go to the wild ass (*gauram āraṇyam*)[74]. The cow is praised as the giver of milk and its distress is directed to the "wild cow-like animal" (*gavayam āraṇyam*), i.e., the Indian bison (*Bos gaurus*). The sheep is here praised as "woolly" (*ūrṇāyu-*), and its distress directed to the wild camel (*uṣṭram āraṇyam*), another animal noted for its wool. The goat's distress is directed to the wild *śarabha-*, an animal whose real identity was mostly forgotten in India in later times (Sāyaṇa, the medieval South Indian commentator of Vedic texts explains it to be an eight-footed lion-killer), which is natural in view of the fact that its habitats were restricted to the mountains of the northwest; the cognates surviving in Nuristani and Dardic languages and in Sindhi and Lahnda reveal it to be 'wild goat': the markhor (*Capra falconeri*), the ibex (*Capra ibex*), or the Sind ibex alias bezoar goat (*Capra aegagrus*) (cf. Turner 1966: no. 12331)[75].

There is thus a clear connection between a given domestic animal and its wild counterpart. This correspondence is even closer when we consider the earliest texts where this twofold list of five animals is presented. In the Maitrāyaṇī Saṃhitā (= MS) 2,7,17, Kāṭhaka-Saṃhitā (= KS) 16,17, and Kapiṣṭhala-Kaṭha-Saṃhitā (= KapS) 25,8 the wild animals are *mayú-*, *gaurá-*, *gavayá-*, *meṣá-* and *śarabhá-*, i.e., the same animals as in the ŚB and the TS, with this exception: instead of the camel (*uṣṭra-*), the wild counterpart of the sheep (*avi-*) is *meṣá-* 'ram'. In the Nuristani Prasun language, the cognate *məṣə* denotes besides 'ram' also 'oorial' (cf. Turner 1966: no. 10334); oorial or urial (*Ovis orientalis vignei*) is one of the mightiest wild sheep, with even one metre long horns (cf. Prater 1971: 249)[76].

Moreover, in the description of the ritual, these older texts (MS 3,2,7; KS 20,8; KapS 31,10; cf. also TS 5,2,8-9) prescribe just the heads of the horse and the cow to be placed in the fire pot, on either side of the human head; the texts use the dvandva compound *go-aśva-*. In ŚB 1,2,3,9, the other impure (wild) animals deprived of sacrificial essence are mentioned one by one, but those corresponding to the horse and cow are mentioned together, with the verb in the dual (*yāv aśvaṃ ca gāṃ ca, tau gauraś ca gavayaś cābhavatām*). Thus the *gaura-* and the *gavaya-* occur together, not because they should both be bovines as has been supposed, but because they are the wild counterparts of the horse and the cow, that is, the wild ass and the gaur bison.

In all of its early Vedic occurrences, *gaura-* as a substantive that refers to a real animal appears to denote exclusively the wild ass. This applies also to the Rigvedic occurrences[77], which mostly ask the gods to drink the sacred drink "like the thirsty *gaura-*" (RV 1,16,5 *gauró ná tṛṣitáḥ piba*; for the other text places see Lubotsky 1997 I: 503). Particularly significant in this connection are the following cases[78]: RV 8,87,1d and 4d (to the two Aśvins) "drink/come like two wild asses at a water-depression of salty soil" (*pātám/gantám gaurāv ivériṇe*)! RV 8,4,3 (to Indra) come to drink Soma "like a thirsting wild ass goes down to a depression of salty soil created by water" (*yáthā gauró apā kṛtám tṛṣyann éty áveríṇam*). (On these passages and on *íriṇa-* n. as a depression of salty soil, cf. Falk 1986: 77-81 and Mayrhofer 1992 I: 196.) The salt desert is the very habitat of the Indian wild ass, and its specially adapted kidneys allow it to drink even salty water without damage.

There is also another factor that makes the wild ass an icon of a thirsty drinker. Most mammals die if they lose more than 20% of their body water. The wild asses are able to lose even 30% of their body water, and like camels, they can stay a long time without drinking. The blood of the camel contains a lot of aluminium and therefore its osmotic pressure is so high that it does not give up water even if the surrounding tissues are lethally dry. Therefore the camel can drink even 100 litres of water in 10 minutes, so that its body weight rises by one third. If a very thirsty human being would drink a corresponding amount of water, this would destroy the red cells of the blood and he or she would die. The wild ass can slake its thirst even quicker than the camel. This has been important in the past to escape the predators, which used to lurk around the water holes (Cf. MacKinnon and MacKinnon 1974: 102-104).

6. South Asian myths related to the wild ass

According to Arrian (*Anabasis* 6,17-19), Alexander the Great and his fleet experienced a very strong ebb and flow of tide in the Indus delta, which along with its capital city was called Patala:

> "17. ... There also arrived the ruler of the land of Patala, which, as I said [in 5,4,1-2] is the delta made by the Indus river and is still larger than the Egyptian delta; he too surrendered all his territory and committed himself and all that he had to Alexander ... When he [Alexander] arrived at Patala, he found the city and land empty... 18. Alexander ordered Hephaestion to fortify the citadel in Patala, and sent out men to the desert in the adjoining country to dig wells and to make the country inhabitable ... Round Patala the stream of the Indus parts into two large rivers, both of these retaining the name Indus till they reach the sea. Here Alexander began to build a ship-station and dockyards, and, when his works had advanced well, he planned to sail down to the outlet of the right-hand stream to the sea... 19. When they had anchored there, the ebb-tide, characteristic of the great sea, followed; as a result their ships were left high and dry. Alexander's men had not known of this before, and it was another thing that gave them a severe shock, repeated with still more force when the time passed and the tide came up again and the ships were lifted up. Ships which the tide found comfortably settled on the mud were lifted off unharmed, and floated once more without sustaining damage; but those which were caught on a drier bottom and were not on an even keel, as the onrushing tide came in all together, either collided with each other or were dashed on the land and shattered" (Brunt1983 II: 151-157).

The Indian tradition ascribes the ebb of tide to a submarine fire[79]. This is imagined to be a mare-faced (*vaḍavāmukha-*) form of Viṣṇu in the netherworld (*pātāla*) who has such an insatiable thirst that it makes him to drink the entire ocean; at the same time, water is conceived to be a libation poured into that submarine fire as a sacrificial offering (fire is the mouth of gods)[80]. Vaḍavāmukha, son of Angry Fire, or Aurva (wrath of angered sage Aurva thrown into ocean), lives in the southern ocean drinking its waters and is the same as the terrible doomsday fire (*saṃvartakāgni-*)[81], which drinks up the waters of deluge (*pralaya-*)[82].

I would like to suggest that the conception of a mare-faced god who in insatiable thirst drinks ocean water and therewith causes the ebb of tide has been inspired by the horse-like wild ass able to drink enormous amounts of salty water[83]. That Vaḍavāmukha was associated with the area of the wild ass in the Indus delta and the Rann of Kutch is supported by the description of India contained in the Mārkaṇḍeya-Purāṇa (58) and Varāhamihira's Bṛhatsaṃhitā (14), where Vaḍavāmukha is placed in the northwest, immediately after Sindhu-Sauvīra (cf. Kirfel 1920: 86).

While Sanskrit *mukha-* has a Dravidian etymology[84], Sanskrit *vaḍavā-* 'mare' is yet another equid-related term of unclear origin, generally considered to be a loanword (cf. Mayrhofer 1996 II: 494). It is attested since the Middle Vedic texts, where it has the shape *váḍabā-*; this *váḍabā-* 'mare' is said to have double seed like the ass, *gardabha-* (Taittirīya-Saṃhitā 7,1,1,2 and Pañcaviṃśa-Brāhmaṇa 6,1,4), and has the attribute 'swift' (*sṛtvarī-*, Maitrāyaṇī Saṃhitā 2,4,4; Kāṭhaka-Saṃhitā 12,11); in the Jaiminīya-Brāhmaṇa, where the word occurs many times, the form is *vaḷabā-*, though in several places, but not always, the manuscripts have the dissimilatory variant reading *viḷabā-* (cf. Oertel 1951 and Ehlers 1988: xxxii); here (in JB 2,115) the goddess Vāc takes the shape of a white mare, which, provided with a halter, is brought as a sacrificial gift to the Angirases (*tebhya etāṃ vācaṃ vaḷabāṃ śvetāṃ bhūtām aśvābhidhānyabhihitām ānayan*); and (in JB 3,23) the prized mares of the king give birth to foals. In Middle Indo-Aryan the word is attested in Pali as *vaḷavā-*, *baḷavā-*, *vaḷabhā(mukha)-*, *vaḷabhī(ratha)-*, in Prakrit as *vaḍavā-*, *valavā-*, *valayā*, but from Neo-Indo-Aryan Turner (1966: no. 11219) records just Sinhalese *veḷamba-*, *veḷemba-* and Tirahi *baṛeṃ*. Sinhalese has come to Sri Lanka from Gujarat, and Tirahi was noted above (4) as a Dardic language of the upper Indus Valley that in *kuzᵊra* 'horse' curiously seems to have preserved an etymon of Proto-Dravidian origin that probably originally denoted the 'wild ass'.

As uncertain cognates Turner adds Sindhi *vaṛu* m. 'sexual heat (of animals)', *vaṛjaṇu* 'to be on heat (of mares)'. These Sindhi words suggest a Proto-Dravidian etymology, if they are related to Kannada *vaḍi* 'heat' and Telugu *vaḍa* 'the hot wind, heat' (DEDR no. 5225). Kālidāsa compares sexual desire directly with the *vaḍavāmukha-* fire: according to him, Śiva in his lovemaking could not get enough of sensual pleasures, as the fire burning under the ocean cannot sate its thirst with the waters of the sea[85].

The association of *vaḍavāmukha-* with the ebb of tide[86] suggests that *vaḍavā-* 'mare' goes back to Proto-Dravidian (and, consequently, that it originally denoted the female of the wild ass), for it is nearly homophonous with the Proto-Dravidian etymon **vaṭi* 'to flow (out), flow in a small stream, trickle, drip', which at least in Tamil and Malayalam is specifically used of the 'ebbing' of tide (DEDR no. 5221). It is clearly in origin the same word as Proto-Dravidian **vaṭi* 'to dry up (as water in a river), be diminished, wither, fade, be thin, weak, poor', and in Gondi at least, 'to be thirsty' (DEDR no. 5222); Burrow and Emeneau connect this with Proto-Dravidian **vāṭu* 'to dry up, wither, pine away, fade, turn pale, diminish' (DEDR no. 5342).

The Vaḍavāmukha myth is not so obviously associated with the wild ass, but there is one Hindu myth that is, namely *Dhenuka-vadha*, 'Killing of (the ass demon) Dhenuka'[87]. The oldest version appears to be chapter 57 of the Harivaṃśa (c. 4th cent. CE), quoted in full in the footnote[88], and paraphrased by me below. Another version is found in Viṣṇu-Purāṇa 5,8 and Bhāgavata-Purāṇa 10,15, these two texts being closely related[89].

Roaming around as small cowherd boys, Kṛṣṇa and his elder brother Balarāma came to a lovely forest of wine palms. The trees were full of nicely smelling ripe fruits. When Kṛṣṇa suggested that they should cause some fruits fall down so that they could drink the sweet juice, his strong elder brother shook the palm trees and made the fruits fall down.

Figure 25 The Dhenukavadha scene, uppermost on a Gupta time (5th century) 366 cm high red sandstone pillar depicting Kṛṣṇalīlā myths, from Mandor near Jodhpur in Rajasthan, at present in the Sardar Museum, Jodhpur. Image courtesy of the American Institute of Indian Studies, Center for Art and Archaeology, Photo Archive (accession no. 15260, neg. no. A15.27)

Figure 26 The palmyra palm capital with a headless ass on top of palm leaves, possibly first century CE, now in the Gwalior Museum. Image courtesy of the American Institute of Indian Studies, Center for Art and Archaeology, Photo Archive (accession no. 40416). Cf. also Banerjea 1956: pl. XXVII, 3

The palmyra forest, however, was occupied and jealously guarded by the fierce ass demon Dhenuka and his large herd of asses[90]. Hearing the sound of ripe fruits falling from palm trees, the huge ass ran to the spot enraged, its mane and face erect with pride, with stiff (unwinking) eyes, neighing sharply, its tail stirred up (*āviddha-puccha-*)[91], tearing earth asunder with its hoofs, its body-hair erect, open-mouthed like the god of death. Rushing on, the ass saw Balarāma standing beneath the wine palm, as if holding the palmyra as his banner. Armed with its teeth, the wicked ass bit the unarmed Balarāma and started kicking him hard on chest with both of its hind legs. Balarāma seized the ass by those very legs, turned around its head and shoulders and flung the ass on the top of a palm tree. The ass fell down with its neck, thigh, hip and back broken and died. Dhenuka's retinue that came to his aid met with the same fate, so that the ground became covered with bodies of dead asses and fallen palmyra fruits. The palm forest, which had been a horrible place while terrorized by the asses, impossible for men to live in, difficult to cross, having great extent and salty soil (*iriṇa-*)[92], being like the haunt of man-eating demons, now became a lovely place where cowherds could roam about with their cattle without fear.

The prominence given to the palmyra alias wine palm alias fan-palm in the Dhenukavadha myth is quite striking and significant. The palm tree figures in many connections, and is mentioned numerous times in the story. It occupies a prominent place also in the two earliest sculptural representations of the Dhenukavadha scene. One is the Gupta period fragmentary stone door-jamb from Mandor, the ancient capital of Marwar near Jodhpur in Rajasthan (cf. Banerjea 1956: 421-422; see Figure 25). The other is a possibly first century wine palm capital (*tāladhvaja*) in the Gwalior Museum, where "a bunch of palm-leaves are very realistically depicted; but what is of particular interest in this sculpture is the headless figure of a donkey which evidently is the ass-demon Dhenuka killed by Balarāma by hurling it against a fan-palm tree" (Banerjea 1956: 424; cf. Kala 1988: 74; and see Figure 26). The wine palm is associated with both the demonic ass who inhabits the forest of wine palms and guards its trees, as well as the killer of the ass, Balarāma, who shakes down fruits of the palm in order to drink their juice. Balarāma also stands beneath the wine palm in such a way that he seems to be holding the palm as his banner. In epic and purāṇic literature, Balarāma's banner has the wine palm as its emblem, and for this reason he has such epithets in Sanskrit as *tāla-ketu-*, *tāla-dhvaja-*, *tāla-lakṣman-*, *tālāṅka-* and *tāla-bhṛt-*. Finally, when Balarāma kills Dhenuka, he throws the demon to the top of the wine palm, from which he falls down, much like the fruit of the palm tree with which he is thus associated.

Megasthenes, who as a Greek ambassador resided in India around 300 BCE, mentions (in fragment 12 = Arrian's *Indica* 7,3) trees called *tála* in the Indian language (καλέεσθαι δὲ τὰ δένδρεα ταῦτα τῇ Ἰνδῶν φωνῇ τάλα). This *tála* tree has been fairly unanimously identified with Sanskrit *tāla-* 'palmyra palm, *Borassus flabelliformis'* (cf. Wirth and Hinüber 1985: 1105; Karttunen 1997: 138). The Sanskrit name of the wine palm, *tāla-*, attested since Manu and the epics, is a loanword (via **tāḷa-/*tāḍa-*)[93] from Proto-Dravidian **tāẓ* 'palmyra palm, *Borassus fabelliformis'* (attested in all branches of Dravidian, cf. DEDR no. 3180; Mayrhofer 1996 II: 242-243; Krishnamurti 2003: 12).

One reason for Balarāma's association with the wine palm[94] is his addiction to drinking palm wine or toddy[95] (referred to also by Kalidāsa in Meghadūta 49)[96]:

> "His palm-sign indicates his love of wine; when described in full, he is half drunk ([Mahabhārata, Bombay ed.] 1,219,7) ... He is as devoted to wine as his brother is to women... Such debauchery in no wise detracts from his divinity... Baladeva's drunkenness is an essential part of his character. Like Indra he gets drunk as a lord as a matter of course." (Hopkins 1915: 212)

Balarāma seems to have inherited his addiction to palm wine from the ass demon whom he kills and replaces in this function. In the Rigveda, the wild ass is the proverbial drinker, with whom Indra should emulate while drinking his Soma. It is significant that the Proto-Dravidian verb **vaṭi* used of the 'ebbing' of tide also denotes 'straining' or 'filtering' liquid (DEDR 5221); in Tamil at least, the corresponding noun *vaṭi(vu)* means both 'outflow' of water in the ebb of tide and 'palm wine, toddy'.

In my opinion, the Dhenukavadha myth epitomizes religious acculturation that is taking place. A demonized older local deity is vanquished and replaced by a younger god, who in some respects is similar to the older god, and who in the process takes over and assimilates functions and attributes of the older god. In addition to being a great drinker, Balarāma shares other features with the wild ass. The wild ass is 'whitish' (*gaura-*) and strong, Balarāma's complexion is white (his colour is usually compared to that of milk or conch) and he has 'strength' (*bala-*).

Balarāma and Kṛṣṇa emerge as syncretistic deities of the early Vaiṣṇava religion around Mathurā region from the fourth century BCE. Balarāma carries a ploughshare as his weapon, and is partly an agricultural deity in origin, while Kṛṣṇa is to a large part a divinized cowherd (cf., e.g., Brockington 1998: 256-267). But the two brothers also have an Indo-European background, brought to South Asia after the collapse of the Indus Civilization, and brought to the Mathurā region by the Yādava tribe of Vedic origin.

In the Mahābhārata, Balarāma's younger brother Kṛṣṇa, whose name means 'Black', acts as the charioteer of Arjuna, the mighty warrior whose name means 'White' and who seems to be a double of the white-complexioned Balarāma. Arjuna marries Subhadrā, the sister of Balarāma and Kṛṣṇa. I have suggested that the early Vaiṣṇava trio (i.e., the white and black brothers and their sister) continues the Vedic trio of the Aśvins and Sūryā: these horse-owning divine twins personify the chariot warrior and his charioteer, while their sister-bride is the solar maiden. The Aśvins, like their Greek counterparts, the Dioskouroi, are connected with the day and night, as are their Vedic doubles, the divine dual kings Mitra and Varuṇa (See Parpola 2005). Two Middle Vedic texts (c. 800 BCE), in their description of the horse sacrifice, prescribe (three) wild asses (which are white) to be immolated to Mitra and (three) water buffaloes (which are black) to Varuṇa (Maitrāyaṇī Saṃhitā 3,14,10 and Vājasaneyi-Saṃhitā 24,28 *mitrāya gaurān [ālabhate], varuṇāya mahiṣān*). This seems to confirm that the Aśvins - horse gods - were in South Asia connected with the wild asses (as suggested in 5), and that one of them (Mitra corresponding to Balarāma) was conceived as white, the other black (cf. Parpola 2005: 18-22).

Surely one indigenous feature in Balarāma's character is his identification with the white cosmic snake Śeṣa or Ananta. The strong Balarāma is said to be a portion of the powerful snake Śeṣa[97]. Balarāma was born of the white hair that Viṣṇu plucked from the body of his white serpent-couch Śeṣa while lying in the cosmic ocean, while Kṛṣṇa was born of the black hair that Viṣṇu plucked from his own dark body[98]. Śeṣa came out as a big white snake from Balarāma's mouth when this died, entered the ocean and was welcomed there by the other divine serpents[99]. Śeṣa is said the support the earth in the netherworld: he is the ruler of Pātāla, the watery realm of the snakes (*nāgaloka*) (cf. Hopkins 1915: 23-26). According to Matsya-Purāṇa 2,5, when the world is destroyed at the end of a cosmic period, the submarine fire will become hostile and shoot out, as also venomous fire emitted from Pātāla from his mouth by Saṃkarṣaṇa (i.e., Balarāma in his manifestation as Snake Śeṣa), and fire from the third eye that has opened on the forehead of Bhava (i.e., Śiva)[100]. It looks as if the submarine *vaḍavāmukha* fire coming from 'mare's mouth' and the fire coming from Snake Śeṣa's mouth from the watery realm of Pātāla were more or less the same thing.

In the Harivaṃśa and the Purāṇas, the story of Dhenukavadha is naturally set in a lovely forest on the banks of the Yamunā river near Mathurā, as are all the other exploits of these two heroic brothers. The original scene of this myth, however, seems to have been the less lovely salt desert (mentioned in Harivaṃśa 57,11) of coastal Sindh and the Rann of Kutch, distinguished as they are by wine palms and wild asses. Arrian and other historians of Alexander inform us that the Indus delta (and its capital city) was called Patala. In the delta of the Indus "the annual inundation covers almost the whole surface of the ground" (Lambrick 1964: 117; cf. also 21), and the same applies to the salt deserts of the Rann of Kutch.

We come now to a further meaning of the wine palm in the Dhenukavadha myth. According to the Rāmāyaṇa, also the thousand-headed snake Ananta (i.e., Śeṣa) who resides near the Vaḍavāmukha, has in his banner a three-headed golden wine palm[101]. It is significant that the snake-ruler of Pātāla has *tāla* 'wine palm' as his emblem, especially when we take into consideration that there are two demon lords, brothers called Pātālaketu[102] and Tālaketu[103]. As noted by Böhtlingk and Roth (1861 III: 314), it can be concluded from the brother's name that the word *tāla* in this case denotes a 'hell' rather than 'wine palm'. The Purāṇa texts in their cosmographic descriptions mention Tāla as the name of one of the 28 hells (*naraka*) that are situated beneath the seven netherworlds (*pātāla*), one of which is called Pātāla, while the names of the other six netherworlds end in *tala-* (cf. Kirfel 1920: 143-152); the word *tala-* means 'level surface, plane'. The word *pātāla-* is not attested in Sanskrit texts before the epics; the traditional etymology derives it from the Sanskrit root *pat-* 'to fall'[104], or the corresponding noun *pāta-* 'fall' + the suffix *-āla* attested in the word *antarāla-* 'interval'[105]; but Mayrhofer (1996 II: 119) is not sure that this is right and declares the word *pātāla-* as "not sufficiently declared". The explanation offered here has not been proposed before.

Proto-Dravidian **tāẓ* 'wine palm' has an exact homophone in the Proto-Dravidian root **tāẓ*, which has such meanings as 'to fall low, be lowered, be(come) low, flow down, descend, go down, fall, decline as the sun, sink in water, plunge, be deep, submerge, immerse, become depressed, decrease', and its nominal derivatives (which include *tāẓam*) 'bottom, low ground, depression, hole, state of being low, sinking, sloping, inferiority, humility', and adverbials 'below, under(neath), down'; the etymon is attested in all branches from Tamil to Brahui (DEDR no. 3178). In Tamil at least, *tāẓ* also means 'to ebb' and *tāẓcci* 'ebb of tide' (cf. Winslow 1888: 418a). As *pātāla-* is known as a netherworld of snakes (which fits the lowland of the Indus delta), it is natural to see in its first component Proto-Dravidian **pāmpu* 'snake', which in several languages has become abbreviated: *pāmu*, *pām*, *pāvu*, *pā*; it has been borrowed into Prakrit as *pāva* (cf. DEDR no. 4085).

Today in Kutch, the water-containing depressions of salt desert, offering drink to the wild asses and other animals, are called *tālāb*. This is an Urdu and Persian word, but Persian *tāl* and *tālāb* 'pond, pool, tank, reservoir of water' are loanwords from Indo-Aryan (cf. Platts 1884: 306a; Steingass 1892: 276b; Ḥasandust 2004: 324), where the etymon is attested as follows (cf. Turner 1966: no. 5742): Western Pahari, Kumaoni, Nepali, Hindi and Marathi *tāl* 'pool, lake', Old Awadhi *tāla* 'pond', Bihari 'canal'; late Sanskrit *talla-* m. 'pond' (writing in Kashmir, Vāmana 2,1,7 records this as a village word c. 800 CE) and late Prakrit *talla-* n. 'pond' (writing in Ujjain, Somadevasūri records the word in his Yaśastilakacampū 951 CE); cf. also Lahnda and Punjabi *tallā* m. 'lowlying land' (Turner 1966: nos. 5731 and 5697). As in the case of Sanskrit *tāla-* 'netherworld, hell', Proto-Dravidian **tāẓ / tāẓam*, which among other things means 'low ground, depression', offers a better etymology than the Sanskrit words *tala-* n. 'level surface, plain' or *taṭāka-*, *taḍāga-*, Pali *taḷāka-* etc. 'pond, pool' (for these earlier suggestions cf. Turner 1966: nos. 5742 and 5635; Mayrhofer 2001 III: 240). For **ẓ* > *l*, cf. Proto-Dravidian **tāẓ* > Sanskrit *tāla-* 'wine palm'.

This examination of what older Indian sources can tell us about the wild ass was prompted by the Indus seal M-290 (see Figure 27), where the inscription begins (on the right in the impression) with a sign that represents the 'hind leg' of a hoofed animal, immediately followed by the sign depicting 'wild ass'. In the seal M-1690 the 'hind leg' sign similarly begins the inscription and is followed by the plain 'fish' sign read in Proto-Dravidian **mīn* 'fish' = **mīn* 'star'. In Old Tamil, *tāḷ* 'leg' denotes a particular star, while its cognate in Toda, *tōḷ*, means 'animal's hind leg'. We set out to find out whether this reading would make any sense in the Indus seal M-290, in the context of the 'wild ass' sign.

Contrary to my expectations, the study of the vocabulary and myths connected with the

Figure 27 Modern impression of the seal M-290 from Mohenjo-daro. Twice the natural size (after CISI 1: 70)

wild ass has given strong support to the pictorial identifications of the 'hind leg' and 'wild ass' signs as well as to the Proto-Dravidian interpretation of the 'hind leg' sign. In the single myth explicitly connected with the wild ass, the ass kicks with its hind legs. The Proto-Dravidian word for 'ass', **kaẓutay*, has also turned out to label this animal as a 'kicker' through its the second component (**utay*), while the first component (**kaẓ*) identifies the animal as the wild ass by mentioning its habitat, the 'salt desert'.

As can be seen from the alphabetical order of the lemma (DEDR no. 3185), Burrow and Emeneau reconstructed **tāḷ* as the protoform of the 'leg' etymon, which on the basis of its distribution goes back to Proto-South-Dravidian only. However, with its basic meaning 'leg, stem or stalk (of plants), trunk (of trees)', this etymon is likely to be the source of Proto-Dravidian **tāẓ* 'wine palm', which is a tree with a very high and prominent trunk[106]; moreover, the protoform is to be reconstructed as **tāẓ*, since Old Kannada *tāẓ* 'stem or stalk of corn, flowers, etc.' has preserved Proto-Dravidian **ẓ*, while *ḷ* is its "widely shared reflex" in South Dravidian (cf. Krishnamurti 2003: 152).

Thus the 'hind leg' sign can be read as an exact homophone of Proto-Dravidian **tāẓ* 'wine palm' > Sanskrit *tāla-*, which figures so prominently in the Dhenukavadha myth. From **tāẓ* comes also the name of 'palm wine, toddy' prepared from the ripe fruits of the tree. The curious detail of the myth which makes the bodies of wild ass fall down from the trees like the ripe fruits suggests that this animal personified the strong drink. Indeed, the enormous capacity of the wild ass to drink even salty water is reflected in the Rigveda, where it is "the drinker" par excellence. The water pools from which the wild ass slakes its thirst were also called **tāẓ* in Proto-Dravidian, so it was natural to think that the ass was drinking palm wine. The myth transferred this addiction to toddy from the ass demon to his killer and successor.

The fact that **tāẓ* in Proto-Dravidian also denoted the 'ebbing' of tide, made people ascribe the sudden outflow of ocean water to an imagined mythical wild ass in the netherworld (again **tāẓ*) who was so thirsty that it tried to drink the entire ocean despite its saltiness. Another Proto-Dravidian word for 'ebbing', **vaṭi*, also means 'to be thirsty' and 'to filter liquid' (more specifically, toddy). As it resembled Proto-Dravidian **vaṭa* 'heat, to be in heat', this myth explaining the ebb came to be connected specifically with the mare of wild ass, whose 'heat' was like fire. The ebb and flow and the wine palms were specific to the coastal zone of the wild ass habitat, the lowland or **tāẓ*.

In connection with the wild ass, the 'hind leg' and 'wine palm' have turned out to be key symbols when studied in their original linguistic context, the Proto-Dravidian language. The clue given by the Indus script has led to better understanding of some rather obscure Hindu myths.

7. The names of the wild ass in Turkic and Mongolic languages

With some important exceptions, Turkic and Mongolic, two unrelated language families, though often viewed together in the context of 'Altaic', share their central zoological terminology on an areal basis. Due to the presence of multiple layers of influences in both directions, it is often extremely difficult to establish from which of the two language families a given word originally derives. In many cases, we have to reckon with the possibility of a third source, unrelated to either Turkic or Mongolic. Also, there is evidence of the existence in the past of subsequently extinct parallel branches of both Turkic and Mongolic (Para-Turkic and Para-Mongolic), which may have participated in the mutual exchange of lexical and grammatical influences. Even so, the most important layer of influences can be dated to the so-called Hunnish period. During this period, it was mainly a form of Pre-Proto-Bulghar-Turkic[107] (presumably, the principal language of the Eastern Huns, or the *Xiongnu* 匈奴 of Chinese sources) that yielded loanwords to Pre-Proto-Mongolic (the language of the 'Eastern Barbarians', or the *Donghu* 東胡 of Chinese sources, later also known as the *Xianbei* 鮮卑). These contacts can be dated to the last centuries BCE and located to the region comprising Mongolia and western and southern Manchuria (for a more detailed ethnohistorical picture, cf. Janhunen 1996: 185-189).

An example of a Turko-Mongolic lexical connection that quite certainly must derive from the Hunnish period is offered by the item for domestic ass or donkey, Turkic (*)*eshek* (with *sh* = *ś*) = Mongolic **eljige/n*. The mutual connection of these words was doubted without reason by Doerfer (TMEN 1: 191-192 no. 68, 2: 65-66 no. 486), but it now has to be recognized as obvious. This must be a case of a borrowing from Pre-Proto-Bulghar-Turkic into Pre-Proto-Mongolic, and the borrowing must have taken place in parallel with the introduction of the domestic donkey to the region, which hardly can have predated the Hunnish period. The same item is also attested in Manchu as *eihen* (Norman 1978: 71), and, as a secondary borrowing from Manchu, in the Mongolic Dagur language as *eigeen* (for a list of all the Mongolic data, cf. Sun 1990: 256). From Turkic (Tatar) the word was borrowed into Russian in the shape *ishák* 'donkey, mule' (Vasmer 1964-1973: 146). Among these, the Manchu data is the most difficult to explain. Most items with a Turkic 'cognate' in Manchu are borrowings transmitted by Mongolic, but in this case a Para-Mongolic source is more likely. This is because the phonological shape of the word in Manchu is clearly aberrant and cannot be explained by any established sound law in any of the languages involved[108].

The relation between Turkic (*)*eshek* and Mongolic **eljige/n* is also inherently ambiguous, in that the sound correspondence is unique and can be explained in several different ways. On the Turkic side, there is a probably more archaic parallel form (*) *eshkek* (= **eshke-k*) > *eshtek* ~ *eshgek* ~ *eshyek*, which suggests that the Turkic item originally contained the cluster **shk*, in which case Mongolic **eljige-* must represent a Turkic original of the type **eshike-* (with a later vowel loss in the second syllable). Even in this case, however, the correspondence between Turkic **sh* and Mongolic **lj* allows several possible reconstructions of the medial consonantism (some alternatives proposed in the past include **sh* **ld* **lj*). The most simple solution would seem to be that the Mongolic cluster **lj* represents a substitution for the Turkic single consonant sound underlying **sh*, which may or may not have been a palato-alveolar sibilant. The question is connected with the much-discussed issue of rhotacism-lambdacism, which happens to be one of the diagnostic features of the Bulghar-Turkic layer of loanwords in Mongolic. In the item for 'donkey', however, the Mongolic representation differs from the 'normal', which would be Turkic **sh* = Mongolic **l* (lambdacism)[109].

For Turkic **esh(k)ek*, two internal etymologies have been proposed: on the one hand, the word has been analyzed as a derivative of the noun **esh* 'mate, pair' (Räsänen 1969: 51, an etymology originally proposed by Willy Bang), while, on the other hand, it has been connected with the verb **esh-* 'to amble (of a horse), to kick (of a horse), to hurry' (Clauson 1972: 255-256, 260, cf. also ESTYa s.vv. *esh-*, *eshek*). The former identification is unlikely[110], while the latter is, at least semantically and derivationally possible. However, an external comparison has also been proposed, originally by Schrader (1901: 205-206, as quoted by Doerfer in TMEN *op. cit.*), with the Indo-European word family for 'donkey' (Latin *asinus* etc.) and its Sumerian source (AN. ŠE or AN.ŠU, as discussed earlier in this paper). In this context, particular attention has been paid to Armenian *êš* (gen. *iš-oy*) 'donkey'[111] as a possible source of the Turkic item, but more likely, the borrowing would have taken place via several other intermediate languages, which makes it impossible to trace the exact route of the word[112]. However this may be, the external etymology appears more attractive than either of the internal ones, especially in view of the fact that donkeys involve the type of cultural innovation that is often borrowed together with the corresponding terminology.

As an appellation of the wild ass, **eshek* is attested only secondarily in the Osman Turkish descriptive phrase *yaban esheği* 'wild ass' (OSTN 3: 275). Otherwise, there is a strict distinction between the domestic donkey and the wild ass. The latter also has a uniform Turko-Mongolic name, reconstructable as **kulan*, the source of the international names of the Transcaspian kulan (*E. hemionus kulan*) and the Mongolian khulan (*E. hemionus hemionus*). In both Turkic and Mongolic, the term can be dated back to the protolanguage level, which for Turkic (in this case, without Bulghar-Turkic) means the language of the ancient Turks of Mongolia and Eastern Turkestan (the latter half of the first millennium CE), and for Mongolic the language of the historical Mongols (the early second millennium CE). Since both Turkic and Mongolic were in those times spoken in a coherent territory centered on eastern Mongolia, the term **kulan* may be identified as originally denoting the Mongolian and Gobi subspecies of the wild ass[113]. The subsequent dispersal of both Mongolic and Turkic has brought the word to the more westerly and southerly parts of Central Eurasia, where it has come to be used also in reference to the Persian and Trans-Caspian subspecies of the animal, as well as to the Tibetan wild ass.

On the Turkic side, **kulan* is documented since the early Middle Turkic period (Makhmud al-Kashgari, cf. DTS p. 465, Clauson 1972: 622, Hauenschild 2003: 149-150)[114], while on the Mongolic side it is attested since Middle Mongol (*Secret History*, cf. Haenisch 1962: 71). Since wild asses are present almost all over the Central Eurasian belt, the word has been preserved in most Turkic and Mongolic languages in living use with only minor variation in shape and meaning. In Kazakh and Kirghiz, for instance, *kulan* (*qulan*) is still used synchronically in its basic meaning and in a virtually unchanged shape (Räsänen 1969: 298)[115]. In modern Mongolian (proper), the word appears in two harmonically differentiated shapes: *xvlen*[116] (< **kulan*, reflecting the original velar vocalism **u-a*) and *xulen* (< **külen*, reflecting a transition to a secondary palatal vocalism **ü-e*) (Lessing 1960: 984 s.v. *xulan* and 499 s.v. *kylen*). From Ordos, the word is only recorded in the combination *xulan jigendii* 'wild ass' (Mostaert 1941-1942: 366), which contains a folk-etymologically distorted form of **eljigen* 'donkey'.

From Turkic, **kulan* was transmitted into Persian in the shape *qūlān* (TMEN 3: 556-557 no. 1574), known to the Persians as the Turkic equivalent of *gōr*, and into Russian in the shape *kulán* (Vasmer 1964-1973: 409), while from Mongolic it was transferred to Manchu in the shape *kûlan* (Norman 1978: 182). Older Russian sources also use the modern Mongolian shape *xulán* (see, e.g., Przheval'skij 1888: 163). It is, however, more difficult to determine what the mutual relationship of the Turkic and Mongolic words is. It has been conventionally assumed that it is a question of a Turkic loanword in Mongolic, but there is no immediate phonological, morphological, semantic, or philological evidence to confirm this (cf. also Rybatzki 2006: 499-500). The earliest data on the word seem to be contained in the Tang-period Chinese encyclopaedic treatise *Tongdian* 通典 (completed in 801 CE), according to which the ancient Turks (*Tujue* 土厥) called the "horse" by the name *helan* 賀蘭 (Liu 1958: 480-481, 498-499 n. 49, also quoted by Doerfer *l.c.*). The meaning 'horse' instead of 'wild ass' must be due to a mistake in the process of compilation of the Chinese work, possibly because the Chinese themselves were unable to make a proper distinction between horses (either wild or domesticated) and wild asses[117].

Several attempts have been made to find an internal etymology for **kulan* (for the most recent summary, see ESTYa s.v. *kulan*), but none of the proposed explanations is without problems. One rather obvious comparison, though rarely mentioned in the etymological literature, would be with Turkic **kulun* 'foal' (ESTYa s.v. *kulun*). The formal difference between **kulan* and **kulun* involves only the vowel of the second syllable, and both words belong to the context of equid terminology. Even so, it is difficult to show any formal derivational connection between these words, and even secondary interference between them is rare, the only example being Osman Turkish *kulan ~ kolan*, which, apart from 'wild ass', is dialectally also attested in the meaning of 'foal of ass' (OSTN 2: 974). Formally, both **kulan* and **kulun* would have to be analyzed as derived words in Turkic, since the primary roots in the language are of the monosyllabic type *CV(:)(C)C. This does not, however, exclude the possibility that words looking like derivatives can also be borrowings.

Another internal point of comparison is offered by Yakut *kulan* 'smart, fast' (also of horses). Since, however, Yakut is a Turkic language spoken in a region (central Siberia) with no wild asses, the semantic development could also have taken place in the opposite direction ('wild ass' > 'fast like a wild ass'). A similar problem is connected with the often-mentioned comparison with the colour term **kula* 'fawn, bay', which is primarily used of light-coloured (yellowish) horses with a dark mane and tail, a combination that is also typical of the wild ass. Although one could here see a semantic parallel to Indo-Aryan *gaura-* 'wild ass', which seems to have developed from a colour term, it is equally possible that the zoological term is primary ('wild ass' > 'coloured like a wild ass'). It happens that the colour term **kula* is another item shared both by Turkic (in this case, with Bulghar-Turkic) and Mongolic. A borrowing from Turkic to Mongolic (and to Persian) has been assumed also in this case (Doerfer TMEN 3: 507-508 no. 1524), but the derivational relationship **kula*: **kulan* would appear to be more natural on the Mongolic side, where a large proportion of nouns end in *-n*[118]. Structurally, **kula* may be compared with **kara* 'black' (also of horses), which is also attested in both Turkic and Mongolic (as well as in Persian, Doerfer TMEN 3: 426-432 no. 1440), but for which the dating and direction of borrowing remains an unsolved issue. The bisyllabic structure CVCV itself is more typical of Mongolic than of Turkic, but in all these cases, the possibility of a third source should also be considered.

When comparing **kula* 'fawn, bay' with **kulan* 'wild ass' it is important to note that **kula* is not a primary colour term in any of the languages concerned. The original system of colour terms in most languages of eastern Eurasia, including Turkic and Mongolic, comprises five members ('white', 'black', 'red', 'blue/green', 'yellow'). As far as applicable, these terms can also refer to the colour of animals, including equids. However, due to the importance of the domestic horse in the pastoral culture of the steppes, there is a large number of secondary terms describing the different shades, patterns, and combinations of colours observed in this particular animal. The term **kula* belongs to this category of secondary colour terms, a circumstance that would seem to support the assumption that it is also secondary to **kulan* 'wild ass'. On the other hand, since the wild ass has been important game in the past, it could have received its current name due to lexical taboo, which could have led to the replacement of a more original term (whatever it was) by a derivative of the secondary colour term **kula*.

Taboo may also be involved in another Central Asian appellation of the wild ass, namely Mongolic **cikitei* (dialectally and in Ordos > **jikitei*) 'the one with ears' (Lessing 1960: 182, from **ciki/n* 'ear(s)', cf. also Rybatzki 2006: 296), which obviously refers to one of the most prominent characteristic features of the wild ass in order to avoid mentioning its actual name. This is the source of the international zoological term *dziggetai* (also written as *chigitai*, *dshiggetai*, *dshikketaei*), although it is not immediately clear from which particular Mongolic language or Mongolian dialect this item was transmitted to the western specialist literature[119]. The word is also present, as a borrowing from Mongolic, in a few Turkic languages, including Teleut *cigettei* 'wild ass' and Osman Turkish *cigetei* 'Syrian wild ass' (OSTN 3: 2114). The Osman Turkish data, which refers to the Syrian wild ass, must reflect a late mediaeval layer of Middle Mongol loanwords, while the Teleut item could also have been borrowed later from early Oirat[120].

8. The name of the Tibetan wild ass and its Central Asian connections

It may be concluded that all that can be said for certain of the zoological term **kulan* is that it seems to be a regional word once used in Mongolia, including the Gobi area, by both Turkic and Mongolic speakers. It is quite possibly connected with the specialized colour term **kula* 'fawn, bay', but the date, place, and direction of the semantic transition cannot be determined. It is also impossible to tell whether the word was first present in Turkic or Mongolic, or in some other (subsequently extinct) local language. In any case, since Proto-Turkic and Proto-Mongolic times, but possibly even earlier, **kulan* has been the basic appellation of the wild ass in the region, and in the linguistic lineages concerned. If there ever existed other, more primary appellations in Turkic or Mongolic, they have been lost without a trace.

There is a possibility of an external connection, however. The Tibetan wild ass (*Equus kiang*, earlier also *Asinus kiang*) has got its name from Tibetan *rkyaṅ* = *rkyang* 'wild ass or horse of Central Asia, Chigitai' (Jäschke 1880: 17). The Tibetan wild ass occurs, or has until recently occurred, in relatively large numbers at altitudes between 2,700 and 5,400 meters all over the Qinghai-Tibetan Plateau, including parts of southern Gansu, southern Xinjiang, northern Pakistan, and northern Nepal (Shah *et al.* 2008, cf. also Denzau and Denzau 1999: 139-163). Correspondingly, the term (*) *rkyang* (orally > *hkyang* > *hcang* > *cang*) seems to be present in most forms of spoken Tibetan, though, unfortunately, there is no detailed dialectological information easily available on the language. There is also no obvious internal etymology for this term, except that it is homonymous with the apparently unrelated Tibetan word *rkyang* 'simple, single, free' (also in reduplication, without prefix, *kyang-kyang* 'only', cf. Jäschke, ibid.). Finally, since there does not seem to exist any wider Tibeto-Burman or Sino-Tibetan etymology for it, it is reasonable to look for an external origin. In this case, (*)*rkyang* should be compared with **kulan*.

It is a generally accepted fact that the Pre-Proto-

Tibetan lexicon underwent a process of phonotactic transformation which, most importantly, involved the loss of the vowel of the initial syllable, resulting in the origination of predominantly monosyllabic roots with initial consonant clusters (*CVCVC > *CCVC). This process may already have been active in Proto-Sino-Tibetan (on the implications of which, see van Driem 2001: 348-407), but it seems to have affected borrowed vocabulary even long afterwards[121]. An example is offered by the East Asian name for the horse, **mVrVn* (Mongolic **mori/n* < **morï/n*), which appears in Sino-Tibetan in the shape **mrang* (> Chinese 馬 *ma*[3], Schuessler 2007: 373). Although this particular item has been lost in modern Tibetan (Old Tibetan still had the metathetic shape **mrang* > *rmang*, cf. Beyer 1992: 78 note 11), it shows that the vowel loss was still active at the time when the horse was introduced to East Asia, which, judging by the archaeological and historical evidence, took place only after the middle of the second millennium BCE. The item for 'horse' is also otherwise instructive, for in a few marginal Tibeto-Burman languages (in the southern Himalayas) it appears in the alternative shape **s-rang*. Obviously, in these languages, the word has undergone a morphological reanalysis, due to which the original initial consonant has been lost and/or replaced by a class marker **s-* for 'animals' (cf. Benedict 1972: 43 and 106-108)[122]. Since the chronology of the underlying cultural innovation is known, all the phonotactic and morphological processes involved must have a relatively shallow history (in any case, less than 3,000 years).

The word for 'horse' also shows that a final dental (or unmarked) nasal **n* can be represented on the Sino-Tibetan side as a velar **ng*. Assuming, then, that the shape **kulan* had been borrowed to some early form of Sino-Tibetan, including, specifically, Pre-Proto-Tibetan, it would have been adapted to something like **klang*. The actually attested shape (*)*rkyang* can be linked to this by assuming two modifications: the adding of a prefixal preinitial (**r*) and the development of the postconsonantal lateral to a palatal glide (**l* > *y*). As far as the preinitial is concerned, the problem is not necessarily big. For one thing, the preinitial could have originated as a mere orthographic complication, for cases of words spelled variably with and without a preinitial, or also with different preinitials, are common in Tibetan since mediaeval times (Beyer 1992: 34-36). The shape *rgyang* (with *g* instead of *k*) in Mahāvyutpatti also appears to involve a scribal error, if it is not a question of a subsequently lost irregular variant, for all other information on the word points unambiguously to an unvoiced consonant (*k*)[123]. On the other hand, if the preinitial is an actual segment, it could also in this case represent a secondarily added class marker (perhaps the very **s-* of 'animals', which in most oral forms of the language is phonetically indistinguishable from **r*).

The representation of the lateral as a palatal glide is, in principle, also possible to explain. The status of a postconsonantal lateral in the Tibetan syllable structure is altogether ambiguous, for it can be analyzed both as a medial (postinitial) and as the actual initial of the syllable. In particular, the sequence **kl* seems to have undergone a series of restructurings, which eliminated most occurrences of this sequence already in Pre-Proto-Tibetan (Beyer 1992: 74-81, especially note 9). It is not too far-fetched to assume that the word **kulan* entered the language at a time when these restructurings were taking place. If this was the case, the development of **klang* to *(*r-*)*kyang* may simply have involved a substitution during the process of borrowing. This substitution may, of course, also have been triggered by specific phonetic circumstances which may have been present in the donor language[124]. While it is likely that Turko-Mongolic **kulan* and Tibetan *(*r-*)*kyang* are etymologically connected, the word may once have been present also in other languages, which may have belonged to entirely different language families. In fact, until mediaeval times, the territories of the Turks and Mongols (in the north) and the Tibetans (in the south) were separated by the people known in Chinese sources as the Tuyuhun 吐谷渾 (Molè 1970). Any words transmitted between Mongolia and Tibet would have passed the Tuyuhun, whose language (of which nothing is known)[125] may well have influenced the phonetic details on the way.

9. Equid terminology, cultural innovation, and linguistic expansions

I have previously shown (Janhunen 1998) that the terms for 'horse' in the languages of Eurasia correlate with the area of domestication of the horse and the routes of diffusion of horse culture. Thus, in the language families originally located relatively close to the primary area of domestication (the steppes between the Black Sea and the Altai mountains) there are several separate language-specific names for the horse. In this area, we observe at least six different early terms, one for each of the following linguistic stocks: Indo-European, Ugric, Samoyedic, Yeniseic, Turkic, and Mongolic[126]. By contrast, most of the languages located to the east of this area show reflexes of only a single term for the horse, identical with the one attested in Mongolic (**morï/n*). This term is present in, at least, five East Asian language families, including Tungusic, Koreanic (Korean), Japonic (Japanese), Amuric (Ghilyak), and Sino-Tibetan[127]. It goes without saying that there are local deviations from this general pattern, one of them being Tibetan, which has the idiosyncratic (possibly also old) term (*)*rta* for the horse.

The situation suggests that the horse was basically introduced from Central Eurasia to East Asia by a rapidly proceeding wave of cultural influence, which reached several linguistic groups in their original homeland regions along the Turkestan-Mongolia-China-Manchuria-Korea axis. This must have happened during the time span between, roughly, 1500 and 0 BCE. For most of the linguistic groups concerned, the adoption of a term for the horse, as well as of other related terminology, was accompanied by the introduction of the animal itself, for no equids, either wild or domestic, had been present east of the steppe and desert belt. Even inside this belt, a need to distinguish between the culturally innovative domestic horse and the local wild horse may have been relevant. Mongolian, in particular, which is the only language spoken in a region where wild horses have existed till modern times, makes still synchronically a terminological difference between the domestic horse (modern Mongolian *mory ~ moer* < **mori/n* < **morï/n*) and the Asian wild horse (*Equus przewalskii*) or *taki* (modern Mongolian *taxy ~ taex* < **taki* < **takï*)[128].

As a technical term, Mongolian taki has also been transmitted to Manchu in the shape *tahi* (Norman 1978: 269), although there have been no wild horses in Manchuria in historical times. More importantly, the word has a counterpart in Turkic *takï* (*taqï*) ~ *tagï* (*taγï* = *taghï*), which, however, seems to be attested only in Middle Turkic and always in combination with *kulan* (*qulan*), as in (*Qutadghu Bilig*) *qulan ya taghï tut* 'catch wild asses and horses!'[129]. For some reason, there is a tradition in western scholarship to interpret the combination *kulan* + *takï* as meaning 'male and female wild asses', which would mean that *kulan* should be understood as a specialized term for 'male wild ass', while *takï* would be the corresponding term for 'female wild ass' (cf., e.g., Hauenschild 2003: 149, Rybatzki 2006: 351). There seems to be no basis for such an interpretation in any living language, and the written documents are ambiguous in this respect. Ligeti (1966: 260), on the other hand, simplifies the issue too much when he translates both *qulan* and *taqï* as 'cheval sauvage'. Quite obviously, the phrase *kulan* + *takï*, at least originally, was intended to mean *both* wild asses *and* wild horses, two closely related but distinct animal species which were native to the same regions, and which were hunted with the same methods. The fact that Turkic *takï* is only known from the combination *kulan* + *takï* may, however, imply that wild horses were rare (or even non-existant) in the regions where Middle Turkic was spoken, which is why the entire phrase may have become obscure to the speakers themselves.

Mongolian *taki* and Turkic *takï* presuppose an original shape of the type **taki*[130]. Unlike **kulan*, which has several possible internal connections especially on the Turkic side, as well as the external connection with Tibetan (*)*rkyang*, **takï* seems difficult to analyze etymologically[131]. Therefore, the proper conclusion is probably that this is another regional word that was once used in the relatively limited (and constantly diminishing) territory where the wild horse has been distributed during the last few millennia. It is possible that, as a regional word, **takï* is older than the appellations used for the domestic horse in Turkic and Mongolic, for the domestic horse may have received its name during the process of domestication, or at the same time as the innovation reached the linguistic lineages of Turkic and Mongolic. In this situation it is again impossible to tell whether **takï* was first present in Turkic or in Mongolic, for both language families were originally located in the vicinity of the region where the wild horse occurs[132]. An unidentifiable third source is also a possibility.

We might say that the terms for the domestic horse, like also those for the domestic donkey, are culturally conditioned, since they are connected with a cultural innovation (domestication of the animals concerned). By contrast, the terms for the wild ass and the wild horse are regionally conditioned, since their relevance is limited to the region(s) where these animals occur, and they do not involve any cultural innovation (no domestication of the animals concerned). Cultural terms can easily move on the map and cross linguistic boundaries from one language or language family into another with the same speed as the underlying cultural innovation proceeds and reaches new regions. In this case, terms move while languages do not. Regional terms can also cross linguistic boundaries, but this happens mainly when new languages or language families expand to the region(s) in question. In this case, languages move while terms do not. Of course, it is also possible that both languages and terms move at the same time and with the same speed: this has happened, for instance, when the expansion of Turkic all over Central Eurasia has brought the term (*)*kulan* from its original area of use in the east (Mongolia and Gobi) far to the western limits of the wild ass (Persia and Syria). Similarly, Indo-Iranian (or Indo-Aryan) **gaura-* as an appellation of the wild ass has reached new areas due to linguistic expansions in the region.

In this connection, it is good to remember that the linguistic map of Central Eurasia, like that of other parts of the world, has undergone major changes until very recent times. Terms for region-specific animal species like the wild ass and the wild horse can have very ancient local roots, which can even precede the 'arrival' of the languages today spoken in the region. In spite of the hostility of the natural environment, even the Gobi Desert and the Tibetan Highlands have since ancient times offered a niche for sparsely distributed human communities. These communities have not always spoken Turkic, Mongolic, or Tibetan, all of which are, as it seems, secondary in their modern areas. What has taken place is linguistic replacement (language shift), in which the earlier inhabitants have lost their original language(s) in favour of new ones introduced from the outside. The analysis and dating of the underlying cultural and ethnic processes is a field to which both linguistics and archaeology can contribute.

10. Summary of the etymological conclusions

This section summarizes our etymological conclusions concerning the asine terminology discussed above. Although the general focus of this paper is on the wild asses and their regionally differentiated names, the present summary will also touch upon some relevant terms denoting the domestic ass (donkey), as well as the wild and, in some cases, the domestic horse.

(1) Sumerian *anše* (AN-ŠE) ~ *anšu* (AN-ŠU) 'domestic ass, donkey'. This is the single most widespread asine term in Eurasia, and there is no doubt that it owes its status to the fact that the domestication of the ass was a major cultural innovation, which spread together with the relevant terminology from the Neolithic and early Metal Age Near East both to the west and to the east. It is likely that the Sumerians were not the first to domesticate the ass, which is why they, too, may have borrowed the term from some other language, possibly ultimately from Africa. Even so, the Sumerian word, either directly or indirectly, was transmitted into several branches of Indo-European, yielding Greek **osónos* > *ónos* and Latin *asinus*. In the west, Latin became the secondary source of the terms for 'domestic ass, donkey' in virtually all European languages, including English *ass*, while in the east, the word is possibly reflected as Turkic **esh(k)ek*, Mongolic **eljigen*, Manchu *eihen*, Dagur *eigeen*, as well as Russian *ishák*. Some of the phonetic correspondences are irregular, suggesting that there may have been several unknown languages that were involved in the transmission process[133].

After its domestication, the domestic ass must have rapidly become the most generally known type of ass, which is why the words for 'domestic ass' are widely used to form secondary expressions denoting the wild ass. This was the case already with Sumerian *anše-edin-na* 'ass of the desert' > 'wild ass', and similar expressions are present in Greek *ónos ágrios* 'ass of the field' > *ónagros* 'Persian wild ass' (*Equus hemionus onager*), Persian *χar-e-daštī* 'ass of the desert', Turkish *yaban esheği* 'wild ass', as well as English *wild ass*. However, in the regions where the wild ass is common, it is normally referred to by regional names independent of the terms used for the domestic ass.

(2-3) Dravidian **kaẓutay* and **kutiray*. Neither of these Dravidian items is synchronically attested in the meaning 'wild ass', but it seems that they originally had exactly this meaning. Reflexes of Proto-Dravidian **kaẓutay* are used for 'domestic ass' in a large number of Dravidian languages, ranging from Tamil *kaẓutai* (at the archaic end) to Parji *gade* (at the innovative end), but it is chronologically unlikely that the Proto-Dravidian speakers could have known the domestic ass. Since the etymon seems to derive from the composite term **kaẓ* + *utay* 'salt-desert' + 'kick' = 'kicker of salt desert', it is likely to have originally denoted the Indian wild ass (*Equus hemionus khur*). As it seems, Proto-Dravidian **kaẓutay*, or one of its post-Proto-Dravidian derivatives, was the source of Indo-Aryan *garda-bha-* 'ass', a word which in Sanskrit is occasionally also used for 'wild ass'.

A comparable change of reference seems to have taken place in Proto-Dravidian **kutiray*, which is probably based on the verb **kuti* 'to leap, to gallop'. In this case, the common secondary reference is 'horse', as attested in a wide range of Dravidian languages, including Tamil *kutirai*. As an early borrowing from Dravidian, this word is also reflected in the shape *kuzᵊra* 'horse' in the Dardic language Tirahi. In principle, both **kaẓutay* and **kutiray* may be understood as general descriptive appellations of equids, but the primary specific reference is likely to have been 'wild ass', since this is the only equid indigenous to the subcontinent.

(4) Originally derivative of the etymon **gav-* 'cow' meaning 'coloured like a cow', Indo-Iranian **gāvra-* > Sanskrit *gaura-* 'yellowish-white, pale, pale red', has become the regular Indo-Iranian term for both the Indian and the Persian wild ass, though it also denotes the Indian bison (*Bos gaurus*). The word is not attested in Old Iranian at all, either as a colour term or as an animal name, while the meaning 'wild ass' is attested in Old Indo-Aryan from the beginning (c. 1000 BCE). Domesticated individuals of the wild ass were imported from the Indus Valley to Persia in the fifth century BCE, so it is possible that Old Iranian had **gaura-* as a borrowing from Indo-Aryan rather than as a retention from Proto-Indo-Iranian. From Middle Persian *gōr* 'wild ass' was borrowed into several other Iranian languages, as well as into Dravidian Brahui. Urdu and Hindi *gōr* 'wild ass' is also probably a borrowing from Persian, though it can also be a direct development of Sanskrit *gaura-*.

A compound literally meaning 'pale donkey' is also encountered in the meaning 'wild ass', attested in Middle Indo-Aryan *gōra-khara-* (79 BCE), Sanskrit *gaura-khara-* (c. 400 CE), Hindi and Urdu *gōr-khar* / *gōr-χar*, and Persian *gōr-χar*. It seems that Old Indo-Aryan received *khara-* 'donkey' as a borrowing from Old Iranian *χara-* as late as during the Achaemenid rule of the Indus Valley, while this word which itself may be of a Semitic origin is widely attested in Iranian languages. This might suggest that the compound **gaura-khara* was originally formed on the Iranian side, but on the other hand **gaura-* is not attested as a colour term in any Iranian language excepting Pashto, which may have borrowed it from Indo-Aryan. Both components were present in the Indus Valley under the Persian rule. In Hindi, the word also occurs in the folk-etymological shape *ghoṛ-khar*, influenced by Hindi *ghoṛā* 'horse'. The scientific name of the Indian wild ass, khur (*Equus hemionus khur*), is based on an Anglicized transcription of (*gōr-*/*ghoṛ-*) *khar*/*χar* 'wild ass'. Sanskrit *khara-gardabha-* (c. 400 CE) > Hindi *khar-gadhā* 'wild ass' is an exclusively Indo-Aryan compound.

Old Indo-Aryan *rāsabha-* 'ass, donkey', from the root *ras-* 'to cry', probably denotes the 'wild ass' in the Ṛgveda (c. 1000 BCE).

(5) Turkic **kulan* = Mongolic **kulan* 'wild ass'. This is the Turko-Mongolic term which originally must have denoted the Mongolian and Gobi varieties of the wild ass, but which, with the expansion of the two language families throughout Central Asia, has also come to denote other varieties of the animal. The word may be connected with the secondary colour term **kula* 'fawn, bay', attested in both Turkic and Mongolic, and it also has several other possible, though unlikely, internal etymologies in the two language families. Most probably, it is an old regional zoological term which might even derive from a third (unknown) language. On an areal basis, possibly as an old borrowing from either Turkic or Mongolic, the word seems to be connected with Tibetan **(r)kyang* 'Tibetan wild ass' (*Equus kiang*). More transparently, it was transmitted from Turkic into Persian as *qūlān* and into Russian as *kulán* ~ *xulán*, and from Mongolic into Manchu as *kûlan*. Via Russian it has become the technical term for the Transcaspian wild ass (*Equus hemionus kulan*).

It has to be noted that Mongolic and Turkic make a clear distinction between 'wild ass' and 'wild horse'. The latter animal is referred to by the Turko-Mongolic term **takï*, which in Turkic sources is commonly attested in the combination **kulan* + **takï* 'wild asses and wild horses'. The distinction between 'wild ass' and 'domestic ass' is also generally strict, though expressions like Ordos *xulan jigendii* 'wild ass' (literally 'wild ass' + 'donkey') suggest that the domestic ass has in some regions become the 'basic' animal to which the wild ass is related.

In addition to the major etymons listed above (1-5), all of which are relatively old and widespread across linguistic boundaries, there are a number of more recent terms used for the the local varieties of the wild ass. Among these, Mongolic **cikitei* 'the one with ears' > 'wild ass', the source of the zoological term *dziggetai* (with various alternative spellings), has been borrowed into Turkic. The Semitic terms used for the Syrian wild ass in the Near East remain outside of the scope of the present paper.

Notes

1) Dr. Richard H. Meadow, Director of the Zooarchaeology Laboratory at the Peabody Museum of Archaeology and Ethnology, Harvard University, has kindly acted as our consultant by both replying to some specific questions and by commenting upon the near-final original version of this paper. We thank him for these contributions, which are reported in the paper.

2) The original version of this paper was in May 2009 submitted for publication in the Sarianidi Festschrift: P. M. Kozhin, M. F. Kosarev and N. A. Dubova (ed.), *Na puti otkrytiya tsivilizatsii: Sbornik statej k 80-letiyu V. I. Sarianidi.* (Trudy Margianskoj arkheologicheskoj èkspeditsii, tom 3) Sankt-Peterburg: Aleteia. As the Festschrift was going to be mainly in Russian and to have a small printrun, we asked its editors for permission to publish a revised version elsewhere, namely in the present publication. After this plan had been approved also by the publisher of the book at hand, Professor Toshiki Osada, Asko Parpola presented his portion of the paper at the Kyoto Session of the 13th Harvard University Round Table on Ethnogenesis of South and Central Asia, held at the Research Institute for Humanity and Nature, Kyoto, on 30-31 May 2009. An abstract entitled "The Asiatic wild ass in Harappan, Dravidian and Indo-Iranian record" (pp. 33-35) was published in the programme booklet of the session, with reference to the forthcoming full paper that includes Juha Janhunen's portion as well. At the Kyoto session J. S. Kharakwal presented a freshly excavated Indus seal from Kanmer, Kutch, Gujarat, with much relevance to our topic, and gave us permission to publish it (see Figure 15). We thank also Gertrud and Helmut Denzau, who in May 2009 kindly permitted us to use one of their photographs in the first version of the paper, and generously sent us several other photographs for this revised version. The new version has benefited from the paper we received from Dan Potts (2002). Jack Hawley, Doris Srinivasan and Vandana Sinha have helped us to obtain Figures 25 and 26. Asko Parpola (2010 a and b) summarized and developed further parts of this study in a paper read at the World Old Tamil Conference held in June 2010 at Coimbatore, and the new insights could still be incorporated here.

3) Latin *pons asinorum*, here implying, as often in Finland, not so much 'a difficult problem' or 'a memory aid' as 'a somewhat clumsy transition to the actual topic'; originally from the popular name of the fifth proposition in Euclid's geometry; cf., e.g., the online version of *Encyclopaedia Britannica* at http://www.britannica.com/EBchecked/topic/724634/The-Bridge-of-Asses

4) Richard Meadow (personal communication, 9 May 2009) notes: "Charring does NOT automatically mean cooking. Cooking has to be demonstrated. There are many ways bones can get charred that do not involve food preparation. Kate Moore's statement about the Gonur material that you quote is, in fact, wrong."

5) According to Meadow (personal communication, 9 May 2009), "the materials that Kate Moore and I are discussing in the 1993 publication are probably different sets of bones, although I do not remember exactly."

6) In his analysis of animal bones recently excavated at Gonur, R. M. Sataev (2008: 138-140) has identified one horse from "the royal grave" ("Tsarskij mogil'nik"). This horse is represented by a single upper second premolar tooth, which belonged to an adult animal perhaps 8-10 years old. From the wear of the badly preserved tooth Sataev proposes that the horse had been ridden, but deplores that he could not check if the wear was actually caused by malocclusion instead of a bit. Richard Meadow

(personal communication, 9 May 2009) comments: "Sataev's identification of a single horse tooth from Gonur is highly problematical because in general identifications based on single teeth in equids are problematical by definition!"

7) "There are great problems in telling much from the photos. They cannot be enlarged enough before they lose definition because of pixelation. Furthermore, there is no scale by which I can reliably judge the size of any of the elements. Equid 1's teeth are shattered and the skull flattened, so without seeing it in person, I can tell very little. It seems like a smallish animal (to judge from the size of people's legs and the ceramics next to it). Thus it could even be a donkey. It is impossible for me to tell without seeing the bones close up and personal, and even then it is sometimes difficult to distinguish between donkeys and onagers. Equid 2 seems better preserved, but again I can say very little without personal acquaintance. Seeing things in person and seeing things from photos are two different things entirely when it comes to bones, although you can tell things from photos of bones if the bones are laid out in a manner so as to permit identification of diagnostic characteristics and if there is a scale from which one can determine size and proportions. I am sorry to be so negative, but when dealing with an issue like this, one needs to be very conservative about identifications." (Richard H. Meadow, personal communication 26 March 2009)

8) Yet the two pairs of Sintashta/Arkaim type cheek pieces along with two bronze bits and a horse-topped bronze scepter found with typical Bactria-Margiana pottery in an aristocratic grave at Zardcha Khalifa in Tajikistan clearly indicates a Ural steppe origin for at least these implied chariot horses. Cf., e.g., Carpelan and Parpola 2001: 138.

9) For a more up-to-date review of the situation in the ancient Near East, which has not essentially changed, see Oates 2003 and Marshall 2007: 383-384, 393-394.

10) Richard Meadow (personal communication, 9 May 2009), points out that in referring to equid hybrids, the male is mentioned first, the female second; he also refers to "an old but useful book titled *Mammalian hybrids* by Annie P. Gray (1954, revised 1972)".

11) The English word *donkey* 'domestic ass', attested since 1785, is supposedly of dialectal or slang origin; it may have been derived, with *-key* as in *monkey*, from the adjective *dun* 'of a dull or dingy or greyish brown colour; dark, dusky', as a substantive "formerly, a quasi-proper name for any horse". Cf. *The Shorter Oxford English Dictionary* (1955 ed.); and *Collins Dictionary of the English Language* (1979).

12) We owe this reference to Marshall's work, and a copy of her paper, to Richard Meadow (personal communication, 9 May 2009); so also Rossel *et al.* 2008, analyzing ten newly found donkey skeletons from Abydos, Egypt, dating from c. 3000 BCE.

13) Reinterpreted as consisting of the masculine article *ho* + *ónos*, the Greek word is supposed to go back, via **ho-onos* < **ohonos*, to a protoform **os(o)nos*. This etymology proposed by Karl Brugmann (1907-08) is preferred by Frisk (1970 II: 397-398) to the older view which connects Greek *ónos* 'donkey' as 'pack-animal' with Latin *onus* 'load, burden', which would have a semantic parallel in New Greek *gomári* 'ass' < *gómos* 'load' and Italian *somaro* 'donkey' via late Latin *sagmarius* from Greek *ságma* 'packsaddle' < *sáttein* 'to pack' (cf. Brugmann 1907-08: 199; Buck 1949: 172).

Latin *onus* (n.) has a cognate in Sanskrit *ánas-* (n.) 'cart for heavy burdens' (attested since the Rigveda) (cf. Mayrhofer 1992 I: 71). Hence the word goes back to Proto-Indo-European, which probably disintegrated with the Late Tripolye culture and the explosive spread of wheeled vehicles c. 3400 BCE (cf. Parpola 2008). It probably is a loanword in origin, as it cannot be derived from any PIE root. Sherratt (2003: 239-242) has underlined the probable spread of the donkey as a pack animal from Mesopotamia to the Caucasus with the Uruk expansion in the fourth millennium BCE (cf. also Oates 2003: 115). It is via this route and at this time that the wheeled vehicles seem to have come from Europe to Mesopotamia (cf. Parpola 2008).

14) The Greek word *hēmí-onos* is first attested in the Iliad (c. 800 BCE). Greek *hēmí-* 'half' is of the same origin

as Sanskrit *sāmi-* and Latin *sēmi-* borrowed into English *semi-* (cf. Risch 1949: 22-23; Frisk 1960 I: 636).

15) The adjective *ágrios*, derived from *ágros* 'field(s), countryside (in contrast to town)', literally meaning 'living in the fields', is used of wild animals and plants (in contrast to domesticated), of 'savage' men living in a wild state, of 'wild, uncultivated' countries, of 'fierce' temper, 'harsh' circumstances, etc. (cf. Liddell and Scott 1940: 15).

16) Sic! This looks like coming from a description of the Persian onager's distribution.

17) It took also a long time until the relatively small genetic difference between the two species was established by zoologists. For instance, in his commentary to Yule's publication of Marco Polo, Cordier writes: "The Wild Ass of Mongolia is... identical with the Tibetan Kyang..." Marco Polo mentions wild asses, "handsome creatures", on two occasions — in Yasdi, Persia, and in Etzina, Province of Tangut (chapters 16 and 45 of Book I), but he does not describe the animal in any detail, nor does he quote its local names (cf. Yule 1903 I: 88, 223-225).

18) As noted by Karttunen (1997: 179), this reference to Prasians reveals that the source here is the fragmentarily preserved description of India by Megasthenes, the Greek ambassador who around 300 BCE visited the capital city Pāṭaliputra (modern Patna in Bihar) of Candragupta Maurya, the king of the "easterners" (Sanskrit *Prācyāḥ*). On Megathenes see Karttunen 1997: 70-94.

19) My (AP) translation of Aelianus, NA 16,9: Ἐν Ἰνδοῖς ἵππων τε ἀγρίων καὶ ὄνων τοιούτων εἰσὶν ἀγέλαι• οὐκοῦν ἀναβαινόντων ὄνων τὰς ἵππους ὑπομένειν ἐκείνας λέγουσιν, καὶ ἥδεσθαι τῇ μίξει, καὶ τίκτειν ἡμιόνους πυρσοὺς τὴν χρόαν, καὶ ἄγαν δρομικούς, δυσλόφους δὲ καὶ γαργαλεῖς ἄλλως. Ποδάγραις δὲ τούτους αἱροῦσιν, εἶτα ἀνάγεσθαι τῷ τῶν Πρασίων βασιλεῖ φασι• καὶ διετεῖς μὲν ἁλωκότας μὴ ἀναίνεσθαι τὴν πώλευσιν, πρεσβυτέρους δὲ μὴ διαφέρειν τῶν καρχάρων θηρίων καὶ σαρκοφάγων μηδὲ ἕν.

20) Jātaka no. 386 p. 278 *rājā c'eva ratheyuttasindhavā... eko ratheyuttasindhavo...* I thank Klaus Karttunen for his reference to this passage.

21) This remarkable correspondence made me wondering if the khur could have been domesticated or cross-bred with the donkey. Richard Meadow in reply to my question commented (personal communication, 27 April 2009): "No, the wild half-ass was never domesticated. The donkey mentioned is probably just another breed of the imported African form. The other possibility is that the authors are grouping both domestic donkeys and the half-ass (khur) all under the term 'donkey' instead of 'ass'. Grouping them together at all is questionable." I am still left wondering is the possibility of cross-breeding with the wild ass really excluded. Has this donkey breed been studied genetically?

22) When in March 2009 I mentioned to Juha Janhunen about my intention to write a paper on the wild asses, Juha told me that for some time he too had intended to write on the same topic, so we decided on a joint study.

23) Many of the signs which I have included as allographs in no. 46 are considered by Bryan Wells (2006: 242-243) as separate graphemes, in my opinion mistakenly (for my criteria for distinguishing between allographs and graphemes see Parpola 1994: 68-69). Some other depictions of a four-legged mammal in the Indus script I have considered to be a separate grapheme, no. 47. It faces left (while no. 46 faces right); there is an upright tail, but it does not show a tuft, and the ears are smaller and upwards or forwards pointing. These characteristics, compared with those of the Harappan animal figurines, have suggested the 'dog' as an interpretation (cf. Possehl 1999: 189-191 on the dog, with illustrations). The differences between the signs 46 and 47 are rather small, however, and new evidence from Kanmer (see Figure 16-17) suggests that both depict the wild ass, and that no. 47 is an allograph of no. 46.

24) For the Dharmasūtra texts and their translation see Olivelle 2000. A Brahmin woman involved in an adultery is to be purified by making her ride naked on an ass in public, see below 5.

25) Rāmāyaṇa 2,63: *14 tvaramāṇaś ca dharmātmā raktamālyānulepanaḥ | rathena kharayuktena prayāto dakṣiṇāmukhaḥ || 15 evam etan mayā dṛṣṭam imāṃ*

rātriṃ bhayāvahām | ahaṃ rāmo 'tha vā rājā lakṣmaṇo vā mariṣyati || 16 naro yānena yaḥ svapne kharayuktena yāti hi | acirāt tasya dhūmāgraṃ citāyāṃ sampradṛśyate || "14. And a righteous man, wearing red garlands and smeared with red cream, was hurrying off toward the south on a chariot yoked with asses. 15. This was the terrifying dream I had last night. Surely I myself, or Rāma, or the king, or Lakṣmaṇa is going to die. 16. For when in dream a man sets out in a carriage yoked with asses, it is not long before a wreath of smoke appears above his funeral pyre." (Transl. Pollock 1984: 218.) Cf. also Brockington 1984: 89.

26) For ass/donkey in the Veda and later Indian culture, see Zimmer 1879: 232-233; Winternitz 1910: 69-70; Macdonell and Keith 1912 I: 214, 221; II: 223; Hopkins 1915: 22, 42, 133, 143, 187, 212, 215, 217; Crooke 1926: 59, 252, 352-353, 434; Meyer 1937 I: 116, 174, 182-183; II: 135; III: 163; and Rau 1980-81.

27) Note that the legs have been added afterwards and that the tail and the ears are broken.

28) Meadow's criticism against charring as an indication of food preparation was cited above in note 4.

29) The onager (*Equus hemionus*) is found widely at archaeological sites in Luristan, and Fars since the Middle Palaeolithic and in Khuzistan since the Aceramic Neolithic. Other equids are attested in Luristan only: the wild horse (*Equus ferus*) since the Middle Palaeolithic, and the domestic horse (*Equus caballus*) just at Godin Tepe in the Chalcolithic period, c. 2000 BCE (cf. Potts 1999: 26-30, tables 2.3-5). In Mesopotamia the earliest evidence of domesticated horse dates from the last century of the third millennium BCE (cf. Oates 2003: 117-120).

30) Tamil *kaẓutai* 'donkey' is attested since the earliest Old Tamil, from c. 200 CE (e.g., Puṟanāṉūṟu 392,9), cf. TL 1928 II: 804a.

31) Cf. Lambrick (1964: 16): "Very characteristic of Sind is the 'kalar', soil which contains an excessive proportion of salts. Its composition has been known to include nearly forty per cent of sodium sulphate. In such ground, almost black in colour, and glutinous, no vegetation can subsist, but in the darkish brown medium kalar several species of salvadora, the Sindhi 'khabar', flourish, particularly in lower Sind. In the north we find wild indigo and a few other small plants in kalar of similar composition. These tracts present a depressing appearance. Often the subsoil water, rising by capillarity to the surface of alkaline soil, carries the salts with it, and these become concentrated by evaporation, producing a crystalline efflorescence highly prejudicial to plant growth."

32) Proto-Dravidian **kaẓ(i)* 'saline soil' seems to be derived, as 'waste land', from the Proto-Dravidian root **kaẓi* 'to be wasted (as time), spent, discharged (as excreta), discarded, cast away, rejected, abandoned, removed, be ruined, expire, die' (DEDR 1356).

33) Gertrud and Helmut Denzau have drawn our attention to the Kurdish expressions for 'wild ass', ***kerê çolî or kerê kûvî*** (cf. Amîrxan 1992: II, 576). Here ***ker*** (cognate of Persian *χar*) is 'ass, donkey', while both ***çolî*** (cf. Amîrxan 1992: I, 98) and ***kûvî*** (I, 260) denote 'wilderness'.

34) I thought to have found an illustration of such an ass fight in the tablet H-180 from Harappa, but a closer inspection of the — all very faintly visible — details (nails in paws, long curled tails, and small ears) suggested to me that M. S. Vats (1940 I: 42) is right in stating that the scene depicts "a pair of tigers standing face to face".

35) Denzau and Denzau (1999: 55) note that P. S. Pallas in 1781 referred to the presence of wild ass on the Malabar coast of South India, and that this is obviously an error that goes back to Barbosa's sailing account from the 16th century. Actually Barbosa ([1518] 1921 II: 34) is speaking of a wild beast that looks like the wild ass and is called "*Cryvamergam*". The context, initiation of the Veda student, makes it quite certain that the black buck (*kṛṣṇamṛga-* in Sanskrit) is meant.

36) "The presence of a bone of *Equus cabal[l]us* in the beginning of this phase at Hallur is suggestive, particularly if it is considered in conjunction with an extensive group of rock paintings showing horses and riders, and with such exotic metal objects as the Kallur swords" (Allchin and Allchin 1982: 287-288). The antennae-hilted bronze swords from Kallur (cf. Allchin and Allchin 1982: 288 fig. 10.21) resemble the antennae-hilted swords of the Gangetic Copper Hoards and the Bactria and Margiana

Archaeological Complex (BMAC) (cf. Parpola 1994: 155 Figure 8.23). It seems to me that the warring traditions reflected in the Old Tamil poems of the Puṟanāṉūṟu came to South India soon after Indo-Iranian speakers brought them to South Asia along with the horse. But these traditions were first Dravidianized in the then predominantly Dravidian-speaking Indus Valley, Gujarat and the Deccan, which even after Aryanization retained poetics similar to the Old Tamil poetry in Hāla's Sattasaī (cf. Hart 1975; 1976).

37) In contrast to *khara-* 'donkey' (which is restricted to the northwestern and western parts of the Indian subcontinent) the cognates of Sanskrit *gardabha-* are widely distributed in South Asia, but are lacking in the Nuristani languages with the exception of Waigali and Tregami, which have borrowed it from Dardic (cf. Turner 1966: no. 4054; Fussman 1972: II, 60-61). Georg Buddruss has suggested that the Dardic languages in the mountainous northern Indus Valley borrowed this word from an Indo-Aryan language of the plains, since dental *d* instead of retroflex *ḍ* in *gadā* does not reflect the normal development of *-rd-*, but Fussman (1972 II: 61 n. 1) points out that actually the treatment of *-rd-* in Dardic and Nuristani languages is obscure.

38) On the mule in Vedic texts, see Rau 1980-81: 186-189. Indo-Iranian **aśvatara-* (cf. New Persian *astar* < Old Persian **asatara-*) 'mule' is formed by adding the suffix *-tara-* to *aśva-* 'horse'; in this connection, the suffix means 'something like, but not quite the same as' the simple noun (cf. Turner 1969). It seems, however, that the construction started with the feminine, *aśvatarī-* going back to **aśvā- starī-* 'sterile mare', cf. Vedic *starī-* f. 'sterile cow' and *dhenu-ṣṭarī-* f. 'cow that stops giving milk' (cf. Debrunner 1954: II.2, p. 603-604, 609; Turner 1969). A similar formation from Indo-Iranian *khara-* 'ass, donkey' is Proto-Iranian **χara-tara-* > Khotanese Saka *khaḍara-* 'mule' and Sogdian (Buddhist) *γrtr'k* > Middle Turkic *qatyr* (on this word cf. Räsänen 1969: 242) > Ossetic (Digor) *qadir* (cf. Turner 1985: 26 no. 3820a; Mayrhofer 1992: I, 447).

39) The Purāṇas are very difficult to date, but the Matsya-Purāṇa has been considered as "one of the best preserved and earliest", and may date from c. 400 CE. (cf. Rocher 1986: 199).

40) *Kutirai* 'horse' is attested in Old Tamil literature (c. 200 CE+), cf. Kuṟuntokai 74,1; Akaṉanūṟu 1,2.

41) The Indus sign no. 216 (cf. Parpola 1994: 74), which in the seal M-1097 precedes the wild ass sign and probably is its attribute, could depict "running legs" and stand for a Proto-Dravidian word meaning 'swift' or 'running, galloping' (cf. DEDR no. 1705 Tamil *kuti* 'leap, gallop, etc.', no. 4087 Tamil *pāy* 'leap, gallop, flee, etc.', no. 5417 Tamil *virai* 'swift, quick', possibly also no. 1041 Tamil *ōṭu* 'to run'). I emphasize that this is nothing but an educated guess, a very tentative working hypothesis to be thoroughly tested in future. The Matsya-Purāṇa 118,61 characterizes the wild ass as 'swift-going' (*turaṃga-*), see above.

42) Gamkrelidze and Ivanov (1995: 480 n. 24) mention *párasvant-* as a Rigvedic term for 'wild ass'; Meulenbeld (1999 IB: 35 n. 526), too, considers this possible, though he also refers to Lüders (see below) and to a medieval gloss *āraṇyamahiṣa-* 'wild buffalo'. The meaning 'wild ass' for *párasvant-* was generally accepted for a long time ever since it was first proposed by Böhtlingk and Roth (1864 IV: 497 "ein best. grösseres Thier, viell. der wilde Esel"). But Heinrich Lüders (1942: 50-56) pointed out that *párasvant-* corresponds to Aśoka's *palasata-* and Pali *phalasata-*, which the commentators explain to be *khagga-miga* 'rhinoceros', and which is clearly identifiable as such on the basis of Jātaka no. 546, which mentions "rhinoceros skin (*phalasataṃ cammam*) carefully wrought by the leather-workers" as "a defence to keep off arrows". As an etymology Lüders suggested *páras-* < Proto-Indo-European **pelos* 'fold' + the suffix of possessive adjective *-vant-*, since the folded skin is one of the distinguishing characteristics of the rhinoceros. Mayrhofer (1996: 88) quotes this (correcting the reconstruction to **péles* 'Falte'), but considers the etymology uncertain. I would like to suggest that the rhinoceros was understood (as the Jātaka passage quoted suggests) to possess 'shields' (which used to be made of skin), connecting the word with Greek

-pélas 'skin', Latin *pellis*, German *Fell*, etc., and Greek *péltē* and *pálmē* both meaning 'light shield', derived from the root **pel-* 'to cover' (cf. Pokorny 1959: 803; Frisk 1970 II: 499). 'Shield' appears to be implied also by the Pali variant *phalasata-*, cf. the following words in this meaning: Sanskrit (and Pali) *phala(ka)-* (from the epics onwards), *sphara(ka)-* (lexica), Buddhist Hybrid Sanskrit *phara-* 'shield', Bengali *phar*, etc., which seem to be loans from Iranian **spara-* 'shield' rather than from Dravidian (Tamil *param* 'armour for the body, a kind of shield' and its cognates in Malayalam and Kannada listed in DEDR no. 3958 are rather loans from Indo-Aryan) (cf. Turner 1966: no. 9054; Mayrhofer 1996 II: 202).

43) The word *rāsabha-* 'ass' is most probably from the OIA verbal root *ras-* 'to cry' [cf. Śatapatha-Brāhmaṇa 6,1,1,11 "and that which, as it were, cried (*ras-*), became the ass (*rāsabha-*)"] + the OIA animal name suffix *-bha-* (cf. Mayrhofer 1996 II: 441, 450).

44) Taittirīya-Saṃhitā 5,1,5,7 says of *gardabha-*: "the sages called it *rāsabha-*" (*rāsabha ity hy etam ṛṣayo 'vadan*); cf. Rau 1980-81: 182 n. 1.

45) RV 8,85,7 *yuñjāthām rāsabham rathe vīḍaṅge vṛṣaṇvasū.*

46) RV 1,116,2 *tad rāsabho nāsatyā sahasram ājā yamasya pradhane jigāya.*

47) The Aśvins are called *surathā rathītamā* in Rigveda 1,22,2; cf. Zeller 1990: 92. Even the aśvamedha hymn RV 1,162 mentions (in verse 22) the yoked *rāsabha-* (of the Aśvins).

48) This however, is not the only reason why the Aśvins are associated with the ass. Another reason is the fame of the ass as a seminator, which plays an important role in marriages and funerals, these being indeed the contexts in which the Aśvins ran their races with the ass-chariot (see Parpola 2005: 29-36). The domestic ass with its darker skin would in its colour suit the funeral context better. Aitareya-Brāhmaṇa 4,9 ends the story of the race by identifying the animal explicitly with the domestic ass by explaining why the ass is the slowest beast of burden: it is because it won, its speed was spent. But in compensation, it possesses twofold sexual power. It mates not only with the she-ass but with the mare as well (cf. Rau 1980-81: 183).

49) The wild ass being famed for its strength and hardiness, the name may also refer to Bahrām's heroic qualities, as noted by C. E. Bosworth (1999: V, 81-82 n. 220) and Potts (2002: 112). Potts points out that Bahrām's name is derived from that of the Old Iranian god of war and victory, Vərəθraγna; he thinks that Bahrām's association with the wild ass might be related to the evidence for ass sacrifice to the god of war in Kerman in eastern Iran, attested in a passage of Strabo's Geography (15,2,14), which very probably goes back to the late 4th century BCE accounts by Alexander's admiral Nearchus and his pilot Onesicritus: "Because of scarcity of horses most of the Karmanians use asses, even for war; and they sacrifice an ass to Ares, the only god they worship, and they are a warlike people" (cf. Potts 2002: 103). Another version is preserved in Aelian's *De natura animalium* (12,34): "The Saracori keep asses, not to carry burdens nor to grind corn but to ride in war, and mounted on them they brave the dangers of war, just as the Greeks do on horseback. And any ass of theirs that appears to be more given to braying than others they offer as a sacrifice to the God of War" (cf. Potts 2002: 105). As Potts (2002: 104-106) notes, the Greek word used in these passages is *ónos*, and hence undoubtedly refers to the donkey, but probably to a superior breed, such as those reported from Iran and Central Asia.

50) Ossetic *χæræg*, *χarag*, Munji *χára-*, Tajik, Baluchi, Pashto, Yaghnobi *χar*, Parachi *khō̆r*, Sanglichi *χor*, *χōr*, Yigdha *χóro*, Ishkashmi, Yazghulami *χůr*, Wakhi *χur*, Kurdish *ker*, (Gurānī) *har*, Sariqoli *čer*, *šer*, Bartangi *šör*, Roshani *šur*, Rushani, Khufi *šōr*, (fem.) *šār* (cf. Horn 1893: 104 no. 473; Steblin-Kamenskij 1999: 409).

51) Gypsy (Palestinian) *ḳar* m. *ḳári* f., (Armenian) *χari*, (Greek) *kher*, (Rumanian) *χerú*, Kati *kur*, Prasun *korū*, Ashkun *kərəṭék*, Shumashti *χareṭá*, Khowar *khairánu* ('donkey's foal'), Bashkarik *kur*, Dameli *khar* m., *khari* f., Tirahi *khar*, Pashai (Laurowani) *khar* m., *khär* f., Kalasha (Urtsun) *khār*, Phalura *khār* m., *khári*, Kashmiri *khar* m., *khürü* f., Sindhi *kharu* m., Lahnda *kharkā* m., *kharkī* f., Panjabi, Gujarati, Marathi, Hindi *khar* m. Old Marathi *khari* f. (Turner 1966 and 1985: no. 3818; McGregor

1993: 230a; a detailed analysis of the Nuristani and Dardic data in Fussman 1972 I: 60-62).

52) English *khur* is at the moment not to be found in *The Oxford English Dictionary* (online), *The Shorter Oxford English Dictionary* (1959), *Webster's new twentieth century dictionary of the English language* (unabridged 2nd ed.) or *Collins Dictionary of the English Language* (1982).

53) Varmmā (1992 II: 141a), however does record Hindi *gōr-khar*, glossing it as a kind of wild ass that is bigger than the donkey but smaller than the horse and is found in northwestern India ("gadhe kī jāti kā ek prakār kā jaṃglī paśu jo gadhe se baṛā aur ghoṛe se choṭā hotā tathā uttar-paścimī bhārat meṃ pāyā jātā hai").

54) Pannavaṇāsutta 1,71: *se kiṃ taṃ egakhurā | egakhurā aṇegavihā paṇṇattā |* taṃ *jahā assā assatarā ghoḍagā gaddabhā gorakharā kaṃdalagā sirikaṃdalagā āvattā je yāva 'ṇṇe tahappagārā | se ttaṃ egakhurā.* (I am obliged to Petteri Koskikallio for sending me the text of this passage.) The first five animals correspond to Sanskrit *aśva-* 'horse', *aśvatara-* 'mule', *ghoṭaka-* 'horse', *gardabha-* 'ass', *gaurakhara-* 'wild ass'. The remaining words are known as names of equids from this passage alone. *kandalaga-* and *sirikandalaga-* have no counterpart in Sanskrit (*kandalaka-* mentioned as such by Sheth 1963: 212a does not exist), but they mean 'the neighing one', and 'the auspiciously neighing', being derived from the Old Indo-Aryan root *krand-* 'to neigh'; *āvatta-* corresponds to Sanskrit *āvarta-*, which does not denote an animal, but the spots of whirling hair on the body of a horse, interpreted as omens (cf. Caland 1911).

55) As noted above, a possible date for this text is 400 CE. (cf. Rocher 1986: 199).

56) The identification of *sṛmara-* as the Kashmir red deer, *Cervus elaphus hanglu* Wagner (see Meulenbeld 1999 IB: 47 n. 615 with further references) is not to be found in Sanskrit dictionaries; Mayrhofer (1996 II: 744) knows it as an unidentified animal frequenting wet places.

57) Since neither Chinese nor Japanese has a native term for the wild ass, the 'glosses' in Sakaki's edition are actually descriptive paraphrases. Edgerton (1953 II: 218a) correctly translates the Japanese paraphrase as "a kind of wild horse found [add: in large numbers] in Central Asia"; and the Chinese paraphrase as "reddish-brown horse, or (2) wild mule (ass?)". The zoological species names used here in Chinese are 馬 *ma3* 'horse' and 騾 *luo2* 'mule'. According to Giles (1909-1912: 912, no. 7290), the Chinese term 騾 *luo*2 'mule' refers specifically to 'the offspring of an ass and a mare'.

58) Professor Tooru Aiba of the Tohoku University in Japan kindly sent a copy of this entry in Sakaki's edition of 1916.

59) According to Denzau and Denzau 1999: 15-16, such early authors as Geoffrey-Saint-Hilaire in 1835, Sclater in 1862, George 1869 speak of *ghor-khur*, as does Blyth 1859 (see 2); cf. in addition *ghor-khar* in Lüders 1942: 53; Prater 1971: 227; Groves 1986: 24; Possehl 1999: 188.

60) Hindi *ghoṛā* goes back to Sanskrit *ghoṭa(ka)-* 'horse', which is first attested in later Vedic texts describing horse-shaped implements connected with the *gharma* or *pravargya* ritual that belongs to the cult of the Aśvins (Āpastamba-Śrautasūtra 15,3,12). The word is considered to be of foreign origin, but the etymology is debated (cf. Mayrhofer 1992 I: 517; Turner 1966: no. 4516; DEDR no. 1711; Krishnamurti 2003: 12). I have suggested that the characteristic 'face urns' with horse-decorated lids of the "Gandhāra Grave" culture of the Swat Valley, introduced around 1500 BCE, are connected with the *gharma* vessel equated in Vedic texts with a hero's head (Parpola 2004; 2009b). As the "Gandhāra Graves" appear to go back to the BMAC culture of southern Central Asia excavated by Viktor Sarianidi, the word *ghoṭa-* may have come to Indo-Aryan from the original BMAC language after the BMAC was taken over by the Indo-Aryan speakers coming from the northern steppes.

61) Klaus Karttunen in a personal communication further suggests that when the Mahābhārata (2,47,17-18) speaks of "wild horses" (*āraṇyān... aśvān*), wild asses are likely to be meant — as there were no wild horses in South Asia.

62) The four social classes of classical India from the highest to the lowest are: (1) *brāhmaṇa* or Brahmin: priests, (2) *kṣatriya*: rulers and warriors, (3) *vaiśya*: peasantry, artisans and merchants, and (4) *śūdra*: serfs.

These four social classes are called *varṇa* 'colour', and four colours are associated with them: (1) white, (2) red, (3) yellow or green and (4) black. The social classes are similarly associated with many other cosmic categories: the directions of space (E - S- W- N), seasons (spring - summer - rains - winter), etc. In the Vedic texts, however, this cosmic classification is complicated by the fact that various texts have different numbers of entities, starting with three (the śūdras are omitted or combined with the vaiśyas in the threefold scheme). Cf. Smith 1994.

63) One manuscript (Ka) out of eight, one (Calcutta) edition out of three, and four commentaries on other Smṛti texts in their quotations of this rule omit *kṛṣṇa*, having just *khara*; but one of these commentaries has *kṛṣṇa* in another quotation of the rule; cf. Olivelle 2000: 692.

64) Two Smṛti text commentaries while quoting this rule omit *gaura*; the commentary on Pārāśara-Mādhavīya in its quotation has *kṛṣṇakhara*; and one manuscript (Ka) as well as the Calcutta edition have *goratha* 'cow-chariot'; cf. Olivelle 2000: 692.

65) The same two commentaries, which in their quotations omit *gaura* in 21,2 also omit *śveta* in this rule (and they omit *kṛṣṇa* in 21,1). Manuscript Ka, the Calcutta edition and one commentary (on Pārāśara-Mādhavīya) read *raktakhara* 'red ass'; one quotation (in Vijñeśvara's commentary on Yājñavalkya-Smṛti) has *gaurakhara*. Cf. Olivelle 2000: 692.

No Sanskrit dictionary records the here occurring compound *śvetakhara*. On this "white ass" cf. the notes on "large white donkey" of Kathiawar above in 2.

66) There is one modification: "donkey" in Olivelle's translation has been replaced with "ass".

67) This etymology seems to be supported by the name *Dhenuka* (from *dhenu-* f. cow) of the demonic wild ass killed by Balarāma; see 6.

68) Cf. Böhtlingk and Roth (1858 II: 826) s.v. *gaura*: "1) adj. weisslich, gelblich, rötlich. 2) m. eine Büffelart, *Bos gaurus*, häufig neben den *gavaya* genannt." Macdonell and Keith (1912 I: 241-242): "*Gaura*, a species of ox (*Bos gaurus*), is frequently mentioned with the *Gavaya* from the Rigveda onwards."

69) Cf. Macdonell and Keith (1912 I: 222): "*Gavaya*, the name of a species of ox (*Bos gavaeus*) occurs frequently from the Rigveda onwards. It is mentioned with *Gaura* and *Mahiṣa* in the Vājasaneyi-Saṃhitā (xxiv.28), where also a wild *Gavaya* is spoken of."

70) The classification into domestic (*grāmya-*) and wild (*āraṇya-*) animals is based on the contrast prevailing between 'village' (*grāma-*) and 'forest, wilderness' (*araṇya-*) in Vedic thought, for which see Malamoud 1976.

71) It seems significant that this early compound synonym of *gaura-* has as its latter member not *khara-* but *mṛgá-*. *Mṛgá-* m. denotes a 'wild animal', especially 'hunted game animal', in particular 'deer' or 'antelope' (cf. the denominative verb *mṛgayati* 'hunts'). The word goes back to Proto-Indo-Iranian, but its origin is unknown (cf. Mayrhofer 1996 II: 370-371). We know that the wild ass was hunted by the kings of ancient Mesopotamia, Egypt and Persia, and in India by the Mughal emperors Babur, Akbar and Jahangir (cf. Denzau and Denzau 1999: 185-200). The cut and charred bones of the wild ass at Gonur and Harappan sites suggest that it was hunted for food. The Middle Vedic texts declare that the meat of the five wild animals listed here may not be eaten, and in later sacred law eating ass, camel and predatory animals is likewise prohibited for a Brahmin (cf. Gautama-Dharmasūtra 23,4). But for instance the Bāhlīka people living in the upper Indus Valley beyond the bounds of orthodox Brahmanism had quite different customs abhorred in the Mahābhārata: "Those who do not eat the meat of the wild boar, the fowl, the cow, the ass, the camel and the goat, their birth is without meaning" (8,30,32 *vārāhaṃ kaukkuṭaṃ māṃsaṃ gavyaṃ gārdabham auṣṭrakam | aiḍaṃ ca ye na khādanti teṣāṃ janma nirarthakam*).

72) The ŚB takes these ritual formulae from Vājasaneyi-Saṃhitā (= VS) 13,41-51; their wording is closely parallelled by the mantras of Taittirīya-Saṃhitā (= TS) 4,2,10.

73) What is meant by *mayu-* and *kiṃpuruṣa-* has been a major problem; the translations offer "monkey", "sham-

man", etc. I have suggested "war-bard", taking *kiṃpuruṣa-* as a folk-etymological transformation of *kinnara-*, which in origin is a Dravidian word for a stringed musical instrument, but is attested in Sanskrit from the epics onwards, mainly denoting a heavenly minstrel (see Parpola 1983: 57-70).

74) That the wild ass rather than the Indian bison is meant in this context has already been suggested by Chlodwig Werba in a personal communication to Manfred Mayrhofer (cf. Mayrhofer 1992 I: 503).

75) Turner quotes Sindhi *sarahu* m. in the meaning 'a kind of mountain goat', but according to Prater (1971: 255) this is the Sindhi name of the Sind ibex. All of these species are distinguished by their mighty horns (cf. Prater 1971, Plate 60), which agrees with the probable etymology for *śarabha-*: *śara-* < Proto-Indo-European **k'er(H2)-* 'horn' + the animal name suffix *-bha-* (cf. Mayrhofer 1996 II: 616).

76) There are six local varieties of the urial; the other subspecies of *Ovis orientalis*, the mouflon (*Ovis orientalis orientalis*), is more westerly distributed (cf. Wikipedia). Although not so recorded in our dictionaries, it is quite probable that the term *meṣá-* 'ram' covered also the mountain sheep or argali (*Ovis ammon*), two subspecies of which live in the highlands of northwestern South Asia, the Marco Polo's sheep (*Ovis ammon polii*) and the Tibetan argali alias nayan (*Ovis ammon hodgsoni*).

77) From references to real animals I exclude RV 4,58,2-3, which speaks of melted butter as a bull (*vṛṣabhá-*) that has four horns, three legs, two heads and seven hands, calling it a "four-horned *gaura*". I suggest a connection with the Iranian Threelegged Ass, cf. the next paper, 4.

78) In later Vedic ritual a reflection of these Rigvedic passages is the following phrase in the *subrahmaṇyā* litany, which is addressed to Indra as an invitation to a Soma sacrifice: "O wild ass rushing down!" (*gaurāvaskandin*). The Jaiminīya-Brāhmaṇa (2,79) explains: "Then he, after having become a wild ass, rushed down to the sea" (*tato haiva gauro bhūtvārṇavam avacaskanda*). The unpublished Anupadasūtra of Sāmaveda in chapter 8,3, on the Agni variant of the subrahmaṇyā litany, records the following reading: *śukrāvaskandinn iti*, and comments it: *śukramṛgo ha sma bhūtvāvaskadyāraṇyād rājānaṃ pibatīti ca karmasāmānyāt*. The word *śukra-* means 'white', being more or less a synonym of *gaura-*: "having become a *śukramṛga-* 'white (game) animal' and rushed down from the wilderness (*araṇya-*) he drinks (Soma, which is called) 'the king'; thus (it is said / one interprets) because of the equality of the action."

79) For a fairly comprehensive survey of Sanskrit literature on the "submarine fire", see O'Flaherty 1971; cf. also O'Flaherty 1979: 13-16.

80) Cf. Brahmāṇḍa-Purāṇa 3,72,17 (speaking of Hari, i.e., Viṣṇu) *yaḥ purā hy analo bhūtvā tv aurvaḥ saṃvartako vibhuḥ | pātālastho 'rṇavagataḥ papau toyamayaṃ haviḥ*. While the mare-faced form of Viṣṇu in Pātāla is connected with the ebb (low) of tide, the flow (high) of tide is ascribed to a horse-headed (*hayaśiras-*) form of Viṣṇu, who stays in the city of Pātāla in the netherworld of the snakes (where a demonic, water-drinking fire is constantly ablaze) and stands up every new and full moon day to fill the world with water. Cf. Mahābhārata 5,97,1 *etat tu nāgalokasya nābhisthāne sthitam puram | pātālam iti vikhyātaṃ daityadānavasevitam ... 3 atrāsuro 'gniḥ satataṃ dīpyate vāribhojanaḥ | ... 5 atra divyaṃ hayaśiraḥ kāle parvaṇi parvaṇi | uttiṣṭhati suvarṇābhaṃ vārbhir āpūrayañ jagat*. Besides *hayaśiras-*, several other expressions meaning 'horse-faced' or 'horse-headed' are used of Viṣṇu as the sun-horse rising from the sea (cf. Hopkins 1915: 203-204): *hayamukha-, hayagrīva-, aśvaśiras*.

81) Cf. Brahmāṇḍa-Purāṇa 2,12,35-36 *putras tv agner manyumato ghoraḥ saṃvartakaḥ smṛtaḥ | pibann apaḥ sa vasati samudre vaḍavāmukhah*; 2,18,78-80 *cakro balāhakaś caiva maināko yaś ca parvataḥ | āyatās te mahāśailāḥ samudraṃ dakṣiṇaṃ prati | cakramainākayor madhye vidiśaṃ dakṣiṇāṃ prati | tatra saṃvartako nāma so 'gniḥ pibati tajjalam | nāmnā samudravāsas tu aurvaḥ sa vaḍavāmukhaḥ*.

82) Cf., e.g., Brahmāṇḍa-Purāṇa 4,1,151-157.

83) Besides these Harappan-Dravidian elements, the concept of the submarine Vaḍavāmukha fire undoubtedly contains elements of Indo-Aryan origin that go back

to Indo-Iranian and Indo-European traditions, but the idea that a mare- or horse-shaped god drinks the ocean to cause the ebb of tide is absent from that mythology. One manifestation of the Vedic fire god Agni is Apāṃ napāt, 'son of waters', but the sea (*samudra-*) is mentioned in the Ṛgveda especially as the birthplace of Agni (cf. RV 1,93,3; 1,163,4; 10,45,1.3; 10,121,7). Apāṃ napāt occurs in the Avesta as well, where he is called Ahura and is coupled with Miθra, thus corresponding to Vedic Varuṇa, the lord of waters, who is associated with the night, while Mitra is associated with the day. In the Veda, Apāṃ napāt is conceived of as a horse-shaped sun-fire in the waters (cf. Findly 1979). I have argued that Mitra and Varuṇa represent the two Aśvins, originally the divinized chariot team (or the pair of chariot horses). The Aśvins circle around the universe in their flying car manifested as the day-sun and the night-sun. The name Aśvin means 'possessor of horses', and these divine twins were born by the wife of the sun-god Vivasvat in the shape of a mare. (See Parpola 2005.) Cf. also Bṛhad-Āraṇyaka-Upaniṣad 1,1: "The head of the sacrificial horse, clearly, is the dawn — its sight is the sun; its breath is the wind; and its gaping mouth is the fire common to all men [i.e., the fire burning inside the body] ... its forequarter is the rising sun; and its hindquarter is the setting sun... the sea is its womb" (transl. Olivelle 1998: 37). In the Harappan religion, it seems, the 'night sun' was conceived of as 'fiery seed' or 'golden embryo' or 'golden egg' in the womb of cosmic waters (cf. Parpola 2009a: 66-68).

84) Sanskrit *múkha-* n. 'mouth, face, beginning' (attested as early as the Rigveda) is a loanword from Proto-Dravidian **mukam* 'mouth, face, front, beginning' (DEDR no. 4889).

85) Kālidāsa, Kumārasambhava 8,91 *na tu suratasukhebhyaś chinnatṛṣṇo babhūva jvalana iva samudrāntargatas tajjaleṣu.*

86) Cf. also the Buddhist Suppāraka-Jātaka (no. 463), which tells of merchants who sailed from the seaport town of Bharukaccha (in Gujarat) but got lost: "After passing the Nalamāli Sea, the merchants came to a sea named Vaḷabhāmukha. Here the water is sucked away and rises on every side; and the water thus sucked away on all sides rises in sheer precipices leaving what looks like a great pit [*mahā-sobbha-* = Sanskrit *śvabhra-* 'hole, (deep) pit'] ... If this ship gets there, she will sink and go to destruction..." (transl. W. H. D. Rouse in Cowell ed. 1901 IV: 89-90).

87) The name *Dhenuka* is derived from *dhenu-* f. '(milch) cow', and seems to refer to the cow-like colour of the wild ass (cf. above 5 on the etymology of *gaura-*).

88) Harivaṃśa 57 (ed. Vaidya 1969 I: 375-377): *1 damite sarparāje tu kṛṣṇena yamunāhrade | tam eva ceratur deśaṃ sahitau rāmakeśavau - 2 jagmatus tau tu saṃraktau godhanaiḥ sahagāminau | giriṃ govardhanaṃ ramyaṃ vasudevasutāv ubhau - 3 govardhanasyottarato yamunātīram āśritam | dadṛśāte 'tha tau vīrau ramyaṃ tālavanaṃ mahat - 4 tau tālaparṇapratate ramye tālavanau ratau | ceratuḥ paramaprītau vṛṣapotāv ivodgatau - 5 sa tu deśaḥ samaḥ snigdho loṣṭapāṣāṇavarjitaḥ | darbhaprāyasthalībhūtaḥ sumahān kṛṣṇamṛttikaḥ - 6 tālais tair vipulaskandhair ucchritaiḥ śyāmaparvabhiḥ | phalāgraśākhibhir bhāti nāgahastair ivocchritaiḥ - 7 tatra dāmodaro vākyam uvāca vadatāṃ varaḥ | aho tālaphalaiḥ pakvair vāsiteyaṃ vanasthalī - 8 svādūny ārya sugandhīni śyāmāni rasavanti ca | tālapakvāni sahitau pātayāvo laghukramau - 9 yady eṣām īdṛśo gandho madhuro ghrāṇasaṃmataḥ | rasenāmṛtakalpena bhaviṣyantīti me matiḥ - 10 dāmodaravacaḥ śrutvā rauhiṇeyo hasann iva | pātayaṃs tālapakvāni cālayām āsa tāṃs tarūn - 11 tat tu tālavanaṃ nṛṇām asevyaṃ duratikramam | nirmāṇabhūtam iriṇaṃ puruṣādālayopamam - 12 dāruṇo dhenuko nāma daityo gardabharūpavān | kharayūthena mahatā vṛtaḥ samupasevate - 13 sa tat tālavanaṃ ghoraṃ gardabhaḥ parirakṣati | nṛpakṣiśvāpadagaṇāṃs trāsayānaḥ sa durmatiḥ - 14 tālaśabdaṃ sa taṃ śrutvā saṃghuṣṭaṃ phalapātane | nāmarṣayata saṃkruddhas tālasvanam iva dvipaḥ - 15 śabdānusārī saṃkruddho darpāviddhasaṭānanaḥ | stabdhākṣo heṣitapaṭuḥ khurair nirdārayan mahīm - 16 āviddhapuccho hṛṣito vyāttānana ivāntakaḥ | āpatann eva dadṛśe rauhiṇeyam avasthitam - 17 tālānāṃ tam adho dṛṣṭvā sadhvajākaram avyayam | rauhiṇeyaṃ kharo duṣṭaḥ so 'daśad daśanāyudhaḥ - 18 padbhyām ubhābhyāṃ ca punaḥ paścimābhyāṃ parāṅmukhaḥ | jaghānorasi daityaḥ*

sa rauhiṇeyaṃ nirāyudham - 19 tābhyām eva sa jagrāha padbhyāṃ taṃ daityagardabham | āvarjitamukhaskandhaṃ prairayat tālamūrdhani - 20 sa bhagnorukaṭigrīvo bhagnapṛṣṭho durākṛtiḥ | kharas tālaphalaiḥ sārdhaṃ papāta dharaṇītale - 21 taṃ gatāsuṃ gataśrīkaṃ patitaṃ vīkṣya gardabham | jñātīṃs tathāparāṃs tasya cikṣepa tṛṇarājani - 22 sā bhūr gardabhadehaiś ca tālapakvaiś ca pātitaiḥ | babhāse channajaladā dyaur ivāvyaktaśāradī - 23 tasmin gardabhadaitye tu sānuge vinipātite | ramyaṃ tālavanaṃ tad dhi bhūyo ramyataraṃ babhau - 24 vipramuktabhayaṃ śubhraṃ viviktākāradarśanam | caranti sma sukhaṃ gāvas tat tālavanam uttamam - 25 tataḥ pravyāhṛtāḥ sarve gopā vananivāsinaḥ | vītaśokā vanaṃ sarve cañcūryante sma te sukham - 26 tataḥ sukhaṃ prakīrṇāsu goṣu nāgendravikramau | drumaparṇāsane kṛtvā tau yathārhaṃ niṣīdatuh.

89) While *gardabha-* is the term for the ass favoured in the Harivaṃśa, the Bhāgavata-Purāṇa uses more *khara-* (*khararūpadṛk* 10,15,23), but also the archaic *rāsabha-* (*asurarāsabhaḥ* 10,15, 29).

90) A herd (*yūtha-* n.) of asses suggests that the wild ass is meant. Richard Meadow (personal communication, 9 May 2009) however reminds that "domestic asses can go feral".

91) As in figures 12-14!

92) This description of the wine palm forest in terms of a salt desert (*iriṇa-*) in HV 57,11 confirms that wild asses are meant. Sanskrit *iriṇa-* denotes 'saline soil' and its 'water depression', where the wild ass drinks. The word *iriṇa-* is also used in Vedic texts of the hole dug for the game of dice (cf. Rigveda 10,34,9 with Falk 1986: 75-86). The Vādhūla-Śrautasūtra (10,7 in Chaubey's ed.) has preserved the information that in the rite of royal consecration, this gaming hole was to be dug beneath an ass chariot (*adhastād rāsabhavāhanasya*) and to be sprinkled with salty water (cf. Falk 1986: 173 with n. 485). According to Harry Falk (1986), originally the ritualistic dice game was played as follows. The gaming hole was filled with 150 'dice', i.e., nuts of the tree called *vibhītaka-*, beleric myrobalan (*Terminalia belerica*); out of these, each player in turn took a handful (*glaha-*) of dice. The number of the nuts in the handful was then counted and divided by four: depending on how many dice were left over, the result (*aya-*) was *kṛtá-* (no remainder), *trétā-* (3 nuts left over), *dvāpára-* (2 nuts left over) and *káli-* (1 nut left over). The game was continued until one of the players got the *káli-* result, which made him to personify Kali, the god of dicing and the divine leader of a band of 150 robbers, a cruel form of Rudra, the killing god of death (cf. Falk 1986: 108-111, 189). The regular place of the dice game was the gambling house (*sabhā-*), which was connected with drinking and the dead (cf. Falk 1986: 84-90, 189). In later texts, the four possible results of the dice game, *kṛtá-*, *trétā-*, *dvāpára-* and *káli-*, are connected with the "world ages", of which the present evil age, Kali-yuga, will end in the destruction of the world (cf. Macdonell and Keith 1912 II: 192-193; Koskikallio 1994). Then the "mare-mouthed" fire will consume the deluge, and from Pātāla snake Śeṣa will emit venomous fire. The etymology of the name *Kali* has remained unexplained (cf. Mayrhofer 1992 I: 322-323); the dice game's connection with *iriṇa-* 'saline soil' = Proto-Dravidian *kaẓi* 'saline soil' (DEDR 1359) suggests Kali's connection with *kaẓi* in the sense of 'death, destruction' (DEDR 1356). *Kaẓi* in the sense of 'discarded waste' (DEDR 1356) could also be behind the Sanskrit name *Śeṣa*, literally '(discarded) left-over'. The wild ass, the 'kicker of salt desert' (**kaẓ-utay*) and the prototypal toddy-drinker, is in the Dhenukavadha myth (HV 57,16) compared with Antaka, the god of death. And according to the Agni-Purāṇa (209,41d-42ab), animals belonging to Yama, the god of death, comprize the horse, any one-hoofer (including the donkey and the wild ass) and the water buffalo (*turago yamadaivataḥ | tathā caikaśaphaṃ sarvaṃ yāmyaś ca mahiṣas tathā*). Nirṛti 'Destruction' rides an ass (cf. above, 3).

93) Proto-Dravidian **-ẓ-/*-ẓ* survives only in some regional and social dialects of Tamil and Malayalam; it is inscriptionally attested in Old Kannada and Old Telugu. Elsewhere it has merged with many other phonemes, especially *ḷ*, *ḍ*, *ṛ* and *r* (see Krishnamurti 2003: 152-153), while in Central and North Dravidian, Proto-Dravidian **-ḷ-/*-ḷ* has mostly merged with *-l-/-l* or become *-ḍ-/-ḍ* (cf.

Krishnamurti 2003: 153). In Vedic and Middle Indo-Aryan, *-ḍ-* > *-ḷ-* and in North Indian manuscripts *ḷ* is regularly written *l* (cf. Hinüber 2001: 166-167).

94) Another reason is Balarāma's great strength (*bala-*). The stem of the palmyra palm is hard as stone, and the Buddha as a young prince alone among several contestants was able to pierce seven palmyra palms that stood in a row with a single arrow (cf. Mahāvastu 2 p. 75-76 and Lalitavistara 2, p. 155; this episode of the Buddha's life is depicted both in cave 16 at Ajaṇṭā and in Borobuḍur, and the trees depicted are clearly palmyra palms). In Rāmāyaṇa 4,11,47 - 4,12,9, Rāma performs the same feat. Many manuscripts here have *tāla* instead of *sāla* in the critical edition and Lefeber's translation (cf Lefeber 1994: 77-78 and 224-226; *sāla* is *Shorea robusta*). It is undoubtedly for such a reason that also Bhīṣma (cf. Mahābhārata 6,44,48) and Kṛṣṇa (Mahābhārata 16,4,5) are said to have the palmyra palm as the emblem on their banner. (See Syed 1990: 311-314 and 323-324 with Abb. 14.6-7.)

95) English *toddy* 'palm wine, fermented juice of the palmyra palm' is derived from Hindi (and Sindhi, Punjabi, Nepali, Bengali, Oriya, Bihari, Bhojpuri, Gujarati) *tāṛī*, Marathi *tāḍī* f., from Prakrit *tāḍī-*, *tālī-* and Sanskrit *tālī-* (cf. Yule and Burnell 1903: 927; Turner 1966: no. 5750; McGregor 1993: 447a).

96) In the iconic representations of Balarāma, the wine cup (*madyapātra-*, *surāmbudhi-*) is one of his standing attributes right from the earliest images of the Kuṣāṇa period (cf. Joshi 1979: 48-49).

97) Mahābhārata 1,61,91 *śeṣasyāṃśas tu nāgasya baladevo mahābalaḥ*.

98) Mahābhārata 1,189,31 *sa cāpi keśau harir udbabarha śuklam ekam aparaṃ cāpi kṛṣṇam | tau cāpi keśau viśatāṃ yadūnāṃ kule striyau rohiṇīṃ devakīṃ ca | tayor eko baladevo babhūva kṛṣṇo dvitīyaḥ keśavaḥ saṃbabhūva*; cf. also Viṣṇu-Purāṇa 5,1.

99) Mahābhārata 16,5,11 *tato gatvā keśavas taṃ dadarśa rāmaṃ vane sthitam ekam vivikte* 12 *athāpaśyad yogayuktasya tasya nāgaṃ mukhān niḥsarantaṃ mahāntaṃ | śvetaṃ* ... 13 ... *taṃ sāgaraḥ pratyagṛhṇān nāgā divyāḥ* ... 15 ... *pratyudgamya svāgatenābhyanandaṃs*.

100) Matsya-Purāṇa 2,5 *aurvānalo 'pi vikṛtiṃ gamiṣyati yugakṣaye | viṣāgniś cāpi pātālāt saṅkarṣaṇamukhacyutaḥ | bhavasyāpi lalāṭotthatṛtīyanayanānalaḥ*.

101) Rāmāyaṇa 4,39,42-47.

102) Mārkaṇḍeya-Purāṇa 21,29 *vajraketoḥ sutaś cogro dānavo 'rividāraṇaḥ | pātālaketur vikhyātaḥ pātālāntarasaṃśrayaḥ* (quoted from Böhtlingk and Roth 1865 IV: 643). Cf. also Prabodhacandrodaya 45 (Böhtlingk 1872 II: 152 no. 2955) *gandharvasya madālasāṃ ca tanayāṃ pātālaketuś chalād daityendro 'pajahāra*.

103) Mārkaṇḍeya-Purāṇa 22,6, quoted from Böhtlingk and Roth 1861 III: 314.

104) According to Mahābhārata 5,97,6, the city of Pātāla in the netherworld is so called because all the waters fall down there: *yasmād atra samagrās tāḥ patanti jalamūrtayaḥ | tasmāt pātālam ity etat khyāyate puram uttamam*.

105) Böhtlingk and Roth 1865 IV: 643; Kirfel 1920: 143; Debrunner 1954: 288; Turner 1966: no. 8054.

106) Cf. also Sanskrit *Tāla-jaṅgha-* 'palm-legged', i.e. having very long legs, as the name of a various demons and of a warrior clan (cf. Böhtlink and Roth 1861 III: 315).

107) Here, the term Bulghar-Turkic is used for the branch of Turkic that has also been called 'Bulgharic' or 'Oghuric'. Although Chuvash, the only surviving language of this branch and a direct descendant of mediaeval Volga Bulghar is today located in the Volga region of eastern Europe, Bulghar-Turkic was originally spoken in eastern Central Asia, where it influenced not only Pre-Proto-Mongolic but also other contemporary languages, notably Pre-Proto-Samoyedic.

108) Rozycki (1994: 67) sees here a parallel with Manchu *aisin* 'gold', which is often identified as a 'cognate' of Turkic (*)*altïn* < **altun* (< **alton*) id. and Mongolic **altan* (< **alton*) id. (cf. further Rybatzki 1994: 202-206), but in which the Turko-Mongolic internal cluster has an aberrant representation in Manchu. The phonological correspondences in the two items are, however, not completely parallel, though in both cases the possibility of Para-Mongolic (or Para-Turkic) languages as intermediaries cannot be ruled out.

109) In reality, the representation depends on contextual

factors on the Turkic side, and it is possible that the correspondence of Turkic **sh* to Mongolic **lj* is in some contexts regular. For a more conventional interpretation, which postulates an original cluster **lj* also for Turkic, cf. Street (1980: 290 n. 24). Altogether, the number of examples of lambdacism between Turkic and Mongolic is very small, and virtually all of them involve a consonant cluster on the Mongolian side. Shcherbak (1997: 116, 151, 178) considers these cases, including (*)*eljigen*, "enigmatic", and, indeed, they have not yet been definitively explained, although there is no question of their loanword status.

110) There is also a possible difference in the vocalism, as pointed out by Erdal (1991: 393), though the issue of the two non-high unrounded front vowels in Turkic (**e* vs. **ä*) is not definitively solved.

111) Armenian *êš*, however, is at least formally an exact cognate of Sanskrit *aśva-* 'horse', from PIE **ékwo-* 'horse'; cf., also for the semantic shift, Watkins (1970: 7). This means that, quite possibly, the Armenian item is not connected with the Near Eastern and Indo-European words for 'donkey'. Even so, it cannot be ruled out that there is a connection with the Turkic item for 'donkey'. In that case, the Turkic word would actually derive from the Indo-European word for 'horse', either via Armenian or via some other ancient Indo-European language. Alternatively, the Turkic item could represent a borrowing from a non-Indo-European source directly connected with the Sumerian data.

112) For this reason, it is also unnecessary to speculate on whether the Turkic medial consonant **sh* (= **š*) and its Mongolic counterpart **lj* incorporate a reflex of the nasal segment present in the Sumerian and Indo-European data. Most likely, the nasal was lost before the word reached Turkic. Accidentally, in some aberrant modern Mongolic languages the word has again come to contain a nasal, as in Shira Yughur *enjigen*, Santa *enzheghe*, Bonan *njige*. This nasal is a secondary reflex of the Proto-Mongolic liquid **l* and has no direct relation to the original shape of the item.

113) As mentioned earlier in this paper, the Mongolian and Gobi varieties of the wild ass are actually likely to represent two areally distinct populations of a single subspecies, rather than two separate subspecies. This taxonomy is supported by Bi Junhuai (2009), who in his recent study of the Gobi wild ass in China identifies the latter by the Latin name *Equus hemionus hemionus*.

114) I thank Volker Rybatzki for directing my attention to Hauenschild's monograph (2003), which deals specifically with the animal names in the dictionary of Makhmud al-Kashgari.

115) The initial velar **k* is in Turkological sources often written with the letter *q*, implying a back velar stop and corresponding to the back velar letter <q> used in most script systems for Turkic. However, the phonemic status of the back velar stop is ambiguous, and in many forms of Turkic it remains an allophone of the general velar stop *k*. In others, it has developed into a velar fricative (*x*).

116) The letter *v* (< **u*) denotes here a somewhat lowered back high rounded vowel which in many forms of modern Mongolian is pharyngealized. The corresponding non-pharyngealized segment *u* (< **ü*) is pronounced as regular back high rounded vowel. Thus, the original palato-velar harmonic correlation has been transformed into an opposition involving both tongue height and pharyngealization.

117) The same Chinese characters are also used to refer the Helan Mountains (Helan Shan 賀蘭山), located immediately to the west of the Yellow River Bend, and to the historical Helan Prefecture in the same region. It is unclear, however, whether there is any connection between these toponyms and the term for 'wild ass'. As far as the name of the Helan Mountains is concerned, other etymologies (not relevant here) have also been proposed, but the ultimate origin of the name remains obscure.

118) Formally, of course, **kulan* is a derivative in **-n* from **kula*, but the difference between the two items may originally have been due to morphological, rather than semantic, factors. Note that there are two types of *-n-* stems in Mongolic: those ending in an unstable *-n* (technically written as */n*), which is lost in certain morphological and syntactic positions, and those ending

in a stable *-n*, which is preserved intact in most positions. Many animal names end in the unstable *-n*, e.g., **mori/n* 'horse', **koni/n* 'sheep', **meci/n* 'monkey', in which it may originally have functioned as some kind of class (possibly gender and number) marker. The **-n* in **kulan* is, however, of the stable type, which is somewhat less common but also attested in animal names, as in **jaxan* 'elephant', a word with widespread connections, including, among others, Chinese *xiang* 象 id.

119) The term seems to have been first used in scholarly literature by Peter Simon Pallas (1774), who in the title of his description of the Mongolian wild ass expressly mentions that "*dshikketaei*" is the Mongolian appellation of the animal. Note that the description by Pallas was published in 1774, but the discovery was internationally acknowledged only in 1775, which is why the animal (subspecies) goes today under the label *Equus hemionus* Pallas 1775.

120) The Osman Turkish data may involve obsolete literary usage and must, in any case, represent a borrowing separate from the Teleut data. The word is not listed by Schönig (2000) in his treatment of Mongolic loanwords in the Western Oghuz branch of Turkic.

121) The same process is attested, as an areally conditioned feature, in most Sino-Tibetan languages, but also in many non-Sino-Tibetan languages that have evolved under the structural influence of Sino-Tibetan (including both Chinese and Tibetan, as well as others). In terms of absolute chronology, the process can be of a very varying age in the different languages in which it has been active.

122) Benedict was not aware of the fact that **mrang* 'horse' is a loanword, so he tentatively proposed an etymological connection with the homonymous Tibeto-Burman word **m-rang* 'high'.

123) It should be noted that the obstruent systems of the languages involved – Turkic, Mongolic, and Tibetan – are very different. For Turkic, only one type of initial velar stop can be reconstructed (**k*), probably originally realized as voiceless segment with or without aspiration. Mongolic, by contrast, has an old distinction between two initial velar stops (**k *g*), distinguished by either voicing or aspiration, or both. Tibetan, finally, has three distinct velar stop segments (**kh *k *g*), distinguished both by voicing (**k* vs. **g*) and by aspiration (**kh* vs. **k*). When preceded by a preinitial, however, the Tibetan initial stops make only a one-way distinction between a strong (unvoiced) and a weak (voiced) segment (**k* vs. **g*). Although we do not know the details, these paradigmatic differences may well have played a role in the transmission of the word from one language family to another.

124) The development **kl* > (*)*ky* represents a universally widespread type of phonetic change (cf., e.g., Mediaeval Latin *clavis* > Italian *chiave* 'key'). Even so, in Tibetan it cannot be regarded as a regular process. Rather, it may have been only one of the ways of doing away with the cluster **kl*.

125) According to a semi-mythical historical tradition, the 'ancestors' of the Tuyuhun had migrated to eastern Central Asia (the modern Gansu-Qinghai region) from southern Manchuria. The ethnohistorical and linguistic implications of this tradition are, however, unclear, and, in any case, it is unlikely that the Tuyuhun in later times spoke a language of a Manchurian origin (cf. Janhunen 2006).

126) Of these, Ugric and Samoyedic are ultimately related with each other in the context of the Uralic language family. The fact that they show different terms for the horse suggests that this animal was of no crucial cultural importance during the Proto-Uralic period, which seems to have been dominated by Mesolithic-level hunting and gathering. Also, the Proto-Uralic speakers may have lived outside of the area of occurrence of the (wild) horse.

127) From Sino-Tibetan, mainly from Chinese, the term has spread further to several other languages and language families of Southeast Asia, including some unclassified languages (Bai, Tujia) with a possible Sino-Tibetan connection (cf. also Huang *et al.* 1992: 90 no. 268).

128) Another possible 'wild' horse breed is the recently discovered Nangchen horse, native to a remote part of the Kham region of Tibet (southeastern Qinghai Province, China), on which cf. Peissel (1997: 229-242). Although the details are still unclarified it seems, however, that this

is a local and possibly archaic variety of the domestic horse (*Equus caballus*), adapted to the extreme conditions of the region. There is no information suggesting the existence of any terminological difference between the Nangchen horse and the regular Tibetan highland horse in the local forms of Tibetan (belonging to the Kham group of Tibetan dialects). Even so, the appearance of the Nangchen horse is surprisingly similar to that of the Mongolian wild horse, as well as to the Palaeolithic depictions of the horse in Europe.

129) Also *qulan ta/da taghï tut*, apparently with *ta/da* = *ya* functioning as a conjunction, if not *-Da* = locative case marker. This somewhat ambiguous expression seems to have given rise to Radloff's entry *qulanta, qulantai* 'wild ass', "*Kulantai*" (OSTN 2: 975), which, at least for this part, must involve a ghost word. In this connection, we also have to consider the Turkic noun (*)*tay* 'two-year old foal' (Clauson 1972: 566). The partial similarity between (*)*taghï* 'wild horse' and (*)*tay* 'foal' reminds of that between (*)*kulan* 'wild ass' and (*)*kulun* 'foal' (younger than *tay*), but it is probably wise not to see any system in this.

130) The variation between (*)*k* (*q*) and (*)*g* (*gh*) in Turkic must reflect a sporadic secondary weakening of the medial consonant. The same alternation is present in the homonymous item *takï* (*taqï*) ~ *tagï* (*taghï*) 'again, also, and' (DTS 527, 536).

131) It would take us too far on the road of speculations if we postulated a connection between **takï* and its semantically unrelated homonyms in Turkic and Mongolic. For instance, the Mongolic verb **taki-* 'to sacrifice, to worship' could offer a potentially interesting point of comparison, but in the absence of any direct evidence in the Mongolian context (in spite of the tradition of horse offerings in Central Eurasia) the comparison cannot be verified, an no further conclusions should be based on it.

132) The bisyllabic structure of the word (CVCV) might support a Mongolic, rather than Turkic origin, since final vowels have normally been dropped in Turkic (> CVC). On the other hand, the Turkic vowel could be a secondary derivative element.

133) The Armenian data often connected with the Turkic item for 'donkey' may or may not be relevant here, as noted above (note 111). In a series of genetic and areal comparisons between Indo-European and Caucasian languages, S. A. Starostin (2009: 80) connects both Sumerian *anše* ~ *anšu* and the Indo-European *equus* family with "Proto-East Caucasian" **ħɨnčwV* 'horse'. Although this comparison is made in a Nostratic spirit, and although the form(s) of the reconstruction(s) may be questioned, some the Caucasian data discussed by Starostin would certainly deserve to be incorporated into the general etymology of the Indo-European 'horse'.

References

Ajithprasad, P. (2002) 'The Pre-Harappan cultures of Gujarat', pp. 129-158, in S. Settar and Ravi Korisettar (eds.) *Protohistory: Archaeology of the Harappan Civilization*. (Indian archaeology in retrospect 2) New Delhi: Manohar.

Ajithprasad, P. (2010) 'Pre-Prabhas', paper read at an *International conference on Gujarat Harappans and Chalcolithic cultures held at Bhuj*, 28-31 January 2010.

Allchin, Bridget and Raymond Allchin (1982) *The rise of civilization in India and Pakistan*. Cambridge: Cambridge University Press.

Amîrxan, [Mustafa] (1992) *Wörterbuch Kurdisch* I: Kurdisch-Deutsch, II: Deutsch-Kurdisch. (Sprachen der Welt) Ismaning: Hueber.

[Anonymous] (1823) 'Der wilde Esel', *Isis* 1823 (7): 764.

Ardeleanu-Jansen, Alexandra (1993) *Die Terrakotten in Mohenjo-Daro: Eine Untersuchung zur keramischen Kleinplastik in Mohenjo-daro, Pakistan (ca. 2300-1900 v. Chr.)*. Aachen: Aachen University Mission.

Ball, Valentin (1885) 'On the identification of the animals and plants of India which were known to early Greek authors', *The Indian Antiquary* 14: 274-287, 303-311 and 334-341.

Banerjea, Jitendra Nath (1956) *The development of Hindu iconography*. Second revised and enlarged edition.

Calcutta: University of Calcutta.

Barbosa, Duarte ([1518] 1918-1921) *The Book of Duarte Barbosa: An account of the countries bordering on the Indian Ocean and their inhabitants, written by Duarte Barbosa, and completed about the year 1518 A.D.* Translated from the Portuguese text, first published in 1812 A.D. by the Royal Academy of Sciences at Lisbon, in Vol. II of its Collection of Documents regarding the History and Geography of the Nations beyond the Seas, and edited and annotated by Mansel Longworth Dames. I-II. (Works issued by the Hakluyt Society, 2nd series, 44 and 49) London: The Hakluyt Society.

Bashir, Elena (2003) 'Dardic', pp. 818-894, in George Cardona and Dhanesh Jain (eds.) *The Indo-Aryan languages*. (Routledge language family series) London & New York: Routledge.

Benecke, N. and R. Neef (2005) 'Faunal and plant remains from Sohr Damb / Nal: A prehistoric site (c. 3500-2000 BC) in central Balochistan (Pakistan)', pp. 81-91, in Ute Franke-Vogt and Hans-Joachim Weisshaar (eds.) *South Asian Archaeology 2003*. (Forschungen zur Archäologie aussereuropäischer Kulturen, 1) Aachen: Linden Soft.

Bennett, Emmett L. (1995) 'Aegean scripts', pp. 125-133, in Peter T. Daniels and William Bright (eds.) *The world's writing systems*. New York: Oxford University Press.

Beyer, Stephan V. (1992) *The classical Tibetan language*. Albany, N.Y.: State University of New York Press.

Bi Junhuai (2009) *Menggu yelü yanjiu, Equus hemionus hemionus, Asiatic wild ass*. Huhehaote: Nei Menggu Daxue Chubanshe.

Blyth, Edward (1859) 'On the different animals known as wild asses', *Journal of the Asiatic Society of Bengal* 28: 229-253.

Böhtlingk, Otto (1870-73) *Indische Sprüche, Sanskrit und Deutsch herausgegeben* I-III. Zweite vermehrte und verbesserte Auflage. St. Petersburg: Kaiserliche Akademie der Wissenschaften.

Böhtlingk, Otto and Rudolf Roth (1855-1875) *Sanskrit-Wörterbuch* I-VII. St. Petersburg: Kaiserliche Akademie der Wissenschaften.

Bökönyi, Sándor (1997) 'Horse remains from the prehistoric site of Surkotada, Kutch, late 3rd millennium B. C.', *South Asian Studies* 13: 297-307.

Boltz, William G. (1986) 'Early Chinese writing', *World Archaeology* 17 (3): 420-436.

Bosworth, C. E. (transl.) (1999) *The History of al-Ṭabarī translated and annotated 5: The Sāsānids, the Byzantines, the Lakhmids, and Yemen*. (SUNY series in Near Eastern Studies; Bibliotheca Persica) Albany: State University of New York Press.

Brockington, J. L. (1984) *Righteous Rāma: The evolution of an epic*. Delhi: Oxford University Press.

Brockington, John (1998) *The Sanskrit epics*. (Handbuch der Orientalistik II.12) Leiden: Brill.

Brugmann, Karl (1907-08) 'Griechisch *ínnos* und *ónos*', *Indogermanische Forschungen* 22: 197-202.

Brunt, P. A. (1976-1983) *Arrian with an English translation* I-II. (The Loeb Classical Library 236, 269) Cambridge, Mass.: Harvard University Press, & London: William Heinemann Ltd.

Buck, Carl Darling (1949) *A dictionary of selected synonyms in the principal Indo-European languages*. Chicago: The University of Chicago Press.

Burrow, T. (1967) 'Review of Turner 1966', *Journal of the Royal Asiatic Society of Great Britain and Ireland* 1967 (1): 39-42.

Burrow, T. and M. B. Emeneau (1984) *A Dravidian etymological dictionary*. Second edition. Oxford: Clarendon Press.

Caland, Willem (1911) 'Over het bijgeloof der haarwervels op het paard', *Verslagen en Mededeelingen van het Koninklijke Akademie van Wetenschappen, Afdeeling Letterkunde*, 4e Reeks, 10e Deel: 177-185.

Carpelan, Christian and Asko Parpola (2001) 'Emergence, contacts and dispersal of Proto-Indo-European, Proto-Uralic and Proto-Aryan in archaeological perspective', pp. 55-150, in : Christian Carpelan, Asko Parpola and Petteri Koskikallio (eds.) *Early contacts between Uralic and Indo-European:*

Linguistic and archaeological considerations. (Mémoires de la Société Finno-Ougrienne, 242) Helsinki: Suomalais-Ugrilainen Seura.

Chakrabarti, Dilip K. (ed.) (2004) *Indus Civilization sites in India: New discoveries.* Mumbai: Marg Publications.

CISI = *Corpus of Indus Seals and Inscriptions.* Vol. 1 (1987): Collections in India, edited by Jagat Pati Joshi and Asko Parpola. Vol. 2 (1991): Collections in Pakistan, edited by Sayid Ghulam Mustafa Shah and Asko Parpola. Vol. 3: New material, untraced objects, and collections outside India and Pakistan, edited by Asko Parpola, B. M. Pande and Petteri Koskikallio, Part 1: Mohenjo-Daro and Harappa, in collaboration with Richard H. Meadow and Jonathan Mark Kenoyer (2010). (Annales Academiae Scientiarum Fennicae, Series B 239-240 & Humaniora 359) Helsinki: Suomalainen Tiedeakatemia.

Clauson, Gerald (1972) *An etymological dictionary of Pre-Thirteenth-Century Turkish.* Oxford: Clarendon Press.

Cowell, E. B. (ed.) (1895-1913) *The Jātaka; or, Stories of the Buddha's former births. Translated from the Pāli by various hands* I-VII. Cambridge: Cambridge University Press.

Crooke, William (1926) *Religion and folklore of northern India.* London: Oxford University Press.

Daniels, Peter T. and William Bright (eds.) (2005) *The world's writing systems.* New York: Oxford University Press.

Debrunner, Albert (1954) *Die Nominalsuffixe* = Jakob Wackernagel [and Albert Debrunner], *Altindische Grammatik* II, 2. Göttingen: Vandenhoeck & Ruprecht.

DEDR = Burrow and Emeneau (1984) *A Dravidian etymological dictionary.* Second edition. Oxford: Clarendon Press.

DeFrancis, John (1989) *Visible speech: The diverse oneness of writing systems.* Honolulu: University of Hawaii Press.

Denzau, Gertrud and Helmut Denzau (1999) *Wildesel.* Stuttgart: Jan Thorbecke Verlag.

Driem, George van (2001) *Languages of the Himalayas: An ethnolinguistic handbook of the Greater Himalayan region* I-II. (Handbuch der Orientalistik II.10/1-2) Leiden: Brill.

DTS = *Drevnetyurkskij slovar'.* Leningrad: Izdatel'stvo "Nauka" (1969)

Dubova, N. A. (2004) 'Mogil'nik i tsarskij nekropol' na beregakh bol'shogo bassejna severnogo Gonura', pp. 254-281, in M. F. Kosarev, P. M. Kozhin and N. A. Dubova (eds.) *U istokov tsivilizatsii: Sbornik statej k 75-letiyu Viktora Ivanovicha Sarianidi.* Moskva: Staryj sad.

Edgerton, Franklin (1953) *Buddhist Hybrid Sanskrit grammar and dictionary* I-II. New Haven: Yale University Press.

Ehlers, Gerhard (1988) *Emendationen zum Jaiminīya-Brāhmaṇa (Zweites Buch).* (Indica et Tibetica 14) Bonn: Indica et Tibetica Verlag.

Erdal, Marcel (1991) *Old Turkic word formation: A functional approach to the lexicon.* (Turcologica 7) Wiesbaden: Otto Harrassowitz.

ESTYa = È. V. Sevortyan *et al.* (1974-2000-) *Ètimologicheskij slovar' tyurkskikh yazykov.* Moskva: Izdatel'stvo "Nauka".

Falk, Harry (1986) *Bruderschaft und Würfelspiel: Untersuchungen zur Entwicklungsgeschichte des vedischen Opfers.* Freiburg: Hedwig Falk.

Feh, C., N. Shah, M. Rowen, R. Reading and S. P. Goyal (2002) 'Status and action plan for the Asiatic wild ass (*Equus hemionus*)', Chapter 5, pp. 62-71, in P. D. Moehlman (ed.) *Equids: Zebras, asses, and horses: Status survey and conservation action plan.* Gland (Switzerland) and Cambridge: IUCN/SCC Equid Specialist Group, IUCN (The World Conservation Union).

Findly, E. Banks (1979) 'The 'Child of the Waters': A revaluation of Vedic Apāṃ Napāt', *Numen* 26: 164-184.

Frisk, Hjalmar (1960-1970) *Griechisches etymologisches*

Wörterbuch I-II. Heidelberg: Carl Winter — Universitätsverlag.

Fuller, Dorian Q. (2003) 'An agricultural perspective on Dravidian historical linguistics: Archaeological crop packages, livestock and Dravidian crop vocabulary', pp. 191-213, in Peter Bellwood and Colin Renfrew (eds.) *Examining the farming / language dispersal hypothesis*. Cambridge: McDonald Institute for Archaeological Research.

Fuller, Dorian Q. (2006a) 'Agricultural origins and frontiers in South Asia: A working synthesis', *Journal of World Prehistory* 20: 1-86.

Fuller, Dorian Q. (2006b) 'Silence before sedentism and the advent of cash-crop: A status report on early agriculture in South Asia from plant domestication to the development of political economies (with an excursus on the problem of semantic shift among millet and rice)', pp. 175-213, in T. Osada (ed.) *Proceedings of the Pre-symposium of RIHN and the 7th ESCA Harvard-Kyoto Roundtable*. Kyoto: Research Institute for Humanity and Nature.

Fuller, Dorian Q., Nicole Boivin and Ravi Korisettar (2007) 'Dating the Neolithic of South India: New Radiometric evidence for key economic, social and ritual transformations', *Antiquity* 81 (313): 755-778.

Fussman, Gérard (1972) *Atlas linguistique des parlers dardes et kafirs* I-II. (Publications de l'École Française d'Extrême-Orient 86) Paris: École Française d'Extrême-Orient.

Gamkrelidze, Thomas V. and Vjačeslav V. Ivanov (1995) *Indo-European and the Indo-Europeans: A reconstruction and historical analysis of a proto-language and a proto-culture* I-II. English version by Johanna Nichols, edited by Werner Winter. (Trends in Linguistics, Studies and monographs 80) Berlin & New York: Mouton De Gruyter.

Gardiner, Alan (1957) *Egyptian grammar, being an introduction to the study of hieroglyphs*. Third edition, revised. London: Oxford University Press.

Geldner, Karl F. (1951-1957) *Der Rigveda aus dem Sanskrit ins Deutsche übersetzt und mit einem laufenden Kommentar versehen* I-IV. (Harvard Oriental Series 33-36) Cambridge, Mass.: Harvard University Press.

Ghosh, A. (ed.) (1989) *An encyclopaedia of Indian archaeology* I-II. New Delhi: Munshiram Manoharlal.

Giles, Herbert A. (1909-1912) *A Chinese-English dictionary*. Second edition, revised and enlarged. Shanghai, Hong Kong, Singapore: Kelly & Walsh Limited.

Glasenapp, Helmuth von (1925) *Der Jainismus: Eine indische Erlösungsreligion, nach den Quellen dargestellt*. (Kultur und Weltanschauung, 1) Berlin: Alf Hägel Verlag.

Gray, Annie P. (1971) *Mammalian hybrids: A check-list with bibliography*. Second, revised, edition. (Technical communication ... of the Commonwealth Bureau of Animal Breeding and Genetics, no. 10) Farnham Royal: Commonwealth Agricultural Bureaux.

Groves, Colin P. (1986) 'The taxonomy, distribution, and adaptations of recent equids', pp. 11-65, in Richard H. Meadow and Hans-Peter Uerpmann (eds.) *Equids in the ancient world* [I]. (Beihefte zum Tübinger Atlas des Vorderen Orients, Reihe A, Nr. 19/1) Wiesbaden: Dr Ludwig Reichert Verlag.

Haenisch, Erich (1962) *Wörterbuch zu Manghol un Niuca Tobca'an (Yüan-ch'ao Pi-shi)*. Wiesbaden: Franz Steiner Verlag GmbH.

Hart, George L. III (1975) *The poems of ancient Tamil: Their milieu and their Sanskrit counterparts*. Berkeley: University of California Press.

Hart, George Luzerne (1976) *The relation between Tamil and classical Sanskrit literature*. (A history of Indian literature, Volume X, Fasc. 2) Wiesbaden: Otto Harrassowitz.

Ḥasandust, Muḥammad (1383 [i.e., 2004]) *Farhang-i rīšašināḫtī-i zabān-i Fārsī (An etymological dictionary of Persian language)* Vol. 1. Tehran: Iranian Academy of Persian language and literature.

Hauenschild, Ingeborg (2003) *Die Tierbezeichnungen bei*

Mahmud al-Kaschgari: Eine Untersuchung aus sprach- und kulturhistorischer Sicht. (Turcologica 53) Wiesbaden: Harrassowitz Verlag.

Hawkins, R. E. (ed.) (1986) *Encyclopedia of Indian natural history.* Delhi: Published on behalf of the Bombay Natural History Society by Oxford University Press.

Hinüber, Oskar von (2001) *Das ältere Mittelindisch im Überblick.* 2., erweiterte Auflage. (Österreichische Akademie der Wissenschaften, Philosophisch-historische Klasse, Sitzungsberichte 467) Wien: Verlag der Österreichischen Akademie der Wissenschaften.

Hinz, Walther (1969) 'Die Schrift der Elamer', pp. 222-227, in Ulrich Hausmann (Hrsg.) *Allgemeine Grundlagen der Archäologie.* München: C. H. Beck.

Hopkins, E. Washburn (1915) *Epic mythology.* (Grundriss der indo-arischen Philologie und Altertumskunde III.1.B) Strassburg: Karl J. Trübner.

Horn, Paul (1893) *Grundriss der neupersischen Etymologie.* (Sammlung indogermanischer Wörterbücher 4.) Strassburg: Verlag von Karl J. Trübner.

Huang Bufan *et al.* (eds.) (1992) *Zang-Mian yuzu yuyan cihui / A Tibeto-Burman lexicon.* Beijing: Zhongyang Minzu Xueyuan Chubanshe.

Jaini, Padmanabh S. (1979) *The Jaina path of purification.* Berkeley: The University of California Press.

Janhunen, Juha (1996) *Manchuria: An ethnic history.* (Mémoires de la Société Finno-Ougrienne 222) Helsinki: The Finno-Ugrian Society.

Janhunen, Juha (1998) 'The horse in East Asia: Reviewing the linguistic evidence', pp. 415-430, in Victor H. Mair (ed.) *The Bronze Age and Early Iron Age peoples of Eastern Central Asia* I. Washington, D.C.: The Institute for the Study of Man.

Janhunen, Juha (2006) 'From Manchuria to Amdo Qinghai: On the ethnic implications of the Tuyuhun migration', pp. 107-119, in Alessandra Pozzi, Juha Janhunen and Michael Weiers (eds.) *Tumen jalafun jecen akû: Manchu studies in honour of Giovanni Stary* (Tunguso-Sibirica 20) Wiesbaden: Harrassowitz Verlag.

Jäschke, H. A. (1881) *A Tibetan-English dictionary with special reference to the prevailing dialects.* London: Trübner & Co.

Joshi, N. P. (1979) *Iconography of Balarāma.* New Delhi: Abhinav Publications.

Kala, Jayantika (1988) *Epic scenes in Indian plastic arts.* New Delhi: Abhinav Publications.

Karttunen, Klaus (1997) *India and the Hellenistic world.* (Studia Orientalia 83) Helsinki: The Finnish Oriental Society.

Keith, Arthur Berriedale (1909) *The Aitareya Āraṇyaka, edited ... with introduction, translation, notes, indexes and an appendix ...* (Anecdota Oxoniensia, Aryan series, 9) Oxford: Clarendon Press.

Kirfel, Willibald (1920) *Die Kosmographie der Inder, nach den Quellen dargestellt.* Bonn: Kurt Schroeder.

Kosarev, M. F., P. M. Kozhin and N. A. Dubova (eds.) (2004) *U istokov tsivilizatsii: Sbornik statej k 75-letiyu Viktora Ivanovicha Sarianidi.* Moskva: Staryj sad.

Koskikallio, Petteri (1994) 'When time turns: Yugas, ideologies, sacrifices', *Studia Orientalia* 73: 253-271.

Krishnamurti, Bhadriraju (2003) *The Dravidian languages.* (Cambridge language surveys) Cambridge: Cambridge University Press.

Kumar, L. S. S., A. C. Aggarwalla, H. R. Arakeri, M. G. Kamath, and Earl N. Moore in collaboration with Roy L. Donahue (1963) *Agriculture in India III: Animals.* London: Asia Publishing House.

Lambrick, H. T. (1964) *Sind: A general introduction.* Hyderabad (Sind): Sindhi Adabi Board.

Lefeber, Rosalind (1994) *The Rāmāyaṇa of Vālmīki, an epic of ancient India IV: Kiṣkindhākāṇḍa. Introduction, annotation and translation.* Edited by Robert P. Goldman. Princeton: Princeton University Press.

Lessing, Ferdinand (ed.) (1960) *Mongolian-English dictionary.* Berkeley and Los Angeles: University of California Press.

Levine, Marsha, Colin Renfrew and Katie Boyle (eds.)

(2003) *Prehistoric steppe adaptation and the horse.* Cambridge: McDonald Institute for Archaeological Research.

Liddell, Henry George and Robert Scott (1940) *A Greek-English lexicon.* A new edition, revised and augmented throughout by Henry Stuart Jones. Oxford: Clarendon Press.

Ligeti, Louis (1966) *Un vocabulaire sino-ouigour des Ming: Le Kao-tch'ang-kouan yi-chou du Bureau des traducteurs.* (Dissertationes sodalium Instituti Asiae interioris 11) Budapestini: Institutum Asiae Interioris.

Liu Mau-tsai (ed.) (1958) *Die chinesischen Nachrichten zur Geschichte der Ost-Türken (T'u-Küe).* (Göttinger asiatische Forschungen 10) Wiesbaden: Otto Harrassowitz.

Lubotsky, Alexander (1997) *A Ṛgvedic word concordance* I-II. (American Oriental Series 82) New Haven: American Oriental Society.

Lüders, Heinrich (1942) 'Von den indischen Tieren', *Zeitschrift der Deutschen Morgenländischen Gesellschaft* 96: 23-81.

Macdonell, A. A. and A. B. Keith (1912) *Vedic index of names and subjects* I-II. London: John Murray.

MacKinnon, John and Kathy MacKinnon (1974) *Animals of Asia: The ecology of the oriental region.* London: Peter Lowe & New York: Holt, Rinehart & Winston.

Maekawa, Kazuya (2006) 'The donkey and the Persian onager in late third millennium B. C. Mesopotamia and Syria: A rethinking', *Nishi Ajia Koukogaku* (Journal of West Asian Archaeology) 7: 1-19 (in Japanese with an English summary).

Malamoud, Charles (1976) 'Village et forêt dans l'idéologie de l'Inde brahmanique', *Archives Européennes de Sociologie* 17 (1): 3-20.

Marshall, Fiona (2007) 'African pastoral perspectives on domestication of the donkey: A first synthesis', pp. 537-594, in T. P. Denham, J. Iriarte and L. Vrydaghs (eds.) *Rethinking agriculture: Archaeological and ethnoarchaeological perspectives.* London: University College London Press.

Mayrhofer, Manfred (1992-2001) *Etymologisches Wörterbuch des Altindoarischen* I-III. (Indogermanische Bibliothek, Reihe 2: Wörterbücher) Heidelberg: Universitätsverlag Carl Winter.

McGregor, R. S. (ed.) (1993) *The Oxford Hindi-English dictionary.* Oxford and Delhi: Oxford University Press.

Meadow, Richard H. (1988) 'La domestication et l'exploitation des plantes et des animaux dans les régions du système de l'Indus du VIIe au IIe millénaire avant notre ère', pp. 38-43, in *Les cités oubliées de l'Indus: Archéologie de Pakistan.* Paris: Association Française d'Action Artistique.

Meadow, R. (1993) 'Continuity and change in the agriculture of the Greater Indus Valley', *International Association for the Study of the Cultures of Central Asia Information Bulletin* 19: 63-77.

Meadow, Richard H. and Ajita K. Patel (1997) 'A comment on "Horse remains from Surkotada" by Sándor Bökönyi', *South Asian Studies* 13: 308-315.

Meadow, Richard H. and Ajita K. Patel (2002) 'From Mehrgarh to Harappa and Dholavira: Prehistoric pastoralism in north-western South Asia through the Harappan period', pp. 391-408, in S. Settar and Ravi Korisettar (eds.) *Protohistory: Archaeology of the Harappan Civilization.* (Indian archaeology in retrospect 2) New Delhi: Manohar.

Meadow, Richard H. and Hans-Peter Uerpmann (eds.) (1986) *Equids in the ancient world* [I]. (Beihefte zum Tübinger Atlas des Vorderen Orients, Reihe A, Nr. 19/1) Wiesbaden: Dr Ludwig Reichert Verlag.

Melchert, H. Craig (1995) 'Anatolian hieroglyphs', pp. 120-124, in Peter T. Daniels and William Bright (eds.) *The world's writing systems.* New York: Oxford University Press.

Meulenbeld, G. Jan (1999-2002) *A history of Indian medical literature* I-III. (Groningen Oriental Studies, 15) Groningen: Egbert Forsten.

Meyer, Johann Jakob (1937) *Trilogie altindischer Mächte*

und Feste der Vegetation: Ein Beitrag zur vergleichenden Religions- und Kulturgeschichte, Fest- und Volkskunde I-III. Zürich und Leipzig: Max Niehans.

Moehlman, P. D. (ed.) (2002) *Equids: Zebras, asses, and horses: Status survey and conservation action plan.* Gland (Switzerland) and Cambridge: IUCN/ SCC Equid Specialist Group, IUCN (The World Conservation Union).

Molè, Gabriella (1970) *The T'u-yü-hun from the Northern Wei to the time of the Five Dynasties.* (Serie Orientale Roma 41) Roma: Istituto Italiano per il Medio ed Estremo Oriente.

Moore, Katherine M. (1993) 'Animal use at Bronze Age Gonur Depe', *International Association for the Study of the Cultures of Cental Asia Information Bulletin* 19: 164-176.

Morgenstierne, Georg (1932) *Report on a linguistic mission to north-western India.* (Instituttet for sammenlignende kulturforskning, Serie C III, 1) Oslo: Instituttet for sammenlignende kulturforskning.

Morgenstierne, Georg (2003) *A new etymological vocabulary of Pashto.* Compiled and edited by J. Elfenbein, D. N. MacKenzie and Nicholas Sims-Williams. (Beiträge zur Iranistik, 23) Wiesbaden: Dr. Ludwig Reichert Verlag.

Mostaert, Antoine (1941-1942) *Dictionnaire ordos.* (Monumenta Serica, Monograph 5) Peking: The Catholic University.

Naissance de l'écriture: Cunéiformes et hiéroglyphes. Paris: Éditions de la Réunion des musées nationaux (1982)

Norman, Jerry (1978) *A concise Manchu-English lexicon.* Seattle and London: University of Washington Press.

Oates, Joan (2003) 'A note on the early evidence for horse in western Asia', pp. 115-125, in Marsha Levine, Colin Renfrew and Katie Boyle (eds.) *Prehistoric steppe adaptation and the horse.* Cambridge: McDonald Institute for Archaeological Research.

Oertel, Hanns (1951) 'Ai. *viḻabā* für *vaḍabā* und *vāgarā* für *vāgurā*', *Zeitschrift für vergleichende Sprachforschung* 69: 29-30.

O'Flaherty, Wendy Doniger (1971) 'The submarine mare in the mythology of Śiva', *Journal of the Royal Asiatic Society of Great Britain and Ireland* 1971 (1): 9-27.

O'Flaherty, Wendy Doniger (1979) 'Sacred cows and profane mares in Indian mythology', *History of Religions* 19 (1): 1-26.

Olivelle, Patrick (1998) *The early Upaniṣads. Annotated text and translation.* New York: Oxford University Press.

Olivelle, Patrick (2000) *Dharmasūtras: The Law Codes of Āpastamba, Gautama, Baudhāyana, and Vasiṣṭha. Annotated text and translation.* Delhi: Motilal Banarsidass Publishers.

Osada, Toshiki (ed.) (2006) *Proceedings of the Pre-symposium of RIHN and the 7th ESCA Harvard-Kyoto Roundtable.* Kyoto: Research Institute for Humanity and Nature.

OSTN = Radloff, Wilhelm [V. V. Radlov] (1893-1911) *Opyt slovarya tyurkskikh narechij* 1-4. S. Peterburg: Tipografiya Imperatorskoj Akademii Nauk.

The Oxford school atlas. 25th ed. Delhi: Oxford University Press.

Pallas, P. S. (1774) 'Equus hemionus, Mongolis dshikketaei dictus', *Novi Commentarii Academiae Scientiarum Imperialis Petropolitanae* 19: 394-417.

Parpola, Asko (1983) 'The Pre-Vedic Indian background of the Śrauta rituals', pp. 41-75, in Frits Staal (ed.) *Agni: The Vedic ritual of the Fire Altar* II. Berkeley: Asian Humanities Press.

Parpola, Asko (1994) *Deciphering the Indus script.* Cambridge: Cambridge University Press.

Parpola, Asko (2004) 'Gandhāra Graves and the Gharma pot, the Nāsatyas and the nose: In pursuit of the chariot twins', pp. 102-128, in M. F. Kosarev, P. M. Kozhin and N. A. Dubova (eds.) *U istokov tsivilizatsii: Sbornik statej k 75-letiyu Viktora Ivanovicha Sarianidi.* Moskva: Staryj sad.

Parpola, Asko (2005) 'The Nāsatyas, the chariot and Proto-

Aryan religion', *Journal of Indological Studies* 16 & 17: 1-63.

Parpola, Asko (2008) 'Proto-Indo-European speakers of the Late Tripolye culture as the inventors of wheeled vehicles: Linguistic and archaeological considerations of the PIE homeland problem', pp. 1-59, in Karlene Jones-Bley, Martin E. Huld, Angela Della Volpe, and Miriam Robbins Dexter (eds.) *Proceedings of the 19th Annual UCLA Indo-European Conference, Los Angeles, November 2-3, 2007.* (Journal of Indo-European Monograph 54) Washington, D. C.: Institute for the Study of Man.

Parpola, Asko (2009a) ''Hind leg' + 'fish': Towards further understanding of the Indus script', *Scripta* 1: 37-76.

Parpola, Asko (2009b) 'The face urns of Gandhāra and the Nāsatya cult', pp. 149-162, in Michael Willis (gen. ed.) *Migration, trade, and peoples* (European Association of South Asian Archaeologists, Proceedings of the Eighteenth Congress, London, 2005), Part 3: Aryans and nomads, edited by Asko Parpola. London: The British Association for South Asian Studies, The British Academy.

Parpola, Asko (2009c) 'The Asiatic wild ass in Harappan, Dravidian and Indo-Iranian record', pp. 33-35, in *13th Harvard University round table Ethnogenesis of South and Central Asia (ESCA), Kyoto session, Research Institute for Humanity and Nature, 30-31 May 2009.* Kyoto: Research Institute for Humanity and Nature.

Parpola, Asko (2010a) 'The Indus script, Harappan Dravidian and the wild ass', paper presented at the *World Classical Tamil Conference in Coimbatore, June 2010.*

Parpola, Asko (2010b) 'The Indus script and the wild ass', *The Hindu* 23 June 2010. http://www.hindu.com/2010/06/23/stories/2010062353871300.htm

Parpola, Asko and Juha Janhunen (2010) 'On the Asiatic wild asses (*Equus hemionus* & *Equus kiang*) and their vernacular names', pp. 423-466, in P. M. Kozhin, M. F. Kosarev and N. A. Dubova (eds.) *Na puti otkrytiya tsivilizatsii: Sbornik statej k 80-letiyu V. I. Sarianidi.* (Trudy Margianskoj arkheologicheskoj èkspeditsii, tom 3.) Sankt-Peterburg: Aleteia. (The first version of the present article, submitted in May 2009)

Peissel, Michel (1997) *The last Barbarians: The discovery of the source of the Mekong in Tibet.* New York: Henry Holt & Company, Inc.

Platts, John T. (1884) *A dictionary of Urdū, classical Hindī, and English.* London: W. H. Allen & Co.

Pokorny, Julius (1959) *Indogermanisches etymologisches Wörterbuch* I. Basel: A. Francke Verlag.

Pollock, Sheldon I. (1984) *The Rāmāyaṇa of Vālmīki, an epic of ancient India II: Araṇyakāṇḍa. Introduction, annotation and translation.* Edited by Robert P. Goldman. Princeton: Princeton University Press.

Pollock, Sheldon I. (1990) *The Rāmāyaṇa of Vālmīki, an epic of ancient India III: Ayodhyākāṇḍa. Introduction, annotation and translation.* Edited by Robert P. Goldman. Princeton: Princeton University Press.

Possehl, Gregory L. (1999) *Indus Age: The beginnings.* New Delhi: Oxford & IBH Publishing Co.

Postgate, Nicholas (1986) 'The equids of Sumer, again', pp. 194-206, in Richard H. Meadow and Hans-Peter Uerpmann (eds.) *Equids in the ancient world* [I]. (Beihefte zum Tübinger Atlas des Vorderen Orients, Reihe A, Nr. 19/1) Wiesbaden: Dr Ludwig Reichert Verlag.

Potts, D. T. (1999) *The archaeology of Elam: Formation and transformation of an ancient Iranian state.* Cambridge: Cambridge University Press.

Potts, D. T. (2006) 'An ass for Ares', *Bulletin of the Asia Institute* 16 (2002): 103-115.

Prater, S. H. (1971) *The book of Indian animals.* Third edition. Bombay: Bombay Natural History Society.

Przheval'skij, N. M. (1888) *Ot Kyakhty na istoki Zheltoi Reki, izsledovanie severnoj okrainy Tibeta i put' cherez Lob-nor po bassejnu Tarima.* S.-Peterburg: Izdanie

Imperatorskago Russkago Geograficheskago Obshchestva.

Räsänen, Martti (1969) *Versuch eines etymologischen Wörterbuchs der Türksprachen.* (Lexica Societatis Fenno-Ugricae XVII) Helsinki: Suomalais-Ugrilainen Seura.

Ratnachandraji Maharaj (1923-38) *An illustrated Ardha-Magadhi dictionary* I-V. Indore: Kesarichand Bhandari.

Rau, Wilhelm (1980-81) 'A note on the donkey and the mule in early Vedic literature', *The Adyar Library Bulletin* 44-45: 179-189.

Risch, Ernst (1949) 'Griechische Determinativkomposita', *Indogermanische Forschungen* 59: 1-61 & 245-294.

Roberts, T. J. (1977) *The mammals of Pakistan.* London: Ernest Benn Limited.

Rocher, Ludo (1986) *The Purāṇas.* (A history of Indian literature, II: 3.) Wiesbaden: Otto Harrassowitz.

Rossel, S., F. Marshall, J. Peters, T. Pilgram, M.D. Adams and D. O'Connor (2008) 'Domestication of the donkey: New data on timing, processes and indicators', *Proceedings of the National Academy of Sciences* 105: 3715-3720.

Rossi, Adriano V. (1979) *Iranian lexical elements in Brahui.* (Istituto Universitario Orientale, Seminario di Studi Asiatici, Series minor 8) Naples.

Rozycki, William (1994) *Mongol elements in Manchu.* (Indiana University Uralic and Altaic Series 157) Bloomington: Research Institute for Inner Asian Studies.

Rybatzki, Volker (1994) 'Bemerkungen zur türkischen und mongolischen Metallterminologie', *Studia Orientalia* 73: 193-251.

Rybatzki, Volker (2006) *Die Personennamen und Titel der mittelmongolischen Dokumente: Eine lexikalische Untersuchung.* (Publications of the Institute for Asian and African Studies 8) Helsinki.

Sakaki, Ryouzaburou (1916) *Bon-Zou-Kan-Wa yon'yaku taikou: Hon'yaku myougi taishuu [Mahāvyutpatti]* I. (Kyouto Teikoku Daigaku Bunka Daigaku Shousho 3) Kyouto: Shingonshuu Kyouto Daigaku.

Sarianidi, Victor (2007) *Necropolis of Gonur.* Athens: Kapon editions.

Sarianidis, V. I. (2008) *Zoroastrianism: A new motherland for an old religion.* Athens: Publishing House Kyriakidis Brothers a.s.

Sataev, R. M. (2008) 'Zhivotnye iz raskopok gorodishcha Gonur-Depe', pp. 138-142, in V. I. Sarianidi (gl. red.) *Trudy Margianskoj arkheologicheskoj èkspeditsii* 2. Moskva: Institut ètnologii i antropologii im. N. N. Miklukho-Maklaya, RAN.

Scheil, Vincent (1923) *Textes de comptabilité proto-élamites (nouvelle série).* (Mémoires de la Mission Archéologique de Perse, Mission de Susiane 17) Paris: Ernest Leroux.

Schmidt, Richard (1928) *Nachträge zum Sanskrit-Wörterbuch in kürzerer Fassung von Otto Böhtlingk.* Hannover: Orient-Buchhandlung Heinz Lafaire.

Schönig, Claus (2000) *Mongolische Lehnwörter im Westoghusischen.* (Turcologica 47) Wiesbaden: Harrassowitz Verlag.

Schrader, Otto (1901) *Reallexikon der indogermanischen Altertumskunde.* Strassburg: Karl J. Trübner.

Schuessler, Axel (2007) *An etymological dictionary of Old Chinese.* (ABC Dictionary Series) Honolulu: University of Hawai'i Press.

Settar, S. and Ravi Korisettar (eds.) (2002) *Protohistory: Archaeology of the Harappan Civilization.* (Indian archaeology in retrospect 2) New Delhi: Manohar.

Shah, N., A. St. Louis, Z. Huibin, W. Bleisch, J. van Gruissen and Q. Qureshi (2008) *Equus kiang.* In IUCN 2008. 2008 IUCN Red List of Threatened Species. <www.iucnredlist.org>.

Shcherbak, A. M. (1997) *Rannie tyurko-mongol'skie yazykovye svyazi (VIII-XIV vv).* Sankt-Peterburg: Rossijskaya akademiya nauk, Institut lingvisticheskikh issledovanij.

Sherratt, Andrew (2003) 'The horse and the wheel: The dialectics of change in the Circum-Pontic region and adjacent areas, 4500-1500 BC', pp. 233-252, in Marsha Levine, Colin Renfrew and Katie

Boyle (eds.) *Prehistoric steppe adaptation and the horse.* Cambridge: McDonald Institute for Archaeological Research.

Sheth, Hargovind Das T. (1963) *Pāia-sadda-mahaṇṇavo: A comprehensive Prakrit-Hindi dictionary.* 2nd ed. (Prakrit Text Society series 7) Varanasi: Prakrit Text Society.

Smith, Brian K. (1994) *Classifying the universe: The ancient Indian varṇa system and the origins of caste.* New York: Oxford University Press.

Sörensen, Sören (1925) *An index to the names in the Mahābhārata.* London: Ernest Benn.

Southworth, Franklin C. (2005) *Linguistic archaeology of South Asia.* London: RoutledgeCurzon.

Southworth, F. C. (2006) 'Proto-Dravidian agriculture', pp. 121-150, in T. Osada (ed.) *Proceedings of the Pre-symposium of RIHN and the 7th ESCA Harvard-Kyoto Roundtable.* Kyoto: Research Institute for Humanity and Nature.

Starostin, S. A. (2009[1988]) 'Indo-European-North Caucasian Isoglosses', *Mother Tongue* (Journal of the Association for the Study of Language in Prehistory) 14. (Originally published in Russian)

Steblin-Kamenskij, I. M. (1999) *Ètimologicheskij slovar' vakhanskogo yazyka.* Sankt-Peterburg: Sankt-Peterburgskij Gosudarstvennyj Universitet.

Steingass, F. (1892) *A comprehensive Persian-English dictionary.* London: Sampson Low, Marston & Company.

Street, John (1980) 'Proto-Altaic *-l(V)b- > Turkic š', *Central Asiatic Journal* 24(3-4): 287-302.

Sun, Zhu (ed.) (1990) *Menggu yuzu yuyan cidian.* Xining: Qinghai Renmin Chubanshe.

Syed, Renate (1990) *Die Flora Altindiens in Literatur und Kunst.* München. (Diss.)

Tegetmeier, W. B. and C. L. Sutherland (1895) *Horses, asses, zebras, mules, and mule breeding.* London: Horace Cox.

Thomas, P. K. (2002) 'Investigations into the archaeofauna of Harappan sites in western India', pp. 409-420, in S. Settar and Ravi Korisettar (eds.) *Protohistory: Archaeology of the Harappan Civilization.* (Indian archaeology in retrospect 2) New Delhi: Manohar.

Tikkanen, Bertil (1987) *The Sanskrit gerund: A synchronic, diachronic and typological analysis.* (Studia Orientalia, 62) Helsinki: The Finnish Oriental Society.

TL = *Tamil lexicon, published under the authority of the University of Madras* I-VI and Supplement, 1924-1939. Madras: University of Madras.

TMEN = Doerfer, Gerhard (1963-1975) *Türkische und mongolische Elemente im Neupersischen* 1-4. Wiesbaden: Franz Steiner Verlag GmbH.

Tod, James (1914[1829-1832]) *Annals and antiquities of Rajast'han, or, The central and western Rajpoot states of India* I-II. Popular edition, with a preface by Douglas Sladen. London: George Routledge & Sons Ltd.

Tod, James (1920[1829-1832]) *Annals and antiquities of Rajasthan, or, The central and western Rajput states of India* I-III. Edited with an introduction and notes by William Crooke. London: Humphrey Milford, Oxford University Press.

Turner, Ralph L. (1966) *A comparative dictionary of the Indo-Aryan languages.* London: Oxford University Press.

Turner, Ralph L. (1969) 'Type aśvatará- in New Indo-Aryan', pp. 319-320, in J. C. Heesterman *et al.* (eds.), *Pratidānam: Indian, Iranian and Indo-European studies presented to Franciscus Bernardus Jacobus Kuiper on his sixtieth birthday.* (Janua linguarum, Series maior 34) The Hague: Mouton & Co.

Turner, Ralph L. (1985) *A comparative dictionary of the Indo-Aryan languages: Addenda and corrigenda.* Edited by J. C. Wright. London: School of Oriental and African Studies, University of London.

Uesugi, Akinori (2010) 'Ceramic styles in the pre-/Early Harappan period in India and Pakistan: A comparative study', paper read at an *International conference on Gujarat Harappans and Chalcolithic cultures held at Bhuj,* 28-31 January 2010.

Vaidya, Parashuram Lakshman (ed.) (1969) *The Harivaṃśa,*

being the Khila or Supplement to the Mahābhārata, for the first time critically edited I. Poona: Bhandarkar Oriental Research Institute.

Varmmā, Rāmcandra (1990-93) *Mānak hindī koś* I-V. 2nd ed. Prayāg: Hindī Sāhitya Sammelan.

Vasmer, Max (Maks Fasmer) (1964-1973) *Ètimologicheskij slovar' russkogo yazyka* 1-4. Perevod s nemetskogo i dopolneniya O. N. Trubacheva. Moskva: Izdatel'stvo "Progress".

Vats, M. S. (1940) *Excavations at Harappa* I-II. Delhi: Manager of Publications.

Watkins, Calvert (1970) 'Language of gods and language of men: Remarks on some Indo-European metalinguistic traditions', pp. 1-17, in Jaan Puhvel (ed.) *Myth and law among the Indo-Europeans.* Berkeley: University of California Press.

Walde, Alois (1938-1954) *Lateinisches etymologisches Wörterbuch.* Dritte, neubearbeitete Auflage von J. B. Hofmann. I-II. (Indogermanische Bibliothek, Zweite Reihe: Wörterbücher) Heidelberg: Carl Winter.

Walser, Gerold (1966) *Die Völkerschaften auf den Reliefs von Persepolis. Historische Studien über den sogenannten Tributzug an der Apadanatreppe.* (Teheraner Forschungen 3) Berlin: Verlag Gebr. Mann.

Watt, George (1889-1896) *A dictionary of the economic products of India* I-VI and Index. Calcutta: Superintendent of Government Printing.

Wells, Bryan Kenneth (2006) *Epigraphic approaches to Indus writing.* (Ph. D. thesis, Harvard University) Cambridge, MA.

Wikipedia: http://en.wikipedia.org/wiki/

Winslow, M., *et al.* (1888) *English and Tamil dictionary for the use of students and colleges.* Third edition, enlarged, improved and romanized by C. Appasamy Pillai. Madras: Higginbotham & Co.

Winternitz, M. (1910) *A general index to the names and subject-matter of the Sacred Books of the East.* (Sacred Books of the East, 50) Oxford: Clarendon Press.

Wirth, Gerhard and Oskar von Hinüber (1985) *Arrian: Der Alexanderzug & Indische Geschichte, Griechisch und deutsch herausgegeben und übersetzt.* (Sammlung Tusculum) München & Zürich: Artemis Verlag.

Yule, Henry (1903) *The Book of Ser Marco Polo the Venetian concerning the kingdoms and marvels of the east, translated and edited, with notes.* Third edition, revised throughout in the light of recent discoveries by Henri Cordier. I-II. London: John Murray.

Yule, Henry, and A. C. Burnell (1903) *Hobson-Jobson: A glossary of colloquial Anglo-Indian words and phrases, and of kindred terms, etymological, historical, geographical and discursive.* New edition edited by William Crooke. London: John Murray.

Zarins, Juris (1986) 'Equids associated with human burials in third millennium B. C. Mesopotamia: Two complementary facets', pp. 164-193, in R. H. Meadow and Hans-Peter Uerpmann (eds.) *Equids in the ancient world [I].* (Beihefte zum Tübinger Atlas des Vorderen Orients, Reihe A, Nr. 19/1) Wiesbaden: Dr Ludwig Reichert Verlag.

Zeller, Gabriele (1990) *Die vedischen Zwillingsgötter: Untersuchungen zur Genese ihres Kultes.* Wiesbaden: Otto Harrassowitz.

The Harappan unicorn in Eurasian and South Asian perspectives

Asko Parpola
University of Helsinki

Abstract

The most frequently occurring iconographic motif of the Indus seals, with thousands of occurrences, is a unicorn bull, a male bovine animal with a single horn. Its exact zoological identity is still controversial, but while some scholars consider it to be a purely fabulous beast, perhaps a conflation of two or more real species, many authorities consider it to represent either the humpless wild cow called aurochs or urus (*Bos primigenius*) or the humpless taurine cow (*Bos taurus*). The religious meaning of the Harappan unicorn has remained unclear as well. The present study tries to solve this problem by considering both Eurasian unicorn myths and those which are particular to South Asia, as well as their historical evolution and context. The evidence strongly suggests that the Harappan unicorn was an integral part of this unicorn mythology, that it stood for male creative power, and that its cult purported to secure rain and fertility for purposes of agriculture and animal husbandry. The Harappan unicorn was probably originally the humpless bull of Western Asia, and then transformed in the Indus Valley into an image of the blue bull, the nilgai antelope (*Boselaphus tragocamelus*).

1. The unicorn myth of medieval European bestiaries

People today probably know the 'unicorn' mainly from Hergé's *Tintin* comic books and from heraldry, especially the royal coat-of-arms of the United Kingdom (Figure 1), whose supporters symbolize the union of England (the lion) and Scotland (the unicorn)[1].

The unicorn[2] was a popular beast in medieval "bestiaries" with their moralizing descriptions of real and mythical animals. It was usually depicted as a real animal (horsc-like, but sometimes as an antelope or a goat) with a long, sharp, twisted horn set in the middle of its forehead. An excellent example can be found in the first printed travelogue, Bernhard von Breydenbach's *Peregrinatio in terram sanctam* of 1486; since the author claims to have seen it in the Holy Land, its model may have been the oryx antelope (Figure 2).

The unicorn was supposed to be very strong, swift and ferocious. It loved solitude and hated male beings. When the unicorn attacked the lion (or a man), the latter typically moved quickly behind a tree at the last moment, so that the unicorn's horn would stick into the tree and get stuck there. Due to its swiftness and ferocity, the unicorn could only be captured by means of trickery. Another common way in medieval tradition to catch a unicorn was with the help of a vestal virgin: upon seeing the virgin, the unicorn would become gentle and lay his head on her lap (Figures 3 and 4). This motif was understood to be an allegory of the Christ and the Virgin, and also as an example of how love softens the fiercest of men.

The unicorn was also a symbol of purity. It was believed that when the unicorn stooped to drink from a pool and dipped its horn into the water, the water was purified and rendered sweet. Furthermore, the unicorn's horn was believed to remove poison. As a result, cups and other instruments allegedly

Figure 1 The royal coat-of-arms of the United Kingdom (after Wikipedia commons)

Figure 2 The unicorn and other animals seen in the Holy Land in the 15th century (after Breydenbach 1486, reproduced in Einhorn 1976: 126, Figure 7)

made of unicorn horn were used to test the food of kings and nobles for poison. Rhinoceros horn and the long tusk of the narwhal (the horn of "sea-unicorn") were highly prized articles of trade, made into talismanic amulets and rings, and ground into medicinal powder[3].

2. The unicorn and the virgin in the Physiologus

The bulk of European unicorn lore is derived from three primary sources of classical antiquity. The most recent of these is the *Physiologus*, a collection of the wonders of natural history written in Greek about 200 CE in Alexandria in Egypt[4], which was an important center of trade between India and the western world at that time. Containing the first Christian interpretation of the unicorn myth, the Physiologus mentions the 'capture by means of a virgin' motif. A significant detail is that after its capture, the virgin leads the unicorn into the palace for the king (Figure 5). While this is not found in earlier classical sources, it is attested in both Indian and Mesopotamian traditions (see below).

> "About the Unicorn. The Psalm [91 (92): 11] says: 'And my horn [*tò kéras mou*] will be raised as (that) of the of the unicorn [*hōs monokérōtos*].' The Physiologus ['the Naturalist'] said about the unicorn that it has this very nature: it is a very little animal, looking like a kid, but very bitter. The hunter cannot approach it because of its enormous strength; it has a single horn in the middle of the head. How can it be caught? They dispose in front of it an undefiled [clothed] maiden, and (the unicorn) leaps upon her bosom [*eis tòn kólpon*, also 'womb'], and the maiden suckles the animal and leads it into the palace for the king [*eis tò palátion tôi basileî*].
>
> Then it is assumed that (this) animal (is) an image of the Saviour, in fact: '(he) raised a horn in the home of David, our father' [Luke 1: 16], and it became for us a horn of safety. The

Figure 3 A unicorn lays his head on the lap of a virgin and is killed. Illustration in an Italian 14th century bestiary manuscript in the Royal collection (973,12) of the British Museum (after Shepard 1930: Plate 2)

Figure 4 Virgin, unicorn and hunter in a German embroidery from c.1375 (after *Encyclopaedia Britannica*, Vol. 9, 1910: 309)

Figure 5 A virgin leads the captured unicorn into the palace for the king (after a medieval manuscript of the *Physiologus* in Schlingloff 1973: Figure 2)

angels and the powers might not rule over him, but he has taken abode in the womb of the true and undefiled virgin Maria [the Mother of God], 'and the Word has become flesh and has taken abode among us' [John 1: 14].[5]"

The Psalm is quoted from the Greek translation of the Old Testament known as the *Septuaginta*, assembled in Alexandria between the 2nd and 4th centuries CE[6]. In eight places, the Hebrew word r^{e}*'ēm* (plural *rēmîm*) 'wild (urus) bull' (cf. Akkadian *rîmu* 'wild bull') was translated with the term *monókerōs* 'unicorn', which was then rendered in the Latin *Vulgate* translation as *unicornis* and in Hiob as

When other animals approach, it does not object but is gentle; with its own kind however it is inclined to be quarrelsome. And they say that not only do the males instinctively butt and fight one another, but that they display the same temper towards the females, and carry their contentiousness to such a length that it ends only in the death of their defeated rival. The fact is that strength resides in every part of the animal's body, and the power of its horn is invincible. It likes lonely grazing-grounds where it roams in solitude, but at the mating season, when it associates with the female, it becomes gentle and the two even graze side by side. Later when the season has passed and the female is pregnant, the male Cartazonus of India reverts to its savage and solitary state. They say that the foals when quite young are taken to the King of the Prasii and exhibit their strength one against the other in the public shows, but nobody remembers a full-grown animal having been captured[17].

Megasthenes is almost certainly the source of this fragment, because it mentions the King of the *Prasii* (= Sanskrit *Prācyāḥ*, 'the Easterners'), by which is meant Candragupta Maurya, Sandrokottos of Megasthenes. What is here said of the foals almost certainly relates to the wild asses; Aelian says practically the same thing about them in *De natura animalium* 16,9[18].

Pliny in his *Naturalis Historia* (8,76) records the following:

"In India there are also solid-hoofed bulls that have a single horn, a beast called axis that has deer-skin having many and rather white spots ... but the most ferocious wild beast is the unicorn, whose body otherwise resembles the horse but whose head is like that of the deer, the legs like those of the elephant, the tail like that of the boar, which has a heavy roar, and one black horn that projects two cubits from the middle of its forehead. They deny the possibility of catching this beast alive[19].

Solinus in *Collectanea rerum memorabilium* (52,39-40) rephrases this:

But the most atrocious is the unicorn, a beast with a horrid roar. It has the body of the horse, the legs of an elephant, the tail of a pig, the head of a deer. From the middle of its forehead protrudes a horn that has miraculous splendour and is four feet long and so sharp that whatever it attacks is easily perforated with its puncture. It does not submit alive to human power; it can be killed, but not captured[20].

Strabo in his *Geography* (15,1,56 p. 710-711) has preserved fragment 27b:

For he [Megasthenes] says that the monkeys are stone-rollers, and, haunting precipices, roll stones down upon their pursuers; and that most of the animals which are tame in our country are wild in theirs. And he mentions horses with one horn and the head of a deer (*híppous te légei monokérōtas elaphokránous*); and reeds, some straight up thirty fathoms in length, and others lying flat on the ground fifty fathoms, and so large that some are three cubits and others six in diameter[21].

Aristotle, *De partibus animalium* 3,2,9 says:

Most of the horned animals are cloven-hoofed, though there is said to be one that is solid-hoofed, the Indian ass, as it is called [*hòn kaloûsin Indikòn ónon*]. The great majority of the horned animals have two horns, just as, in respect of the parts by which its movement is effected, the body is divided into two—the right and the left. And the reason in both cases is the same. There are, however, some animals that have one horn only, e.g. the oryx (whose hoof is cloven) and the so-called Indian ass (whose hoof is solid). These creatures have their horn in the middle of the head[22].

A variant of this is in Aristotle's *Historia animalium* 2,1 p. 446b:

> Further, some animals are horned, some hornless. Most of the horned ones are cloven-hoofed, e.g., the ox, the deer, and the goat; we have seen no solid-hoofed animal with a pair of horns. But a few, e.g., the Indian ass, have a single horn and are solid-hoofed. The oryx has a single horn and cloven hooves. The only solid-hoofed animal with a huckle-bone is the Indian ass[23].

Philostratus (c. 165-250 CE)[24] in his *Vita Apollonii* (3,2) remarks:

> And they say that the wild asses [*toùs ónous dè toùs agríous*] are also to be captured in these marshes, and these creatures have a horn upon the forehead, with which they butt like a bull and make a noble fight of it; the Indians make this horn into a cup, for they declare that no one can ever fall sick on the day on which he has drunk out of it, nor will any one who has done so be the worse for being wounded, and he will be able to pass through fire unscathed, and he is even immune from poisonous draughts which others would drink to their harm. Accordingly, this goblet is reserved for kings, and the king alone may indulge in the chase of this creature. And Apollonius says that he saw this animal, and admired its natural features; but when Damis asked him if he believed the story about the goblet, he answered: 'I will believe it, if I find the king of the Indians hereabout to be immortal; for surely a man who can offer me or anyone else a draught potent against disease and so wholesome, will he not be much more likely to imbibe it himself, and take a drink out of this horn every day even at the risk of intoxication? For no one, I conceive, would blame him for exceeding in such cups.'[25]

4. The Iranian Bundahišn

Ctesias got his information on the Indian unicorn in the capital of Persia. As soon as the unicorn bulls of Persepolis (Figure 6) became known, Carsten Niebuhr (1778) connected them with the unicorn described by Ctesias/Aristotle, arguing that the artist had wanted to represent this beast. Eb. Schrader (1892) in turn proposed that Ctesias got his idea of the Indian unicorn from the sculptures that he would have seen in Susa or Persepolis. These views have been rejected[26], but in my opinion there is an indirect connection (see section 10).

Ctesias' account of the horned wild ass and its purifying function has counterparts in Zoroastrian literature. These have as their background a single brief reference in the Avesta, namely Yasna 42,4: "we worship the pious Ass (*xara-*) which stands in the middle of the Sea Vourukaša"[27].

The *Mēnōg ī Xrad* (62,26-27) notes:

> "26. The Three-legged Ass[28] sits in the middle of the Sea Walkaš. 27. (It) completely polishes and purifies with (its) watchfulness (*pad wēnišn*) all the water which rains on the dead matter (*nasā*), on the menstruation (*daštān*) and on the other excrement (*hixr*) (—and on the filth—) when it arrives to the Three-legged Ass."[29]

Figure 6 Lion attacks unicorn bull in a sculpture in Persepolis (after Shepard 1930: Plate 18)

The *Bundahišn* (ch. 24 D in Iran) contains a long and elaborate commentary:

> "10. As regards the Three-legged Ass, (He) says: 'It stands in the middle of the Sea Frāxwkard and has three feet, six eyes, nine testicles, two ears, one horn, a dark-blue head, white body, and spiritual food, (and he is) holy. 11. And of those its six eyes, two are in the eye-sockets, two on the top of the head, two on the hump, and by means of those six eyes it overcomes [the danger and] the worst destruction. 12. And of those nine testicles, three are on the head, three on the hump, and three inside the flanks; and each testicle is as large as a house and as big as the Mount Xvanvant (in Pāzand). 13. And when each one of those three feet has been placed, it covers as much ground as when a thousand sheep sit down in a circle by sitting together; a pastern of (its) foot is such as a thousand men with horses and a thousand chariots can pass in through. 14. And those two ears surround the districts of Māzandarān. 15. That one horn is as it were golden and hollow (or, golden like a horn-trumpet). Another thousand horns have grown therefrom, some of which are as big as a camel, some (are) as big as a horse, some as big as an ox and some as big as an ass, great as well as small; by means of that horn it destroys and shatters all that worst pest of the fighting *xrafstars*. 16. When that Ass takes a round in the sea (and) bends its ears, all the waters of the Sea Frāxwkard furiously tremble, (and) (its) sides and centre are in turmoil. 17. When it brays, all the Ohrmazdean female water-creatures become pregnant, and all the pregnant *xrafstars* of the water, when they hear that bray, cast as corpses (their young). 18. When it stales in the sea, all the water in the seas — which is in the seven Kišwars of the earth — becomes purified. For this reason all the asses, when they see water, they stale in it.' 19. As (He) says: 'If the Three-legged Ass would not have purified the water, all the waters would have perished because of the contamination which the Evil Spirit (*Gannāg Mēnōg*) had brought on the water for the death of the creatures

of Ohrmazd. 20. Tištar can seize more water from the sea with the assistance of the Three-legged Ass. And ambergris — it is known — is the dung of the Three-legged Ass; for, (even) if its food is mostly spiritual, the moisture and the nutrition of the water goes to (its) body through the pores and (the Three-legged Ass) casts (it) away as urine and dung.'"[30]

The Tištar mentioned here is the star Sirius, who in the Iranian tradition is the liberator of waters (comparable to Vedic Indra, the god of thunder and war)[31]. Tištar's association with the Three-legged Ass is also mentioned in the Iranian version of the Bundahišn in chapter 21,5-6:

"5. When it rains owing to the defilement of the demons with excess and deficiency, (and with) harm, damage and contamination of the various divisions (of the earth), Tištar takes water from the entire Frāxwkard Sea. 6. As (He) says: 'The Three-legged Ass, which causes to move (the waters) in the Frāxwkard Sea, and agitates all the water of the sea, pours down the water on the sides of the sea. Tištar descends with the help of the *frawahr* of the right ones and also of the other celestial divinities'."[32]

The ass is also linked with atmospheric phenomena in the *Pahlavi Rewāyat* accompanying the *Dādestān ī Dēnīg* (35a5-6):

"5. (Zoroaster asked:) 'What (is) this thunderbolt which falls from the cloud?'
6. Ohrmazd said: 'This is a stone; when the cloud draws (up) water (from the sea), through the power of the wind and the movement of the Three-legged Ass which stands in the middle of the sea, it [i.e. the water] goes up (to) the atmosphere and burns and is heated severely, when it falls on men and beneficent animals it kills them, and Ahriman becomes more oppressive.'"[33]

James Darmesteter has assumed that the Three-legged Ass is a celestial animal, whose urine is rain possessed with the power to kill demons. Darmesteter points out that this mythical animal of Iran thus corresponds to the heavenly bull, which many peoples have imagined as urinating rain[34].

The Three-legged Ass's purification of water by means of its horn has been compared to Atharvaveda (Śaunaka-Saṃhitā) 3,7,1-2, where the horn (*viṣāṇā-*) of the swift-running gazelle (*hariṇa-*) is a remedy against a disease[35].

While discussing the Ṛgvedic references to the wild ass, I maintained that whenever *gaura-* is mentioned as a real animal, it denotes the 'wild ass'. "From references to real animals I exclude RV 4,58,2-3, which speaks of melted butter as a bull (*vṛṣabhá-*) that has four horns, three legs, two heads and seven hands, calling it a 'four-horned *gaura*'."[36] This mythical wild ass of the Ṛgveda with its three legs is rather similar to the Three-legged Ass of the Bundahišn!

The Iranian Three-legged Ass is a "hyper-phallic animal", "with its 9 (pair of) testicles" and "its three legs clearly an allusion to its virile member, as in the case of the three-legged Priapus"[37]. Priapus was not only a three-legged phallic god, but also an ass-god[38].

5. An Indian 'unicorn' (*ekaśṛṅga*): The Ṛṣyaśṛṅga legend

Ever since 1875, the European lore of capturing the unicorn by means of a maiden (which dates back to the Physiologus) has been connected with the Indian Ṛṣyaśṛṅga legend[39]. The principal variants of this legend are found in the Mahābhārata (3,110-113), the Rāmāyaṇa (1,8-10), the Padma-

Purāṇa (Pātāla-khaṇḍa 13), the Skanda-Purāṇa, Kṣemendra's Bhāratamañjarī (3,758-795), the Alambusā-Jātaka (Jātaka no. 523), the Naḷinikā-Jātaka (Jātaka no. 526), the Mahāvastu (141-152), the Bhadrakalpāvadāna (33), Kṣemendra's Bodhisattvāvadānakalpalatā (65), the Kanjur (IV, Dulva, fol. 136-137), and the Jaina legend of Valkalacīrin in Vasudevahiṇḍī (16,16-50,2, quoted verbatim in Āvaśyaka-Cūrṇi 456-460), found also in the Āvaśyaka-niryukti (1164), and in Hemacandra's Sthavirāvalīcarita, Pariśiṣṭaparvan (1,90-258); in addition, there are numerous short passages in various texts and Chinese translations of Buddhist texts. There are several extensive and penetrating studies of the Ṛṣyaśṛṅga legend[40]. I present here a selection of variants in already published summaries; my own contribution to the Ṛṣyaśṛṅga research follows, in studies of the legend's Vedic and Harappan background (see also section 13).

Among the oldest versions are two Jātaka texts. No. 523 repeats the theme of an ascetic's seduction by a prostitute, which is quite prominent in Indian literature, and which implies the concept that an ascetic who remains celibate accumulates creative power for himself.

> "A Brahmin ascetic lived in the forest. A doe drank water mixed with his semen, fell in love with him, and gave birth to a male child named Isisinga [= Pāli form of Sanskrit Ṛṣyaśṛṅga 'Antelope-horn']. When the boy came of age, his father warned him against the wiles of women, initiated him into the practice of asceticism, and died. Isisinga practiced such fierce asceticism that Indra [the king of gods], fearing that the sage would depose him, sent the *apsaras* [heavenly nymph] Alambusā to seduce him. When Isisinga saw her, he immediately desired her and pursued her; she embraced him and his chastity was destroyed. For three years he made love to her, but then he came to his senses and realized that he had neglected his duties. He gave up the path of desire, and he forgave and blessed the *apsaras*. When she returned to heaven, Indra offered to grant her any wish, and she chose never to be made to tempt another sage."[41]

No. 526 includes the theme of drought that is found in most versions:

> "Indra feared that the powers of a certain great sage posed a threat to him, so he sent an *apsaras* to seduce the sage, who shed his seed at the sight of her. A gazelle ate some grass and water mixed with the sage's seed and became pregnant. She brought forth a son named Isisinga, who was raised by the sage in seclusion in the forest (Figure 7).
>
> Isisinga performed such great *tapas* [asceticism, literally '(solar) heat'] that Indra

Figure 7 Ṛṣyaśṛṅga's conception and birth from a doe
A medallion at the stūpa of Bhārhut, second century BCE
(after Sivaramamurti 1981: Figure 46)

was shaken and determined to break down his virtue. For three years Indra sent no rain, advising the king, 'Send your daughter Naḷinikā to break the virtue of Isisinga and it will rain, for his fierce *tapas* has caused the rain to stop.' She went to him and enticed him, and he thought her to be some marvellous ascetic. His virtue was overcome, his meditation broken off, and he made love to her. Then she ran away from him, and Indra sent rain that day. Isisinga longed for Naḷinikā, still thinking that she had been an ascetic, until his father realized from Isisinga's tale that a woman had broken his virtue. He told his son, 'This was a female demon. You must always avoid them.' Then Isisinga returned to his meditation."[42]

In the Kanjur version, it is quite clear that the drought is due to Ṛṣyaśṛṅga's ascetic powers, and that the drought ends in rain when he is seduced to shed his seed:

"One day when Ṛṣyaśṛṅga was carrying a pitcher of water, rain fell in such torrents that the pitcher broke. In anger, Ṛṣyaśṛṅga cursed the gods to send no rain for twelve years. Famine arose, and the priests told the king, 'This drought is due to the anger of a sage. If his *tapas* is destroyed, Indra will send rain.' The king sent his daughter, Śāntā, to Ṛṣyaśṛṅga, who gave himself up to pleasure with the woman, and his magic power vanished. Rain fell. Śāntā, having conquered the sage with love, brought him to the king, who gave her to him as his wife."[43]

In a version preserved in the Chinese Tripiṭaka, Ṛṣyaśṛṅga is called Ekaśṛṅga 'Unicorn'[44] (Figure 8) and Śāntā is the name of a courtesan (Figure 9)[45]:

"The sage Ekaśṛṅga [Ṛṣyaśṛṅga] had obtained the five supernatural faculties [*abhijñās*]. One day when the rain had made the ground slippery on the mountain where he lived, the

Figure 8 Ṛṣyaśṛṅga dressed in barkcloth (*valkala*) garment of a celibate student with a single horn on his forehead. Stūpa relief from the Caubārā mound near Mathurā, now in the Mathurā Museum (after Sivaramamurti 1981: Figure 45)

Figure 9 Illustration of the Ṛṣyaśṛṅga legend at Mathurā: (above) women going to the hermitage in a ship, (middle) conversation with the seductress, (below) seduction (after Schlingloff 1973: Figure 6)

sage slipped and fell; and, since he had the feet of a deer and was clumsy, he injured one of his feet. Irritated, he used a magic formula to prevent the Nāgas from sending rain for twelve years. A great famine arose, and the king of Benares proclaimed, 'If anyone can make this hermit fall from his supernatural faculties and become an ordinary subject, I will give him half of my kingdom.' ... Śāntā, a courtesan, took 500 of her women to the forest, where they plied the sage with wine and 'pills of joy'. They all bathed together, and when the women touched him, Ekaśṛṅga conceived sensual desires in his heart. He lost all of his supernatural faculties, and rain fell from the sky for seven days and seven nights."[46]

In the Mahābhārata, a prostitute brings Ṛṣyaśṛṅga to the palace of the king:

> "An *apsaras* was cursed to become a female deer and to remain in this form until she bore a son to a sage. One day the sage Vibhāṇḍaka, the son of Kaśyapa, caught sight of another *apsaras* and shed his seed. The female deer drank his seed and bore Ṛṣyaśṛṅga, who had a horn on his head.
>
> Years later, a certain king transgressed against a Brahmin, and so Indra sent no rain in his land. The king's ministers advised him to bring to the palace the sage Ṛṣyaśṛṅga, who had lived in complete chastity in the forest all his life and had never seen a woman. They said, 'If Ṛṣyaśṛṅga may be enticed and lured into your kingdom, Indra will send rain immediately.' The king sent a prostitute to the forest, and Ṛṣyaśṛṅga, thinking her to be a new, delightful sort of ascetic, invited her to perform *tapas* with him. She served him and plied him with garlands, drinks, and embraces, until he was overpowered with love for her, emotionally aroused, and maddened with passion. When he described to his fathers the qualities of this 'ascetic', 'his' beautiful 'rosaries' (garlands) and 'matted locks' (long hair perfumed and bound with gold), his father warned him against such demons. Nevertheless, the young ascetic took

advantage of his father's temporary absence and followed the prostitute to the women's quarters of the palace, and the rain fell. The king gave his daughter, Śāntā, to Ṛṣyaśṛṅga in marriage.

When Vibhāṇḍaka returned and saw that his son had gone, he became furious and went to the palace to burn the king with his *tapas*. The king, however, having foreseen the wrath of Vibhāṇḍaka, had given much land and cattle to Ṛṣyaśṛṅga, and when Vibhāṇḍaka saw his son's wealth he was pacified. He said to Ṛṣyaśṛṅga, 'When a son is born, let the two of you come to the forest.' Ṛṣyaśṛṅga agreed, and he later returned to the woods, with his wife Śāntā, to become a forest-dweller."[47]

Virtually the same story is told in the first book of the Rāmāyaṇa (chapter 8), with an expansion on the methods by which the courtesans succeeded in bringing Ṛśyaśṛṅga (chapter 9). The epic goes on to describe (in chapters 10-17) how the childless King Daśaratha invites Ṛśyaśṛṅga to perform the horse sacrifice on his behalf and then the son-producing sacrifice (*putrīyeṣṭi*). In this latter ritual, the king's three queens are given divinely charged porridge to eat, which impregnates them and causes them to give birth to four sons[48]. In the Buddhist Mahāvastu, the drought motif is missing, but instead the king has Ekaśṛṅga brought to him in order to have offspring. As a result, the queens give birth to a hundred sons, and the king's daughter to 32 sons[49].

The Jaina version in Saṅghadāsa's Vasudevahiṇḍī also involves seduction by a prostitute, but here the hero is the lost brother of the king (and he is not horned):

"A boy Valkalacīrin ['clothed in bark garments'] lives in a hermitage with his father who is not a brahmin ascetic but an abdicated king. On growing old, he had handed over his kingdom to the eldest son and had taken abode in the jungle with his wife. The queen died after the birth of her son Valkalacīrin. Hence the boy has grown up in the solitude of the jungle educated by only his father. He has never seen a female. However, his brother, the reigning king of the country, is longing for him. He sends courtesans to the hermitage who infatuate the boy with female charm and sweets. They make their escape before the father returns. Valkalacīrin goes in search of the so-called ascetics and finally reaches the city of the king. He arrives at the house of the courtesans and is washed and dressed by them. Finally his brother the king finds him, receives him with great joy and gives him in marriage."[50]

All the known versions of the Ṛṣyaśṛṅga date from the post-Vedic period: "Though Lüders believes that there may be some old elements contained in the name Ṛśyaśṛṅga, there is no Vedic text to support this epic legend."[51] In fact, Lüders (1940: 1) pointed out that the name occurs in the teacher genealogies of the two Sāmavedic schools. According to the Jaiminīya-Upaniṣad-Brāhmaṇa (3,40), Ṛśyaśṛṅga[52] Kāśyapa received the immortal gāyatra *sāman* [ritual song] from Kāśyapa (who had learnt it from Indra) and in turn handed it down to Devataras Śyāvasāyana Kāśyapa. In the Vaṃsa-Brāhmaṇa of the Kauthuma–Rāṇāyanīya school, Ṛṣyaśṛṅga Kāśyapa is the son and pupil of Kaśyapa and the father and teacher of Vibhaṇḍaka[53]. In addition, Lüders felt sure that this Sāmavedic Ṛṣyaśṛṅga can be considered to be the same person as the Ṛśya, who in the Ārṣeya-Brāhmaṇa (3,6,10 in the Kauthuma version, 1,9,2 in the Jaiminīya version) is mentioned as the seer of a sāman in the Āraṇyaka-Gāna[54].

I would like to expand here on this sāman[55] and the context in which it is used in the Vedic ritual, given its relevance to the Ṛsyaśṛṅga legend. In the Kauthuma-Rāṇāyanīya school of Sāmaveda, this sāman is recorded in Āraṇyaka-Gāna 5,1,22[56]. Its name is *Ṛsyasya vratam*, but according to the Jaiminīya school of Sāmaveda, either *Ṛśyasya vratam* or *Bhūtecchandasāṃ vratam*[57], its seer is Kaśyapa, its metre anuṣṭubh, and its deity Indra. The first part of the sāman is composed on the verse recorded in Āraṇyaka-Saṃhitā 4,9 and in Jaiminīya-Saṃhitā 2,4,3[58]; the second part, which is composed on chanted interjections (*stobha*) that do not form regular phrases, is recorded in Stobhagrantha 2,6[59] and in Jaiminīya-Saṃhitā 2,4,4[60]. These stobhas start with the word *ṛśyāsaḥ* '(O) antelope bulls', followed by vocatives addressed to Indra that are separated by the interjection[61] *bhuṅ*, which is undoubtedly derived from the verbal root *bhuj-* 'to enjoy'[62].

According to Pañcaviṃśa-Brāhmaṇa 5,4,13, with the chant of Ṛśya they address the *gārhapatya* [fire(place)]."[63] The text goes on to explain this in 14: "All beings (once upon a time) praised Indra with a chant; Ṛśya noted that one of his (viz. Indra's) members had been omitted in (these) chants; praising that one member, he reached the place dear to Indra. Through this (chant) they reach the place dear to Indra." The medieval commentator Sāyaṇa clarifies that by the "one member" (*ekam aṅgam*)[64] is meant "the secret place of enjoyment" (*bhogasādanaṃ guhyarūpam*), undoubtedly the male organ[65]. Sāyaṇa also quotes a passage from the Śāṭyāyanaka (i.e., the lost earlier version of the Jaiminīya-Brāhmaṇa); the passage quoted is actually found in JB 2,403, though with slightly variant readings[66]. The key passage is difficult to interpret, but seems to gloss the immediately preceding verse composed with stobhas. Its final phrase describes "Indra who has his shuttle cleansed (*trasarapūta-*)". Indra is "one who has his 'shuttle' (the stick that goes back and forth in the act of weaving) (*tasara-* or *trasara-*)[67] again and again[68] in the 'buttocks'[69]. The meaning of this is further clarified in the Jaiminīya-Brāhmaṇa with the explanation that his unpraised single member was in the 'buttock' (*sphigau, locative*)[70].

This ritual chant of Ṛśya belongs to the last part of the thirteen sāmaparimāds sung around the sacrificial area. They form an extension of the mahāvrata laud chanted at noon on the mahāvrata day at the end of a year-long sacrificial session. At this juncture, various rarely performed ritual actions take place, in particular the sexual union of a prostitute (*puṃścalū*) and a student of religion (*brahmabandhu*) who hails from the eastern country of Magadha. This action is prescribed in the Jaiminīya-Brāhmaṇa (2,404) and in the Jaiminīya-Śrautasūtra[71], but not in the Pañcaviṃśa-Brāhmaṇa; the Śāṅkhāyana-Śrautasūtra (17,6,2) prohibits its performance as an obsolete practice[72]. The participants are supposed to scold each other (for scolding is a purifying activity). The prostitute blames the student for breaking his vow of celibacy, while the student mocks the prostitute for cleansing every man's member[73].

The antiquity and agricultural affinity of the religious conceptions and practices connected with the ritual intercourse of the celibate student and the prostitute in the mahāvrata and in the Ṛśyaśṛṅga legend can be gleaned from a verse in the Atharvaveda (Śaunaka-Saṃhitā 11,5,12; Paippalāda-Saṃhitā 16,154,2): "Roaring, thundering, the ruddy, whitefooted[74] [*brahmacārin*] has inserted a great penis into the ground. The *brahmacārin* pours semen over the surface, the earth. By that the four directions live."[75] The term for the student's celibate asceticism is *tapas*, literally '(solar) heat': it parallels the scorching heat of the sun, which culminates at the summer solstice (quite probably the day on which the mahāvrata was celebrated)[76]. The monsoon rains which end the long period of drought are symbolized by the celibate ascetic's shedding of his seed in the "divine union" of the sky and earth that is crucial for farming and animal husbandry. In archaic farming communities, it was common to perform ritual sexual unions as primitive fertility magic to induce rain[77].

6. The Gilgamesh epic of Mesopotamia

The Ṛṣyaśṛṅga legend was first compared with the Enkidu and Hierodule episode of the Gilgamesh epic by Edward Lehmann in a personal communication to Hugo Gressmann, published in 1911[78]. Peter Jensen, who translated the Gilgamesh epic, believed that the Indian legend was derived from it[79], but his enthusiastic inclination to ascribe a Mesopotamian origin to most of mankind's cultural achievements was not the best endorsement for his opinions. Nevertheless, we can affirm that "the hypothesis of the correspondence of the Indian tale to the Gilgamesh epic is highly probable"[80] and even that "the cycle of Ṛṣyaśṛṅga with its variants cannot be separated from that of Enkidu; the patterns of both cycles show too many parallels and no historical, geographic or cultural element prohibits such a connection."[81]

The hero of the world's oldest epic is Gilgamesh (Gilgāmeš), the legendary fifth ruler of the Sumerian city of Uruk. He likely lived between 2800 and 2600 BCE, but was later considered to be a divinity, along with his friend and companion Enkidu (Enkīdu) (Figure 10). Sumerian epic poems were at first oral; some half dozen separate works were first written down in Sumerian around 2100-2000 BCE. The actual Gilgamesh epic was composed in Akkadian in the Old Babylonian period (c 1600 BCE). The epic evolved over time into its Standard version (divided into tablets I-XII), which was probably composed around 1250 BCE. Yet it mainly came to be known from the cuneiform tablets of the library of King Assurbanipal (668-627 BCE) in Niniveh. Copies of the epic were made even after this, the latest known dating from 130 BCE. The oldest Sumerian poems recount the feats of the heroic king, with Enkidu as his servant. In the Standard Babylonian version, however, Gilgamesh is a mystic searching for eternal life. Enkidu is the friend and "brother" whose death greatly shocks the hero[82].

In tablet I, the goddess Aruru takes clay and throws it to the steppe, thus creating the wild man Enkidu in order to control Gilgamesh, the arrogant king of Uruk. Enkidu's whole body was covered with

Figure 10 Gilgamesh and Enkidu killing the monster Humbaba. Impression of cylinder seal VA4215 in the Vorderasiatisches Museum, Berlin (after Simo Parpola 1997a: cover)

hair. He did not know any human beings, but ate grass with the gazelles and cattle and came to drink at the river with the herds. A hunter who saw him at the drinking place was horrified. Telling his father of this terrifically strong wild man who had prevented his hunting by filling the trap pits and by tearing the trap snares, he confessed that he dared not try to stop him. On his father's advice, the hunter went to Uruk to petition Gilgamesh for aid. The king had been counseled in dream by his divine mother that he would be finding a strong companion and friend from the steppe. The hunter was sent home with the prostitute (*harimtu*) Shamhat, who seduced Enkidu. After the wild man had had sex with her for six days and seven nights, his strength was sapped and the gazelles ran away from him. Shamhat told him about Gilgamesh and his dream, and led him to the city of Uruk.

In tablet I, Enkidu's mother is the goddess Aruru. But tablet VIII gives a variant genealogy, which is rather striking in relation to the unicorn myths[83]: "Enkidu, your mother, the gazelle (*ṣabītu*), and your father, the wild ass (*akkannu*), have generated you."[84] In the same tablet (lines 49-50), Gilgamesh addresses Enkidu as follows: "Enkidu, O my friend, rejected mule (*kūdanu ṭardu*)[85], wild ass (*akkannu*) of the mountains, panther (*nimru*) of the steppe."

The wild ass was much admired for its strength and sexual potency, and in both respects corresponds to Enkidu's qualities. In tablet I (lines 161-162), the prostitute Shamhat "saw him, the primordial man, the young whose sexual virility (comes) from the deep of the steppe."[86]

7. The Harappan 'unicorn': is it a real or a fabulous animal and does it come from Western Asia?

With thousands of occurrences, the so-called 'unicorn bull' (Figure 11) is by far the most frequently occurring iconographic motif of the Indus seals[87]. The first published report of excavations at Mohenjo-daro naturally referred to the "Indian one-horned ox" described by the classical Greek and Roman authors[88]. It was also clear from the beginning that the Sumerian seals with their unicorn bulls constituted another parallel to the Indus unicorns. But are they really related? Did the Harappans borrow the unicorn motif from Western Asia or did they invent it on their own?[89] In addition to these questions, there is one more much discussed and still debated issue: does the 'unicorn' represent a real or a fantastic animal? The question is quite relevant: some Indus seals depict clearly fantastic beasts, whose bodies are made up of body parts belonging to two or more different animals, some of which (like the elephant) are clearly South Asian[90] (Figure 12)[91].

One early opinion on these topics was formulated as follows:

> "The favourite animal ... was the beast shown with one horn only. ... It is not yet certain that this animal was purposely represented as having a single horn; in all probability, owing to the difficulty of drawing in perspective, one horn is supposed to be behind the other. This method of portraying horns is well known on archaic Sumerian seals, the same animal being indifferently portrayed with two horns or one. For instance, [seals] Nos. 234 and 359 [in Mackay 1938: II] distinctly show an animal, which is definitely of the type that is usually portrayed with one horn, possessed of two horns though of a rather different shape."[92]

The two seals referred to here are illustrated in Figures 13 and 14.

John Marshall made sound statement on several basic issues concerning the Indus unicorn. Referring

Figure 11 Unicorn bull on seal M-18 from Mohenjo-daro (after CISI 1: 377)

Figure 12 Fabulous beast comprised of body parts belonging to different animals. Indus seal M-300 (after CISI 3.1: 388)

Figure 13 "Two-horned unicorn" on seal M-232 and its impression (after CISI 1: 57)

Figure 14 "Two-horned unicorn" on seal M-1077 and its impression (after CISI 2: 109)

to a tablet from Harappa (see Figure 15), he wrote:

> "This animal is depicted with two horns instead of one, and it is just within the bounds of possibility that the single horn is due merely to the engravers having portrayed the animal in profile, with one horn concealed behind the other; in which case it may have belonged to some actual breed of cattle then familiar in the Indus Valley. Examples of two-horned animals

Figure 15 "Two-horned unicorn" on tablet H-697 B (after CISI 2: 316)

portrayed in this manner could, of course, readily be cited from other countries. If, however, we compare these unicorns with the buffaloes, gaurs, and humped bulls ... we see at once that the engravers of Mohenjo-daro (and it was the same at Harappā) made a practice of showing both horns, even when the animal was in profile, and that they could do this with consummate skill. In face of this we are bound, I think, to conclude that a one-horned creature is intended to be understood on these seals, and ... we must regard this creature as fabulous. The unicorn was, of course, a familiar creature of Indian folk stories, and Vishnu's title of *Ekaśriṅga* may conceivably embody some memory of this prehistoric beast, though it is just as likely that it owed its origin to the rhinoceros, from which also the unicorn we are discussing may ultimately have been derived. Whatever its origin, however, it seems clear from the large number of amulet seals on which this creature is portrayed that ... it was more popular than any other animal among the Indus people."[93]

Here "the difficulty of drawing in perspective" argument is effectively refuted[94]. The matter is clinched by the existence of several three-dimensional terracotta statuettes of 'unicorn' bulls with just one horn (Figure 16), while similar terracotta statuettes of the zebu bull, for instance, have two horns[95]. This undeniably proves that the Harappans intentionally and with preference represented this bovid animal with a single horn.

On the other hand, it is likewise undeniable that the above-mentioned two-horn variants[96] feature an animal that has two horns resembling those of the humped cattle, but in all other respects is similar to the 'unicorn' (including the distinctive "complicated, roughly heart-shaped decoration reaching from the withers to the top of the front legs"[97] and the occasional collar[98], plus the presence of the 'cult stand' that is almost invariably placed in front of the 'unicorn' but only very exceptionally in front of other animals)[99]. In my opinion, these two-horned variants indicate, as Marshall suggested, some actual animal species that for ideological reasons was represented as a unicorn. The boar incarnation of Viṣṇu, also mentioned by Marshall, supplies a good parallel: the boar is a real animal, but is represented in images as having just one tusk. Likewise, the elephant-headed god Gaṇeśa reflects a real animal (i.e., the elephant), yet usually —but not always!— the elephant head of the deity has just one tusk. In order to better understand what emphasis on a single horn in the case of the unicorn bull might have meant to the Harappans, we shall examine these later Indian parallels in detail.

One broken round Indus seal from Mohenjo-daro, M-417 (Figure 17), shows animal foreparts (protomes) arranged in a whorl[100]. The animals preserved include the tiger, the Indian bison, the 'unicorn' bull, and the "'unicorn' with two zebu-like horns". The occurrence of both one- and two-horned bulls does not prove, as has been claimed, that they are two different animal species. Though in Mesopotamian iconography the bull is also often depicted with a single horn, the artists there were not prevented from representing the bull with two horns as well; both variants are found in one and the same picture. Nor does the predominance of unicornity in the Indus Valley prove that the Harappans did not copy the motif from Western Asia; to the contrary, it may work the other way around, since the same emphasis on unicornity is found there as well.

Considering the fact that the Harappans borrowed other art motifs from Mesopotamia, it seems more likely than not that they borrowed the motif of a single horn as well. The connection between the Ṛśyaśṛṅga legend and the Gilgamesh epic adds to this likelihood.

8. The single horn in Indian mythology

The depiction of the 'unicorn bull' with a single horn is clearly intentional in the Indus Civilization and presumably also in ancient Western Asiatic[101] art, although this has not prevented representations of the bull with two horns in either context. The divinities and kings of many ancient peoples, including those of Western Asia and Egypt, wore horned headgear as symbols of power and strength. On warriors' helmets, bull horns represent destructive power, as the horns are the instruments with which the wild beast butts and tosses its adversary and tears up its body[102]. The bull and the goat, in particular, are paragons of male sexual power: the single horn is a device for emphasizing masculine prowess. The single 'horn' of the rhinoceros (called also *ekaśṛṅga-mṛga-* in Sanskrit)[103] as a phallic symbol of erect virility[104] is highly esteemed as an aphrodisiac, not only in classical antiquity (see the Kyranides quoted in section 2) but also in Chinese medicine, where it is known as 'dragon's tooth' and is one of the "eight treasures"[105]. "*Corno* ['horn'] in Italian argot means phallus."[106] The male sex of the unicorn is emphasized in some Indus seals by the addition of testicles to a consistently prominent pizzle (penis)[107]. 'Horn' or 'tusk' in Sanskrit is *śṛṅga-*; and its derivative[108] *śṛṅgāra-* has as one of its principal meanings 'erotic love, sexual passion'[109].

Shubhangana Atre (1985: 5-6), synthesizing ideas of Moti Chandra (1966), S. A. Dange (1970) and M. K. Dhavalikar (1983), has made the following valuable comment on the symbolism of the single horn with regard to the Ṛṣyaśṛṅga legend and the Harappan unicorn:

> "Moti Chandra thinks that the horn [of sage Ṛṣyaśṛṅga] must have been of an antelope as Ṛṣyaśṛṅga was born of a hind. The Ṛṣyaśṛṅga story also resembles the Sumerian story of Enkidu in the Gilgamesh epic. Enkidu, a half-human and half animal was born of a gazelle and was civilized by a courtesan. Significantly

Figure 16 One-horned unicorn statuette from Chanhu-daro, now in Museum of Fine Arts, Boston (after Kenoyer 1998: 220 no. 132)

Figure 17 Animal rhomb on seal M-417 (after CISI 1: 378)

unicorn also bears an antelope's horn on his forehead. Does this antelope / hind / gazelle motif run a common thread of symbolism binding these legends together? Dange ... points out that 'the ploughshare and the horn appear to be identified...' ... He is of the opinion that the sage Ṛṣyaśṛṅga probably did not have an original horn on the head but a horn was attached, in view of the belief in the power of fertility and virility in the horn. He has cited many examples where horn was used as a symbol of status and masculinity. He observes that the bāśiṅga (dvi-śṛṅga, literally two horns) of the bridegroom is indicative not only of his status but also is the sign of masculine power. Interestingly, Moti Chandra has arrived at a conclusion which can be supported by archaeological evidence also. He states, ' ... that the antelope horn at some distant past was used for tillage and therefore it symbolizes a good harvest bringing wealth in its turn.' Antlers have been found at Inamgaon, a chalcolithic site in Maharashtra which 'could have been used as a hand-plough because they are almost identical with that which was in use in Maharashtra in the last century. It was used more in hilly regions where it was made to work by dragging.' Once the horn is identified with a plough-share the phallic value of the horn-symbol no longer remains a mystery as to why the mythical unicorn should carry only one horn and combine the features of the animals belonging to the group of ruminants only. ... The association of a virgin with the unicorn is explained by the fact that mythologically the Earth is considered as the eternal virgin."

As the following myths demonstrate, the Ṛṣyaśṛṅga legend is not the only case in Indian tradition to support such a sexual connotation of the single horn or tusk.

The 'unicorn' hog: Prototypal ploughman and mate of the earth

Ekaśṛṅga- and *ekaśṛṅgin-*[110] 'unicorn, having (just) a single tusk' is the epithet of the wild boar (*varāha-*) in the shape of which Viṣṇu lifted up the earth that had sunk into the nether regions[111]. In the iconographic representations of this myth, the boar is rarely depicted in animal shape; usually Viṣṇu appears as a man with the head of a boar (Figure 18)[112]. In the Rāmāyaṇa, the wild boar is not an incarnation of Viṣṇu, but a manifestation of the creator god Brahmā, who in this shape raised the earth from the primeval ocean[113]. This version dates back to early Vedic versions of the myth. According to the Taittirīya-Saṃhitā, "This (universe) was in the beginning just water. The creator god Prajāpati moved there in the shape of the wind. He saw this (earth). Having become a boar, he lifted it up. As Viśvakarman (the demiurge), he (Prajāpati) wiped her dry. She extended herself (*prath-*) and became 'the broad one', i.e. the earth (*pṛthivī*)."[114] The Taittirīya-Brāhmaṇa relates the story, similarly providing an etymology for another term for 'earth', namely *bhūmi*, which is derived from the root *bhū-* 'to become'[115]. According to the Taittirīya-Āraṇyaka, the boar which lifted up the earth was black and had a hundred (TĀ 10,1,8) or a thousand (TĀ 1,10,8) arms[116]. In the Śatapatha-Brāhmaṇa, "a boar, called Emūṣa[117], raised her [i.e., the earth] up, and he was her husband Prajāpati: with that mate, his favourite abode, he [i.e., the Adhvaryu priest taking earth dug up by a boar] thus supplies and completes him [i.e., Prajāpati][118].

In the Viṣṇu-Purāṇa (5,29,23), the goddess Earth says to Viṣṇu after the god has killed the demon Naraka (his own son): "when you, assuming the form of a boar (*śūkara-*) lifted me up, this son, begotten through the contact with you, was born from me."[119] The relatively recent Śākta tantric text

Figure 18 Boar-shaped Viṣṇu lifts Goddess Earth. Udayagiri, Madhya Pradesh, c. 400 CE (after Kramrisch 1954: Plate 47)

Kālikāpurāṇa[120] provides more details on this variant of the myth. The god Śiva blames Viṣṇu for having committed a transgression when in boar shape he violated the goddess Earth in the water, while she was having her monthly period. By the boar's seed the Earth became pregnant, and she carried in her womb a frightful embryo[121]. The gods tried to prevent the birth of this demonic son, which was engendered by sexual union with the Earth when she was in an impure state. The Earth suffered greatly, and was hardly able to bear the long delay[122]. Eventually a son, the demon Naraka, was born in the same sacrificial place[123], that King Janaka ('Progenitor') tore up with his ploughshare (receiving from the resulting furrow his daughter Sītā ('Furrow'), who was given to him by the goddess Earth)[124]. Naraka was brought up by King Janaka as his adopted son.

The connection between the divine boar's "violation" of the earth (evidently with its single tusk) and the "tearing up" of soil by means of the ploughshare (associated with the sowing of seed in the field) makes it quite clear that the boar's tusk symbolizes the plough and the male organ[125]. The earth is spoken of here as *dharṣitā* 'violated' by the boar (i.e., her husband) in a sexual sense: she becomes pregnant. In Sanskrit, the word *potra-* primarily denoting 'pig's snout' is also used for the 'ploughshare'[126], while *lāṅgala-* 'plough' is also used for 'penis'[127]. In the Śatapatha-Brāhmaṇa (7,2,2,5), it is expressly stated that the furrow is the vulva (*yoni*) of the earth and the seed sown therein is the sperm. The verb **uẓu*, which goes back to Proto-Dravidian (which, in my opinion, was spoken in the Indus Civilization), is used in many Dravidian languages for ploughing as well as pigs' digging up of soil[128]. The idea that the earth sank into water and was then "brought up" by the boar, being in this process "violated" and "fertilized" during the menstruation period of the goddess, appears to reflect the "disappearance" of soil during the rainy season—which is the peak breeding time of the wild boar[129]—and its subsequent "surfacing" (and being ploughed) when the waters recede.

According to the Śatapatha-Brāhmaṇa, the earth was lifted up by her husband, Prajāpati, in the form of a boar. By virtue of his name, King Janaka is associated with this creator god. Ploughing the earth, Janaka symbolically unites with the earth or the furrow he creates (which is then identified with his daughter)[130]. According to Aitareya-Brāhmaṇa 3,33, Prajāpati united with his own daughter and thereby gave birth to all beings; he was then killed by the terrible god Rudra in punishment for his sin of incest. In connection with the construction of the Vedic fire altar, it is said that Prajāpati (who is equated with the year) became so exhausted from creating the world that he fell apart; by building the fire altar, he is put together again. Prajāpati is the "Primeval Man or Male" (*puruṣa*), sacrificed by the gods in the beginning so that the cosmos could be created out of his body parts[131]. In the Kālikāpurāṇa, Viṣṇu in his boar incarnation is killed by Śiva because his body had become impure through union with a menstruating woman: this is the reason (not mentioned in other sources) for his appearance as the *yajña-varāha* 'sacrificial boar', whose body parts were assumed as the various sacrifices and their implements (e.g., his three destructive boar sons became the three sacrificial fires)[132].

The son of the goddess Earth by Viṣṇu's boar incarnation is named Naraka, a word which otherwise denotes 'hell' or 'infernal region'. It is etymologically related to Greek *nérthe* 'below' and *nérteroi* (= Latin *inferi*) 'those below, the dead'[133]. Naraka is a chthonic deity of vegetation associated with the spirits of the dead[134] and manure[135]:

> "The divine power or being going by the name of Naraka is mainly a representative of dung, 'der Genius des Misthaufens', 'the demon of filth or manure', 'the god of the filth of the farm-yard'. As such he is also a 'Genius der Trieb- und Zeugungskraft der Erde'. Filth and manure, the favourite home of hogs and their relatives, actually are a product of the earth and the rooting and messing activities of these animals: no wonder that Naraka should have been a son of the goddess Earth and a god in the form of a boar" (Gonda 1954: 141).

The prolific offspring of the pig makes it a paragon of fertility, and the Kālikāpurāṇa stresses that sexual union with the sow-shaped earth could not satisfy the passion of the primeval boar. These swine parents and their sons wallowed in mud and filth in their 'dirt play' (*kardamakrīḍā*, *kardamalīlā*)[136]. Bones of the wild pig (*Sus scrofa*), which is nowadays distributed throughout the Indus Valley[137], have been found in a number of Harappan sites (Meadow 1991: 55)[138]. This animal is not represented in the iconography, however, probably because of its ominous connection with the dead and the dirt (as is also the case of the wild ass)[139].

The 'unicorn' elephant: ekadanta Gaṇapati

Naraka's association with dirt connects him with the elephant-headed god Gaṇapati, another one-tusker, whom the goddess Pārvatī fashioned out of her own bodily dirt (*mala*)[140]. More specifically, *mala* denotes menstrual blood (e.g., a menstruating woman is *malinī-* 'impure'). In this context, the Goddess' bodily dirt is also called *rajas* (i.e., 'dust', as well as 'menstrual discharge'). Gaṇeśa's origin from menstrual blood parallels Naraka's origin from the primeval boar's intercourse with the menstruating goddess. It also seems to be the reason why Gaṇeśa is connected with the red planet Mars, why he wears a red garment, and why he is smeared with red paste[141]. On the other hand, the goddess' dirt out of which she fashioned her son also seems to refer to her excreta; Gaṇeśa is also worshipped in the form of images made of cow dung[142]. In this case, the goddess is found in the shape of a cow, an important mother symbol. The Tamils worship Piḷḷaiyār 'son, child' (Gaṇeśa) in the shape of cow dung balls, which are set on fire to cook a pot of milk during the cow-festival (*māṭṭu-p-poṅkal*) at the new year[143]. This South Indian festival is related to two northern Indian festivals that also involve fire and cattle, namely Holī and Divālī. The latter of these two includes the *narakacaturdaśī*, the last day of the dark half of the month connected with the killing of the demon Naraka. On the following new moon day, models of mountains and cattle are made of cow dung[144]. The Tamil festival undoubtedly goes back to the pastoralist Southern Neolithic culture (c. 2500-1500 BCE), the ash mounds of which were excavated by Raymond Allchin[145], and which seems to be derived from the Early Harappan cultures[146].

The name Gaṇapati or Gaṇeśa 'host leader' and his retinue of the 'mother' goddesses are features suggesting that he is a double (probably the lunar double)[147] of Śiva's other son, Skanda (who is firmly associated with the morning or vernal sun); this god is the divine Senāpati 'army leader', accompanied by the 'mothers' associated with the Pleiades, his birth star. Both gods go back to the earlier class of Vināyakas, evil spirits who lead hosts of ghosts, and to the 'terrible' Vedic god Rudra, the lord of robber bands and spirits of the dead[148]. The Rigveda (1,114,5) speaks of Rudra as the "ruddy boar of the sky" (*divo varāham aruṣam*), which is likely to refer to the red rising sun[149], the planet Mars, or lightning[150]. On the other hand, Skanda is the overlord of the planet Mars[151], who is said to be the son of the earth[152] like 'terrible' Naraka, the son of the earth and the primeval boar: this detail of planetary mythology is clarified by the 'terrible' Naraka's association with Rudra-Skanda-Gaṇapati[153].

The elephant-headed Hindu god Gaṇapati (alias Gaṇeśa) is described as having just one tusk, two tusks or four tusks[154]. The one-tusked variety (Figure 19) is called *eka-danta-* or *eka-daṃṣṭra-* 'one-toothed'. Iconographic manuals such as the Śrītattvanidhi prescribe that Ekadanta-Gaṇapati should have a dark body and a large and clearly visible tusk in his right hand[155]. There are many different myths explaining why Gaṇapati is one-tusked[156]. One popular myth connects it with the moon (whose crescent resembles the broken tusk):

> Gaṇeśa had overeaten balls of sweets (*modaka*, *laḍḍu*) of which he is very fond. His belly became quite round and eventually burst when Gaṇeśa fell off his rat-mount as this became frightened at the sight of a snake. The undigested balls fell on the ground, and the moon, seeing this, burst into laughter. His laughter hurt Gaṇeśa, who pulled out one of his tusks and threw it at the moon. It caused a total eclipse and darkness. Eventually Gaṇeśa relented so that the moon only suffers from waxing and waning[157].

The single tusk of Gaṇapati is also a male symbol. According to a 'fine saying' (*subhāṣita*) found in many works, Gaṇeśa as an androgyne has a tusk only on his male (right) side, the female (left) side being without a tusk:

> "May the single-tusked Gaṇeśa guard the universe, who imitates his parents' custom in that his bride, it seems, has been allowed to take that half of him wherein his face is tuskless."[158]

The verse refers to the androgynous form of Śiva

Figure 19 One-tusked Gaṇeśa holding his missing tusk in one of his four hands. Miniature of the Nurpur school dating from c. 1810 in the Museum of Chandigarh (after Martin-Dubost 1997: 64 Figure 29)

Figure 20 Śiva and the Goddess as an androgynous deity (after Moor 1810: Plate 24, 1 and 2)

as Ardhanārīśvara. Significantly, illustrations of this manifestation of the great god of Hinduism and his consort include also their symbolic animals, which, like those of the principal divine couples of ancient Western Asia (see section 10), are the bull (male) and the lion or tiger (female) (Figure 20).

The word *ekadanta-* 'single-tusked' is used in Sanskrit also for the plough. With its large male organ, the elephant is one of the male prototypes in the erotic sciences; the god Gaṇapati has erotic manifestations, too.

The dark colour of the elephant's body and its trumpeting have made it a favourite symbol for rain clouds. A very popular iconographic motif is Gaja-Lakṣmī, the Goddess of Wealth (Earth), sprinkled with water by two overarching elephants (Figure 21).

9. The Harappan 'unicorn' as the auroch (urus) or taurine bull

The Harappan unicorn bull does not have a hump (like that of the Indian zebu bull), leading Cunningham to conclude that the very first known Indus seal was a foreign import[159].

Zoologists have established that modern humped zebu cattle (*Bos indicus*) are descendants of the wild *Bos namadicus* (short for *Bos primigenius namadicus*), known from Indian Pleistocene fossils. Modern humpless taurine cattle (*Bos taurus*) have been linked to the extinct wild *Bos primigenius* (short for *Bos primigenius primigenius*)—called aurochs or urus—that lived in Europe (until 1627 CE), North Africa, and Western Asia (Figure 22). Mitochondrial DNA and nuclear microsatellites have moreover indicated a pre-domestication divergence of about 200,000 years between *Bos namadicus* and *Bos primigenius*, and separate radiations for them since domestication[160].

Figure 21 Gaja-Lakṣmī. Medallion of the stūpa at Bhārhut, second century BCE (after Sharma 1994: 29)

In bone finds from Mehrgarh in Pakistani Baluchistan, truly wild taxa constituted approximately 55% of the material around 6000 BCE, while by 5000 BCE the portion of protodomesticates was as much as 80%. During this period, the ratio of cattle rose from 38% to 65%, and simultaneously the size of the animals grew smaller. This is clear evidence of local domestication[161].

> "The form of cattle present in the greater Indus region was presumably the zebu (*Bos indicus*). Representation of humped cattle dominate the coroplastic art of the region, while the distinctively cleft dorsal spines of thoracic vertebrae turn up occasionally in the faunal collections together with zebu-like skull pieces. Also depicted on Indus seals, however, are non-humped cattle. Although it is not presently possible to determine from the available faunal material whether this latter form is represented or not, it was probably never particularly common in the area. In addition, there is now evidence that cattle could have been brought under human control locally and, once domesticated, were maintained at a size significantly above that of contemporary cattle in Europe and Anatolia."[162]

Recently analyzed genetic data of South Asian cattle indicate introgression between taurine and zebu cattle that could have began by the third millennium BCE. Dorian Fuller concludes:

> "Depictions on Harappan seals indicate that some humpless taurine cattle had spread into South Asia from the west by this time (Zeuner 1963). Thus, sometime between the period of zebu domestication in Pakistan and the urban Harappan civilization (from the mid Third Millennium BC), the introgression between West Asian and South Asian cattle had begun, a process that remains detectable in the genes of modern cattle populations (Kumar *et al.* 2003)."[163]

Although the domesticated humped zebu spread from Pakistan to the Iranian plateau[164] and even to Mesopotamia[165], it is humpless taurine cattle that predominate in the ancient Near East. Genetic studies point towards the Neolithic Near East as the centre of origin for *Bos taurus*[166]. In glyptics of the ancient Near East, depicted cattle are regularly humpless, usually shown in profile so that only one horn is visible. This applies to scenes of both domesticated cattle (Figures 23-24) and wild cattle (Figure 25). Even after the domestication of cattle,

Figure 22 The aurochs or urus (*Bos primigenius primigenius*) in a 19th century copy of a 16th century European painting (after *Brehms Thierleben* (1927 ed.), from Wikipedia commons)

wild cattle (*Bos primigenius*) could still be found throughout the Near East:

> "They still roamed the plains of north-western Mesopotamia as late as Neo-Assyrian times, when they were hunted by Assyrian kings. The wild bull must have been a truly awe-inspiring beast, six feet tall at the shoulder and with an enormous pair of wide-sweeping horns. Domestic cattle were tiny by comparison. As a visual and literary image of power and strength, wild cattle preoccupied the Mesopotamian imagination, a metaphor for deity or a suitable comparison for heroes or kings."[167]

Eminent archaeozoologists thus identify the Indus 'unicorn' as a type of humpless cattle. Its Near Eastern origin coincides with the artistic convention of showing them in profile with one horn visible, a fashion which is likewise of Mesopotamian origin. This interpretation of the Indus 'unicorn' has been held and continues to be held by a number of scholars[168].

Harappan sailors may have imported aurochs or taurine cattle in very small numbers—too few to survive for long—from Mesopotamia to the Indus Valley[169]. It is also possible that visiting Harappan craftsmen borrowed just the 'unicorn' motif at the same time (in the Late Early Dynastic period or Early Akkadian period) as other Near Eastern motifs (e.g., the 'contest', the 'double-bun hair style' of warrior kings, the victory pose of placing the foot upon the defeated)[170].

Some taurine cattle could also have made it overland to the Indus Valley by the time of the Indus Civilization, and in greater numbers a little later. The "Bactria and Margiana Archaeological Complex" (BMAC) alias "Oxus Civilization", dated c. 2400-1500 BCE[171], had humpless domestic cattle used for ploughing (Figure 26); golden images of such bulls (Figure 27) were found in the Quetta treasure left behind by BMAC people who came to the Indus Valley around the 20th century BCE[172]. These BMAC immigrants were probably a vanguard of Aryan-speaking pastoralists coming with taurine cattle from the Eurasian steppes to Iran and India via Central Asia; they appear en route to have taken over the rule of the BMAC[173].

Figure 23 Humpless taurine cattle and wheat on a Sumerian cylinder seal of c. 3000 BCE in the Louvre Museum (after Parrot 1960: 88 no. 108)

Figure 24 Domestic taurine cattle in the sacred precincts, Sumerian cylinder seal from c. 3000 BCE in the Baghdad Museum (after Parrot 1960: 89 no. 113)

Figure 25 Sumerian king hunts wild bulls. Cylinder seal c. 3200 BCE (after Amiet 1980: no. 1614)

Figure 26 Feasting and ploughing on a BMAC silver vase, early 2nd millennium BCE (after Ligabue and Salvatori 1989: 136, Figure 9)

Figure 27 Bull-shaped golden pendants from the BMAC treasure found at Quetta, Pakistan (after *Les cités oubliées* 1988: 124 nos. 153-154)

10. The lion-bull combat and the 'sacred marriage' in Western Asia

Mark Kenoyer (2009) presents an argument against the Mesopotamian origin of the unicorn, citing the regular combination of the unicorn bull with the lion in Western Asiatic art (cf. Figures 6, 28, 29). He points out that the Indus 'unicorn' is not associated with the lion and, furthermore, that the lion in fact is nowhere to be seen in Harappan art. Kenoyer is right about the close association between the unicorn bull and the lion in Western Asiatic art, but it actually supports (rather than detracts from) a Mesopotamian derivation of the unicorn bull. To back up this statement, it is necessary to discuss at some length the lion and bull motif, as it is fundamentally important for an understanding of the symbolism of the bull and its horns, and the unicorn in general[174].

In the Mesopotamian art of the Late Uruk period (c. 3400-3100 BCE), the king is represented as hunting lions (Figure 28) and wild bulls (Figure 25). The king is also shown holding back a rearing lion on either side with his bare hands (Figure 29). These scenes depict the king as a match for—or even more powerful than—the mightiest of beasts. In the Uruk-inspired art of Predynastic Egypt (c. 3200-3000 BCE), the king of Upper Egypt is depicted as a giant lion as well as a giant wild bull when defeating his human enemies. In Proto-Elamite art (c. 3100-2700 BCE), the fashion of representing humans in animal shape is generally extended from kings to all other people. One can expect that in royal hunting scenes, therefore, the lion and the bull as royal animals would come to be adversaries with one another. The combat between the lion and the bull is a much repeated theme in Western Asiatic art in general, but it does not merely repeat the natural enmity between these mighty animals in nature. On one Proto-Elamite seal (Figure 30)[175], an enormous bull masters two small lions and a giant lion dominates two small bulls. The lion and the bull are personifications of opposite cosmic forces, whose symmetrically balanced victories and defeats symbolize the equilibrium that manifests itself in the cycle of seasons or the alternation of night and day[176].

On another Proto-Elamite seal with two antithetic scenes, a standing lion shoots a squatting bull and a standing bull clubs a squatting lion (Figure 31). With its yellowish colour and mane of ray-like hair, the lion is a good symbol for the sun[177] and, accordingly, the day. The bull, with its darker skin and horns resembling the sickle moon, symbolizes night. Standing up and sitting down can refer to sunrise and sunset, or the appearance and disappearance of the moon and the stars: it is at these moments of dawn and dusk that day takes over the night and vice versa. The lion and the bull can represent various opposing but complementary forces of nature, such as, day and night :: light and darkness :: life and death :: summer and winter :: heat and cold :: fire and water. The corresponding members of these oppositions can be homologized (bull = moon = night = darkness = death = winter = cold = water; lion = sun = day = light = life = summer = heat = fire) with everything reduced to a basic dualism that is characteristic of Iranian religion in later times as well.

Lion and bull as symbols of female earth and male sky

On the first of the above-mentioned Proto-Elamite seals with antithetic combats between lion and bull (Figure 30), as well as on several other Proto-Elamite seals where the lion in an Atlas-like pose holds up mountains and trees (Figure 32), one finds next to the lion a pictogram that replicates the Archaic Sumerian script sign for the word KI 'earth'[178]. In these representations (and Proto-Elamite art in general), the lion is often female; in this regard,

Figure 28 Sumerian king hunts lions. Stela from Uruk, c. 3200 BCE (after Aruz (ed.) 2003: 22, Figure 5)

Figure 29 Sumerian king holds back two lions. Handle of the flint knife from Jebel el-Araq, Upper Egypt (after Parrot 1960: 80 no. 99)

Figure 30 Lion—bull contest on a Proto-Elamite seal from Susa, c. 3000 BCE (after Amiet 1980: no. 585)

Figure 31 Lion and bull in combat with each other. Proto-Elamite seal, c. 3000 BCE (after Amiet 1980: no. 591)

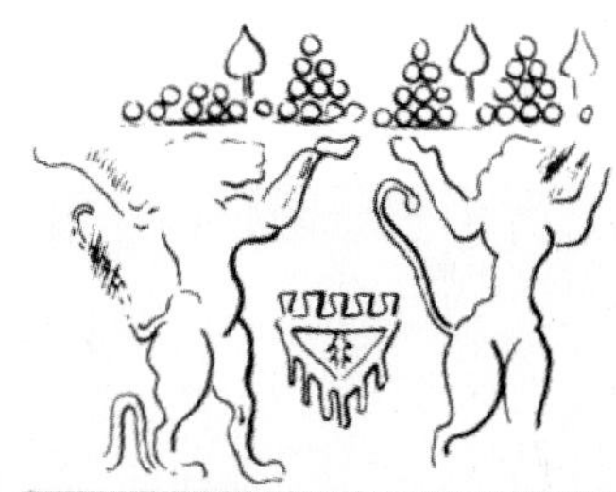

Figure 32 Goddess Earth as lioness holding up mountains. Proto-Elamite seal, c. 3000 BCE. (after Amiet 1980: no. 577)

the lion represents the earth conceptualized as a goddess. The depiction of mountains in this context is natural, since in nature mountains are often the lion's habitat. This interpretation agrees with the cuneiform tradition: "*Ki* is the Sumerian word for earth, and was sometimes personified as a goddess and female counterpart to An (heaven). In some Sumerian accounts, An copulates with Ki to produce a variety of plants."[179] That the bull in the lion-bull combat represents the sky is in agreement with the early Mesopotamian concept of the "Bull of Heaven"[180] discussed below. The thundering and raining sky-god is many archaic religions conceived to be a roaring bull, whose semen fertilizes the earth[181].

Anatolian cult of the lion-escorted goddess and her slain bull-husband in Anatolia

Representing the earliest Neolithic cultures in which agriculture and animal husbandry began in Western Asia are the sites of Çatal Hüyük and Hacilar in Anatolia. Here impressive shrines datable to c. 7000

BCE attest to the cult of the great earth goddess who had the lion as her symbolic animal (Figure 33) and to whom bulls were sacrificed. More than 5000 years later, this Anatolian goddess was known to the Hittites as Kubaba and still later to the Greeks and Romans as Kybele. In the first millennium BCE, she was worshipped with an orgiastic cult in which her priests were castrated like Attis, the young lover of the goddess in the myth. An important part of Kybele's mystic cult was the taurobolium (Figure 34), which involved sacrifice of a bull whose blood was poured on the worshipper to cleanse him or her of sins and whose testicles were eaten in a sacramental meal. This "mother of the gods" had also a martial aspect: her lions guarded the city gates, while walls built on high mounds surrounding the city formed the mural crown on the head of this earth goddess. A as long as she stood for the defense, the city walls remained impregnable[182].

The lion-escorted goddess and her bull-husband in Syrian religion

The religion of ancient Syria[183] gives further background that is useful for understanding the Mesopotamian religion, with which the Harappans primarily had contact. According to Lucian, who wrote an account "Of the Syrian Goddess" in c. 150 CE, the chief goddess of many Syrian towns was Atargatis. Her throne in the temple was buttressed by lions, while the throne of her husband Baᶜal-Hadad was supported by bulls. Like the earlier Canaanite goddess ᶜAθtart (Astarte) and ᶜAnat, the chief goddess of Ugarit (Ras Shamra) in the 14th century BCE, Atargatis symbolized nature's power of reproduction and her cult culminated in her sacred marriage. Hadad was the god of thunder and rain; his other name, Baᶜal, means 'husband, owner' (the husband who had paid the bride-price owned his wife). He owned the cultivated land and was called "the husband of furrow".

Figure 33 Mother Earth seated on a lion throne and giving birth. Çatal Hüyük, Turkey, c. 7000 BCE (after Vermaseren 1977: Plate 5)

Figure 34 Taurobolium (after Vermaseren 1977: Figure 30)

In Ugarit, the year had three seasons, ruled by three gods in turn. The thunder god Baᶜal ruled the season of inseminating rains, fresh vegetation and growth. When it was his time to abdicate, Baᶜal descended to the netherworld. After a short interregnum by ᶜAθtar, shown sitting like a small boy on Baᶜal's throne, there followed the rule of Mot, the god of the drying wind and drought (which makes everything fade and die, but also ripens the corn and yields full harvest). Baᶜal's sister-beloved, the "virgin ᶜAnat", would try to rescue Baᶜal. The cycle closed with her furiously attacking Mot, cutting his head like ripe corn, so that Baᶜal might return and ascend his throne to the joyous shouts of the gods. This moment coincides with the new year festival and the sacred marriage of Baᶜal and ᶜAnat'. ᶜAnat's title of 'virgin' expresses her ability to renew her virginality for a new sacred marriage. In one myth, Baᶜal as a bull mates with ᶜAnat in the shape of a cow. After the death of Baᶜal, ᶜAnat would give birth to a male calf, the young Baᶜal, with whom she apparently was expected to unite in a sacred marriage the next year.

The Mesopotamian counterpart of the Anatolian goddess and her sacred marriage

In Mesopotamian religion, the Anatolian goddess had a counterpart in the Sumerian Inanna and Akkadian Ištar (earlier Eštar), related to Syrian goddess Astarte and to ᶜAθtar, the male god of war and the planet Venus in Pre-Islamic South Arabia. The most important Mesopotamian goddess of all times, Inanna-Ištar was the goddess of sexual love and prostitutes, as well as a bloodthirsty warrior deity who was fond of battle and stood by her favourite kings in battle. Her totem was the lion and her astral manifestation was the planet Venus[184]. At least one local variant of Ištar, the goddess of Mari in Syria, was called 'Mistress of the city wall' (*bêlêt ḫiṣâri*)[185].

The mystic cult of this goddess also included a 'sacred marriage', in which the Sumerian king was ritually married to the goddess Inanna (the king being identified with the goddess's young lover and husband, Dumuzi). Described as a shepherd (and in one cult song as a warrior hero), Dumuzi was a god of the pastoralists. When Inanna visited the underworld, she could not return without a substitute to take her place. Therefore, demons came to fetch Inanna's beloved young husband to replace her. Thus Dumuzi died and became a god of the underworld. Ritual lamentation for the death of Dumuzi was part of the cult[186]. The fertility of vegetation, animals and humans was believed to depend upon the union of Inanna and Dumuzi[187]. The union was enacted by priestly personnel, and then in later times with cult statues of the gods. People in general took part in the festival that included processions, dance, music and banquets. The sacred marriage was celebrated at least on the new year's day, but could be performed also monthly on the "day of the disappearance of the moon". "It is commonly thought that, as Dumuzi's mythological half-year imprisonment in the Netherworld ended around the New Year, his ascent probably included a sacred marriage with his spouse Inanna."[188] The Sumerian king was equated with "Inanna's *mes*-tree", a cosmic tree that "unites heaven and earth". In later Assyrian royal ideology and Jewish mysticism, the tree symbolizes the main god of the pantheon as Perfect Man, who combines the powers of all the great gods and righteously distributes divine blessings on earth[189].

11. The lion-bull combat and the 'sacred marriage' in ancient South Asia

Transfer of the cult of the lion-escorted goddess to Afghanistan and India

The classical Mesopotamian goddess Inanna-Ištar represents a syncretization of many local deities of her description, one of these being Nanaya[190]. Around 2000 BCE, Nanaya's cult spread via Elam to Afghanistan[191], where she is depicted in Mesopotamian dress and flanked with lions on the compartmented metal seals of the BMAC culture (Figure 35). The cult of Nanaya or Nana was adopted by the Iranian-speaking tribes of Kuṣāṇas upon their arrival in Afghanistan around the beginning of the Christian era; the goddess is then represented as seated on a lion and wearing a mural crown (Figure 36). Nana is still worshipped in some places in Afghanistan as "Bibi Nani"[192].

When the Kuṣāṇas conquered northwestern India, their cult of the lion-escorted goddess is first attested there in Kuṣāṇa sculptures of the Mahiṣasuramardinī, 'Crusher of the buffalo demon'. This is the standard epithet of Durgā, whose myths surface in texts from the 5th century CE onwards. Her main feat is depicted in the magnificent Pallava granite panel at Māmallapuram (c. 700 CE), which greatly resembles the above-discussed Proto-Elamite sealing: the lion-riding goddess Durgā uses bow and arrows on her opponent, the buffalo demon Mahiṣa Asura who has the club as his weapon (Figure 37). The Buffalo demon is described as a great warrior, who on the point of being defeated changes his shape into various mighty animals, ending with that of a human warrior. In some variants of the myth the demon is hopelessly in love with the goddess, reaching union with her (touching her female organ) only at the moment of death[193].

Durgā's main festival is the navarātri festival culminating on the "tenth day of victory". This is around the autumnal equinox, when the rains end [i.e., the thundering Heavenly Bull dies!], the roads become passable, and war expeditions traditionally began. In earlier times, another navarātri was celebrated six months later at the vernal equinox (the new year). The orgiastic navarātri festival includes feasting with strong drinks and the meat of the various animals sacrificed to the goddess, especially the water buffalo; in olden times, human victims were decapitated. One must behave like a *śabara* ('savage') on the final day:

> "People should be engaged in amorous play with single women, young girls, courtesans and dancers, amidst the sound of horns and

Figure 35 Lion-escorted Goddess on a golden BMAC seal from Afghanistan (after Ligabue and Salvatori 1989: 202, Plate 58)

Figure 36 Goddess Nana from Kuṣāṇa period Afghanistan (after Azarpay 1976: Figure 6)

Figure 37 Lion-riding Goddess Durgā defeating the buffalo demon. Rock-panel, Mamallapuram, South India, c. 700 CE (after Kramrisch 1954: Plate 86)

> instruments, and with drums and kettle-drums, with flags and various sorts of cloths covered with a miscellany of parched grain and flowers; by throwing dust and mud; with auspicious ceremonies for fun; by mentioning the female and male organs, with songs on the male and female organs, with words for the female and male organs, until they have enough of it. If one is not derided by others, if one does not deride others, the Goddess will be angry and utter a very terrible curse."[194]

In Nepal, this festival is celebrated in a fortress. Many names of this martial goddess, starting with Durgā, are directly related to words denoting 'fortress'[195]. In South Indian villages, the yearly marriage of the guardian goddess involves the sacrifice of a water buffalo representing her husband. In the associated myths, the high caste bride discovers that the groom has deceived her by concealing his lowly birth and kills him; the husband is converted into a tree[196].

Durgā's predecessors in the Veda

A predecessor of Durgā had come to India already much earlier. In the Vedic texts, her manifestation is Goddess Vāc, who secures victory and is addressed as *siṃhī* 'lioness', *mahiṣī* 'she-buffalo', and *aṣāḍhā* 'invincible'. Several archaic rituals connected with her cult are described. One is on the *mahāvrata* day (either a solstice or equinox). A man of high birth and a man of low birth fight for a bull hide that represents the sun, and the former wins. A chariot warrior shoots three arrows at the hide of a sterile cow. All sorts of musical instruments representing the goddess are played, especially a thundering 'earth drum' which is covered with a bull's hide.

and beaten with its tail. (The words "beat" and "tail" have a sexual as well as violent connotation) A priestly ascetic who has practiced celibacy and a prostitute unite sexually and scold each other for misbehaviour[197]. The *vrātyastoma* rituals performed before and after raiding expeditions closely resemble the later navarātris. Particularly important is the horse sacrifice (*aśvamedha*). The chief victim, a stallion, is "escorted" by an army on a year-long war expedition; its celibacy ends in a 'sacred marriage' with the chief queen of the sacrificing king. The bridegroom of this 'marriage', who is killed, was supposed to have fertilized the queen and the earth. The queen's title, *mahiṣī* 'she-buffalo', connects her with the goddess Vāc; this suggests that the sacrificed male victim representing her husband was *mahiṣa* 'water buffalo bull' before it was transformed into a horse, the most important animal for the Vedic Aryans. The carver of the horse, a virginal youth, was garlanded; he was lamented, as if he was to die, for in former times he himself was cut up, probably as the chief victim of the obsolete human sacrifice (*puruṣamedha*), where the victim represented the Primeval Man (*puruṣa*) out of whose severed limbs the world came into being[198]. — Evidence for the practice of similar 'sacred marriage' in Harappan religion is a seal from Chanhu-daro depicting a sexual intercourse between a bison and a prostrate woman with an elaborate headdress and outspread legs (Figure 38)[199].

The Dāsas, who were enemies of the Rigvedic Aryans, had 'autumnal' fortresses (*śāradī pur*), which were probably venues of the autumnal festival of the Goddess, like the present-day fortress called Śār(a)dī in Kashmir. The Dāsa chief Śambara shares the same name as the fierce form of the god Śiva in Hindu and Buddhist Tantrism; this name evokes the *śabara* 'savage' figuring in the autumnal navarātri[200].

The Harappan goddess of war

The Harappans had a goddess of war connected with the tiger, another large feline that was once native to the Indus Valley. On a cylinder seal from Kalibangan (Figure 39), a goddess in long skirt and plaited hair holds the hands of two warriors in the process of spearing each other. Next to this scene, the same deity is shown with an elaborate horn crown and the back part of a tiger as a continuation of her body. The hair of the two warriors is arranged into the 'double bun' or chignon at the back of the head, characteristic of Late Early Dynastic Mesopotamian kings on the warpath. As in the later South Asian tradition, this tiger-riding goddess of war apparently received water buffaloes in sacrifice. There are several Harappan images of a man who spears a water buffalo while placing one of his feet on the head of the beast. This pose came to signify 'victory' in Mesopotamian glyptic art during the reign of Sargon the Great (2334-2279 BCE)[201].

The aurochs and lion in Western Asia = the wild water buffalo and tiger in South Asia

In India, the wild water buffalo is the most dangerous animal besides the tiger. There is

Figure 38 Intercourse of bison and priestess on an Indus seal from Chanhu-daro. (Cf. Figure 44!) (after Mackay 1943: Plate 51, 13)

Figure 39 Warriors spearing each other and tiger-goddess on a cylinder seal from Kalibangan, K-65 (after CISI 1: 311)

Figure 40 Contest with bulls and lions, Fara period cylinder seal, c. 2500 BCE (after Amiet 1980: no. 893)

direct glyptic confirmation that these two natural enemies actually form the Indian counterpart to the aurochs and lion, the main characters of the 'contest' motif on Western Asiatic glyptics. In the Late Early Dynastic period, the fight between the lion and the bull on Proto-Elamite seals developed into the 'Gilgamesh and Enkidu'[202] type of contest, which was the most important motif of the royal seals in the Akkadian period (Figure 40). During the sixty year long rule of Sargon the Great, the aurochs bull is suddenly replaced with the water buffalo in this 'contest' scene (Figure 41). Sargon boasts that ships from the far-off land of Meluhha (nowadays fairly unanimously considered to denote the Greater Indus Valley) came to his new capital Akkad. These ships probably brought some water buffaloes as gifts to Sargon's royal park. Before this time, the water buffalo is not attested in the Mesopotamian fauna (with neither bone finds, nor pictorial representations). On the other hand, in the Harappan version of the 'contest' motif (Figure 42), the hero holds back two tigers (instead of lions) the Mesopotamian origin of which is clear from the hairstyle of the Harappan hero (either 'six locks of hair' or the 'chignon'). The establishment of this correspondence (aurochs and lion = water buffalo and tiger) makes it impossible to cite the absence of lion in Harappan art as an argument against the Western Asiatic origin of the unicorn motif.

12. The Bull of Heaven and astral symbols and myths

In Mesopotamia, the 'Bull of Heaven' (Sumerian GU_4-AN-NA = Akkadian *ālu*) is mentioned both in the Sumerian poem "Gilgamesh and the Bull of Heaven" and in tablet VI of the Babylonian Gilgamesh Epic. After Gilgamesh (the King of Uruk) rejects the marriage proposal and sexual

Figure 41 Contest with water buffalo and lion, Akkadian seal, c. 2300 BCE (after Aruz (ed.) 2003: 218 no. 146)

advances of Ishtar (the guardian goddess of the city), citing the fate of her other lovers who have lost their lives in such a marriage, the spurned goddess asks her father (the Sky god An) to send his demonic bull to destroy the city of Uruk. The bull causes much destruction, but is eventually killed by Gilgamesh with the assistance of his friend Enkidu[203].

In Mesopotamia, the lion and bull myth was transferred to the sky: the zodiacal constellation Taurus was also called 'Bull of Heaven' (Sumerian ^{mul}GU$_4$-AN-NA)[204]. Dating to 4000 BCE is an astral myth that apparently involves the killing of the bull by the lion: when the zodiacal sign of Lion (Sumerian ^{mul}UR.GU.LA 'lion') with its "royal star" (*šarru* = Regulus = alpha Leonis) stood at the zenith (thereby displaying its maximum power), the Bull (comprising "the Bull's eye" = Aldebaran = alpha Tauri and the Pleiades with Alcyone = ēta Tauri) set heliacally under the western horizon; remaining invisible for a period of forty days, it was then "reborn", rising again heliacally at the spring equinox[205].

Apparently the rosette on the forehead of many Western Asiatic and related bull statuettes (Figure 43) represents the red star Aldebaran as the eye of the Heavenly Bull in the constellation Taurus. Such a "third eye" is depicted on the forehead of some bull images of the Indus Civilization and the related Kulli culture. Later in South Asia, water buffalos with three eyes are depicted in wrathful tantric images of the god Śiva and other deities (Figure 44)[206].

Sumerian sculptures of a reclining bull covered with inlaid trefoils and quatrefoils have plausibly been interpreted to represent the 'Bull of Heaven'[207]. Such statues are known both from the Jemdet Nasr period (c. 3100-2900 BCE) (Figure 45) and from the Neo-Sumerian time (c. 2100-1900 BCE) (Figure

Figure 42 Harappan version of the contest motif: hero with tigers on seal M-308 (after CISI 1: 384)

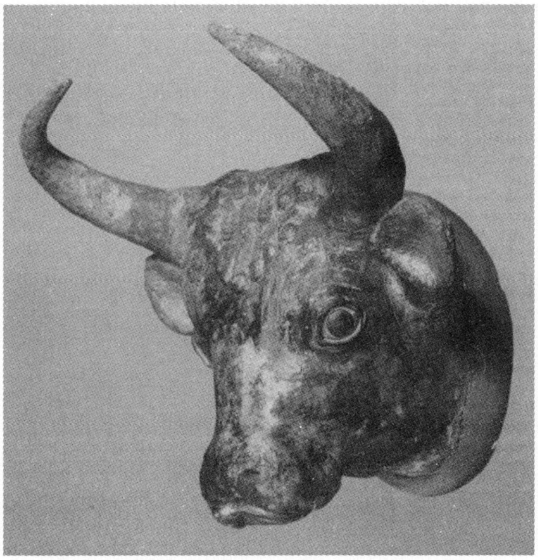

Figure 43 Silver bull's head with a star-like rosette on its forehead. Queen Puabi's tomb chamber, Ur, c. 2400 BCE. Now in the University Museum, Philadelphia (after Aruz (ed.) 2003: 115 no. 65)

Figure 44 God of Death as a water buffalo with three eyes, riding a buffalo that copulates with and tramples a prostrate human being. (Cf. Figure 38!) (after Grünwedel 1900: 168, Abb. 142)

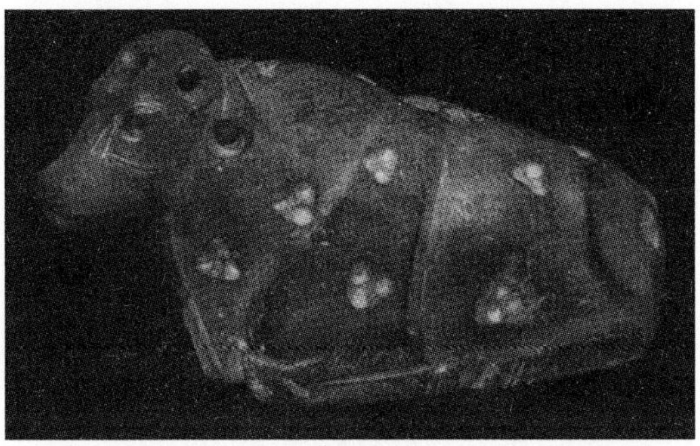

Figure 45a An early Sumerian statuette of the Bull of Heaven, made of blue lapis lazuli, c. 3000 BCE (after *La Mésopotamie* 2000: no. 46)

Figure 45b An early Sumerian statuette of the Bull of Heaven from Uruk, c. 3000 BCE. Now in the Vorderasiatisches Museum, Berlin (after Aruz (ed.) 2003, 17 no. 2b)

46) (Parpola 1985: 26-29). A mosaic of a reclining bull covered with trefoils was found in the 'palace' of the BMAC site Dashly-3 in northern Afghanistan (Figure 47)[208]. From Mohenjo-daro comes a fragmentary steatite sculpture of an animal covered with red-coloured trefoils and figures-of-eight. Though its head and feet are missing, the animal can be identified as a bull; the space on its underside with holes for attaching separate sexual organs is too narrow for udders, but sufficient for testicles and penis (Figure 48)[209].

The hypothesis that the quatrefoils, trefoils,

figures-of-eight and dots-in-circle of these bull sculptures represent constellations is supported not only by such parallels as the trefoils covering the body of the cow-shaped Egyptian "Lady of Heaven" in Tutankhamon's tomb[210]. The trefoil motif corresponds to the Sumerian pictogram consisting of three stars placed in a triangle: this sign expresses the word MUL 'constellation'[211]; it is also the name of the Pleiades (^{mul}MUL) as the constellation par excellence[212]. The dress of the famous 'Priest-king' statue from Mohenjo-daro—decorated with red-coloured trefoils, figures-of-eight and dots-in-circle (Figure 49)—has been compared to the festive clothes of Near Eastern gods and divine kings onto which were sewn golden stars, rosettes, and so forth and called 'sky-garments' (Sumerian AN.MA = Akkadian *nalbaš šamê*)[213]. In the 5th century CE, the Egyptian author Nonnos (writing in Greek) describes a temple of the Syrian city of Tyrus and calls its deity 'Starclad God' (Βὴλ ἀστροχίτων), "clad in a patterned robe like the sky, and image of the universe" and "called Starclad, since by night starry mantles illuminate the sky."[214]

Related Harappan traditions seem to have survived in India until Vedic times; at the royal consecration, the king was invested with a *tārpya* garment with images of sacrificial fireplaces (*dhiṣṇya*) sewn onto it. According to the Mahābhārata (3,43), stars are the fireplaces (*dhiṣṇya*) of pious ancient Sages in the sky. This is the same dress worn by the divine King Varuṇa, who is associated with the night sky[215]. In the royal horse sacrifice (and the parallel human sacrifice, obsolete in Vedic times), in his 'sacred marriage' with the king's chief queen, the male victim is enveloped in the *tārpya* garment[216].

Astral myth of the primeval incest and the killing of the male creator in Vedic India

In the Vedic texts, there are several variants in which the creator god Prajāpati creates the goddess Vāc out of himself and then seeks to pair with this daughter. She tries to escape his incestuous advances by assuming the female form of one animal species after another, while Prajāpati chases her by assuming the shape of the corresponding male. In this way, they create all of the different kinds of animals in the world. According to the Aitareya-Brahmana

Figure 46 A Neo-Sumerian statue of the Bull of Heaven from Tello, c. 2000 BCE, now in the Louvre, Paris (after Parrot 1960: 225 no. 276a)

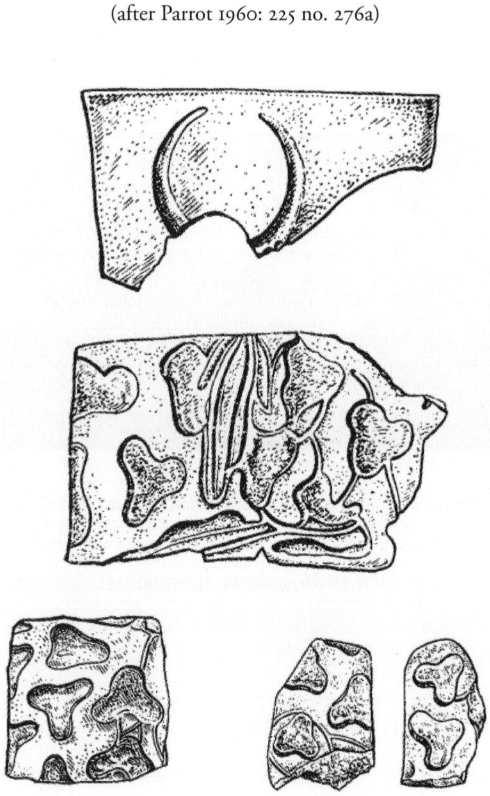

Figure 47 Mosaic of a reclining bull decorated with trefoils from the BMAC site Dashly-3 in northern Afghanistan, c. 2000 BCE (after Parpola 1985: Figure 21 (from Sarianidi 1977: Figure 19))

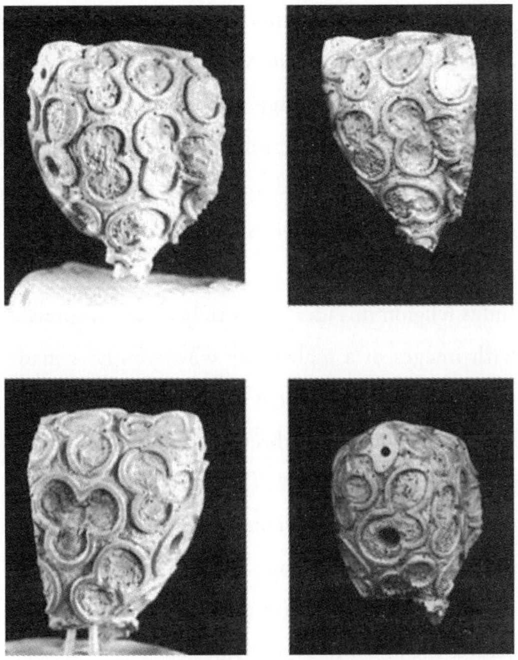

Figure 48 Fragment of a Harappan bull statuette, decorated with trefoils and figures-of-eight (after Parpola 1985: 35)

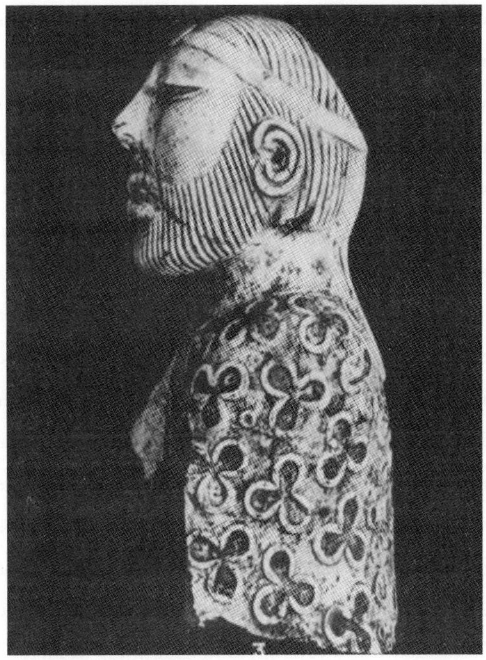

Figure 49 The 'Priest-King' statuette from Mohenjo-daro (after Marshall (ed.) 1931: III, Plate 98,3)

(3,33), "Prajāpati conceived a passion for his own daughter... Having become an antelope stag [*ṛśya-*] he approached her in the form of a doe [*rohit-*]."[217] Wanting to punish Prajāpati for this sin of incest, the gods created the 'terrible' Rudra to pierce him with an arrow. The chapter identifies the various participants of this myth (the doe, the stag, the arrow and the hunter) with constellations of the Vedic star calendar, starting with Aldebaran[218] (called *rohiṇī* 'red' in Sanskrit; this word also denotes a virginal girl at the time of her first menstruation)[219]. In this version, Prajāpati is the antelope stag (*ṛśya-*), represented by the constellation named *mṛgaśīrṣa-*, 'antelope's head', situated in the Orion system. If this union with the *ṛśya-* initiated rains at the summer solstice (as does Ṛśyaśṛṅga's union in many versions of the legend; compare also the union of the celibate student and the prostitute at the mahāvrata), the heliacal rising of the *mṛgaśīrṣa-* at the summer solstice could mark this event astronomically, dating it to around 2000 BCE[220].

13. Identification of the Harappan 'unicorn' as the nilgai antelope

While many archaeozoologists have identified the Indus unicorn as humpless cattle, this identification is not without its difficulties: "The presence of so much imagery of unhumped cattle in the Mature Harappa, in the absence of confirming osteological evidence, is one of the unresolved issues of the Indus Age."[221] Caroline Grigson, who wrote her Ph.D. on the skulls of the taurine and zebu cattle and their wild ancestors (1973), is one archaeozoologist who is not happy with the urus identification. Having studied the various distinguishing features of the Indus 'unicorn', she has found that in many respects the representations of the 'unicorn' do not accurately depict the *Bos primigenius*. But while other bovid species which could possibly have served as models (the Indian gaur, buffalo, black buck, nilgai, the Middle Eastern hartebeest and oryx, and even the Tibetan antelope) "resemble the unicorn in some ways, they all differ from it even more than *Bos primigenius* does."[222] In Grigson's opinion, the most likely interpretation is that "while being based on *Bos primigenius* these seals have been copied again and again *in the absence of the original animal*. And in the process of being copied, either from a depiction of the actual animal or from a remembered animal, many of its features became distorted or perhaps replaced with those of other species."[223] Grigson concludes that "depictions of the unicorn, far from proving that *Bos primigenius* was living in the Indus Valley, are evidence that it was *not*. If it had been present, and therefore available as a living model, it would, like the humped ox, have been much more carefully and accurately depicted" (Grigson 1984: 168).

As Grigson notes, this possibility had in fact already been suggested by Ernest Mackay: "the one-horned beast, which is not far removed from an actual animal, might easily have assumed from constant copying the form we now see on the seals, the animal itself having become rare or extinct."[224] Mackay decided to "term it a 'urus bull'", but he qualified this with a reservation: "I do not think these animals are the ordinary ox. The head is much too small and pointed."[225]

I accept the hypothesis that the 'unicorn' bull originally represented the *Bos primigenius* of Western Asia. Adopted from Mesopotamia by the Harappans, in the Indus Valley this imported image was largely remodeled after a local animal that occupied an important position in the Harappan religion. Its symbolism and function should have been at least partially similar to those of the wild bull in Mesopotamia, which represented the thundering "Bull of Heaven", the husband of the earth goddess, whom he fertilized with rain-seed. As we have seen, one South Asian animal that was certainly a counterpart of the urus bull of Western Asia is the water buffalo. This is one of the strong male animals surrounding the buffalo-horned "Proto-Śiva" in seal M-304 from Mohenjo-daro (see Figure 56 of the crocodile paper). In Harappan as well as in Vedic and Tantric religions, all male animals were apparently considered to be manifestations of the singular primeval male, the creator god, the husband and opponent of the Goddess[226]. In the Indus religion this idea seems to have been expressed with images of a male deity whose body is made up of parts from different animals (cf. Figure 12). Another example is a three-headed bovine animal with a single body: each of the three animals joined together perhaps represents the primeval male at a particular time of the daily and/or yearly cycle. One of the three bovine animals united in this single beast is the unicorn (Figure 50).

The unicorn thus appears to be just one of several potential counterparts of the urus bull of Western Asia. Based on the later religious and literary traditions of India, one of the foremost local animals that could have altered the 'unicorn' image in the Indus Valley is the *ṛśya / ṛṣya*, which in the Ṛṣyaśṛṅga legend is expressly connected with the concept of 'unicorn' (*ekaśṛṅga*). This animal also personifies the creator god Prajāpati in the above-discussed pivotal Vedic myth of primeval incest in Aitareya-Brāhmaṇa 3,33. But which animal is *ṛśya / ṛṣya*? The Sanskrit dictionaries render the word as 'the male of a kind of antelope', but which antelope? Etymologically the word goes back to Proto-Aryan; the Iranian cognates (Khotan Saka *rūś* and Wakhi *rūš*) denote 'a wild mountain sheep, *Ovis poli*'[227]. The etymon may ultimately go back to Proto-Indo-European **el-* (from which English *elk* is derived)[228], and the original meaning may have been 'reddish' or 'brown' (PIE **el-*) animal[229]. A variant form *ṛśa-* occurs in the Śaunaka version of the Atharvaveda (4,4,7 and 6,101,3) in a charm for the recovery of virility: "I make thy member taut, like a bowstring on a bow; mount, as it were a stag a doe, unrelaxingly always (?)."[230] Here, as in the myth

Figure 50 Seal M-1171 with a composite bovine uniting protomes of the bison, the unicorn and the gazelle (after CISI 2: 136)

Figure 51 Male and female nilgai (after Prater 1971: pl. 61)

of primeval incest in AB 3,33, the female antelope corresponding to the male *ṛś(y)a-* in Sanskrit is called *rohit-*, literally 'red'. Many dictionaries again give the meaning just as 'a kind of deer', but in Marathi the cognate *rohī* denotes the 'slate-coloured or white-footed antelope'[231]. Derived from Old Indo-Aryan **rohya-*, also originally denoting a 'red' animal, are Sindhi *rojhu* m. *rojha* f., Punjabi *rojh* f., and Hindi and Gujarati *rojh* m., all denoting 'the white-footed or painted antelope'[232]. This antelope is better known as the nilgai (*Boselaphus tragocamelus*, in older terminology *Antelope picta*). The Hindi name *nīlgāy* means 'blue cow', yet the females (which are hornless) and immature males are yellowish brown or reddish -fawn and only the bulls are blue-grey (Figure 51)[233].

Ernest Mackay thought that the Indus 'unicorn' is "a composite of the ox and the antelope"[234]. He based this suggestion on the following observations:

> "In some respects the body of this beast, which is always a male, resembles that of an antelope of heavy build, such as the eland or oryx, and in others that of an ox. The long tufted tail may belong to either class. The horn is sometimes smooth (Nos. 2, 4, 15, 18, etc.); sometimes it has transverse ridges (Nos. 6, 9, 11, etc.). In the latter case, the possibility of the creature being an ox is ruled out. The long pointed ears are also a characteristic of an antelope."[235]

One more distinctive feature mentioned by Mackay can be added:

> "A prominent feature about this beast is the striking eye and the well-marked eye-lid above it... definitely cow-like and, moreover, set in their proper place in the head", but in other instances "the eye is entirely different and has something of the camel's eye about it."[236]

The eyes of the nilgai are indeed camel-like, and the camel figures also in the scientific name of the nilgai (*Boselaphus tragocamelus*) (Figure 52).

In all these respects and in some other important ones, the nilgai fits perfectly with the antelope features of the unicorn. I would like to draw particular attention to the nilgai's being like "a horselike cow... an adult bull is a handsome

Figure 52a Antelope-like unicorn on seal H-6 from Harappa (after CISI 3.1: 367)

Figure 52b Antelope-like unicorn on seal Nd-1 from Nindowari (after CISI 2: 419)

and impressive antelope. They are sturdy animals with stout legs and rather long sloping horselike necks... The whole head is long and narrow, almost horselike... The adult males are bigger than the females with noticeably higher sloping shoulders and very thick muscular necks... The horns of the male are cowlike in appearance, being black ... [but] despite the large size of the animal generally measure only 15.2—17.8 cm (6—7 in.) though 30 cm (11 ¾ in.) is on record..."[237] As in the case of the hatchings of the neck, the natural muscular patterns of the shoulders (clearly visible in Figures 53-54) perfectly explain "the curious markings that occur on the shoulders of these animals, and of these alone," which Mackay thought "to represent trappings of some kind rather than muscles or wrinkles in the skin."[238] The length of the unicorn's horn differ's from that of the nilgai, but it can be understood either as a urus heritage or as a wish to emphasize this important symbol of virility; in any case, the shape is similar.

So here is the original beast behind the classical and medieval unicorn legend: in *ṛś(y)a- / ṛṣya-* = nilgai we have an *Indian* animal, which is *horselike*, has a *deerlike head with black horns*, and is explicitly represented as ***unicorn*** both in Indian folklore (Ṛṣyaśṛṅga Ekaśṛṅga) and in Indus iconography. Moreover, being so cowlike as to be called ***nīl-gāy*** 'blue cow', and identified with the wild cow of Western Asia by the Harappans, this animal was worshipped as sacred[239]. The nilgai "bulls generally remain solitary"[240], yet another characteristic of the classical unicorn. The unicorn and lion fight has a counterpart in the fact that the nilgai's' "main predators are tigers and lions."[241] "A hundred years ago Nilgai were frequently hunted by British sportsmen on horseback and armed with spears (...). Despite their ungainly looking gallop Nilgai have great endurance and are fast runners so that this must have been a difficult sport requiring considerable skill."[242] This and the nilgai's horselike appearance are likely to have contributed to its confusion with the wild ass, which can drink brackish water and is therefore thought to be able to remove poison from water. "Blue bulls can survive for days without water, but they live close to waterholes."[243] Accordingly, a comparison usually connected with the wild ass in the Ṛgveda[244] is also applied to the nilgai: Indra is invited to come and drink Soma "like a thirsting *ṛśya-* (comes to drink water)"[245].

Figure 53 Nilgai bull. Photo Toby Sinclair (after Israel and Sinclair (eds.) 1989: 53)

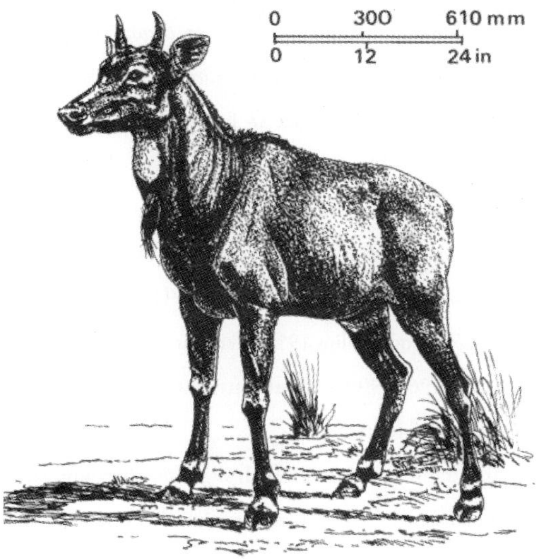

Figure 54a Nilgai bull (after Roberts 1977: 176, ill. 52)

Figure 54b Nilgai bull. Mughal painting by Mansur, c. 1610, now in Fitzwilliam Museum in Cambridge (after *In the image of man* 1982: 104, Figure 38)

Finally, the nilgai is a *paragon of virile power* and represents the creator god, who has *sexual intercourse* with his own *virginal* daughter. The blue colour of the nilgai bull connects it with the rainclouds and thus the drought and rain motif of the Ṛśyaśṛṅga legend; moreover, "breeding can probably occur throughout the year..., though there appears to be a peak breeding season with more young being born at the beginning of the Monsoon season."[246]

In the vocabulary of Dravidian languages there is only one etymon[247] which is likely to represent the Proto-Dravidian appellation of the nilgai. Since the nilgai is not found in southernmost India, it is not surprising that these native terms come only from the tribal languages of Central India:

Parji *guḍva* 'nilgai'
Gondi dialects:
(Mu.) *koḍa (māv)* 'a kind of deer'
(L.) *koḍā māv* 'blue bull'
(SR.) *khoḍḍa māv* 'blue bull'
(Ko.) *guṛiya māv* 'nilgai'

Gadaba *guri goḍ* 'bison'
Konḍa *gura* 'bison'

In Gondi, the name of the nilgai ends in the word *māv* (from Proto-Dravidian **māku*) 'animal, beast, deer, antelope'[248], suggesting that the foregoing word **kuṭV-* is a qualifying attribute. It could be Proto-Dravidian **kuṭV(-kuṭV)*, which denotes a rapidly repeated rumbling or grumbling and rattling sound and is often used of thunder; it also means, among other things, a 'stamping noise in running' (used in Toda for buffalo), which in my opinion describes the nilgai very well, having personally seen nilgais at Dholavira, Kutch, Gujarat[249]. These words have coincidental homophones that probably have caused certain associations in Proto-Dravidian speakers and may have influenced their views of the nilgai, and which do remind one of details in the Ṛśyaśṛṅga legend: **kuṭV* 'waterpot' (in Tamil also 'ascetic's pitcher')[250], **kuṭV* 'to drink'[251], and **kuṭV* 'hut, house, abode, home, household, family' (in South Dravidian languages also 'servant, landholder, tenant, farmer')[252].

My conclusion is that the Indian Ṛśyaśṛṅga legend goes back to the Harappan religion, where the unicorn bull depicted on thousands of seals represents a real local animal, the nilgai antelope, called *ṛśya* in Sanskrit. His single horn, the length of which is exaggerated, has a phallic connotation and emphasizes the importance of this animal as a symbol of fertility. His cult purported to secure abundant rains that were vital for agriculture and animal husbandry, the foundations of Harappan economy. Such a role can best explain the overwhelming popularity of the unicorn as the favourite deity of many Indus seal owners.

Notes

1) The unicorn supporter first appears on the gold coins of King James III of Scotland (c. 1480). It is supposed to have been introduced into Scotland with the marriage of James I to Jane Beaufort, since the Beauforts as dukes of Somerset used the unicorn as a supporter on their coat-of-arms. After the Union, the unicorn became the left-hand supporter in England; in Scotland it was placed on the right. (Phillips 1911: 582.)
2) All words used for the unicorn in European languages are translation loans going back to Classical Greek *monókerōs*, being based on a learned literary tradition (Güntert 1929-30: 710): German *Einhorn*, English *unicorn*, Latin *unicornis*, French *licorne*, *lincorne*, Italian *licorno*, *liocorno*, *leocorno*, *leoncorno* and (most commonly used) *alicorno*, Portuguese *alicornio*, and Modern Greek *liokórno*. The French and Italian words have the Romance article (affected by the word for 'lion', *leone*, *lion*) prefixed to Latin *cornu* 'horn', while Italian *alicorno* and Portuguese *alicornio* in addition have the Arabic definite article *al-* prefixed to them (Shepard 1930: 141-142).
3) On the lore of the medieval unicorn, see especially Shepard 1930 and Einhorn 1976 (with extensive bibliography of further literature); Güntert 1929-30: 708-710 and Phillips 1911 offer short summaries.
4) Lesky 1963: 909 and Panaino 2001: 154, n. 39 with further references.
5) This translation is taken with slight modifications from Panaino 2001: 155, where the original Greek text is also given.
6) Lesky 1963: 854.
7) Psalms 21 (22): 22; 28 (29): 6; 77 (78): 69; 91 (92): 11; Numeri 23: 22; 24: 8; Deut. 33: 17; Hiob 39: 9; Einhorn 1976: 42-44; and Panaino 2001: 156, with the Greek and Latin translations of many of these passages cited in notes 49-53. See also Schrader 1892: 573 and 580-581, and Phillips 1911: 581. Phillips suggests that "the medieval conception of the unicorn as possessing great strength and fierceness may have been partly due to" these translations. She also points out that while the Revised Version has 'wild ox', the Authorized Version of the English Bible also has 'unicorn', "though in Deut. XXXIII.17 it obviously refers to a two-horned animal"

(see also Schrader 1892: 580).

8) Translation from Panaino 2001: 169-170, where the Greek original is also given. Panaino notes that a related source, the (fictitious) description of the Marmara Sea by the Dutch priest Johannis Witte de Hese from the year 1389 more clearly reflects the Zoroastrian source, the tradition of the Three-legged Ass in the Bundahišn (see below), including the dualistic opposition of good and bad animals: "He says that still at his time some poisonous animals (*animalia venemosa*) come at twilight to infect the waters of the Sea and that the good animals (*animalia bona*) cannot drink any water; but each day, after dawn, the unicorn comes and he enters the waters purifying them from the poison and allowing other animals to drink during the day."

9) Modified from the translation of Panaino (2001: 156), who gives the original Greek text and further references.

10) On Ctesias, see Karttunen 1989: 80-85.

11) Photius, *Bibliotheca* 72, 45, translated by Freese 1920. Aelianus, *De natura animalium* 4,52, gives a slightly more extensive version, which essentially agrees with Photius. The Greek originals of these two versions are given by Jacoby 1958: III C no. 688, pp. 505-506.

12) See the summary given by Karttunen 1989: 168-171; 1997: 184-186. See also Panaino 2001: 156 and 161.

13) Steier 1935: 1781-2; Karttunen 1989: 168 n. 95; Panaino 2001.

14) On Megasthenes, see Karttunen 1997: 69-94.

15) On account of these uncertainties, some of these fragments are not included in the fragments of Ctesias nor Megasthenes in Felix Jacoby 1958: IIIC.

16) On *kartázōnos*, which denotes the rhinoceros, see Karttunen 1997: 185; Panaino 2001: 161.

17) Translated by Scholfield 1958: III, 289 and 291, quoted with the Greek text by Panaino 2001: 159. This is Megasthenes fragment 15 in Schwanbeck 1846: 104, but is not included in Jacoby 1958: IIIC no. 715.

18) See the paper on the wild asses, above, p. 66.

19) My translation. The Latin text is quoted by Panaino 2001: 160, n. 65: *in India et boves solidis ungulis, unicornes, et feram nomine axin hinnulei pelle pluribus candidioribus maculis, sacrorum Liberi patris—(Orsaei Indi simias candentes toto corpore venantur)—asperrimam autem feram monocerotem, reliquo corpore equo similem, capite cervo, pedibus elephanto, cauda apro, mugitu gravi, uno cornu nigro media fronte cubitorum duum eminente. hanc feram vivam negant capi.*

20) My translation. The Latin text is quoted by Panaino 2001: 160, n. 65: *sed atrocissimus est monoceros, monstrum mugitu horrido, equino corpore, elephanti pedibus, cauda suilla, capite cervino. cornu e media fronte eius protenditur splendore mirifico, ad magnitudinem pedum quattuor, ita acutum ut quidquid impetat, facile ictu eius perforetur. vivus non venit in hominum potestatem et interimi quidem potest, capi non potest.*

21) Transl. Jones 1930: VII, 92-93, quoted with the Greek text by Panaino 2001: 159-160. See Jacoby 1958: IIIC2, 631 no. 715 F 27b.

22) Slightly modified from the translation by Peck (1961: 218-221), quoted with the Greek text by Panaino 2001: 160, n. 64.

23) Translation by Peck (1965: 88-89), quoted with the Greek text by Panaino 2001: 160, n. 64.

24) Lesky 1963: 893.

25) Text and transl. Conybeare 1969: 234-237, quoted by Panaino 2001: 160, n. 65.

26) Cf. Einhorn 1976: 33 and Panaino 2001: 157, n. 59, both with further references.

27) The Iranian sources are cited here in (minimally modified) translations presented by Antonio Panaino (2001: 162-167), who also quotes and comments on the original texts.

28) Panaino (2001: 166): "The direct identification between the *xara-* of Yasna 42 and the *xar ī se pāy* is undisputed among Iranologists" (in note 160, Panaino quotes Windischmann, W. Geiger, Darmesteter, Jackson, Nyberg and Voigt).

29) Panaino 2001: 166.

30) Panaino 2001: 164-165.

31) Tištar is the Avestan Tištrya, who is represented by a white horse with golden ears. Panaino (2001: 167 n. 168) lists a number of features and functions in which

Tištrya parallels the Three-legged Ass. There clearly has been some mutual adjustment between the earlier cults connected with the ass and the Irano-Aryan traditions connected with the horse.

32) Panaino 2001: 167.

33) Translation of A. V. Williams, quoted by Panaino 2001: 167.

34) Panaino 2001: 166, n. 162, quoting Darmesteter 1877: 147-148.

35) Einhorn 1976: 32; Panaino 2001: 168.

36) Parpola and Janhunen 2011 (in this book), note 77.

37) Panaino 2001: 173; the three-legged Priapus was connected with the Iranian Three-legged Ass by Albright (1920: 333).

38) Albright 1920: 331-332. In Lydia and Mysia (Lampsacus), the ass was sacrificed to Priapus, and in some myths he was the son of an ass. "The association of the ass with fecundity might be illustrated by a mass of evidence, mythological, pornographic, and philological. The quasi-divine nature of the ass appears in Juvenal's statement (6,334) that prominent Roman matrons consorted with the animal at the orgies of the 'Bona Dea'. That bestiality of this sort was practised elsewhere is clear from Apuleius, *Met.*, 10, 22 and Lucian's *Loúkios ē ónos*, which draws freely from Syro-Anatolian tales and customs."

39) Beal 1875: 124 n. 2: "The connection of this myth with the medieval story of the Unicorn being capable of capture only by a chaste maiden is too evident to require proof." See Lüders [1898] 1940: 25 n. 3. The objections made against this connection by Heinrich Günter (1922: 65-74) were annulled by Schlingloff 1973: 301-302.

40) The fundamental study is Lüders 1898 and 1901, reprinted in 1940: 1-43 and 47-73; see also Schroeder 1908: 292-303; Przyluski 1929; Meyer 1930: II, 540-548; Schlingloff 1973, O'Flaherty 1973: 42-52; Vasil'kov 1979; Jain 1981: 196; Simson 1986; Della Casa 1986; Panaino 2001: 150-153.

41) O'Flaherty 1973: 43.

42) O'Flaherty 1973: 43.

43) O'Flaherty 1973: 45.

44) Also in the Mahāvastu the son of the sage Kāśyapa and a doe is named Ekaśṛṅga, the reason given being that he had a single horn on his forehead. Elsewhere two horns are mentioned. See Lüders 1940: 65.

45) On the basis of textual history, Lüders (1940: 14, 25) thought that in the original version of the story it was the king's daughter that fetched Ṛṣyaśṛṅga. In the opinion of Moriz Winternitz (1908: I, 344, n. 2), later bards or copyists of the story found it offensive that a princess should have seduced Ṛṣyaśṛṅga and substituted her with a courtesan. Schlingloff (1973: 303), however, has pointed out that for a Brahmin, union with a courtesan is a bigger offence than the union with a princess that ended in marriage. "On the other hand, if in the original version a courtesan was the seductress, the Buddhists had a very obvious reason to replace her with a king's daughter. The Buddhists interpreted this story as a Jātaka, an event from one of the previous lives of the Buddha. The young ascetic was identified with the Buddha and his mate accordingly with his wife. Thus the seductress could not very well be a courtesan but had to be of royal blood like the wife of the Buddha." Simson (1986: 207-208) suggests that the story may have involved two women from the beginning, the courtesan seducing Ṛṣyaśṛṅga and bringing him to the king's palace, where the princess married him and got children: the marriage motif is well attested, and no version has the courtesan bringing Ṛṣyaśṛṅga to the palace and marrying him there. Schroeder (1908: 300) derives the two women from the archaic cultic drama of the mahāvrata, where a prostitute performs the sexual union; he suggests that here the prostitute personifies the king's daughter. I would like to point out that in a parallel 'sacred marriage' of the Vedic horse sacrifice, the king's chief queen (who represents the earth goddess) lies down with the sacrificed stallion that has remained celibate for one year until that point.

46) O'Flaherty 1973: 45-46.

47) O'Flaherty 1973: 44.

48) Lüders 1940: 16-18; Przyluski 1929: 333-337; Goldman 1985: 74-76, 139-161 and 292-323; Simson 1986: 206-

207.

49) Simson 1986: 206.

50) Schlingloff 1973: 304-305: "Here we have a version where the abduction to the city is well motivated. The king allures the jungleman to win him over as brother and friend. This exactly is the motive in the Enkidu episode of the Gilgamesh epic" (p. 305). Simson (1986: 219-221), however, thinks that this version is not particularly old (and that it may be a psychologically motivated transformation of the Mahāvastu version).

51) Sivaramamurti 1981: 15.

52) The JUB has the older Vedic spelling of the name, Ṛśyaśṛṅga, with a palatal sibilant instead of the later retroflex sibilant of Ṛṣyaśṛṅga.

53) Hermann Berger (1971) has proposed a Dravidian etymology for the name Vibhāṇḍaka; Simson (1986: 203 and 223) accepts this, but I find it unconvincing.

54) Lüders (1940: 1) points out that the Ṛṣya mentioned in Bhāgavata-Purāṇa 9,22,11 is a different person, since he is the son of Devātithi. Lüders likewise dismisses the Ṛṣyaśṛṅga mentioned in the Sarvānukramaṇī as the seer of Ṛgveda 10,136,7, since he and his six brothers are said to be sons of Vātaraśana. Simson (1986: 223) thinks that on the basis of the verse's content the author may nevertheless be associated with the Ṛṣyaśṛṅga of the legend, but does not go further into the matter. I would like to point out that the 'sages having ropes of the wind' mentioned in the verse can be linked with the cosmic banyan tree growing up to the pole star, which holds up the stars and planets with its invisible aerial 'ropes of wind' bound to the heavenly bodies (Parpola 1994: 244-245; 1998: 258). That the Harappan religion included the concept of a heavenly banyan or pipal tree is suggested by an Indus tablet (H-179), where a fig tree with a deity inside is surrounded on either side by a star figure (Parpola 1994: 244, fig. 14.5). In the Indus seal M-296, a unicorn protome sticks out of a pipal tree that tops the 'sacrificial stand' regularly placed in front of the unicorn.

55) Simson (1986: 223) has already pointed out that the probable connection of this sāman with the male member in PB 5,4,13-14 can be a further testimony of Ṛṣyaśṛṅga's connection with the sexual sphere.

56) Ed. Sámaśramí 1876: II, 324.

57) Burnell's edition of the Jaiminīya-Ārṣeya-Brāhmaṇa reads *bhūteśaṃ ca sāma vā*, while the manuscripts of Jaiminīya-Āraṇyaka-Gāna 1,9,4 have *ṛśyasya vrataṃ bhūtecchandasāṃ vā* (Caland 1907: 25 and Makarabhūṣaṇa 2000: 33). In connection with the mahāvrata, Taittirīya-Saṃhitā 7,5,9,4 mentions *bhūtechadāṃ sāmāni*, Śāṅkhāyana-Āraṇyaka 1,4 *bhūtecchadāṃ* (variant readings: *bhūtecchaṃdāṃ*, *bhūtecchaṃdāṃsi*, *bhūtecchaṃdasāṃ*, see Bhim Dev 1980: 5) *sāma* (adding: *priyam indrasya dhāmopajagāmeti*). See Caland 1931: 79-80. Outside Sāmaveda, the term *bhūte-cchád-* is used of the Atharvavedic verses 20,135,11-13 belonging to the *kuntāpa* verses and employed at the mahāvrata; the expression *bhūte-cchád-* is not found in these verses, but Aitareya-Brāhmaṇa 6,36,1-2 glosses them with *bhūtaṃ chādayitvā* (see Debrunner 1957: 63), which Keith (1920: 287) translates "having obscured the might (of the [demonical] Asuras)".

58) This verse is as follows: *harī ta indra śmaśrūṇy uto te haritā harī | taṃ tvā stuvanti kāravaḥ puruṣāso vanargavaḥ ||* "Tawny are your beard-hairs, O Indra, and tawny are your two steeds; singers, *men roaming in the wilds (or: in the forest)*, praise you as such."

59) Ed. Sámaśramí 1876: II, 538.

60) The stobha text runs as follows: *ṛśyāsa indra bhuṅṅ iti maghavann indra bhuṅṅ iti pra bhuṅṅ iti indras tasarapūtaḥ ||*

61) Renou 1952: 109.

62) Caland 1931: 78 on PB 5,4,14.

63) This fire(place), from which all other sacrificial fires are taken, represents the womb; such symbolism seems significant in the present context.

64) Note that in Ṛgveda 10,109,5 the celibate student (*brahmacārin-*) "becomes one member (*ekam aṅgam*) of the gods". On this verse, the only one in the Ṛgveda to have the word *brahmacārin-*, see Kajihara 2001: 28 and 35-37.

65) Caland 1931: 78.

66) Cf. Jaiminīya-Brāhmaṇa 2,403: *yad v eva prati bhūtechandasāṃ vratena stuvate / harī ta indra śmaśrūṇy uto te haritā harī / taṃ tvā stuvanti kāravaḥ puruṣāso vanargavaḥ // ṛśyāsa indra bhuṅṅ iti maghavann indra bhuṅṅ iti pra bhuṅṅ itīndras trasarapūtaḥ* (*tasarapūtaḥ* is the original reading of the Śāṭyāyanaka according to Sāyaṇa) // *iti* (thus Sāyaṇa : *sphigi* JB) *punaḥ punas tasarasphigir iti / etāvadd ha vā asyaikam aṅgam anāstutam āsa yat sphigau / anāstutenainam aṅgena stuvanti / ṛddhiṣṇavo ha bhavanty enena tuṣṭuvānāḥ*.

67) On *tasara-* and its (later) variant *trasara-*, see Mayrhofer 1992: I,639-640.

68) "Again and again" appears to refer to the repeated interjection *bhuṅ*.

69) I take *tasarasphigir* as a bahuvrīhi compound.

70) The dictionaries give only the meanings 'buttock' and 'hip' for Sanskrit *sphigī-* and *sphij-* (on this etymon, see Mayrhofer 1996: II, 777). Here it should refer to the female organ where Indra's member is understood to be (like Greek, *pugē'*, English *behind* and Finnish *perse*, all primarily denoting 'buttocks').

71) The passage is in the unpublished Paryadhyāya section that I am currently in the process of editing: JŚS 3,39,19 *māgadhaṃ ca puṃścalūṃ ca dakṣiṇe vedyante mithunā upakalpayanti*, 20 *tāv abhimantrayate ahaṃ daivyaṃ mithunaṃ gāsyāmi yuvaṃ mānuṣaṃ mithunaṃ caratam iti*, 21 *yadā sāma prastūyātā atha saṃvartayātād iti*, 22 *atha yadi sāmaparimādaḥ kuryād etasmin kāle kuryād*, 23 *yathā bhavati brāhmaṇam*. According to this text, the performance of even the sāmaparimāds was optional; this probably means that they were becoming obsolete.

72) Caland 1931: xx.

73) Cf. Lāṭyāyana-Śrautasūtra 4,3,10-11: *sā brūyād duścaritinn avakīrṇinn iti / dhik tvā jālmi puṃścali grāmasya mārjani puruṣasya puruṣasya śiṣṇapraṇejanīti brahmacārī*. See Rolland 1973: 66.

74) *śitiṅga-* 'whitefooted': could this refer to the nilgai, which is also called 'whitefooted antelope' (on account of the prominent white spots in its feet)?

75) Kajihara 2002: 116 and 126-129.

76) According to Hillebrandt (1890) and Schroeder (1908: 298), the mahāvrata celebrated the summer solstice: this would agree with the symbolism involved here (i.e., a long period of heat/ascetic celibacy (*tapas*) ending with the rains/shedding of seed. Other scholars, however, connect the mahāvrata with the beginning of the year and the winter solstice (see Rolland 1973: 58-60). Similar sexual symbolism was indeed connected with the beginning of the year, which in my opinion was originally connected with the vernal equinox: the birth of Rudra/Skanda is associated with the Pleiades (see Parpola 1994: 205-206).

77) Schroeder (1908: 298-302) interpreted the Ṛṣyaśṛṅga legend as a poetic version of this sexual union in the Vedic mahāvrata ritual, which he considered to be a dramatized rain charm performed at the summer solstice. While some scholars approve of the connection between the Ṛṣyaśṛṅga legend and the mahāvrata (O'Flaherty 1973: 51; Simson 1986: 224), others find it far-fetched (Panaino 2001: 151 n. 20). The express connection of the sage Ṛśya with a sexually loaded song, chanted during the union of the ascetic student and the prostitute at the mahāvrata, makes the connection rather compelling.

78) Ungnad and Gressmann 1911: 95, n. 2.

79) Jensen 1913: 528; 1928: II, 108-112.

80) Schlingloff 1973: 305.

81) Panaino 2001: 170, with reference to Della Casa 1986: 17, 23-24. See also Albright 1920: 329-330 (quoted below in note 81) and O'Flaherty 1973: 50: "Much of the Ṛṣyaśṛṅga story resembles the tale of Enkidu in the Gilgamesh Epic ... There may be a historical link between the myths of Enkidu and Ṛṣyaśṛṅga ... for ties have been established between the Indus Valley and Babylonian civilizations."

82) Hämeen-Anttila 2000: 9-29.

83) This removes Albright's (1920: 331) objection against the assumption that the Ṛṣyaśṛṅga legend is a direct loan from the Gilgamesh epic: "Jensen is certainly wrong in seeing here a direct loan from GE, as the gazelle-mother does not occur in the latter. But it is very probable that our story goes back eventually to a Mesopotamian

origin; in no other case that I have seen is the likelihood so great."

84) Tablet VIII, lines 3-4 [d]EN.KI.[DÙ] AMA-*ka ṣa-bi-ti* / *ù a-ka-a-nu a-bu-ka ib-[nu]-ka ka-a-šá*; cf. Simo Parpola 1997a: 99 and Panaino 2001: 149 and 153 with further references.

85) This probably refers to Enkidu's auto-castration connected with the esoteric cult of the Goddess, which seems to be implied in tablet VI of the epic: Enkidu cuts off the "right hand" of the Bull of Heaven and flings it at the face of Goddess Ištar; cf. Simo Parpola 1997b: xcii-xciii, xcvi-xcvii, notes 119 and 139-140; Panaino 2001: 172.

86) Panaino 2001: 173, n. 190.

87) Mackay 1931: II, 382. According to Atre (1985: 1), 70% all square seals at Mohenjo-daro with a boss have the 'unicorn' motif; at Harappa the number is 77%. According to Franke-Vogt (1991: I, 62), the 'unicorn' constitutes 58.3% of all identifiable main motifs on the seals of all types excavated at Mohenjo-daro, and 80% of those excavated at Chanhu-daro.

88) Marshall 1931: I, 69 n. 1: "According to Pliny, the oryx, the Indian ass, and an Indian ox were all one-horned (NH. viii.30; xi.106)." Marshall comments on Schrader's (1892) suggestion that Ctesias wrote of the unicorn bulls of Persepolis: "But it is now obvious that the idea of a one-horned ox is much older than Achaemenian times."

89) In his recent, still unpublished paper, Mark Kenoyer (2009) argues that the Harappans independently from the West invented a mythical animal with just one horn.

90) Exclusive connections with South Asian fauna, however, do not preclude the possibility that the underlying concept was borrowed from Western Asia and adjusted to the local environmental conditions by means of suitable replacements.

91) The fabulous animal in Figure 12 has "the horns of the zebu, the face of man, the tusks and the trunk of the elephant, the neck and front legs of the goat, the middle body of the 'unicorn', the hind legs of the tiger, and the snake for a tail" (CISI 1: xxxi). In my opinion, this composite animal represents the creator god of the Harappans, the primeval male, who, like the Vedic Puruṣa-Prajāpati, is the male of all animal species; the various male beasts surrounding the seated 'Proto-Śiva' on the well-known Indus seal M-304 convey the same message. On the copper tablets from Mohenjo-daro there are a number of other composite animals, such as the zebu (the horns) + the tiger (the head and front part of the body) + the rhinoceros (the back part of the body); the markhor goat + the 'unicorn' (see CISI 1: xxxi).

92) Mackay 1938: I, 326.

93) Marshall 1931: I, 68-69.

94) See also Franke-Vogt 1991: I, 62.

95) These unicorn statuettes form one of the focal points of Kenoyer's 2009 paper. The first to be excavated was found in 1929 at Chanhu-daro by M. G. Majumdar (1934: pl. XXI: 4), who already commented that that the 'unicorn' "may after all have been intended for an one-horned animal, not a two-horned creature seen in profile." In 1935-36, Ernest Mackay found further examples at Chanhu-daro, comparing them to the unicorn ass of Ctesias and other classical authors (Mackay 1943: 157 and pl. LV: 10, 11, 13-15 and LVI: 2; Franke-Vogt 1991: I, 62 n. 15) (Figure 16). There are examples from Mohenjo-daro and Harappa as well (Kenoyer 1998: Figure 5.15).

96) In the CISI, these two-horned variants have been erroneously conflated with a somewhat similar animal with two long somewhat forward-bending horns. This animal, which is usually without the 'cult stand' of the unicorn (though M-233 has it), has been correctly identified by Franke-Vogt (1991: I, 69, motif 8b, no. 168) as an antelope or gazelle, most probably the Indian gazelle alias chinkara (*Gazella gazella bennetti*) that she mentions as a possible model for this motif.

97) Grigson 1984: 168.

98) There is considerable variation in the depiction of the 'unicorn' and the 'cult stand'; see Franke-Vogt 1991: I, 113-118; II, Plate 43-44, and CISI 2 (1991): xxxi and 433.

99) The 'cult stand' is only very exceptionally placed in front of other animals, such as the rhinoceros in M-1135, the elephant in one roughly made terracotta seal from Allah-dino (Ad 8 in CISI 2: 388), a 'horned tiger' in a seal from Banawali (B-17 in CISI 1: 346), and the goat on a seal from Lothal (L-48). Animals other than the 'unicorn', even wild animals like the tiger and the rhinoceros, usually have what looks like a trough in front of them. In the copper tablets from Mohenjo-daro, such a trough is placed also in front of the unicorn (cf. M-519 and M-520 in CISI 1: 130 and Parpola 1994: 111-112, Figure 7.14 ('unicorn' in type B1).

100) This whorl composition resembles the 'radial and whorl compositions' of the later (early second millennium BCE) Dilmun type seals of the Gulf (Laursen 2010: 109-110). There is much evidence of a close contact between the Harappans and the peoples of eastern Arabia, where the circular 'Gulf type' seal developed under Indus influence c. 2100-2000 BCE (Laursen 2010). Most of the Indus seals found in the Gulf are circular and have as their iconography the Indian bison or gaur (*Bos gaurus*), which has been adopted also in the 'Gulf type' seals. I have wondered if "perhaps it was in Iran (Susa) that the Near Eastern Indus traders first adopted the local circular form for their seals, which were then to become the models of the Gulf seals" (Parpola 1994: 315). Laursen (2010: 129) has now further evidence pointing in this direction. Circular seals are rare in the Indus Valley, and M-417 has been long considered to be due to western influence on Harappan iconography. It seems significant that the closest early Western Asiatic parallel appears to be supplied by a Proto-Elamite seal coming from ancient Anshan (present Tell-i Malyan) in western Iran (Amiet 1980: 510-511 Plate 126 no. 1688).

101) As noted earlier (in section 2 above), the Septuaginta translation of the Old Testament renders the Hebrew word for 'wild bull' with Greek *monókerōs* 'unicorn'.

102) Scheftelowitz 1912; MacCulloch 1913.

103) Somadeva's Yaśastilaka of the 10th century (ed. Kāvyamālā 70, Vol. I, p. 461, lines 7-8), glossed with the word *gaṇḍaka* by the commentator Śrutadeva (quoted from Simson 1986: 217 and 226, note 48).

104) On the horn as a phallic symbol, see Einhorn 1976: 264-269 with further literature; Panaino 2001: 153.

105) Beer 2003: 48.

106) Shepard 1930: 292, n. 133.

107) Kenoyer 2009.

108) Vārttika 3 on Pāṇini 5,2,122 (*śṛṅgavṛndābhyām ārakan*) derives *śṛṅgāraka-* from *śṛṅga-*.

109) Reference to this is made also by Simson 1986: 217.

110) Mahābhārata (Bombay ed. 3,142,28-47, crit. ed. app. 16,56-95) *idaṃ dvitīyam aparaṃ viṣṇoḥ karma prakāśate / naṣṭā vasumatī kṛtsnā pātāle caiva majjitā / punar uddhāritā tena vārāhenaikaśṛṅgiṇā / ... / tato varāhaḥ saṃvṛtta ekaśṛṅgo mahādyutiḥ / ... / sa gṛhītvā vasumatīṃ śṛṅgenaikena bhāsvatā / yojanānāṃ śataṃ vīra samuddharati so 'kṣaraḥ*. In 13,149,70, this boar incarnation is *mahāśṛṅga-*.

111) In the Mahābhārata (3,142,28ff. and elsewhere), the sinking of the earth is ascribed to the increase of living beings on the earth to such an extent that the supporter of all beings became unable to bear such a heavy load; see Gonda 1954: 139-140; Gail 1977: 134. According to most classical accounts of Viṣṇu's boar incarnation, the evil demon Hiraṇyākṣa ('having golden eyes') had seized the earth and carried it down to the bottom of the ocean; Viṣṇu then became a boar, dove into the ocean, slew the demon, and rescued the earth by raising her up. For a detailed text-historical study of the variants, see Gail 1977.

112) See Gail 1977: 145-166 for the iconography and its evolution.

113) Rāmāyaṇa 2,102,2 *imaṃ lokasaṃpattiṃ lokanātha nibodha me / sarvaṃ salilam evāsīt pṛthivī yatra nirmitā / tataḥ samabhavad brahmā svayambhūr daivataiḥ saha, 3 sa varāhas tato bhūtvā projjahāra vasuṃdharām / asṛjac ca jagat sarvaṃ saha putraiḥ kṛtātmabhiḥ*.

114) Taittirīya-Saṃhitā 7,1,5,1-2.

115) Taittirīya-Brāhmaṇa 1,1,3,5-6.

116) In Mahābhārata 3,272,54, Viṣṇu in the shape of a boar roars like thunderclouds and is as black as they

are. In northern Europe, too, grunting hogs and boars were believed to represent thunderclouds and their tusks lightning; see Gonda 1954: 129.

117) The name Emūṣa is taken from another myth associated with the wild boar, where the boar killed by Indra is a sacrificial victim; the Sacrifice (*yajña*) is equated here with Viṣṇu (who in this role undoubtedly has succeeded the creator god Prajāpati). This myth is found in the four oldest texts of the Black Yajurveda, among them Maitrāyaṇī Saṃhitā 3,8,3 and Taittirīya Saṃhitā 6,2,4,2-3, and then continued in Purāṇic texts (Macdonell 1895: 180-181; Gonda 1954: 137-138; Gail 1977: 128-130). The name Emūṣa consists of three syllables, of which the middle one is long, a pattern that together with the suffix *-ūṣa-* suggests its origin in the language of the Bactria and Margiana Archaeological Complex, or BMAC (see Lubotsky 2001: 303 with Parpola 2002c: 92-94). The boar has a prominent place in the BMAC iconography.

118) Śatapatha-Brāhmaṇa 14,1,2,11 *atha varāhavihatam / iyaty agra āsīd* (VS 37,5) *itīyatī ha vā iyam agre pṛthivy āsa prādeśamātrī tām emūṣa iti varāha ujjaghāna so 'syāḥ patiḥ prajāpatis tenaivainam etan mithunena priyeṇa dhāmnā samardhayati kṛtsnaṃ karoti.*

119) Gonda 1954: 142: The Mahābhārata, too, depicts Naraka as a demon who is the son of the Earth; in 12,209,7 Naraka is the first of the demons to be destroyed by Viṣṇu in his boar shape.

120) For a summary, partial translation and discussion of this version of the myth, see Meyer 1937: II, 51-56. Meyer's references differ from the Kālikāpurāṇa editions by B. Śāstrī (1972 and 1991) used here; the latter one includes an introduction (which among other things discusses the Naraka myth) and an English translation. The Naraka myth is also narrated in the Old Javanese Bhomakāwya (2,1-9) and its Malay version (on these see Gonda 1954: 143).

121) Kālikāpurāṇa 29,23-26 *viśeṣatas tvayā pṛthvī sakāmādharṣitā jale / strīdharmiṇī tvattejobhiḥ sādhāḍ garbhaṃ ca dāruṇam / rajasvalā kṣamā garbhaṃ yam ādhatta jagatpate / tasmād yas tanayo bhāvī so 'py ādāsyati duryaśaḥ / eṣa prāpyāsuraṃ bhāvaṃ devagandharvahiṃsakaḥ / bhaviṣyatīti lokeśaḥ prāha māṃ dakṣasannidhau / malinīratisaṃjātaṃ duṣṭaṃ te 'niṣṭakārakam / kāmukaṃ tyaja lokeśa vārāham kāyam īdṛśam /*

122) Kālikāpurāṇa 36,28-32 *pṛthivy uvāca: na garbhabhāraṃ saṃvoḍhuṃ mādavāhaṃ kṣamādhunā / bhṛśaṃ nityaṃ viṣīdāmi tasmāt tvaṃ trātum arhasi / tvayā varāharūpeṇa malinī kāmitā purā / tena kāmena kukṣau me yo garbho 'yaṃ tvayāhitaḥ / kāle prāpte 'pi garbho 'yaṃ na pracyavati mādhava / kaṭhoragarbhā tenāhaṃ pīḍitāsmi dine dine / yadi na trāhi māṃ deva garbhaduḥkhāj jagatpate / na cirād eva yāsyāmi mṛtyor vaśam asaṃśayam / kayāpi nedṛśo garbhaḥ pūrvaṃ mādhava vai dhṛtaḥ / yo 'calāṃ cālayati māṃ sarasīm iva kuñjaraḥ.*

123) Kālikāpurāṇa 37,33 *gatvā videharājasya yajñabhūmiṃ tadā kṣitiḥ / suṣuve tanayaṃ vīraṃ yatra sītā purābhavat.*

124) Kālikāpurāṇa 37,12-15 *nāradasyopadeśena yajñabhūmiṃ tato nṛpaḥ / halena dārayām āsa yajñavāṭāv adhi svayam / tad bhūmijātasītāyāṃ śubhāṃ kanyāṃ samutthitām / lebhe rājā mudā yuktaḥ sarvalakṣaṇasaṃyutām / tasyāṃ ca jātamātrāyāṃ pṛthivy antarhitā svayam / jagāda vacanaṃ cedaṃ gautamaṃ nāradaṃ nṛpam / eṣā sutā mayā dattā tava rājan manoharā / enāṃ gṛhāṇa subhagāṃ kuladvataśubhāvahām.*

125) The phallic significance of the single tusk (and the single horn; see Meyer 1937: III,301) is "in perfect harmony with the generative function of the boar" (Gonda 1954: 144, n. 93). Defourny (1976: 19, n. 7) refers to the authorities just quoted, but curiously maintains that "rien dans le mythe de Varāha ne permet d'assimiler la corne au phallus." His rather peculiar suggestion is that the horn in general, and the single horn in particular (due to its vertical nature, pointing towards the sky), is "salvatrice ... ou signe du salut." In the case of the boar myth, the key passage for Defourny is the identification of the single horn of the sacrificial boar with the sacrificial stake (*yūpadaṃṣṭraḥ* in Matsya-Purāṇa 248,67), which is "unique et vertical lui aussi" (Defourny 1976: 21): the sacrificial stake is the axis mundi that connects the world to heaven (p. 22).

126) Gonda 1954: 134.

127) Gonda 1954: 133.

128) Burrow and Emeneau 1984: 67, DEDR no. 688. According to German folklore (which has counterparts elsewhere), the boar by rooting up the soil taught the art of ploughing to man (cf. Gonda 1954: 133).

129) Roberts 1977: 166.

130) On the birth of Sītā out of the furrow ploughed by King Janaka (related in Rāmāyaṇa 1,66,14-15) in terms of an incestuous sexual intercourse, and on Janaka's identity with Prajāpati (alias Brahmā) and Bala-Rāma who uses the plough as his weapon (= Rāma, the husband of Sītā), see Parpola 2002b: 367.

131) Cf. Rigveda 10,90 and Parpola 2007: this idea is behind the human sacrifice (*puruṣamedha*), which has existed in India but not during early Vedic times.

132) Cf. Kālikāpurāṇa 29-31 and Meyer 1937: II, 54-55.

133) Mayrhofer 1996: II, 37.

134) Naraka got his name when as a newborn baby he was found lying on Janaka's sacrificial ground with his head on a human skull (Kālikāpurāṇa 38,2 *narasya śīrṣe svaśiro nidhāya sthitavān yataḥ / tasmāt tasya muniśreṣṭho narakaṃ nāma vai vyadhāt*).

135) See also Meyer 1937: II, 41-56.

136) Cf. Kālikāpurāṇa 29,24-31 *vārāho 'pi svayaṃ gatvā lokālokāhvayaṃ girim / vārāhyā saha reme sa pṛthivyā cārurūpayā / sa tayā ramamāṇas tu suciraṃ parvatottame / nāvāpa toṣaṃ lokeśaḥ potrī paramakāmukaḥ / pṛthivyāḥ potrīrūpāyā ramayantyās tataḥ sutāḥ / trayo jātā dvijaśreṣṭhās teśāṃ nāmāni me śṛṇu / suvṛttaḥ kanako ghoraḥ sarva eva mahābalāḥ / śiśavas te merupṛṣṭhe kāñcane vaprasaṃstare / remire 'nyonyasaṃsaktā gahvareṣu saraḥsu ca / sa taiḥ putraiḥ parivṛto vārāho bhāryayā svayā / ramamāṇas tadā kāyatyāgaṃ naivāgaṇad dhiyā / kadā cic chiśubhis tais saṃśliṣṭaḥ kardamāntare / cakāra kardamakrīḍāṃ bhāryayā ca mahābalaḥ / sapaṅkalepaḥ śuśubhe varāho madhupiṅgalaḥ*. Cf also Meyer 1937: II, 55.

137) Roberts 1977: 165, map 64.

138) Whether the Harappans had domestic pigs is uncertain. "Domestic pigs are identified (2-3 per cent) at Harappan sites mostly from the Mature Harappan and Post-Urban periods... Both at Kuntasi and Shikarpur, piglets were killed in large numbers." (Thomas 2002: 411)

139) See section 3 as well as footnote 25 in the wild ass paper contained in this book. Footnotes 32 and 92 discuss the Proto-Dravidian word **kaẓ(i)* 'saline soil', the habitat of the wild ass (apparently forming the first part of the Proto-Dravidian name **kaẓutai* of the wild ass), as well as its likely derivation as 'waste land' from the Proto-Dravidian root **kaẓi*, the meanings of which include 'wasting, discarding, excreta, becoming ruined' and 'dying', and which may be connected with Kali, the god of gambling and ruin.

140) See Krishan 1999: 39-40 for quotations from many Purāṇa texts using the term *mala*.

141) Dange 1987: II, 577.

142) A Proto-Dravidian word for 'rubbish heap' is **kumppV* (DEDR 1731, 1741), which has also denoted the swelling protuberance of the male gharial's snout (which has a phallic connotation). The same Proto-Dravidian word is very probably also the source of Sanskrit *kumbha-* when it refers to the two protuberances on the upper part of the elephant's forehead, which swell in the rutting season (see the discussion of Sanskrit *kumbhīra-* in the crocodile paper in this book). *Kumbha* and *Nikumbha* are known as the names of two demon brothers, and at least Nikumbha is among the names of the elephant-headed god Gaṇeśa (see Krishan 1999: 127 quoting Vāyu-Purāṇa 2,30). In Tamil, *kuppam* 'dungheap' has a male proper name Kuppan derived from it: parents who have lost many babies may give it to their newborn son to avert the interest of evil spirits seeking after the blood of newborn babies.

143) Allchin 1963: 133-135.

144) Allchin 1963: 127-133.

145) Allchin 1963.

146) See section 4 in the wild ass paper.

147) Lunar features in Gaṇeśa include his round stomach full of sweets; the special day of his worship is the 4th day of the bright half of the month, when the sickle of the new moon appears.

148) For these features uniting Rudra, the Vināyakas, Skanda and Gaṇapati, see Krishan 1999: 20-22, 55 and 126-135.

149) Gonda (1954: 139 n 62, with many references) has pointed out that "the sun-god (or a god related to the sun) not seldom marries the earth."

150) See Macdonell 1895: 185 with n. 3.

151) Gaṇeśa, too, is connected with the planet Mars; the auspicious weekday associated with him is Tuesday, the day of the planet Mars.

152) The planet Mars (whole names include *Rudhira-* 'red', 'blood') was born out of a drop of the Goddess' menstrual blood, which fell to earth during her sexual union with Śiva. Cf. Bhaviṣya-Purāṇa, Brāhma-khaṇḍa, 31,17-18: *purā maithunam āśritya sthitābhyāṃ tu himācale / bhīmomābhyāṃ mahābāho raktabinduś cyutaḥ kṣitau / medinyā saprayatnena sukhena vidhṛto 'nayā / jāto 'syāḥ sa kujo vīraḥ rakte raktasamudbhavaḥ.*

153) According to the Rāmāyana (4,42), the wicked demon Naraka lived in the golden town of Prāgjyotiṣa, the name of which refers to the 'light of the east'. This associates him with Skanda, who among other things symbolizes the young morning sun. According to the Mahābhārata, Naraka stole the pair of ear-rings from Aditi (the mother of gods) and kept them at Prāgjyotiṣa (5,48,80), whence they were recovered by Kṛṣṇa (3,12,17) and given to the sun-god Sūrya (3,307,21) (Gonda 1954: 142, n. 81). A pair of earrings appears to be the pictorial meaning of the Indus sign used as a rebus (Proto-Dravidian **muruku* 'ear-ring, bangle') to signify the name of the god Muruku "Youth" (who in the Tamil religion is the counterpart of Rudra and Skanda, both called Kumāra 'Youth'; see Parpola 1994a: 225-230).

154) Krishan 1999: 47.

155) Martin-Dubost 1997: 218 and 228.

156) See Krishan 1999: 45-48.

157) Condensed from Krishan 1999: 46, based on Rao 1914: I (1), 50-51; the myth is said to be found in the Brahmavaivarta-Purāṇa.

158) *ekaḥ sa eva parpālayatāj jaganti / gaurīgirīśacaritānukṛtiṃ dadhānaḥ / ābhāti yo daśanaśūnyamukhaikadeśa- / dehārdhahāritavadhūka ivaikadantaḥ //* Translated by Daniel H. H. Ingalls (Sternbach 1980: IV, 1861 no. 7437; Krishan 1999: 47-48 and 65 n. 37).

159) Cunningham 1875: 108.

160) Fuller 2006: 25-26; Wikipedia s.v. Aurochs.

161) Meadow and Patel 2002: 396; Fuller 2006: 26.

162) Meadow 1986: 54-55.

163) Fuller 2006: 26.

164) The zebu has been identified inter alia at Tepe Yahya and Shahr-i Sokhta; see Meadow 1987: 898 and Grigson 1996: 43-44.

165) Bökönyi 1997; Fuller 2006: 26.

166) Edwards, Magee, Park *et al.* 2010.

167) Black and Green 1992: 103.

168) F. E. Zeuner (1963: 236-238), Raymond and Bridget Allchin (1974: 71 n. 1) and Gregory L. Possehl (1999: 175; 2002: 131). Ute Franke-Vogt (1991: I, 62-64), providing comprehensive coverage of the data relating to the 'unicorn' and their interpretation, also identifies the animal as the urus (*Bos primigenius primigenius*), although she confesses that this is controversial.

169) It is almost certain that Harappan sailors did import a small number of water buffaloes from the Indus Valley to Mesopotamia during the reign of Sargon the Great (2334-2279 BCE); this is the period when the water buffalo suddenly replaced the humpless *Bos primigenius* in Akkadian glyptics (Boehmer 1975; Parpola 1984; 1994: 246-256).

170) Cf. Parpola 1984; 1994: 246-256; 2011.

171) Francfort and Tremblay 2010: 104.

172) Jarrige 1988; Parpola 2005a.

173) Parpola 1988; 2005b; 2009.

174) I have written on this theme many times since the early 1980s (Parpola 1984a; 1984b; 1985; 1988: 252-263; 1992; 1994: 246-272; 1999; 2002a; 2002b; 2011) and hope to be excused for repeating here what I have said before (especially in my retreatment of the 'contest' motif in 2011). I shall try to restrict myself to the essentials.

175) Amiet 1980: no. 585.

176) Porada 1950; Amiet 1980: 109.

177) In the Sanskrit epics of India, the warrior kills with arrows "like the sun" (kills with arrow-like hot rays) (Hopkins 1915: 85).

178) Amiet 1980: 109.

179) Black and Green 1992: 112-113. "A variety of cosmological ideas were current at different periods of Mesopotamian history. The earlier, Sumerian, view of cosmology seems to have been one of a dipartite universe consisting of *an* (heaven) and *ki* (earth, including the underworld) (see *Du-ku*). Originally united and inhabited only by gods, they were at a primordial time separated from each other." (Black and Green 1992: 52)

180) Amiet 1980: 137 with references in n. 46.

181) For example, in Sanskrit 'rain' is *varṣa-*, from the same root as *vṛṣan-* m. 'manly animal, bull, stallion and *vṛṣabha-* m. 'bull' (Mayrhofer 1996: II, 522f. and 575f.).

182) On the Kubaba/Kybele and her cult, see Vermaseren 1977.

183) For the following, see especially Maag 1961 and Hörig 1979.

184) Black and Green 1992: 108-109.

185) Hörig 1979: 187.

186) Black and Green 1992: 72-73.

187) Black and Green 1992: 158.

188) Lapinkivi 2004: 245.

189) Lapinkivi 2004: 247-248.

190) Black and Green 1992: 108-109.

191) Potts 2001.

192) Potts 2001.

193) Stietencron 1983.

194) Kālikā-Purāṇa 63, 19-23, transl. Kooij 1972: 121.

195) Parpola 2002: 260-291.

196) Beck 1981.

197) Rolland 1973; Parpola 1999.

198) Parpola 2007.

199) Cf. Allchin 1985; Parpola 1994: 256, with further literature on p. 300.

200) Parpola 2002a.

201) Cf. Parpola 1984.

202) The popular identification of the two heroes in the 'contest' motif as Gilgamesh and Enkidu is considered incorrect (Black and Green 1992: 91).

203) Black and Green 1992: 49; 89-90, 109; Leick 1991: 70.

204) Borger 1975: 413.

205) Hartner 1965: 16; 1985: 737-738; Panaino 2001: 157, n. 59.

206) On Aldebaran and the 'third eye', see Parpola 1994: 261-272; 1998: 240-252.

207) C. J. Gadd quoted by Mackay 1931: I, 356 n. 2; Wheeler 1968: 87.

208) Sarianidi 1979: 654; Parpola 1985: 75.

209) Ardeleanu-Jansen 1989; Parpola 1985: 156.

210) Wheeler 1968: 87.

211) Parpola 1985: 78-79.

212) Hartner 1965: 8.

213) Oppenheim 1949; Parpola 1985: 31-37.

214) Parpola 1985: 157.

215) Parpola 1985: 37-75.

216) Parpola 1985: 66-68.

217) The Bṛhad-Āraṇyaka-Upaniṣad (1,4) has preserved another version of this myth, where the first animals created by Prajāpati and Vāc are the cow and the bull.

218) Weber 1862: II, 368-371.

219) Here we have the virgin of the unicorn legends. On *rohiṇī*, see Parpola 1998: 239-252.

220) Simson 1986: 216 and 223-224.

221) Possehl 1999: 175.

222) Grigson 1984: 168.

223) Grigson 1984: 168, with her emphasis.

224) Mackay 1931: II, 392.

225) Mackay 1938: I, 326 and note 1.

226) Parpola 1992 and the Indus script section of the crocodile paper in this book.

227) Mayrhofer 1992: I, 260.

228) Pokorny 1959: I, 303-304.

229) Pokorny 1959: I, 302.

230) AVŚ 4,4,7 *ahaṃ tanomi te paso adhi jyām iva dhanvani / kramasva rśa iva rohitam anavaglāyatā sadā*, translated by Whitney 1905: 151. The commentator takes *sadā* to

mean 'always', but, as Whitney notes, the word might be instrumental of *sad-* 'position in coitus' as suggested by Böhtlingk and Roth 1875: VII,603: "2. *sad-* ... 2. m. das Besteigen (des Weibchens) AV. 4,4,7". The verse is not found in the Paippalāda version of the Atharvaveda.

231) Molesworth 1857: 703c; Turner 1966: 628 no. 10865.

232) Turner 1966: 628 no. 10870.

233) Roberts 1977: 175-176.

234) Two species are combined in the genus name of the nilgai: *Bos-elaphus*, literally 'cow-deer' (although the nilgai is not a deer but an antelope).

235) Mackay 1931: II, 382.

236) Mackay 1931: II, 383.

237) Roberts 1977: 175-176.

238) Mackay 1931: II, 382.

239) Cf. Roberts 1977: 177a "They are believed to be much reduced in numbers in all these regions despite being regarded as sacred by most of the Hindu farming population." Krishna 2010: 48: "The nilgai or blue bull is actually a species of antelope, commonly seen all over north India. It looks like a cow, hence its name (nil means blue, gai means cow). The blue bull is regarded as a bovine animal, leading to the local belief that the nilgai is a cow and hence sacred. This has protected it form hunters."

240) Roberts 1977: 177a.

241) Krishna 2010: 48. "As a result of the reduction of the tiger population, the population of the nilgai has multiplied considerably."

242) Roberts 1977" 177b.

243) Krishna 2010: 48.

244) See the paper on the wild asses, section 5.

245) Ṛgveda 8,4,10a *ṛśyo na tṛṣyann avapānam ā gahi.*

246) Roberts 1977: 177b.

247) DEDR no. 1664.

248) Cf. DEDR no. 4780.

249) Cf. DEDR no. 1659.

250) Cf. DEDR no. 1651. Waterpot reminds one of water, one of the main issues in the Ṛśyaśṛṅga legend, which also contains the motif of 'pot birth' common in ancient Indian mythology. Ṛśyaśṛṅga was born when the nilgai doe drank semen shed into a waterpot by his father.

251) Cf. DEDR no. 1654.

252) Cf. DEDR no. 1655.

References

Albright, W. F. (1920) 'Gilgames and Engidu, Mesopotamian Genii of Fecundity', *Journal of the American Oriental Society* 40: 307-335.

Allchin, Bridget (ed.) (1984) *South Asian Archaeology 1981.* (University of Cambridge Oriental Publications 34) Cambridge: Cambridge University Press.

Allchin, F. R. (1963) *Neolithic cattle-keepers of South India: A study of the Deccan ashmounds.* (University of Cambridge Oriental Publications 9) Cambridge: Cambridge University Press.

Allchin, F. R. (1985) 'The interpretation of a seal from Chanhudaro and its significance for the religion of the Indus Civilization', pp. 369-384, in Janine Schotsmans and Maurizio Taddei (eds.) *South Asian Archaeology 1983.* I-II. (Istituto Universitario Orientale, Dipartimento di Studi Asiatici, Series Minor 23) Naples: Istituto Universitario Orientale.

Allchin, Raymond and Bridget Allchin (1974) 'Some new thoughts on Indian cattle', pp. 71-77, in J. E. van Lohuizen-de Leeuw and J. M. M. Ubaghs (eds.) *South Asian Archaeology 1973.* Leiden: E. J. Brill.

Amiet, Pierre (1980) *La glyptique mesopotamienne archaïque.* Deuxième édition revue et corrigée avec un supplément. Contribution pour les inscriptions de Maurice Lambert. Paris: Éditions du Centre National de la Recherce Scientifique.

Ardeleanu-Jansen, Alexandra (1989) 'A short note on a steatite sculpture from Mohenjo-Daro', pp. 196-210, in Karen Frifelt and Per Sørensen (eds.) *South Asian Archaeology 1985.* (Scandinavian Institute of Asian Studies, Occasional Papers 4). London: Curzon Press.

Aruz, Joan (ed.) (2003) *Art of the first cities: The third millennium B.C. from the Mediterranean to the Indus.* New York: Metropolitan Museum of Art, &

New Haven: Yale University Press.

Atre, Shubhangana (1985) 'The Harappan riddle of 'unicorn'', *Bulletin of the Deccan College Research Institute* 44: 1-7 and figures 1-14.

Azarpay, G. (1976) 'Nanā, the Sumero-Akkadian goddess of Transoxiana', *Journal of the American Oriental Society* 96: 536-542.

Beck, Brenda E. F. (1981) 'The goddess and the demon: A local South Indian festival and its wider context', pp. 83-136, in Madeleine Biardeau (ed.) *Autour de la Déesse hindoue: Études reunies*. (Puruṣārtha 5) Paris: Éditions de l'École des Hautes Études en Sciences Sociales.

Beer, Robert (2003) *The handbook of Tibetan Buddhist symbols*. Chicago: Serindia Publications.

Berger, Hermann (1971) 'The Ṛṣyaśṛṅga story — a Dravidian rain myth', pp. 158-161, in R. E. Asher (ed.) *Proceedings of the Second International Conference Seminar of Tamil Studies, Madras 1968*, Volume I. Madras: International Association of Tamil Research.

Bhim Dev (1980) *Śāṅkhāyanāraṇyakam, critically edited*. (Vishveshvaranand Indological series 70) Hoshiarpur: Vishveshvaranand Vedic Research Institute.

Black, Jeremy and Anthony Green (1992) *Gods, demons and symbols of ancient Mesopotamia: An illustrated dictionary*. Illustrations by Tessa Rickards. London: British Museum Press.

Boehmer, Rainer Michael (1975) 'Das Auftreten des Wasserbüffels in Mesopotamien in historischer Zeit und seine sumerische Bezeichnung', *Zeitschrift für Assyriologie* 64: 1-19.

Böhtlingk, Otto und Rudolph Roth (1852-1875) *Sanskrit-Wörterbuch* I-VII. St. Petersburg: Kaiserliche Akademie der Wissenschaften.

Bökönyi, Sándor (1997) 'Zebus and Indian wild cattle', *Anthropozoologica* 25-26: 647-654.

Borger, Rykle (1975) 'Himmelsstier', pp. 413-414, in *Reallexikon der Assyriologie und vorderasiatischen Archäologie* IV (6-7). Berlin: Walter de Gruyter.

Burrow, Thomas and M. B. Emeneau (1984) *A Dravidian etymological dictionary*. Second ed. Oxford: Clarendon Press. (= DEDR)

Caland, Willem (1907) *Die Jaiminīya-Saṃhitā mit einer Einleitung über die Sāmavedaliteratur*. (Indische Forschungen 2) Breslau: Verlag von M. und H. Marcus.

Caland, Willem (1931) *Pañcaviṃśa-Brāhmaṇa: The Brāhmaṇa of Twenty Five Chapters, translated*. (Bibliotheca Indica, Work 255) Calcutta: The Asiatic Society of Bengal.

Carpelan, Christian, Asko Parpola and Petteri Koskikallio (eds.) (2001) *Early contacts between Uralic and Indo-European: Linguistic and archaeological considerations*. (Mémoires de la Société Finno-Ougrienne 242) Helsinki: Suomalais-Ugrilainen Seura.

CISI = *Corpus of Indus Seals and Inscriptions. 1: Collections in India*, edited by Jagat Pati Joshi and Asko Parpola, 1987. *2: Collections in Pakistan*, edited by Sayid Ghulam Mustafa Shah and Asko Parpola, 1991. *3: New material, untraced objects, and collections outside India and Pakistan*, edited by Asko Parpola B. M. Pande and Petteri Koskikallio, *Part 1: Mohenjo-daro and Harappa*, in collaboration with Richard H. Meadow and Jonathan Mark Kenoyer, 2010; *Part 2: Global supplement*, in preparation. (Annales Academiae Scientiarum Fennicae, B 239, 240, Humaniora 359) Helsinki: Suomalainen Tiedeakatemia.

Conybeare, F. C. (1969) *Philostratus, The Life of Apollonius of Tyana. The epistles of Apollonius and the treatise of Eusebius, with an English translation* I-II. (The Loeb classical library 16-17) London: Heinemann & Cambridge, Mass: Harvard University Press.

Cunningham, Alexander (1875) 'Harapâ', pp. 105-108 and Plate XXXII-XXXIII, in *Archaeological Survey of India, Report for the year 1872-73*. ([Reports, Old series] Vol. V) Calcutta: Office of the Superintendent of Government Printing.

Dange, Sadashiv Ambadas (1970) *Pastoral symbolism from*

the Ṛgveda. (The Bhau Vishnu Ashtekar Vedic Research Series 3) Poona: University of Poona.

Dange, Sadashiv Ambadas (1986-1990) *Encyclopaedia of Puranic beliefs and practices* I-V. New Delhi: Navrang.

Darmesteter, James (1877) *Ohrmazd et Ahriman: Leur origines et leur histoire*. (Bibliothèque de l'École des Hautes Études, Sciences Religieuses 29) Paris: Wieweg.

Debrunner, Albert (1957) *Nachträge zu Band I der Altindischen Grammatik* von Jakob Wackernagel [und Albert Debrunner]. Göttingen: Vandenhoeck & Ruprecht.

DEDR = Burrow and Emeneau (1984)

Defourny, Michel (1976) 'Note sur le symbolisme de la corne dans le Mahabharata et la mythologie brahmanique classique', *Indo-Iranian Journal* 18 (1-2): 17-23.

Della Casa, Carlo (1986) 'Contatti tra popoli e scambi culturali: La leggenda dell' unicorno', pp. 11-24, in *Contributi de orientalistica, glottologia e dialettologia*. (Quaderni di Acme 7) Milano: Facoltà di Lettere e Filosofia dell'Università degli Studi di Milano.

Dhavalikar, M.K. (1978) 'Proto-Paśupati in Western India', *East and West* NS 28: 203-211.

During Caspers, Elisabeth C. L. (1991) 'The Indus Valley 'unicorn': A Near Eastern connection?', *Journal of the Economic and Social History of the Orient* 34 (2): 312-350.

Edwards, Ceiridwen J., David A. Magee, Stephen D. E. Park, Paul A. McGettigan, Amanda J. Lohan *et al.* (2010) 'A complete mitochondrial genome sequence from a Mesolithic wild aurochs (*Bos primigenius*)', *PLoS ONE* 5 (2): e9255. doi:10.1371/journal.pone.0009255.

Einhorn, Jürgen W. (1976) *Spiritalis unicornis: Das Einhorn als Bedeutungsträger in Literatur und Kunst des Mittelalters*. (Münstersche Mittelalter-Schriften 13) München: Wilhelm Fink Verlag.

Fortelius, Walter (1999) 'Kaksituhatta vuotta yksisarvisia', *Tieteessä tapahtuu* 1999 (6). http://www.tieteessatapahtuu.fi/996/fortelius.htm

Francfort, Henri-Paul et Xavier Tremblay (2010) 'Marhaši et la Civilisation de l'Oxus', *Iranica Antiqua* 45: 51-224.

Franke-Vogt, Ute (1991) *Die Glyptik aus Mohenjo-Daro. Uniformität und Variabilität in der Induskultur: Untersuchungen zur Typologie, Ikonographie und räumlichen Verteilung* I-II. (Baghdader Forschungen 13) Mainz: Verlag Philipp von Zabern.

Freese, J. H. (1920) *The Library of Photius* [edited and translated] Vol. 1. (Translations of Christian literature, Series 1: Greek texts 2) London: Society for Promoting Christian Knowledge & New York: Macmillan Company.

Fuller, Dorian Q. (2006) 'Agricultural origins and frontiers in South Asia: A working synthesis', *Journal of World Prehistory* 20 (1): 1-86.

Gail, Adalbert J. (1977) 'Viṣṇu als Eber in Mythos und Bild', pp. 127-168, in *Beiträge zur Indienforschung, Ernst Waldschmidt zum 80. Geburtstag gewidmet*. (Veröffentlichungen des Museums für Indische Kunst Berlin 4) Berlin: Museum für Indische Kunst Berlin.

Goldman, Robert P. (1985) *The Rāmāyaṇa of Vālmīki: An epic of ancient India* Vol. I: *Bālakāṇḍa*. Introduction and translation by Robert P. Goldman, annotation by Robert P. Goldman and Sally J. Sutherland. (Princeton Library of Asian translations) Princeton: Princeton University Press.

Gonda, Jan (1954) *Aspects of early Viṣṇuism*. Utrecht: Oosthoek.

Grigson, Caroline (1973) 'The comparative craniology of *Bos taurus* L., *B. indicus* L., *B. primigenius* Boj. and *B. namadicus* Falc. Unpublished Ph. D. thesis, University of London.

Grigson, Caroline (1984) 'Some thoughts on unicorns and other cattle depicted at Mohenjo-daro and Harappa', pp. 166-169, in Bridget Allchin (ed.)

South Asian Archaeology 1981. (University of Cambridge Oriental Publications 34) Cambridge: Cambridge University Press.

Grigson, Caroline (1996) 'Early cattle around the Indian Ocean', pp. 41-74, in Julian Reade (ed.) *The Indian Ocean in antiquity*. London & New York: Kegan Paul International.

Günter, Heinrich (1922) *Buddha in der abendländischen Legende?* Leipzig: H. Haessel Verlag.

Güntert, Hermann (1929-30) 'Einhorn', Columns 708-712, in Hanns Bächtold-Stäubli (Hrsg.) *Handwörterbuch des deutschen Aberglaubens*, Band II. Berlin und Leipzig: Walter de Gruyter & Co.

Hämeen-Anttila, Jaakko (suom.) (2000) *Gilgamesh: Kertomus ikuisen elämän etsimisestä*. Helsinki: Basam Books.

Hartner, Willy (1965) 'The earliest history of the constellations in the Near East and the motif of the lion-bull combat', *Journal of Near Eastern Studies 24* (1-2): 1-16 and Plate I-VI.

Hartner, Willy (1985) 'Old Iranian calendars', pp. 714-792, in *The Cambridge History of Iran* Vol. 2: *The Median and Achaemenian periods*, edited by Ilya Gershevitch. Cambridge: Cambridge University Press.

Hillebrandt, Alfred (1890) 'Die Sonnwendfeste in Alt-Indien', pp. 299-340, in *Festschrift für Konrad Hofmann zum 70sten Geburtstag 14. November 1889 gewidmet von seinen Schülern*. (Romanische Forschungen 5) Erlangen und Leipzig: Andr. Deichert'sche Verlagsbuchhandlungs Nachfolger.

Hopkins, E. Washburn (1915) *Epic mythology*. (Grundriss der Indo-Arischen Philologie und Altertumskunde III: 1: B) Strassburg: Karl J. Trübner.

Hörig, Monika (1979) *Dea Syria: Studien zur religiösen Tradition der Fruchbarkeitsgöttin in Vorderasien*. (Alter Orient und Altes Testament 208) Kevelaer: Verlag Butzon & Bercker, & Neukirchen-Vlyun: Neukirchener Verlag.

In the image of man: The Indian perception of the universe through 2000 years of painting and sculpture. London: Weidenfeld and Nicolson (1982)

Jacoby, Felix (1958) *Die Fragmente der griechischen Historiker (FGrHist)* 3. Teil: *Geschichte von Städten und Völkern (Horographie und Ethnographie)*, C: *Autoren über einzelne Länder Nr. 608a-856* I-II. Leiden: E. J. Brill.

Jain, Jagdishchandra (1981) *Prakrit narrative literature: Origin and growth*. New Delhi: Mushiram Manoharlal.

Jarrige, Catherine and Vincent Lefèvre (eds.) (2005) *South Asian Archaeology 2001* I-II. Paris: Éditions Recherche sur les Civilisations.

Jarrige, Jean-François (1988) 'Le complexe culturel de Mehrgarh (période VIII) et de Sibri. Le "trésor" de Quetta', pp. 111-116, in *Les cités oubliées de l'Indus*. Paris: Association Française d'Action Artistique.

Jensen, Peter (1913) 'Review of Ungnad & Gressmann 1911', *Zeitschrift der Deutschen Morgenländischen Gesellschaft* 67: 503-529.

Jensen, Peter (1928) *Das Gilgamesch-Epos in der Weltliteratur* II. Marburg a. L.: Ebel.

Jones, H. L. (1930) *The Geography of Strabo, translated* VII. (The Loeb classical library 241) London: William Heinemann Ltd. & Cambridge, Mass.: Harvard University Press.

Jones, J. J. (1949-1956) *Mahāvastu, translated from the Buddhist Sanskrit* I-III. (Sacred Books of the Buddhists 16, 18, 19) London: Luzac & Co.

Kajihara, Mieko (2002) The *brahmacārín* in the Veda: The evolution of the "Vedic student" and the dynamics of texts, rituals, and society in ancient India. (Doctoral thesis, Department of Sanskrit and Indian Studies, Harvard University.)

Karttunen, Klaus (1989) *India in early Greek literature*. (Studia Orientalia 65) Helsinki: The Finnish Oriental Society.

Karttunen, Klaus (1997) *India and the Hellenistic world*. (Studia Orientalia 83) Helsinki: The Finnish Oriental Society.

Keith, Arthur Berriedale (1920) *Rigveda Brahmanas: The*

Aitareya and Kauṣītaki Brāhmaṇas of the Rigveda,, translated from the original Sanskrit. (Harvard Oriental Series 25) Cambridge, Mass.: Harvard University Press.

Kenoyer, Jonathan Mark (1998) *Ancient cities of the Indus Valley Civilization.* Karachi: Oxford University Press.

Kenoyer, Jonathan Mark (2009) 'Harappan iconography of the unicorn: Origins and legacy', Powerpoint presentation, *Society for American Archaeology*, Session in honor of G. L. Possehl entitled "Complexity and technology in South Asia and the Old World", Atlanta, GA, April 23, 2009.

Kooij, Karel van (1972) *Worship of the Goddess according to the Kālikāpurāṇa* I: *A translation with an introduction and notes of chapters 54-69.* (Orientalia Rheno-Traiectina 14) Leiden: E.J. Brill.

Kramrisch, Stella (1954) *The art of India: Traditions of Indian sculpture, painting and architecture.* London: Phaidon Press.

Krishan, Yuvraj (1999) *Gaṇeśa: Unravelling an enigma.* Delhi: Motilal Banarsidass.

Krishna, Nanditha (2010) *Sacred animals of India.* New Delhi: Penguin Books India.

Krishna Murthy, K. (1985) *Mythical animals in Indian art.* New Delhi: Abhinav Publications.

Kumar, P., A. R. Freeman, R. T. Loftus, C. Gaillard, D. Q. Fuller and D. G. Bradley (2003) 'Admixture analysis of South Asian cattle', *Heredity* 91: 43-50.

La Mésopotamie. Tokyo: NHK (2000)

Lapinkivi, Pirjo (2004) *The Sumerian sacred marriage in the light of comparative evidence.* (State Archives of Assyria Studies Vol. 15) Helsinki: The Neo-Assyrian Text Corpus Project.

Laursen, Steffen Terp (2010) 'The westward transmission of Indus Valley sealing technology: Origin and development of the 'Gulf Type' seal and other administrative technologies in Early Dilmun, c. 2100-2000 BC', *Arabian Archaeology and Epigraphy* 21: 96-134.

Law, Randall William (2011) *Inter-regional interaction and urbanism in the ancient Indus Valley: A geologic provenience study of Harappa's rock and mineral assemblage.* (Linguistics, archaeology and the human past, Occasional Paper 11) Kyoto: Indus Project, Research Institute for Humanity and Nature.

Leick, Gwendolyn (1991) *A dictionary of ancient and Near Eastern mythology.* London and New York: Routledge.

Les cités oubliées de l'Indus: Archéologie du Pakistan. Musée National des Arts Asiatiques Guimet, 16 novembre 1988 --- 30 janvier 1989. Paris: Association Française d'Action Artistique, 1988.

Lesky, Albin (1963) *Geschichte der griechischen Literatur.* Zweite, neu bearbeitete und erweiterte Auflage. Bern und München: Francke Verlag.

Ligabue, Giancarlo and Sandro Salvatori (eds.) (n.d. [1989]) *Battriana: Una antica civiltà delle oasi dalle sabbie dell' Afghanistan.* (Studi e Documenti 3) Venezia: Erizzo.

Lubotsky, Alexander (2001) 'The Indo-Iranian substratum', pp. 301-317, in C. Carpelan *et al.* (eds.) *Early contacts between Uralic and Indo-European: Linguistic and archaeological considerations.* (Mémoires de la Société Finno-Ougrienne 242) Helsinki: Suomalais-Ugrilainen Seura.

Lüders, Heinrich (1897) 'Die Sage von Ṛṣyaśṛṅga', *Nachrichten von der Königlichen Gesellschaft der Wissenschaften zu Göttingen, Phil.-hist. Klasse*, 1897: 87-135. Reprinted, pp. 1-43, in Lüders (1940)

Lüders, Heinrich (1901) 'Zur Sage von Ṛṣyaśṛṅga', *Nachrichten von der Königlichen Gesellschaft der Wissenschaften zu Göttingen, Phil.-hist. Klasse*, 1901: 28-56. Reprinted, pp. 47-73, in Lüders (1940)

Lüders, Heinrich (1940) *Philologica Indica: Ausgewählte kleine Schriften von Heinrich Lüders. Festgabe zum siebzigsten Geburtstage am 25. Juni 1939 dargebracht von Kollegen, Freunden und Schülern.* Göttingen: Vandenhoeck & Ruprecht.

Maag, Victor (1961) 'Syrien — Palästina', pp. 448-604, in Hartmut Schmökel (ed.) *Kulturgeschichte des Alten Orient.* (Kröners Taschenausgabe 298) Stuttgart: Kröner.

MacCulloch, J. A. (1913) 'Horns', pp. 791b-796a, in James Hastings (ed.) *Encyclopaedia of Religion and Ethics* VI. Edinburgh: T. and T. Clark.

Macdonell, A. A. (1895) 'Mythological studies in the Rigveda, II: The mythological basis in the Rigveda of the Dwarf and Boar Incarnations of Viṣṇu', *Journal of the Royal Asiatic Society of Great Britain and Ireland* 1895: 165-189.

Mackay, Ernest J. H. (1931) 'Seals, seal impressions, and copper tablets, with tabulation', pp. 370-405 (chapter XXI), in J. Marshall (ed.) *Mohenjo-daro and the Indus civilization* II. London: Arthur Probsthain.

Mackay, Ernest J. H. (1937-38) *Further excavations at Mohenjo-daro* I-II. Delhi: Manager of Publications, Government of India.

Mackay, Ernest J.H. (1943) *Chanhu-daro excavations* 1935-36. (American Oriental Series 20) New Haven, Conn.: American Oriental Society.

[Makarabhūṣaṇam, T. N. (ed.)] (2000) *Ārana Ganam of Talavakara Sakha of Jaiminiya Sama.* Chennai: Veda Rakshana Nidhi Trust.

Marshall, John (1931) 'Religion', pp 48-78 (chapter V), in J. Marshall (ed.) *Mohenjo-daro and the Indus civilization* I. London: Arthur Probsthain.

Marshall, John (ed.) (1931) *Mohenjo-daro and the Indus civilization* I-III. London: Arthur Probsthain.

Martin-Dubost, Paul (1997) *Gaṇeśa: The enchanter of the three worlds.* (Project for Indian cultural studies publication 6) Mumbai: Franco-Indian Research Pvt. Ltd.

Mayrhofer, Manfred (1992-2001) *Etymologisches Wörterbuch des Altindoarischen* I-III. (Indogermanische Bibliothek, Reihe 2: Wörterbücher) Heidelberg: Universitätsverlag Carl Winter.

McGregor, R. S. (ed.) (1993) *The Oxford Hindi-English dictionary.* Oxford and Delhi: Oxford University Press.

Meadow, Richard H. (1986) 'Faunal exploitation in the Greater Indus Valley: A review of recent work to 1980', pp. 43-64, in Jerome Jacobson (ed.) *Studies in the archaeology of India and Pakistan.* New Delhi: Oxford & IBH Publishing Co. and American Institute of Indian Studies.

Meadow, Richard (1987) 'Faunal exploitation patterns in eastern Iran and Baluchistan: A review of recent investigations', pp. 881-916, in Gherardo Gnoli and Lionello Lanciotti (eds.) *Orientalia Iosephi Tucci memoriae dicata* II. (Serie Orientale Roma 56.2) Roma: IsMEO.

Meadow, Richard H. (1991) 'The domestication and exploitation of plants and animals in the Greater Indus Valley, 7th-2nd millennium B.C.', pp. 51-58, in Michael Jansen, Máire Mulloy and Günter Urban (eds.) *Forgotten cities on the Indus: Early civilization in Pakistan from the 8th to the 2nd millennium B.C.* Mainz: Verlag Philipp von Zabern.

Meadow, Richard H. and Ajita K. Patel (2002) 'From Mehrgarh to Harappa and Dholavira: Prehistoric pastoralism in north-western South Asia through the Harappan period', pp. 391-408, in Settar, S. and Ravi Korisettar (eds.) *Protohistory: Archaeology of the Harappan Civilization.* (Indian archaeology in retrospect Vol. II) New Delhi: Indian Council of Historical Research & Manohar.

Meyer, Johann Jakob (1930) *Sexual life in ancient India: A study in the comparative history of Indian culture* I-II. London: George Routledge & Sons.

Meyer, Johann Jakob (1937) *Trilogie altindischer Mächte und Feste der Vegetation: Ein Beitrag zur vergleichenden Religions- und Kulturgeschichte, Fest- und Volkskunde* I-III. Zürich und Leipzig: Max Niehans.

Molesworth, James T. (1857) *A dictionary, Marathi and English.* Assisted by George and Thomas Candy. 2nd revised and enlarged edition. Bombay: Bombay Education Society's Press.

Moor, Edward (1810) *Śrī sarvvadevasabhā: The Hindu Pantheon*. London: J. Johnson.

Moti Chandra (1966) 'Nidhiśṛṅga (Cornucopia): A study in symbolism', *Bulletin of the Prince of Wales Museum of Western India* 9: 13.

O'Flaherty, Wendy Doniger (1973) *Asceticism and eroticism in the mythology of Śiva*. London: Oxford University Press.

Panaino, Antonio (2001) 'Between Mesopotamia and India: Some remarks about the Unicorn cycle in Iran', pp. 149-179, in R. M. Whiting (ed.) *Mythology and mythologies: Methodological approaches to intercultural influences*. (Melammu symposia 2) Helsinki: The Neo-Assyrian Text Corpus Project.

Parpola, Asko (1984) 'New correspondences between Harappan and Near Eastern glyptic art', pp. 176-195, in Bridget Allchin (ed.) *South Asian Archaeology 1981*. (University of Cambridge Oriental Publications 34) Cambridge: Cambridge University Press.

Parpola, Asko (1984) 'From Ištar to Durgā: Sketch of a prehistory of India's feline riding and buffalo-slaying goddess of victory', (Unpublished manuscript of 70 pages and 9 figures)

Parpola, Asko (1985) *The Sky-Garment: A study of the Harappan religion and its relation to the Mesopotamian and later Indian religions*. (Studia Orientalia 57) Helsinki: The Finnish Oriental Society.

Parpola, Asko (1988) 'The coming of the Aryans to Iran and India and the cultural and ethnic identity of the Dāsas', *Studia Orientalia* 64: 195-302.

Parpola, Asko (1992) 'The metamorphoses of Mahiṣa Asura and Prajāpati', pp. 275-308, in A. W. van den Hoek, D. H. A. Kolff and M. S. Oort (eds.) *Ritual, state and history in South Asia: Essays in honour of J. C. Heesterman*. (Memoirs of the Kern Institute 5) Leiden: E. J. Brill.

Parpola, Asko (1994a) *Deciphering the Indus script*. Cambridge: Cambridge University Press.

Parpola, Asko (1994b) 'Harappan inscriptions: An analytical catalogue of the Indus inscriptions from the ancient Near East', pp. 304-315 and 483-492 (bibliography), in Flemming Højlund and H. Hellmuth Andersen, *Qala'at al-Bahrain, I: The northern city wall and the Islamic fortress*. (The Carlsberg Foundation's Gulf Project) (Jutland Archaeological Society Publications 30: 1) Aarhus: Jutland Archaeological Society.

Parpola, Asko (1998) 'Sāvitrī and resurrection', pp. 167-312, in Asko Parpola and Sirpa Tenhunen (eds.) *Changing patterns of family and kinship in South Asia*. (Studia Orientalia 84) Helsinki: The Finnish Oriental Society.

Parpola, Asko (1999 [2000]) 'Vāc as a Goddess of Victory in the Veda and her relation to Durgā', *Zinbun: Annals of the Institute for Research in Humanities, Kyoto University* 34 (2): 101-143.

Parpola, Asko (2002a) 'Pre-Proto-Iranians of Afghanistan as initiators of Śākta Tantrism: On the Scythian/Saka affiliation of the Dāsas, Nuristanis and Magadhans', *Iranica Antiqua* 37: 233-324.

Parpola, Asko (2002b) 'Pandaíē and Sītā: On the historical background of the Sanskrit epics', *Journal of the American Oriental Society* 122 (2): 361-373.

Parpola, Asko (2002c) 'From the dialects of Old Indo-Aryan to Proto-Indo-Aryan and Proto-Iranian', pp. 43-102, in Nicholas Sims-Williams (ed.) *Indo-Iranian languages and peoples*. (Proceedings of the British Academy 116) London: Oxford University Press for the British Academy.

Parpola, Asko (2005a) 'Administrative contact and acculturation between Harappans and Bactrians: Evidence of sealings and seals', pp. 267-274 in: C. Jarrige and V. Lefèvre (eds.) *South Asian Archaeology 2001* I. Paris: Éditions Recherche sur les Civilisations.

Parpola, Asko (2005b) 'The Nāsatyas, the chariot and Proto-Aryan religion', *Journal of Indological Studies* 16 and 17 (2004-2005): 1-63. Kyoto.

Parpola, Asko (2007) 'Human sacrifice in India in Vedic times and before', pp. 157-177, in Jan N.

Bremmer (ed.) *The Strange World of Human Sacrifice.* (Studies in the History and Anthropology of Religion 1) Leuven: Peeters.

Parpola, Asko (2009) 'The face urns of Gandhāra and the Nāsatya cult', pp. 149-162, in Michael Willis (gen. ed.) *Migration, trade, and peoples (European Association of South Asian Archaeologists, Proceedings of the Eighteenth Congress, London, 2005)* Part 3: *Aryans and nomads,* edited by Asko Parpola. London: The British Association for South Asian Studies, The British Academy.

Parpola, Asko (in press) 'Motifs of early Iranian, Mesopotamian and Harappan art (and script), reflecting contacts and ideology', In Toshiki Osada and Michael Witzel (eds.) *Cultural relations between the Indus and the Iranian Plateau during the third millennium BCE.* (Harvard Oriental Series, Opera Minora 7) Cambridge, MA: Department of Sanskrit and Indian Studies, Harvard University.

Parpola, Simo (1997a) *The Standard Babylonian Epic of Gilgamesh: Cuneiform text, transliteration, glossary, indices and sign list.* With the assistance of Mikko Luukko and Kalle Fabritius. (State Archives of Assyria Cuneiform Texts 1) Helsinki: The Neo-Assyrian Text Corpus Project.

Parpola, Simo (1997b) *Assyrian prophecies.* Illustrations edited by Julian Reade and Simo Parpola. (State Archives of Assyria 9) Helsinki: Helsinki University Press.

Parrot, André (1960) *Sumer.* Translated by Stuart Gilbert and James Emmons. (The arts of mankind 1) London: Thames and Hudson.

Peck, A. L. (1937) *Aristotle, Parts of animals, with an English translation.* (The Loeb classical library 323) London: Heinemann.

Phillips, Catherine Beatrice (1911) 'Unicorn', pp. 581-582, in *The Encyclopaedia Britannica,* Eleventh edition, Vol. 27. Cambridge: University Press.

Porada, Edith (1950) 'A leonine figure of the Protoliterate period of Mesopotamia', *Journal of the American Oriental Society* 70: 223-226.

Possehl, Gregory L. (1999) *Indus age: The beginnings.* Philadelphia: University of Pennsylvania Press & New Delhi: Oxford & IBH Publishing Company Pvt. Ltd.

Possehl, Gregory L. (2002) *The Indus Civilization: A contemporary perspective.* Walnut Creek, CA: AltaMira Press.

Potts, Daniel T. (2001) 'Nana in Bactria', *Silk Road Art and Archaeology* 7: 23-35.

Przyluski, Jean (1929) 'La légende de Ṛṣyaśṛṅga', *Journal Asiatique* 214: 328-337.

Renou, Louis (1952) 'List of words and forms in the Sāmaveda (both in Kauthuma and in Jaiminīya Saṃhitās which are missing in the Ṛgveda or are given there with a various reading)', *Vāk* 2: 100-116. Poona.

Roberts, T. J. (1977) *The mammals of Pakistan.* London & Tonbridge: Ernest Benn Limited.

Rolland, Pierre (19739 'Le Mahāvrata: Contribution à l'étude d'un rituel solennel védique', *Nachrichten der Akademie der Wissenschaften in Göttingen* I (Philologisch-historische Klasse) 1973.3: 51-79.

Sámaśramí, Satyavrata (1874-1878) *Sáma Veda Sañhitá. With the commentary of Sáyaṇa A'chárya, edited.* I-V. (Bibliotheca Indica, Work 71) Calcutta: The Asiatic Society of Bengal.

Sarianidi, Viktor I. (1979) 'New finds in Bactria and Indo-Iranian connections', pp. 643-659, in Maurizio Taddei (ed.) *South Asian Archaeology 1977* Vol. II. (Istituto Universitario Orientale, Seminario di Studi Asiatici, Series Minor 6). Naples: Istituto Universitario Orientale.

Śāstrī, Biśwanārāyaṇ (ed.) (1972) *Kālikāpurāṇam.* (The Jaikrishnadas-Krishnadas Prachyavidya Granthamala 5) Varanasi: The Chowkhamba Sanskrit Series Office.

Scheftelowitz, I. (1912) 'Das Hörnermotiv in den Religionen', *Archiv für Religionswissenschaft* 15: 451-487.

Scholfield, A. F. (1958) *Aelian, On the characterisrtics of animals, translated* I-III. (The Loeb Classical

Library) London: William Heinemann Ltd. & Cambridge, Mass.: Harvard University Press.

Schlingloff, Dieter (1973) 'The unicorn: Origin and migrations of an Indian legend', pp. 294-307 (with 7 figures), in *German scholars on India: Contributions to Indian Studies*, edited by the Cultural Department of the Embassy of the Federal Republic of Germany, New Delhi, I. Varanasi: The Chowkhamba Sanskrit Series Office.

Schrader, Eb. (1892) 'Die Vorstellung vom μονόκερως und ihr Ursprung', pp. 573-581 and Tafel 5, in *Sitzungsberichte der Königlich Preussischen Akademie der Wissenschaften zu Berlin*, Jahrgang 1892 II. Berlin: Verlag der Königlichen Akademie der Wissenschaften.

Schroeder, Leopold von (1908) *Mysterium und Mimus im Rigveda*. Leipzig: H. Haessel Verlag.

Schwanbeck, E. A. (1846) *Megasthenis Indica*. Fragmenta collegit, commentationem et indices addidit E. A. Schwanbeck. Bonnae: Pleimesius.

Sharma, R. C. (1994) *Bharhut sculptures*. New Delhi: Abhinav Publications.

Shastri, Biswanarayan (1991-92) *The Kālikāpurāṇa (text,, introduction & translation in English)* I-III. Delhi: Nag Publishers.

Shepard, Odell (1930) *The lore of the unicorn*. London: George Allen & Unwin Ltd.

Simson, Georg von (1986) 'Ṛśyaśṛṅga: Ursprung und Hintergrund', pp. 203-228, in Eivind Kahrs (ed.) *Kalyāṇamitrārāgaṇam: Essays in honour of Nils Simonsson*. Oslo: Norwegian University Press and The Institute for Comparative Research in Human Culture.

Sivaramamurti, C. (1981) *Rishis in Indian art and literature*. New Delhi: Kanak Publications.

Sternbach, Ludwik (1974-2007) *Mahā-subhāṣita-saṃgraha* I-VIII. (Vishveshvaranand Indological Series 64, 69, 71, 73, 75, 80, 83, 88) Hoshiarpur: Vishveshvaranand Vedic Research Institute.

Steier, August (1935) 'Nashorn', col. 1780-1784, in Wilhelm Kroll *et al.* (Hrsg.) *Paulys Real-Encyclopädie der classischen Altertumswissenschaft*, Neu Bearbeitung begonnen von Georg Wissowa, Bd. 16. Stuttgart: Metzler.

Stietencron, Heinrich von (1983) 'Die Göttin Durgā Mahiṣāsuramardinī: Mythos, Darstellung und geschichtliche Rolle bei der Hinduisierung Indiens', *Visible Religion* 2: 118-166.

Thomas, P. K. (2002) 'Investigations into the archaeofauna of Harappan sites in western India', pp. 409-420, in S. Settar and Ravi Korisettar (eds.) *Protohistory: Archaeology of the Harappan Civilization*. (Indian archaeology in retrospect Vol. II) New Delhi: Indian Council of Historical Research & Manohar.

Turner, Ralph L. (1966) *A comparative dictionary of the Indo-Aryan languages*. London: Oxford University Press.

Ungnad, Arthur and Hugo Gressmann (1911) *Das Gilgamesch-Epos*, neu übersetzt von Arthur Ungnad und gemeinverständlich erklärt von Hugo Gressmann. (Forschungen zur Religion und Literatur des Alten und Neuen Testaments 14) Göttingen: Vandenhoeck & Ruprecht.

Vasil'kov, Ya. V. (1979) 'Zemledel'cheskij mif v drevne-indijskom èpose: Skazanie o Rish'yashringe', pp. 99-133, in G. A. Zograf and V. G. Èrman (eds.) *Literatura i kul'tura drevnej i srednevekovoj Indii: Sbornik statej*. Moskva: Akademiya Nauk SSSR, Institut vostokovedeniya.

Weber, Albrecht (1860-62) *Die vedischen Nachrichten von den naxatra (Mondstationen)* I-II. (Abhandlungen der Königlichen Akademie der Wissenschaften zu Berlin, aus dem Jahre 1860: 282-332 and 1861: 267-400) Berlin: Druckerei der Königlichen Akademie der Wissenschaften.

Whitney, William Dwight (1905) *Atharva Veda Samhita translated*. Edited by C. R. Lanman. I-II. (Harvard Oriental Series 7-8) Cambridge, Mass.: Harvard University Press.

Winternitz, Moriz (1908-1922) *Geschichte der indischen Litteratur* I-III. (Litteraturen des Ostens in Einzeldarstellungen 9) Leipzig: C. F. Amelang.

Zeuner, Frederick E. (1963) *A history of domesticated*

animals. London: Hutchinson & Co.

UNICORN, MAMMOTH, WHALE
Mythological and etymological connections of zoonyms in North and East Asia

Juha Janhunen
University of Helsinki

Abstract

Although the unicorn is a mythological animal, it has prototypes in the world of real animals. These prototypes, which have historically varied from region to region, have also affected the names used for the unicorn in different cultural spheres. The present study examines, in particular, the mythological and etymological background of the Chinese unicorn in relation to several other extant or extinct animals in North and East Asia. Though their connection with the unicorn has previously been neglected, the two most important animals taken up in this context are the mammoth and the whale.

An examination of names used for the mammoth by the Siberian aboriginal peoples, many of whom are familiar with fossilized mammoth skeletons, carcasses, and tusks, reveals a diversity of terms. While some of these are transparent, others are not. There is, however, a single widespread term for the whale, which in some languages also denotes the mammoth. It is not impossible that this word, reconstructable as **kalimV* ~ **kalay-*, is the indirect source of the Chinese term **kilin* > *qilin* 'unicorn'. On the other hand, there might also be a connection with the European words for 'whale', including Germanic **hwalaz* and Greek *phállaina.*

Irrespective of etymological connections, which will remain uncertain until confirmed by additional evidence, it is a fact that the Siberian aboriginal peoples traditionally conceive of the mammoth as an aquatic beast with a single horn. This "horn" (i.e., the tusk of the mammoth) has since ancient times been an important commodity exported from Siberia to China. It is therefore very likely that the trade in mammoth tusks and ivory has nourished and strengthened the unicorn myth. In its later evolution, however, the Chinese unicorn becomes differentiated into several types, which collectively represent a highly variegated unicorn fauna.

0. On the sources of the unicorn

Connecting the origin of the unicorn myth with a single animal species appears to be a hopeless task, for the myth may be very old, quite possibly dating back to the Palaeolithic. Depending on region and time, zoological associations vary widely. These must have been inspired by almost all animals, especially terrestrial mammals with pointed protuberances on the head such as horns, antlers or tusks. In some cases, pointed ears may also have been significant enough of an attribute to suggest the idea of "horn".

The most obvious source of the unicorn is, of course, the rhinoceros (*Rhinocerotidae spp.*). Relevant already in Palaeolithic times, today there are five living species of rhinoceros with either one (Indian, Javan) or two (African White and Black, Sumatran) central horns. However, many mammals with paired horns or antlers (such as goats and antelopes) have also influenced the unicorn myth. The reindeer (*Rangifer tarandus* Linnæus 1758), which has a complex system of antlers with a forward-protruding centralized section, may have been relevant in some regions. Moreover, for various reasons, mammals without horns (especially equids such as the horse and the wild ass) have quite certainly served as general prototypes for the unicorn as far as its body

Figure 1 The unicorn in Conrad Gesner's *Historia animalium* (1551) corresponds to the prototypical European image of the animal as an equid, though with cloven hooves, with a narwhal tusk on the forehead

shape and physical attributes are concerned, perhaps because of their protruding ears[1]. Finally, one can point to horns which have come from beasts which have not been immediately available to observation, but which nonetheless have been conceived of as "unicorns", the most important example being the narwhal (*Monodon monoceros* Linnæus 1758)[2].

Judging by many classic depictions of the animal (especially from the late Middle Ages and the Renaissance), the prototypical Western—or European—unicorn could perhaps best be described as an equid with a narwhal tusk on the forehead. There are, however, other syncretic features that make the zoological classification more complex. For instance, the hooves of the animal are often cloven (like those of an ox), while the mane is reminiscent of that of a lion (Figure 1)[3]. Against this background, the following treatise will examine in greater detail the possible sources of the Eastern—or Chinese—unicorn, as well as its mythological and etymological counterparts in the neighbouring regions, especially Siberia, Manchuria, Mongolia, and Eastern Central Asia.

1. The unicorn in China

The Chinese unicorn, commonly known by the name *qilin* 麒麟 (Wade-Giles: *ch'i-lin*)[4], is by definition a hybrid animal having "a single horn on its forehead, a yellow belly, a multicoloured back, the hooves of a horse, the body of a deer, and the tail of an ox" (*Encyclopædia Britannica*, online edition). The *qilin* is traditionally listed as one of the four auspicious beasts of Chinese mythology—the others being the dragon, the phoenix, and the turtle (Einhorn 1976: 38). Of these, only the turtle is a real animal, its mythological status being based on deep-rooted cosmological conceptions (Allan 1991: 103-111)[5], as well as on the practical fact that turtle bones were used as instruments of divination in Shang China. On the other hand, the dragon, the phoenix, and the unicorn, are mythological animals known both in China and in the West, though their origins and manifestations may differ from one end of the continent to the other.

There are also, however, many other animals with auspicious or mythological connotations in

Figure 2 A dragon-like manifestation of the *qilin*, with two horns, scales, and a dorsal fin (from Gao Guopei (1991: 234))

China; these vary depending on the context. The animals marking the cardinal points of the compass, for instance, include the dragon (east), the phoenix (south), and the turtle in combination with the snake (north). In this system, the fourth animal is not the *qilin* but the tiger (west). The dualistic opposition of *yang* 陽 vs. *yin* 陰 is also represented by a pair of animals: dragon *long* 龍 (east) vs. tiger *hu* 虎 (west). This combination dates back to the Neolithic. Most significant is the absence of the *qilin* in such fixed pairs or sets, suggesting that in some respects it may be secondary or historically more isolated than other auspicious or mythological animals in China[6].

Whether the *qilin* can actually be classified as a "unicorn" is sometimes in question. Nor is it immediately clear whether the creature has a direct connection with the unicorn motif of Europe and India. The one certain thing is that the unicorn in China shows considerable variation in its external appearance. For this reason, it would be better to speak not of a single Chinese unicorn but rather of an entire unicorn fauna. While the *qilin* is prototypically a hoofed animal with an equid or cervid general appearance, some of its manifestations have paws which look more feline or canine, coming close to the mythological representations of the lion *shizi* 狮子 (also known as *fogou* 佛狗 'Buddha dogs' or, in Japan, as *komainu* 狛犬 'Korean dogs'). The primary difference between these and the *qilin* is the horn: if there is a horn, the animal must be classified as a *qilin*, irrespective of how feline or canine it might otherwise look.

On the other hand, there are not large differences between the *qilin* and the dragon. Many representations of the *qilin* include a dragon's head and body, including scales and a dorsal fin; in fact, scales may be regarded as one of the features of the prototypical *qilin*. The dragon itself is highly variable in its appearance, with many of the varieties having specific names in Chinese (Carr 1990). While there are both horned and hornless dragons, the horned varieties, also known as *jiaolong* 角 龍 (ibid. 153) normally have two horns, not one. However, because dragon-like specimens of the *qilin* can also have two horns, the hooves are the only unambiguous differentiator vis-à-vis the dragon (Figure 2). Moreover, both the dragon and the *qilin* can have wings[7]. As a hoofed and winged animal, the *qilin* possesses aspects reminiscent of the Pegasus, though it appears impossible to show any direct connection between the two.

It may be concluded that the *qilin* can possess features of both dragon and mammal. A full taxonomy of the different manifestations of the *qilin* and their distribution across time and place remains to be constructed, but relevant variables include scales, hooves, fins, and wings, all of which can

Figure 3 Ink rubbing of a unicorn from the Eastern Han period. Nanyang, Henan. Depicted and discussed in Parker at http://www.chinese-unicorn.com/qilin/book

Figure 4 Wooden sculpture of a unicorn from the Eastern Han period. Wuwei, Gansu. Depicted and discussed in Parker (online)

either be present or absent. A horn is an attribute that cannot be absent, but in some cases the single horn is replaced by a pair of horns; here the animal still remains a *qilin*. The general shape of the body can be feline, canine, equid, cervid, or even bovine. Only some of these manifestations are externally reminiscent of the European unicorn, while others are conspicuously different. In particular, the double-horned varieties of the *qilin* cannot be classified as "unicorns" in the technical sense of the word, though they remain within the overall range of variation of Chinese unicorn fauna.

It seems certain that many of the later (Ming-Qing) representations of the *qilin* are the result of further syncretic evolution, which has added new features to the animal from other real and mythological contexts (and perhaps removed other features). In some of the oldest depictions of the unicorn in China, dating from the Eastern Han period (1st to 3rd cc. CE), the animal has a rather massive and bovine general structure with hooves (possibly not cloven, like those of a horse), wings, and a single long horn (Figure 3). From a two-dimensional side-view it is, of course, technically impossible to verify that the animal has only a single horn, but the general iconographic approach of the ancient artist would strongly seem to suggest this. Many of the attributes of the prototypical *qilin*, including scales and fins seem to be absent at this stage.

The presence of a single horn is confirmed by a famous three-dimensional image from the same period (Figure 4), though this specimen lacks wings. On the basis of this evidence, it has been questioned whether these are actually depictions of the *qilin*, as the animal later comes to be known, or of some earlier prototypical unicorn, which has been identified with the zoonym *zhi* 廌 (Parker online). The latter seems originally to have denoted a real goat-like animal (perhaps an antelope) that was hunted in large numbers by the kings of the Shang dynasty. By the Han period it had come to denote a mythical beast characterized by a single long horn. It appears likely that the animal underlying the zoonym *zhi* 廌 was indeed *one* of the sources of the Chinese unicorn, which later evolved into the prototypical *qilin*. Even so, it was not the only source.

A common property of the mythical *zhi* 廌 and the *qilin* is that both are able to tell right from wrong. There may be many factors behind this property, one factor (confirmed by Chinese legends) being the belief that the single horn can function as a symbolic pointer that reveals truth (or guilt)[8]. Otherwise, little is known of the *zhi* 廌 . The habits of the *qilin* are much better known. Like the dragon,

Figure 5 A bronze *xiniu* with bovine features, one central horn and wings indicated by narrow coral-like lines The back is decorated with an auspicious lingzhi mushroom and a moon crescent. Dresden, Haus Kühl (from Einhorn (1976, Plate 9))[10]

the *qilin* can both swim and fly, as well as move on land (without trampling the grass). However, while the Chinese dragon is basically a "meteorological" animal connected with water and wind[9], the *qilin* is less clearly linked to any particular environment and more clearly defined by its moral qualities and capabilities.

Though the bovine manifestation of the Chinese unicorn is often identified as the *qilin*, it is also known as the "rhinoceros-unicorn" or *xiniu* 犀牛 (literally 'rhinoceros-ox'). This type survives in later bronzes, where its external features—with the exception of the horn—are often indistinguishable from those of regular bovines (Figure 5). This confirms that the rhinoceros, especially the Indian variety (*Rhinoceros unicornis* Linnæus), long remained an important source of Chinese unicorn fauna. The rhinoceros was once relatively common in China; in Shang times, it was an object of royal hunts. It is also depicted in archaic bronzes in a naturalistic and correct way. During later periods, after it had already become extinct, it was given mythical connotations. Its evolution into the "rhinoceros-unicorn" provided one of the sources for the *qilin*.

2. The names of the Chinese unicorn

It may be concluded from the preceding that the Chinese unicorn fauna, variable as it is, is derived from at least two source animals: the rhinoceros and the goat-like animal (antelope?) connected with the zoonym *zhi* 廌 . Both of these were real animals with horns, and both were hunted in ancient China for purposes of ritual and prestige. Both also ultimately lost their connection with the real world and entered the realm of mythology, either by way of local extinction (the rhinoceros) or due to the loss of cultural relevance (the goat-like animal corresponding to the zoonym *zhi* 廌). The other creatures that have participated in the evolution of the Chinese unicorn fauna are either mythical or "meteorological" in origin (the dragon) or surviving as real animals up to the present day (cervids, bovines, felines, canines).

The Chinese term for the rhinoceros is *xi* (*xī*) 犀 (Wade-Giles *¹hsi*). There is no doubt that this was originally used as the appellative name of a real animal present in the natural environment, as is evident from extant archaic bronzes (Figure 6). The character 犀 combines the pictograms for 'bovine'

Figure 6 A naturalistic rhinoceros in bronze, Shang period (c. 1100-1050 BCE). Avery Brundage Collection, Asian Art Museum, San Francisco (picture from: www.asianart.org/newlightgallery/newlightgallery.htm)

('ox, cow, cattle') 牛 *niu* and 'tail' 尾 *wei*, with the latter itself being a compound of the pictograms for 'body' 尸 *shi* and 'hair' 毛 *mao* (Karlgren 1923: 236 no. 784, 192 no. 601). In the character for rhinoceros, the element 牛 is probably used as a classifier (radical). Importantly, the other elements are also not used in a phonetic function, implying that 犀 is a semantic-only character belonging to the oldest layer of Chinese writing (present already in the oracle bone inscriptions).

The word *xī* (< **siei*) 'rhinoceros' is connected with other Sino-Tibetan languages, including Tibetan (*)*bse* 'rhinoceros' (Schuessler 2007: 523), although it is not immediately clear whether these connections are based on an inherited cognateship or on secondary borrowings within the Sino-Tibetan family (and beyond). The original meaning of the word may have been 'large animal (in general)', but in Chinese, at least, the reference must quite early have been confined specifically to the rhinoceros. The binome *xiniu* (*xīniú*) 犀 牛 'rhinoceros-ox' is best seen as a result of the general bisyllabicization of Chinese vocabulary conditioned by the increasing number of homonyms, and also by the disappearance of the rhinoceros from the immediate environment of China. Of course, the Chinese never really lost the rhinoceros from their cultural consciousness, since its horn has always served as a ritual and medicinal object imported to China via trade routes from India and Southeast Asia[11].

Similarly, the term *zhi* 廌 seems to have originally denoted a real animal, although the exact zoological reference remains a mystery. The character 廌 is apparently a pictogrammatic representation of the animal (Parker online); it may also contain the character 鹿 *lu* 'deer' (or the upper part of it) as a semantic component (Karlgren 1923: 348 no. 1226). On the other hand, 廌 seems to be fully interchangeable with 豸 , which is of unambiguous pictogrammatic origin (Karlgren 1923: 328 no. 1160)[12]. The two characters 廌 and 豸 may originally have denoted different animals, but they became confused to the extent that both can be used in reference to the same range of vague folkloric and mythical beasts[13].

This leaves only the term *qilin* 麒麟 as a true *terminus technicus* for the Chinese unicorn. Unlike *xi* 犀 and *zhi* 廌 (豸), *qilin* is not attested as denoting a real animal, except that it came to be used for the giraffe (*Giraffa camelopardalis* Linnæus 1758) when the first specimens of this African mammal were brought to China by the seafarers of the early Ming

Figure 7 A giraffe in a Ming period Chinese court painting. In spite of the generally naturalistic approach of the artist, the animal is coloured more in the style of a *qilin*, with a scale-like pattern (from http://iberianature.com/wildworld/giraffes-in-imperial-china/, See also Wilson 1992)

period (early 15th century). In fact, the giraffe was sufficiently exotic to correspond to the definition of a *qilin*: it has (cloven) hooves, a long tail (with a conspicuous tuft, more or less like an ox), bright and motley colouring, and the general appearance of something between a deer and a horse. Most importantly, it has a pair of horns, a feature that fits with the broad definition of a *qilin*. Very probably, the image of the *qilin* influenced some of the early depictions of the giraffe in China (Figure 7).

Chinese *qilin* (*qílín*) 麒麟 is a bisyllabic word composed of two otherwise meaningless syllables *qi* (*qí*) 麒 and *lin* (*lín*) 麟 , both of which are written with secondary compound characters containing the deer radical 鹿 *lu*. Alternatively, the horse radical 馬 *ma* can also be used, yielding *qilin* (*qílín*) 騏驎 with no difference in sound or meaning. According to one popular explanation, however, the syllable *qi* 麒 denotes a male *qilin*, while the syllable *lin* 麟 denotes its female counterpart (see, e.g., *Encyclopædia Britannica*, online edition). Comparable explanations exist for the elements *qi* 騏 and *lin* 驎 as well, though they can also have horse-related meanings. Such explanations very likely reflect secondary scholastic attempts to "understand" the otherwise obscure bisyllabic word.

Although the interference of real monosyllabic etymons cannot be ruled out, there is no overruling evidence against *qilin* 麒麟 ~ 騏驎 in the meaning of 'unicorn' being a single etymologically indivisible bisyllabic entity[14]. In fact, differentiation by gender does not seem to have been an original feature of the Chinese unicorn fauna, though secondary examples of paired items (one being male and the other being female) are not uncommon among the depictions of the feline type of *qilin*[15].

Figure 8 The *kirin* of Kirin Beer (Kirin Brewery Company Ltd., Japan) contains many characteristic features of the prototypical Chinese *qilin*: (cloven) hooves, scales (combined with the underbelly of a reptile, like that of a dragon), wings (like flames or branching coral), and a single horn. The general appearance is somewhat reminiscent of a goat

As a composite word, Chinese *qilin* 麒麟 ~ 騏驎 is well attested already in the Pre-Qin classics (5th to 3rd c. BCE). The elements *qi* 麒 ~ 騏 and *lin* 麟 ~ 驎 are also attested separately in this early material, but there is no indication of an original gender differentiation[16]. Rather, the single characters are used as abbreviations of the original bisyllabic word. A common combination is *fenghuang qilin* 鳳凰麒麟 'the phoenix and the unicorn' ~ *qilin fenghuang* 麒麟鳳凰 'the unicorn and the phoenix', which is often abbreviated as *linfeng* 麟鳳 [17]. The original status of *qilin* as an indivisible bisyllabic entity is also suggested by the fact that the characters 麒 ~ 騏 and 麟 ~ 驎 share a secondary composite origin (semantic + phonetic). In all likelihood, this is a word that did not belong to the most ancient inherited vocabulary of Old Chinese.

Phonetically, Modern Mandarin *qilin* [tɕ^{h}ilin] goes back to earlier (*)*kilin* < Late Middle Chinese [kɦilin] (Pulleyblank 1991: 245, 194). The earlier Mandarin shape is reflected by European variant spellings like *kilin* ~ *kylin* ~ (Spanish) *quilin*, which are occasionally still used today. The Late Middle Chinese (8th to 11th c.) and/or Early Mandarin (12th to 16th c.) shape was also transmitted to several neighbouring languages, in which it is represented as Sino-Japanese *kirin*, Sino-Korean *girin* (in Yale Romanization: *kilin*), Sino-Vietnamese *kỳ lân*, and Manchu *kilin*. Together with the word, the concept of the animal and the underlying beliefs concerning its properties were transmitted as well. This is why unicorn mythology and iconography throughout East Asia is remarkably homogeneous (Figure 8). The occurrence of the unicorn in combination with other auspicious symbols shows some variation, however. In Japan, for instance, the *kirin* is combined in varying sets with the lion, phoenix, bamboo, and paulownia (tree) (Baird 2001: 145).

Due to the dominance of China in East Asian conceptions of the unicorn, local languages have rarely introduced independent terms for the creature. An exception is Manchu, which in addition to Chinese *kilin* also uses the native expressions *sabitun* 'male unicorn' and *sabintu* 'female unicorn' (Norman 1978: 229). These must be artificial and probably very late creations, based on the noun *sabi* '(auspicious) sign, omen', in reference to the belief that sighting a unicorn brings good luck. Furthermore, in Mongolian the unicorn can be referred to as (*)*bilig-tü* (male) vs. (*)*bilig-tei* (female) *görüxesü/n*, literally 'the knowledgeable beast'

(Sinor 1960: 173), though in spoken language the modern Mandarin word *qilin* → (*)*ciiling* is more commonly used (Mostaert 1941: 704). It is likely that the necessity to distinguish between male and female unicorns arose in connection with literary translations from Chinese, which had introduced the likewise artificial distinction between *qi* 麒 and *lin* 麟 [18].

Going further back in the reconstruction of Chinese *qilin*, the Early Middle Chinese shape of the word (5th to 7th c. CE) would appear to have been **gilin* ~ **gïlin* (Pulleyblank), while the Old Chinese shape (mid 1st millennium BCE) may have been something like **gərin* (Schuessler)[19]. In light of the difficulties encountered in the traditional reconstruction of Chinese (mainly with the help of rhymes), too much weight should not be placed on the phonetic details. We do not know, for instance, the exact value of the liquid reconstructed as **r*, nor do we know the extent to which the initial velar stop reconstructed as **g* was voiced (or otherwise marked). The phonetic and phonemic properties of the vowel system are particularly open to discussion.

Among the languages adjacent to Chinese, attention may be given to Ancient Uighur *kilän* ~ *kelän* (*kälän*) 'unicorn' (Räsänen 1969: 270; see also Sinor 1960: 168-169). Although this must also be a loanword from Chinese, dating back roughly to the Tang period (7th to 10th c. CE), the vocalism of the Uighur word is somewhat unexpected, with the low vowel *e* (*ä*) in either the second syllable or in both syllables[20]. If it is not a question of a borrowing received from an early aberrant form of Chinese, and if the word was not borrowed via a third language, the low vowel could possibly also be due to folk-etymological confusion with one or more native Turkic words, including (*)*kilä-* 'to wish, to search' and (*)*kälä-* 'to speak', both of which would correspond to the truth-telling properties of the Chinese unicorn. The final *-n* in the Uighur item could well have been reanalysed as a suffix (participle marker, if the root was understood as a verb). It is, then, possible that the Ancient Uighur speakers interpreted the word as meaning literally 'the one who searches (the truth)' or 'the one who tells (the truth)'[21].

Another item that should be considered in this context is Mongolian (*)*kers* ~ (*)*keris* ~ (*) *kiris* > *xirs* 'rhinoceros, unicorn' (Lessing 1960: 458, 472), also (*)*kers+eber-tü* id., with (*)*eber-tü* 'having horns'. In modern Mongolian, this word is used as a regular zoological term for the rhinoceros (Jigmitdurzi, Vurta and Nuvgnajizabe 1986: 1574-1575)[22]. Unfortunately, little is known of the history of the word, and it is also unclear what kind of "unicorn" it has referred to in the past. Since the rhinoceros is not attested in Mongolia in historical times, the term is not actively used in spoken dialects in terms of its zoological meaning. The word is apparently unknown in the more marginal Mongolic languages, and it does not seem to have any verified areal parallels in Turkic or Tungusic (Manchu)[23]. Even so, by both form and meaning the word is close enough to the reconstructed shapes of Chinese *qilin* to suggest a connection. Until more information surfaces, the details remain unclear[24].

3. The mammoth in Siberia

An important mammal often neglected in the context of the unicorn is the mammoth, an extinct genus of proboscideans whose most recent and best known representative is the "woolly mammoth" (*Mammuthus primigenius* Blumenbach 1799). This exceptionally large and woolly elephant was once common all over Pleistocene Northern Eurasia and North America (Kurtén and Anderson 1980: 353-354). Inhabiting the tundra and forest tundra zones in herds, the mammoth was the largest and most important terrestrial mammal hunted by Palaeolithic man during his migration from Eurasia to the Americas. It was long believed that the mammoth became extinct with the end of the latest glacial period (some 11,000 years ago), but recent discoveries have shown that the animal survived several thousand years into the Holocene on the Arctic islands off Northeastern Siberia (notably Wrangel Island)[25].

During a period of over 100,000 years, millions of mammoths were buried in the Pleistocene tundra zone, part of which is still comprised of permafrost. As a result, many mammoth individuals have been preserved even up to the present day with their soft parts intact (including intestines, skin, and residues of woolly fur). Only a dozen of these have become available for scientific documentation, however, the most famous ones being the Berezovka Mammoth (also known as the mammoth of Herz and Pfitzenmayer), discovered in 1900 (Pfitzenmayer 1926, Figure 9), and the Kirgilyakh Baby Mammoth (also known as the Magadan Baby Mammoth or the mammoth of Logachev), which was discovered in 1977 (Vereshchagin *et al.* 1981)[26]. Of many mammoths, of course, only skeletal remains (including tusks) are preserved. Entire skeletons being rare, mammoth bones are most often found in isolation or in randomly accumulated aggregations. Mammoth remains are typically brought to light by the natural process of erosion from river banks collapsing during annual springtime flooding.

Due to its importance to Ice Age man, the mammoth is depicted in numerous naturalistic paintings and engravings preserved on the walls of caves in both Europe and Siberia. Many of these depictions are well-known works of Palaeolithic art (Figure 10). Occasional miniature sculptures representing the mammoth have also been discovered. However, after the extinction of the animal, concrete knowledge of its appearance and proportions must have disappeared rapidly in most places. What remained was a vague memory of a giant animal, whose bones and tusks could still occasionally be found. There is no doubt that the mammoth has influenced mythological traditions local to its previous habitats (and beyond), though its full impact on the belief systems of humans remains to be explored.

As in Siberia, in permafrost zones where mammoth carcasses are found relatively often, knowledge of the actual animal likely survived much longer among the aboriginal populations. Local inhabitants must have come across numerous well-preserved mammoths even after the extinction of the animal. One possibly authentic case of a discovery of a mammoth carcass has been recorded

Figure 9 The Berezovka mammoth, partly reconstructed, and now exhibited at the Zoological Museum of the Russian Academy of Sciences, St. Petersburg (picture from Pfitzenmayer 1926)

Figure 10 A Palaeolithic depiction of a mammoth on the wall of a cave in Combarelles, Southern France (today dated at c. 14,000 BP) (from Pfitzenmayer 1926: 17[27])

by the Chukchee of Northeastern Siberia. While the story includes folkloric elements and references to traditional customs, including the hunting ritual of putting together the bones of the animal, its background may be factual:

> Chukchee: "[S]ome Chukchee men found two mammoth-tusks protruding from the earth. They began to beat the drum, and performed several incantations. Then the whole carcass of the mammoth came to sight. The people ate the meat. It was very nutritious, and they lived on it all winter. When the bones were stripped of all the meat, they put them together again, and in the morning they were again covered with meat." (Boas 1904-1906: 326)[28].

Even where no soft parts have been preserved, the abundance of mammoth bones and tusks has stimulated aetiological explanations concerning the taxonomy and habitat of the mammoth. In general, the mammoth is conceived of as a large subterranean or aquatic beast that can be dangerous to humans. The mammoth may also represent the transformation of other animals. According to a late 19th-century Khanty (Ugric Ostyak) informant from Northwestern Siberia, an old elk, when reaching the age of 25 years, becomes a mammoth, with "stocks" of a diameter of half an ell (ca. 30 cm) growing out of its nostrils (Karjalainen 1918: 401)[29]. The following stories and reports from Northwestern Siberia are also typical in their genre:

> Mansi (Vogul): "The mammoth lives in a deep whirlpool: it has the shape of a fish, elk, bear, or horse. Animals and fish, when they become old and are about to die, fall into the whirlpool and are transformed into mammoths by the shaman of the Sky God [...]. Nowadays we do not see mammoths any more. The Sky God has doomed them to death. Only their horns, marrow bones and ribs can be found in sandy river banks." (Kálmán 1976: 78)[30].

> Ket (Yenisei Ostyak): "[T]he ear of the mammoth [...] is the name of the part of a forest, in a place [...] where a river [...] forms a curve. The water is very deep in this place, and a mammoth is believed to have lived there in ancient times. [It is generally believed that the mammoth lives under the ground and in the water.]"[31]

Although the mammoth in the stories above is assumed to be extinct, several aboriginal populations of Northern Siberia have until recently believed that it is still a living animal, which dies when it accidentally comes to the surface. This is a rational explanation, given that only bones, tusks, skeletons, and carcasses of the mammoth can be observed today. It is also commonly believed that the tusk of the mammoth is actually a "horn", and that the mammoth has only a single "horn". Another related belief, documented from Northwestern Siberia, is that the mammoth, when swimming in deep water in autumn, uses its "horn" to break the ice from below (Kannisto 1958: 233-236).

In general, it may be noted that Siberian aboriginal peoples conceive of the mammoth on one hand as a real animal, while on the other hand it is a very special animal with mythical properties. In the latter capacity it may be compared with other mythical animals. Similar to what one finds among the Khanty people, these can include a lizard (or snake) and a giant bird (Karjalainen 1918: 402-405). Analogies and probable external sources of these other animals are not difficult to penetrate: the lizard (or snake) is quite possibly related to the mythical reptiles (crocodile, dragon) of the more dominant cultures, while the giant bird combines motifs from the realm of avian mythology (*garuḍa*, but also the phoenix). The triplet mammoth-lizard-bird is not so different from, for instance, the Chinese set unicorn-dragon-phoenix. What is important, however, is that the conceptualization of mammoth as unicorn seems to be a specifically Siberian phenomenon, firmly anchored in the fossil fauna of the region.

As a mythical beast, the mammoth has also a strong connection with shamanism. The mammoth functions, for instance, as one of the helping animals of the Siberian shaman. In a Yukaghir tale about two duelling shamans, one shaman "conjured the soul of the mammoth, sat down astride its back and [...] made the soul of the mammoth swim across the lake" (Jochelson 1926: 214-215). In a Tundra Nenets (Yurak Samoyed) tale, one of the two men living at the time of creation was captured by the Creator God. The other man searched for him, performing shamanic rituals on a mythical drum made of mammoth bone (Lehtisalo 1924: 12). On a practical note, pulverized mammoth bone has been used medicinally by several peoples (in Northwestern Siberia, at least) to stop bleeding[32].

Most interestingly, the mammoth is depicted along with other animals on a "plank" found in a collection of shamanic paraphernalia in Northeastern Siberia (Figure 11):

> "In 1897 I found the dress of a shaman and several drums in an old, long-forgotten storehouse near the village of Pyatistennoye, on the Large-Anui River. The district has a scanty population, a mixture of Yukaghir and Yakut, by this time thoroughly Russianized. With the drums was a birch plank covered with drawings scratched in with the sharp point of a knife. The plank was an elongated rectangle divided into two equal parts. One part was painted with red ochre, and represented day; and the other, painted with graphite, represented night. With the drawing in proper position, the red part would be at the right hand of a person looking down on the plank, and the black at his left hand. On the border, two indentations were scraped out for the insertion of pieces of silver, according to the statement made by some old men of the village. On the red part were scratched animals, birds, and plants, and in front of them a human figure riding a reindeer. On the black part were images of a dog and horse, and on the front of them a mammoth with a strange figure standing on its back. The figure had two birds in its hands. [...] I was told that the board was used by shamans for calling the spirits. The red part represented white shamanism, and was used for cures; and the dark one represented black shamanism, and was used for evil charms." (Boas 1904-1909: 326-327).

In this depiction, the mammoth clearly has a single "horn", which incidentally shows the typical curvature of a mammoth tusk. In other respects, the mammoth is depicted as having rather generic mammalian features that are difficult to classify with any certainty. Rather curiously, the mammoth has a mane, while the horse in the same picture does not have one[33]. The fact that the mammoth is placed on the "night" side of the "plank" is, of course, connected with its subterranean habitat; this is also reflected by its status as a basically "evil" beast[34].

4. The names of the mammoth

As a partly real and partly mythical animal that is well known to the aboriginal peoples of Siberia

Figure 11 Shaman's "plank" from Northeastern Siberia. 18th-19th c. Depicted in Boas (1904-1906: 327). The animal immediately left of the central line is a mammoth

(especially in the northern parts of the region), it is natural that the local languages have native terms for the mammoth. The languages in which such terms are found represent four families; from west to east, these are: Uralic, Yeniseic, Yukaghiric, and Tungusic. Of these, the Uralic family has the greatest diachronic depth and is represented in Siberia by two separate branches: Ugric and Samoyedic[35]. Not all languages of each family or branch have terms for the mammoth, however. There exists data for the following languages: (Ugric:) Mansi, Khanty; (Samoyedic:) Tundra and Forest Nenets, Tundra and Forest Enets, Nganasan, Selkup; (Yeniseic:) Ket, Yugh; (Yukaghiric:) Tundra and Forest Yukaghir; and (Tungusic:) Ewenki, Ewen (Lamut). Some of these reflect further dialectal differences.

It is important to note that all of the languages spoken today in the permafrost zone in Siberia are secondary in their present area of distribution. The modern language families and their branches have spread from the south in a series of relatively recent processes of expansion: Ugric from the region between the Southern Urals and the Irtysh, Samoyedic and Yeniseic from the Upper Yenisei region, and Tungusic from the Middle Amur region. Only the former homeland of Yukaghiric remains difficult to locate, but there are indications that even this family has moved from south to north relatively recently[36]. This means that the ancestral forms of all these languages were spoken south of the permafrost zone and may not have included original terms for the mammoth. Therefore, most terms attested in the modern languages are likely innovations. As such, they are either independent creations (in which case they are often semantically transparent) or borrowings from the earlier languages once spoken in the permafrost zone (in which case they are semantically opaque).

Among the semantically transparent terms, there exists data from Mansi, Khanty, and Tundra Nenets (all of which are spoken in Northwestern Siberia). In these languages, the concept of 'mammoth' can be expressed by the descriptive phrase 'earth bull, bull of the earth', while 'mammoth tusk' is the 'earth bull's horn' or simply the 'horn of the earth' (Figure 12):

(1) Mansi *maa+xar* = Khanty *muw+xar* 'earth bull' (both with dialectal variants), with *maa* = *muw* 'earth' and *xar* 'bull, ox' (in reference to male cervids, especially reindeer), Mansi *maa+xar+aañt* 'earth-bull horn' (Kálmán 1986: 289, 298; Steinitz 1966-1993: 535, 899)[37]. Although the elements *maa* = *muw* and *xar* are etymologically identical in the Mansi and Khanty data, the concept of 'mammoth' must have arisen separately in the two languages under conditions of secondary mutual interaction[38]. Importantly, the Russian word *mámont* 'mammoth', which has served as the basis for the international and zoological names of the animal, is also derived from Mansi. There is a large amount of literature on the word with a range of hypotheses[39], but the most likely explanation is that the

Figure 12 The term 'horn of the earth' is well justified in the tundra zone, where mammoth tusks can still be found simply lying on the ground. This picture (photo: Lev Veisman) is from Wrangel Island (Veisman, Zlotin and Bobrov 1986: 51)

Russians adopted it in the 16th century in the Ural region from the otherwise unattested Mansi expression *maa-ng+aańt* 'earthen horn' (Helimski 1990 [2000]: 353-354), in which *-ng-* functions as a denominal derivative suffix for adjectival nouns.

(2) Nenets **ya-n+kora* > Tundra Nenets *ya-ng+kora* = Forest Nenets *jaa+koora* 'bull of the earth', Nenets **ya-n+nyamt°* > Tundra Nenets *ya+nyamt°* = Forest Nenets *jaa+nyaamt°* 'horn of the earth' (Lehtisalo 1956: 86-87). These expressions seem to have a limited distribution in Forest Nenets (only in the Western dialects), but since Tundra Nenets and Forest Nenets are two closely related languages it is possible that the data derive from their common protolanguage, which was once spoken in the region between the lower courses of the Ob and the Yenisei. It may also be noted that the word **kora* 'bull, ox' is an etymological cognate of the Mansi and Khanty word *xar* (with variants) as discussed above; this has, however, no implications on the age of the expressions connected with the mammoth[40]. Interestingly, in accordance with the definition of the mammoth as a 'bull', the Nenets also speak of the 'hooves of the mammoth'[41].

The other names used for the mammoth and/or mammoth tusks in Siberian languages are semantically either partly or completely opaque. There is, therefore, a chance that some of these may be very old and possibly derived from local substratal languages:

(3) Mansi *wit-kaś* 'mammoth' (with dialectal variants) (Kálmán 1986: 729). This item is also translated as 'water monster', with *wit* 'water', in reference to the belief that the mammoth is an aquatic beast, but the latter component *-kaś* has no independent meaning or known etymology. In some dialects, *wit-kaś* may have been confused with the somewhat similarly sounding word *utśi* 'benevolent forest spirit' (with variants, ibid. 709), which can also refer to the mammoth. An original connection between these two etymons seems unlikely. Obviously, as a mythical beast, the mammoth can easily be referred to by various taboo expressions whose primary meaning is something else (such as 'spirit', 'giant', 'monster').

(4) Khanty *wes* 'mammoth' (with dialectal variants), also *yəngk+wes* 'water mammoth', *wes+ăngət* 'mammoth horn', *wes-lŏg* 'mammoth bone' (Steinitz 1966-1993: 1631-1632). This looks like a simple basic word with no other reference than the mammoth, though this animal can be conceptualized vaguely as a mythical beast with various shapes and origins. The word has also been transmitted to Forest Nenets as *wees°*, where the meaning is explained as 'mit dem Hochwasser ankommender Geist, der die Weiden- und Birkenwurzeln anfrisst und dadurch den Einsturz der Ufer verursacht' (Lehtisalo 1956: 68). In one (Northern) Khanty dialect the plural is recorded as *wens-ə-t* (with *-t* functioning as the regular plural marker), which might mean that the earlier shape of the word was **wens(ə)*.

(5) Selkup *kośar* 'mammoth' (Alatalo 2004: 320 no. 2179). This item, restricted to a single Samoyedic language (with dialectal variants), is likewise an etymologically indivisible word referring specifically to the mammoth or also, as in Khanty, to 'the spirit that makes river banks collapse'. It happens that Selkup *ś* (= *š*, *sh*) in intervocalic position represents earlier

*ns, while an initial *k* (*q*) can stand for both original **k* and **w*[42]. This means that the Selkup word might theoretically go back to a shape like **wVnsV-*, making it compatible with the Khanty term for 'mammoth'. Since Khanty and Selkup are adjacent languages, there is a strong possibility that we here have an old term for the mammoth that is local to the region between the middle courses of the Ob and the Yenisei. If it is a question of a Khanty loanword in Selkup, or vice versa, the borrowing must have taken place a relatively long time ago.

(6) Ket ^{1}*tel* (*te·l'*), Yugh ^{1}*cel* 'mammoth' (Werner 2002, Vol. 2: 260), Ket *tel-də qo'-ng* 'mammoth horns', with ^{2}*qo'* : plural *qo'-ng* 'horn' (Donner 1955: 89). These seem to be the only mammoth-related lexical data recorded from the Yeniseic languages. The word for 'mammoth', a first-tone monosyllabic masculine noun, is attested in Ket and Yugh, two closely related Northern Yeniseic languages that are spoken immediately east of Selkup. In view of the plural forms (Ket ^{1}*tekng* ~ ^{1}*tel ang* = Yugh ^{1}*cekng* ~ ^{1}*cel-ïng*), it may be assumed that the original shape of the stem was of the type **tekəl*[43]. No further etymology of the word is known, but the phrase 'mammoth horn' seems to have been transmitted from some Yeniseic language into Shor (a Yenisei Turkic language), in which it is attested as *täkkä ang* 'mammoth' (Stachowski 1998: 111-112)[44].

(7) The two Samoyedic languages Enets and Nganasan share a term for the mammoth, attested as Forest Enets *kario*, Tundra Enets *kali* ~ *kari* (Katschmann and Pusztay 1978: 85 no. 462), and Nganasan <*kalája*> (Castrén 1855: 47). Another source on Nganasan has <*kalám+ńarymtýma*> 'mammoth-reindeer, on which the helping spirits of a shaman travel' (Kortt and Simčenko 1985: 123). An immediate observation regarding these items is that the vowels of the initial syllable are not in a regular correspondence: Nganasan a would suggest an earlier **ä*, while Enets *a* goes back to **a*, a different Proto-Samoyedic vowel. It is therefore possible that the word has been transmitted as a loan from Enets to Nganasan, or vice versa. Assuming that the Enets shape is more original, the word may be reconstructed approximately as **kalVyə*[45].

(8) Ewenki *selii* [səli:] 'mammoth' (with dialectal variants), also **seelir* > *xeelir* (Cincius 1975-1977, Vol. 2: 140)[46]. This item is attested both in the northwestern and northeastern dialects of Ewenki, but not in the more southerly dialects, nor in the closely related Ewen language. This means that the term may have originated after the break-up of Proto-Ewenki (a language with a history of less than 1,000 years) during the initial stage of the Ewenki expansion from the Middle Amur region across Siberia. No internal or external etymology is known for the word, but the same item is also attested (in one dialect) as referring to a shamanic object described as "a figure with two heads: the one of the heads is that of a fish, and the other one is that of an elk."

(9) Ewen *kiami* [ke:mi ~ qæ:mi] 'mammoth tusk; ivory; mammoth' (Cincius 1975-1977, Vol. 1: 388). It is not immediately clear whether the original meaning of this item was 'mammoth' or 'mammoth tusk'. The latter possibility is suggested by the fact that the word can also be used in reference to light brown (= mammoth-tusk-colour) reindeer. The word is not attested in Ewenki, which means that it is very probably a recent Ewen innovation; while

it is perhaps a borrowing, the background and source remain unknown.

(10) Tundra Yukaghir (Wadul) *qolghut* = Forest (Kolyma) Yukaghir (Odul) *qolghol* (with minor phonetic and dialectal variation) 'mammoth', Tundra Yukaghir *qolghud+enmur* 'mammoth horn' (Nikolaeva 2006: 384 no. 2056). The data would seem to suggest a root of the type **qolq* (Nikolaeva) with the meaning 'mammoth', though it might also be a question of repetition of the primary root *qol* → *qol&qol*. No further etymology is known.

As may be seen, the above ten native names for the mammoth (or, in some cases, for the mammoth tusk) used in the aboriginal languages of Northern Siberia are basically independent local expressions, which rarely have deep diachronic roots in the languages concerned. There is a clear areal link between the semantically transparent terms 'earth bull' > 'mammoth' and 'earth horn' > 'mammoth tusk', as attested in the languages of Northwestern Siberia (Mansi, Khanty, Nenets), but this link must be chronologically shallow. The only case of a relatively deep etymological link in this corpus of names is the possible relationship between the semantically opaque terms Khanty *wes* and Selkup *kośar* (both possibly < **wVnsV-*).

Due to its vague mythical content, the concept of 'mammoth' can also be connected with the names of other large and/or mythical animals. In such cases, the lexicographically registered meaning 'mammoth' may be secondary or even questionable, since its implications to the speakers are not known. Udeghe, for instance, uses the etymologically opaque zoonym *egule* with the meaning of both 'bear' and 'mammoth' (Girfanova 2001: 360). However, since Udeghe speakers live in a region (the Ussuri taiga in Northeastern Manchuria) where mammoth-related finds are not common, it is unlikely that this is a primary name for the mammoth. Rather, it is one of the many expressions used in general for 'large animal', 'giant' or 'monster'. When referring to the bear, it is also one of the many taboo expressions for that animal, which has a very important place in Udeghe mythology[47].

5. The mammoth and the whale

In spite of the fact that its horn significantly influenced European depictions of the unicorn, the narwhal (Figure 13) is historically of secondary significance as regards the evolution of that mythical animal. Because the narwhal inhabits Arctic waters far from the cultural centres of both Europe and Asia, its role in the formation of the Chinese unicorn is particularly marginal. Narwhal tusks were extremely rare before the Age of Exploration, and an understanding of their connection with the actual animal was only formed when commercial whaling developed in the 17th century. Only after that did the role of the narwhal as the "sea unicorn" (*unicorno del mare*) become consistently established[48].

Even after the introduction of commercial whaling, however, conceptions concerning the appearance of the narwhal remained distorted for a long time; the animal was confused with other marine mammals and fish. A typical report is that of Pierre Martin de la Martinière, who writes of a "Sea Horse" (Cheval-Marin) somewhere between a fish and a walrus (Fig. 14). From his description of the hunting process and the "tooth" or "horn" of the animal, it is clear that the animal was a narwhal:

> "La pesche de ce poisson ne se faisant que pour avoir ses dents, qui servent à faire toutes sortes d'ouvrages, comme l'yvoire & se vend la livre beaucoup plus cher, tant à cause de sa blancheur, qui surpasse celle de l'yvoire, qu'à cause aussi que les ouvrages qui en sont faits ne se roussissent pas

Figure 13 Narwhals "tusking" (communicating with their tusks) (picture from: http://news.nationalgeographic.com/2005/12/photogalleries/narwhals/)

Figure 14 Catching the "Sea Horse" (i.e. the narwhal). Picture from de la Martinière (1671: 140). The narwhal is depicted as a scaly fish with a reptile-like head. Note that the tusk is placed incorrectly Discussed also by Shepard (1930, Plate 23)

si tôt." (de la Martinière 1671: 141).

Of far greater significance for the unicorn myth are other types of whales. Whales (*Cetacea*) have always been well known to coastal inhabitants, particularly those of the Arctic Ocean and the Northern Pacific. Coastal whaling in open boats developed early on among native communities living in the longitudinal belt between the Bering Strait to the north and the Japanese Islands to the south. Whales are also well known to the populations living on the continental shores of the Sea of Japan. Early whaling also extended in the latitudinal belt from the Barents Sea and White Sea in the west to the Kara Sea off of Northwestern Siberia. It is very probable that the native populations engaged in whaling in these regions inherited the tradition from their local predecessors, who spoke other languages which have subsequently been lost. Whaling is closely connected with the hunting of other sea mammals, including seals and walruses[49].

Whales need not necessarily be hunted, as they sometimes simply drift ashore for various reasons, sometimes even collectively. Because a single whale can provide food for an entire community for a long time, the "arrival of the whales" (whales migrate seasonally) has been regarded as a divine favour of immense proportions. The lack of appearance of the whales, on the other hand, is a tragedy that can bring hunger and starvation to a community[50]. In fact, whales are the only animals today that match the mammoths of the Pleistocene in size and significance. Therefore, whale-hunting populations are, in some respects, the closest equivalents to the mammoth hunters of the past.

There are, however, other parallels between the whale and the mammoth. The whale, like the mammoth in the past, has been for coastal populations a source of large bones, which have been used since Palaeolithic times as materials for dwellings, utensils, and ritual structures. The most famous ritual structure made of whalebones is the so-called "Whalebone Alley" (*Kitovaya alleya*), discovered in Chukotka in the region of Cape Chaplin (Indian Point) in 1976 and tentatively dated to c. 1300 CE (Arutyunov, Krupnik and Chlenov 1982). The monument was built using different types of massive bones from bowhead whales (*Balaena mysticetus*), including skulls and jawbones (Figure 15)[51].

While the whale is a known category of animals for coastal peoples, with many different species used for a variety of purposes, inland populations with no direct access to the sea have a less specific understanding of these creatures. It is curious, then, that many inland populations—such as those in Central Asia and continental Siberia—are familiar with the general concept of 'whale' (or at least have a word that is lexicographically registered as meaning 'whale', even if the word may also denote a vague mythical animal). Even more interestingly, many Inner Asian languages use a single widespread etymon for 'whale'. This etymon is represented in five different language families:

(1) Amuric: Ghilyak (Nivkh) *qalm* '(small) whale' (Savel'eva and Taksami 1970: 147). Ghilyak is the only surviving member of a previously probably larger language family (termed Amuric) whose territory may have extended down to Central Manchuria. Since modern Ghilyak is spoken on the coast, in the Amur Delta region and on Northern Sakhalin, Ghilyak speakers know whales from personal experience. Sea mammal hunting is an integral part of Ghilyak culture (Taksami 1975: 26-40). Among the animals hunted are both various types of seals and small whales, especially the belukha whale (*Delphinapterus leucas*)[52]. Larger whales are not hunted by the Ghilyak. The language has several terms for different types of whale, of which *qalm* is probably the culturally most important, though it does not seem to denote a specific species of whale. Since Ghilyak has undergone a process of vowel loss in non-initial syllables, the earlier shape of the word may be reconstructed as < **kalVmV*[53].

(2) Tungusic: Northern Tungusic (Ewenic: Ewenki-Ewen-Neghidal) *kalim* (*kalïm*) 'whale', dialectally also 'walrus', Amur Tungusic (Nanai-Ulcha-Orok, Udeghe-Oroch) *kalima* (*kalma*) ~ *kaalima* (*kaalma*), Manchu *kalimu* (*qalimu*) (Cincius 1975-1977, Vol. 1: 367). All of these are compatible with Ghilyak **kalVmV*, but the vowel correspondences within Tungusic are not regular. Very probably, the forms with a long vowel (*kaalima*, *kaalma*) and the forms with a medial vowel loss (*kaalma*, *kalma*) are secondary. The final vowel loss in the Northern Tungusic forms (*kalim*) is regular and suggests an original high vowel (**u*). This leaves the two reconstructions **kalimu* (Manchu and Northern Tungusic) ~ **kalima* (Amur Tungusic)[54]. Since Tungusic-speaking populations are generally not engaged in sea mammal hunting[55], it is likely that the word is a borrowing from Amuric to Tungusic, rather than vice versa (Doerfer 1985a: 197-198). This pattern may also hold for several other marine

Figure 15 The Whalebone Alley in Chukotka. A line of bowhead whale jawbones standing erect (picture from http://www.phorus.ru/page7-r661.html)

and aquatic terms in Tungusic[56].

(3) Mongolic: (*)*kalimu* (*qalimu*) > modern (Buryat) *xalim* > (Khalkha) *xalyem* ~ (Khorchin) *xaelem* 'whale' (Lessing 1960: 920, Cheremisov 1973: 538). The Mongolic form corresponds exactly to the Tungusic reconstruction **kalimu*. Although in general Mongolic has provided a large number of loanwords to Tungusic, aquatic terminology shared by the two language families often seems to be of Tungusic origin (Doerfer 1985b: 247-251). Quite possibly, the Tungusic homeland extended east to the Sea of Japan, while the Mongolic homeland was located in Southwestern Manchuria, north of the Bohai Gulf. It is therefore more likely that **kalimu* was transmitted from Tungusic to Mongolic, rather than vice versa. Even so, Tungusic itself seems to have received at least some of its maritime terminology from Amuric.

(4) Turkic: Yakut *xaalïm* 'whale', also *xaalïm+balïk* 'whale-fish' (Pekarskij 1927: 3275). The word seems to be obsolete in modern Yakut but must have had an earlier concrete meaning; the compound phrase *xaalïm+balïk* 'whale-fish' clearly identifies it as denoting an aquatic animal. Yakut is basically an inland language, which expanded from the Baikal region to the Middle Lena basin roughly between 1300 and 1500 CE. Soon after that, Yakut speakers reached the coast at both the Okhotan Sea and at the Arctic Ocean. Being cattle nomads, however, the ethnic Yakut have not engaged in whaling. Since the word is not attested in any other Turkic language, it must be a relatively recent borrowing in Yakut. Formally, the source could be either Mongolic (Buryat) or Tungusic (Ewenki-Ewen), but in view of the cultural situation the Tungusic source appears more likely. The long (double) vowel in the Yakut data must be secondary (as in Amur Tungusic), but its exact background remains unknown[57].

(5) Samoyedic: Tundra Nenets *xalaeh*: *xalae*°- = Forest Nenets *kaalae(ng)*: *kaalae*°- 'whale' (Lehtisalo 1956: 165). The word can be derived from Proto-Nenets **kalayəng* or possibly **kalayng*, suggesting that the concept of 'whale' is not quite recent in Nenets[58]. Indeed, the Tundra Nenets, who live partly at the Arctic coast (of the Kara Sea), are locally engaged in sea mammal hunting, including whaling (Khomich 1960: 75-81), although their dominant subsistence economy is based on reindeer herding. Since Proto-Samoyedic was spoken far to the south, however, the word for 'whale' (at least in this meaning) is probably a Post-Proto-Samoyedic innovation. The similarity with the Amuric-Tungusic-Mongolic-Yakut items discussed above is conspicuous, suggesting that there is an etymological connection.

The Nenets word for 'whale' also has another connection: it is a direct cognate of the Enets and Nganasan words for 'mammoth', as discussed above. The reconstructions **kalay(ə)ng* 'whale' and **kalVyə* 'mammoth' are formally compatible, though there may be a difference in the structure of the non-initial syllables[59]. A semantic link is shown by the fact that the mammoth is, in fact, conceived of as an aquatic animal (or even as a fish). In this mythological framework, a semantic transition from 'mammoth' to 'whale' would be equally possible as 'whale' to 'mammoth'. However, the formal connection of the word with the Inner Asian etymon for 'whale' suggests that this meaning might be more primary in Samoyedic. Of course, it is also possible that the word has undergone two semantic transitions, first from 'whale' to 'mammoth' (at some early stage of Samoyedic) and then back from 'mammoth' to 'whale' (in Nenets only) when the Nenets speakers came into contact with real whales, which may have happened a few hundred years ago.

Among the Inner Asian words for 'whale', as far as the form is concerned, the Samoyedic are somewhat idiosyncratic. While the other data are basically all derived from the reconstructed form **kalimV*, which very probably was transmitted first from Amuric to Tungusic and then from Tungusic to both Mongolic and Turkic (Yakut), the Samoyedic data cannot be directly linked to Tungusic or Mongolic (which would otherwise be the most probable sources). We should therefore consider the fact that the Tungusic expansion in Siberia is a very recent development, datable to the first half of the second millennium CE. Before Tungusic, other subsequently lost languages were spoken in Central and Eastern Siberia. Some of these may well have functioned as intermediaries when the word for 'whale' was transmitted to Samoyedic[60].

In this context, it is also necessary to recall two European words for 'whale', Germanic **hwalaz* and Greek *phállaina*. Germanic **hwalaz* (English *whale*, also in nar*whal*, *wal*rus, see Klein 1966-1967, Vol. 2: 1738) has been compared with Old Prussian *kalis* 'shad' (a fish of the herring family) and Latin *squalus* 'large fish, shark', yielding hypothetical Proto-Indo-European *(*s*)*k*^{w}*alo-s* ~ *(*s*)*k*^{w}*ali-s* (Rodriguez 1989). These comparisons are not particularly convincing, however, given the considerable semantic differences and the ad hoc derivative devices (*s mobile* and the stem vowel variation). For the same reasons, the Germanic word can hardly be derived from Uralic **kala* 'fish' (see Itkonen and Kulonen 1992-2000, Vol. 1: 282), though such a possibility has occasionally been proposed[61]. It is worth noting, however, that the Germanic item for 'whale' has been transmitted to the Finnic and Saamic branches of Uralic (e.g., Finnish *valas* (ibid., Vol. 3: 397)); this suggests that in the Baltic region, Germanic speakers preceded Finnic and Saamic speakers to the sea.

As for Greek *phállaina* 'whale', which was borrowed (though apparently with the intermediation of other languages) into Latin as *balaena*, an etymological comparison with *phallós* has been made, the idea being that whales are "phallic" in shape (Beekes 2010: 1549-1550). This is a rather far-fetched proposal, which does not seem to be corroborated by any independent evidence. Rather, we should consider the possibility that Greek *phállaina* is connected, via an areal link, with Germanic *hwalaz*. The phonetic similarity of the roots is rather obvious and comprises the labial element (*p* ~ *w*), the aspiration element (*h*), and the sequence *ala*. We might go even further, drawing a connection with the Inner Asian words for 'whale', which differ from the European ones only in the aspect of the initial consonant (velar vs. labial). Although this remains at present a mere hypothesis, it might be a question of a trans-Eurasian cultural word with both zoological and mythological connections[62].

6. Bone, horn, and ivory

Large animals such as the whale and the mammoth may be said to have three types of potential value to human communities: subsistence value, cognitive value, and commodity value. Subsistence value is the greatest for those communities that actually catch the animal and use it for food, clothing, and other practical applications. Cognitive value is relevant to all those who know of the animal and use it as an element to support their worldview and belief systems. Commodity value becomes relevant when the animal has parts that can be transported over long distances and exchanged for other commodities. Regular bones are rarely precious enough to function as exchangeable commodities, but horns and tusks have been sold and bought since Palaeolithic times.

If we disregard symbolic applications (e.g., medicinal or ritual), the inherent value of horns and tusks is found in the properties of the material; it is solid, hard and relatively heavy, but easy to carve and not too brittle. There are, of course, many types and sources of horns and tusks, the three basic types being bone (like the antlers of cervids), keratin (like the horns of bovids and the rhinoceros), and dentine (like the tusks of elephants, walruses and the narwhal). Due to differences in rarity, size, technical workability, and aesthetic properties, there have always been differences in the price-setting of horns and tusks, the two most desired types being rhinoceros horn and elephant ivory. The tusks of the walrus (*Odobenus rosmarus* Brisson 1762) provide a good local alternative for elephant ivory (especially in the Bering Sea region)[63], but the materials are not identical, as there are differences in their technical properties[64].

As the extant resources of horns and tusks have always tended to be exploited more rapidly than they are renewed, fossil resources have been prized since ancient times. For rhinoceros horns, fossil resources are unfortunately very limited (Pallas 1769, Tolmachoff 1929, Mikael Fortelius 1983), but not non-existent. Siberia was once the home of not only the woolly mammoth, but also the woolly rhinoceros (*Coelodonta antiquitatis*); its fossilized horns are known from various finds (Figure 16). By contrast, mammoth tusks are found in abundance all over Siberia, especially in the permafrost zone. They must have been exported in considerable quantities to the neighbouring regions, including China, since Neolithic times at least.

Although technically distinguishable from the ivory of elephant species still surviving today, of which only that of the African elephant (*Loxodonta africana*) has been widely exploited by global trade networks, mammoth ivory has basically the same properties and can be used for the same purposes as regular elephant ivory[65]. The principal difference is in the state of preservation; many fossilized mammoth tusks are severely weathered, which reduces their practical value. On the other hand, mammoth tusks are considerably larger than those of contemporary elephants. A single tusk, when not overly affected by the weathering process, typically has a length of approximately three meters and weight of 30 to 50 kg (Figure 17). Some of the largest specimens observed are up to four meters long and can weigh over 100 kg (Pfitzenmayer 1926: 257).

The commercial excavation and exportation of mammoth tusks from Siberia, especially from Yakutia, intensified in the 19th and early 20th centuries, when huge numbers of tusks were exported all over the world. The transportation and exportation of tusks was facilitated by the completion of the Trans-Siberian Railroad in 1903. The annual output traded in Yakutsk between 1825 and 1831 has been estimated at around 1,500 to

Figure 16 The horn of a woolly rhinoceros from Siberia. 19th century (picture from Nordenskiöld (1880, Vol. 1: 392))

2,000 *pood* (that is, approximately 24,000 to 32,000 kg). The output remained at similar (or even higher) levels until the Russian Revolution in 1917, with some of the largest importers being England (Figure 18) and Japan (Pfitzenmayer 1926: 255-256). After a decline during the Soviet period, the situation today is again comparable with that before the Revolution: 15 tons of tusks are excavated annually in Yakutia alone, corresponding to some 500 medium-sized tusks (30 kg on average)[66].

China has always been a major importer of mammoth ivory. This is simply because China has no indigenous elephant populations of her own, and fossil ivory is rare due to climatic, vegetational, and soil conditions. As a precious and prestigious material, ivory (*xiangya* 象牙) has been used in China since the Neolithic to produce a variety of objects with practical and decorative value (Laufer 1926)[67]. It is, however, difficult to estimate the proportion of mammoth ivory to total ivory used at any given time in the past, as no systematic distinction has been made between the two types of ivory. Only very recently, in connection with the Convention on International Trade in Endangered Species (CITES), which restricted access to elephant ivory, has mammoth ivory been fully recognized as a distinct material[68]. China is now the largest consumer of mammoth ivory (though regular elephant ivory—both legal and illegal—is also used, depending on availability).

This brings us finally back to the question of the Chinese unicorn and its connection with the mammoth and the whale. As has been shown above, the concepts of unicorn, mammoth, and whale are often confused in the mythological traditions of aboriginal populations who are only vaguely familiar with the underlying real animals. Thus, both the unicorn and the mammoth are thought to be animals with a single horn, while both the mammoth and the whale are conceptualized as aquatic beasts. Although the whale is an extant real animal (or, zoologically speaking, an order of animals), it remains for inland populations an abstraction, in this respect being no different from the extinct mammoth or the truly mythical unicorn.

On the other hand, of the three animals, the mammoth is the only one that yields real "horns" in the form of actual fossilized tusks (we may here ignore the narwhal). Compared with African and Indian elephant ivory, which had to be transported overland or via the sea across long distances to China, samples of Siberian mammoth tusks must have already been much closer at hand in ancient times and must have been known to the

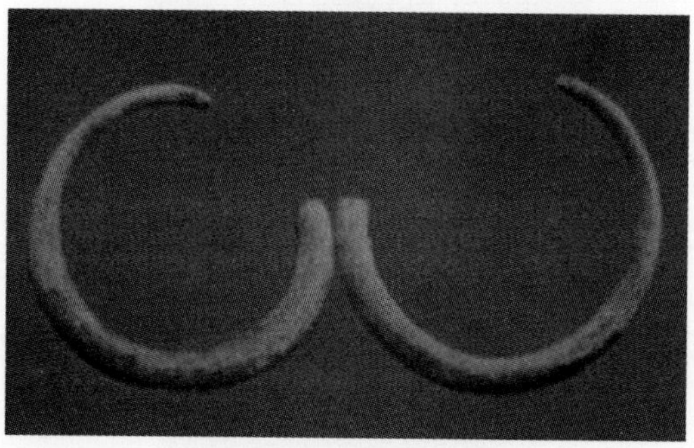

Figure 17 A medium-sized pair of exceptionally circular mammoth tusks from Siberia. Length of each tusk 2,79 m, weight 32 kg (from Pfitzenmayer (1926: 257 and Plate))

Figure 18 Siberian mammoth tusks at the ivory warehouse of London Docks
National Maritime Museum, London (online)
Originally published in *Illustrated London News* (1873)

Chinese as a source of ivory. One possible trade route from Siberia to China could have passed through Manchuria. While there appears to be no information as to how the ancient Chinese conceived of the mammoth, neither is there any indication that they thought of it as an elephant (which was an animal that they knew)[69].

It may well be, therefore, that the mammoth held for the ancient Chinese both commodity value as a source of ivory and cognitive value as a mythical animal, which could have easily been confused with other mythical or semi-mythical animals, including the whale. Since many Siberian populations understood the mammoth to be an animal with a single horn, it is quite possible that the Chinese also thought of it as a kind of unicorn. Together with the other animals discussed earlier— the rhinoceros, cervids, and bovines—the mammoth may well have served as one of the sources and prototypes for the Chinese unicorn, even if the Chinese only knew its "horns" and had no idea of its actual appearance.

Against this background, we should reconsider the Chinese term for the unicorn, *qilin* 麒 麟 . Since this is a bisyllabic item composed of two originally meaningless syllables, and written with two characters specially designed for writing this particular word, it is very probably a loanword of a type that is common in the cultural vocabulary of Chinese, a language which in its historically attested forms otherwise operates with monosyllabic roots. It is also possible that the word originally meant 'ivory' or 'tusk', a meaning which could easily have been adopted to denote the animal which supposedly yielded such material[70]. However this might be, the Chinese term for the unicorn could well be a borrowing from regions where mammoth ivory has been imported to China. Of course, borrowing need not have taken place from the ancestor of any extant modern language, considering that the languages and language families attested north of China today represent only part of the former linguistic diversity.

This being the case, we might tentatively compare Chinese *qilin* < **kilin* with the Inner Asian words denoting both 'whale' and 'mammoth', as discussed above. The formal and semantic similarity between **kilin* < **gilin* ~ **gïlin* 'unicorn' and **kalimV* 'whale' (but also Samoyedic **kalay-* 'mammoth') is sufficient to support, though perhaps not confirm, the hypothesis of an etymological connection. This possibility may, of course, have implications for the reconstruction of the Old Chinese shape of the word for 'unicorn', and perhaps also a connection with Mongolian (*)*kers* ~ (*)*keris* ~ (*)*kiris* 'rhinoceros'.

Another line of comparison would be to consider the actual Chinese word for 'whale' (modern Mandarin *jīng* ~ *qíng* 鯨 < **king*), reconstructed for Old Chinese as **grang* (Schuessler 2007: 316). While as a monosyllabic item it is clearly older than the bisyllabic term for 'unicorn', ultimately Chinese monosyllables are derived from bisyllables, which in this particular case would imply a shape of the type **gVrang*. Assuming that Chinese (Sino-Tibetan) was originally spoken in an inland environment[71], the word for 'whale' would have to be a borrowing received at the time when contact was established with the coast. In principle, both **kilin* < **gərin* 'unicorn' and **king* < **g(V)rang* 'whale' could be compared with the Inner Asian words for 'whale' and 'mammoth'. Both comparisons could be relevant, although the underlying chronological settings would have to have been different.

Unfortunately, no certain conclusion can be made at this stage. Not all of the items discussed above need be mutually connected, and for the moment we cannot say which items exactly go together. Even so, the zoological and mythological background that links the items with one another and makes etymological comparisons possible is there. Proceeding along these lines, we may someday be able to say more.

Notes

1) Most of these well-known sources of the unicorn (though not the reindeer) are also mentioned in the Wikipedia entry on "Unicorn" at http://en.wikipedia.org/wiki/Unicorn.

2) Narwhal tusks were traded as decorative objects and sources of ivory as soon as they became more widely accessible due to European seafaring activities. Even so, most of the people who came into contact with narwhal tusks probably had no clear idea of the external appearance and taxonomic status of the actual animal. The role of the narwhal in the formation of the unicorn myth will be discussed later in the present study.

3) I thank Mikael Fortelius for turning my attention to the unicorn depictions in Gesner's treatise. For the purpose of the present paper, it is irrelevant to discuss in detail the somewhat varying definitions, descriptions and depictions of the animal in the different editions of Gesner's work, also known as the *Thierbuch*. In the revised German edition (1669), the unicorn is confused with the onager (Waldesel), although the depictions of this animal incorporate features of the rhinoceros (Fortelius and Fortelius 1989: 162-171, see also Gratz 2005). On the European (and Indian) unicorn, see also Walter Fortelius (1999).

4) In the present text, the Chinese tones are marked in Romanization only when relevant to the discussion, as in the etymological excursions.

5) Allan (1991) also discusses the mythological face motif *taotie* 饕餮, which may or may not have a horn or horns. The *taotie* seems to have represented a wide range of animals, including insects. There is, however, no clear evidence that suggests its connection with the unicorn.

6) The secondary status of the *qilin* is possibly also signalled by its multicoloured appearance, with the other auspicious animals normally appearing in varying monochromatic manifestations. In particular, each of the animals marking the cardinal points of the compass is associated with a specific basic colour: green (dragon), red (phoenix), white (tiger), and black (turtle and snake).

7) In later (Song-Yuan-Ming-Qing) depictions of the Chinese unicorn fauna, the wings are often reduced to narrow stripes resembling branching coral, starting at the front and back legs. Similar attributes often accompany depictions of the dragon. It is, of course, difficult to say to what extent these may be regarded as "wings", as they also have other decorative and symbolic functions. In multicoloured depictions of the *qilin* (such as those found on cloisonné objects), the stripes are often red, confirming the connection with coral. In some cases, the red colour may also convey the notion of flames.

8) According to Schuessler (2007: 620), the truth-telling property of the *zhi* 廌 may actually be due to a philological misunderstanding in the transmission of the classics. This animal is also referred to by the binome *xiezhi* 解廌, in which the character *xie* 解 may stand for a real phonetic syllable, but it may also be used semantically to mean 'to distinguish, to understand'. If this is so, the connection with truth, law and righteousness would have been secondarily transferred from the *zhi* to the *qilin* type of Chinese unicorn.

9) Andersson (1932: 397-400) explains the origin of the Chinese dragon from the whirlwind (tornado), associated with thunder and rain. According to him, the related dragon motif is already present in Neolithic pottery decorations. Iconographically, of course, the dragon has also many other sources, including the crocodile.

10) Einhorn identifies this animal as a *qilin*, though it corresponds more closely with the definition of the *xiniu*. The object is a mirror stand, probably from the Song-Yuan period (if it is not a later copy from the Ming period). Similar mirror stands with a *xiniu* motif are commonly encountered (see Kerr 1990: 100-103 Figure 87). One also finds the regular two-horned variety of bovine in repose with an auspicious *lingzhi* 靈芝 mushroom on its back.

11) By far the best known and most sophisticated expression of the Chinese appreciation for rhinoceros horn is the tradition of the exquisitely carved rhinoceros horn cups, on which see Chapman (1999).

12) The interchangeability does not extend to the use of 豸 as a radical (no. 153 in the Kangxi system) in a number

of compound characters, many of which denote medium-sized mammals (including 豹 *bao* 'leopard', 豺 *chai* 'jackal', 貂 *diao* 'marten', and 貉 *he* 'badger'). In many of these, 豸 is interchangeable with 犬 *quan* 'dog' (no. 94 in the Kangxi system), as in 貍 ~ 狸 *li* 'raccoon dog'.

13) Karlgren (1923) glosses 廌 as 'elk; unicorn' and 豸 as 'elk; unicorn; feline animals; crawling creatures'. It is possible that the meaning 'crawling creatures' (= reptiles, worms, insects) was originally specific only to the character 豸 , although early pictogrammatic forms of this character nevertheless suggest a mammal with four feet and a head. It may be noted that the character 豸 , when used as a radical, is variously known in Japan either as the "badger radical" (*mujina hen*) or as the "reptile radical" (*ashinakimushi hen*).

14) The dissection of the bisyllabic word *qilin* 麒 麟 into two semantic components distinguished by gender may have been stimulated by similar compositions, either real or illusory, of names for other mythical animals. A well-known example is offered by the term *fenghuang* 鳳 凰 'phoenix', which is allegedly composed of the elements *feng* 鳳 'male phoenix' vs. *huang* 凰 'female phoenix'. In general, there is a lot of scholastic invention involved in the names of mythical animals. This may also be the reason why the elements *qi* 騏 and *lin* 驎 , containing the horse radical, are lexicographically attested in meanings such as 'étalon blanc avec une raie noire sur la dos, qui peut parcourir mille 里 *li*[3] en jour' for *qi* 騏 and 'cheval gris fer, tacheté de noir; étalon; beau cheval' for *lin* 驎 (*Dictionnaire Ricci de caractères chinois*, nos. 1088 and 7149).

15) The University of Pennsylvania, for instance, offers on its web pages an early pair of large stone *qilin* (objects C656 and C657, Henan, 4th to 5th c. CE), which must have functioned as guardians. Both of these are of the feline type with wings, and should perhaps be classified as "lions" rather than as *qilin* in the strict sense of the word. However this may be, one of the items has two horns and appears to represent a female; the other has no prominent horn at all, but is apparently a male (see http://www.flickr.com/photos/pennmuseum/3687883506/). It would, however, be a mistake to classify all specimens of *qilin* with two horns as females. The gender differentiation of feline guardians is later often made by standard attributes (a cub for the female and a ball for the male).

16) It may be added that Chinese, like most other East Asian languages, also otherwise avoids making lexical gender differentiations in animal names. Thus, zoonyms like *niu* 牛 'cow, ox', *ma* 馬 'horse' (both 'stallion' and 'mare'), and *xi* 犀 'rhinoceros' are inherently gender-neutral.

17) A search of Pre-Qin material in the Chinese Text Project (online) gives 64 occurrences for 麒 , 227 occurrences for 麟 , and 60 occurrences for the compound 麒 麟 . The sequences 鳳凰麒麟 and 麒麟鳳凰 are both attested four times, while the abbreviation 麟 鳳 is attested 27 times. See http://ctext.org/pre-qin-and-han?searchu=%E9%BA%92%E9%BA%9F&page=6.

18) It may noted that from Ming period Jurchen (16th c.), the direct ancestor of Manchu, a word glossed as Chinese *qilin* 麒麟 is recorded as 阿撒郎 *asalang*, which, however, represents the widespread Eurasian word (*)*arsalan* 'lion' (Kane 1989: 221). This data may be due to confusion between the two animals, but it may also reflect the fact that many feline representations of the Chinese unicorn are actually very lion-like in their general appearance. The word *qilin* is attested in another source on Jurchen, where it is transcribed as 其里因 *qiliyin* (Grube 1896: 95 and no. 167).

19) Neither *qi* 麒 nor *lin* 麟 as such can be phonetically reconstructed for Old Chinese, but the values of both syllables can be approached with the help of the phonetic components of the written characters. Thus, the value of *qi* 麒 must have been identical with (or close to) that of *qi* 其 (modal particle) < **gə*, while *lin* 麟 may be compared with *lin* 鱗 'scale (of fish or reptile)' < **rin* (both reconstructions from Schuessler). In this context, it is interesting to note the homonymy of the syllables *lin* 麟 (second syllable of *qilin*) and *lin* 鱗 'scale'. It is difficult to say whether this pun has had any influence on the fact that the prototypical *qilin* is depicted as having scales.

20) It is unnecessary here to go into the question concerning the possible distinction and positional relations between

the two vowels (*)*e* vs. (*)*ä* in Turkic.

21) The situation is slightly complicated by the fact that the verb (*)*kälä-* 'to speak' is areally connected with the Mongolic nomenverbum **kele-* 'to speak' = **kele/n* 'tongue'. It may actually be an early Mongolic loanword in Turkic (see also Räsänen 1969: 248). There is, however, no indication that Mongolic would have been involved in the transmission of the Chinese word into Turkic.

22) Another (albeit obsolete) name of the rhinoceros in Mongolian is (*)*serü* (Lessing 1960: 691), a borrowing from Tibetan *bse-ru* (cf. also Sinor 1960: 171-172).

23) Mongolian *kers* is discussed in some detail by Sinor (1960: 169-171), who compares the word with data from Uighur and Arabic. The Uighur data is, however, poorly verified (= probably false), while the Arabic item (*ḥarīš*) is semantically vague and, in any case, geographically too far to provide a credible direct connection for the Mongolian word. As long as the word is not reliably documented from any of the intermediate languages (e.g., Persian, Sogdian, Uighur), the connection remains unlikely.

24) Technically it could be postulated that the word was originally transmitted from Chinese into Mongolic with the meaning 'unicorn', which later changed to the meaning 'rhinoceros' as that animal became known to the Mongols. The chronological and phonological details remain to be clarified, however. The medial *-r-* in the Mongolian word is reminiscent of the reconstructed Old Chinese **-r-* in the same position, but the significance of this correspondence is difficult to assess. Also, the final *-s* in the Mongolian data remains unexplained. — I thank Volker Rybatzki for consultation on this item.

25) As is often the case, the last population of mammoths on Wrangel Island was characterized by insular dwarfism. Dwarf mammoths seem to have survived as late as 2000 BCE or even somewhat later (S. L. Vartanyan, Kh. A. Arslanov, T. V. Tertychnaya and S. B. Chernov 1995).

26) Both of these mammoth carcasses date from c. 40,000 BP (on the Kirgilyakh mammoth, see Shilo, Lozhkin, Titov and Shumilov 1983: 88-91). Both were discovered in local river beds in Northeastern Siberia; this area continues to have the largest number of mammoth finds. Well-preserved mammoths or mammoth parts have, however, also been discovered further to the west. The partially preserved carcass of an adult mammoth, subsequently known as the Yuribei Mammoth and dated to circa 10,000 BP, was found in the Yuribei river basin on the Gydan Peninsula in 1979 (Sokolov *et al.* 1982). An exceptionally well-preserved baby mammoth from about the same absolute age came to light as recently as 2007 in the basin of another river, also called the Yuribei, on the Yamal Peninsula (see http://news.bbc.co.uk/2/hi/science/nature/6284214.stm). For a general review of the dating of mammoth remains, see Stuart *et al.* (2002). An early discussion of mammoth finds in Siberia is provided by Nordenskiöld (1880, Vol. 1: 383-399).

27) The picture is originally based on a sketch made by Henri Breuil, one of the discoverers of the Combarelles cave in 1901 (see http://leseyzies-tourist.info/dordogne_tourist_attractions/les-combarelles). For a comparison of data from the Southern Urals, see Ščelinskij and Širokov (1999) and especially the paper by Bosinski (ibid. 139-166).

28) It is, of course, questionable whether mammoth meat preserved in permafrost is edible. The fact remains, however, that mammoth carcasses emerging from beneath the earth are often consumed by wild animals and birds before they can be collected for research purposes. This partially occurred with the Berezovka mammoth.

29) Karjalainen assumes that the idea of "stocks" growing out of the elk's nostrils might derive from Russian stories about elephants. It appears more likely, however, that it is a question of local knowledge based on actual sightings of well-preserved mammoth skeletons or carcasses.

30) The story was originally published by Bernát Munkácsi, from whom it was adapted by Kálmán (1971/1976). Here it is translated into English from the original Mansi and the accompanying German version. The story is also paraphrased by Karjalainen (1918: 401).

31) This information was recorded by Donner from a Ket student named I. F. Dibikov, who visited Finland from St. Petersburg (Leningrad) in 1928. The information was not new to Donner, who himself had carried out field work on the Ket and their neighbours in Siberia in 1911-1913.

32) This use of mammoth bone is reported both by Kannisto (1958: 235) and Donner (Alatalo 2004: 320). These reports do not specify, however, whether it is mammoth bone (proper) or mammoth ivory. In any case, the external use of pulverized material to stop bleeding must have a simple mechanic effect; the fact that it is made of mammoth bone adds a mythological dimension to the treatment. The practice is reminiscent of the Chinese tradition of using pulverized "dragon bones" 龍骨 *longgu* for medicinal purposes, though in China pulverized bone is used internally (and apparently with no effect other than psychological stimulus).

33) Boas' informants were apparently unable to comment on these details. For some reason, he speaks of (two) "tusks", though the picture suggests rather unambiguously a single thick "horn", drawn with two parallel lines. The summary Boas (1904-1906: 326) gives of the Chukchee conception of the mammoth also mentions "tusks", which either "stand off from [the mammoth's] nose, or protrude from his nose." It is, of course, possible that some Chukchee were so familiar with mammoth carcasses, skeletons, or skulls that they knew the anatomy of the animal better than the aboriginal populations of Northwestern Siberia.

34) It is more difficult to explain why the horse is also found on the "evil" side. Boas suggests that the object may have been used by reindeer-herding people, but the implications of this remain ambiguous. It may be more relevant to note that, according to Boas, the Chukchee regard the mammoth as the "ke´let's reindeer", "ke'le" (= *kelə* : plural *kelə-t*) being the Chukchee term for a category of evil spirits or idols (Fortescue 2005: 130).

35) The status of Ugric as a single branch has been contested and may turn out to be false. In any case, in a binary division, the "Ugric" languages in Siberia belong to the Finno-Ugric branch of Uralic, as opposed to Samoyedic. This issue is not relevant to the present discussion.

36) The present discussion is not concerned with Mongolic, which has a consistently southern location in Siberia, nor with Turkic, which has only very recently spread to Northern Siberia (Yakut and Dolgan). Other families not considered here are Kamchukotic (Chukchee-Kamchadal) and Eskaleutic (Eskimo-Aleut), both of which are located in the far northeast of the region with possible early Trans-Beringian connections.

37) The linguistic data from the Siberian languages is presented in a phonemically adequate but graphically simplified transcription, which may deviate from that used in the quoted sources.

38) All the elements contained in the Mansi and Khanty data have also wider etymological connections within Uralic. These are, however, irrelevant to the present discussion.

39 Earlier literature on the Russian word includes Räsänen (1951-1952), Unbegaun (1954), Vasmer 1964-1973 Vol. 2: 566, and Heaney (1976); for a general survey, see Stachowski (2000). It appears that the earliest attestation of *mámont* (in the adjectival form *mámontov-*) dates from 1578.

40) The split between Tundra Nenets and Forest Nenets precedes the arrival of the Russians (in the 16th century), but probably not by more than a few hundred years. This was probably also the time when Mansi and Khanty expanded to their present-day northern locations. The age of the descriptive expressions for the 'mammoth' in all these languages may therefore be estimated roughly at 1000 CE.

41) Lehtisalo (1956: 488b and 492b) quotes the folkloric expression *ya-ng+kora xabt° tob°-ta tideru-q to-won-toh* 'man hört das Trappeln der Hufe des Mammutochsen herankommen', in which the term *ya ng+kora* is followed by the noun *xabt°* 'castrated male (reindeer)' and the singular 3rd person possessive genitive plural form of *toba* 'hoof' (: 'his hooves'). This suggests that the Nenets may have thought of the mammoth as some kind of subterranean reindeer.

42) These and other sound laws quoted in the present paper are well established in the study of the languages concerned. However, due to the technical nature of the issues, no references will be given here.

43) The reconstruction of earlier forms of Yeniseic is not yet fully reliable. From the areal point of view, the Yeniseic languages likely represent a relatively recent secondary

intrusion into Siberia. Among other things this is signalled by their phonological and morphological structure, which includes features such as grammatical gender and tones. Note that these are not attested in the neighbouring ("Ural-Altaic") languages.

44) The Shor data may involve a folk-etymological distortion due to association with Turkic *täkä* 'goat'. It may be noted that Shor is spoken in the Kuznetskij Alatau region of Southern Siberia. In general, words for the 'mammoth' have not been recorded in languages spoken this far south. The historical and cultural background of the Shor data remains, therefore, unknown.

45) The Nganasan data from Kortt and Simčenko (1985) is phonologically unreliable, which is to some extent also true of data from Castrén (1855). The exact phonological shape of the Nganasan item remains therefore uncertain, at least as far as the quality of the vowels of the non-initial syllables is concerned. There is, however, no question concerning the vowel of the initial syllable and its diachronic incompatibility with the Enets data; this suggests a borrowing. The Enets data are also not fully sufficient to provide an unambiguous reconstruction of the word structure, leaving open, in particular, the quality of the vowel of the second syllable.

46) The phonological relationship between (*)*selii* and (*)*seelir* is not regular, and the latter data may involve notational mistakes (in the quality of vowels). The final *-r* looks like the plural suffix of nasal-stem nouns, but its appearance in this case is irregular (since the singular stem has no final nasal).

47) Girfanova suggests that Udeghe *egule* may be etymologically connected with Common Tungusic **xegdi* > Udeghe *egdi* 'large, abundant'. In spite of the possibility of an associational relationship, the derivational pattern is not regular; it may be a case of two originally different etymons.

48) For the sake of curiosity it may be mentioned that, in rare cases, a narwhal can have two tusks. Such a specimen can be found at the Zoological Museum of Hamburg (http://en.wikipedia.org/wiki/Narwhal).

49) There is a geographical gap in the sea-mammal hunting traditions of Northern Eurasia, in that the coastal section of the central part of the continent, marked by the Taimyr Peninsula, has not been inhabited by human populations in historical times. The indigenous peoples of Taimyr—notably the Nganasan Samoyeds—are basically wild reindeer hunters. Recently also reindeer herders, they do not engage in sea mammal hunting (Simchenko 1976). The opposition between the sea-mammal hunting and reindeer-herding cultural adaptations has divided some linguistic groups, especially the Chukchee, into two culturally different sections (on the Chukchee, see Boas 1904-1906: 25-32 *et passim*).

50) In a modern interpretation, this motif was taken up by the Chukchee writer Yurij Rytkheu in his well-known short story "When the whales leave" (*Kogda kity ukhodyat*, 1977).

51) Ethnically and linguistically, the Whalebone Alley appears to have been built by early Asiatic Eskimos (ancestors of the Siberian Yupik), whose territory has gradually been reduced at the expense of the expanding area occupied by Chukchee speakers. Although the Maritime Chukchee are also whale hunters whose culture is directly inherited from the earlier populations of the region, some traditions (including those connected with the Whalebone Alley) were lost in the process of language change.

52) The belukha whale is also known in English as the "white whale" or the "beluga whale" (see the Wikipedia entry at http://en.wikipedia./wiki/Beluga_whale). Both terms, *belúga* and *belúkha*, are derived from Russian *bélyi* 'white', but strictly speaking *belúga* refers to the "white sturgeon" (*Acipenser transmontanus*), while the "white whale" is properly termed *belúkha* in Russian. The belukha whale is a close relative of the narwhal (the *Monodontidae* family), but lacks its tusk.

53) The velar consonants *q* (back) and *k* (front) are originally allophones, and even synchronically they do not contrast in native words in initial position.

54) Technically, since Tungusic (like Mongolic) has vowel harmony, the vowel of the second syllable should be reconstructed as *ï (back *i*). The distinction between **i*

and *ï is automatic in this position, however, and has even been phonetically neutralized in most modern forms of Tungusic (and Mongolic).

55) An exception is formed by the Ulcha (in the Amur Delta region) and Orok (on Sakhalin), who share considerable parts of their culture with the Ghilyak. These groups may essentially be viewed as "Tungusized" Ghilyak; as populations, they retain their cultural continuity but have changed their language.

56) Doerfer considers the difference in the final vowel of **kalimu* vs. **kalima* as indicative of the loanword status of the item. It is indeed likely that the shape **kalimu* represents an older layer (perhaps borrowed earlier from Amuric) than **kalima* (perhaps borrowed later from a different chronological stage of Amuric). The difference may, however, also be due to an internal irregularity within Tungusic.

57) Yakut (like Amur Tungusic) makes a rather strict distinction between short (single) and long (double) vowels, the long vowels being either "original" (from Proto-Turkic) or of contractive origin. In Ewenki-Ewen, vowel length is a more unstable property (the diachronic background of which is still unknown), which is why it is possible that the Yakut data reflects some non-functional detail of the Northern Tungusic dialectal pronunciation of the word.

58) The final nasal **ng* developed into the so-called nasalizable glottal stop *h* in Tundra Nenets. While this is a regular development, there are a few other issues that make the reconstruction of the Proto-Nenets shape of this word difficult, one of them being the representation of the medial liquid in Forest Nenets. In a majority of cases, Proto-Nenets **l* (voiced lateral) yields *lh* (voiceless fricolateral) in Forest Nenets. There are exceptions, however, and the word for 'whale' belongs to these. — My thanks go to Tapani Salminen for consultation on this item.

59) The final nasal (*)-*ng* in Nenets may, in any case, be a derivative element. The vowel of the second syllable is difficult to reconstruct, since this word type is rare. The alternatives would be **kalay-* / **kalayə-* / **kaləyə-*, but each of these involves some unconfirmed details. Even so, there is no need to assume a borrowing between Nenets and Enets; rather, it is a question of shared heritage from the protolanguage. The Nganasan data, by contrast, would seem to involve a borrowing from Enets, as was pointed out earlier.

60) It may nevertheless be noted that Samoyedic **kalay(ə)ng* 'whale' is not formally very far from **kalimV*, for the two reconstructions share not only the initial section **kal-* but also the palatal element (**y* ~ **i*) and the nasal consonant (**ng* ~ **m*). The nasal in the Nenets data may, of course, also be secondary, since it is absent in the corresponding Enets and Nganasan items.

61) In Nenets, the items *xalaeh* 'whale' and *xalya* 'fish' (here in their Tundra Nenets shapes) are conspicuously close to one another. Even so, there seems to be no reason to consider the word for 'whale' as a derivative of 'fish'; furthermore, there are no indications that the two words are confused in the consciousness of native speakers.

62) This Eurasian etymon for 'whale' might have also other pendants. Cincius (1975-1977, vol. 1: 366-367) proposes a connection with Korean *korae* 'whale'. By the regular sound laws of Korean, this would presuppose an earlier shape of the type **kula-i* (which might be compatible with **kalimu*, etc). If we also consider the words for 'mammoth', there are possible connections with the Yukaghir root *qol(q)-*. It is, however, best not to proceed too far down this path without further evidence.

63) Trade in walrus tusks on a large scale, as well as their use for artistic and souvenir purposes, arose only in the 19th century when Russian, Western European, and North American activities intensified in Alaska and Chukotka. A special genre, formed in connection with the souvenir industry, was (and still is) the decoration of whole walrus tusks with pictures by Chukchee and Eskimo artists. Many collections of these decorated tusks exist in museums. For an early collection, formed by the Finnish traveller and archaeologist Sakari Pälsi in 1917, see Janhunen (1983).

64) As can be seen from the description of de la Martinière (Figure 14), narwhal tusks were in his time the most desired source of ivory in Europe. Even so, they were

never able to replace elephant tusks as the most widely traded type of ivory. Compared with elephant ivory, which has a homogeneous structure throughout the substance and an easily recognizable pattern known as Schreger lines (http://en.wikipedia.org/wiki/Schreger_line), walrus ivory has a grainy core with no lines, which is somewhat harder to carve or polish.

65) The main difference is that mammoth ivory is slightly harder and has greater density than regular elephant ivory. Technically, the difference can be seen in the angles formed by the Schreger lines. For practical step-by-step instructions on the identification of different types of ivory (and synthetic materials), see http://www.asianartmall.com/refivory.htm. In the case of an intact piece, a mammoth tusk can be easily distinguished by a brown layer of "bark" formed on its surface. The interior of a well-preserved mammoth tusk, however, can be even whiter than typical elephant ivory.

66) The mammoth tusk business involves legal problems, of course. These include smuggling and other attempts to avoid state control and international authorities. In a recent case in January 2011, Russian customs seized three tons of mammoth ivory on the way to the export market (http://www.sify.com/news/russia-seizes-three-tonnes-of-ancient-mammoth-tusks-news-international-lbvi4ccdffa.html).

67) Strictly speaking, both the rhinoceros and the elephant were found in parts of China until Neolithic times and possibly until the Bronze Age, as is confirmed by both palaeontological and historical data (see also Bishop 1921, Chang 1926). The native elephants became extinct before the rhinoceros, however.

68) Trade in ivory from living elephants was officially banned in 1990, but the implementation of the ban has not been complete, partly due to resistance from African countries (http://en.wikipedia.org/wiki/Ivory_trade, http://www.cites.org/). Due to the ban, some African countries have ended up with unsold ivory stockpiles of several dozens of tons—much more than the annual "production" of mammoth ivory.

69) The Chinese term for 'elephant', *xiang* 象 , is a well-known and widespread Eurasian *Wanderwort*, the discussion of which remains outside of the scope of the present paper; see Schuessler (2007: 534-535).

70) Similar examples can be found in the names of other materials. The concept of 'glass, glaze', for instance, is expressed by the bisyllabic loanword *liuli* 琉 璃 , which was borrowed ultimately from Middle Indian *veluria ~ verulia ~ velulia* [various kinds of jewel] = Greek *bēr͞yllos* (see, e.g., Kryukov 1986).

71) On the position of Chinese with regard to Sino-Tibetan and Tibeto-Burman, cf. van Driem (2001: 348-388). Of the homeland hypotheses presented for Sino-Tibetan, the Sichuan version appears as one of the most plausible. If so, Chinese would not have reached the Pacific coast before Shang times (late 2nd millennium BCE).

References

Alatalo, Jarmo (2004) *Sölkupisches Wörterbuch aus Aufzeichnungen von Kai Donner, U. T. Sirelius und Jarmo Alatalo*. Lexica Societatis Fenno-Ugricae 30. Helsinki.

Allan, Sarah (1991) *The Shape of the Turtle: Myth, Art, and Cosmos in Early China*. SUNY Series in Chinese Philosophy and Culture. New York: State University of New York Press.

Andersson, J. Gunnar (1932) *Den gula jordens barn: Studier över det förhistoriska Kina* [Children of the Yellow Earth: Studies in Prehistoric China]. Stockholm: Albert Bonniers förlag.

Arutyunov, S. A., I. I. Krupnik and M. A. Chlenov (1982) *"Kitovaya alleya": Drevnosti ostrovov proliva Senyavina*. Moskva: Izdatel'stvo "Nauka".

Baird, Merrily (2001) *Symbols of Japan: Thematic Motifs in Art and Design*. New York: Rizzoli International Publications, Inc.

Beekes, Robert (2010) *Etymological Dictionary of Greek* Vols. 1-2. Leiden Indo-European Etymological Dictionary Series. Leiden: Brill.

Bishop, Carl W. (1921) 'The elephant and its ivory in Ancient China', *Journal of the American Oriental Society* 41: 290-306.

Bogoras, W[aldemar] (1904-1909) *The Chukchee—Material Culture, Religion, Social Organization.* The Jesup North Pacific Expedition. Memoirs of the American Museum of Natural History 11, parts 1-3. Leiden: E. J. Brill.

Carr, Michael (1990) 'Chinese dragon names', *Linguistics of the Tibeto-Burman Area* 13 (2): 87-189.

Castrén, M. Alexander (1855) *Wörterverzeichnisse aus den samojedischen Sprachen.* Im Auftrage der Kaiserlichen Akademie der Wissenschaften bearbeitet von Anton Schiefner. St. Petersburg: Buchdruckerei der Kaiserlichen Akademie der Wissenschaften.

Chang, H. T. (1926) 'On the question of the existence of elephants and rhinoceros in North China in historical times', *Bulletin of the Geological Society of China* 5: 99-105.

Chapman, Jan (1999) *The Art of Rhinoceros Horn Carving in China.* London: Christie's Books Ltd.

Cheremisov, K. M. (1973) *Buryatsko-russkii slovar'.* Moskva: Izdatel'stvo "Sovetskaya ènciklopediya".

Cincius, V. I. (ed.) (1975-1977) *Sravnitel'nyi slovar' tunguso-man'chzhurskikh yazykov,* Vols. 1-2. Leningrad: Izdatel'stvo "Nauka", Leningradskoe otdelenie.

Doerfer, Gerhard (1985a) 'Terms for aquatic animals in the Wu T'i Ching Wên Chien', pp. 190-220, *in Proceedings of the International Symposium on B. Piłsudski's Phonographic Records and the Ainu Culture.* Sapporo: Hokkaido University.

Doerfer, Gerhard (1985b) *Mongolo-Tungusica.* Tungusica 3. Wiesbaden: Otto Harrassowitz.

Donner, Kai (1933) *Ethnological Notes about the Yenisey Ostyak (in the Turukhansk Region).* Mémoires de la Société Finno-Ougrienne 66. Helsinki.

Donner, Kai (1955) *Ketica: Materialien aus dem Ketischen oder Jenisseiostjakischen.* Bearbeitet und herausgegeben von Aulis J. Joki. Mémoires de la Société Finno-Ougrienne 108. Helsinki.

van Driem, George (2001) *Languages of the Himalayas,* Vols. 1-2. Handbuch der Orientalistik, Abt. 2, Band 10. Leiden: Brill.

Einhorn, Jürgen W. (1976) *Spiritalis unicornis: Das Einhorn als Bedeutungsträger in Literatur und Kunst des Mittelalters.* München: Wilhelm Fink Verlag.

Fortelius, Mikael (1983) 'The morphology and paleobiological significance of the horns of Coelodonta antiquitatis (Mammalia: Rhinocerotidae)', *Journal of Vertebrate Paleontology* 3(2): 125-135 (September 1983).

Fortelius, Walter (1999) 'Kaksituhatta vuotta yksisarvisia [Two thousand years of unicorns]', *Tieteessä tapahtuu* 6/1999: 35-42. Helsinki.

Fortelius, Walter and Mikael Fortelius (1989) 'Om enhörningens ensamhet [On the loneliness of the unicorn]', *Nordenskiöld-samfundets tidskrift* 49: 151-176. Helsingfors.

Fortescue, Michael (2005) *Comparative Chukotko-Kamchatkan Dictionary.* Trends in Linguistics, Documentation 23. Berlin: Mouton de Gruyter.

Gao Guopei (ed.) (1991) *A Chinese-English Glossary and Illustrations of Antique.* Hong Kong: The Woods Publishing Co.

Gesner [Gessner], Conrad (1551) *Conradi Gesneri medici Tigurini Historiae Animalium Lib. I de Quadrupedibus uiuiparis.* Tiguri apvd Christ. Froschvervm.

Girfanova, A. Kh. (2001) *Slovar' udègejskogo yazyka.* Sankt-Peterburg: Nauka.

Gratz, Pascal (2005) *De monocerote: Zur Rezeptionsgeschichte des Einhorns.* Wettbewerbsarbeit "Schweizer Jugend forscht". Winterthur. Online version at: http://www.summagallicana.it/unicorno.

Grube, Wilhelm (1896) *Die Sprache und Schrift der Jučen.* Leipzig: Kommissions-Verlag von O. Harrassowitz.

Heaney, M. (1976) 'The implications of Richard James '*maimanto*', Oxford Slavonic Papers 9: 102-109.

Helimski, Eugene (1990) 'Rossica: Ètimologicheskie zametki', *Issledovaniya po istoricheskoj grammatike i leksikologii.* Moskva, pp. 30-42, [Reprinted in:] E. A. Khelimskij, *Komparativistika, uralistika: Lekcii i stat'i.* Yazyki russkoj kul'tury. Moskva (2000), pp. 353-357.

Itkonen, Erkki and Ulla-Maija Kulonen (eds.) (1992-2000) *Suomen sanojen alkuperä* [Finnish Etymological Dictionary], Vols. 1-3. Helsinki: Suomalaisen Kirjallisuuden Seura and Kotimaisten kielten tutkimuskeskus.

Janhunen, Juha (1983) 'Sakari Pälsi—collector of Artic art', *Suomen Museo* 90: 131.136. Helsinki.

Jigmitdurzi, vUrta and Nuvgnajizabe (1986) *vAmidav u Jiruqdu Tuli* [Illustrated Dictionary of Animals]. Tuivgliyuu [Tongliao]: vUibur Muvgqhul uv Surqhav Guimuzil uv Gablal uv Qurii e.

Jochelson, Waldemar (1926) *The Yukaghir and the Yukaghirized Tungus*. The Jesup North Pacific Expedition. Memoir of the American Museum of Natural History 9. Leiden: E. J. Brill.

Kálmán, Béla (1971/1976) *Chrestomathia Vogulica*. Egyetemi segédkönyv. [Quoted according to the second edition.] Budapest: Tankönyvkiadó.

Kálmán, Béla (1986) *Wogulisches Wörterbuch*. Gesammelt von Bernát Munkácsi. Budapest: Akadémiai kiadó.

Kane, Daniel (1989) *The Sino-Jurchen Vocabulary of the Bureau of Interpreters*. Indiana University Uralic and Altaic Series 153. Bloomington, Indiana: Indiana University.

Kannisto, Artturi (1958) *Materialien zur Mythologie der Wogulen*. Bearbeitet und herausgegeben von E. A. Virtanen und Matti Liimola. Mémoires de la Société Finno-Ougrienne 113. Helsinki.

Karjalainen, K. F. (1918) *Jugralaisten uskonto* [The Religion of the Ob-Ugrians.] Suomen Suvun uskonnot 3. Porvoo: Werner Söderström Osakeyhtiö.

Karlgren, Bernhard (1923) *Analytic Dictionary of Chinese and Sino-Japanese*. Paris: Librairie orientaliste Paul Geuthner.

Katzschmann, Michael and János Pusztay (1978) *Jenissej-Samojedisches (Enzisches) Wörterverzeichnis*. Fenno-Ugrica 5. Hamburg: Helmut Buske Verlag.

Kerr, Rose (1990) *Later Chinese Bronzes*. Victoria and Albert Museum, Far Eastern Series. London: Bamboo Publishing Ltd.

Khomich, L. V. (1960) *Nency: Istoriko-ètnograficheskie ocherki*. Moskva & Leningrad: Izdatel'stvo "Nauka".

Klein, Ernest (1966-1967) *A comprehensive Etymological Dictionary of the English Language* Vols. 1-2. Amsterdam: Elsevier Publishing Company.

Kortt, I. R. and Ju. B. Simčenko (1985) *Wörterverzeichnis der Nganasanischen Sprache*. Teil 1: Nganasan-Deutsch-Russisches Glossar. Systemata mundi. Institut zur Erforschung fremder Denksysteme und Organisationsformen. Materialien 1. Berlin.

Kryukov, M. V. (1986) 'The Silk Road—the Glass Road', pp. 119-125, in Ildikó Lehtinen (ed.) *Traces of the Central Asian Culture in the North*. Mémoires de la Société Finno-Ougrienne 194. Helsinki.

Kurtén, Björn and Elaine Anderson (1980) *Pleistocene Mammals of North America*. New York: Columbia University Press.

Laufer, Berthold (1925) *Ivory in China*. Field Museum of Natural History, Department of Anthropology, Leaflet 21.

Laufer, Berthold (1928) *The Giraffe in History and Art*. Field Museum of Natural History, Popular Series, Anthropology Leaflet 27.

Lehtisalo, Toivo (1924) *Entwurf einer Mythologie der Jurak-Samojeden*. Mémoires de la Société Finno-Ougrienne 53. Helsinki.

Lehtisalo, Toivo (1956) *Juraksamojedisches Wörterbuch*. Lexica Societatis Fenno-Ugricae 13. Helsinki.

Lessing, Ferdinand D. (ed.) (1960) *Mongolian-English Dictionary*. Berkeley and Los Angeles: University of California Press.

de la Martinière, Pierre Martin (1671) *Voyage Des Païs Septentrionavx: dans le quel se void les mœurs, maniere de vivre, & superstitions des Norweguiens, Lappons, Kiloppes, Borandiens, Syberiens, Samojedes, Zembliens, & Islandois*. A Paris: chez Louis Vendosme.

Mostaert, Antoine (1941) *Dictionnaire ordos*. Peking: the Catholic University. [Reprint:] New York & London: Johnson Reprint Corporation (1968).

Nikolaeva, Irina (2006) *A Historical Dictionary of Yukaghir*.

Trends in Linguistics, Documentation 25. Berlin: Mouton de Gruyter.

Nordenskiöld, A. E. (1880) *Vegas färd kring Asien och Europa jemte en historisk återblick på föregående resor längs gamla verldens nordkust* [Voyage of the Vega] Vols. 1-2. Stockholm: F. & G. Beijers förlag.

Norman, Jerry (1978) *A Concise Manchu-English Dictionary.* Seattle and London: University of Washington Press.

Pallas, P. S. (1769) 'De ossibus Sibiriae fossilibus craniis prasertim rhinocerotum atque buffalorum, obervationes', *Novi Commentarii Academiae Petropolitanae* 13: 436-477.

Parker, Jeannie Thomas (online: n.d.) *Chinese Unicorn.* http://www.chinese-unicorn.com/qilin/book.

Pekarskij, È. K. (1907-1927) *Slovar' yakutskogo yazyka* Vols. 1-3. Trudy yakutskoj ekspedicii. St. Peterburg / Petrograd / Leningrad.

Pfitzenmayer, E. W. (1926) *Mammutleichen und Urwaldmenschen in Nordost-Sibirien.* Leipzig: F. A. Brockhaus.

Pulleyblank, Edwin G. (1991) *Lexicon of Reconstructed Pronunciation in Early Middle Chinese, Late Middle Chinese, and Early Mandarin.* Vancouver: UBC Press.

Rodriguez, Martin Sevilla (1989) '*Indo-European *(s)kwalo/i-s* "sheat-fish"', *Journal of Indo-European Studies* 17: 177-180.

Räsänen, Martti (1951-1952) 'Das Wort Mammut', *Zeitschrift für slavische Philologie* 21: 293-295.

Räsänen, Martti (1969) *Versuch eines etymologischen Wörterbuchs der Türksprachen.* Lexica Societatis Fenno-Ugrica 17. Index (1971). Helsinki.

Savel'eva, V. N. and Ch. M. Taksami (1970) *Nivkhsko-russkij slovar'.* Moskva: Izdatel'stvo "Sovetskaya ènciklopediya".

Ščelinskij, Vjačeslav E. and Vladimir N. Širokov (1999) *Höhlenmalerei im Ural: Kapova und Ignatievka. Die altersteinzeitlichen Bilderhöhlen im südlichen Ural.* Herausgegeben, aus dem Russischen übertragen und mit einem Beitrag von Gerhard Bosinski. Sigmaringen: Jan Thorbecke Verlag.

Schuessler, Axel (2007) *ABC Etymological Dictionary of Old Chinese.* Honolulu: University of Hawai'i Press.

Shepard, Odell (1930) *The Lore of the Unicorn.* London: George Allen & Unwin Ltd.

Shilo, N. A., A. V. Lozhkin, È. È. Titov and Yu. V. Shumilov (1983) *Kirgilyakhskij mamont.* Moskva: Izdatel'stvo "Nauka".

Simchenko, Yu. B. (1976) *Kul'tura okhotnikov na olenej Severnoj Evrazii: Ètnograficheskaya rekonstruktsiya.* Moskva: Izdatel'stvo "Nauka".

Sinor, Denis (1960) 'Sur les noms sino-altaïques de la licorne', *Wiener Zeitschrift für die Kunde des Morgendlandes* 56: 168-176.

Sokolov, V. E. *et al.* (ed.) (1982) *Yuribejskij mamont.* Moskva: Izdatel'stvo "Nauka".

Stachowski, Marek (1998) 'Notizen zur schorischen und tschulymischen Etymologie', *Studia Etymologica Cracoviensia* 3: 107-123. Kraków.

Stachowski, Marek (2000) 'Das *Wort* Mammut in etymologischen Wörterbüchern', *Folia Orientalia* 36: 301-314. Studia in honorem Stanislai Stachowski dicata. Kraków.

Steinitz, Wolfgang (1966-1993) *Dialektologisches und etymologisches Wörterbuch der ostjakischen Sprache.* Berlin: Akademie-Verlag.

Stuart, Anthony J., Leopold D. Sulerzhitsky, Lyobov A. Orlova, Yaroslav V. Kuzmin and Adrian M. Lister (2002) 'The latest Woolly Mammoths (*Mammuthus primigenius* Blumenbach) in Europe and Asia: a review of the current evidence', *Quaternary Science Reviews* 21: 1559-1569.

Tolmachoff, I. P. (1929) 'The carcasses of the mammoth and rhinoceros found in the frozen ground of Siberia', *The American Philosophical Society*, Vol. 23/1.

Unbegaun, B. (1954) 'Zum russischen Namen des Mammuts', *Zeitschrift für slavische Philologie* 22: 150-151.

Vartanyan, S. L., Kh. A. Arslanov, T. V. Tertychnaya and S. B. Chernov (1995) 'Radiocarbon dating evidence for mammoths onWrangel Island, Arctic Ocean, until

2000 BC', *Radiocarbon* 37:1-6.

Vasmer, Max [Maks Fasmer] (1964-1973) *Ètimologicheskij slovar' russkogo yazyka*. Perevod s nemeckogo i dopolneniya O. N. Trubacheva, Vols. 1-4. Moskva: Izdatel'stvo "Progress".

Veisman, Lev, Roman Zlotin and Aleksandr Bobrov (1986) *Samyj severnyj zapovednyj ostrov Vrangelya*. Moskva: Sovetskaya Rossiya.

Vereshchagin, N. K. *et al.* (1981) *Magadanskij mamontenok: Mammuthus primigenius* (Blumenbach). Leningrad: "Nauka", Leningradskoe otdelenie.

Werner, Heinrich (2002) *Vergleichendes Wörterbuch der Jenissei-Sprachen*, Vols. 1-3. Wiesbaden: Harassowitz Verlag.

Wilson, Samuel M. (1992) 'The Emperor's Giraffe', *Natural History* 101(12): 22-26. [Reprinted in:] Id. (1999). *The Emperor's Giraffe and Other Stories of Cultures in Contact*. Boulder, Colo.: Westview Press.

The Harappa Culture in North Gujarat: a Regional Paradigm

P. Ajithprasad and V. H. Sonawane
The M.S. University of Baroda

Abstract

The paper presents the regional identity and distinctive features of a group of non-Harappan pottery associated with the Harappan affiliated Chalcolithic settlements in North Gujarat. The regional tradition in pottery has been equated with a distinct socio-economic group within the Chalcolithic society. The regional model questions the concept of a homogeneous Harappan society and elucidates the nature of diverse socio-economic strands in the making of the integrated Harappan society of North Gujarat.

Until a decade and a half ago, North Gujarat was considered to be the backwaters of the Harappa culture; a region not particularly preferred by the Harappan agricultural communities to settle down in. A series of explorations and excavations since 1978 have dramatically changed this belief after the discovery of more than hundred Harappan affiliated Chalcolithic sites in this region (IAR 1978-79, 1982-83, 1984-85 to 1994-95; Hegde and Sonawane 1986, Bhan 1994). Six sites among these have so far been excavated (see Hegde *et al.* 1988, IAR 1984-85 to 1990-91, 1992-93 to 1994-95). Artefact assemblages from many of these explored and excavated sites include a few pottery types, which are different from the Harappan pottery. These distinct non-Harappan pottery types are characteristic of the North Gujarat region and, therefore, can be named the "Anarta" tradition after the traditional name of North Gujarat. The Anarta tradition not only had an independent existence prior to the spread of Harappa culture but also was associated with the Mature/Urban and later Phases of the Harappa culture.

Much of the pottery belonging to the Anarta tradition had already been identified earlier in the excavation at Surkotada in Kachchh district (Joshi 1972:122-26)[1]. In spite of this, it was only after the excavation at Nagwada in Surendranagar district in the late 1980's (Hegde *et al.* 1988: 60-62), which had revealed a ceramic assemblage predominated by the regional Anarta pottery types, the need to investigate the significance of this non-Harappan tradition was fully recognized. A cursory glance through the published literature on the Harappa culture in Gujarat may indicate that almost all important excavated sites like Lothal, Surkotada, Somnath (Prabhas Patan), Rojdi, Nagwada etc. (Figure 1), have brought to light cultural relics, predominantly pottery, that are different from the Harappan. The non-Harappan pottery types, which are found independently as well as in association with the Harappan relics, vary in quality and quantity from those of the Harappan. No serious attempt has been made so far to evaluate the significance of these non-Harappan components in the making of the Harappan society and culture. One way of addressing this issue is by studying the non-Harappan traits as the expression of a local tradition peculiar to a geographically and culturally circumscribed region within the large cultural domain of the Harappa culture. It is in this context the Harappan affiliated Chalcolithic settlements in North

Figure 1 Location of North Gujarat and major Harappan/Chalcolithic sites mentioned in the paper
The box in the map is expanded in Figure 31

Gujarat become significant.

Problems and Perspectives

The regional paradigm for understanding the cultural dynamism of the Harappa culture in North Gujarat is essentially based on two important assumptions, both to a large extent dependent on the ceramic assemblage from North Gujarat sites. To begin with, we assume pottery as a group identifier. The group, by and large, could be a social group (we would not like to call it an ethnic group as it has wider connotations) or sometimes it could also be an economic group. It is not an easy task to distinguish and discriminate the two archaeologically. The truth of our interpretation, therefore, depends up on how correctly we are able to distinguish the two. One way to understand some of the general features of the model through which this complicated issue can be addressed is an ethno-archaeological investigation of pottery-using societies. Problem oriented studies, such as the recent ethnographic study on Kachchh potters by Chokshi (1995), focussing on the above features for understanding the social configuration are very much a desideratum in Harappan studies.

Very often, social and economic groups could be mutually inclusive; but not necessarily always so. One may come across two distinctive social groups having the same economic status or conversely, a single social group may have different economic strata within it. It is not our intention to reify inanimate objects like pottery at this juncture, and we are also aware of the inherent difficulties in such an attempt. But, in view of paucity of workable leads towards a better understanding of the Harappan society, it is important to have such paradigms. Changes within the conceptual frame of reference could be incorporated as we move further and as and when it is necessary.

Secondly, we assume that the Harappan pottery was heterogeneous. This, therefore, questions the homogeneous nature of the Harappan pottery and society. Most of the studies in Harappan pottery are to a great extent influenced by the meticulous description of pottery from Mohenjodaro and Chanhudaro by E.J.H. Mackay (1931, 1938, 1943) and in Gujarat by a generalized scheme of chronological framework proposed by S.R. Rao (1963: 20-25). Both studies have their merits and demerits. Mackay's description followed by Wheeler's writings (see Wheeler 1947, 1960) catered to an impression that the Harappan ceramics at Mohenjodaro and Harappa formed a homogeneous assemblage. We do not know how far the two scholars were overawed by the fine features of the well made Harappan pottery and overlooked the coarse variety in the assemblage. In any case, their writings led to the impression of an over-standardized pottery assemblage, probably at best, applicable to the urban centres and urban economy. The standard features thus became a rooted position and a touchstone for generations of archaeologists for referring to Harappan ceramic assemblages from several sites located in different parts of the large Harappan cultural domain.

When S.R. Rao started excavating at Rangpur in the 1950's, he was faced with issues which were of a totally different nature. Two earlier excavations at the site in the 1930's by M.S. Vats (1935) and G. Ghurye (1939) had proclaimed its Harappan character and were able to propose the southward extension of the Harappa culture into Gujarat. On the other hand, M.G. Dikshit (1950), after the renewed excavation of the site in 1947, had found it difficult to ascertain the Harappan features of the assemblage. Rao took up the excavation at this ambivalent juncture to ascertain the nature of Chalcolithic settlement at the site (Rao 1963:8). While he was able to ascertain the Harappan remains unearthed in the excavations at Rangpur from 1953 to 1956, he had also reported significantly different material remains from the site which was not fitting into the homogeneous Harappan model (Rao 1963: 13-25). Rao observed that, stratigraphically the variant materials, especially pottery, were predominant in the later levels. This led to the original three fold division of the Harappa culture in Gujarat into Mature, Late and Post-Harappan. One of the merits of this framework was that it clearly defined for the first time, even though somewhat inflexibly, the three phases of the Harappa culture in terms of ceramic and other cultural indices at a time when the Harappan cultural milieu was growing into a jungle of confusion. The division is essentially chronological and to a large extend overlooks all other aspects of cultural variation. In spite of this drawback, initially, the concept of a uni-linear evolution of pottery illustrated through specific attribute variations did help to categorize sites into different periods of cultural developments within this broad framework. In the absence of absolute dates from most of the surface sites the new scheme became an extremely useful tool in the chronological classification of Harappan sites in Gujarat. As a result, those simple criteria of chronological divisions were followed or are still being followed in Harappan site classification without considering other factors that can contribute towards variation in material culture.

Generally speaking, these two concepts – the concept of Harappan homogeneity and Rao's ideas of regional evolution – somewhat contradictory though, have greatly influenced the development of various research models on the Gujarat Harappan. During our excavation in 1985 at Nagwada in North Gujarat (Figure 1) we, however, found that neither of these concepts could be directly adopted to study the material remains, especially pottery, from the site. This realization became stronger in the subsequent excavations and explorations in the region. The amount of Mature Harappan pottery at Nagwada is meagre, constituting hardly 20% of the total collection. Yet, the site has yielded most of the characteristic remains which we generally associate with the Classical/Mature Harappan including a terracotta sealing having an inscribed seal impression. No real "Late Harappan" pottery, as described by Rao (1963), is found at the site. Instead, the assemblage is dominated by the Gritty Red ware and a few other pottery types that showed little resemblance to the Classical Harappan pottery. In fact, the new types belonged to a ceramic tradition confined to the North Gujarat region. The ceramic tradition has an individuality of its' own in terms of techniques used in clay preparation and pottery production. The individuality is visible in the vessel forms, surface treatment and even in the quality of their firing. Very often in the assemblage one comes across imitations of Harappan vessels in the Gritty Red ware. Besides, there is also another distinct set of pottery confined only to the burials excavated at the site. The burial pottery is not only different from the Mature Harappan but also from the above regional pottery types. Clearly, none of these were fitting into the conservative homogeneous Harappan model. It is at this time we started thinking of the existence of a regional Chalcolithic tradition within the wider cultural mosaic of the Harappan tradition in North Gujarat.

In view of the above variations within the cultural remains in North Gujarat, it would be worthwhile to investigate how the variations came into being and in what way would the studies on these varying components affect our overall understanding of the Harappa culture. Proper identification of regional traditions and understanding their origin, integration and survival become important in the Harappan studies in this context. The immediate premise of our further studies would, therefore, be that the Harappan society was not a homogeneous one, but a tapestry consisting of many individual strands forming an integrated whole, probably held together by common cultural ethos. By trying to separate the elements of regional tradition we are only trying to understand and evaluate how each of these individual strands interact with and integrate into the Harappa culture. And, it is within this frame of reference we treat distinctive pottery types in a region as the material representative of a social group. The validity of this assumption could be tested by further specific studies designed for that purpose.

The pottery type vis-à-vis social/economic group equation needs further clarification. It is not our intention to treat every single and simple variation in pottery as representative of a separate social group. It is an accepted fact that a given type of pottery shows some amount of variation within a site and between sites. Such variations are a common denominator for all types of pottery. Moreover, in order to identify a group of pottery as a regional tradition, it should be distinct from the mainstream Harappan ceramic types in their form, clay texture and surface treatment and in the decorative patterns painted on the vessels. It should also be represented by varieties of vessel forms. Besides, to designate such distinctive pottery types as part of a regional pottery tradition, it should also have a regional or geographical identity; that is, it should be present not just at one site, but in an appreciable number of sites in the region. Precisely, these are the different aspects which distinguish the non-Harappan pottery types of North Gujarat as a distinct regional pottery tradition.

North Gujarat Environmental Setting

Gujarat constitutes three important physiographic regions: Kachchh, Saurashtra and the mainland of Gujarat. The narrow corridor which connects the mainland of Gujarat with Kachchh, bordered in the northwest by the Rann of Kachchh and in the southeast by the Sabarmati, is known as North Gujarat (Figure 1). It is traditionally known by the name "Anarta" (Majmudar 1960). North Gujarat is a semiarid, sandy plain, dotted with fossil sand-dunes. The region extends in the north from the southern Rajputana and gradually merges into the alluvial plains of Saurashtra and central Gujarat. North Gujarat includes Banaskantha and Mehsana districts and the northern parts of Surendranagar, Sabarkantha and Ahemdabad districts. It is drained by the Banas, the Sarasvati, the Rupen, the Sabarmati and their tributary streams. Except the Sabarmati which flows into the Gulf of Cambay, all other rivers flow into the Little Rann of Kachchh. Except the Sabarmati, no other rivers in this region are perennial; yet, during the monsoon, they drain a large volume of water into the Rann. Also, most of these rivers and their tributaries at present contain brackish water for the major part of the year. The Banas and the Sarasvati which flow in the northern part of the region are heavily silted and have a broad and shallow channel. It is difficult to assess precisely when actually the silting started, as the region is not well studied with that as a focal point. Silting is relatively less evident in the Rupen which, on the other hand, forms deep channel by cutting the alluvium. At places, the river section has a height of 6 to 8 m indicating a deep entrenchment of the channel.

The newly discovered Chalcolithic settlements in North Gujarat are located in the estuaries of the Rupen, the Banas and the Sarasvati forming the eastern margin of the Little Rann of Kachchh and on both side of the narrow creek-like depression that connects the Little Rann and the Great Rann. The entire area is covered by a thick deposit of sandy loams and appears dead flat except for a few stabilised sand dunes and the attendant shallow blow-outs. These inter-dunal depressions accumulate rainwater and many a times retain the water throughout the year. Since water in these village ponds remains potable, they are an important source of water for people as well as livestock.

The climate in the region is characterised by hot summers and cold winters and, therefore, a dry weather prevails in the region during most part of the year. Being situated in a climatic zone of 600 mm isohyets (Figure 1), rainfall in this region is sparse and irregular. Because of the unpredictability and the uneven distribution of rainfall, drought in this region is a recurrent phenomenon, the latest of which occurred during the year 1986 to 1990. Nearly ninety percent of the soil in this region is sandy. The black cotton soil is also not uncommon in some parts. In many areas, the soil is poor and saline and the subsoil water is brackish. The salinity rises up in summer and does not go back to the original low level because of low and scanty rainfall. At many places, such lands have developed into rich pastoral fields.

All these environmental factors have considerable influence on the subsistence activities of the present day population of North Gujarat. Millet, especially *bajri* (pearl millet) and cotton are the two important crops grown in the region, as these two do not need much moisture and, therefore, are suited to the environment. In fact *bajri* is the staple food of rural folks in North Gujarat, Kachchh and Saurashtra today. Vast pastoral grassland and fallow-land in the region support a large population of cattle, sheep and goat. In fact, pastoralism and agriculture are the two important components of the village economy of North Gujarat at present. We will see later that the pattern was not much different during the Chalcolithic period too.

Chalcolithic Settlements and Ceramic Assemblages

As has been mentioned in the beginning, more than a hundred Chalcolithic sites have so far been located in North Gujarat (see Appendix). The artefact assemblages from these explored sites and a few excavated ones in the region show an assortment of pottery, lithic and shell artefacts and a few terracotta objects. Most of these sites are affiliated at varying degrees to different periods of the Harappa culture. In order to understand the pattern of settlement distribution during different periods, it is necessary to classify them according to their cultural affiliation. Pottery being the most abundant and chronologically sensitive artefact in most of the sites, the classification has been practically based on the presence/absence or relative abundance of chronometric pottery type-fossils belonging to different periods. Besides, rare specimens of the Reserved Slip ware sherds, triangular terracotta cakes and characteristic shell artefacts, agate weights and Rohri chert blades from the sites also helped to substantiate the classification.

Based on these considerations the entire collection of pottery from the above sites can be divided into two major categories: (a) the Harappan types and (b) the regional type or the Anarta Pottery tradition peculiar to North Gujarat and southeastern parts of Kachchh. In addition to these, there are two more important ceramic industries associated with the above assemblages: the Micaceous Red ware and the Black and Red ware of Saurashtra. Since these two industries are not necessarily confined to North Gujarat, and have their origin outside North Gujarat, they are not part of the Anarta tradition.

The Harappan Pottery

The majority of pottery collected from the sites in this region belonged to the following successive Periods/ Phases of the Harappa culture in Gujarat: (a) the Mature/Classical Harappan, (b) the Sorath Harappan characterised by the Rojdi A, B and C (Possehl and Raval 1989, Possehl and Herman 1990) and the Rangpur Period-IIA and IIB pottery and (c) the Post-Urban Harappan represented by the Rangpur Period-IIC and Period-III pottery, particularly the Lustrous Red ware (Rao 1963: 20-25). Sites belonging to the first two periods essentially belong to the Urban Phase of the Harappa culture. General features of the Harappan pottery from these three periods are so well known and therefore no attempt is made to describe them here. The Harappan pottery includes the Red ware, Buff ware, Coarse Red ware and Coarse Grey ware with or without incised decoration and the Lustrous Red ware. Associated with them are found the Black and Red ware and rare specimens of the Micaceous Red ware in some of the sites. The vessels are similar to those from other Harappan sites in Saurashtra and their forms vary, corresponding to the Period to which the site belongs. While the type-fossils of the Classical/Mature Harappan shapes are found only at a few sites like Nagwada (Figures 2 and 3), a majority of sites belonged to the Sorath Harappan and the Late Sorath Harappan. The Lustrous Red ware of the Post-Urban, Rangpur Period III, is one of the important ceramic types reported from the sites in the region.

In addition to the above types, the Harappan pottery includes a few sherds of the Reserved Slip ware and Rusticated Red ware. Although reported only from a few sites the Reserved Slip ware sherds

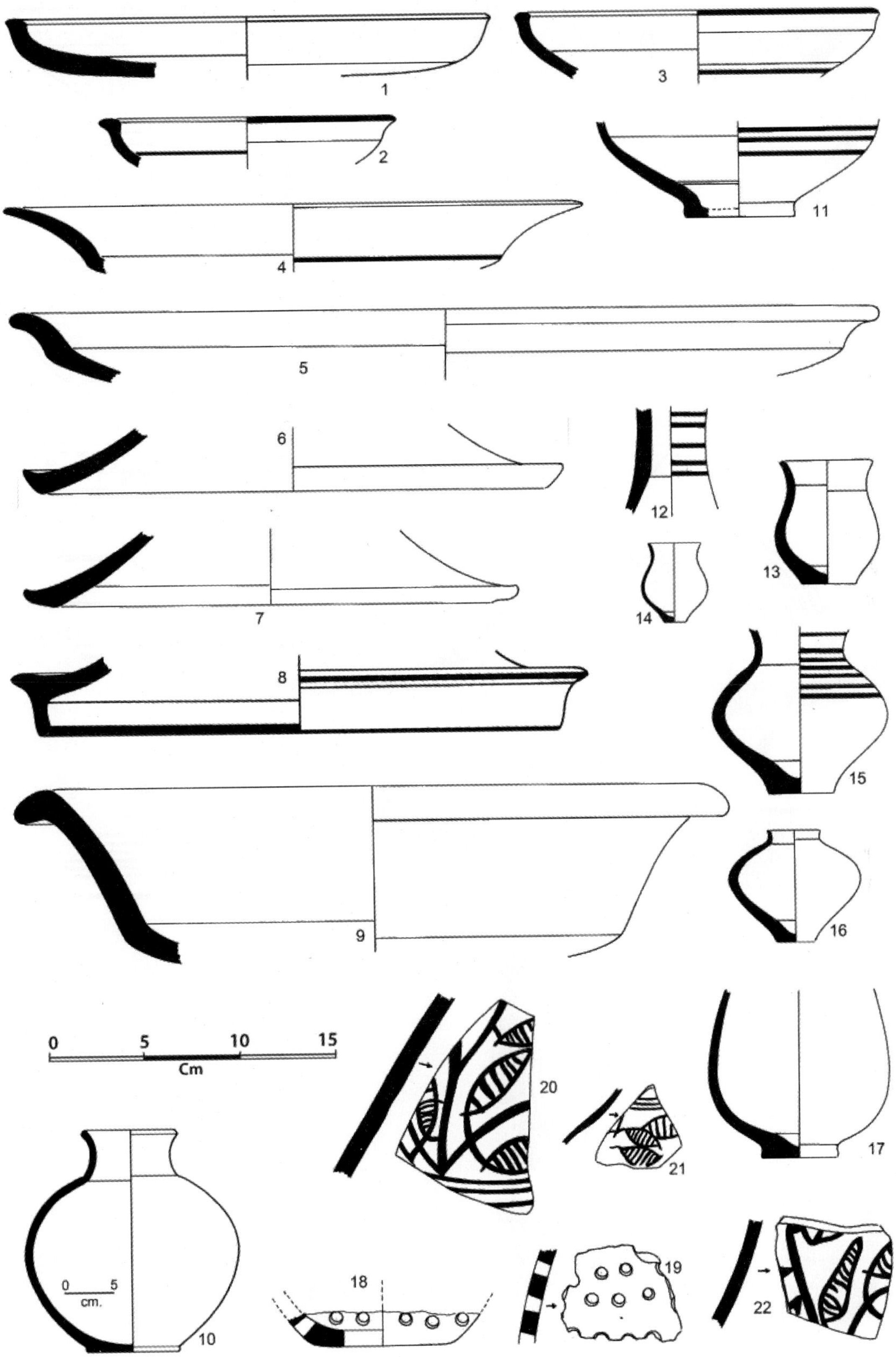

Figure 2 The Classical Harappan pottery from Nagwada excavation

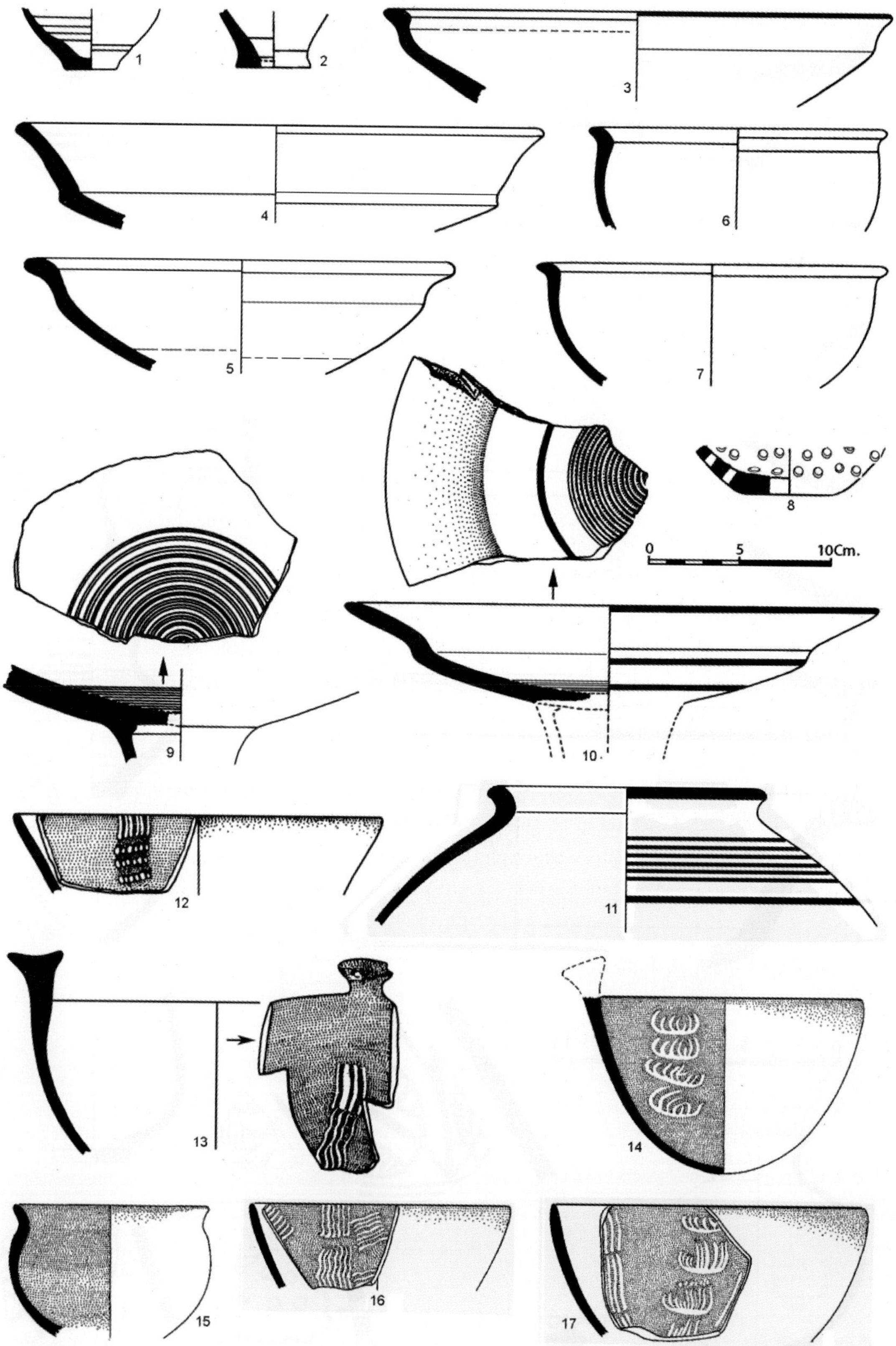

Figure 3 The Harappan pottery from Nagwada excavation: 1-3, 8 Classical Harappan; 4, 5, 9, 10 imitation of Harappan shapes in the Anarta pottery; 6 and 7 Nageshwar bowls affiliated to the Classical Harappan; 11-17 affiliated to the Sorath Harappan (12-16 Black and Red ware)

have a steel grey core, a black first slip and a bluish-grey second slip. The second slip was removed from the surface to form either parallel or wavy line pattern in the usual reserved slip technique. An appreciable number of rusticated sherds are found in the Late Sorath (Rangpur Period IIC, Rojdi C) or/and Post-Urban Harappan sites. These are the sherds of Red ware pots whose external surface was roughened with the application of sand while the clay was wet and plastic.

Anarta Pottery: The Regional Pottery Tradition of North Gujarat

The regional pottery tradition of North Gujarat needs detailed description as it is peculiar to this region. As has been mentioned earlier much of our understanding about the features of this non-Harappan pottery tradition is based on the excavations at Nagwada and Loteshwar. Although the Mature Harappan pottery and other type-fossils of the Classical Harappan are recovered from Nagwada, the ceramic assemblage is predominated by the non-Harappan pottery types of the Anarta tradition which constituted more than 80% of the assemblage. A Fine Red ware, Gritty Red ware, Burnished Red ware and a Burnished Grey/Black ware are the important types so far identified in this ceramic tradition from Nagwada. The Anarta pottery at Loteshwar includes potsherds with incised decoration.

The Gritty Red ware is the most important and characteristic type of the Anarta ceramic tradition. While the Fine Red ware is found in considerable quantity, the Burnished Red ware and the Burnished Grey/Black wares are rare in the collection. That, all these different types belong to the same ceramic tradition is evident from the common shapes, decorative patterns and other features of the vessels. The division, however, is made on the basis of relative fineness of the clay, variation in surface treatment and sometimes on the basis of the colour of the pottery. The Fine Red ware and the Gritty Red ware show remarkable conformity in shape and decoration. Besides, a few Harappan type-fossil vessels like the dish-on-stand and perforated jar were imitated in both the types at Nagwada (Figure 3). Small or medium size pots are the only shape so far identified in the case of Burnished Red ware and the Burnished Grey ware. Features of the pot in these two types are similar to the small and medium pots of the Gritty Red ware and the Fine Red ware.

The Gritty Red Ware

This is the most abundant and popular pottery type of the Anarta tradition present in the North Gujarat Chalcolithic sites. It occurs in different vessel forms like pots/jars, bowls and basins, and has painted decorations different from the Classical Harappan (Figures 4-11). The clay used in the preparation of these vessels was not sufficiently elutriated and refined. As its name implies, the core has a gritty appearance because of the admixture of a considerable amount of sand. According to the size and the relative abundance of sand particles present in the clay this pottery can be further classified into a fine and a coarse variety. The vessels of the Fine Gritty Red ware, in general, have a thin body and a good coating of slip. They are decorated with paintings and well fired too. On the other hand, the Coarse Gritty Red ware generally has a thick body and was coated with a thin wash of slip or no slip at all. Often the coarse variety was indifferently fired and painted were done more casually than the fine variety.

Mode of Production

The Gritty Red ware vessels are either hand modelled or made on a slow turn-table; for the striations on the interior of the vessels are short, irregular and zigzag. However, many of the vessels show a wheel turned rim

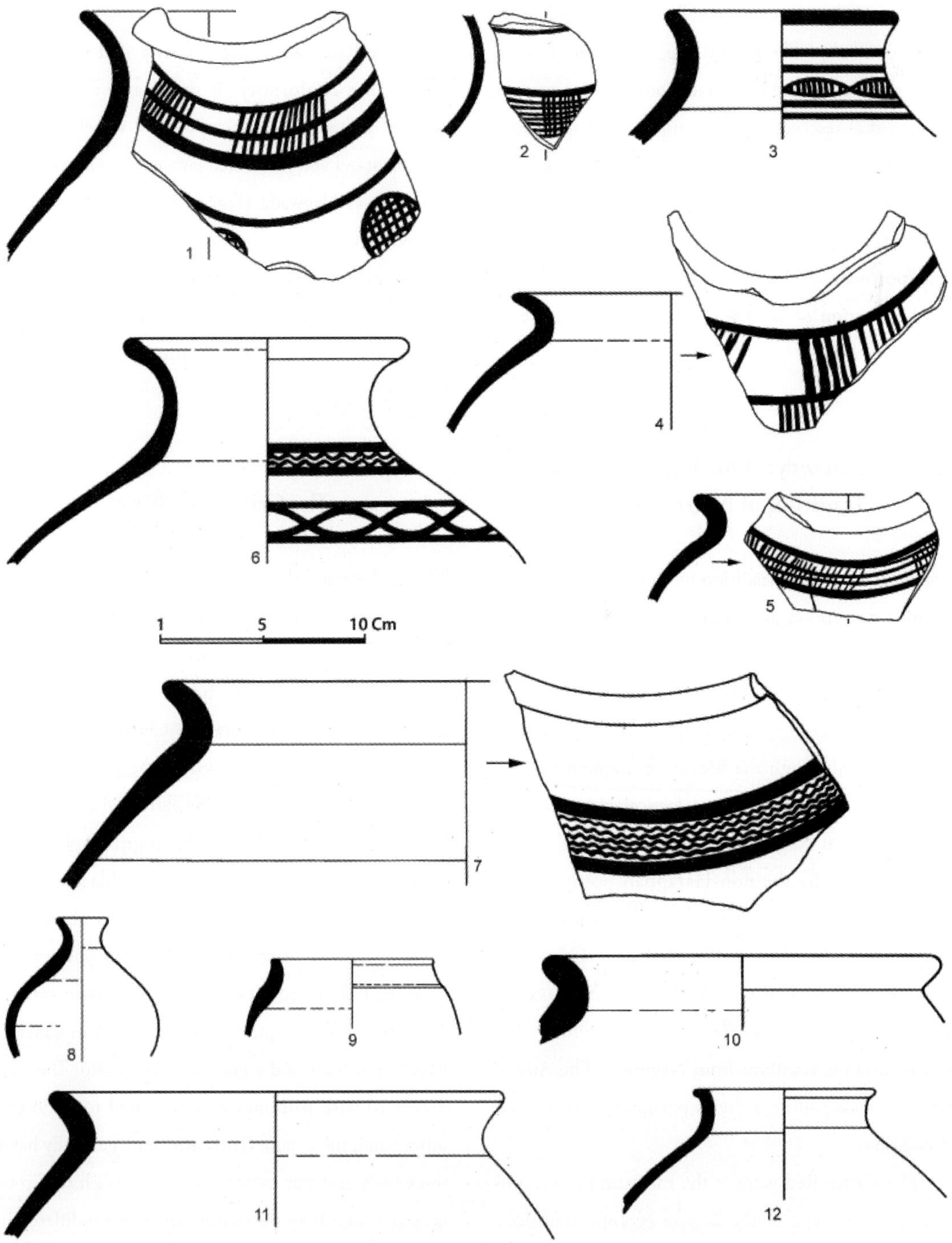

Figure 4 The Anarta pots/jars from Nagwada: 1-9 Gritty Red ware; 10,11 Coarse Grey ware; 12 Grey ware: (1, 2, 5 Cream slip)

luted to a hand modelled body. Very rarely, specimens of wheel made vessels in the Gritty Red ware are also found. For example, when the Harappan shapes like the dish-on-stand is imitated in the Gritty Red ware, they are wheel thrown. Such imitations are met with only in assemblages that were associated with the Classical/Mature Harappan sites; for instance at Nagwada and Zekhada

The vessels show a general crudeness and coarseness in spite of various surface treatments. Two types of

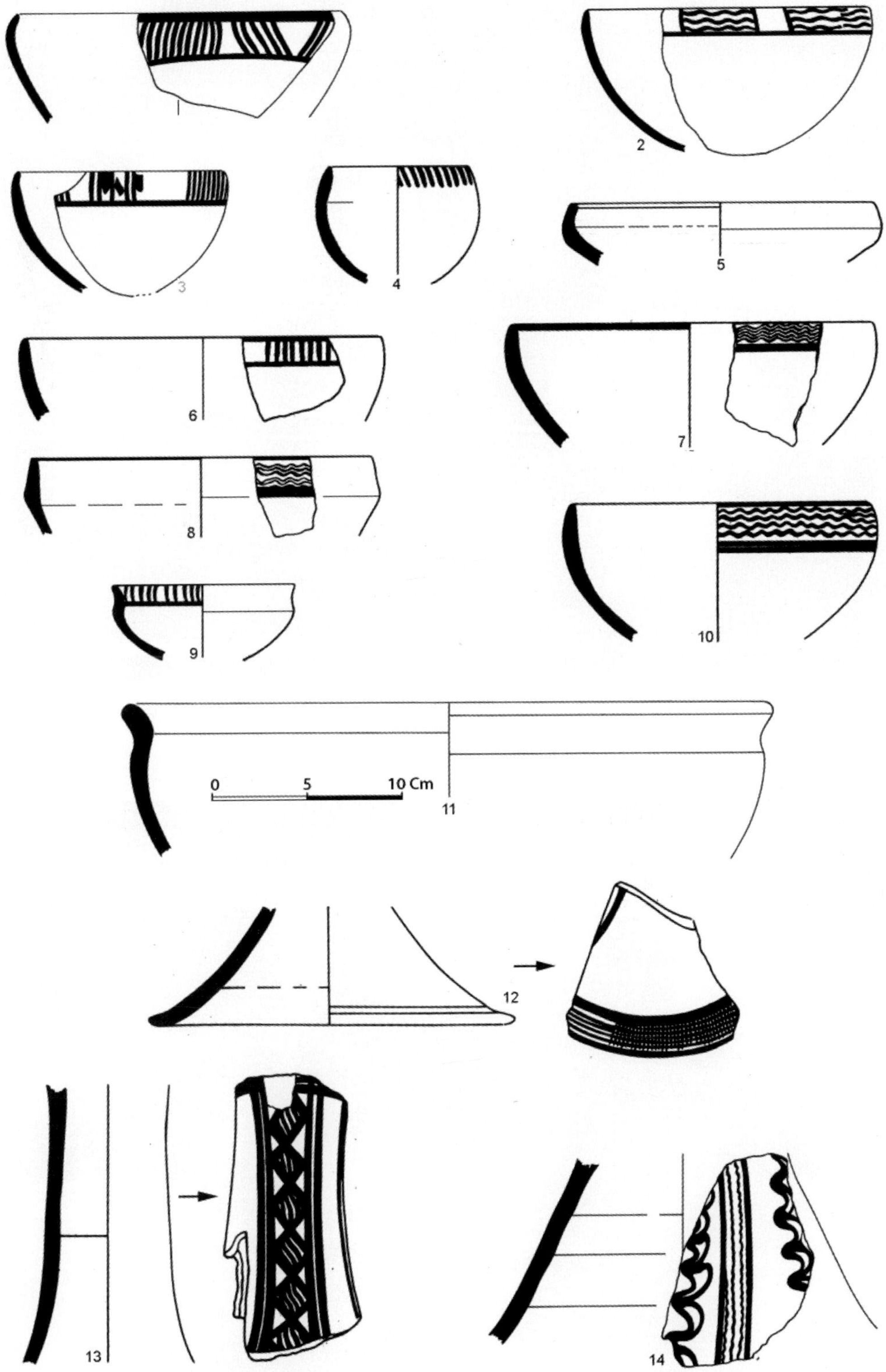

Figure 5 The Anarta pottery from Nagwada: 1 Fine Red ware; 2-14 Gritty Red ware (2, 7, 8 bichrome paintings, 3 and 5 dark brown slip, 12-14 cream slip

Figure 6 The Gritty Red ware and the Fine Red ware pot/jar from Loteshwar (photo by Akinori Uesugi)

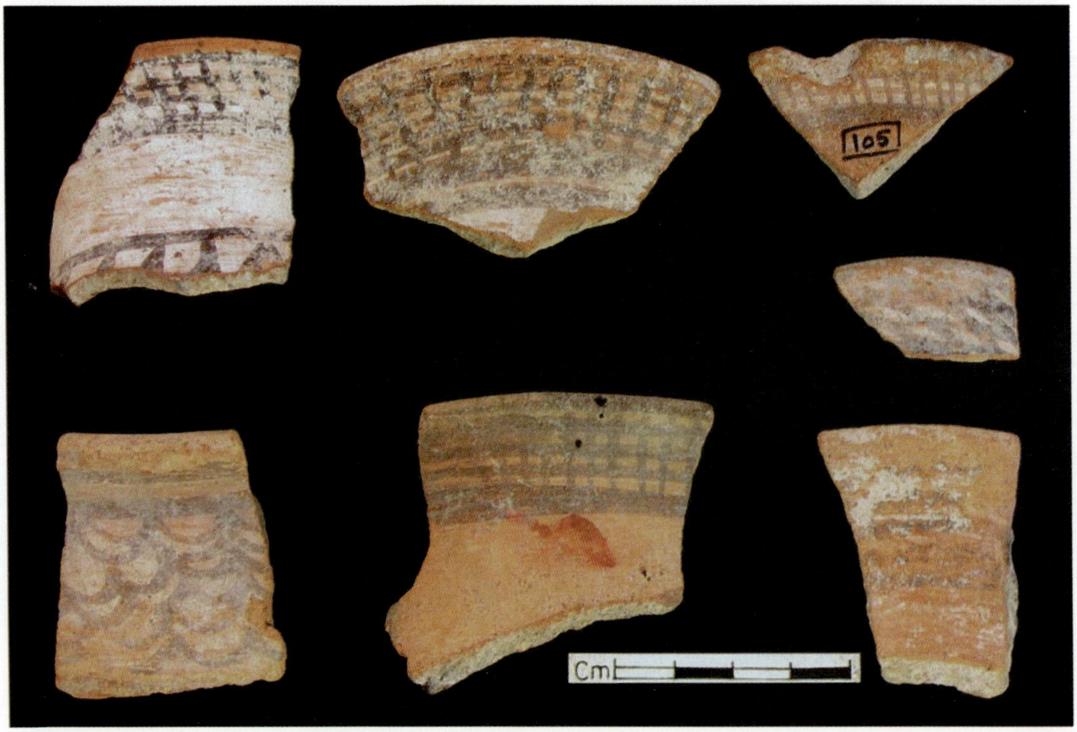

Figure 7 Pots/jars of the Gritty Red ware and Fine Red ware from Loteshwar showing the whitish background in which the paintings are executed

Figure 8 The Gritty Red ware bowls and basins from Nagwada (photo by Akinori Uesugi)

Figure 9 The Gritty ware bowls from Loteshwar

Figure 10 Basins/large bowls of the Gritty and Fine Red ware of the Anarta pottery from Loteshwar
The samples at the bottom row are light greyish and buff in colour

surface treatments can be identified in this pottery: (a) vessels coated with a slip and (b) vessels having no slip. In the latter case, the vessels are just left alone in their coarse condition, without applying any kind of slip. Large and medium size thick walled vessels generally belong to this category. Vessels in the first category are coated either with a thin wash of the slip solution or with a regular thick slip having varying shades of red, chocolate, buff or cream. In many specimens, while the whole vessels were coated with a red slip, zones at the rim, neck or at the shoulder were applied with either a cream or white slip and then painted in red or black pigment. The slip was smeared carelessly on many, especially on vessels having a chocolate slip, leaving behind the marks of the rag with which the slip was applied. Besides, vessels treated with buff and cream slip are also common in the Gritty Red ware. The vessels of the fine Gritty Red ware are generally treated with a normal thick slip of dark brown or red colour in a similar manner. The vessels treated with a wash of slip have a drab red appearance. Many of the large and medium size pots, bowls and basins were treated with a thin slip solution. In addition to the Gritty Red ware, rare instances of Buff or Grey ware with a gritty core are also found in the assemblage. This Gritty Buff ware is similar to the Gritty Red ware except for the buff colour. Considering its small number, the ware seems to be an aberration of the Gritty Red ware than an intentional creation of the potter.

Vessel Shapes

Pots/jars, bowls and basins are the common vessels of the Anarta pottery tradition. The most popular and characteristic shape in the Gritty Red is a small or medium size pot/jar with a bulbous body, elongated and constricted neck and a widely flaring out rim (Figures 4, 6, 7, 14). Pots of similar shape are common in the Fine Red ware, Burnished Red ware and in the Burnished Grey/Black ware, indicating their popularity in the regional pottery tradition of

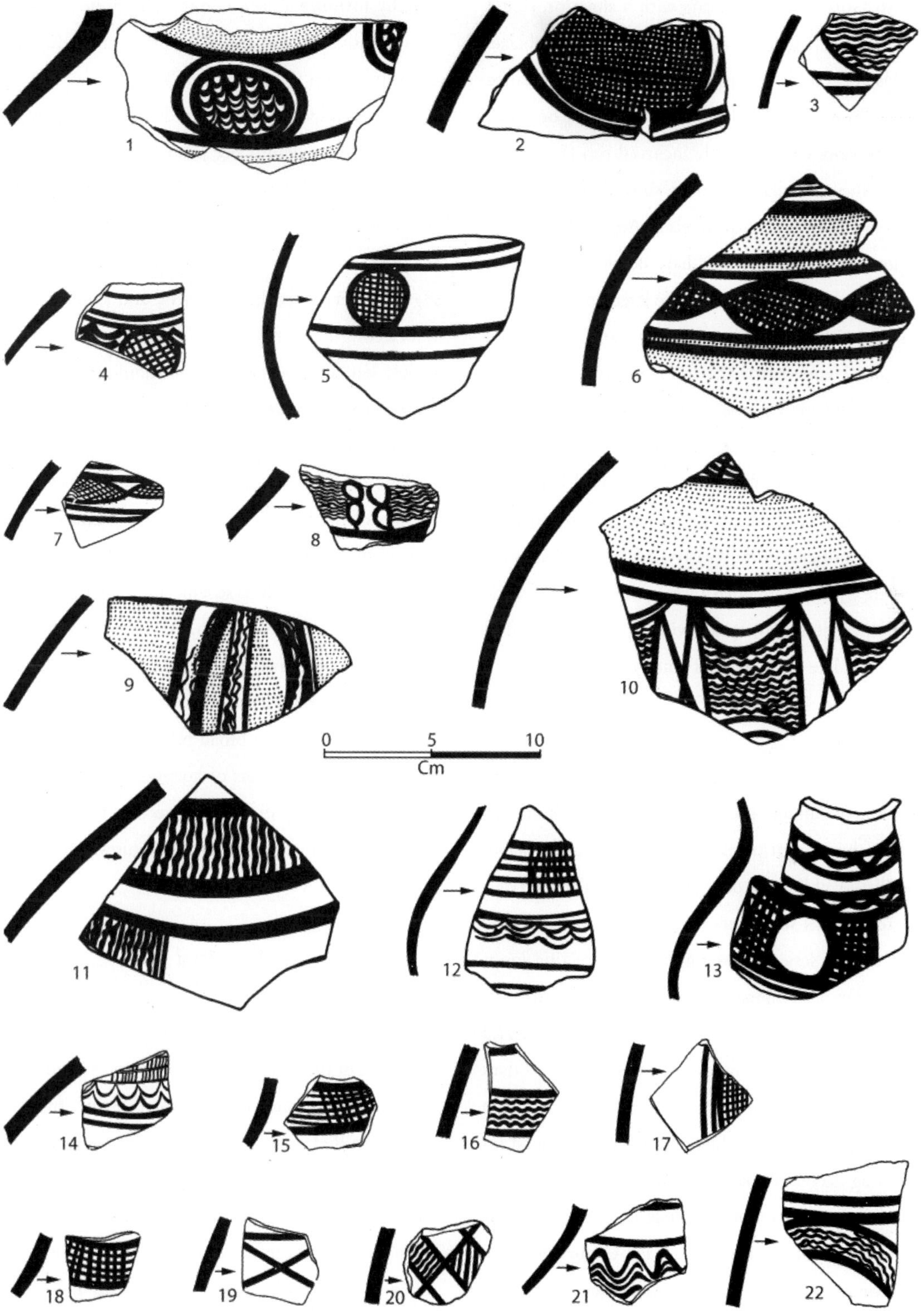

Figure 11 Painted decorations on the Anarta pottery from Nagwada: 1-6, 8-11, 14-22 Gritty red ware; 7, 12, 13 Fine Red ware: 1, 6, 9, 10, 22 bichrome (black/red in cream background); 4, 8, 11, 16, 19 cream slip

North Gujarat. Pots and jars with a short projected out or straight rims are also found in the assemblage. Bowls and Basins are second in the popularity range of Anarta pottery. Bowls have either convex or short, straight sides with a slightly incurved rim (Figures 5, 8, 9). These peculiar shapes are similar to those from the Pre-Urban Harappan levels at Amri (Casal 1964: Figures 38 and 39) or may have derived from them. Basins in the Gritty Red ware are large open-mouthed vessels with slightly convex sides and a rounded bottom (Figure 5.10). The rim is thick and projected out and there is a gentle carination where the curved rim joins the body.

In addition to the above forms, typical Harappan shapes like the dish-on-stand and the perforated jars are imitated in the Gritty Red ware at Nagwada (Figure 3). Such imitated forms were generally made of relatively fine clay, coated with slip and well fired so as to look like the Harappan pottery.

Decorations

The Gritty Red ware vessels are generally painted with varieties of complex geometric patterns, which include sets of horizontal parallel lines with another set of vertical or oblique strokes over it at regular intervals, sets of parallel wavy lines, hatched diamonds, squares and circles, series of hanging and intersecting loops and different combinations of vertical and horizontal straight or/and wavy lines (Figure 11). Black and shades of red, which ranged from bright red to dark brown, are the pigments generally used in such paintings. Sometimes white pigment was also used for painting decorative patterns and also as a background for dark brown paintings (Figures 12 and 13). The use of white painting seems to be a Pre-Urban Harappan tradition in ceramic decoration well footed in the early Chalcolithic cultures of Sindh and Rajasthan (Mughal 1974, Lal 1979). The paintings are generally confined to the rim, neck and the shoulder parts of the vessels. Very often, besides the customary red slip, a cream slip was applied either at the rim or at the shoulder thereby forming a cream zone. This zone was then painted either in red or in black pigment producing a bi-chrome effect (Figures 4 and 7).

There is a specific scheme of design that repeatedly occurs on the medium size jars/pots with a long and narrow neck at many sites. This popular pattern is a combination of a set of thin horizontal lines intersected by another set of vertical strokes at regular intervals at the rim, neck and shoulder, and intersecting loops filled in with either wavy lines or simple hatching, just below the shoulder. The loops are generally bordered by thick lines or bands. Many a times the painted designs are executed in a cream background. This design scheme is found repeated on the jars of the Fine Red ware and the Burnished Red ware of the Anarta tradition (Figures 4 and 14).

A comparable colour scheme and pattern of design are found on the bowls too. Both the interior and exterior of the bowls are treated with slips having shades of red colour. A cream zone is produced at the rim by applying a broad band of cream slip, and over this are painted sets of horizontal wavy lines and vertical or oblique strokes, intersecting hatched loops etc., in panels at regular intervals (Figures 5, 6, 7).

The Fine Red Ware

In its general features like shape and decoration, the Red ware of the regional ceramic tradition is similar to the Gritty Red ware and, therefore, distinct from the Harappan Red ware. Unlike the Gritty Red ware, the Anarta Fine Red ware was made of well elutriated, fine clay. More often than not, the clay contained abundant mica particles. As in the case of the Gritty Red ware, the vessels are either hand modelled or made on a turn-table. The vessels are generally treated with a red or dark brown slip on the exterior. Buff or cream slip is also equally common. The Fine Red ware shapes are identical with the Gritty Red ware and include pots, jars, basins and bowls (Figures 4 and 5). The pattern

Figure 12 The Gritty and Fine Red ware sherds with bichrome paintings from Loteshwar

Figure 13 Bichrome painted pottery of the Gritty Red ware and the Fine Red ware of the Anarta tradition at Loteshwar

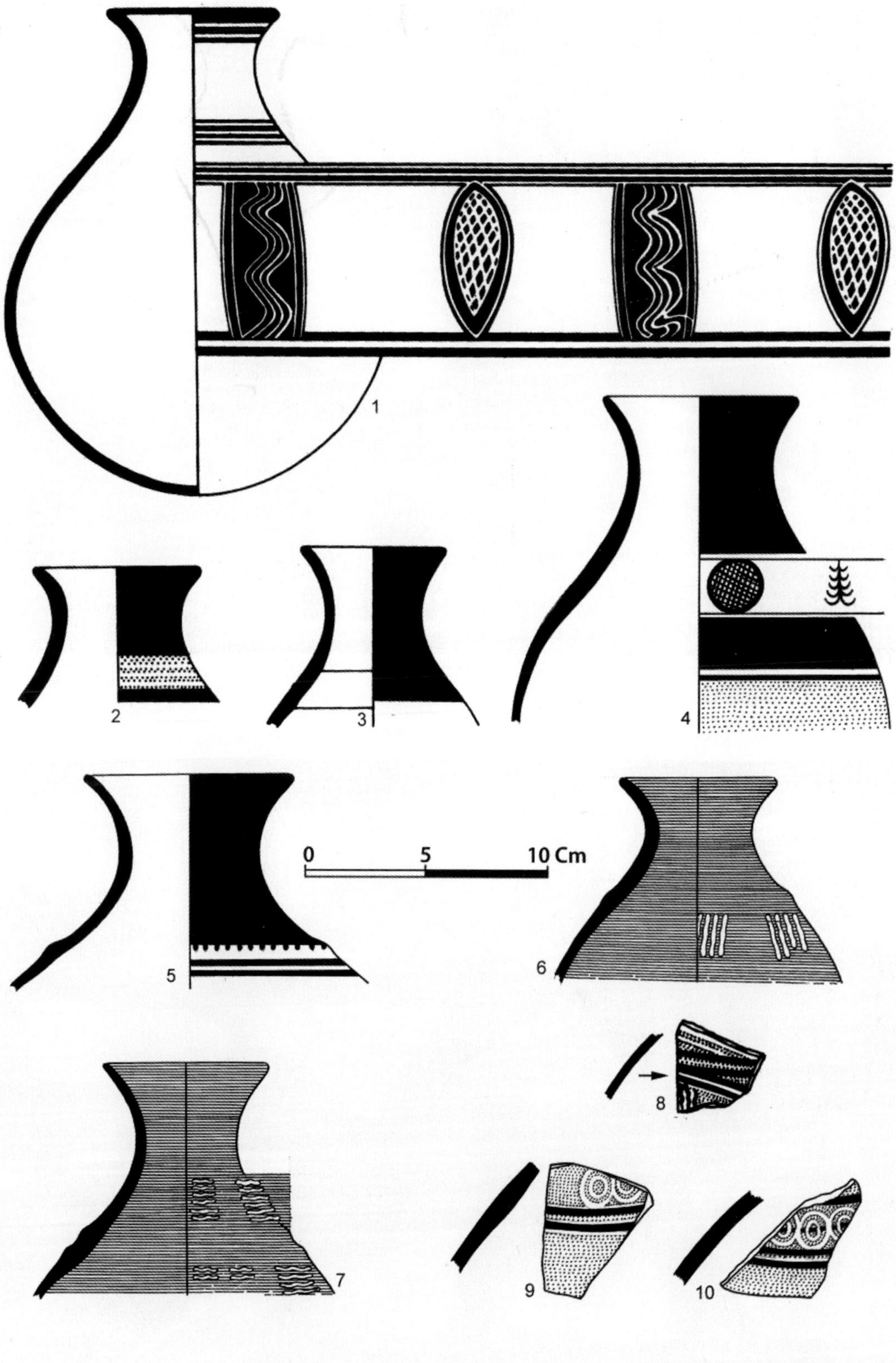

Figure 14 The Anarta pottery from Nagwada: 1, 4 Burnished Red ware; 2, 3, 8 Fine Red ware; 5, 9, 10 Gritty Red ware (5 cream slip); 6 and 7 White painted Burnished Grey/Black ware (1, 2, 4, 8-10 bichrome painting)

and colour scheme of painted designs on the vessels are also similar. These overall similarities may indicate that the Fine Red ware and the Gritty Red ware are the fine and coarse varieties of the same ceramic tradition. Sometimes, especially at Nagwada, characteristic Harappan shapes were also imitated in the Anarta Fine Red ware, which are difficult to distinguish from the real Classical Harappan vessels.

The Burnished Red Ware

The Burnished Red ware and the Burnished Grey/Black ware are distinguished on the basis of surface colour and decoration. The Burnished Red ware is so far reported only in small pots/jars: a standard shape common in the Gritty Red ware and in the Fine Red ware. It has a flaring out rim, long and constricted neck, elongated, bulbous body and a round base (Figures 14 and 15). These are thin walled vessels having a thickness ranging from 2 to 4 mm. The pot is generally hand modelled in two halves and luted at the shoulder. The upper half, especially the rim, is sometimes slow-wheel turned. It is treated with a bright red slip and burnished to produce a smooth shining surface. Some of the vessels are treated with a fine dark chocolate slip up to the shoulder. Decorative patterns are painted on the burnished surface of the pot. The pattern and scheme of paintings are the same as that of the Gritty Red ware. On some vessels a buff or a cream zone is produced at the shoulder by applying a cream slip and the patterns are executed on that background. A few pots in this type have bichrome painted decoration drawn in white on a black background too.

The Burnished Grey/Black Ware

Except for its colour, which is either grey or black, this pottery is similar to the Burnished Red ware. Pots/jars of small size are the only shape so far found in this type, and that too are very few. The pots have a flaring out rim, long and constricted neck, and bulbous body (Figures 14 and 16). Some of them are cordoned with a ridge at the shoulder. Being fired in a reducing atmosphere the whole pot is either grey or black. A generic resemblance with the black and red ware is evident not only in the technique of firing but also in the painted patterns on the exterior of the vessel. These vessels have a well burnished exterior surface which was painted with parallel horizontal lines or sets of four or five wavy lines and dots in fugitive white pigment at regular intervals around the neck or shoulder.

Apart from the above pottery types, the assemblage at Nagwada incorporates a large number of Black and Red ware. The Black and Red ware is generally represented in large bowls having short stud-handles similar to the stud-handled bowls of the Saurashtran Harappa sites (Figure 3). These bowls are made of relatively well elutriated clay and have a burnished, smooth surface and decorated with vertical strokes, wavy lines, dots and a comb-like pattern painted in a fugitive white pigment on the black interior.

Stratigraphy and Chronology

The Anarta pottery is associated with the Mature Harappan remains at Nagwada from the earliest level onwards. No appreciable variation in their relative abundance vis-à-vis the Classical Harappan pottery is apparent in the four successive layers, although the second layer incorporates the maximum number of Harappan artefacts. A single radiocarbon date from this layer indicates c. 2200 BCE for the deposit at Nagwada (Table 1). Many of the above pottery types like the Gritty Red ware and Fine Red ware are analogous with the non-Harappan Polychrome, Bichrome and Coarse Red ware pottery excavated from Surkotada and some of the painted Coarse

Figure 15 Burnished red ware, Nagwada

Figure 16 The Burnished Red and Burnished Grey/Black wares from Loteshwar (Photo by Akinori Uesugi)

Table 1 Radiocarbon dates from Nagwada and Loteshwar

Site	Period	Sample no.	Date BC half life 5730	Calibrated dates		
				1σ	2σ	Intercept
Nagwada	IB	A 4555	1860±80 BC	2349BC(59.4%)2138BC	2470BC(95.4%)2033BC	2205calBC
Loteshwar	II (Anarta)	PRL 1564	2510±110 BC	3340BC(30.0%)3202BC 3199BC(38.2%)3018BC	3377BC(92.7%)2889BC	3090calBC
		PRL 1565	3100±110 BC	3959BC(61.3%)3760BC	4056BC(95.3%)3636BC	3790calBC
	I (Mesolithic)	PRL 1567	4060±120 BC	5053BC(64.6%)4767BC	5221BC(95.4%)4610BC	4912calBC

Calibrated using IntCal09, Calib Rev 6.0.1

Red ware from Lothal (Hegde *et al.*, 1988: 62). At Surkotada, in the south-eastern part of Kachchh, the "non-Harappan" pottery types occur in the early levels, Period-IA, dated to c. 2500 BCE along with the Mature/Urban Harappan remains. In the succeeding Period-IB, the non-Harappan Coarse Red ware outnumbers even the Harappan pottery (Joshi 1972: 129), indicating its remarkable influence on the Harappa culture at the site. Similarly, the painted Coarse Red ware vessels reported from Lothal (Rao 1985) along with the Micaceous Red ware and the Mature Harappan wares from the earliest level onwards are comparable with the Gritty Red ware, particularly in their shape and painted decoration.

The use of white colour both as a pigment as well as a background for paintings is common in the Stage-I and II, which precede the Mature Harappan Stage, at Dholavira (Bisht 1989, 1994). A similar correspondence with the Pre-Harappan Chalcolithic pottery reported from Binjor-I, RD-89 and other sites in Rajasthan by Dalal (1980, 1981, 1987) can also be cited to illustrate the general ambiance of the tradition[2]. It should also be noted that the Anarta pottery shows several shared features, especially in the painted decorations and shapes, with the Early Harappan pottery reported from Jalilpur by Mughal (1974). It is therefore obvious that certain vessel forms in the Anarta pottery tradition, like the bowls, and the use of white pigment in painted decoration are more akin to the Pre-Urban Harappan ceramic traditions of the Indus and the Ghaggar-Sarasvati basins, than the Urban/Mature Harappan tradition. Therefore, a generic kinship of the Anarta tradition of the North Gujarat region with that of the Pre-Urban Harappan traditions can be tentatively proposed (Ajithprasad 2002). It is noteworthy that many features of the Gritty Red ware show close resemblance, especially the vessel shapes, patterns of decorations and overall techniques of production, with the Padri ware (Shinde and Kar 1992) dating back to the second half of the fourth millennium BCE, excavated at Padri in the Saurashtra coast of Bhavnagar district. It can be, suggested that most of these regional ceramic traditions were an integral part of the Western Indian Pre-Urban Harappan village cultures of the fourth and the early third millennium BCE (Sonawane and Ajithprasad 1994). This has been validated by the excavations at Loteshwar in North Gujarat.

Anarta Tradition and Loteshwar

The Anarta tradition had an independent existence much earlier than the beginning of Mature Harappan in North Gujarat. In a few sites in the vicinity of the Khari stream, a small tributary of the Rupen, the Anarta pottery is not associated with the Harappan remains (Figure 31). Subsequent excavation in one of such sites at Loteshwar, in Mehsana (now Patan) district in 1991, revealed its independent existence prior to the beginning of the Urban Harappa culture. All the pottery types of the Anarta that are described above have also been reported from Loteshwar-I (Figures 17-19, also Figures 6, 7, 9, 10). In fact,

Figure 17 Gritty Red ware, Loteshwar

varieties of shapes and painted decorations, particularly the white/bichrome painted ones, are much more in the Loteshwar assemblage than in Nagwada (Figures 20 and 22, also Figures 12 and 13). In addition to these, the assemblage included a few sherds of Coarse Red ware and Coarse Grey ware with incised decoration and sherds of the Gritty Red ware vessels decorated with the "Reserved Slip" technique (Figures 21 and 22). These are different from the Reserved Slip ware found in the Classical Harappan context. They in fact are close to the Reserved Slip ware reported from the Chalcolithic assemblage dating back to 3500 BCE at Balathal in southern Rajasthan (Misra 2005), probably indicating incidents of early Chalcolithic inter-regional interaction.

Another type of pottery that is identified in the Anarta pottery collection of Loteshwar is a Coarse Red ware with matt surface (Figure 23). Sometimes a few samples of this pottery in grey colour are also found in the collection. It was made of a clay paste containing a lot of coarse sand and was reasonably well-fired. Generally, sections of broken potsherds of this category have a uniform reddish colour indicating complete oxidation of the clay. It resembles the common Coarse Red ware in overall appearance, but has a matt external surface that was intentionally produced by scraping and paring. Medium to large size pots are the only type of vessels found in this category.

The excavation at Loteshwar revealed that the habitation deposit at the site formed discrete clusters of artefact concentrations whose depositional history could not be adequately ascertained. The overall Chalcolithic deposit at the site is meagre, ranging from hardly 20 to 40 cm. However, a conspicuous feature of the non-Harappan occupation is the presence of a number of roughly circular pits varying from 0.50 to 2.00 m in diameter and a corresponding variation in depth from 0.50 to 2.00 m. It is interesting to note that similar pits have been unearthed at Nagwada as well as in the excavation at Santhli, another site belonging to the Anarta tradition in Banaskantha (now Patan) district. The pits at Loteshwar are filled with plenty of ash and other debris of occupation including sherds of pottery, skeletal elements of the exploited animals, steatite micro-beads, terracotta objects and burnt clay lumps having reed impressions, presumably the remains of clay plaster over wattle and daub structures. A few shell beads and semiprecious stone beads are also found in the excavation. Radiocarbon assay of the charcoal samples from this deposit suggests a date c. 3600 - 3000 BCE (Table 1) thereby indicating an early beginning of the Anarta tradition in North Gujarat.

Loteshwar has a very rich and substantial deposit of Mesolithic occupation, underlying the Chalcolithic deposit. Radiocarbon date from this deposit is one of the earliest, 4700 BCE, in Western India[3]. A preliminary assessment of the rich collection of faunal remains from the Mesolithic deposit indicates high abundance of a few wild species of animals, especially blackbuck (*Antelope cervicapra*). This would suggest that the hunter-gatherers had probably practiced selective hunting. Whether the selective hunting eventually led to the beginning of herding and early stages of organized food production is not clear at present. In any case, this preliminary assessment

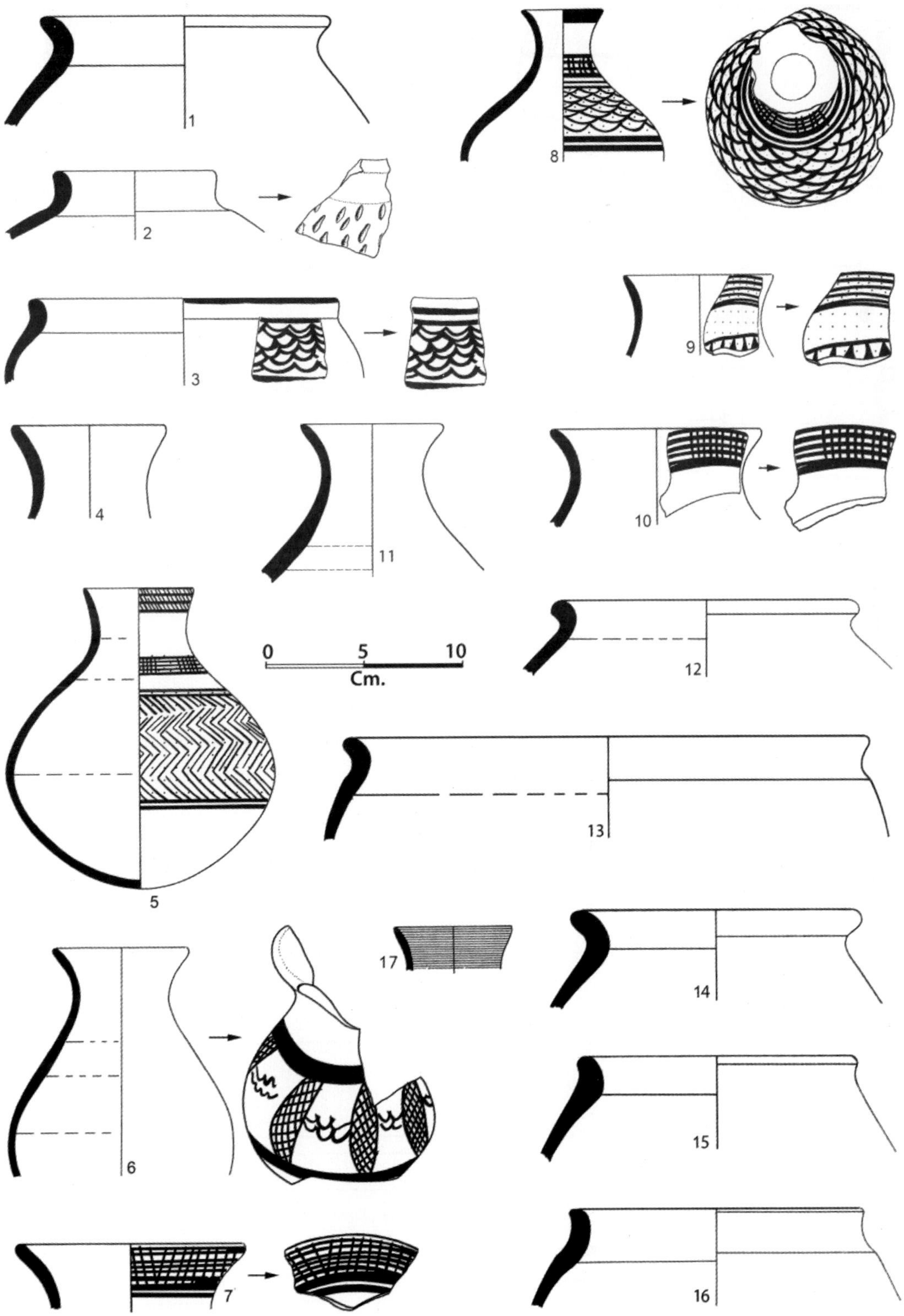

Figure 18 Loteshwar-I Anarta pottery: 1 Coarse Red ware with matt surface; 2 Coarse Grey ware (incised); 3, 4, 6, 10-15 Gritty Red ware; 5, 7-9 Fine Red ware (bichrome: black on white); 16 Coarse Red ware; 17 Burnished Grey/Black ware

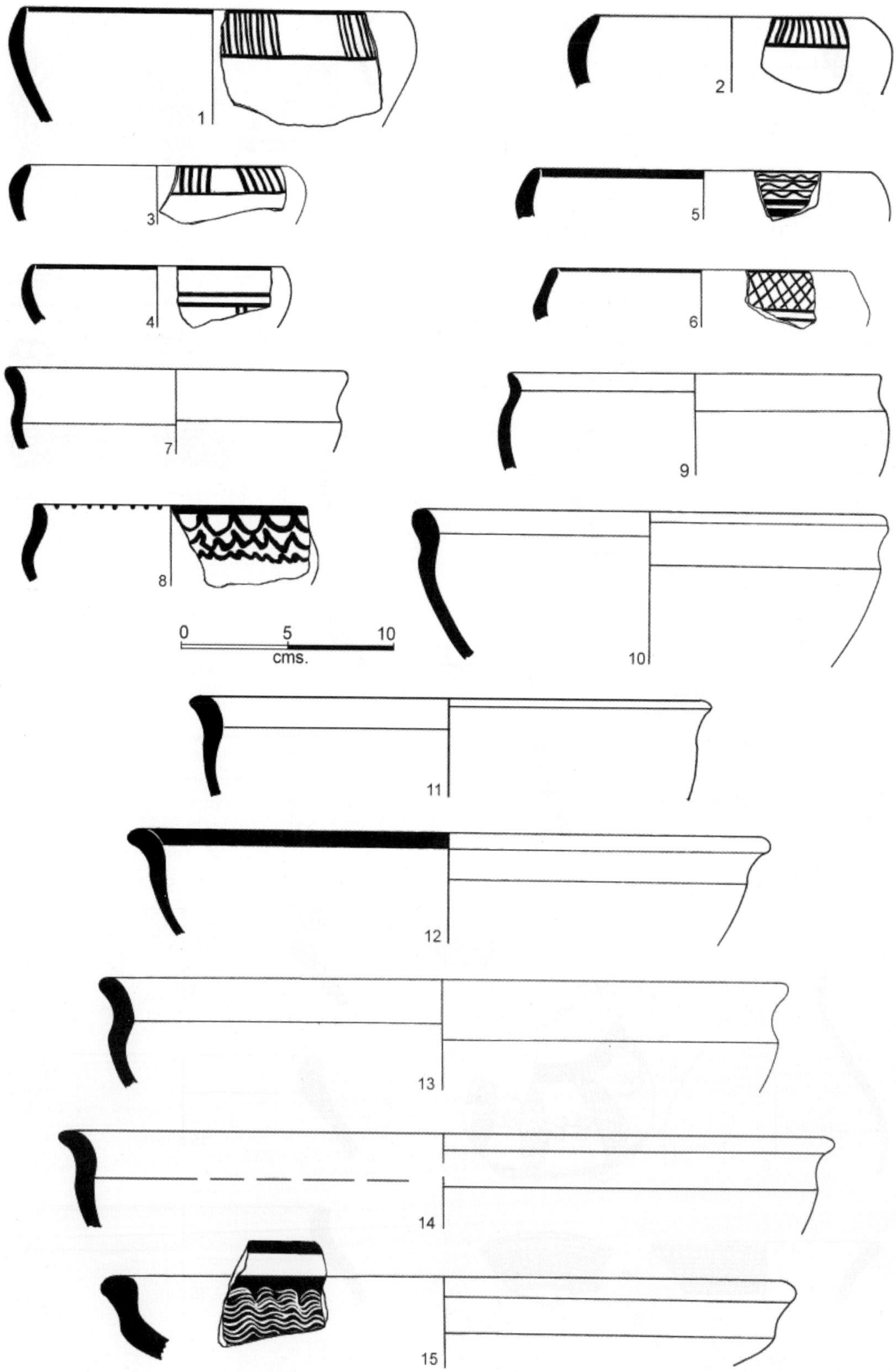

Figure 19 Loteshwar-I Anarta pottery: 1, 2, 6-8, 10, 13, 14 Gritty Red ware, 3-5, 9, 11, 12, 15 Fine Red ware (3 cream slip, 4, dark brown slip, 5 bichrome: black on cream; 15 Reserved slip)

Figure 20 White painted decorations on the Anarta pottery from Loteshwar

Figure 21 TAnarta pottery from Loteshwar having Reserved slip and incised decoration

Figure 22 The Anarta Pottery from Loteshwar-I: 1, 2, 6, 12 Fine Red ware; 3-5, 7, 8, 11 Gritty Red ware; 9 Grey ware; 10 Coarse Red ware; (1-3, 5, 8 bichrome: white on black; 4 cream slip; 9 and 10 incised; 11 and 12 Reserved slip)

needs to be ascertained by further detailed analysis of the faunal remains[4]. The presence of a large number of grinding stones in quartzite, sandstone and other rocks, and the evidence of grinding and polishing to produce a smooth and bluntly pointed stone implement of unknown function in a fine siltstone from the Mesolithic level may imply intensive food processing as well as innovations in lithic technology during the period. Stratigraphically, the Chalcolithic deposit directly overlies the Mesolithic deposit without any break. However, there are no conclusive indications of a cultural continuity from the

Figure 23 Coarse Red ware with matt surface from Loteshwar

Figure 24 Terracotta animal figurine from Nagwada

Figure 25 Terracotta Female figurine from Nagwada

Mesolithic to the Anarta Chalcolithic at the site.

Very little is known about other cultural materials associated with the Anarta pottery apart from the steatite micro-beads, and a few beads of shell, amazonite and carnelian; terracotta beads, pellets and pottery discs recovered from Loteshwar. A few copper wires and a large number of lithic blade tools and debitage are also part of the assemblage. The lithic

Figure 26 Early Harappan pot-burial in Nagwada

debitage and the tools recovered from the site do not reveal any evidence of the application of crested ridge technique in the blade production. Probably the early Chalcolithic community at Loteshwar was not acquainted with this technique. The assemblage also had oval and square shaped terracotta lumps and a small terracotta animal figure (Figure 24). A female figurine measuring hardly 5cm is reported from the Anarta assemblage at Nagwada (Figure 25). Decorated with steatite beads, this figurine is quite different from those found in the Classical Harappan context. Simple and minimalistic modelling style of this female figure bespeaks the individuality of the Anarta tradition.

It is apparent that the Anarta tradition continued to survive even after the Mature/Urban Phase of the Harappa culture. In many of the sites in the region the Anarta pottery is found associated with the so called "Late Harappan" pottery belonging to the Period-IIB and Period-IIC of the Rangpur sequence. It is also found associated with the Post-Urban Harappan context indicating a long period, spanning from 3600 B.C. to c. 1700 B.C. The pottery tradition goes through perceptible changes during this long period of time. For example, the Fine Red ware and the Burnished Red ware with bichrome decoration are found only in the early stages and associated with the Mature Phase of the Harappa culture. Similarly, the use of white pigment for painting and as a background also disappeared in the later period. The scheme of yellowish slip and yellow as background colour however survived in the Sorath Harappan pottery tradition. Similarly, the Burnished Grey ware continued even in the later period but, new vessel forms were adopted. Generally, the Gritty Red ware with simple painted decoration is the only type of Anarta pottery present in the later period sites.

The Anarta Pottery and the Chalcolithic Burials of North Gujarat

A new dimension to the regional Chalcolithic tradition is added with the discovery of Anarta pottery in association with the Earl Harappan/Chalcolithic

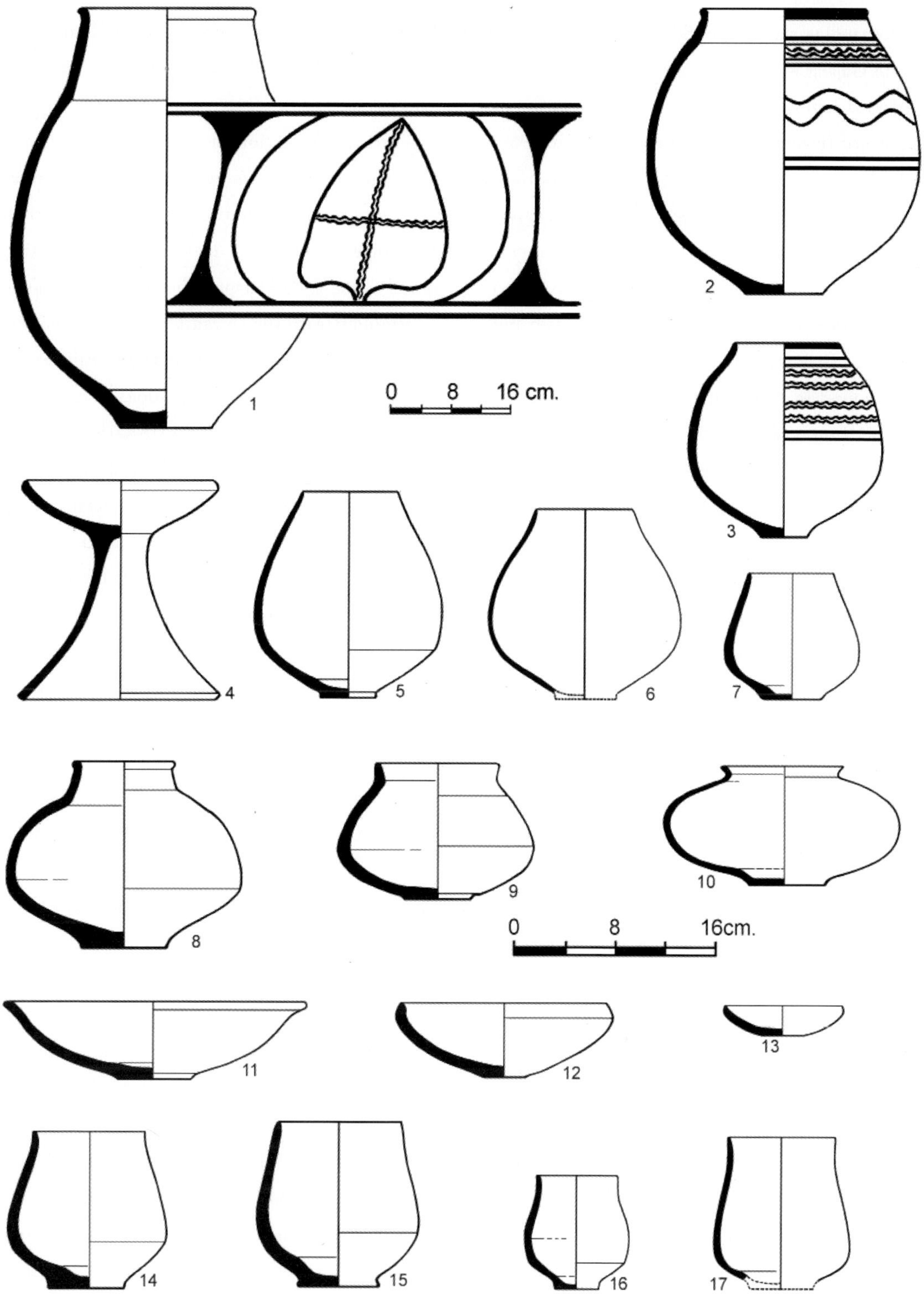

Figure 27 Early Harappan pottery from the Nagwada-I burials: 1-3, 5-7, 9, 11-17 Red ware (3 bichrome painting); 4 and 8 Grey ware; 10 Buff ware (1-6, 8, 9, 11-17 from pot-burial, 7-10 from extended burial)

burials of North Gujarat. This interesting evidence for understanding the Chalcolithic/Harappan society of North Gujarat was first brought to light from the two extended inhumation burials and three pot-burials unearthed (Figure 26) at Nagwada in the late 1980's (Hegde *et al.*, 1988: 58-59). The burials invariably contained pottery as burial good interred in the grave. The potteries that are found in these two burial types are similar, even though the number of vessels in each burial varied considerably. Red ware, a pinkish Buff ware and Grey ware are the three important pottery types found in these burials (Figure 27). They are distinct from the Harappan pottery and the non-Harappan, Anarta pottery types and are not found in the regular habitation layers at the site. The clay used in their production was well elutriated and the vessels were slipped and painted even though the slip and painting had almost completely peeled off. Characteristic shapes in the burial pottery are a large bulbous pot, flasks or beaker-shaped vases with sides converging into a rather narrow opening, beakers with slightly flaring rim, dish-on-stand, the dish with no carination and shallow bowls. The large bulbous pot has a narrow flat base, a short and straight neck and a flat rim. It is painted at the rim and sometime up to the neck with thick dark bands and at the shoulder with horizontal and wavy lines. A stylized pipal leaf motif on one of the large pots is also noteworthy (Figure 27.1).

The shapes and the decorations of the burial pottery do not resemble the shape and decoration of the Urban Harappan pottery; rather they resemble similar vessels from the Early Harappan levels at Kot Diji (Khan 1965), Amri (Casal 1964: Figure 62), and Balakot (Dales 1974, Frank-Vogt 1997, Possehl 2006). Besides, similar pot-burials were found in association with Pre-Urban Harappan sites at Nal and Damb Bhuti (Piggott 1952). Analogous pottery types have also been reported from the pot-burials unearthed from the cemetery at Surkotada by Joshi (1972) suggesting very clearly the spread of the tradition towards the north into Kachchh. Joshi (1990) has compared the pottery from the burials with the Pre-Urban/Early Harappan pottery of Sindh and Balochistan.

Further exploration in the region in the early 1990's revealed eight more sites that incorporated the Early Harappan burial pottery types in their assemblage (Figure 31). In fact, the geographical spread of the Early Harappan burial pottery is found coterminous with the spread of the Anarta pottery tradition in the region (Sonawane and Ajithprasad 1994, Ajithprasad 2002). Excavations at two of the above sites, Moti-Pipli in 1993 (IAR-1992-93) and Santhli in 1994 (IAR-1993-94), in Banaskantha (now Patan) district, have revealed further details of the Chalcolithic community who had buried the dead with the pots (Majumdar 2001). Of the two extended burials excavated at Santhli, one is a joint/double burial with five distinct vessels similar to those found in the Nagwada burials. However, no substantial habitation deposit of the Chalcolithic community is reported from the site. This is a feature which is common to most of the above sites in North Gujarat. Moti-Pipli, on the other hand, showed a substantial (about 1.00 m) habitation deposit even though no burials were unearthed in the excavation. The site not only has all the already reported `Early Harappan burial pottery' types in the habitation levels but also several new shapes (Figures 28 and 29) which are analogous to the Early-Harappan vessels from Kot Diji, Balakot and other sites in Sindh and Baluchistan. The Early Harappan strata at these sites have been dated from the middle of the fourth millennium B.C. to the first half of the third millennium B.C. (Possehl 1994). This evidence has important historical significance in understanding the movement of early Chalcolithic cultures as it suggests that, the Pre-Urban Harappan settlements of Sindh and Baluchistan extended further southwards into the northwestern part of Gujarat during this period (Hegde *et al.*, 1988, Majumdar and Sonawane 1996-97, Possehl 2006).

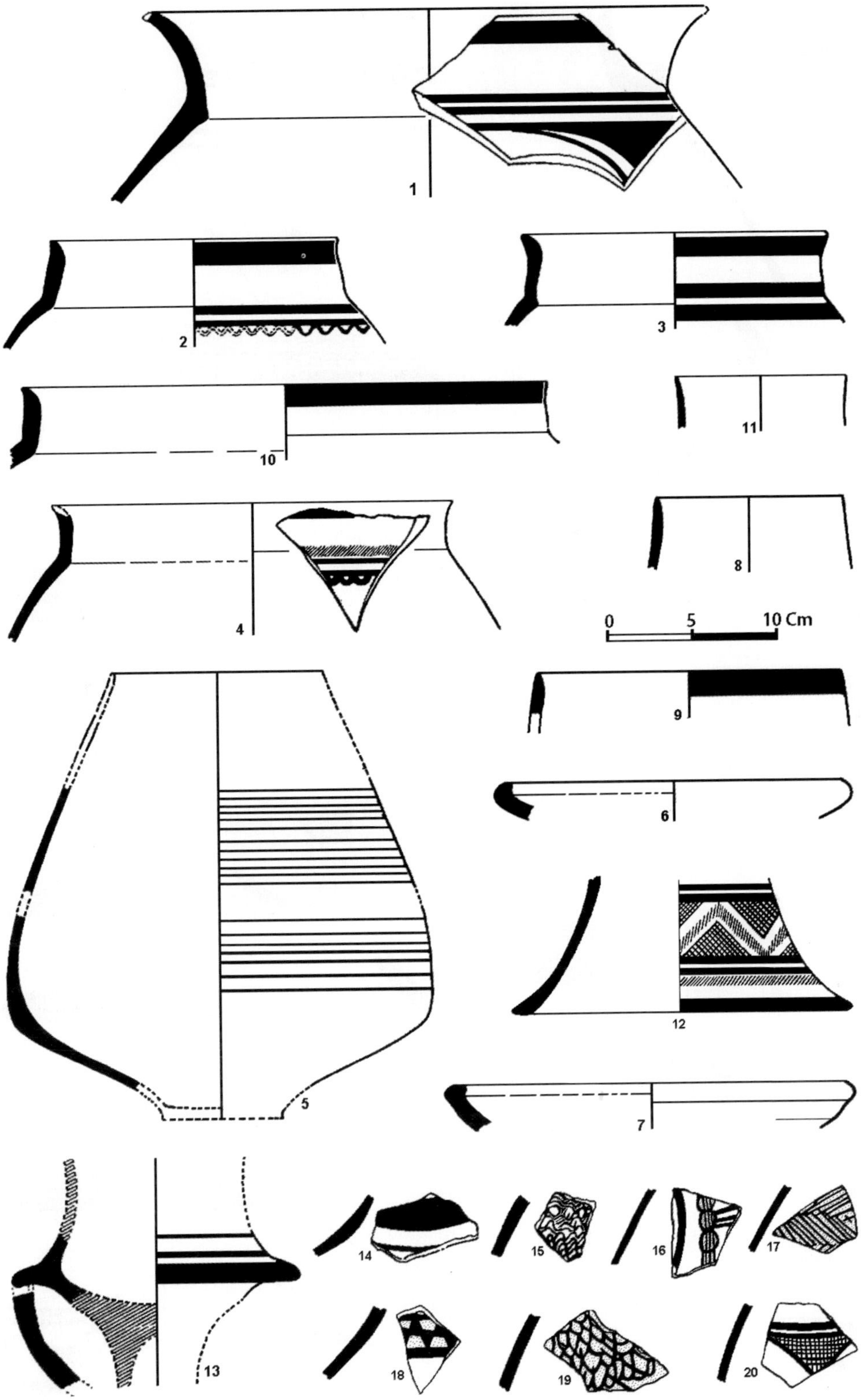

Figure 28 The Early Harappan pottery from Motipipli in North Gujarat: 1-9, 12 Red ware; 10 and 11 Buff ware; 14-20 Anarta Red ware (11 dark brown slip, 12 Bichrome painting, 16-19 cream slip)

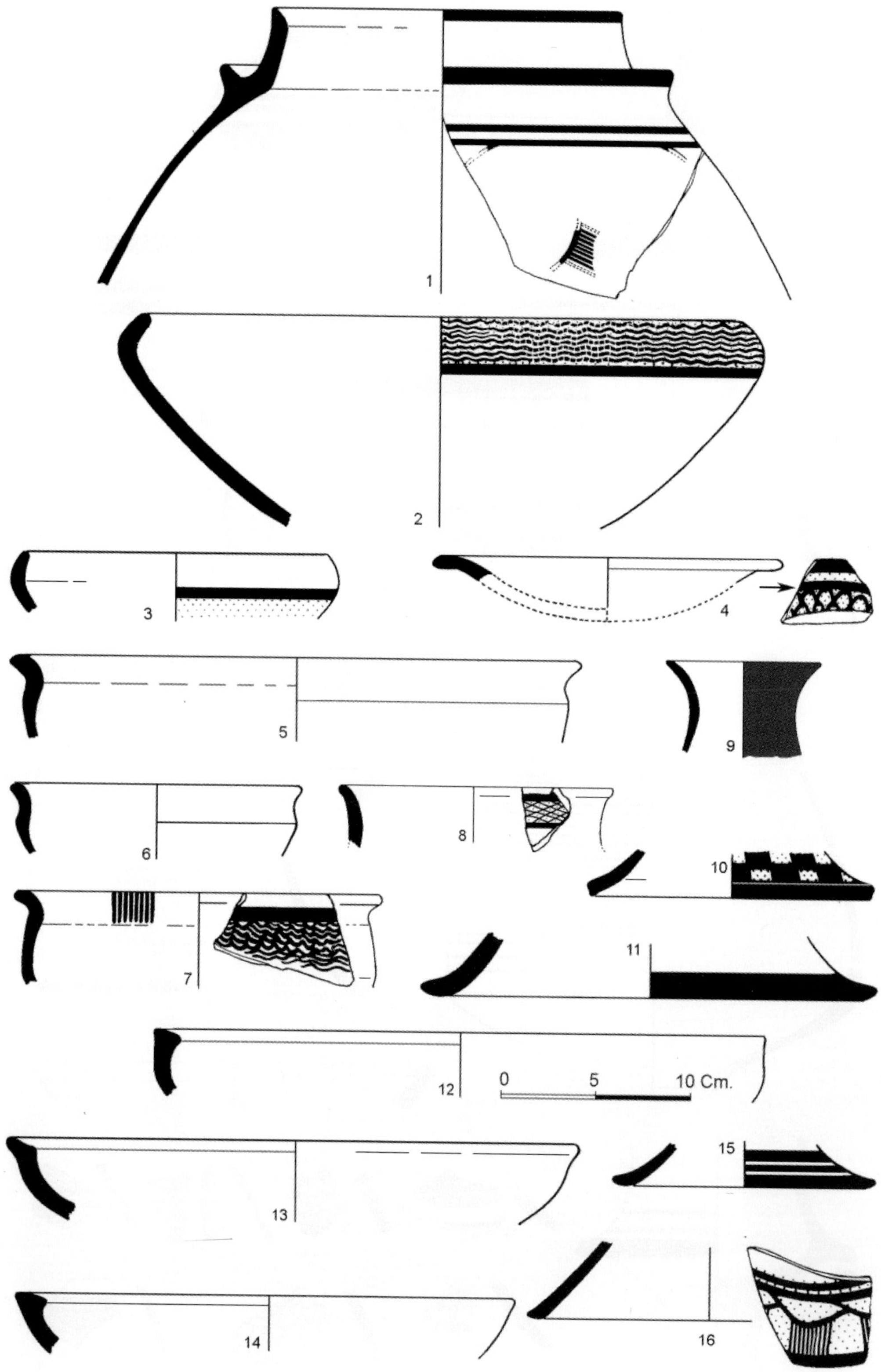

Figure 29 Motipipli, the Early Harappan (1, 3, 11-16) and Anarta pottery (2, 4-10): 1, 5, 12, 13, 16, Fine Red ware; 2, 4, 6, 10 Gritty Red ware; 3, 11, 14, 15 Buff ware (2, 4, 7, 8, 10, 16 bichrome; 3 and 14 dark brown slip)

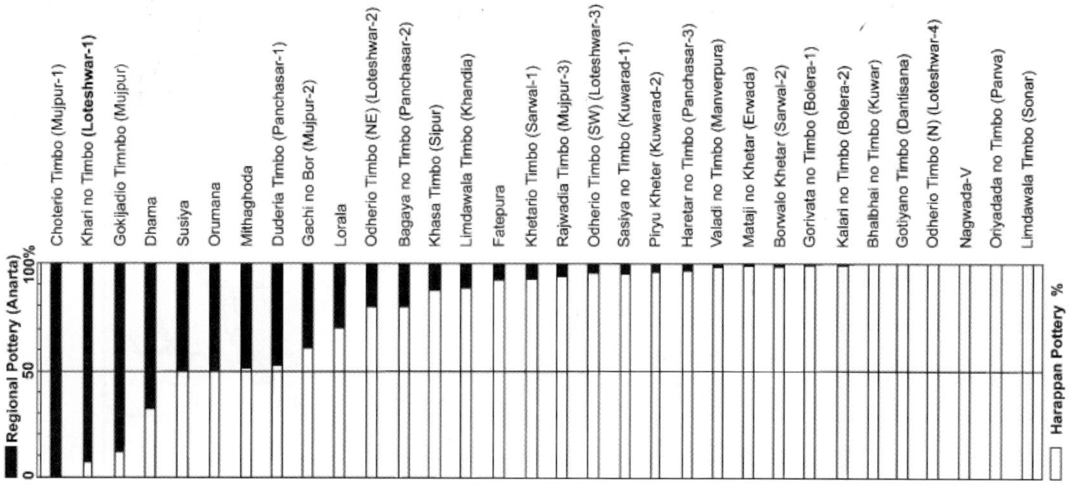

Figure 30 Relative abundance of the Anarta and the Harappan pottery in North Gujarat sites

Geographical Extension and Cultural Affiliation

In order to ascertain the regional character of the non-Harappan Anarta pottery tradition, it is also necessary to trace the geographical extension and assess their relative abundance in the Chalcolithic settlements of North Gujarat. The ceramic assemblages of 62 sites among the hundred sites so far located in this region are found to incorporate the Anarta pottery types (see Appendix). However, the relative abundance of the Anarta pottery in these assemblages varied considerably (Figure 30). The chart shows the distribution of Anarta pottery from the sites in the Rupen estuary. Sites situated further northwest in Banaskantha district were discovered later and their systematic classification is not included in the chart.

In some of the sites such as Choterio timbo and Loteshwar-I, the Anarta pottery is the most predominant pottery if not the only one. However, in the majority of sites it varied from 20 to 60% and in a few sites its presence is less than 10% of the total collection. Sites, which incorporated the Anarta pottery 10% and above are designated as affiliated to the Anarta tradition (Mahida 1992). On the basis of the above criteria two distinct cultural contexts to which the Anarta pottery is associated with can be identified: (a) independently in the Pre-Urban Harappan context and (b) affiliated to the Urban Harappan and later context which can be further classified corresponding to the fourfold Rangpur sequence of S. R.Rao (1963). The cultural affiliation and the distribution of sites in different periods of occupation are shown in the Figure 31.

In the Pre-Urban Harappan context, the Anarta pottery is found independently at least in four sites: at Loteshwar-I, Choterio timbo (Munjpur), Go-khijadio timbo (Munjpur) and at Santhli-I. The first three sites are located along the banks of the Khari stream, a small tributary of the Rupen, within a distance of one to three kilometres. Santhli-I, on the other hand, is situated about 60 km northwest of Loteshwar. Another rich assemblage of the Anarta pottery is found at Naeka, about 8 km northwest of Loteshwar. Similarly, Moti-Pipli, about 6km southwest of Santhli-I, and Santhli-II also show a large number of Anarta pottery in association with the Early Harappan Sindh related pottery which, are similar to those found in the burials at Nagwada. In the Urban Harappan and later context, the regional pottery is associated with different Phases of the Harappa culture, starting from the Mature Phase. As has been mentioned earlier, the Harappan ceramics from these sites are classified according to

Figure 31 Locations of Chalcolithic sites in North Gujarat showing their cultural affiliation

the Rangpur Period IIA, IIB, IIC and Period III (Rao 1963: 59-137) and Rojdi Period- A, B and C (Possehl and Herman 1990, Herman 1989) classification. However, it became abundantly clear in the course of the study that, an over-simplified classification of sites following the above schemes is not feasible in the case of North Gujarat, as there are many sites in this region which show the beginning of occupation during the Rangpur IIC Period and continued to be occupied during the succeeding Post-Urban Harappan Period marked by the Lustrous Red ware.

Sites affiliated to the Anarta tradition and the Mature Harappan together are few and far between in North Gujarat. Nagwada-I is the most important site of this category showing predominance of the Anarta pottery associated with all the Classical Harappan remains. Other sites like Zekhada and Nagwada-IV can also be included in this category although they incorporate only a few type-fossils of the Mature Phase. Similarly, only very few sites show the Anarta pottery affiliated with the Urban Phase Sorath Harappan pottery of the Rangpur IIB or the Rojdi A&B types (Figure 31). In many sites, the Anarta pottery is associated either with the Rangpur IIC or with the assemblages incorporating both Rangpur IIC and III Period pottery. 26 sites in the region belong to this category. And, only in 5 sites the Anarta pottery is associated with the Post-Urban Rangpur III elements. However, in these Post-Urban sites the Anarta pottery is represented by less than 10%. It is, therefore, clear that the Anarta tradition had an independent origin and existence, but became an important component in the Harappan settlements of North Gujarat during the Mature and the early phase of the Post-Urban Harappan or the so called 'Late Harappan' period. The tradition, however, started losing its ground in the Post-Urban Phase of the Harappa culture.

Settlement Pattern

Chalcolithic sites in North Gujarat are located not very far away from the eastern margin of the Little Rann of Kachchh. In fact, some of them are located on all along the edge of the Rann. Almost all of them are situated at the top of fossil sand-dunes which form gentle natural eminences in an otherwise flat landscape. In the vicinity of these Chalcolithic sites are found a number of Mesolithic sites. Sometimes, the same site was occupied successively by both the Mesolithic and the Chalcolithic communities. Close to the eastern margin of the Rann the Mesolithic sites are sparsely scattered. As one moves east towards Harij and further, the Mesolithic sites outnumber the Chalcolithic ones. It may be noted that the western alluvial plain gradually merges with the rugged and severely undulating topography further east of Harij. This eastern rugged land is more thickly vegetated than the western part and was inhabited by the Mesolithic hunter-gatherers for a long time before the Harappans came in the scene. Mesolithic sites in this area are rich in microlithic artefacts and show substantial habitation deposits. The two major excavated Mesolithic sites, Langhnaj in the southeast of Loteshwar in Mehsana district and Bagor, further northeast in southern Rajasthan, are located within this geographic context. These two sites have illustrated some good evidence of Mesolithic – Chalcolithic interaction that was going on in the region (Misra 1973, Sankalia 1965). Nevertheless, it seems the Harappan peasants had penetrated probably not much further east of Harij. It is obvious that the Mesolithic hunter-gatherers and the Harappan agriculturalists coexisted in the region exploiting the same echo-niche for a long period of time. Probably, in due course of time, these two communities may have had a symbiotic existence; details of which remains to be investigated properly (Possehl and Kennedy 1979).

A feature that is been shared by many of the Chalcolithic sites of different cultural affiliation in this region is their small size (see Appendix). Most of the sites in the region measure less than 3 hectares. Many of the sites around Loteshwar and Santhli measured around half a hectare only. In general, the size varied from a minimum of 0.02 hectare at Ghachi-no bor (Munjpur) to 7.00 hectare at Bagayano timbo (Panchasar). In fact, many of the relatively large sites like Panchasar and Fatepura show discrete clusters of artefacts, each one of which may be hardly a little more than 0.10 hectare. It is possible that such clusters of artefact concentration might have been occupational areas separated sufficiently by time. Large size therefore does not necessarily always indicate a single large settlement. Besides, none of the settlements appears to have a substantially thick habitation deposit either. The excavated sites in this region have shown a deposit varying from 0.20 m to a little more than 1.00 m. Some of the explored sites like Dhama, Nagwada-V,

Jhandada-II, Varanasri etc. (see Appendix), show only superficial deposit spreading to a small area. Such sites might have been seasonal settlements connected with the pastoral and agricultural activities of the Chalcolithic community.

The surface assemblages from North Gujarat sites do not reveal much evidence of structural remains or the type of dwelling structures built by the early Chalcolithic community. However, excavations at Nagwada, Loteshwar and Santhli have revealed a few tangible remains of the dwelling structures of the community. Structures in the Mature Harappan Phase at Nagwada were built of rubble stones and moulded mud-bricks. Remains of post-holes unearthed in the excavation would also suggest the presence of wattle and daub structures in the early stages of habitation at the site. Remains of clay plaster with reed impressions, probably used for plastering the structures of wattle and daub, belonging to the Anarta pottery tradition prior to the Urban Harappa culture have been excavated from Loteshwar and Santhli. Some of the dark and dense mud-walls and rubble stone structural remains unearthed from Nagwada (Hedge *et al.* 1988) may also belong to this tradition. Remains of similar wattle and daub circular structures are found at Zekhada (IAR 1977-78, Momin 1983) in the Mature/ Urban Harappan Phase and at Ratanpura (IAR 1984-85, Bhan 1989) in the Post-Urban Phase, suggesting a long surviving tradition of circular huts.

Another important feature related to the distribution of the sites is their location close to the landforms which are designated as 'salty waste'. These are slightly low-lying, flat wastelands which are generally marshy throughout the year and partially covered with a salt efflorescence with the onset of summer. Although they are unsuitable for agriculture, contiguous land around such depressions forms good pastoral land for cattle and sheep, as they support many types of edible grass. Fringes of these salty wastes are generally found occupied by Chalcolithic settlements. Sites around such depressions in the middle course of the Rupen river and near Vaghel show a close clustering during different periods of Chalcolithic occupation (Figure 31). Clustering of sites could also be seen around Korda and Jhandada, on either side of a very large natural depression locally known as Sandher. Besides these, a similar pattern of site dstribution is observed in the margins of the eastward extension of the depression which connects the Great and the Little Rann. It should also be noted that many of these depressions retain potable water till the months of December and January and become brackish only with the onset of summer. In the light of considerable silting that had been happening in many of the rivers in the region, it is also possible that these depressions might have been a little more deep and retained potable water a little longer than today during the 4th and 3rd millennium BCE.

Agricultural and cattle breeding must have been the two important components of the subsistence activity of the Chalcolithic community in the region. Nevertheless, none of the sites in the region have yielded direct evidence of grain cultivation. The large faunal collection from the sites included skeletal remains of wild animals like gazelle (*Gazalla sp.*), blackbuck (*Antelope sp.*), sambar (*Cervus sp.*), nilgai (*Boselaphas tragocamelus*), chital (*Axis axix*), wild boar (*Sus scrofa*) etc. associated with the remains of the domesticated cattle (*Bos indicus*), sheep (*Ovis sp.*) and goat (*Capra sp.*). It also included the remains of aquatic fauna like fish and turtle. A large collection of cattle and sheep/goat bones recovered from the excavated and explored sites may indicate the importance of these animals in the economy of the Chalcolithic settlements in this region. Cattle bones constituted about 70% followed by sheep/goat bones represented by 20% of the total collection from different sites in the region (Patel 1989, Pratapachandran 1984, Subbarao 1984, Battacharya 1981). Besides the natural grass, to a certain extent, cattle population is known to depend on the by-products of agricultural production. In fact, even at present, pastoralism is an important occupation of a section of the agrarian population in North Gujarat.

The surface spread of the artefacts, the thickness of habitation deposit and the presence of durable structures are considered indices of the size, intensity and duration of occupation at a site, apart from its economic status. The habitation features of North Gujarat sites do not indicate the presence of a large site in the region; nor do they indicate prolonged occupation at any of the sites. The features, in fact, indicate that almost all the sites were dependent on subsistence farming and stock raising rather than a surplus economy. In a region that had been continuously fraught with poor soil and low rainfall, development of large settlements based on surplus agricultural products would have been difficult, unless they depend on production of some such industrial craft products that can be traded and exchanged far and wide, which would have brought in the necessary economic stability. Incidentally, Nagwada was a rural centre for the production of semiprecious stone beads, steatite beads and shell ornaments during the Mature Phase of the Harappa culture (Hegde *et al.* 1988). Consequently, the economic stability and wellbeing of the settlement are reflected on the large structures of both mud-bricks and rubble stones unearthed at the site.

It can be summarized that, the economic activities of the Chalcolithic peasant communities of North Gujarat had been delimited by severe geographical and environmental constraints. The nature and distribution pattern of the sites in the region may therefore, be viewed as a reflection of the strategies adopted to overcome these constraints. It appears that the prolonged occupation at a site was influenced by at least three major factors: (a) easy access to constant source of potable water, (b) a good, fertile agricultural field around the settlements and (c) the presence of good grasslands for livestock rising. A negative shift in any one of these factors would have adversely affected the economic equilibrium resulting into either abandoning the site or shifting off a part of the population into a more favourable location as it happens today.

Summary

The picture that emerges from the foregoing is that there seems to be two groups of pottery either associated with or affiliated to the Harappa culture in North Gujarat. These two are represented by (a) the Anarta group of pottery and (b) the Early Harappan group of pottery primarily confined to the burials. Both of these had an existence prior to the beginning of the Urban Harappa culture in the region and dated to a period at the very beginning of or even earlier than the 3rd millennium BCE. The burial pottery has a limited distribution and their origin can be traced into the Pre-Urban/Early Harappan cultures of Sindh and Balochistan. However, the mechanism of their expansion into Gujarat has not been satisfactorily explained. A study of this burial pottery together with the skeletal features of the human beings represented in the burials is expected to throw much light on the social structure of the Harappan Chalcolithic community in Gujarat.

The Anarta pottery tradition, on the other hand, is more widely spread both in time and space. Although a remote generic resemblance with certain features of the Pre-Urban Harappan pottery traditions of Sindh and Rajasthan has been alluded to, nothing concrete can be said about its origin. The pottery had an independent existence in North Gujarat prior to the beginning of Urban Harappa culture. A few more regional Pre-Urban Harappan ceramic traditions contemporary to the Anarta have been reported from Prabhas Patan and Padri in the Saurashtra coast. It can, therefore, be suggested that different regional ceramic traditions, like the Anarta tradition along with the Pre-Prabhas and the Padri assemblage, formed part of the Pre-Urban Harappan cultural mosaic during the fourth and the early third millennium BCE in Western India. Rooted firmly in North Gujarat, the Anarta pottery tradition constitutes an important socio-economic group in the integrated Harappan society during the Mature and the later Phase of the Harappa culture in Gujarat. The tradition, however, asserts itself only when the strong urban ethos of the Harappa culture started declining towards the end of the Mature/Urban Phase, and during the period that immediately followed the Mature Harappan.

Acknowledgements

A short form of this paper was originally presented in a seminar on Gujarat Harappans held at Deccan College, Pune, in 1993 and was subsequently submitted for publication. For reasons beyond the control of the authors the paper however remained unpublished since then. Our understanding of the Harappan/Chalcolithic cultural scene in Gujarat has undergone dramatic changes since then with several new excavations. The new studies have in fact validated the core ideas expressed in the paper. The paper is updated by adding new data and references. The authors are thankful to Professor T. Osada and other members of the Indus Project of the Research Institute for Humanity and Nature, Kyoto, Japan, for their continued cooperation for the Harappan research in Gujarat. The primary data presented here are collected in a series of exploratory surveys and excavations carried in North Gujarat in the late 1980's and early 1990's. The authors have received help and support from several colleagues in the Department of Archaeology and the Archaeological Survey of India (ASI) – Prof. V.S. Parekh, Prof. K.K Bhan, Prof. K. Krishnan and Prakash Chaudary, and Dr. R. S. Bisht, former Joint Director General (ASI), New Delhi – at different stages of the study. We are thankful to Miss. Bhamini Mahida, currently Curator at the Surat Museum, Gujarat, for classification of the ceramic collection from North Gujarat sites.

The archaeological research in North Gujarat leading to this paper was supported by the Ford Foundation through a Research Grant to the Department of Archaeology, the M.S. University of Baroda. Thanks are also due to the "Indus Project" of the RIHN, Kyoto, Japan for providing financial support for resurveying the sites and updating the list of sites by correcting the geo-coordinates recorded by GPS.

Notes

1) Recent excavations at Bagasra (Sonawane *et al.* 2003) in the northeastern tip of Saurashtra in Rajkot district and Kanmer (Kharakwal *et al.* 2008) and the ongoing M.S. University excavations at Shikarpur in the eastern margin of Kachchh district bordering North Gujarat have also revealed the Anarta pottery from the early layers onwards showing a wider geographical extension of the tradition than what had earlier been thought of.
2) Potteries quite similar to the Anarta pottery are reported in the recent studies from Baror in Rajasthan (Urmila *et al.* 2005), and Bhirrana (Rao *et al.* 2005) and Girawad (Shinde *et al.* 2008) in Haryana. Certain amount of similarity in the scheme and pattern of paintings and the choice of colours with the Anarta pottery are apparent in the Ravi Phase pottery reported from the excavations at Harappa (Kenoyer and Meadow 2000). These would confirm our position that the Pre-Urban Harappan societies of North Gujarat and that of the Indus and the Ghaggar – Sarasvati basins had several shared and common cultural traits reflected in their material remains.
3) A series of subsequent AMS estimation of samples collected from the Mesolithic and the Chalcolithic levels at the site has confirmed the 3600 BCE date of Anarta Chalcolithic. The new series of dates has shown that the beginning of Mesolithic at the site goes back to 7000 BCE (Patel 2008). This is one of the earliest dates for Mesolithic occupation in Western India. See Patel A.K (2008, 2009) for detailed discussion on dating and related issues regarding the Mesolithic and Chalcolithic habitation remains at Loteshwar.

4) Systematic study of the faunal remains from the site recently has brought to light the importance of faunal collection from the site in understanding the beginning of farming communities in region. Specially, important are the presence of a few wild cattle bones in the Mesolithic strata followed by the domesticated cattle bones in the Chalcolithic layers. The study has argued that North Gujarat is a potential region for investigating localized beginning of cattle pastoralism (Patel 2009). The high abundance of blackbuck bones in the Mesolithic fauna would suggest a preference for hunting this animal.And, this should be seen as an adaptive strategy of the Mesolithic hunter-gatherers in articulation with expanding food base during the early half of the Holocene. In the light of all these, it is necessary to investigate different modules of environmental resource management by the Mesolithic hunter-gatherers that would allow expansion of resource base for intensive food gathering and eventually the emergence of farming in the region.

References

Ajithprasad, P. (2002) 'The Pre-Harappan Cultures of Gujarat', in S. Settar and Ravi Korisettar (eds.) *Indian Archaeology in Retrospect Vol. II Protohistory: Archaeology of the Harappan Civilization.* ICHR and Manohar, New Delhi, pp. 129-158.

Bhan, K.K. (1989) 'Late Harappan Settlements of Western India, with Specific Reference to Gujarat', in J.M. Kenoyer (ed.) *Old Problems and New Perspectives in the Archaeology of South Asia.* Wisconsin Archaeological Report 2: 219-242.

Bhan, K.K. (1994) 'Cultural development of the Prehistoric period in North Gujarat with reference to Western India', *South Asian Studies* 10: 71-90.

Bhattacharya, Bandana (1981) Animal Remains from Zekhada. M.A. Dissertation, Department of Archaeology, M.S. University of Baroda.

Bisht, R.S. (1991) 'Dholavira: A New horizon of the Indus Civilization', *Puratattva* 20: 71-82.

Bisht, R.S. (1994) Urban Planning at Dholavira: A Harappan City. Unpublished paper presented at the seminar on "*The City and the Stars: Cosmic Urban Geometries of India*" at Indira Gandhi National Centre for the Arts. New Delhi

Choksi, Archana (1995) 'Ceramic Vessels: Their Role in Illuminating Past and Present Social and Economic Relationships', *Man and Environment* 20(1): 87-108.

Casal, J.M. (1964) *Fouilles D'Amri* 2 Vol. Paris. De La Commission des Fouilles Archaeologique, Fouilles de Pakistan: Figures 38, 39, 62.

Dalal, Katy Feroze (1980) 'A short history of archaeological exploration in Bikaner and Bahawalpur along the 'lost' Sarasvati River', *Indica* 17(1): 3-40.

Dalal, Katy Feroze (1981) 'RD 89: A new Hakra Ware site?', *Man and Environment* 5: 77-86.

Dalal, Katy Feroze (1987) 'Binjor l: A Pre-Harappan site on the Indo-Pak border', in B.M. Pande and B.D. Chattopadhyaya (eds.) *Archaeology and History: Essays in memory of S. A. Ghosh.* 2 Vols., Agam Kala Prakashan, Delhi. pp. 75-111.

Dales, G.F. (1974) 'Excavations at Balakot, Pakistan 1973', *Journal of Field Archaeology* 1: 3-22, Figure 8.

Dikshit, M.G. (1950) 'Excavations at Rangpur, 1947', *Bulletin of the Deccan College Research Institute, Pune.* XI: 3-55.

Franke-Vogt, Ute (1997) 'Reopening Research on Balakot: A summary of Perspectives and First Results', in Raymond Allchin and Bridget Allchin (eds.) *South Asian Archaeology 1995.* Proceedings of the 13th Conference of the European Association of South Asian Archaeologists, Cambridge, 5-9 July, 1995. pp. 217 – 237.

Ghurye, G.S. (1939) 'Two sites in Kathiawar', *Journal of the University of Bombay* 8(1): 3-12.

Hegde, K.T.M. and V.H. Sonawane (1986) 'Landscape and Settlement Pattern of the Harappa Culture Villages in the Rupen Estuary', *Man and Environment* X: 23-31.

Hegde, K.T.M., V.H.Sonawane, D.R.Shah, K.K.Bhan, P.Ajithprasad, K. Krishnan, and S. Pratapachandran (1988) 'Excavations at Nagwada-1986 & 1987: A Preliminary Report', *Man and Environment* XII: 55-

65.

Herman, C.F. (1989) 'Rojdi material culture: The Sorath Harappan Ceramics Harappan', in G.L. Possehl and M.H. Raval (eds.) *Civilization and Rojdi*. Oxford and IBH Publishing Co. New Delhi. pp. 53-140.

IAR (*Indian Archaeology A Review: Annual Report of the Archaeological Survey of India*). 1977-78:20-21; 1978-79:6-7; 1982-83:28; 1984-85:17-19; 1987-88:19-20; 1988-89:13-17; 1992-93:15-19; 1993-94:25-27; 1994-95:11-18.

Joshi, J.P. (1972) 'Exploration in Kutch and Excavation at Surkotada and New Light on Harappan Migration', *Journal of the Oriental Institute, M.S.U. Baroda* 22: 98-144.

Joshi, J.P. (1990) 'Excavations at Surkotada 1971-72 and Exploration in Kutch', *Memoirs of the Archaeological Survey of India* 87: 363-371.

Kenoyer, J.M. and R.H. Meadow (2000) 'The Ravi Phase: a New Cultural Manifestation at Harappa', in M. Taddei and G. De Marco (eds.) *South Asian Archaeology 1997* Vol. 1. Rome. pp. 55-76.

Khan, A.R. (1965) 'Excavations at Kot Diji', *Pakistan Archaeology* 2: 11-85, Figure 76-77.

Kharakwal, J.S., Y. S. Rawat, and T. Osada (2008) 'Preliminary Observations on the Excavations at Kanmer, Kachchh, India 2006-2007', in T. Osada and A. Uesugi (eds.) *Linguistics,Archaeology and the Human Past. Occasional Papers* 5. Indus Project, Research Institute for Humanity and Nature, Kyoto. pp 5-23.

Lal, B.B. (1979) 'Kalibangan and Indus Civilization', in D.P. Agrawal and D.K. Chakrabarti (eds.) *Essays in Indian Protohistory*. ISPQS History and Archaeology Series 5: 65-97.

Mackay, E.J.H. (1931) *Mohenjo daro and the Indus Civilization.* Vol. I. in John Marshall (ed.) Arthur Probsthain, London.

Mackay, E.J.H. (1938) *Further Excavations at Mohenjo daro* Vol. I. Delhi: 175-256.

Mackay, E.J.H. (1943) *Chanhudaro Excavations 1935-36.* Bharatiya Publishers, Delhi (reprint 1976). pp. 65-103.

Mahida, Bhamini (1992) Chalcolithic settlements of North Gujarat: A Study of Regional Tradition in the Rupen Estuary. M. A Dissertation, Department of Archaeology, The M.S. University of Baroda.

Majmudar, M.R. (1960) Historical and Cultural Chronology of Gujarat. The M. S. University Oriental Institute Publication, Baroda: (Preface XVII).

Majumdar, A. (2001) 'Emergence of the Early Harappans in North Gujarat', *Man and Environment* 26: 23-38.

Majumdar, A and V.H. Sonawane (1996-97) 'Pre-Harappan Burial Pottery from Moti-Pipli: A New Dimension in the Cultural Assemblage of North Gujarat', *Pragdhara* 7: 11-17.

Mehta, R.N. 1982) 'Some Rural Harappan Settlements in Gujarat', in G L Possehl (ed.) *Harappan Civilization: A Contemporary Perspective*. Oxford Press, New Delhi. pp. 167-174.

Misra V.N. (1973) 'Bagor - a Late Mesolithic settlement in North-West India', *World Archaeology* 5: 92-110.

Misra V.N. (2005) 'Radiocarbon chronology of Balathal, District Udaipur, Rajasthan', *Man and Environment* 30(1): 54-60.

Momin, K. N. (1983) 'Excavation at Zekhada', *Puratattva* 12: 120-125.

Mughal, M. R. (1974) 'New Evidence of the Early Harappan Culture from Jalilpur, Pakistan', *Archaeology* 27 (2): 106-113.

Patel, A.K. (1989) Vertebrate Archaeofauna from Nagwada: A Preliminary Report. M.A. Dissertation, Department of Archaeology, The M.S. University of Baroda.

Patel, A.K. (2008) 'New Radiocarbon Determinations from Loteshwar and their Implications for Understanding Holocene Settlement and Subsistence in North Gujarat and Adjoining Areas', in Ellen M. Raven (ed.) *South Asian Archaeology 1999*. Proceedings of the Fifteenth International Conference of the European Association of South Asian Archaeologists, the Universiteit Leiden, 5-9 July, 1999. pp. 123-134.

Patel, A.K. (20099 'Occupational Histories, Settlements, and Subsistence in Western India: What Bones and Genes can tell us about the Origins and Spread of

Pastoralism', *Anthropozoologica* 44(1): 173-188.

Piggott, Stuart (1952) *Prehistoric India*. Penguin Books, Hammondsworth.

Possehl, G. L. (1994) *Radiometric Dates for South Asian Archaeology* (compiled by G.L. Possehl). An Occasional Publication of the Asia Section. University of Pennsylvania Museum of Archaeology and Anthropology.

Possehl, G. L. (2006) 'The Harappan Settlements in Gujarat', in E.C. Stone (ed.) *Settlement and Society: Essays dedicated to Robert McCormick Adams*. Cotsen Institute of Archaeology, Los Angeles. pp. 297-328.

Possehl, G.L. and C.F. Herman (1990) 'The Sorath Harappan: A new Regional Manifestation of the Indus Urban Phase', Maurizio Taddei (ed.) *South Asian Archaeology 1987*. Naples: Instituto Universitario Orientale di Studi Asiatica. pp. 295-321.

Possehl, G. L and K. A.R. Kennedy (1979) 'Hunter-Gatherer/ Agriculturalist Exchange in Prehistory: An Indian Example', *Current Anthropology* Vol. 20(3): 592-593.

Possehl, G.L. and M.H. Raval (1989) *Harappan Civilization and Rojdi*. Oxford and IBH Publishing Co. New Delhi.

Pratapachandran, S. (1984) Archaeology of Panchasar. M.A. Dissertation, Department of Archaeology, The M. S. University of Baroda.

Rao, L.S., Nandini B. Sahu, Parvas Sahu, Samir Diwan, and U.A. Shastry (2005) 'New Light on the Excavation of Harappan settlement at Bhirrana', *Puratattva* 35: 60 -68.

Rao, S.R. (1963) 'Excavations at Rangpur and other Explorations in Gujarat', *Ancient India* 18-19: 5-207.

Rao, S.R. (1985) 'Lothal: A Harappan Port Town 1955-62', *Memoirs of the Archaeological Survey of India* No 78, Vol. II: 393-407.

Sankalia, H.D. (1965) *Excavations at Langhnaj: 1944-63, Part I. Archaeology*. Deccan College Postgraduate and Research Institute, Poona.

Shinde, V and S.B. Kar (1992) 'Padri Ware: A New Painted Ceramic Found in the Harappan Levels at Padri in Gujarat', *Man and Environment* XVII (2): 105-110.

Shinde, V., S.S. Despande and Y. Yasuda (2004) 'Human response to Holocene climatic change: A case study of western India between 5th and 3rd millennia BC', in Y. Yasuda and V. Shinde (eds.) *Monsoon and Civilization*. International Research Center for Japanese Studies. Lustre Press; Roli Books, New Delhi. pp. 383-406.

Shinde, V., T. Osada, M.M. Sharma, A. Uesugi, T. Uno, H. Maemoku, P. Shirvalkar, S.S. Despande, A. Kulkarni, A. Sarkar, A. Reddy, V. Rao and V. Dangi (2008) 'Excavation at Girawad' in T. Osada and A. Uesugi (eds.) *Exploration in the Ghaggar Basin and Excavations at Girawad, Fermana (Rothak dist.), and Mitathal (Bhiwani dist.) Hariyana, India, Occasional Paper* 3. Research Institute for Humanity and Nature, Kyoto, Japan. pp. 95-131.

Sonawane, V.H., P. Ajithprasad, K.K. Bhan, K. Krishnan, S. Pratapachandran, A. Majumdar, A.K. Patel and J. Menon (2004) 'Excavations at Bagasra 1996-2003: A Preliminary Report', *Man and Environment* XXXIII (2): 21-50.

Sonawane, V.H. and P. Ajithprasad (1994) 'Harappa Culture and Gujarat', *Man and Environment* XIX (1-2): 129-139.

Subbarao, K.V. (1984) Archaeology of Bolera. unpublished M.A. Dissertation, Department of Archaeology, The M.S. University of Baroda.

Urmila Sant, T.J. Baidya, N.G. Nikoshey, N.K. Sinha, S. Nayan, J.K. Tiwari and J. Arif. (2005) 'Baror – A new Harappan Site in Ghaggar Valley – A Preliminary Report', *Puratattva* 35: 50-59.

Vats, M.S. (1935) 'Trial Excavations at Rangpur, Limdi state, Kathiawar', *Annual Report of the Archaeological Survey of India* 1934-35: 348.

Wheeler, R.E.M. (1947) 'Harappa 1946: The Defense and Cemetery R-37', *Ancient India* 3: 59-130.

Wheeler, R.E.M. (1960) *The Indus Civilization*. (second edition) Cambridge University Press, Cambridge.

Appendix: List of Chalcolithic/Harappan Sites in North Gujarat[1]

No.	Site Name[2]	Coordinates	Viillage	Taluka, District	Size (m) Ha.	Period/Culture	Bibliography, Source
1	GenghdaThumdo	23°49'35.1"N 71°21'28.6"E	Bambnoli	Santalpur, Patan	30×20 0.06	Anarta[3], RGP[4] IIC	IAR 1992-93: 23, Ajithprasad and Sonawane (site list 1993)
2	Ori no Thumdo	23°50'04.2"N 71°07'55.6"E	Barara	Santalpur, Patan	70×60 0.42	Anarta, RGP IIC, RGP III / LRW[5]	IAR 1992-93: 25, Ajithprasad and Sonawane (site list 1993)
3	Gorivatano Timbo (Bolera-I)	23°29'14.8"N 71°45'54.0"E	Bolera	Sami, Patan	80×80 0.64	RGP IIC, RGP III / LRW, BRW[6]	IAR 1982-83: 28, Hegde and Sonawane 1986: 30
4	Kalari no Timbo (Bolera-II)	23°30'21.2"N 71°45'43.4"E	Bolera	Sami, Patan	135×100 1.35	RGP IIC, RGP III / LRW	IAR 1982-83: 28, Hegde and Sonawane 1986:30, Bhan 1994:86-7
5	Chaniyathar no Thumdo (Thunda Timbo)	23°43'49.9"N 71°31'01.0"E	Chaniyathar	Radhanpur, Patan	120×105 1.26	RGP IIC, RGP III / LRW	IAR 1991-92: 19, Bhan 1994: 86-7, Ajithprasad and Sonawane (site list 1993)
6	Garasyano Thumdo (Charandha-I)	24°00'38.4"N 71°29'45.7"E	Charandha	Santalpur, Patan	40×30 0.01	RGP IIB, RGP IIC	IAR 1992-93: 23, Ajithprasad and Sonawane (site list 1993)
7	KanakrialoThumdo (Charandha-II)	24°01'09.3"N 71°28'48.6"E	Charandha	Santalpur, Patan	60×50 0.30	Anarta, RGP IIB, RGP IIC	IAR 1992-93: 24, Ajithprasad and Sonawane (site list 1993)
8	Chipa no Godh (Chhanasara-I)	23°45'20.2"N 71°16'30.0"E	Chhanasara	Santalpur, Patan	120×100 1.20	RGP IIC, RGP III / LRW	IAR 1992-93: 22, Ajithprasad and Sonawane (site list 1993)
9	Ishwar ghod (Chahanasara-II)	23°45'56.4"N 71°16'45.2"E	Chhanasara	Santalpur, Patan	30×30 0.09	RGP IIC	IAR 1992-93: 23, Ajithprasad and Sonawane (site list 1993)
10	Godha	23°40'44.6"N 71°35'50.4"E	Dadka	Sami, Patan	55×67 0.37	RGP III / LRW	IAR 1991-92: 19, Bhan 1994: 86-7, Ajithprasad and Sonawane (site list 1993)
11	Vokda-no Thumdo	23°50'20.4"N 71°19'27.6"E	Daldi	Santalpur, Patan	50×40 0.20	Anarta, RGP IIB, RGP IIC	IAR 1992-93: 26, Ajithprasad and Sonawane (site list 1993)
12	Godhiyano Timbo	23°30'10"N 71°53'30"E	Dantisana	Sami, Patan	100×100 1.00	RGP III / LRW	Hegde and Sonawane 1986: 30, Ajithprasad and Sonawane (site list 1993)
13	Datrana IX (Randia no Thumdo)	23°47'03.6"N 71°08'08.7"E	Datrana	Santalpur, Patan	9×6 0.005	RGP IIC	IAR 1994-95: 18
14	Datrana X (Vanta no Thumdo)	23°45'46.0"N 71°06'28.5"E	Datrana	Santalpur, Patan	22×17 0.038	Anarta, RGP IIB, RGP IIC	IAR 1994-95: 18
15	Datrana-I (Ghorapir nu Khetar)	23°46'48.2"N 71°07'53.4"E	Datrana	Santalpur, Patan	90×70 0.63	RGP IIC, RGP III / LRW	IAR 1992-93: 22, Ajithprasad and Sonawane (site list 1993)

Notes

1) The list was originally compiled in 1993 and was updated periodically as and when new sites were located in subsequent surveys. In March 2011 we completed a resurvey of North Gujarat Harappan sites in collaboration with the "Indus Project" of the Research Institute for Humanity and Nature, Kyoto, Japan; and were able to revisit most of the sites and record their correct geo-coordinates using GPS. The site list refers corrected GPS co-ordinates, except for a few sites which we were not able to trace.We have also tried to avoid repetition of same site in different names in the list, as it often happens due to variations in recording vernacular names by different researchers, by cross checking with published and unpublished records available to us. The list is sorted in the ascending order of village names rather than the site names. We think this would enable readers to quickly refer the number and types of sites that are found in and around a village.2) Names in parenthesis are additional/alternate names of the same site.

3) Anarta refers to the Anarta pottery tradition of North Gujarat.

4) RGP IIB, RGP IIC and RGP III refer to the Rangpur Period IIB, Period IIC and Period III respectively of the Rangpur sequence.

5) LRW refers to the Lustrous Red ware pottery.

6) BRW refers to the Black and Red ware pottery.

No.	Site Name	Coordinates	Viillage	Taluka, District	Size (m) Ha.	Period/Culture	Bibliography, Source
16	Datrana-II (Haren Thumdo, Ravaichi mata)	23°46'52.4"N 71°07'33.5"E	Datrana	Santalpur, Patan	80×70 0.56	RGP IIC, RGP III / LRW, Microliths[7]	IAR 1992-93: 23, Ajithprasad and Sonawane (site list 1993) Excavation in 1995
17	Datrana-III	23°46'51.6"N 71°07'55.9"E	Datrana	Santalpur, Patan	20×20 0.04	RGP IIC, RGP III / LRW, Microliths	IAR 1992-93: 22, Ajithprasad and Sonawane (site list 1993)
18	Datrana-IV (Hadkawala Timbo, Vadkiwalu khetar-II)	23°46'14.7"N 71°07'26.2"E	Datrana	Santalpur, Patan	700×500 35.00	Mesolithic[8]/ microliths, Anarta, Early Harappan[9], Pre-Prabhas	IAR 1992-93: 26, Ajithprasad and Sonawane (site list 1993) Excavtion in 1994, 1995, 2010
19	Datrana-V (Patel no Khetar, Vadkiwalu khetar-I)	23°46'12.6"N 71°07'25.5"E	Datrana	Santalpur, Patan	100×70 0.70	Mesolithic / microliths, Anarta, Pre Prahbas	IAR 1992-93: 26, Ajithprasad and Sonawane (site list 1993); Excavation in 1995
20	Datrana-VI	23°46'50.5"N 71°07'55.9"E	Datrana	Santalpur, Patan	15×10 0.02	Anarta, RGP IIC, Microliths,	IAR 1992-93: 22, Ajithprasad and Sonawane (site list 1993)
21	Datrana-VII	23°46'52.1"N 71°07'55.8"E	Datrana	Santalpur, Patan	20×15 0.30	Anarta, RGP IIB, RGP IIC	IAR 1992-93: 23, Ajithprasad and Sonawane (site list 1993)
22	Datrana-VIII	23°46'51.7"N 71°07'57.6"E	Datrana	Santalpur, Patan	40×30 0.12	Mesolithic / microliths, RGP IIC, RGP III	IAR 1992-93: 23, Ajithprasad and Sonawane (site list 1993)
23	Datrana IX (Sutaria no Thumdo)	23°45'59.6"N 71°07'21.5"E	Datrana	Santalpur, Patan	95×65 0.62	Early Harappan, Pre-Prabhas	Survey 2010 (NoGAP)
24	Ganario no Thumdo (Dehisar-I)	23°55'31.6"N 71°30'23.5"E	Dehisar	Santalpur, Patan	60×40 0.24	Mesolithic / microliths, Anarta	IAR 1992-93: 26, Ajithprasad and Sonawane (site list 1993)
25	Haiduk no Thumdo (Dehisar-II)	23°55'20"N 71°30'20"E	Dehisar	Santalpur, Patan	60×40 0.24	RGP III / LRW	IAR 1993-94: 32,
26	Dhama-ni Timbo	23°23'56.8"N 71°39'33.9"E	Dhama	Dasada, Surendranagar	10×10 0.01	Anarta, RGP IIC, BRW, Microliths	Bhan 1994: 86-7, Ajithprasad and Sonawane (site list 1993)
27	Dhanora Timbo (Deriwalu Khetar -I)	23°30'24.7"N 71°55'28.8"E	Dhanora	Dasada, Surendranagar	85×65 0.55	RGP IIC, RGPIII, BRW, Microliths	Hegde and Sonawane 1986: 30, Ajithprasad and Sonawane (site list 1993)
28	Kachha no Timbo	23°59'05.4"N 71°20'17.6"E	Dudasan	Vav, Banaskantha	10×10 0.01	RGP IIC, RGP III / LRW	IAR 1992-93: 24, Ajithprasad and Sonawane (site list 1993)
29	Sai Timbo	23°37'59.1"N 71°41'09.3"E	Dudkha	Sami, Patan	150×100 1.50	Anarta, RGP IIB, RGP IIC, RGP III / LRW	IAR 1978-79: 6-7, Bhan 1994: 86-7, Ajithprasad and Sonawane (site list 1993)
30	Janoyano Timbo (Erwada-I)	23°25'31.1"N 71°51'37.9"E	Erwada	Dasada, Surendranagar	80×60 0.48	Mesolithic / microliths, RGP III / LRW	IAR 1982-83: 28, Hegde and Sonawane 1986:31, Bhan 1994: 86-7, Ajithprasad and Sonawane (site list 1993)
31	Mataji-no Timbo (Erwada-II)	23°25'35"N 71°51'50"E	Erwada	Dasada, Surendranagar	100×100 1.00	RGP III / LRW, BRW	IAR 1982 83, Hegde and Sonawane 1986: 31, Bhan 1994: 86-7
32	Ranol-no Tekro (Ranolno Ghod)	23°23'49.9"N 71°38'37.1"E	Fatepura	Dasada, Surendranagar	200×200 4.00	Anarta, RGP IIB, RGP IIC	IAR 1984-85:19, Bhan 1994: 86-7, Ajithprasad and Sonawane (site list 1993)
33	Kachha no Thumdo	23°53'08.3"N 71°24'41.4"E	Gadha	Santalpur, Patan	10×10 0.01	RGP IIC, RGP III / LRW	IAR 1992-93: 24, Ajithprasad and Sonawane (site List 1993)
34	Timbo-I (Godhana-I)	23°42'56.7"N 71°36'34.0"E	Godhana	Sami, Patan	93×77 0.72	RGP IIC, RGP III / LRW	IAR 1991-92: 19, Bhan 1994: 86-87, Ajithprasad and Sonawane (site list 1993)
35	Timbo-II (Godhana-II)	23°43'05.2"N 71°36'41.9"E	Godhana	Sami, Patan	93×68 0.63	RGP III / LRW	IAR 1991-92: 20, Bhan 1994: 86-87,Ajithprasad and Sonawane (site list 1993)
36	Inderwa no Timbo-I (Inderwa-I)	24°00'20.0"N 71°29'30.4"E	Inderwa	Bhabhar, Banaskantha	80×50 0.40	RGP IIC, RGP III / LRW	IAR 1992-93: 19, Ajithprasad and Sonawane (site list 1993)
37	Inderwa no Timbo-II (Inderwa-II)	24°00'10.0"N 71°29'11.2"E	Inderwa	Bhabhar, Banaskantha	50×30 0.15	Mesolithic / microliths, RGP IIC	IAR 1992-93: 19, Ajithprasad and Sonawane (site list 1993)
38	Indranagar no Thumdo	23°54'38.3"N 71°34'48.8"E	Indranagar	Radhanpur, Patan	20×10 0.02	RGP IIB, RGP IIC	IAR 1993-94: 32, Ajithprasad and Sonawane (site list 1993)
39	Sankatrawalo Thumdo	23°53'45.6"N 71°19'53.4"E	Jamwada	Santalpur, Patan	60×50 0.30	Anarta, RGP IIB, RGP IIC	IAR 1992-93: 25, Ajithprasad and Sonawane (site list 1993)
40	Javantri	23°54'30"N 71°33'30"E	Javantri	Radhanpur, Patan	20×10 0.20	Anarta, RGP IIC	IAR 1993-94: 32, Ajithprasad and Sonawane (site list 1993)

7) Microliths at the end of the sequence refers to the micro-blade artefacts found with Chalcolithic remains.

8) Mesolithic/microliths in the beginning of the sequence refer to the possible Mesolithic substratum at the site.

9) Early Harappan refer to the Early Harappan Sindh type pottery reported from the burials at Nagwada and Santhli.

No.	Site Name	Coordinates	Viillage	Taluka, District	Size (m) Ha.	Period/Culture	Bibliography, Source
41	Soont no Timbo	23°56'12.1"N 71°19'37.1"E	Jhajham	Santalpur, Patan	20×15 0.30	Anarta, RGP IIC	IAR 1992-93: 25, Ajithprasad and Sonawane (site list 1993)
42	Bhamaria Thumdo (Jhandada-III)	23°54'02.1"N 71°27'01.0"E	Jhandada	Santalpur, Patan	36×22 0.79	Early Harappan, RGP IIC	IAR 1993-94: 32, Ajithprasad and Sonawane (site list 1993)
43	Jhandada no Thumdo-I (Jhandada-I)	23°54'25.0"N 71°27'17.4"E	Jhandada	Santalpur, Patan	100×80 0.80	Anarta, RGP IIC, RGP III / LRW	IAR 1992-93: 24, Ajithprasad and Sonawane (site list 1993)
44	Jhandada no Thumdo-II (Jhandada-II)	23°54'10.4"N 71°26'21.8"E	Jhandada	Santalpur, Patan	10×10 0.01	Anarta, RGP IIC, microliths	IAR 1992-93: 24, Ajithprasad and Sonawane (site list 1993)
45	Thumba Timbo	23°48'41.4"N 71°27'17.2"E	Jorawargadh	Santalpur, Patan	47×36 0.17	Anarta	Survey 2010 (NoGAP)
46	Thikariya no Timbo	23°31'13.2"N 71°45'06.1"E	Khandia	Sami, Patan	240×120 2.88	Anarta, RGP IIB, RGP III	Hegde and Soanawane 1986: 30, Bhan 1994:86-7, Ajithprasad and Sonawane (site list 1993)
47	Bajaniyano Thumdo (Koliwada-III)	23°49'54.8"N 71°29'27.8"E	Koliwada	Radhanpur, Patan	40×30 0.12	Mesolithic / microliths, Early Harappan	IAR 1993-94: 32, Ajithprasad and Sonawane (site list 1993)
48	Patel no Khetar (Koliwada-I)	23°49'45.5"N 71°29'42.4"E	Koliwada	Santalpur, Patan	40×40 0.16	Anarta, RGP IIC	IAR 1992-93: 22, Ajithprasad and Sonawane (site list 1993),
49	Shiharu no Thumdo (Koliwada-II)	23°50'30.2"N 71°29'58.4"E	Koliwada	Santalpur, Patan	100×30 0.30	Anarta, RGP IIC	IAR 1993-94: 32, Ajithprasad and Sonawane (site list 1993)
50	Harharino Thumda (Hariharno Thumda)	23°53'00.0"N 71°23'15.8"E	Korda	Santalpur, Patan	80×70 0.56	Mesolithic / microliths, Anarta, RGP IIC	IAR 1992-93: 23, Ajithprasad and Sonawane (site list 1993)
51	Bhalibhai no Timbo Bhalbhai no Timbo	23°32'26.9"N 71°36'30.2"E	Kunwar	Sami, Patan	160×90 1.44	RGP III / LRW, BRW	IAR 1978 79: 6-7, Bhan 1994: 86-7, Ajithprasad and Sonawane (site list 1993)
52	Piriya no Timbo (Kunward-II)	23°31'40.1"N 71°51'20.2"E	Kunward	Sami, Patan	140×100 1.40	RGP IIC, RGP III / LRW	IAR 1982-83: 28, Hegde and Sonawane 1986:30, Bhan1994:86-7, Ajithprasad and Sonawane (site list 1993)
53	Sasiya no Timbo -I (Kunward-I)	23°32'31.6"N 71°52'20.4"E	Kunward	Sami, Patan	150×150 2.25	RGP IIC, RGP III / LRW	IAR 1982-83: 28, Hegde and Sonawane1986: 30, Bhan 1994: 86-7, Ajithprasad and Sonawane (site list 1993)
54	LimbadkaThumdo	23°53'40.5"N 71°30'48.7"E	Limbadka	Radhanpur, Patan	60×50 0.30	Anarta, RGP IIC	IAR 1992-93: 22, Ajithprasad and Sonawane (site list 1993)
55	Limbuni no Ghod (Suigam -I)	24°08'27.4 "N 71°21'54.0"E	Limbuni	Vav, Banaskantha	30×30 0.09	RBP IIC, Microliths	IAR 1993-94: 33, Ajithprasad and Sonawane (site list 1993)
56	Lolara (Lolada)	23°32'28.9"N 71°41'44.5"E	Lolara	Sami, Patan		Anarta, RGP IIC	IAR 1978 79: 6-7, Bhan 1994: 86-7, Ajithprasad and Sonawane (site list 1993)
57	Loteshwar-I (Khari no Timbo-I)	23°36'01.8"N 71°50'11.8"E	Loteshwar	Sami, Patan	135×135 1.82	Mesolithic / microliths, Anarta	IAR 1982-83: 28, Hegde and Sonawane 1986: 30, Bhan 1994: 86-7, Ajithprasad and Sonawane (site list 1993), Excavation 1991 & 2009
58	Loteshwar-II (Odherio Timbo)	23°36'08.6"N 71°49'11.6"E	Loteshwar	Sami, Patan	150×100 1.50	Anarta, RGP IIC	IAR 1990-91: 17, Bhan 1994:86-7, Ajithprasad and Sonawane (site list 1993)
59	Valivada no Timbo (Vadadi no Timbo)	23°33'38.2"N 71°53'41.7"E	Manverpura	Sami, Patan	100×50 0.50	RGP III / LRW, BRW	IAR 1982-83: 28, Hegde and Sonawane 1986:30, Bhan 1994:86-7, Ajithprasad and Sonawane (site list 1993)
60	Kanthoda no Thumdo (Mathutra -III)	23°44'27.4"N 71°06'05.3"E	Mathutra	Santalpur, Patan	14×12 0.013	RGP IIB, RGPIIC	IAR 1994-95: 18
61	Madhvya no Timbo (Mathutra -I)	23°44'42.7"N 71°05'23.1"E	Mathutra	Santalpur, Patan	40×30 0.12	Early Harappan	IAR 1992-93: 25, Ajithprasad and Sonawane (site list 1993)
62	Pagiyawala no Thumdo (Mathutra -IV)	23°44'47.4"N 71°06'31.6"E	Mathutra	Santalpur, Patan	11×7 0.008	RGP IIB, RGP IIC	IAR 1994-95: 18
63	Talavadi no Thumdo (Mathutra -V)	23 44'32.6"N 71 07'11.9"E	Mathutra	Santalpur, Patan	8×7 0.006	RGP IIC	IAR 1994-95: 18
64	Vaditalavdi no Thumdo (Mathutra -II)	23°44'02.1"N 71°06'20.2"E	Mathutra	Santalpur, Patan	10×8 0.008	RGP IIB, Early Harappan	IAR 1994-95: 18
65	Gomsar no Timbo	23°16'22.8"N 71°41'14.6"E	Mithagoda	Dasada, Surendranagar	250×200 5.00	Anarta, RGP IIB, RGP IIC, Microliths	Bhan 1994: 86-7, Ajithprasad and Sonawane (site list 1993)
66	Solariya Timbo	23°16'41.8"N 71°42'04.2"E	Mithagoda	Dasada, Surendranagar	162×102 1.65	Anarta, Classical Harappan, BRW, Microliths,	Survey 2010 (GHSGP)

No.	Site Name	Coordinates	Viillage	Taluka, District	Size (m) Ha.	Period/Culture	Bibliography, Source
67	Moti Pipli (Shakatri Timbo)	23°49'24.9"N 71°30'01.8"E	Moti-Pipli	Radhanpur, Patan	255×120 3.06	Anarta, Early Harappan, Classical Harappan	IAR 1991-92: 19, Bhan 1994: 86-7, Ajithprasad and Sonawane (site list 1993), Excavation in 1993
68	Barvadno Timbo	23°33'54.4"N 71°51'30.02"E	Munjpur	Sami, Patan	70×65 0.46	Mesolithic / microliths, Anarta, Medieval	Survey 2010 (NoGAP)
69	Gachi no Bor (Munjpur-II)	23°36'17.8"N 71°53'07.5"E	Munjpur	Sami, Patan	20×20 0.04	Anarta, Classical Harappan.	IAR 1990-91: 17, Ajithprasad and Sonawane (site list 1993)
70	Gokhijadio Timbo	23°36'53.8"N 71°52'38.7"E	Munjpur	Sami, Patan	100×75 0.75	Anarta	IAR 1990-91: 17, Bhan 1994: 86-7, Ajithprasad and Sonawane (site list 1993)
71	Choteria Timbo (Munjpur-I)	23°36'05.7"N 71°51'07.3"E	Munjpur/ Mujpur	Sami, Patan	70×45 0.32	Anarta, Classical Harappan?.	IAR 1990-91: 17, Bhan 1994: 86-7, Ajithprasad and Sonawane (site list 1993)
72	Rajwadio Timbo-II (Munjpur -III)	23°35'00"N 71°51'10"E	Munjpur/ Mujpur	Sami, Patan	65×50 0.33	RGP IIC, RGP III / LRW	IAR 1990-91: 17, Bhan 1994:86-7, Ajithprasad and Sonawane (site list 1993)
73	Nagwada-I (Ghod)	23°18'38.8"N 71°42'59.6"E	Nagwada	Dasada, Surendranagar	140×110 1.54	Anarta, Early Harappan burial, Classical Harappan	IAR 1984-85: 19, IAR 1985-86: 20-1, Hegde et al 1988:55, Ajithprasad and Sonawane (site list 1993); Excavation 1986 to1990
74	Nagwada-II (Bhoirawalu Ghod)	23°18'38.1"N 71°43'02.7"E	Nagwada	Dasada, Surendranagar	200×150 3.00	Anarta, RGP IIC, RGP III, BRW	IAR 1984 85:19, Bhan 1994: 86-7, Ajithprasad and Sonawane (site list 1993)
75	Nagwada-III	23°18'19.7"N 71°42'38.9"E	Nagwada	Dasada, Surendranagar	100×70 0.70	RGP IIC, RGP III / LRW, Microliths	IAR 1985-86: 20-1, Hegde *et al.* 1988:55, Bhan 1994: 86-7, Ajithprasad and Sonawane (site list 1993)
76	Nagwada-IV	23°17'17.7"N 71°41'45.2"E	Nagwada	Dasada, Surendranagar	100×80 0.80	Anarta, Classical Harappan.	IAR 1985-86: 20-1, Hegde *et al.* 1988:55, IAR 1984 85, Bhan 1994: 86-87
77	Nagwada-V (Mullada -II)	23°17'50"N 71°43'00"E	Nagwada	Dasada, Surendranagar	30×25 0.08	RGP IIC, RGP III / LRW	Bhan 1994:86-7, Ajithprasad and Sonawane (site list 1993)
78	Nani Chandur	23°35'00"N 71°37'00"E	Nani-Chandur	Sami, Patan	50×25 0.13	Mesolithic / microliths, Anarta, RGP IIC	IAR 1991-92: 19, Bhan 1994:86-7, Ajithprasad and Sonawane (site list 1993)
79	Footeriya	23°37'10.6"N 71°43'25.6"E	Nayka	Sami, Patan	30×8 0.02	Anarta	IAR 1991-92: 19, Bhan 1994: 86-7, Ajithprasad and Sonawane (site list 1993)
80	Orumana	23°35'39.6"N 71°52'58.2"E	Orumana	Sami, Patan	75×60 0.45	Anarta, RGP IIC	IAR 1990-91: 17, Bhan 1994: 86-7, Ajithprasad and Sonawane (site list 1993)
81	Bagayano Timbo (Panchasar-I)	23°25'07.2"N 71°49'38.7"E	Panchasar	Dasada, Surendranagar	100×100 1.00	Anarta, RGP IIC, RGP III / LRW, Microliths	IAR 1982-83: 28, Hegde and Sonawane 1986: 31, Bhan 1994: 86-7, Ajithprasad and Sonawane (site list 1993)
82	Duderiya Timbo (Panchasar-II)	23°26'01.0"N 71°48'17.4"E	Panchasar	Sami, Patan	60×50 0.30	Mesolithic / Microliths, Anarta, RGP IIC,	IAR 1982-83: 28, Hegde and Sonawane 1986: 31, Bhan 1994: 86-7
83	Harthar no Timbo (Panchasar-II)	23°26'09.3"N 71°48'54.3"E	Panchasar	Sami, Patan	250×200 5.00	Mesolithic, Early Harappan, RGP IIC, RGP III, BRW	IAR 1982-83: 28, Hegde and Sonawane 1986:31, Bhan 1994: 86-7, Ajithprasad and Sonawane (site list 1993)
84	Oriyadada no Timbo	23°23'50.9"N 71°48'27.8"E	Panva	Dasada, Surendranagar	160×160 2.56	RGP IIC, RGP III / LRW, BRW, Microliths	Hegde and Sonawane 1986: 31, Bhan 1994:86-7, Ajithprasad and Sonawane (site list 1993)
85	Godha II	23°36'00"N 71°28'00"E	Pati	Santalpur, Patan	70×60 0.42	RGP IIB, RGP IIC	IAR 1991-92: 19, Bhan 1994: 86-7, Ajithprasad and Sonawane (site list 1993)
86	Pirojpur	23°30'44.8"N 71°42'09.8"E	Pirojpur	Dasada, Surendranagar	50×50 0.25	RGP III / LRW	IAR 1978 79: 6-7, Bhan 1994: 86-7, Ajithprasad and Sonawane (site list 1993)
87	Jamathar no Thumdo	23°45'24.3"N 71°13'58.4"E	Rajusar	Santalpur, Patan	100×100 1.00	RGP IIB, RGP IIC	IAR 1992-93: 24, Ajithprasad and Sonawane (site list 1993)
88	Lavanano Godh	23°50'39.6"N 71°35'13.4"E	Randhanpur	Radhanpur, Patan	70×60 0.42	Anarta, RGP IIC	IAR 1992-93: 22, Ajithprasad and Sonawane (site list 1993)

No.	Site Name	Coordinates	Viillage	Taluka, District	Size (m) Ha.	Period/Culture	Bibliography, Source
89	Lakahar no Thumdo	23°46'05.3"N 71°08'40.2"E	Ranmalpura	Santalpur, Patan	13×9 0.121	RGP IIC	IAR 1994-95: 18
90	Mepla no Thumdo (Ranmalpura -I)	23°46'24.4"N 71°09'24.2"E	Ranmalpura	Santalpur, Patan	80×60 0.48	Anarta, RGP IIB, RGP IIC	IAR 1992-93: 25, Ajithprasad and Sonawane (site list 1993)
91	Moda no Thumdo (Ranmalpur -III)	23°47'45.1"N 71°08'35.8"E	Ranmalpura	Santalpur, Patan	65×48 0.312	Anarat, RGP IIB	IAR 1994-95: 18
92	Panchahari no Thumdo (Ranmalpur -II)	23°45'48.8"N 71°08'28.3"E	Ranmalpura	Santalpur, Patan	12×9 0.011	RGP IIC, RGP III	IAR 1994-95: 18
93	Duwala Timbo	23°32'55.6"N 71°48'58.5"E	Ranod	Sami, Patan	38×25 0.095	RGP IIB, Microliths	Survey 2010 (NoGAP)
94	Tokariya Timbo (Ratanpura)	23°28'36.3"N 71°48'55.5"E	Ratanpura	Sami, Patan	500×200 10.00	Mesolithic / microliths, RGP IIC, RGP III / LRW, BRW	IAR 1982-83: 28, IAR 1984-85: 17-8, Hegde and Sonawane 1986: 30, Bhan 1994: 86-7, Excavation in 1985
95	Lakneyani Thumdo-I (Thumda 1)	23°39'00"N 71°34'00"E	Rupnagar	Sami, Patan	30×24 0.07	RGP IIC, RGP III / LRW	IAR 1991-92: 19, Bhan 1994: 86-7, Ajithprasad and Sonawane (site list 1993)
96	Santhli-I (Santhli no Thumdo)	23°53'24.9"N 71°30'09.6"E	Santhli	Radhanpur, Patan	90×70 0.63	Anarta	IAR 1992-93: 22, , Ajithprasad and Sonawane (site list 1993)
97	Santhli-II (Ghachiyawado)	23°54'16.7"N 71°29'37.1"E	Santhli	Radhanpur, Patan	96×65 0.62	Mesolithic/microliths, Early Harappan Burial	IAR 1993-94: 30, Ajithprasad and Sonawane (site list 1993), Excavation in 1994
98	Santhli-III (Vajiyasri no Thumdo)	23°51'27.8"N 71°28'30.2"E	Santhli	Radhanpur, Patan	21×10 0.02	Mesolithic/microliths, Anarta?	IAR 1993-94: 32, Ajithprasad and Sonawane (site list 1993)
99	Santhli-IV (Navod no Thumbo)	23°54'36.7"N 71°28'30.6"E	Santhli	Radhanpur, Patan	10×10 0.01	Mesolithic / microliths, Ealy Harappan	IAR 1993-94: 32, Ajithprasad and Sonawane (site list 1993)
100	Santhli-V (Kalatalavdi no Thumdo)	23°54'40.2"N 71°29'54.4"E	Santhli	Radhanpur, Patan	60×50 0.30	Mesolithic / microliths, RGP IIC	IAR 1993-94: 32, Ajithprasad and Sonawane (site list 1993)
101	Santhli-VI (Haiduk no Thumdo-I)	23°54'30.6"N 71°29'30.8"E	Santhli	Radhanpur, Patan	60×50 0.30	Mesolithic / microliths, RGP IIC	IAR 1993-94: 32, Ajithprasad and Sonawane (site list 1993)
102	Borawalu Khetar (Sarwal-II)	23°42'00"N 71°51'00"E	Sarwal	Harij, Patan	100×100 1.00	RGP IIC, RGP III / LRW	IAR 1982 83: 28, Hegde and Sonawane 1986: 31, Bhan 1994: 86-7
103	Khathariya no Timbo (Sarwal-I)	23°42'15"N 71°51'20"E	Sarwal	Harij, Patan	150×100 1.50	RGP IIC, RGP III / LRW	IAR 1982-83: 28, Hegde and Sonawane 1986: 31, Bhan 1994: 86-7
104	Kasha no Timbo (Kacho timbo)	23°31'14.2"N 71°39'33.6"E	Sipur/Sibpur	Sami, Patan	130×120 1.56	Anarta, RGP IIC, RGP III / LRW, Microliths,	IAR 1978-79: 7 Bhan 1994: 86-7, Ajithprasad and Sonawane (site list 1993)
105	Limdavalo Timbo	23°40'56.6"N 71°45'06.7"E	Sonar/Sonur	Sami, Patan	100×100 1.00	RGP III / LRW, BRW	IAR 1982-83: 28, Hegde and Sonawane 1986: 30, Ajithprasad and Sonawane (site list 1993)
106	Jakhra Pir no Thumdo (Suigam -II)	24°09'16.4"N 71°22'12.0"E	Suigam	Vav, Banaskantha	100×70 0.70	Anarta, RGP IIC, Microliths	IAR 1993-94: 33, Ajithprasad and Sonawane (site list 1993)
107	Khari-no Khetar (Suneth-II)	23°58'56.6"N 71°26'00.0"E	Suneth	Vav, Banaskantha	60×50 0.30	Anarta	IAR 1992-93: 26, Ajithprasad and Sonawane (site list 1993)
108	Mata no Thumdo (Suneth-I)	23°58'41.6"N 71°26'8.7"E	Suneth	Vav, Banaskantha	120×90 1.08	Anarta, RGP IIB, RGP IIC	IAR 1992-93: 26, Ajithprasad and Sonawane (site list 1993)
109	Gordhan Timbo (Govardhaniya Timbo)	23°28'01.1"N 71°53'57.2"E	Susiya	Dasada, Surendranagar	200×150 3.00	Anarta, RGP IIC, BRW	Hegde and Sonawane 1986: 31, Ajithprasad and Sonawane (site list 1993), Bhan 1994: 86-7
110	Bhutawed no Godh (Unrot-II)	23°50'40.8"N 71°29'56.7"E	Unrot	Santalpur, Patan	60×50 0.30	Anarta, RGP IIC, RGP III / LRW	IAR 1992-93: 22, Ajithprasad and Sonawane (site list 1993)
111	Pepadia Timbo (Unrot-I)	23°49'58.5"N 71°21'38.6"E	Unrot	Santalpur, Patan	40×30 0.12	RGP IIB, RGP IIC	IAR 1992-93: 25, Ajithprasad and Sonawane (site list 1993)
112	Vadgam	23°21'00"N 71°48'10"E	Vadgam	Dasada, Surendranagar	100×100 1.00	RGPIIC, RGP III / LRW	IAR 1964-65: 11, Bhan1994: 86-7, Ajithprasad and Sonawane (site list 1993)
113	Veranath Timbo (Atariyano Hanuman)	23°38'13.8"N 71°54'57.2"E	Vaghel	Sami, Patan	130×120 1.56	RGP III / LRW	IAR 1982-83: 28, Hegde and Soanawane 1986: 30, Bhan 1994: 86-7, Ajithprasad and Sonawane (site list 1993)
114	Haji no Kachha (Varanasri-II)	23°53'45.9"N 71°19'51.3"E	Varanasri	Santalpur, Patan	70×60 0.42	Anarta, Microliths	IAR 1992-93: 23, Ajithprasad and Sonawane (site list 1993)
115	Katadia no Thumdo (Varanasri-I)	23°54'48.3"N 71°20'17.4"E	Varanasri	Santalpur, Patan	20×20 0.34	RGP IIC	IAR 1992-93: 24, Ajithprasad and Sonawane (site list 1993)

No.	Site Name	Coordinates	Viillage	Taluka, District	Size (m) Ha.	Period/Culture	Bibliography, Source
116	Kasano Relo (Ghod, Kasna Relo	23°26'34.2"N 71°34'37.8"E	Visnagar	Dasada, Surendranagar	125×125 1.56	RGP III/LRW	Bhan 1994: 86-7
117	Lakhetra no Timbo (Visnagar-I)	23°28'16.5"N 71°34'05.9"E	Visnagar	Dasada, Surendranagar	62×54 0.34	RGP III / LRW	IAR 1991-92: 20, Bhan 1994: 86-7, Ajithprasad and Sonawne (site list 1993),
118	Linedoriwalo Khetar (Visnagar-II)	23°27'43.9"N 71°33'47.0"E	Visnagar	Dasada, Surendranagar	67×54 0.36	RGP IIC, RGP III / LRW	IAR 1991-92: 19, Bhan 1994: 86-7, Ajithprasad and Sonawane (site list 1993)
119	Zekhada (Amasrino Tekra, Jhekhda)	23°52'40.8"N 71°27'30.6"E	Zekhada	Santalpur, Patan	300×150 4.50	Anarta, Classical Harappan.	IAR 1977-78: 20, Mehta 1982, Momin 1983: 120, Ajithprasad and Sonawane (site list 1993)

The following sources are used to compile the list:

Ajithprasad and Sonawane (site list 1993): A list (unpublished) of prehistoric and Historic Period sites in North Gujarat prepared by P. Ajithprasad and V. H. Sonawane in 1993. It lists Mesolithic, Harappan/Chalcolithic and Historic period sites.

IAR 1978-79: Survey by C. Margabandhu and K. Raghavachari of the Archaeological Survey of India and K.T.M Hegde and A. M Thakkar of the M. S. University of Baroda

IAR 1982-83: Survey by K.T.M. Hegde, V.H. Sonawane and K.N. Momin, Department of Archaeology and Ancient History, The M.S. University of Baroda

IAR 1984-85: Survey by K.T.M. Hegde, V.H. Sonawane, and P. Ajithprasad, Department of Archaeology and Ancient History, The M.S. University of Baroda

IAR 1990-91: Survey by V.S. Parekh, V.H. Sonawane, P. Ajithprasad and K.K. Bhan, Department of Archaeology and Ancient History,The M.S. University of Baroda.

IAR 1991-92: Survey by V.S. Parekh, V.H. Sonawane and K.K. Bhan, Department of Archaeology and Ancient History, The M.S. University of Baroda

IAR 1992-93: Survey by V.S. Parekh, P. Ajithprasad and P.C. Chaudhary, Department of Archaeology and Ancient History, The M.S. University of Baroda

IAR 1993-94: Survey by V.S. Parekh, V.H. Sonawane, P. Ajithprasad and P.C. Chaudhary, Department of Archaeology and Ancient History, The M.S. University of Baroda

IAR 1994-95: Survey by V.S. Parekh, V.H. Sonawane, P. Ajithprasad and P.C. Chaudhary, Department of Archaeology and Ancient History, The M.S. University of Baroda

Survey 2009, 2010 (NoGAP): Survey by the North Gujarat Archaeological Project (NoGAP), a collaborative research programme between the Department of Archaeology and Ancient History, The M.S. University of Baroda, India and the Department of Archaeology and Anthropology, IMF, CSIC, Barcelona, Spain

Survey 2010 (GHSGP): Survey by the Gujarat Harappan Site Gazetteer Project (GHSGP), a collaborative research programme between the Department of Archaeology and Ancient History, The M.S. University of Baroda, India and the "Indus Project" of the Research Institute for Humanity and Nature, Kyoto, Japan